Out in Psychology

Out in Psychology
Lesbian, Gay, Bisexual, Trans and Queer Perspectives

Edited by

Victoria Clarke
University of the West of England, UK
and
Elizabeth Peel
Aston University, UK

John Wiley & Sons, Ltd

Other Wiley Editorial Offices

John Wiley & Sons Inc., 111 River Street, Hoboken, NJ 07030, USA

Jossey-Bass, 989 Market Street, San Francisco, CA 94103-1741, USA

Wiley-VCH Verlag GmbH, Boschstr. 12, D-69469 Weinheim, Germany

John Wiley & Sons Australia Ltd, 42 McDougall Street, Milton, Queensland 4064, Australia

John Wiley & Sons (Asia) Pte Ltd, 2 Clementi Loop #02-01, Jin Xing Distripark, Singapore 129809

John Wily & Sons Canada Ltd, 6045 Freemont Blvd, Mississauga, ONT, L5R 4J3, Canada

Wiley also publishes its books in a variety of electronic formats. Some content that appears in print may not
be available in electronic books.

Anniversary Logo Design: Richard J. Pacifico

Library of Congress Cataloging-in-Publication Data

Out in psychology : lesbian, gay, bisexual, trans, and queer perspectives /
edited by Victoria Clarke, Elizabeth Peel.
       p.   cm
   Includes bibliographical references and index.
   ISBN 978-0-470-01287-1 (cloth : alk. paper)
1. Sexual minorities–Psychology.   2. Gays–Psychology.   3. Sexual
minorities–Mental health services.   4. Gays–Mental health services.   I. Clarke,
Victoria, Ph.D.   II. Peel, Elizabeth.
   HQ73.O88 2007
   155.3′4–dc22

                                                                    2006036089

British Library Cataloguing in Publication Data

A catalogue record for this book is available from the British Library

ISBN 978-0-470-01287-1

Typeset in 10/12 pt Times by SNP Best-set Typesetter Ltd., Hong Kong
Printed and bound in Great Britain by Antony Rowe, Chippenham, Wiltshire
This book is printed on acid-free paper responsibly manufactured from sustainable forestry in which at least
two trees are planted for each one used for paper production.

Contents

About the Editors

Victoria Clarke is a Senior Lecturer in social psychology at the University of the West of England, Bristol, UK. She has published a number of papers on lesbian and gay parenting, same-sex relationships, the history of LGBTQ psychologies, and qualitative methods in journals such as *Sexualities, British Journal of Social Psychology, Qualitative Research in Psychology* and *Lesbian & Gay Psychology Review*. She has edited (with Sara-Jane Finlay and Sue Wilkinson) two special issues of *Feminism & Psychology* on marriage, and edited (with Elizabeth Peel) special issues of *Feminism & Psychology, Journal of Gay & Lesbian Psychotherapy, Lesbian & Gay Psychology Review* and *Psychology of Women Section Review* on LGBTQ psychologies. She is also the editor with Elizabeth Peel and Jack Drescher of *British LGB Psychologies: Theory, research and practice* (Harrington Park Press, 2007). She is a member of the British Psychological Society's Lesbian & Gay Psychology Section and Qualitative Methods in Psychology Section. She is an editorial board member of the *Journal of Gay & Lesbian Psychology*, the *Journal of GLBT Family Studies*, and *Feminism & Psychology*. She is currently conducting British Academy funded research on civil partnership (with Elizabeth Peel) and co-authoring a textbook (with Sonja J. Ellis, Elizabeth Peel and Damien W. Riggs) entitled *LGBTQ Psychologies: Themes and perspectives* (Cambridge University Press).

Elizabeth Peel is a Lecturer in psychology in the School of Life and Health Sciences, Aston University, Birmingham, UK. She has published a number of articles about heterosexism, diversity training and lesbian and gay relationships in journals such as *Discourse & Society, Feminism & Psychology, Lesbian & Gay Psychology Review* and *Women's Studies International Forum*. She is the editor with Victoria Clarke and Jack Drescher of *British LGB Psychologies: Theory, research and practice* (Harrington Park Press, 2007). She has also edited (with Victoria Clarke) special issues of *Feminism & Psychology, Journal of Gay & Lesbian Psychotherapy, Lesbian & Gay Psychology Review* and *Psychology of Women Section Review* on LGBTQ psychologies. She is a chartered psychologist and a member of the British Psychological Society's Lesbian and Gay Psychology Section and Qualitative Methods in Psychology Section. She is former editor of *Lesbian & Gay Psychology Review* and editorial board member of the *Journal of Gay & Lesbian Psychotherapy*. Her current research centres on the management of chronic illness (especially diabetes), understandings of health-related technologies (such as neuroimaging techniques), same-sex relationships and the intersections of LGBTQ psychologies and critical health psychology. She is currently editing (with Michael Thomson) a special issue of *Feminism & Psychology* on LGBTQ health psychologies and is co-authoring a textbook (with Victoria Clarke, Sonja J. Ellis and Damien W. Riggs) entitled *LGBTQ Psychologies: Themes and perspectives* (Cambridge University Press).

List of Contributors

Jeffery Adams is undertaking his PhD in (Critical) Psychology at the University of Auckland. His research is concerned with gay men's health and well-being – particularly focusing on gay men's discourse around health, health-related practices and masculinity, and seeking to understand how these affect health-related practices and outcomes. He is also researcher at the Centre for Social and Health Outcomes Research and Evaluation, Massey University.

Sydney Bayley is a Specialist Educational Psychologist working largely within the Child and Adolescent Mental Health Services (CAMHS) in the North Essex Mental Health Partnership Trust, UK. Sydney works with young people on issues affecting their lives, including sexuality, and also with schools on mental health issues, including those arising from homophobic bullying and negative attitudes towards different sexualities.

Meg Barker is a Senior Lecturer at London South Bank University, UK. She teaches the psychology of sex and gender, critical psychology, counselling, and qualitative and quantitative methods. She researches sexual identities, practices and communities with a particular focus on bisexuality, polyamory and sadomasochism. She has published in both academic journals and popular magazines including *Journal of Constructivist Psychology, The Psychologist* and *Diva Magazine*. Meg is the honorary secretary for the Lesbian and Gay Psychology Section of the British Psychological Society and is co-editor of the Section's journal *Lesbian & Gay Psychology Review.*

Christopher Bennett is a Consultant Clinical Psychologist working in a medium secure unit for people with learning disabilities, part of Hertfordshire Partnership NHS Trust, UK. His doctoral dissertation explored the psychological and emotional impact for men with learning disabilities who were gay or who were exploring a gay identity. Within his clinical work he has facilitated a support group for gay men with learning disabilities as well as providing psychotherapy to gay men. He also provides supervision to an organization working with people with learning disabilities who identify as gay, lesbian, bisexual or transgender.

Jerry J. Bigner, PhD, is Professor Emeritus, Department of Human Development and Family Studies, Colorado State University. He is the editor of the *Journal of GLBT Family Studies* and editor of the *Haworth Series in GLBT Family Studies*. He is a member of the Editorial Board of the *Journal of Couple and Family Therapy*. His principle research area is in parent–child relations with an emphasis on GLBT parenting. He is the author of *Parent-Child Relations* (7th edn, 2006, Prentice Hall), and is the author of two lifespan development texts. He has over 50 research publications and 20 chapters in texts relating to parent–child relations as well as gay and lesbian family issues. He has provided expert testimony in Canadian same-sex marriage litigation and his research served as part of the plaintiff's cases in the Hawaii, Massachusetts and Vermont same-sex marriage litigation. He is a research member of the American Family Therapy Academy and is a member of the National Council on Family Relations. He is a 2006 Centennial Laureate of the College of Human Sciences, Florida State University.

Jo Bower, PhD, is currently a Research Consultant. Her research has focused on post-modern and discursive approaches to deconstructing gender and sexuality, relying primarily on Foucauldian analysis and feminist epistemologies. Specific research projects have included identity construction in bisexual women and lesbians in the military.

Virginia Braun is a Senior Lecturer in the Department of Psychology at the University of Auckland, where she teaches social psychology, gender, sexuality and qualitative methodology. Her research interests encompass sex, sexuality, bodies and health. Current projects include 'sex in long-term relationships', the social contexts of STI transmission, and 'female genital cosmetic surgery'.

Carol Burgoyne is a Senior Lecturer and member of the Economic Psychology Research Group in the School of Psychology, University of Exeter, UK. She is on the editorial boards of the *Journal of Economic Psychology*, the *Journal of Community and Applied Social Psychology* and is a member of the International Association for Research in Economic Psychology. Her current research includes an ESRC-funded study of money management in lesbian and gay relationships; a study funded by the DfES on money management and commitment in heterosexual couples, and a Leverhulme-funded project on beliefs about the allocation of money in marriage.

Maree Burns is the co-ordinator of the Eating Difficulties Education Network in Auckland, New Zealand. She recently completed ESRC-funded research on money management in same-sex relationships with Carole Burgoyne and Victoria Clarke at the University of Exeter. Maree has also published several articles on discourses of the 'eating disorder' bulimia. She is currently co-editing two books: *Critical Feminist Perspectives on Eating Dis/Orders* (Routledge & Psychology Press) and *Critical Bodies: Representations, practices and identities of weight and body management* (Palgrave Macmillan).

Clair Clifford is a Clinical Psychologist with Birmingham and Solihull Mental Health Trust, working at The Cystic Fibrosis Unit. Her doctoral research addressed 'The experience of social power in the lives of people who define as transgendered' and was completed at the University of Birmingham, UK.

Adrian Coyle is Senior Lecturer in the University of Surrey's Department of Psychology. He was one of a group of psychologists whose campaigning efforts resulted in the establishment of a Lesbian & Gay Psychology Section within the British Psychological Society in 1998 and was a founding co-editor of its publication, *Lesbian & Gay Psychology Review*. With Celia Kitzinger, he was editor of *Lesbian & Gay Psychology: New Perspectives* (BPS Blackwell, 2002). His other publications have addressed various issues within lesbian and gay psychology with a focus on identity issues, psychological well-being and experiences of therapy.

Bramilee Dhayanandhan, BA, is a Research Analyst for the Centre for Addiction and Mental Health, Canada. Her current research projects focus on the concurrence of domestic violence, substance use, anger and problem gambling. Other research interests include resiliency and motivational factors among youth and women in disadvantaged communities.

Sonja J. Ellis is a social psychologist and Senior Lecturer at Sheffield Hallam University, UK where she teaches Social Psychology, Social and Psychosocial Perspectives on Young People, and Qualitative Research Methods – all with a healthy dose of lesbian and gay perspectives! She completed her PhD on support for and reasoning about lesbian and gay rights issues in 2001, which has been published as a number of papers including a chapter in *Lesbian and Gay Psychology: New Perspectives* (edited by Coyle and Kitzinger, 2002). Her more recent work has focused on contemporary issues in the lives of lesbians and gay men, and she is currently undertaking exploratory work on homophobia among students. She is currently co-authoring a textbook (with Victoria Clarke, Elizabeth Peel and Damien W. Riggs) entitled *LGBTQ Psychologies: Themes and perspectives* (Cambridge University Press).

Richard Green obtained his medical degree from Johns Hopkins. Psychiatry training was at the University of California, Los Angeles and the National Institute of Mental Health. Legal training was at Yale (all in the USA). He co-edited the first multi-disciplinary text on transsexualism in 1969, *Transsexualism and Sex Reassignment*. He has been Professor of Psychiatry at the University of California and the State University of New York (USA) and Imperial College (UK). He has been on the law faculty of the University of California and Cambridge University. He was Research Director or Head of the Gender Identity Clinic, Charing Cross Hospital, 1994–2006. He has 180 publications.

Maria Gurevich, PhD, is Assistant Professor in Psychology at Ryerson University, Canada. Her research has focused on lesbian and bisexual women's health, community, identity and sexuality. Current research interests also include traumatic stress in medical populations, emergency medical personnel and residential youth.

Gareth Hagger-Johnson is a PhD candidate in the Department of Psychology, University of Edinburgh, UK. His research interests are in personality, individual differences and health psychology.

Rosie Harding is currently a PhD student in the AHRC Centre for Law, Gender and Sexuality at the University of Kent after completing an LLM in Gender, Sexuality and Human Rights at Keele University. Her research interests include the intersection of law and psychology, the legal regulation of lesbian and gay relationships, anti-discrimination law, employment law and legal consciousness and law in everyday life. Her work has been published in *Feminism & Psychology*, *Lesbian & Gay Psychology Review* and *Social & Legal Studies*.

Peter Hegarty received his PhD in psychology from Stanford University and taught at City University of New York and Yale University before his current appointment as Lecturer in the Psychology Department at the University of Surrey in 2002. His research focuses on the intersections of sexual politics and scientific work, drawing on both social psychology and the history of psychology and has been published in such journals as *Journal of Personality and Social Psychology, Psychological Science, Feminism & Psychology* and the *Journal for the History of Sexuality*. He is currently Chair of the British Psychological Society Lesbian & Gay Psychology Section.

Katherine Johnson is Senior Lecturer in psychology in the School of Applied Social Science, University of Brighton, UK. Her research interests straddle theoretical and methodological debates in psychology and sociology with a focus on notions of self, identity and embodiment, particularly in relation to gender and sexuality. She has published articles in *British Journal of Social Psychology, Social Alternatives, Qualitative Research in Psychology* and the *Journal of Lesbian Studies*, and is an Associate Editor of the *Psychology of Women Section Review*. She is currently working on a collaborative, community-based study of LGBT suicidal distress and she is writing a book *On Sexualities* (tentative title) (Polity).

Kerrie Kauer is an Adjunct Faculty at Smith College in the Exercise and Sport Studies department and at Bay Path College in the Liberal Arts Program, USA. Her research, grounded in queer and feminist cultural studies theories, focuses on identity and identification, heteronormativity and social justice in sport. Dr Kauer recently completed her PhD at the University of Tennessee in the Cultural Studies of Sport program and she is also a Certified Consultant, AAASP.

Celia Kitzinger is Professor of Conversation Analysis, Gender and Sexuality in the University of York's Department of Sociology. She was one of a group of psychologists whose campaigning efforts resulted in the establishment of a Lesbian & Gay Psychology Section within the British Psychological Society in 1998 and, with Adrian Coyle, she was editor of *Lesbian & Gay Psychology: New perspectives* (BPS Blackwell, 2002). She married her long-term partner, Sue Wilkinson, in Canada in 2003 when equal access to marriage was granted to same-sex couples in British Columbia, and Sue and Celia subsequently petitioned the British government for recognition of their Canadian marriage. They lost their High Court case in July 2006, when the judge declared that marriage was, by traditional definition, a union of a man and a woman and that civil partnership is an 'expressly different' institution. More information is available at www.equalmarriagerights.org.

Vikki Krane is the Director of the Women's Studies Program and a Professor in the School of Human Movement, Sport, and Leisure Studies at Bowling Green State University, USA. Her research, grounded in social identity theory, specifically focuses on heterosexism in sport and is published in the *Journal of Applied Sport Psychology, Quest, Research Quarterly for Sport and Exercise*, and *Sex Roles*. She is the Editor of the *Women in Sport and Physical Activity Journal*, former editor of *The Sport Psychologist* and is on the editorial board of the *Journal of Applied Sport Psychology*. Dr Krane also is a Fellow of the Association for the Advancement of Applied Sport Psychology (AAASP) and a Certified Consultant, AAASP.

Victoria Land was a doctoral student, supervised by Celia Kitzinger, in the Department of Sociology at the University of York, UK, but is now at the University of Surrey, UK. Her research uses conversation analysis to explore how and why sexuality is relevant in talk-in-interaction. She is using a naturalistic data set (150 telephone conversations to and from five lesbian households) to investigate how sexuality and sexual identity become relevant in these ordinary mundane interactions. Her work contributes to our knowledge about the basic organisation of talk in interaction (including membership categorization, person reference, repair and correction), to sociology more broadly (including work on language, identity and stigma management), and to interdisciplinary lesbian and gay studies.

Lih-Mei Liao is a Consultant Clinical Psychologist who works with women presenting atypical genitalia. Employed by Camden and Islington Mental Health and Social Care Trust, she leads Psychological Services to Women's Health at University College London Hospitals, Whittington Hospital and Royal Free Hospital. As Honorary Senior Lecturer at University College London, her academic activities have a broader focus. Key themes in her research include: (1) social constructions in women's health complaints and decisions to undergo complex treatments; (2) models of sexuality in clinical/social practices.

Becky J. Liddle is currently a contractual Associate Professor at the University of Toronto, Ontario Institute for Studies in Education. She recently relocated to Canada after 14 years on the faculty of Auburn University (USA). She has served on various editorial boards including *Journal of Counseling Psychology*, *Psychology of Women Quarterly*, and *Journal of Lesbian Studies*. She publishes in LGBTQ psychology and has also had a private practice specializing in counselling LGBTQ clients.

Bonita C. Long is Professor of Counselling Psychology at the University of British Columbia, Canada. Her main areas of research and publication focus on the influence of personality and contextual factors on the health of individuals who experience chronic psychosocial stress (e.g. occupational stress, chronic illness). Her work examines conceptual and theoretical aspects of stress and coping processes, as well as person-environment interactions. In addition, Dr Long and her colleagues have conducted research on lesbians' experiences of disclosing their sexual orientation. She also has supervised research focused on same-sex immigrant partners and the career development of lesbians who are leaders in their field. She has published numerous journal articles and book chapters. Among her publications is the book *Women, Work, and Coping* (1993). Professor Long is a Fellow in the Canadian Psychological Association.

Sara MacBride-Stewart is a Research Fellow in the School of Social Sciences at Cardiff University, Wales. She is currently leading a research programme on professionalism, feminisation and general practice. Sara has related research work and publications in the areas of heteronormativity and cervical screening, dental dams, critiques of 'queer science' and biocultural understandings of chronic pelvic pain.

Cynthia M. Mathieson, PhD, is Professor of Psychology at UBC Okanagan, USA. Her research interests include women's health, narratives of chronic illness and qualitative research methodologies.

Tim McCreanor is a social science researcher in Whariki Research Group and the Centre for Social and Health Outcomes Research and Evaluation at Massey University in Auckland, New Zealand. He also lectures in the Psychology Department at Massey University's Albany Campus in Auckland. Current research projects are in race relations, the linkages between health and place, positive youth development, and impacts of marketing on youth identities.

Jeremy J. Monsen has been involved in training educational and child psychologists in the Psychology Department at University College London for 11 years and is an Assistant Principal to the Kent County Council's Educational Psychology Service. Jeremy works with schools and other agencies to address issues associated with intolerance and ignorance around the experience of LGBTQ young people. Current research projects involve the exploration of children's, parents' and school staff's attributions of sexuality and homophobic bullying and identifying those factors that support more positive experiences of school.

Jim Orford is Professor of Clinical and Community Psychology and Head of the Alcohol, Drugs, Gambling and Addiction Research Group in the School of Psychology at the University of Birmingham, UK. He has promoted the development of community psychology in Europe, and was coordinator of the European Network of Community Psychology between 2003 and 2005. His published works include: *Community Psychology: Theory and Practice* (Wiley, 1992) and he is working on a sequel, as well as books and articles on addiction.

Damien W. Riggs is an ARC postdoctoral fellow in the School of Psychology, University of Adelaide, Australia. He is the National Convenor of the Australian Psychological Society's 'Gay and Lesbian Issues in Psychology' Interest Group and is the Editor of its *Gay and Lesbian Issues and Psychology Review*. He has published in the areas of lesbian and gay psychology and critical race and whiteness studies in *Psychoanalysis, Culture and Society, Journal of Community & Applied Social Psychology, Lesbian & Gay Psychology Review, Culture, Health and Sexuality* and *International Journal of Critical Psychology*. He is the editor of two books: *Out in the Antipodes: Australian and New Zealand perspectives on gay and lesbian issues in psychology* (with Gordon Walker, 2004, Brightfire Press), and *Taking up the Challenge: Critical race and whiteness studies in a postcolonising nation* (2006, Crawford Publishers). His new book, *Priscilla, (White) Queen of the Desert: Queer rights/race privilege* (Peter Lang) was published in 2006 and he is completing work on a second, due out in 2007, entitled *Becoming Parents: Lesbians, gay men, and family* (Brightfire Press). He is currently co-authoring a textbook (with Victoria Clarke, Sonja J. Ellis and Elizabeth Peel) entitled *LGBTQ Psychologies: Themes and perspectives* (Cambridge University Press).

Ian Rivers is Professor of Community and Applied Psychology, and Head of Psychology at Queen Margaret University College, Edinburgh, UK. He is the author of over 80 articles and chapters focusing on homophobia in schools and its long-term effects, and has presented at over 150 international and national conferences. Ian is the recipient of the British Psychological Society's 2001 Award for Promoting Equality of Opportunity in the United Kingdom through his work as a researcher and psychologist, and currently serves as deputy chair of the Society's Standing Committee for the Promotion of Equal Opportunities. Previously Ian was Professor of Applied Psychology at York St John University College, and co-ordinator of the Social Inclusion and Diversity Research Unit – a facility developed to support health, education and voluntary sector organizations evaluate and develop their services for lesbians, gay men, bisexual and transgender women and men.

Suzanna M. Rose, PhD, is Chairperson and Professor of Psychology and also Director of the Women's Studies Center at Florida International University, Miami. Dr Rose's research focuses on how gender, sexual orientation and race affect relationships and sexuality and on gay and lesbian issues more generally, as well. She has published extensively on love scripts and friendships in psychology journals and co-authored or edited several books and journal special issues, including *Lesbian Love and Relationships* (Haworth, 2002) and *Innovations in Lesbian Psychology*, a special section of the *Psychology of Women Quarterly* (June, 2005).

Faith Rostad gained her PhD in counselling psychology from the Department of Educational and Counselling Psychology at the University of British Columbia, Canada (November, 2002). Her dissertation research explored the occupational experiences of a diverse sample of lesbians in order to understand how they succeeded. Dr Rostad is presently working as a registered psychologist in private practice as well as a counsellor in a public high school where she works with students on issues such as 'coming out' and 'handling homophobia'.

Glenda M. Russell, PhD is a psychologist who has been involved in clinical practice, research, theory-building, teaching and activism. Her work has centred on the psychological impact of anti-gay politics, out-group activism and social constructionist approaches to sexual orientation. She is the author of *Voted Out: The Psychological Consequences of Anti-gay Politics* (2000) and, with Janis Bohan, of *Conversations about Psychology and Sexual Orientation* (1999).

Susan A. Speer is a Senior Lecturer in Language and Communication in the School of Psychological Sciences at the University of Manchester, UK. Her research focuses on topics and debates at the intersection of feminism and conversation analysis. She has published articles in *Sociology, Discourse & Society, Discourse Studies, Journal of Sociolinguistics, Feminism & Psychology* and *Theory & Psychology*. Her book *Gender Talk: Feminism, discourse and conversation analysis* was published by Routledge in 2005. She is currently Principal Investigator (with Prof Richard Green, Imperial College School of Medicine) on a three-year ESRC-funded project 'Transsexual Identities: Constructions of gender in an NHS gender identity clinic', which is part of the Social Identities and Social Action Research Programme (award number RES-148-0029). She spent the 2005–2006 academic year as a Visiting Scholar in the Sociology Department at UCLA, funded by an ESRC-SSRC Collaborative Visiting Fellowship. She is currently collaborating with Elizabeth Stokoe (Loughborough University, UK) on an edited collection, *Conversation and Gender* (Cambridge University Press).

Foreword

Jerry J. Bigner, Professor Emeritus
Department of Human Development and Family Studies
Colorado State University, USA

The year 1983 is indelibly imprinted on my life as the year I came out to several family members and friends and started my life as an authentic person for the first time since my birth, a gay man who was also a father. It was a tumultuous time that began the process of letting go of illusions and developing a new identity. I was giving up what I misperceived as an appropriate way of life for me – believing I was successfully passing as heterosexual by being married to a woman, being the father of three children, and developing my professional life as an academic behavioral scientist working in the fields of human development and family studies. Up until that time, my life, both personally and professionally, had been governed by the awesome fears generated by internalized homophobia and heterosexism.

In those days, one did not come out publicly as a professional, for to do so was to commit suicide regarding one's respect and acceptance in academia – at least, where I was teaching and working as a researcher. So, like many others, I continued to hold private my personal identity at a cost to my integrity. Coming out completely was stymied by maintaining one foot in the closet to keep some semblance of security for myself and my children.

In the beginning of my coming out process, I prepared for my divorce by searching the literature about what research showed about gay fathers. My search took place very quickly since there was only a handful of studies that had been conducted prior to 1984. The works of Fred Bozett were almost the only ones that the search produced as he was the pioneer researcher on gay fathering (Bozett, 1980, 1981). While I found Fred's works to be reassuring, I fretted that there were no empirically-based studies nor were there any that utilized the experimental-control group methodology that was based on acceptable sampling procedures. Knowing that it was possible that I (as well as countless other gay and lesbian parents) could be denied holding joint custody of our children by a court (despite the fact that I had authored three editions of my parent–child relations text and one edition of my lifespan development text), I set out to rectify this glaring gap in the literature about gay fathers. The studies that I produced with a colleague, with graduate students and with Fred resulted in some of the first studies of gay fathers based on acceptable, quantitative behavioral science methodology (Bigner & Bozett, 1989; Bigner & Jacobsen, 1989a, 1989b). We also turned our attention to studying lesbian mothers (Miller, Jacobsen & Bigner, 1981; Siegenthaler & Bigner, 2000). Thankfully, over the years, we were joined by an increasing number of researchers who hammered out similar findings using a wide variety of instrumentation, data collection and analyses (e.g. Patterson, 1995; Tasker, 1999, 2002). Armed with this sound databank, I and other research colleagues began testifying on behalf of US gay and lesbian parents in legal custody proceedings. In my personal life, it was this path of research that eventually enabled me to come out publicly as a professor, a researcher and a father (and grandfather).

As I reflect on the past 30 years of works produced by what is now an army of researchers instead of only a few, I acknowledge the position taken by Stacey and Biblarz (2001) that heterosexism thwarted intellectual progress in the early path that research programmes in lesbian, gay, bisexual, trans and queer (LGBTQ) family studies followed. This was apparent in claims that LGBTQ parents were no different than heterosexual ones; that children were not harmed by being reared by LGBTQ parents. In acknowledging this, however, it is important to emphasize that there was very good reason for the heterosexist bend in the research path followed by myself and most of the other early researchers: the political atmosphere of the legal system and of the court of public opinion heavily discriminated against LGBTQ parents. It was this atmosphere that necessitated this stance. More pointedly, we needed acceptable, scientifically valid proof that would stand up in court that refuted the myths, stereotypes and misconceptions about ourselves as parents and how we influenced our children. We deeply feared losing them from our lives and needed data proving we were not different significantly from heterosexual parents; essentialism 'rather naturally spring[s] from hostile times' (Bohan & Russell, 1999, p. 184).

Today, because of the path followed by early research, sexual orientation of parents is no longer considered a viable factor in court proceedings regarding fitness to care for children; adoption is made easier in most US states; legal issues surrounding surrogacy and non-biological parenthood have been examined; same-gender marriage is definitely a hot political, social and religious issue; and the path is now clear for new directions of enquiry. We've learned that we no longer need to fear admitting our differences from heterosexuals – and that these differences are good and positive ones.

The works you are about to read here represent a new era for the future in which psychology, in particular, can lead the way for more adventurous and fearless research about LGBTQ issues. Taken together, the chapters in this book show the multifarious nature of the issues at hand. What is particularly unique about this volume is that it serves as a showcase for current directions in *international* LGBTQ psychologies. The international perspectives found here are frequently lacking in other collections on LGBTQ issues. The volume is also valuable in demonstrating inclusiveness by integrating all of the communities represented in the acronym LGBTQ, particularly bisexual, transgender and queer communities and perspectives. Such inclusion is difficult to achieve in a single collection of works and not usually accomplished by others. The editors should be congratulated in this achievement. A further important aspect of this volume is the use and examination of a variety of theories, methods and approaches employed to research LGBTQ communities. This book is a much needed addition to the field. Perhaps the true value of this volume is that it demonstrates how LGBTQ psychologists are leading the way applying research findings to the practical worlds in which we all live.

The authors of these works open up the closet that has hidden the controversies within the LGBTQ communities for years, not only in the scientific world but in the political and social worlds as well. Just as the path now diverges into novel branches of enquiry about LGBTQ parenting, it diverges now into novel directions in relation to the discipline of

LGBTQ psychologies, as the contributors to this volume aptly demonstrate. Indeed, they provide encouragement, thoughtful reflection and an adamant call to action to address the new world of enquiry that lies ahead.

REFERENCES

Bigner, J. J. & Bozett, F. W. (1989). Parenting by gay fathers. *Marriage and Family Review,* **14**(3), 155–176.

Bigner, J. J. & Jacobsen, R. B. (1989a). The value of children to gay and heterosexual fathers. *Journal of Homosexuality,* **18**(1/2), 163–172.

Bigner, J. J. & Jacobsen, R. B. (1989b). Parenting behaviors of homosexual and heterosexual fathers. *Journal of Homosexuality,* **18**(1/2), 173–186.

Bozett, F. W. (1980). Gay fathers: How and why they disclose their homosexuality to their children. *Family Relations,* **29**(2), 173–179.

Bozett, F. W. (1981). Gay fathers: Identity conflict resolution through integrative sanctioning. *Alternative Life-Styles,* **4**(1), 90–107.

Bohan, J. & Russell, G. (1999). Afterword: The conversation continues. In J. Bohan & G. Russell (Eds), *Conversations about Psychology and Sexual Orientation* (pp. 183–210). New York: New York University Press.

Miller, J. A., Jacobsen, R. B. & Bigner, J. J. (1981). The child's home environment for lesbian versus heterosexual mothers: A neglected area of research. *Journal of Homosexuality,* **7**(1), 49–56.

Patterson, C. J. (1995). Sexual orientation and human development: An overview. *Developmental Psychology,* **31**(1), 3–11.

Siegenthaler, A. & Bigner, J. J. (2000). The value of children to lesbian and nonlesbian mothers. *Journal of Homosexuality,* **39**(2), 73–92.

Stacey, J. & Biblarz, T. J. (2001). (How) does the sexual orientation of parents matter? *American Sociological Review,* **66**(2), 159–183.

Tasker, F. (1999). Children in lesbian-led families: A review. *Clinical Child Psychology & Psychiatry,* **4**(2), 153–166.

Tasker, F. (2002). Lesbian and gay parenting. In A. Coyle & C. Kitzinger (Eds), *Lesbian and Gay Psychology: New perspectives* (pp. 81–97). Malden, MA: Blackwell.

CHAPTER 1

Introducing *Out in Psychology*

Victoria Clarke
University of the West of England, UK
and
Elizabeth Peel
Aston University, UK

'If we are liberated we are open with our sexuality. Closet queenery must end. *Come out.*'[1]
'We're out. Where the fuck are you?'
'Nobody knows I'm a lesbian.'
'We're here. We're queer. Get used to it'.
'Trans, out and proud.'
'Blatantly bisexual.'

These pride slogans and rallying cries for lesbian, gay, bisexual, trans[2] and queer (LGBTQ) movements – at once celebratory and confrontational – highlight the importance of 'outness' and visibility across a range of political eras and agendas. The title of this volume *Out in Psychology: Lesbian, gay, bisexual, trans and queer perspectives*, draws attention to the centrality of visibility for LGBTQ psychologies[3], movements and politics. We chose this title to signal the presence, and increasing validation and acknowledgement, of research, theory and practice on LGBTQ concerns across the discipline of psychology. We are 'outing' psychology as a discipline that already, if sometimes ambivalently or unwillingly, incorporates LGBTQ perspectives. Although it is important to have a separate space to pursue research and practice, it is vital that we engage with, and contribute to, the broader discipline (Dworkin, 2002). LGBTQ psychologies of all varieties aim to support social change. This goal is realised both through making or assisting interventions

---

[1] These slogans are all general LGBTQ pride slogans with no specific source, other than the first (Wittman, 1997/1969–70, p. 383, emphasis in original) and second (Queer Nation, 1990).

[2] We use the term 'trans' as an umbrella term for those people whose gender presentation or behaviour conflicts with or exists outside of dominant sex/gender norms (see the Press for Change web site: http://www.pfc.org.uk).

[3] We use the label 'LGBTQ psychologies' with some caution. We think that it is not possible to confidently identify the existence of a coherent LGBTQ psychology (as opposed to lesbian and gay psychology) in the UK or internationally. We view this book, and the use of the term 'LGBTQ' in this book, as a step towards LGBTQ psychologies rather than a declaration or celebration of their establishment. As such, we shift between using LGBTQ, LGBT, LGB and lesbian and gay in order to avoid using the less established labels in a meaningless way. We considered adding 'I' onto 'LGBTQ' in this chapter (and including the word 'intersex' in the title of the book), but, ultimately, it seemed problematic to include 'I' when only one chapter in *Out in Psychology* addresses intersex concerns.

Out in Psychology: Lesbian, gay, bisexual, trans and queer perspectives. Edited by Victoria Clarke and Elizabeth Peel.
© 2007 John Wiley & Sons, Ltd.

into the world outside of academic psychology and through turning our attention back onto psychology and interrogating and challenging the homophobia and heteronormativity[4] embedded in the discipline (see Hodges & McManus, 2006). We have come a long way in this endeavour (Greene, 2000), but there is still a long way to go.

To give some examples of progress and of the challenges that remain, we draw on our own experiences of teaching on undergraduate (British Psychological Society [BPS] accredited[5]) psychology programmes. In these programmes, LGBTQ issues are virtually only mentioned when *we* mention them. Our students receive lectures on social psychology, developmental psychology, health psychology, and sport psychology, to name but a few areas of the curriculum. These are all areas of the discipline where LGBTQ concerns are highly relevant, and LGBTQ psychology is largely not taught in these areas, unless we are there to teach it. This is not intended as a criticism of our colleagues but rather to point out how easy it is, even for people who ascribe to broadly pro-gay principles, to ignore, exclude and marginalize LGBTQ concerns (Peel, 2001). When we do teach a 'token' lecture about, for instance, same-sex relationships on a core psychology course, we are sometimes faced with a half-empty classroom. We have experienced resistance, hostility and abuse from heterosexual students, and some of our LGB students have told us that they have felt extremely anxious and exposed before, during and after attending core lectures on LGBTQ issues. These students have also spoken to us about the hidden curriculum of heteronormativity (Epstein, O'Flynn & Telford, 2003) they are compelled to negotiate in the psychology classroom. For example, they frequently encounter situations where teaching staff or students assume that everyone in the classroom is heterosexual. This means that they constantly face dilemmas about whether to come out or to leave such assumptions unchallenged. We have also at times felt that some of our colleagues are bewildered by our sexuality and/or our research interests and we have on occasion been told that sexuality is not a workplace issue.

At the same time, we both teach elective courses on sexuality and many of our colleagues and the students who take these courses are supportive of these additions to the psychology programme. Every year we are delighted by students sharing their enthusiasm for these courses and the insights they have developed about heteronormativity or the limits of a binary gender system. We are also approached annually by students – both heterosexual and LGB – who are keen to undertake a research project on LGBT issues for their final year dissertation, and colleagues have been extremely supportive when we have been subject to homophobic abuse.

These positive and negative experiences suggest that it is vitally important to continue to seek transformation of the discipline of psychology. LGBTQ psychologists must push for inclusive curricula, teaching materials and practices; we must challenge others to revise heteronormative theories and research processes; and we must promote the field as a vital and necessary element of the discipline, rather than a, at best, marginal 'specialist' concern. Although, as we noted above, our presence is increasingly acknowledged, and occasionally welcomed, there is a danger of the field becoming a mere 'add on' to the discipline. LGBTQ psychologies offer crucial challenges to the discipline, ones that must be reckoned with and eventually actualized. Therefore, central to the realization of LGBTQ psychologies in this

---

[4] We use heteronormative to signal assumptions, norms and values based on traditional conceptions of heterosexuality.
[5] For the benefit of readers outside of the UK, most psychology programmes in the UK are accredited by the BPS, which means that students follow a core psychology curriculum for at least the first two years of their degree (and many students study only psychology). Some of the experiences we discuss are shared and some are not.

book is a dual focus on providing a variety of psychological perspectives on LGBTQ concerns and a variety of LGBTQ perspectives on the discipline of psychology.

ADDRESSING ABSENCES AND FORGING NEW DIRECTIONS

This is the second British-edited collection on lesbian and gay psychology. The first (Coyle & Kitzinger, 2002) was a groundbreaking celebration of the establishment of lesbian and gay psychology as a legitimate area of psychological research and practice in the UK. Five years on, this collection documents and showcases the development and diversification of the field, and in particular a move from lesbian and gay psychology to LGBTQ psychologies. This collection also has an international focus – with contributions from Australia, New Zealand, Canada and the USA, in addition to primarily the UK. We use the term 'psychologies' throughout this introductory chapter to capture the multiplicity of perspectives and approaches to LGBTQ research, theory and practice that constitute the text. As we discuss in more detail below, it is no longer possible to claim that lesbian and gay psychology is predominantly practised within positivist-empiricist and liberal-humanistic frameworks. As well as drawing on a diverse array of perspectives, the chapters address a diverse array of concerns, offering insights into topics ranging from how gay men with intellectual disabilities develop and maintain a gay identity (Christopher Bennett and Adrian Coyle) to how lesbian athletes and coaches cope with heteronormative sports climates (Vikki Krane and Kerrie Kauer) – both neglected topics in lesbian and gay psychology. Other chapters interrogate areas of psychological practice including the ways in which psychology textbooks (re)produce heteronormativity and, in particular, the invisibility of bisexuality (Meg Barker), and the ways in which LGB psychological discourses on 'ethnic minorities' serve to disappear the race and privilege of white lesbians, gay men and bisexuals (Damien Riggs). *Out in Psychology* seeks to acknowledge and begin to challenge absences in lesbian and gay psychology, and the discipline of psychology more broadly. These absences include the marginality of bisexuality in psychology, and the neglect of the lives and experiences of bisexual and lesbian women, gay men with disabilities, trans people, and heteronormativity/heterosexual privilege and whiteness/race privilege in lesbian and gay psychology.

The one theme that all the chapters speak to directly or indirectly is inclusivity. The contributors offer different answers to questions of inclusivity: some advocate giving specific and sole attention to the experiences of lesbians (Sara MacBride-Stewart, Faith Rostad and Bonita Long), gay men (Jeffery Adams, Timothy McCreanor and Virginia Braun), trans people (Clair Clifford and Jim Orford), and bisexual women (Maira Gurevich, Jo Bower, Cynthia Mathieson and Bramilee Dhayanandhan). Others champion an inclusive coalition of lesbian and gay (Victoria Clarke, Carol Burgoyne and Maree Burns), LGB (Sonja Ellis, Gareth Hagger-Johnson, Rosie Harding and Elizabeth Peel), or LGBTQ (Peter Hegarty, Riggs) psychologies. In the following chapter we argue that a move from lesbian and gay psychology to LGBTQ psychologies requires some reflection on the meaning and politics of inclusivity. We explore tensions within lesbian and gay, and between lesbian and gay, bisexual, trans and queer psychologies, movements and politics and suggest that in the immediate future LGBTQ psychologists should pursue both separatist and coalitional strategies.

We are delighted that *Out in Psychology* includes chapters specifically focused on bisexuality (Barker, Gurevich et al.), on trans (Clifford and Orford, Katherine Johnson,

Susan Speer), and on the possibilities of queer theory (Gurevich et al., Hegarty, MacBride-Stewart). These chapters stand alongside a number of others that engage more broadly with LGB, LGBT or LGBTQ concerns (Hagger-Johnson, Hegarty, Ellis, Jeremy Monsen and Sydney Bailey, Harding and Peel, Riggs). The chapters focused on trans exemplify different traditions in this area of research. Some social scientists have long been interested in transgender and transsexuality (and intersexuality) because they facilitate an examination of the social construction of sex, gender and sexuality (e.g. Garfinkel, 1967; Kessler & McKenna, 1978). Both Speer's and Johnson's chapters fit into this broad tradition of work and are examples of a critical psychology of trans as a social, political and historical phenomenon. Johnson adopts a social constructionist perspective to explore the historical development of 'transsexualism' as a diagnostic and identity category distinct from homosexuality and other iterations of trans, such as transvestism. Using an ethno-methodological/conversation analytic approach, Speer analyses an actual interaction between a psychiatrist and a male-to-female transsexual in a gender identity clinic. The focus of her analysis is on how the trans-woman's gender identity gets constructed and displayed in a segment of interaction. The third chapter (Clifford and Orford) represents a very different and neglected approach to the psychology of trans in that it focuses on the lived experiences of women and men who identify as trans. Clifford and Orford explore the processes through which people come to an identity as trans, and how social power (people's access to social, material and other types of resources that influence individual life chances) informs this process.

As we discuss in the next chapter, until recently, lesbian and gay psychology has resisted the seductive advances of queer theory. Three chapters in *Out in Psychology* specifically showcase the potential of queer theory for LGBTQ psychologies and demonstrate the ways in which the influence of queer theory is now increasingly felt in some areas of psychological research on sexuality and gender. Gurevich et al. provide an analysis of women's accounts of what it means to disclose bisexual identities informed by post-structuralist and queer theorizing. Hegarty's chapter centres on a queer informed critique of the ways in which social constructionism and discourse analysis are positioned as the self-evidently radical frontier of (British) LGBTQ psychology. He interrogates the heteronormative assumptions underpinning a prominent debate about conversation analysis, critical discourse analysis and ways of reading gender from conversations, and explores other formations of the social beyond the textual. MacBride-Stewart examines feminist social constructionist and queer theorizing about lesbian identity. She notes that whereas feminist social constructionist work retains 'lesbian' as an identity category (while acknowledging its constructed status), queer posits that identity categories are regulatory fictions that reproduce heteronormative concepts of sex and gender. She considers what each approach can learn from the other and what both can offer lesbian health research.

Many of the chapters in *Out in Psychology* emphasize the importance of new intersections with other disciplines (and between areas of psychology such as LGB psychology and personality and individual differences research [Hagger-Johnson]). As well as highlighting the possibility of productive links between queer theory and LGBTQ psychologies, contributors demonstrate the value of connecting critical psychology and critical legal studies (Harding and Peel), and psychology and sociology (Clarke et al.). Contributors also call for, and highlight, new approaches to clinical/professional practice in domains such as educational psychology and LGB youth (Monsen and Bailey), and clinical psychology and heterosexuality-identified intersex women (Lih-Mei Liao). There are many visions and versions of LGBTQ psychologies in circulation: *Out in Psychology* offers readers an unapologetically socially and politically engaged LGBTQ psychology, one that identifies productive links with LGBTQ scholarship outside the often narrow confines of psychology.

OUT ACROSS THE SPECTRUM

The chapters address a range of areas of the mainstream discipline, including: health psychology (MacBride-Stewart, Adams et al.); counselling and clinical psychology (Johnson, Liao, Speer); educational psychology (Monsen and Bailey); social psychology (Hagger-Johnson); sport psychology (Krane and Kauer); family psychology (Clarke et al., Ellis); qualitative and critical psychology (Barker, Bennett and Coyle, Clarke et al., Clifford and Orford, Ellis, Gurevich et al., Harding and Peel, Hegarty, Victoria Land and Celia Kitzinger, MacBride-Stewart, Riggs, Speer); and occupational psychology (Ellis, Harding and Peel, Rostad and Long). Until recently, there has been an emphasis on research, theory and practice in the areas of social, health, developmental, counselling and clinical psychology within lesbian and gay psychology texts. *Out in Psychology* incorporates fields and areas of research not typically considered under the banner of lesbian and gay psychology, and these include sport, qualitative and critical psychology.

There is an increasing acknowledgement of the important differences in approach between US, and UK and Australasian LGBTQ psychologies. Whereas in the USA there continues to be a strong engagement with positivist-empiricist frameworks (Clarke & Peel, 2007; Russell & Gergen, 2004), in the UK and Australasia qualitative and critical LGBTQ psychologies are gaining momentum (Coyle, 2000), as *Out in Psychology* demonstrates. Critical psychology is a developing area of research, theory and practice, and the label 'critical psychology' is regarded as an 'umbrella term' (Walkerdine, 2001) for a wide variety of radical perspectives on the discipline. As the editors of a key collection – Prilleltensky and Fox (1997) – outlined, critical psychologists 'believe that psychology's traditional practices and norms hinder social justice, to the detriment of individuals and communities in general and of oppressed groups in particular' (p. 3). Critical psychologists argue that – echoing the authors of early UK lesbian and gay psychology texts, such as Hart and Richardson (1981) and Kitzinger (1987) – psychology is not a neutral endeavour conducted by researchers and practitioners detached from the larger social and political context. Moreover, the theories and practices of mainstream psychology are value-laden and reinforce an unjust status quo. By contrast, the central themes of critical psychology are the explicit pursuit of social justice, the promotion of the well-being of communities and in particular of oppressed and marginalized groups, and changing the status quo of society and of psychology. It is crucial to note, however, that critical psychology is not all that LGBTQ psychologies are or should be. As Hegarty (Chapter 3) cautions, we should be suspicious of any approach to LGBTQ psychology that announces itself as radical. *Out in Psychology* aims to bring critical and qualitative psychology to the table, not to replace other approaches to this area of psychology, but to contribute to the diverse buffet that is LGBTQ psychologies.

The following 20 chapters span a broad range of theoretical/epistemological approaches: from positivist or essentialist perspectives (e.g. Hagger-Johnson) to experiential or contextual perspectives (e.g. Ellis, Rostad and Long), to critical, constructionist and discursive perspectives (e.g. Land and Kitzinger). However, there is an emphasis on qualitative and critical approaches. The chapters that fall under this banner demonstrate a range of different approaches to qualitative and critical research, including: conversation analysis (Land and Kitzinger, Speer); thematic and thematic decomposition analysis (Clarke et al., Ellis, Gurevich et al.); phenomenological analysis (Bennett and Coyle, MacBride-Stewart); textual analysis (Barker, Riggs); and grounded theory (Clifford and Orford, Rostad and Long). Some authors also develop novel combinations of different qualitative and critical approaches (e.g. Gurevich et al., Ellis). The empirical chapters draw on a variety of data sources including more traditional sources such as interviews (Bennett and Coyle, Ellis, Gurevich et al., Clarke et al., Rostad and Long, Harding and Peel) and case notes (Liao, Monsen and Bailey), and more innovative sources (ones that are new to LGBTQ psychologies), such as email interviews (Clifford and Orford), psychological literature (Barker, Riggs) and 'naturalistic' data collected from lesbian and gay awareness training sessions (Harding and Peel), psychiatric assessment sessions (Speer) and telephone calls going in and out of lesbian households (Land and Kitzinger). The chapters also use a range of theoretical models including social power (Clifford and Orford), identity process theory (Bennett and Coyle), and social identity theory (Krane and Kauer). Together the chapters provide a range of empirical, theoretical and reflective insights into contemporary LGBTQ psychologies.

THEMES IN *OUT IN PSYCHOLOGY*

In this final section, we outline the themes, structure and organization of *Out in Psychology*. In addition to two introductory chapters, there are four thematic sections: (1) histories and commentaries, (2) lives and experiences, (3) work and leisure and (4) health and practice. Each section includes a commentary written by a leading scholar in the associated field of research. The chapters that constitute the first section 'histories and commentaries' provide a range of critical reflections on the historical and contemporary practices of psychology in general and LGBTQ psychologies in particular. Riggs interrogates discourses of race in LGB psychology, Barker probes the invisibility of bisexuality in psychology textbooks, Hagger-Johnson examines the intertwining histories of LGB psychology and personality and individual differences research, and Hegarty offers a queer informed critique of the increasingly common presentation of social constructionism and discourse analysis as representing the radical frontier of (British) LGBTQ psychology.

The chapters in 'lives and experiences' highlight the continuing importance of examining the everyday experiences, realities and perspectives of LGBTQ people. The chapters explore the lived experiences of specific groups of LGBTQ people – gay men with intellectual disabilities (Bennett and Coyle) and trans people (Clifford and Orford) – as well as specific aspects of our everyday existence. Land and Kitzinger provide a fine-grained analysis of telephone conversations between lesbians, gay men and their partners and family members, and show how these testify to the continuing importance of 'the closet' and visibility in the everyday interactions of lesbians and gay men. Clarke et al. enter the hotly contested terrain of same-sex relationship recognition and offer an empirical exploration of lesbian and gay couples' views on civil partnership and marriage. Until recently work in this area has been dominated by academic debates about legal recognition, Clarke et al.'s analysis provides an examination of the discourses informing accounts of legal recognition grounded in the personal and political experiences of lesbian and gay couples.

The chapters in 'work and leisure' continue the focus on the everyday experiences of LGBTQ people, but in relation to the specific domains of work and leisure. Ellis offers a holistic appraisal of contemporary issues in the lives of lesbians, gay men and bisexuals living in Britain – her analysis centres on the workplace, relationship recognition and the LGB community. She argues that greater inclusion of LGB people in mainstream society and culture has led to the loss of distinct and vibrant LGB community spaces. Ellis queries whether it is time to revive such spaces and debates about the goals of LGBT movements and communities. Harding and Peel examine heterosexism in the workplace and the strengths and weaknesses of a two-pronged strategy for tackling the marginalization that LGB people experience in their working lives. This strategy involves structural challenges (through anti-discrimination law) and individual challenges (through education and training). As noted above, their chapter provides an example of a productive intersection between critical psychology and critical legal studies aimed at the interrogation of LGB marginality. Rostad and Long continue the focus on the workplace with an analysis of the experiences of a group of high achieving lesbians. These women have attained significant levels of workplace success and their stories provide an insight into successful career development in heteronormative working environments. In addition, Krane and Kauer, as previously noted, examine the experiences of lesbians in sport.

The chapters in the final section, 'health and practice', shift the focus to the applied domain of LGBTQ psychologies. MacBride-Stewart explores lesbians' accounts of what it means to be a 'healthy lesbian', Adams et al. examine the public health implications of marketing alcohol directly to gay men, and Liao outlines a clinical psychological approach to the sexual concerns of heterosexually-identified intersex women. Monsen and Bailey, drawing on their experiences as practising educational psychologists, explore the practical implications of the dilemmas associated with developing an LGB identity in school. They develop recommendations for interventions at the level of the individual (with LGB pupils) and the institutional (working within and attempting to change the homophobic school environment), and highlight the importance of the latter. As noted above, both the chapter by Speer and the chapter by Johnson fall into the critical social science tradition of interrogating the historical, social and political meanings of trans and what trans reveals about the social construction of sex/gender.

The gaps and absences in *Out in Psychology* suggest some priorities for future research in LGBTQ psychologies. We are very pleased that *Out in Psychology* has an international focus; however, this is limited to a small number of countries located in the cultural west. There is much potential for international dialogue beyond these rather narrow confines. There needs to be a greater acknowledgement and examination of the diversity within LGBTQ communities, although *Out in Psychology* makes some considerable leaps forward in this respect, there is still much work to be done. We also hope that our examination of the dilemmas and tensions underlying the reconstitution of the field as LGBTQ psychologies in the following chapter prompts further consideration of who we include in and exclude from our research and why. This is an exciting time for the field and we are delighted that *Out in Psychology* forms part of the cutting edge of LGBTQ psychologies.

ACKNOWLEDGEMENTS

This book has been a long time in the making. We first mooted the possibility of editing a 'follow-up' collection to Coyle and Kitzinger (2002) when it was still in preparation in 2001. Six years later *Out in Psychology* has finally come to fruition. This book would never have happened without the assistance and support of the following (in no particular order): our editors at Wiley; Bramble, Diesel and Amber; noodle-based dishes; Celia Kitzinger; Julia Lawton; Sue Wilkinson; John Fenaughty; Peter Hegarty; Meg Barker; Adrian Coyle; Damien Riggs; Sonja Ellis; members of the BPS Lesbian & Gay Psychology Section; our colleagues at Aston University and the University of the West of England; and those lovely, lovely people who straddle the friend/colleague divide and provide us with much needed support, encouragement and the occasional smile (you know who you are!).

Thanks to all the contributors for graciously (and in some cases patiently) dealing with our, at times, no doubt rather 'enthusiastic' editorial feedback. Thanks to the commentary writers for agreeing to come aboard the good ship *Out in Psychology* just before it set sail. Rosie Harding deserves an extra special thank you for supplying the noodle-based dishes, for walking the dog (and performing a myriad of other mundane tasks so that we could keep sitting at our computers), and for never being afraid to ask 'how's it going?'.

With regard to this and the following chapter, thanks to Sonja Ellis and Rosie Harding for their helpful comments on earlier versions, thanks also to Damien Riggs, Peter Hegarty and Meg Barker for advice and suggestions on various aspects of Chapter 2.

REFERENCES

Clarke, V. & Peel, E. (2007). LGBT psychosocial theory and practice in the UK: A review of key contributions and current developments. *Journal of Gay & Lesbian Psychotherapy*, **11**(1/2).

Coyle, A. (2000). Qualitative research and lesbian and gay psychology in Britain. *Lesbian & Gay Psychology Section Newsletter*, **4**, 2–5.

Coyle, A. & Kitzinger, C. (Eds) (2002). *Lesbian and Gay Psychology: New perspectives*. Oxford: BPS Blackwell.

Dworkin, S. H. (2002). Guess who's coming to dinner? The future of LGB psychology. Presidential Address to Division 44, American Psychological Association Convention, Chicago, Illinois, August. Available from http://www.apadivision44.org/events/address_dworkin.doc

Epstein, D., O'Flynn, S. & Telford, D. (2003). *Silenced Sexualities in Schools and Universities*. Stoke-on-Trent: Trentham Books.

Garfinkel, H. (1967). *Studies in Ethnomethodology*. Englewood Cliffs, NJ: Prentice-Hall.

Greene, B. (2000). Beyond heterosexism and across the cultural divide: Developing an inclusive lesbian, gay, and bisexual psychology: A look to the future. In B. Greene & G. L. Croom (Eds), *Education, Research and Practice in Lesbian, Gay, Bisexual, and Transgendered Psychology: A resource manual* (pp. 1–45). Thousand Oaks, CA: Sage.

Hart, J. & Richardson, D. (Eds) (1981). *The Theory and Practice of Homosexuality*. London: Routledge & Kegan Paul.

Hodges, I. & McManus, J. (2006). Psychology at the crossroads. *The Psychologist*, **19**(1), 24–26.

Kessler, S. J. & McKenna, W. (1978). *Gender: An ethnomethodological approach*. New York, NY: John Wiley & Sons.

Kitzinger, C. (1987). *The Social Construction of Lesbianism*. London: Sage.

Peel, E. (2001). Mundane heterosexism: Understanding incidents of the everyday. *Women's Studies International Forum*, **24**(5), 541–554.

Prilleltensky, I. & Fox, D. (1997). Introducing critical psychology: Values, assumptions, and the status quo. In D. Fox & I. Prilleltensky (Eds), *Critical Psychology: An introduction* (pp. 3–20). London: Sage.

Queer Nation (1990). *The Queer Nation Manifesto*. Available from: http://www.sterneck.net/cybertribe/gender/queer-nation-manifesto/index.php

Russell, G. & Gergen, K. J. (2004). The social construction of lesbianism: Resistance and reconstruction. *Feminism & Psychology*, **14**(4), 511–514.

Walkerdine, V. (2001). Editorial. *International Journal of Critical Psychology*. Retrieved 3 September 2002 from http://www.l-w-bks.co.uk/journals/archive/ctri-psych/Crit-psych1_Editorial.htlm

Wittman, C. (1997/1969–70). A gay manifesto. In M. Blasius & S. Phelan (Eds), *We are Everywhere: A historical sourcebook of gay and lesbian politics* (pp. 380–88). New York, NY: Routledge.

CHAPTER 2

From Lesbian and Gay Psychology to LGBTQ Psychologies: A Journey into the Unknown (or Unknowable)?

Victoria Clarke
University of the West of England, UK
and
Elizabeth Peel
Aston University, UK

TOWARDS LGBTQ PSYCHOLOGIES?

Our argument in this chapter is that a move from lesbian and gay psychology to LGBTQ psychologies requires some reflection on the meaning and politics of inclusivity and on lesbians, gay men, bisexual, trans and queer (and pro-LGBTQ heterosexual) people being part of the same field, as its 'subjects' and/or as its researchers and practitioners. For many LGBTQ psychologists, the tensions between and among lesbian, gay, bisexual, trans and queer communities have personal and political as well as professional dimensions. Although there is no requirement for LGBTQ psychologists to be LGBTQ-identified (as Hegarty [2004] pondered 'how would we check?'), there is an implicit acknowledgement that: 'most people studying human sexuality tend . . . to be "non-straight" themselves' (Bell et al., 2002, p. 54). As will become clear from our discussion of these tensions, emotions often run high because of the personal issues at stake. Weiss's (2003) work on biphobia and transphobia (see below) provides a useful framework for exploring the divisions between the different groups under the LGBTQ umbrella. She argues that individualizing and psychologizing explanations of tensions between members of LGBTQ communities are largely fruitless. Although it is important to air and hear personal concerns, a respectful appreciation of the broader historical, cultural, social and political

Out in Psychology: Lesbian, gay, bisexual, trans and queer perspectives. Edited by Victoria Clarke and Elizabeth Peel.
© 2007 John Wiley & Sons, Ltd.

contexts and processes that give rise to particular fractures is vital for productive debate.

Our intention in this chapter is not to argue for or against inclusivity, but to consider what it might mean for people with conflicting experiences, perspectives and agendas to be part of the same field. Our argument is that simply adding 'BTQ' to 'LG' is not enough, we must consider what it means to reconstitute the field as 'LGBTQ psychologies' and to reflect on the past in order to secure a workable approach to inclusivity for the future. There is a thundering silence around this issue, an apparent unwillingness to explore the strains and contradictions that exist between LGBTQ lives, politics and psychologies. We hope to initiate the discussion in this chapter by reviewing reflections on lesbians and gay men working together, tensions between lesbian and gay, and bisexual and trans communities, and between lesbian and gay, and queer politics. These reflections relate to tensions in lesbian and gay psychology in particular and academia in general, as well as wider LGBTQ movements and communities, and are drawn from psychology, sociology, history, feminist theory and politics and interdisciplinary LGBT studies. In addition to exploring the inclusion of BTQ people under the rainbow umbrella of lesbian and gay psychology, we explore the inclusion of other forms of social marginalization. As we outline further below, sexuality is frequently assumed to be the primary, and even sole, basis of oppression for non-heterosexuals, and the intersections between sexuality and other forms of marginalization and privilege are too often overlooked. Our review of the limited literature that directly engages with these issues suggests that these two strands of inclusivity are intertwined. Opening the door of lesbian and gay psychology to BTQ (and heterosexual [Dworkin, 2002]) psychologies compels us to consider other forms of diversity (Humphrey, 1999). Likewise engaging with issues of gender, race, culture, class and ability creates an onus to consider seriously the concerns of bisexual and trans people, alongside queer challenges to fixed identities.

The rest of this chapter is organized as follows. First, we consider the privileging of younger, white, middle-class, able-bodied, urban-dwelling gay male experience in lesbian and gay psychology and argue for the importance of 'working through the hyphens' that separate and connect sexuality, gender, race, culture, class, age and ability. Then we consider the importance of getting past 'divide and conquer' politics (Hegarty, 2004) in LGBTQ psychologies. To do so, we explore, in turn, the historical and contemporary tensions and divisions within lesbian and gay, and between lesbian and gay and bisexual, lesbian and gay and trans, and lesbian and gay and queer politics, communities and psychologies.

THE MEANINGS AND POLITICS OF INCLUSIVITY

Working Through the Hyphens?

Lesbian and gay psychology has predominantly focused on the lives and experiences of younger, white, middle-class, able-bodied, urban dwelling gay men and, to a lesser extent, lesbians (Greene, 2000).[1] The field has failed to reflect aspects of diversity among LGBTQ

---

[1] Fox (1995) similarly noted that research on bisexuality has focused on young, white, middle-class women and men and called for more research on older, working-class, non-white bisexuals and the ways in which gender, age, ethnicity and social class affect the experience of bisexuality.

people – such as gender, race, culture, class, age, ability – and the complex interaction of multiple or intersectional[2] oppressions. There has been a concomitant failure to acknowledge the ways in which some LGBTQ people embody social privilege in relation to, for example, race and sexuality (Riggs & Choi, 2006). In short, contemporary lesbian and gay psychology has not acknowledged or examined, in a synthesized way, the heterogeneity of LGBTQ experiences and as such it leaves us with an incomplete picture of LGBTQ lives (Greene, 1998; 2000). An exclusive focus on heterosexism 'as the primary locus of oppression for all lesbians and gay men presumes that it is experienced in the same way for all group members and that it has the same meaning and consequences for them' (Greene, 2000, p. 2). We must consider how LGBTQ people's positioning in relation to hierarchies of race, culture, gender, class, age, and ability intersects with and transforms their experiences of heterosexism. LGBTQ psychologists need to ask questions about what it means to be LGBTQ in a wide range of cultural, political and social contexts (Greene, 2000). Alongside heterosexism, classism, racism, sexism and other forms of oppression are embedded in mainstream psychological practices and LGBTQ psychologies must be at the forefront of challenges to these practices.

When aspects of diversity such as race or class are addressed in lesbian and gay psychological research, usually the fact that very few participants were members of marginalized groups is mentioned but the implications of this information does not merit any discussion (Gabb, 2004; Greene, 2000). As Greene (1998) pointed out, the inadequacies of samples are rarely highlighted in the titles of papers or in discussions about the limitations of findings (e.g. papers entitled 'same-sex couples' views on . . .' could more often be accurately titled 'white, middle-class, able-bodied lesbian and gay couples' views on . . .'). There is a tendency to report research as if it is automatically relevant to groups not included in the sample, and to all lesbians and gay men in the same way. Such practices contribute to the invisibility of marginalized groups and allow lesbian and gay psychologists to avoid examining the operation of forms of oppression and privilege other than heterosexism. The findings of research on privileged groups of lesbians and gay men cannot necessarily translate to members of marginalized groups, or in the same way to all members of privileged groups. We cannot assume that members of, for instance, particular 'racial' groups experience their racial identity in the same way (Greene, 1998; see also Riggs, Chapter 4).

Non-white, disabled and working-class LGBTQ people and white, 'abled' and middle-class LBTQ women are often doubly marginalized in psychology. For instance, psychological research on race typically ignores LGBTQ issues, and lesbian and gay psychology, as noted above, ignores issues of race and focuses on the experiences of white gay men. It is important to make connections between different experiences of oppression and privilege, while retaining a sense of distinct experience (as individual members of particular groups) (Corbett, 1994). To this end, a three-pronged approach to inclusivity within LGBTQ psychologies seems appropriate: in order to redress the marginality of some aspects of LGBTQ experience, these require specific attention. For instance, just as 'lesbian experience' needs separate consideration, so do the experiences of particular

---

[2] As Phoenix (2006) notes, the term 'intersectional' was coined by Crenshaw (1989) to conceptualize for the legal field how categories of difference intersect in institutional arrangements, social practices and cultural discourses. This concept provides a way of working through the hyphens of, and analysing the complex and contradictory processes of, simultaneous oppressions in local contexts.

groups of lesbians (or particular groups of GBTQ people). At the same time, the diversity within LGBTQ communities must be consistently acknowledged. We must learn from the phenomenon of the 'token lesbian chapter' (Kitzinger, 1996), and not solely relegate the experiences of the more marginalized members of the LGBTQ community to 'special' spaces. Phoenix (2006) also urges us to avoid dealing with the simultaneity of oppression in tokenistic and ritualistic ways. Finally, as Riggs and Choi (2006) argue, we need to pay heed to the ways in which norms around race and sexuality (and, we add, other dimensions of experience such as gender and class) serve to privilege particular groups of people. This necessitates an interrogation of the intertwined positions of heterosexuality, whiteness and masculinity (among other privileged identity categories); these should not be preserved as 'silent, natural positions' (Phoenix, 2006, p. 5). It is important not to lose sight of the fact that being positioned in relation to race, culture, gender, class, age and ability is relevant to all members of LGBTQ communities.

Black lesbian feminist theorist Barbara Smith (Diehl & Smith, 2000) has been critical of the economically privileged, white gay movement for its narrow focus on 'gay rights', that is, 'those things that concern wealthy white gay men'. She argues that the mainstream gay movement is not concerned with racism, poverty, and violence against women (among many other issues) and urges a move away from single issue, reformist and assimilationist politics to a more inclusive and radical movement for social and economic justice. Smith's work highlights the need to forge links with black feminist theory (see Phoenix, 2006), critical race and whiteness studies (see Riggs, Chapter 4) and queer theory (see Dworkin, 2002, Hegarty, Chapter 3) in order to effectively interrogate normative positionings.

Intersections of Sexuality and Social Class

We now consider the example of social class in order to provide a brief but focused examination of the ways in which lesbian and gay psychology (and related disciplines, such as sociology) fails to acknowledge the ways in which non-heterosexual identities intersect with other axes of social marginality and privilege.

Questions regarding social class are rarely posed in lesbian and gay psychology, which perhaps reflects the invisibility of working-class people in LGBTQ communities (Hennessy, 2000). Although many studies suggest that lesbian and, particularly, gay respondents have higher than average educational and income levels, this may be a reflection of our chosen recruitment strategies rather than a real reflection of the lesbian and gay community (Greene, 2000). Research recruitment often takes place in universities, large urban areas and the 'gay scene'. Income may determine access to higher education and to the gay scene (and whether we can be a 'gay consumer'), and thus the likelihood of participating in lesbian and gay psychological research. Concerns about job/income security also might lead some lesbians and gay men to remain closeted and to be unwilling to participate in research (see Carrington, 1999). In addition, the high levels of 'snowball sampling' (or 'friendship pyramiding') in lesbian and gay research may lead to the exclusion of working-class lesbians and gay men. As Dunne (1997) noted, snowball samples tend to reflect the social positioning (and privilege) of researchers. The invisibility of working-class lesbians and gay men 'shapes and perhaps even distorts what we presume to know about lesbians and gay men and socio-economic class issues among this group' (Greene, 2000, p. 20). Gabb (2004) argues that it is time for sexuality researchers to 'reconsider *how* and *whom* we research' (p. 176, emphasis in original). She calls for researchers to acknowledge the limitations of commonplace methodologies, particularly the tendency for such methodologies to exclude certain members of lesbian and gay communities.

Interestingly, research that does take account of class has produced very different findings from that which does not. For example, lesbian and gay family research on the division of domestic labour and childcare that takes account of social class and other potential sources of power imbalances has produced very different findings from research that emphasizes the ways in which lesbian and gay families embody gender-sameness and equality. Studies that are based on data collected from white, middle-class couples (and that emphasize the couples' gender-sameness) typically find couples to divide domestic labour equally (e.g. Kurdek, 1993), studies based on more diverse samples and/or that take account of differences between couples typically find less evidence of equality (e.g. Carrington, 1999; Gabb, 2004).

There is an increasing interest in redressing the neglect of class and other aspects of diversity in LGBTQ communities (Kitzinger & Coyle, 2002). Critical challenges are necessary to defend against lesbian and gay psychology privileging some voices and neglecting others. Lesbian and gay psychologists should learn from experiences of marginalization in relation to the discipline of psychology – it is problematic to criticise the mainstream for ignoring lesbian and gay experiences and then proceed to ignore some LGBTQ voices (Kitzinger & Coyle, 2002). It is sometimes suggested that the field should be labelled 'psychology of sexuality' (Kitzinger & Coyle, 2002) or 'queer psychology' (Petford, 2003). Such names imply either a narrow focus on sexual practices that ignores the broader range of psychosocial issues that constitute the field or a political homogeneity that belies the diversity within LGBTQ communities (Kitzinger & Coyle, 2002; cf. Hegarty, Chapter 3). We agree with Kitzinger and Coyle that such a narrow focus would make it harder to forge links with analyses of gender, race and class.

Some commentators caution that conducting inclusive research is not easy and it requires active engagement on the part of researchers. Researchers must reflect on their own positioning and how this might shape or limit their research, use their privilege constructively, and be accountable to social groups (Greene, 2000; Phoenix, 2006; Riggs, 2006). Phoenix (2006, p. 2) argues that 'dialoguing within differences' requires us to confront 'uncomfortable conversations and contradictions'.

To conclude this section, lesbian and gay (and LGBTQ) psychological research is impoverished by a sole focus on, and homogenous understanding of, sexuality as *the* axis of oppression for lesbians and gay men. Research based on the experiences of privileged groups of white, middle-class, able-bodied, younger, urban dwelling gay men and lesbians give us only a limited picture of lesbian and gay lives. Furthermore, even within these select groups, there are varied experiences of privilege and marginalization, the implications of which are rarely considered. Throughout the history of lesbian and gay psychology, it seems that we have often sought to tell particular, publicly acceptable stories about lesbian and gay lives and experiences at the expense of the most marginalized members of LGBTQ communities. We need to reflect on the ways in which lesbian and gay psychology has failed to be inclusive of diversity and interrogate privilege, and to actively address those failures.

Getting Past Divide and Conquer?

Peter Hegarty (2004), writing as chair of the British Psychological Society (BPS) Lesbian & Gay Psychology Section, argued for the importance of getting past 'divide and conquer' politics. However, he acknowledged that any attempt to define the remit of lesbian and gay psychology highlights the tensions and divisions that exist within and between LGBTQ communities. This area of psychology 'does not yet have a coherent theory of how to think about the relationship between bisexual and transgender psychologies and lesbian and gay psychologies' (Hegarty, 2004, p. 5). We explore these dilemmas in this section of the chapter: which histories, meanings and exclusions are associated with defining the domain of this area of psychology as lesbian and gay, LGB, LGBT or LGBTQ? What is the relationship between these different psychologies and the politics, communities and peoples to which they relate? As we noted above, a more inclusive LGBTQ psychology needs to appreciate the ways in which experiences of privilege and oppression are filtered through many 'different lenses and realities' (Greene, 2000, p. 38). We must simultaneously avoid universalizing LGBTQ experience and not retreat from:

> the difficult tensions that disrupt the false sense of harmony and security that often exists between members of disadvantaged groups. The result is a failure to give voice to the ways that lesbians and gay men may engage in oppressive behaviour toward other lesbians, gay men, bisexual men and women, and transsexual and transgendered men and women both personally and institutionally. (Greene, 2000, p. 38)

Weiss (2003) discusses the 'myth' of GLBT community togetherness: 'the "GLBT community" appears monolithic. The quadratic formula of "GLBT", adding together several second-order elements to create a single, defined community, suggests communal interests' (p. 28). The reality is, she argues, far more complex. The very creation of the GLBT or LGBT acronym suggests that each category is 'clearly defined, separate and mutually exclusive' (p. 29), rather than one and the same. The conflicts that 'seethe beneath the surface' (p. 29) of the LGBT community call into the question the very idea of such a community. As Alexander and Yescavage (2003) note in relation to the US context:

> Now more than ever we need to dialogue about our continued strategy for liberation. Do we dive into the assimilationist, erroneous 'melting pot' of America? Or, do we strive to be tossed into the 'salad' of a truly pluralistic society, where each group (or individual) adds its own unique and recognisable flavours? (p. 21)

To stretch the metaphor further, the question is will this salad be too challenging to prepare or taste unpalatable? Some lesbian and gay psychologists have certainly warned against drawing the boundaries of the field too narrowly. Kitzinger and Coyle (2002), for instance, noted that, despite the name, 'lesbian and gay psychology', this area of psychology has always, if minimally, included research on bisexual and transsexual/transgender (and heterosexual) issues. Moreover, many relevant organizations have expanded or chosen their names to explicitly include bisexuality and transgender in their remit. For instance, Division 44 of the American Psychological Association (APA) – Society for the Psychological Study of Lesbian, Gay and Bisexual Issues – originally included only 'lesbian and gay' in its title. The equivalent grouping within the Canadian Psychological Association (CPA) has had the title 'Sexual Orientation and Gender Identity Issues' since its inception in 2002. By contrast the parallel section within the BPS includes only 'lesbian and gay', as does the interest group within the Australian Psychological Society (APS),[3] however a more inclusive title has been called for in both countries.[4] We now consider the friction that exists between different groups under the LGBTQ umbrella in more detail, starting with the relationship between lesbian psychology and gay psychology, and more broadly between lesbian politics and communities and gay politics and communities.

Lesbian Psychology and Gay Psychology: Never the Twain Shall Meet?

The Lesbian/Gay Movement

As we noted above, lesbian and gay psychology privileges the experiences of (younger, white, middle-class, able-bodied, urban-dwelling) gay men, and lesbians are often only a footnote to research on gay men (Edwards, 1994). If we examine the history of the broader western lesbian/gay movement, it doesn't take long to uncover evidence of conflicts between lesbians and gay men (Blasius & Phelan, 1997). This history (which can be told in any number of ways) provides different answers to questions such as: are lesbians and gay men a natural community? Should lesbians ally with heterosexual women or with gay men? Are lesbians' and gay men's gender differences greater than their shared rejection of heterosexuality? Are lesbians' experiences of oppression more similar to or different from those of gay men?

The modern post-Stonewall lesbian/gay movement incorporates moments of deliberate and default separatism and moments of alliance. Gay liberation politics, for instance, represented a brief moment of lesbian and gay unity, but many lesbians were rapidly disillusioned by the behaviour of their gay 'brothers' (Blasius & Phelan, 1997). Ward (2000) argued that gay men are often treated as exemplars of reconstructed men; however, for many lesbians, gay men proved to be just as sexist as were heterosexual men. As Blasius and Phelan (1997) outlined, lesbian feminism grew out of lesbians' twin dissatisfaction with gay liberation and feminism: in many feminist groups, lesbians were asked to remain in the closet for the 'greater good' of women. Throughout the 1970s, lesbian feminism offered women a vision of the lesbian nation, a woman-centred, separatist utopia, 'a sort of haven in a heartless (male/heterosexual) world' (Stein, 1998/1992, p. 553). Lesbian feminists were critical of the sexual practices of gay men and of the politics of sexual freedom (for many lesbians and gay men, the division between the lesbian feminist vision of a safer world for women and the gay male vision of sexual liberation for men remains today). Lesbian feminists argued that gay male culture was hostile to women. Some gay men countered with the argument that feminists seek to eliminate all that makes gay men *gay* and fail to recognize that gay men are also oppressed by hegemonic masculinity and heterosexuality (Preston, 1997/1981). Edwards (1994) argued that feminist critiques of gay male culture presented it as unvaried, and did not allow for the possibility of gay men rebelling against this culture or being influenced by lesbians

---

[3] The terms of reference for the APS group mention bisexual and 'gender issues related to sexual orientation' as do the web pages of the BPS section.

[4] It was a requirement of the BPS that the proposers of the lesbian and gay psychology section were able to demonstrate the existence of relevant bodies of work, particularly UK-based work. Until the last few years, there has been little in the way of bisexual or transgender psychology, so the name of the section was limited to 'lesbian and gay psychology' (Kitzinger & Coyle, 2002).

and feminism (see Jensen, 2004, for an account of why gay men should engage with radical feminism).

Just as the promise of gay liberation was short-lived, so was that of the lesbian nation. In the 1980s challenges from black and working-class lesbians and the so-called lesbian 'sex-wars' led some lesbians to re-open their alliances with gay men. These women found more support and community among gay men than among lesbian feminists (there was a developing gap between lesbian feminists and those lesbians [and gay men] who engaged in and defended certain practices such as sadomasochism (S/M) and pornography, Blasius & Phelan, 1997). The AIDS epidemic and the tide of homophobia it unleashed, especially from the increasingly vocal and powerful new right, also reshaped the terrain of lesbian and gay politics: for many lesbians it served to emphasize their shared rejection of heterosexuality with gay men. Moreover, as Stein (1998/1992, p. 560; see also Rudy, 2001) noted, 'as the withered body of the person with AIDS replaced the once-pervasive image of the all-powerful male oppressor, the sense of male threat which underlay lesbian-feminist politics diminished further'. Many lesbians joined predominantly gay organizations and worked with gay men to increase lesbian and gay visibility and challenge the heterosexual assumption. The lesbian and gay coalitions that began with AIDS activism and extended beyond this, although far from unified, began to experience increased political power. It is this context, in the late 1990s, which gave rise to many of the lesbian and gay organizations that exist today – including the groups within the APA, BPS, APS and CPA – and the cogency of a lesbian and gay standpoint. The 'gender chasm' (Humphrey, 2000) has been covered over for the sake of political cohesion.

One of these organizations is the National Lesbian and Gay Committee (NLGC) in the UK's public sector trade union, UNISON (Humphrey, 2000). As Humphrey (2000) outlines, in the NLGC lesbians and gay men work together (because they are assumed to share sufficient commonality to render this a meaningful strategy), but the coalition sometimes nurtures tensions left over from the separatist politics of the 1970s. Gender differences between lesbians and gay men are positively acknowledged to prevent gender inequality, while, at the same time, some gay men negatively attempt to subvert lesbians' pursuit of separate spaces (to redress the gender divide) or themselves pursue separatism by default because of their greater social and economic resources.

Humphrey maintains that some gay men within the NLGC have learnt to see themselves differently through a feminist lens. At the same time, she argues, there needs to be greater acknowledgement that gay men are both victim and perpetrator in the matrix of sexism and heterosexism; they have a unique double-consciousness that a pure feminist lens cannot make sense of. There also needs to be an acknowledgement that lesbians can be oppressive towards other lesbians and towards gay men. Humphrey argues that for lesbian and gay coalitions like the NLGC to work, lesbians' and gay men's political common interests have to be viewed as more important than their cultural and gender differences.

Lesbian/Gay Psychology

Similar divisions and deliberate and default separatism are evident within lesbian and gay psychology. In her groundbreaking text, *The Social Construction of Lesbianism*, Celia Kitzinger (1987) was critical of the male bias of the then emerging field of 'affirmative gay psychology'. She explained that she chose to focus exclusively on lesbian identities because of important differences between lesbians and gay men. She saw few signs of reciprocity between lesbian and gay male communities and argued that many lesbians had left lesbian and gay organizations because of gay men's sexism and liberal conformism.

Since the publication of *The Social Construction of Lesbianism* there has been little discussion or even acknowledgement of tensions and gender differences between lesbians and gay men, and of the emphasis on gay male experience within lesbian and gay psychology. There have been some attempts by lesbian psychologists to establish a separate psychology of lesbianism (see Rothblum's, 1992, call both for separate organizations to promote lesbian research and for the integration of lesbian research under the banner of feminist *and* lesbian and gay organizations). Most notably there were two unsuccessful attempts by a small group of British lesbian psychologists to establish a formal Psychology of Lesbianism Section within the BPS in the late 1980s and early 1990s (Comely, Perkins & Wilkinson, 1992). Some of these women later joined forces with gay psychologists to campaign (successfully) for a Lesbian and Gay Psychology Section. The book *Lesbian Psychologies* (Boston Lesbian Psychologies Collective, 1987) grew out of the authors' frustrations with the limited opportunities for lesbians in psychology to discuss their work and a feminist analysis of lesbian experience. However, the push for such opportunities appears not to have extended beyond the publication of this book.

Some lesbian and gay psychologists continue to call for separate research on lesbians (and on gay men). For instance, Rothblum (2004), in a commentary on *The Social Construction of Lesbianism*, argues for the importance of research about lesbians by lesbian researchers. Rothblum is critical of research ostensibly on lesbians that includes women who identify as non-heterosexual or bisexual:

> We must continue to ask ourselves what it means to be a lesbian, and not dilute our research by combining lesbians with the experiences of individuals with other sexual orientations, behaviors, and gender identities . . . we need to publicise the voices of lesbians themselves, to keep a perspective on the unique and changing lives of women in our lesbian communities. (p. 505)

Wilkinson (2002) has also called for a separate lesbian health psychology (see MacBride-Stewart, Chapter 20). She argues that lesbian health is ignored in the mainstream health literature (when women's health is studied, there is little attention paid to diversity among women, the focus is on the most privileged [heterosexual] women) and lesbian health is subsumed under 'lesbian and gay' health research. This literature predominantly focuses on (gay men's) sexual health, which affects few lesbians directly. She calls for a separate focus on lesbian and gay health issues: 'there is a need to disaggregate lesbian and gay health' (p. 129) and to diversify the study of women's health in order to acknowledge and examine the concerns of a variety of lesbians.

Taking Gender Seriously

Kitzinger and Coyle (2002, p. 4) argue for greater alliances between lesbian and gay psychology and the psychology of gender, and caution against drawing the boundaries of the field around sexuality: 'lesbian and gay issues have always been deeply implicated with notions of gender (as in the stereotype of "mannish" lesbian women and "effeminate" gay men)'. Taking gender seriously also makes it easier to build connections between lesbian and gay psychology and transgender psychology.

Research on gender in related disciplines, such as sociology, provides productive insights into how an analysis of gender might proceed within LGBTQ psychology. Oerton's (1998) sociological research on lesbian families suggests that acknowledging gender in lesbian and gay psychology need not translate into a sole focus on gender differences between lesbians and gay men (indeed, gender is often assumed only to operate in contexts of gender difference).[5] It is also important to examine lesbian and gay men as gendered beings: we emphasize how lesbians and gay men negotiate living in a heterosexist world, and neglect how they live as women and men in a gendered world (Ward, 2000). In lesbian and gay family research, lesbian and gay households are typically assumed to be 'empty' of gender processes and practices. Gender is not thought to have any role in, for instance, the division of domestic labour in lesbian households. There is also little consideration of the possibility that partners in same-sex couples might identify their gender in different ways or that other elements of privilege or marginalization might shape relationship or family dynamics. The absence of men supposedly strips lesbian households of gendering processes, so housework becomes egalitarian by virtue of being done on the basis of skills or preferences. Oerton argues that gender still exists in contexts of supposed gender equality/sameness – lesbians are women – and gender is central to the organization of work in lesbian households. Lesbians might not be 'housewives', but lesbians still do housework labour, which is gendered labour: 'no woman escapes the processes and practices which constitute women (even lesbians) as having a *gendered* relationship to family and household work' (p. 79).

With regard to the tensions between lesbian psychology and gay psychology and between lesbians and gay men, it seems important to acknowledge and examine the social and historical processes that have given rise to these tensions. Moving toward a more intersectional approach to LGBTQ psychologies requires us to pay attention to the gender divide between lesbians and gay men, and the ways in which (individual) lesbians and gay men (and BTQ people) are differently (and similarly) positioned in relation to gender and heteronormativity. There is also a need to acknowledge the different ways in which lesbians' and gay men's oppression functions: for gay men overt visibility often leads to oppression, for lesbians oppression often hinges on invisibility (Edwards, 1994). Both arguments for separating lesbian psychology and gay psychology (to acknowledge lesbians' and gay men's different positioning in relation to gender and redress lesbians' marginality under the banner of lesbian and gay psychology) and for including lesbians and gay men in a rainbow coalition (that acknowledges similarities and differences) are compelling. It seems that the best way forward for LGBTQ psychologies in the foreseeable future is to use either or both strategies where appropriate, and to do so in a conscious and reflective manner in order to avoid the default separatism and privileging of gay male experience that defines lesbian and gay psychology.

We now consider the tensions and divisions between lesbian and gay, and bisexual psychology, and between lesbian and gay, and bisexual politics and communities.

---

[5] This is one of many potential approaches to analysing gender in LGBTQ psychologies: see, for instance, Jalas (2004) for an alternative queer account of how gender norms shape lesbian experience.

Lesbian and Gay Psychology and Bisexual Psychology: Bye, bye binary?

Bisexuality and Psychology

Bisexuality has typically occupied a marginal (or even invisible) position in lesbian and gay psychology (Coyle, 2003; Fox, 1995; Petford, 2003). The name of the BPS Lesbian & Gay Psychology Section (and the APS Gay and Lesbian Issues and Psychology [GLIP] interest group) seems to embody and institutionalize this state of affairs. In most edited collections on lesbian and gay and LGB psychology bisexuality is overlooked. For instance, none of the chapters in Coyle and Kitzinger (2002) specifically address bisexual concerns, and there are only six references to bisexuality listed in the index (ironically, three of which are to a brief comment on the marginalization of bisexuality, and the other three to passing mentions of bisexuality). In many other edited collections, although some chapter titles might include bisexuality (and there might be a 'token bisexual chapter') there is little direct or specific consideration of bisexual concerns and of the similarities and differences in lesbian, gay and bisexual experiences in the text. This could be dubbed 'empty inclusivity' (Clarke & Rúdólfsdóttir, 2005) or inclusivity in name only (Barker & Yockney, 2004; Petford, 2003). Barker and Yockney (2004) note that it is important for organizations to change their name to include bisexuals, but, even though this signals a positive commitment, this is the least challenging part of the process. Bisexuals must be included in word *and* in deed.

A number of commentators have reflected on why bisexuality occupies a position of neglect in this area of psychology and in the wider discipline. Petford (2003) maintains that the marginalization of bisexuality in psychology reflects the broader invisibility of bisexuality in society. She argues that bisexuality does not exist as an identity in the present, it either belongs to the past (a pre-adult Freudian 'polymorphous' sexuality, a transitory stage on route to a fully realized and mature monosexuality) or the future (a utopian sexuality that exists beyond gender and sexuality oppression). Although the argument goes that if the feminist and lesbian and gay movements succeeded, the gay/straight binary would disappear, as Orlando (1997/1991) noted, 'belief in bisexuality as utopian potential has not always coincided . . . with support for and acceptance of bisexuals' (p. 803). Fox (1995) contended that the dominance of a dichotomous model of sexual orientation has constrained the development of research on bisexuality. Cass's (1979) classic stage model of homosexual identity development provides a clear example of the peripheral position of bisexuality in the binary framework of lesbian and gay psychology. This model presented bisexuality as an example of 'identity foreclosure' – something that delays or prevents the development of a positive homosexual identity (Fox, 1995; see also Rivers, 1997). Bisexuality is merely a transitional stage – a passing phase – on the path to a permanent homosexual identity. Because many lesbians and gay men experience bisexuality as a stage, this fuels the belief that real bisexuality doesn't exist (Orlando, 1997/1991).

Bisexuality and the Lesbian and Gay Movement

Some commentators conceptualize bisexual oppression in terms of a 'double-bind' (Barker & Yockney, 2004): bisexuals experience both hostility within the larger (heterosexual) society and hostility within the lesbian and gay community. The wider lesbian and gay/

bisexual movement provides clear examples of the marginality of bisexuality and tensions between lesbian and gay, and bisexual politics and communities. Various social and political forces have created splits between lesbian and gay, and bisexual communities. Orlando (1997/1991) argued that the lesbian and gay community:

> abounds with negative images of bisexuals as fence-sitters, traitors, cop-outs, closet cases, people whose primary goal in life is to retain 'heterosexual privilege,' power-hungry seducers who use and discard their same-sex lovers like so many Kleenex . . . These stereotypes result from the ambiguous position of bisexuals, poised as we are between what currently appear as two mutually exclusive sexual cultures, one with the power to exercise violent repression against the other. (p. 803)

Although many lesbians and gay men see bisexuals as part of their community, others see them as separate and distinct, and see their inclusion as detrimental to the social and political acceptance of lesbians and gay men (Weiss, 2003). In a number of lesbian and gay groups and organizations, the addition of 'B' to 'LG' has been the subject of angry debate (Alexander & Yescavage, 2003). Some members of these organizations have questioned whether lesbians and gay men and bisexuals are natural allies because they are all victimized by a heteronormative conception of sexuality. Furthermore, lesbian and gay groups often disappear bisexual specificity by assuming that bisexual issues are subsumed under lesbian and gay ones, and that bisexuals will be liberated at the same time as lesbians and gay men (Weiss, 2003). In the context of lesbian feminism (which promoted lesbianism as a political choice that all women could make, e.g. Rich, 1980/1987) bisexual women were viewed as traitors who refused to shift their alliances away from men (Blasius & Phelan, 1997; Hartman, 2005; Humphrey, 1999; Rust, 1995). During the 1980s and 1990s, when the AIDS epidemic and the homophobic backlash from the new right led lesbians and gay men to reform their old alliances, the potential for coalitions with bisexuals was foreclosed by an emphasis on sexual immutability. In this context, bisexuals were vilified as confused because of the desire for fixed categories around which to organize politically (Blasius & Phelan, 1997).

Weiss (2003) argues that concerns about bisexuality and bisexuals remain alive and well within the lesbian and gay community. The positioning of 'BT' last in the LGBT acronym is not accidental and reflects on-going conflicts between and within LGBT communities. Tensions abound between the interest group politics and assimilationist claims of the white, middle-class lesbian and gay movement and the sexual freedom agenda of some bisexuals (particularly in relation to S/M and non-monogamy) (Barker & Yockney, 2004; Weiss, 2003). The marginalization of bisexuals can be seen as 'an accommodationist attempt to disavow these more "radical" forms of sexuality' (Weiss, 2003, p. 27). Alexander and Yescavage (2003) describe bisexuality as 'heretical' and as a 'radical border crossing', disrupting binary understandings of sexuality and the notions of categories altogether. They argue that 'B' and 'T' are not 'mere "additions" tacked onto LG' (p. 4); rather they have much to say to lesbian and gay communities. Cooper (2003) observes that 'it's not surprising that the big, starchy, lesbian and gay dinosaurs of the scene wouldn't want to include those queers who brought the dignity of homosexual identity into disrepute with their salacious behaviour' (p. 90).

A number of commentators like Cooper are critical of the traditional lesbian and gay movement and what they view as exclusionary practices such as single-gender spaces and 'dykes express[ing] horror that a boyfriend might want to watch them get it on' (p. 90).

Gay and, especially, lesbian politics are viewed as overly 'politically correct', boring and prudish. Humphrey (1999) argued that opening the door to bisexual people facilitates the forming of coalitions across other forms of differences and prevents the exclusion of the most marginalized members of LGBT communities. For instance, she suggested that some black gay men might identify as bisexual because of homophobia in black communities and racism in gay communities (likewise some gay men in non-western countries have learnt to express their homosexuality in trans communities) (cf, Riggs, Chapter 4).

The Multiple Meanings of Bisexuality

Some commentators have suggested that a one-way analysis of the relationship between lesbian, gay and bisexual politics, communities and psychologies (and the concept of biphobia) is, however, problematic. The instability and invisibility of the categories 'gay' and, especially, 'lesbian' might give rise to what is conceptualized as biphobia. Certainly, as we noted above, the backlash politics of the 1980s and 1990s sent lesbians and gay men running for cover under the shelter of clearly demarcated identities. Weiss (2003) argues that biphobia within the lesbian and gay community is not an actual irrational fear; rather, it mirrors political and cultural fractures with the LGBT community. Locating this issue at the level of the individual is, she maintains, problematic: 'we will not repair our divisions by ignoring them and attributing them to psychological abberation' (p. 30). Lesbians and gay men who marginalize bisexuals might be reacting rationally to social and political pressures not psychological ones. As such it seems problematic to dismiss some political analyses of bisexuality as evidence of psychological phobias.

Bisexuals can embody both heterosexual privilege and queer marginalization. Bisexuals are viewed as both too straight (normative) and too different (transgressive) (Hemmings, 2002), as reifying and as exploding gender/sexual binaries. Alexander and Yescavage (2003) argue that some bisexuals, like some lesbians and gay men, seek assimilation into mainstream society and others seek to create separate queer spaces. It is clear that there is no one meaning or politics of bisexuality. Some commentators call for a growth of academic work based on a positive acceptance of bisexuality as a legitimate identity (Barker & Yockney, 2004) (this position broadly maps onto, but also potentially troubles, a more traditional lesbian and gay identity politics agenda). Whereas other theorists argue that it is precisely the indeterminacy of bisexuality that holds its radical potential, and any attempt to pin the meaning of bisexuality and shore up its status as a 'legitimate' identity will foreclose this radical potential (see Gurevich et al., Chapter 11) (this position broadly maps onto a queer agenda).

Alexander and Yescavage (2003) call for mutual understanding between and appreciation of the lesbian and gay and the bisexual community, they emphasize the value of learning from each other and from the turf wars that have divided the LGBT community. It is important to acknowledge and to redress the neglect of bisexuality in lesbian and gay psychology. It is also necessary to recognize and examine bisexual specificity and the similarities and differences between lesbians', gay men's, bisexual men's and bisexual women's experiences, and the multiple meanings of bisexuality.

We now consider the relationship between lesbian, gay and trans psychology, and lesbian, gay and trans politics and communities.

Lesbian and Gay Psychology and Trans Psychology: Transforming Sex, Gender and Sexuality?

Trans occupies a position of even greater marginality within lesbian and gay psychology than that of bisexuality or lesbianism. This perhaps reflects the fact that there is arguably less public acceptance of trans people than of lesbians and gay men, especially of those lesbians and gay men that seek traditional lifestyles defined by marriage (Coombs, 1997). Very few edited collections on lesbian and gay (and LGB, and even LGBT) psychology incorporate transgender psychology in anything other than a minimal fashion.

As Kitzinger and Coyle (2002) point out, the field of lesbian and gay psychology has always, if minimally, encompassed work on trans (right from the birth of scholarship in this area and the work of early sexologists and sexual reformers such as Krafft-Ebing and Havelock Ellis). Some commentators argue that the socio-political histories of trans and homosexuality have much in common (Gainor, 2000).

As Weiss (2003) outlines, until the 1950s people now labelled transgendered were classified as homosexual and it is only in the past 50 or so years that transgender has been understood as conceptually and phenomenologically distinct from homosexuality. Weiss argues that a 'fault line' emerged between gay men/lesbians and transgendered people through the development of a sex orientation/gender identity dichotomy (particularly in the work of early sexologists such as Magnus Hirschfeld). This dichotomy was, she argues, deepened when homosexuality was separated into male and female forms. Gender-separate organizations such as The Mattachine Society and The Daughters of Bilitis (established in the USA in 1950 and 1955 respectively) encouraged their members to be 'normal' and fit in. Lesbians and gay men in these organizations campaigned for acceptance on the basis that they were 'just the same' as heterosexuals; such campaigns highlighted fractures between the accommodationist strands in lesbian/gay communities and gender ambiguity. Meyerowitz (2002) reports on the heated debates that took place within the homophile movement about whether or not to support Christine Jorgensen, the first transperson to receive widespread media attention (see Johnson, Chapter 21). Gender ambiguity 'channeled the stigma of illegitimacy' according to Weiss (2003, p. 38), so it is not surprising that some lesbians and gay men chose to lessen that stigma by rejecting 'inappropriate' gender behaviour. At the same time some trans people sought to distance themselves from the stigma of homosexuality. Coombs (1997) has similarly noted that the marginalization of transgender people within the lesbian and gay community has been a process of omission rather than commission.

Some members of LGB communities struggle to understand and to welcome trans people because trans works at the level of sex/gender not sexuality (Alexander & Yescavage, 2003). Although, some trans women and men identify as lesbian, gay or bisexual, the argument goes that trans oppression is better dealt with under the rubric of gender oppression (which is the domain of feminism). So, the marginalization of trans in lesbian and gay psychology is not theorized solely in terms of transphobia, but uncertainty about whether lesbian and gay psychology is the rightful home of trans psychology.

For some commentators (e.g. Dreschler, 2003), lesbian and gay expectations have taken the place of heteronormative ones in LGBT communities, and lesbian and gay identities are privileged over BTQ identities. Furthermore, some lesbians and gay men share straight perceptions of trans people, and subscribe to the belief that only a person born male or female is a 'true' lesbian or gay man. As Alexander and Yescavage (2003) note, like bisexuals, trans people are also accused of fence-sitting by members of lesbian and gay (and straight) communities – they are sometimes alleged to be suffering from internalized homophobia, and to change sex rather than live as a lesbian or gay man. Trans (like bisexuality) potentially shakes the ground on which (immutable) lesbian and gay identities are built.

Any move to locate trans under the umbrella of gender studies is complicated by the fact that feminism is not always a welcoming space for trans people. Some of the most trenchant critiques of trans come from feminists, particularly radical feminists (e.g. Jeffreys, 2003; Raymond, 1979). This does not of course mean that all feminists are critical of trans (see Johnson, Chapter 21, Speer, Chapter 16). Finding a home for trans within academia is also complicated by the fact that trans is far from a unitary phenomenon, and not all trans people identify with LGB communities (Alexander & Yescavage, 2003). Indeed, just as there are multiple meanings and politics of bisexuality (and homosexuality/lesbianism), there are multiple meanings and politics of trans. Some trans people identify with normative values and have no desire to be 'gender terrorists'; other trans people seek to (visibly) disrupt existing norms around sex/gender.

Common Battles and Strategic Coalitions

A number of commentators have argued that trans people and lesbians and gay men often share common battles and can benefit from strategic coalitions. Furthermore, trans and homosexuality are linked politically because they are treated as linked, as different aspects of the same deviance, by the dominant heteronormative society[6] (which is not to lose sight of the important differences between homosexuality and trans) (Coombs, 1997; Gainor, 2000). Gainor (2000), for instance, discusses the homophobia evident in the treatment of childhood gender identity disorder (GID) – a diagnostic category parallel to ego-dystonic homosexuality (EDH), in that both GID and EDH fail to take account of an oppressive social context. She argues that the current approach to treating GID is aimed at the preventing the development of homosexuality in adults. The fear is that gender nonconforming children will become lesbians/gay men. Gainor argues that GID is socially constructed to maintain a patriarchal social system and that lesbians, gay men and transgendered people have a stake in challenging this system.

Coombs (1997) urged lesbians and gay men to learn from the exclusion of lesbians from feminism, which, she argues, was a political 'mistake'. Feminism is only strengthened if it is inclusive of all women, while at the same time recognizing that the category 'woman' includes a diverse group of people whose interests only partially overlap. The exclusion of transgendered people from the lesbian and gay movement would also be a political mistake.[7] She argues that both lesbian and gay and transgender communities are coalitional: both include people who have different understandings of the identity category around which they bind (people who see themselves as 'normal' and people who want to be radical/queer activists). Moreover, lesbians and gay men are more likely than heterosexuals to be gender non-conformists and to be aware of the complexity of sexual/

---

[6] Beliefs persist that gay men want to be women, and lesbians want to be men.
[7] The exclusion of trans people is especially problematic given that they were at the forefront of the Stonewall riots that triggered the development of the modern lesbian and gay movement (Gainor, 2000).

gender identity, indeed, the two communities overlap (some LGBTQ people might consider themselves to be members of both communities). A more inclusive approach
to LGBTQ psychologies that takes seriously the ways in which sexuality and other axes
of social oppression intersect, and the close relationship between sexual and gender
marginalization, creates a strong impetus for including trans under the umbrella of
lesbian and gay psychology and for not excluding political analyses of the phenomenon
of trans.

Phoenix (2006, p. 2) argues that the history of feminism is one of 'negotiating boundaries, difference, commonality and diversity', this could become the history of LGBTQ
psychologies. An approach that encourages those who exist outside of sexual and gender
norms to work together and to prioritize what unites rather than what divides them is
queer theory. It is to queer theory that we now turn in the final part of this chapter.

Lesbian and Gay Psychology and Queer Psychology

As we noted above, the fracturing of lesbian feminism and the AIDS epidemic led to
the regeneration of lesbian and gay coalitions in the 1980s and 1990s, and these coalitions gave birth to queer activism and, hot on its heels, queer theory. Queer theory has
taken (some sections of) academia by storm, but, until recently (see Barker & Hegarty,
2005; Hegarty, 1997; Hegarty & Massey, 2006; Jalas, 2004; Minton, 1997; O'Rourke,
2005; Speer, 2005; Warner, 2004) queer theory has passed by the heavily policed
boundaries of psychology (Hegarty & Massey, 2006).[8] This is symptomatic perhaps of
lesbian and gay psychology's lack of engagement with interdisciplinary LGBT studies
(Hegarty, 2004). Hegarty and Massey (2006) point to the disjunction between queer
theory's concern for psychoanalysis and the dominance of the cognitive-behavioural
paradigm in psychology. They argue that lesbian and gay psychology is a 'more cautious
disciplinary project' (p. 19) than queer theory; for instance, queer theorists have focused
on sexual practices, whereas lesbian and gay psychologists have prioritized sexual
identity.

Any attempt to define queer theory is, as any queer theorist worth their salt will tell
you, bound to falter because the 'essence' of queer theory (and one thing that queer's
detractors find deeply irksome) is its refusal of fixed definitions. As Warner (2004, p. 322)
notes 'there is not one queer theory, but many queer theories'. Nonetheless, for readers
unfamiliar with queer theory, we will offer a, necessarily brief and simplified, account of
what queer is or might be (for an accessible introduction to queer, see Sullivan, 2003;
Warner, 2004). The coining of the term 'queer theory' is credited to Teresa de Lauretis
(1991) and oft claimed as 'the founding moment of queer theory' (Gamson, 1995, p. 394)
is the publication of Eve Kosovsky Sedgwick's (1990) *Epistemology of the Closet*. Minton
(1997) argued that the key to understanding queer theory is its reclamation of the
word queer, which signifies something different and peculiar (and also some*one* non-
heterosexual). As such, queer has become a site for transforming and resisting heteronormativity. Queer has defined itself against conventional lesbian and gay, and feminist

---

[8] However, it is possible to read as queer or detect the influence of queer in a larger number of lesbian and gay psychological
publications (e.g. Braun, 2000; Riggs, 2005; Riggs & Walker, 2006). Thanks to Peter Hegarty for drawing our attention to
this point.

politics (Gamson, 1995), and more specifically against identity politics, so much so that some commentators have argued that it makes an enemy of feminism (Walters, 1996), even though it has strong roots in feminist theory. There are no clear membership criteria for queer (Rudy, 2001); queers are not defined by their sexual identity, but by their opposition to heteronormativity, which raises the – for some, uncomfortable (Walters, 1996) – possibility of straight queers (O'Rourke, 2005). Queer only has meaning in relation to its opposition to that which is normative (Minton, 1997). Queer, thus, draws the boundaries of its membership more inclusively than the lesbian and gay movement, including potentially anyone, such as bisexual, trans and heterosexual people, who rejects heteronormative conceptions of sex/gender and sexuality.

Prominent queer theorists include (among many others) Judith Butler (1990, 1993), Eve Kosofsky Sedgwick (1990) and Michael Warner (1993), but the grand daddy of queer is the French post-structuralist theorist, Michel Foucault (1978). As Minton (1997) outlined, Foucault challenged traditional understandings of power as a possession, instead conceiving of power as a relation. Power is everywhere, freedom cannot operate outside of power, we can never achieve freedom *from* power, thus the goal of oppositional politics is not liberation but resistance. Queer theorists have used Foucault's conceptualization of power to theorize resistance to heteronormativity.

One of the most well known and widely used, and misused, queer concepts is Butler's (1990) notion of the performativity of gender (something that she has revisited in her subsequent work, see Butler, 1993, 2004). To simplify Butler's rather complex and subtle argument, categories like gender are neither natural nor essential but are nonetheless foundational, and occupy the status of social norms that serve particular regulatory purposes. Gender is the discursive effect of reiterative 'acts', acts that are repeated within a highly ordered frame and which 'congeal over time to produce the appearance of a substance, of a natural sort of being' (1990, p. 33). Butler uses the concept of performativity, rather than performance, to avoid the connotations of intentionality: there is no agent who performs; rather, the agent is constituted in and through the performative processes (Sullivan, 2003). If gender is a cultural fiction, then so are heterosexuality and homosexuality. Power/knowledge regimens – such as psychology – do not simply describe identities; rather, they produce identities in the service of particular projects. Butler and other queer theorists aim to 'denaturalize' sex, gender and sexuality and the relationships between them.

Queer theory 'shakes the ground on which lesbian and gay politics has been built' (Gamson, 1995, p. 390); there is a tension between the lesbian and gay movement's concern to shore up identity categories and the queer impulse to deconstruct them. As Gamson (1995) outlined, the lesbian and gay movement is based on the assumption that clear collective identity categories are necessary for political action. By contrast, queer challenges the content *and* utility of identity categories: power operates through very the production of sexual categories as well as through their repression, therefore deconstructing identity categories is the key to meaningful resistance. As Butler (1990, pp. 13–14) argued, 'identity categories tend to be instruments of regulatory regimes, whether as the normalising categories of oppressive structures, or as the rallying points for a liberatory contestation of that very oppression'. Queer can be viewed as a contemporary anti-assimilationist politics, opposed to mainstream lesbian and gay inclusionary (but not inclusive) identity/rights politics. Queer's more inclusive politics requires 'not simply an expansion of identity, but a subversion of it' (Gamson, 1995, p. 399).

The Pitfalls of Queer Theory

Since the mid-1990s, outside (and occasionally inside [see Kitzinger & Wilkinson, 1997, Wilkinson & Kitzinger, 1996]) of psychology, queer theory has been the subject of much debate and vociferous critique. Lesbian feminists feature prominently among queer's detractors (e.g. Jeffreys, 1994, 1996, 2003; Walters, 1996). Gamson (1995) argued that because of the greater invisibility and fragility of the category 'lesbian' there have been greater levels of anxiety about its deconstruction, than about the deconstruction of the category 'gay man'. Some critiques are forwarded by authors who are not wholly unsympathetic to the project of queer theory (e.g. Jackson, 1999; Walters, 1996), whereas others are forwarded by those who see little promise in a queer future (Jeffreys, 2003). To provide a sense of some of the possible limitations of engaging more thoroughly with queer theory in lesbian and gay psychology we briefly outline some of the key themes in critiques of queer that have emerged from feminism and sociology. Writers, both sympathetic and hostile to queer, highlight the potential for the boundaries of queer's inclusionary politics to be drawn so wide as to be meaningless, to erase internal differences (Gamson, 1995; Gamson & Moon, 2004), and to create a new and reductive binary of everything queer/heteronormativity. Many critics, and some queer theorists, argue that just like gay liberation, queer is synonymous with white, gay male experience (Barnard, 2004; Riggs, 2006), so much so that a number of lesbian feminists have revived their earlier critiques of 'homosexual patriarchal culture' (Jeffreys, 2003, p. 3). Queer theory is said to be male centred, to 'disappear' lesbians and assimilate them into gay male culture and politics and to ignore the specificity of lesbian experience (Jeffreys, 1994; Rudy, 2001; Wilkinson & Kitzinger, 1996). Queer implicitly and explicitly portrays lesbians and feminists as boring, prudish and politically correct. Walters (1996, p. 844) most vividly captures this objection to queer:

> Once upon a time there was this group of really boring ugly women who never had sex, walked a lot in the woods, read bad poetry about goddesses, wore flannel shirts, and hated men (even their gay brothers). They called themselves lesbians. Then, thankfully, along came these guys named Foucault, Derrida, and Lacan dressed in girls' clothes riding some very large white horses. They told these silly women that they were politically correct, rigid, frigid, sex-hating prudes who just did not GET IT – it was all a game anyway, all about words and images, all about mimicry and imitation, all a cacophony of signs leading back to nowhere. To have a politics around gender was silly, they were told, because gender was just a performance anyway, a costume one put on and, in drag performance, wore backward. And everyone knew boys were better at dress up.

Moreover, queer is said to ignore or reverse feminist critiques of S/M, pornography, transsexualism, bisexuality and heterosexuality (Wilkinson & Kitzinger, 1996) and to be generally hostile to feminism (Walters, 1996). Queer is argued to prioritize a male sexual freedom agenda, and to immunize gay male sexual practices from political critique (Jeffreys, 2003). Some lesbian feminists maintain that gay men, bisexuals and transgenderists/transsexuals do not share political ground with lesbians (Jeffreys, 2003). Many critics allege that queer is fundamentally elitist, an obfuscatory, unintelligible political theory, that is accessible only to some (predominantly privileged, white, middle-class) academics (Jeffreys, 2003; Walters, 1996). Queer replaces the meaningful programme for social change developed by feminists and others with political quietism (Murray, 1997, cited in Jeffreys, 2003), and romanticizes transgression – 'a pleasure of the powerful' (Jeffreys, 2003, p. 43) – and playing with or 'fucking' gender (feminists, by contrast, argue that gender should be resisted and eliminated).

Queer is also alleged to be unoriginal, parasitically laying claim to insights that are more appropriately credited to others (Epstein, 1996; Jackson, 1999; Jeffreys, 2003) or incorporating the work of feminists (see, for examples, Minton, 1997; Sullivan, 2003), without fully taking account of their opposition to the queer project. Queer places 'a fashionable intellectual gloss on old-fashioned liberalism and individualism' (Jeffreys, 1996, p. 372) and ignores the material realities of oppression (Jackson, 1999; Jeffreys, 2003; Wilkinson & Kitzinger, 1996). Some writers have asked where 'the actual vulgar oppression of women fits into all this' (Jeffreys, 1996, p. 361). Related to this, queer is argued to provide an impoverished understanding of the social – some commentators express concern about the utility of a political theory that emanates from the arts, rather than the social sciences (Gamson & Moon, 2004; Jackson, 1999; Jeffreys, 2003). Jackson (1999) argues that queer theory works at the level of the cultural/discursive, and reduces the social to this level (sometimes practices are included, as in Butler's [1990, 1993] discussion of performativity, but these are not located in their interactional or institutional setting). Some feminists have called for a reinvigoration of micro-sociological perspectives that account for agency and structure, everyday interaction and its institutional settings, and the ways that interaction is furnished with and shaped by the meanings it has for participants, such as ethnomethodology, interactionism and phenomenology (Jackson, 1999; Speer, 2005). Gamson and Moon (2004) argue that since the late 1990s there has been something of a reconciliation between queer theory and sociology, and sociological theory provides an empirical anchor for queer's abstract theorizing.

There are many other critiques of queer in circulation, perhaps the most fundamental is that queer signs the death warrant of a lesbian and gay rights agenda, and, moreover, the categories 'lesbian' and 'gay' (Gamson, 1995; Humphrey, 1999). The deconstruction of identity categories makes meaningful political action difficult, if not impossible (Jeffreys, 2003), and denies a voice to those who have only just begun to acquire one as a result of their deployment of particular categories (Gamson, 1995; Jeffreys, 1996).

The Possibilities of Queer Theory

Other commentators have argued that queer theory has much to offer theory, research and practice in a number of different domains, including psychology. Some lesbian and gay psychologists have called for a more meaningful engagement with queer theory (Barker & Hegarty, 2005). Warner (2004) argues that research that seeks to define the psychology of 'normal' lesbians and gay men 'can never produce ultimately liberatory knowledge' (p. 326) because there are no such things as 'normal' lesbians and gay men, these categories are the products not the precursors of research. A psychology of 'normal' lesbians and gay men may benefit those who are able to fall within the boundaries of the normal that are produced through the research (which, as we established above, tends to be white, middle-class, gay men), but succeeds only in further oppressing the already marginalized. We now outline two examples of queer re-interpretations of lesbian and gay psychological research to provide an indication of what queer theory might offer this field.

Warner (2004; see also Hegarty, 2003) queerly interrogates how Hooker's (1957) groundbreaking research on homosexuality established the ways in which 'queers were made intelligible to the psychological gaze' (Warner, 2004, p. 326). The choices Hooker made in collecting and presenting her data constructed the 'normal male homosexual', an identity 'within the matrix of intelligibility' (Warner, 2004, p. 327) that dominates contemporary LGBT research. Hooker sought to locate a sample of 'pure' homosexuals (men with no heterosexual experience); thus she defined homosexuality negatively, as not heterosexual. Warner argues that a true homosexual (or heterosexual) 'cannot be known outside of someone's identifying with the identity' (2004, p. 329), sexual behaviour is linked to identity through the assumption that a pure homosexual core is organizing a person's behaviour. In the absence of this assumption, the behaviour could be organized in any number of other ways. Hooker sought to avoid homosexuals of less than 'average adjustment' (such as prisoners), but, Warner argues, given that her aim was to show no personality differences between homosexuals and heterosexuals, she could have used a prison population. If she had made this choice she could have avoided making any statement about norms and avoided dehumanizing prison populations, but Hooker also aimed to show that homosexuals are 'normal'. The population of men from which Hooker drew her sample were largely white, middle-class, urban-dwelling, self-identifying homosexuals and members of the Mattachine Society. As Warner notes, this population was far from representative or normal. By selecting her sample from this population, Hooker created a norm against which other queers were going to be judged and that new queers could strive for.

Hegarty and Massey (2006) reinterpret the findings of experimental social psychological research on the behavioural effects of anti-homosexual prejudice within what Sedgwick (1990) called a universalizing view (the assumption that sexual definition is an issue for all people, rather than just for the homosexual minority). Hegarty and Massey ask to what 'are the anti-homosexual attitudes which social psychologists have measured opposed? Is the homosexuality in question a minority group, a form of sexual practice, an identity performance, or a political moment?' (p. 50). Research on the behavioural effects of anti-homosexual prejudice involves participants making judgements about a target individual whose perceived sexual orientation is experimentally manipulated. Target individuals perform homosexuality (and straightness) in a variety of ways, including through direct disclosure and wearing gay pride badges. Such performative processes constitute identities, rather than report the same core identity. Participants' responses to these processes have been understood as reactions to lesbians and gay men versus heterosexuals. But Hegarty and Massey argue these may also be understood as assessing different responses to out and passing lesbian/gay individuals, to ways of performing minority sexual identities, rather than to lesbians and gay men versus heterosexuals. Hegarty and Massey suggest that future experiments that acknowledge the performativity of identity could examine if different sexual identity performances regulate the relationship between participants' attitudes and behaviours, and what particular performative processes accomplish. They conclude that queer theory enables social psychologists to use and deconstruct the technologies of attitude research, to work with and acknowledge the contingency of psychological knowledge, and to pursue anti-homophobic inquiry 'within mutually incompatible epistemologies' (p. 62).

Warner (2004) advocates the use of qualitative approaches because these 'have a better chance of accounting for queer experiences in the same terms as the actual people living these experiences' (p. 335). Hegarty and Massey (2006), by contrast, do not consider quantitative/experimental research as 'devoid of epistemic value'. In their view, queer theory does not require a rejection of scientific epistemology.

To Queer or Not to Queer?

We tentatively suggest queering lesbian and gay psychology with caution, mindful of queer's own distrust of anything that positions itself as inherently radical (Hegarty, Chapter 3). A number of commentators (e.g. Gamson, 1995; Humphrey, 1999) have argued for the need to both shore up and deconstruct identity categories (stable identities are necessary for specific purposes[9]) because different forms and sites of oppression require different political strategies. Gamson (1995) argued that the label 'LGBTQ' orients to both strategies (which is why we chose it for this chapter), highlighting both the strategic importance of identity categories and the need to undermine those categories. Humphrey (1999, p. 239) similarly argued against collapsing lesbian, gay and queer politics into one another:

> since our oppression is multidimensional, we can ill afford to sacrifice one set of insights or strategies to another, and if we succumb to the temptation, we may delude ourselves that the battle has been won, when in fact the sites and symptoms have been displaced.

Analyses of eroticism outside of the west suggest that it may also be necessary on occasion to bring together queer, feminist, lesbian and gay analyses. For instance, in his work on discourses of gender and eroticism in Thailand, Peter Jackson (2000) argues that in order to understand these and other non-western patterns of eroticism it is necessary to integrate feminist theories of gender and queer theories of sexuality 'so as to offer a unified account of the eroticization of gender, and the gendering of eroticism' (p. 405).

To conclude this section and the chapter, we reiterate Humphrey's (1999, p. 240) caution that justice for lesbians and gay men is a step not the final goal, and 'quite simply, it is difficult to justify any vision of justice for lesbian woman and gay men [or indeed BTQ people] if the pursuit of this vision, and its end product, entails injustices against other sexual and gendered minorities'.

REFERENCES

Alexander, J. & Yescavage, K. (2003). Bisexuality and transgenderism: InterSEXions of the others. *Journal of Bisexuality*, **3**(4), 1–23.

Barker, M. & Hegarty, P. (2005). Queer science, queer politics. *Psychology of Women Section Review*, **7**(2), 71–79.

Barker, M. & Yockney, J. (2004). Including the B-word: Reflections on the place of bisexuality within lesbian and gay activism and psychology. *Lesbian & Gay Psychology Review*, **5**(3), 118–122.

Barnard, P. (2004). *Queer Race: Cultural interventions in the racial politics of queer theory*. New York, NY: Peter Lang.

---

[9] This chimes with some lesbian feminists' theorization of the category 'lesbian' as a strategically useful social construction (Jeffreys, 1996).

Bell, S., Kitzinger, C., Hodges, I., Coyle, A. & Rivers, I. (2002). Reflections on 'science', 'objectivity' and personal investment in lesbian, gay and bisexual psychology. *Lesbian & Gay Psychology Review*, **3**(3), 91–95.

Blasius, M. & Phelan, S. (Eds) (1997). *We are Everywhere: A historical sourcebook of gay and lesbian politics*. New York, NY: Routledge.

Boston Lesbian Psychologies Collective (1987). *Lesbian Psychologies: Explorations and challenges*. Urbana, IL: University of Illinois Press.

Braun, V. (2000). Heterosexism in focus group research: Collusion and challenge. *Feminism & Psychology*, **10**(1), 133–140.

Butler, J. (1990). *Gender Trouble: Feminism and the subversion of identity*. New York, NY: Routledge.

Butler, J. (1993). *Bodies that Matter: On the discursive limits of 'sex'*. New York, NY: Routledge.

Butler, J. (2004). *Undoing Gender*. New York: Routledge.

Carrington, C. (1999). *No Place like Home: Relationships and family life among lesbians and gay men*. Chicago, IL: University of Chicago Press.

Cass, V. C. (1979). Homosexual identity formation: A theoretical model. *Journal of Homosexuality*, **4**(3), 219–235.

Clarke, V. & Rúdólfsdóttir, A. G. (2005). Love conquers all? An exploration of guidance books for parents, family and friends of lesbians and gay men. *Psychology of Women Section Review*, **7**(2), 37–48.

Comely, L., Kitzinger, C., Perkins, R. & Wilkinson, S. – Lesbians in Psychology Sisterhood (LIPS) (1992). Lesbian psychology in Britain: Back in the closet? *Feminism & Psychology*, **2**(2), 265–267.

Coombs, M. (1997). Transgenderism and sexual orientation: More than a marriage of convenience. *National Journal of Sexual Orientation Law*, **3**(1), 4–30. Available at: http://www.ibiblio.org/gaylaw/issue5/coombs.html.

Cooper, C. (2003). Swing it baby! *Journal of Bisexuality*, **3**(3/4), 87–92.

Corbett, J. (1994). A proud label: exploring the relationship between disability politics and gay pride. *Disability & Society*, **9**(3), 343–357.

Coyle, A. (2000). Qualitative research and lesbian and gay psychology in Britain. *Lesbian & Gay Psychology Section Newsletter*, **4**, 2–5.

Coyle, A. (2003). Editorial. *Lesbian & Gay psychology Review*, **4**(2), 3–4.

Coyle, A. & Kitzinger, C. (Eds) (2002). *Lesbian and Gay psychology: New perspectives*. Oxford: BPS Blackwell.

Crenshaw, K. (1989). *Demarginalising the Intersection of Race and Sex: A black feminist critique of antidiscrimination doctrine, feminist theory and antiracist politics*. Chicago, IL: University of Chicago Legal Forum.

de Lauretis, T. (1991). Queer theory: Lesbian and gay sexualities. *Differences*, **3**, iii–xviii.

Diehl, K. & Smith, B. (2000). 'Here's the movement, let's start the building': An interview with Barbara Smith. *Colorlines: Race, class, action*, **3**(3). Available from http://www.arc.org/C_Lines/CLArchive/story3_3_05.html.

Dreschler, C. (2003). We are all others: An argument for queer. *Journal of Bisexuality*, **3**(3/4), 265–276.

Dunne, G. A. (1997). *Lesbian Lifestyles: Women's work and the politics of sexuality*. London: Macmillan.

Dworkin, S. H. (2002). Guess who's coming to dinner? The future of LGB psychology. Presidential Address to Division 44, American Psychological Association Convention, Chicago, Illinois, August. Available from http://www.apadivision44.org/events/address_dworkin.doc.

Edwards, T. (1994). *Erotics and Politics: Gay male sexuality, masculinity and feminism*: London: Routledge & Kegan Paul.

Epstein, S. (1996). A queer encounter: Sociology and the study of sexuality. In S. Seidman (Ed.), *Queer Theory/Sociology* (pp. 144–167). Cambridge, MA: Blackwell.

Foucault, M. (1978). *The History of Sexuality: An Introduction*. New York, NY: Vintage.

Fox, R. C. (1995). Bisexual identities. In A. R. D'Augelli & C. J. Patterson (Eds), *Lesbian, Gay, and Bisexual Identities over the Lifespan: Psychological perspectives* (pp. 48–86). New York, NY: Oxford University Press.

Gabb, J. (2004). Critical differentials: Querying the incongruities within research on lesbian families. *Sexualities*, **7**(2), 167–182.

Gainor, K. A. (2000). Including transgender issues in lesbian, gay and bisexual psychology: Implications for clinical practice and training. In B. Greene & G. L. Croom (Eds), *Education, Research and Practice in Lesbian, Gay, Bisexual, and Transgendered Psychology: A resource manual* (pp. 131–160). Thousand Oaks, CA: Sage.

Gamson, J. (1995). Must identity movements self-destruct? A queer dilemma. *Social Problems*, **42**(33), 390–407.

Gamson, J. & Moon, D. (2004). The sociology of sexualities: Queer and beyond. *Annual Review of Sociology*, **30**(1), 47–64.

Greene, B. (1998). Family, ethnic identity, and sexual orientation: African-American lesbians and gay men. In C. J. Patterson & A. R. D'Augelli (Eds), *Lesbian, Gay, and Bisexual Identities in Families: Psychological perspectives* (pp. 40–52). New York, NY: Oxford University Press.

Greene, B. (2000). Beyond heterosexism and across the cultural divide: Developing an inclusive lesbian, gay, and bisexual psychology: A look to the future. In B. Greene & G. L. Croom (Eds), *Education, Research and Practice in Lesbian, Gay, Bisexual, and Transgendered Psychology: A resource manual* (pp. 1–45). Thousand Oaks, CA: Sage.

Hartman, J. E. (2005). Another kind of 'chilly climate': The effects of lesbian separatism on bisexual women's identity and community. *Journal of Bisexuality*, **5**(4), 63–76.

Hegarty, P. (1997). Materializing the hypothalamus: A performative account of the 'gay brain'. *Feminism & Psychology*, **7**(3), 355–372.

Hegarty, P. (2003). Contingent differences: An historical note on Evelyn Hooker's uses of significance testing. *Lesbian & Gay Psychology Review*, **4**(1), 3–7.

Hegarty, P. (2004). Getting past 'divide and conquer': A statement from the new Chair of the Section. *Lesbian & Gay Psychology Review*, **5**(1), 4–5.

Hegarty, P. & Massey, S. (2006) Anti-homosexual prejudice . . . as opposed to what? Queer theory and the social psychology of anti-homosexual attitudes. *Journal of Homosexuality*, **52**(1/2), 47–71.

Hemmings, C. (2002). *Bisexual Spaces: A geography of sexuality and gender*. New York, NY: Routledge.

Hennessy, R. (2000). *Profit and Pleasure: Sexual identities in late capitalism*. New York, NY: Routledge.

Hooker, E. (1957). The adjustment of the male overt homosexual. *Journal of Projective Techniques*, **21**, 18–31.

Humphrey, J. C. (1999). To queer or not to queer a lesbian and gay group? Sexual and gendered politics at the turn of the century. *Sexualities*, **2**(2), 223–246.

Humphrey, J. C. (2000). Cracks in the feminist mirror? Research and reflections on lesbians and gay men working together. *Feminist Review*, **66**(1), 95–130.

Jackson, P. (2000). An explosion of Thai identities: Global queering and re-imagining queer theory. *Culture, Health & Sexuality*, **2**(4): 405–424.

Jackson, S. (1999). Feminist sociology and sociological feminism: Recovering the social in feminist thought. *Sociological Research Online*, **4**(3). Available from http://www.socresonline.org.uk/socresonline/4/3/jackson.html.

Jalas, K. (2004). Butch lesbians and the struggle with recognition. *Lesbian & Gay Psychology Review*, **5**(1), 15–21.

Jeffreys, S. (1994). The queer disappearance of lesbians: Sexuality in the academy. *Women's Studies International Forum*, **17**(5), 459–472.

Jeffreys, S. (1996). Return to gender: Post-modernism and lesbianandgay theory. In D. Bell & R. Klein (Eds), *Radically Speaking: Feminism reclaimed* (pp. 359–374). London: Zed Books.

Jeffreys, S. (2003). *Unpacking Queer Politics: A lesbian feminist perspective*. Cambridge: Polity Press.

Jensen, R. (2004). Homecoming: The relevance of radical feminism for gay men. *Journal of Homosexuality*, **47**(3/4), 75–81.

Kitzinger, C. (1987). *The Social Construction of Lesbianism*. London: Sage.

Kitzinger, C. (1996). The token lesbian chapter. In S. Wilkinson (Ed.), *Feminist Psychologies: International perspectives* (pp. 119–144). Buckingham: Open University Press.

Kitzinger, C. & Coyle, A. (2002). Introducing lesbian and gay psychology. In A. Coyle & C. Kitzinger (Eds), *Lesbian and Gay Psychology: New perspectives* (pp. 1–29). Oxford: BPS Blackwell.

Kitzinger, C. & Wilkinson, S. (1997). Virgins and queers: Rehabilitating heterosexuality? In M. M. Gergen & S. N. Davis (Eds), *Toward a New Psychology of Gender: A reader* (pp. 403–420). New York, NY: Routledge.

Kurdek, L. A. (1993). The allocation of household labour in gay, lesbian, and heterosexual married couples. *Journal of Social Issues*, **49**(3), 127–139.

Meyerowitz, J. (2002). *How Sex Changed: A history of transsexuality in the United States*. Cambridge, MA: Harvard University Press.

Minton, H. L. (1997). Queer theory: Historical roots and implications for psychology. *Theory & Psychology*, **7**(3), 337–353.

Oerton, S. (1998). Reclaiming the 'housewife'? Lesbians and household work. *Journal of Lesbian Studies*, **2**(4), 69–83.

Orlando, L. (1997/1991). Loving whom we choose. In M. Blasius & S. Phelan (Eds), *We are Everywhere: A historical sourcebook of gay and lesbian politics* (pp. 802–808). New York, NY: Routledge.

O'Rourke, M. (2005). On the eve of a queer-straight future: Notes towards an antinormative heteroerotic. *Feminism & Psychology*, **15**(1), 111–116.

Petford, B. (2003). Power in the darkness: Some thoughts on the marginalization of bisexuality in psychological literature. *Lesbian & Gay Psychology Review*, **4**(2), 5–13.

Phoenix, A. (2006). Centring marginality? Otherness, difference and the 'psychology of women'. *Psychology of Women Section Review*, **8**(1), 2–11.

Preston, J. (1997/1981). Goodbye to Sally Gearhart. In M. Blasius & S. Phelan (Eds), *We are Everywhere: A historical sourcebook of gay and lesbian politics* (pp. 511–521). New York, NY: Routledge.

Raymond, J. (1979). *The Transsexual Empire: The making of the she-male*. Boston, MA: Beacon Press.

Rich, A. (1980/1987). Compulsory heterosexuality and lesbian existence. In Adrienne Rich (Ed.), *Blood, Bread and Poetry: Selected prose 1979–1985* (pp. 23–75). London: Virago.

Riggs, D. W. (2005). Locating control: Psychology and the cultural production of 'healthy subject positions'. *Culture, Health & Sexuality*, **7**(2), 87–100.

Riggs, D. W. (2006). *Priscilla, (White) Queen of the Desert: Queer rights/race privilege*. New York, NY: Peter Berg.

Riggs, D. W. & Choi, P. Y. L. (2006). Heterosexism, racism and psychology. *The Psychologist*, **19**(5), 288–291.

Riggs, D. W. & Walker, G. A. (2006). Queer(y)ing rights: Psychology, liberal individualism and colonisation. *Australian Psychologist*, **41**(2), 95–103.

Rivers, I. (1997). Lesbian, gay and bisexual development: Theory, research and social issues. *Journal of Community & Applied Social Psychology*, **7**(5), 329–343.

Rothblum, E. (1992). We may be your worst nightmare, but we are also your future. *Feminism & Psychology*, **2**(2), 271–274.

Rothblum, E. (2004). 'Out'standing in her field: Looking back at Celia Kitzinger's *The Social Construction of Lesbianism*. *Feminism & Psychology*, **14**(4), 503–506.

Rudy, K. (2001). Radical feminism, lesbian separatism, and queer theory. *Feminist Studies*, **27**(1), 190–224.

Rust, P. (1995). *Bisexuality and the Challenge to Lesbian Politics: Sex, loyalty, and revolution*. New York, NY: New York University Press.

Sedgwick, E. K. (1990). *Epistemology of the Closet*. Berkley, CA: University of California Press.

Speer, S. (2005). *Gender Talk: Feminism, discourse and conversation analysis*. London: Routledge.

Stein, A. (1998/1992). 'Sisters and queers': The decentering of lesbian feminism. In P. M. Nardi & B. E. Schneider (Eds), *Social Perspectives in Lesbian and Gay Studies* (pp. 553–563). New York, NY: Routledge.

Sullivan, N. (2003). *A Critical Introduction to Queer Theory*. Edinburgh: Edinburgh University Press.

Walters, S. D. (1996). From here to queer: Radical feminism, postmodernism, and the lesbian menace (or, why can't a woman be more like a fag?). *Signs: Journal of Women in Culture and Society*, **21**(4), 830–869.

Ward, J. (2000). Queer sexism: Rethinking gay men and masculinity. In P. Nardi (Ed.), *Gay Masculinities* (pp. 152–74). Thousand Oaks, CA: Sage.

Warner, D. N. (2004). Towards a queer research methodology. *Qualitative Research in Psychology*, **1**(4), 321–337.

Warner, M. (Ed.), (1993). *Fear of a Queer Planet: Queer politics and social theory*. Minneapolis, MN: University of Minnesota Press.

Weiss, J. T. (2003). GL vs. BT: The archaeology of biphobia and transphobia within the US gay and lesbian community. *Journal of Bisexuality*, **3**(3/4), 25–55.

Wilkinson, S. (2002). Lesbian health. In A. Coyle & C. Kitzinger (Eds), *Lesbian & Gay Psychology: New perspectives* (pp. 117–134). Oxford: BPS Blackwell.

Wilkinson, S. & Kitzinger, C. (1996). The queer backlash. In D. Bell & R. Klein (Eds), *Radically Speaking: Feminism reclaimed* (pp. 375–382). Melbourne: Spinifex Press.

PART I

Histories and Commentaries

Power, Invisibility and Heteronormativity: Invitations to Paradox

Glenda M. Russell

Institute for Gay and Lesbian Strategic Studies, USA

The four chapters in this section serve as an introduction to a slice of lesbian, gay, bisexual, transgender and queer (LGBTQ) psychologies. The essays represent a varied amalgam of theoretical analyses, methodological enactments, methodological critiques, and reflexive exercises. They showcase the breadth of approaches and productions that occur within the rubric of LGBTQ psychologies; at the same time, they highlight the tensions and the contradictions between and among these approaches. Readers in search of a single position from which to view LGBTQ *psychology* may be frustrated and will surely be challenged by the diversity of perspectives these chapters represent. A similar fate awaits those who seek a coherent agreement running through the collection of chapters, as they are rife with oppositions and apparent incongruities – as is befitting a text where coherence is less a goal than is multiplicity and conscientious reflexivity.

Thus, rather than homogeneity, the reader will find here four chapters portraying ambiguity and even argument rather than consensus. In some cases, an argument made in one chapter appears to disqualify a position advocated in another; even more challenging are such apparent disqualifications within a single chapter. These conflicts and complexities demonstrate both the value of and the difficulties that ensue from following Celia Kitzinger's (1997) counsel to employ methodological, theoretical, and epistemological plurality (see Hagger-Johnson, Chapter 5). A pluralistic vision inspires innovation and also allows for dissension; it proffers opportunities to stretch boundaries precisely by encouraging ambiguity. These chapters, collectively, are testimony to that vision.

The internal contradictions and the nuanced twists and turns of meanings and arguments that arise within these chapters at once reflect and exemplify the degree to which psychology's consideration of LGBTQ themes has reached a point where it can turn its gaze on itself – a position that is apparent throughout this section. This is remarkable to those of us more enmeshed in US psychology, where similar reflexivity is often lacking. Arguing in favor of this self-reflective stance, Gareth Hagger-Johnson cautions us about radical claims made for any approach. In a specific enactment of this position, Peter

Hegarty (Chapter 3) simultaneously privileges a particular approach and offers a critique of the products of that very approach. Thus, the first dominant impression left by this group of writings is the openness to – indeed, the commitment to – a critical stance vis-à-vis one's preferred approach and the products of one's work.

Within and surrounding these conflicts and incongruities, two themes appear again and again throughout the histories and commentaries section. One theme speaks to the meaning of visibility and invisibility in the experiences of LGBTQ people and to the interplay between in/visibility and power. As explicated in these chapters, the relationship between power and visibility or invisibility is not altogether stable or predictable. On the one hand, Meg Barker's research (Chapter 6) points to the invisibility of lesbian and gay people in psychology textbooks – and the even greater invisibility of bisexual people; in this case, invisibility is regarded as clearly a mark of powerlessness. On the other hand, Damien Riggs (Chapter 4) discusses how the elusive nature both of whiteness and of heteronormativity renders them powerful in the social sphere – paradoxically, by making their power invisible. The meaning and the power valence of visibility depend, it becomes clear, both on context and on the subjectivity of the observer. This dance between visibility and invisibility, between power and powerlessness occurs throughout this section of *Out in Psychology*. The tension is fitting, as a similar dance winds persistently through the lives of lesbian, gay, bisexual, trans and queer people and through psychology's study of us.

The other recurrent theme that suffuses these chapters is the pervasive impact of heteronormativity. The chapters collectively demonstrate the impact of heteronormativity – and of homophobia and heterosexism – both on the lives of LGBTQ people and on the work of LGBTQ psychologists. We cannot talk about LGBTQ people without speaking of this triad of oppressive forms. Conversely, our efforts to describe or understand LGBTQ people will always be framed by the limits of our own understanding of the role of heteronormativity, homophobia and heterosexism. It is an odd paradox that our efforts to free LGBTQ people and LGBTQ psychologies from the throes of heteronormativity are inevitably framed by that very heteronormativity. Given that fact, how could the introductory section of a text on LGBTQ psychologies not be riddled with tensions and contradictions? Welcome to the dance.

REFERENCE

Kitzinger, C. (1997). Lesbian and gay psychology: A critical analysis. In D. Fox & I. Prilleltensky (Eds), *Critical Psychology: An introduction* (pp. 202–216). London: Sage.

CHAPTER 3

What Comes After Discourse Analysis for LGBTQ Psychology?

Peter Hegarty
University of Surrey, UK

In recent years, *discourse analysis* has become a popular approach both in British social psychology in general, and in British LGBTQ psychology in particular.[1] Practitioners of discourse analysis are reluctant to define the approach too narrowly, but rather call attention to the many ways that critical analysis can address questions about talk and text as forms of social action. Coyle's (2000a, p. 251) introduction to the field is typical:

> Discourse analysis is a field of inquiry that traces its roots to various domains such as speech act theory, ethnomethodology, conversation analysis and semiology. It owes a particular debt to post-structuralism which holds as a central tenet that meaning is not static and fixed but is fluid, provisional and context dependent. However, discourse analysis does not fit easily within any particular disciplinary boundaries.

'Discourse analysis' has also, on occasion, come to define *British* LGBTQ psychology against its US-based counterparts. In the foreword to the volume *Lesbian and Gay Psychology: New perspectives*, D'Augelli (2002, p. xv) notes that there may be a 'critical distinction between British lesbian and gay psychology and its American counterpart' due to the former's use of qualitative methods and 'an explicitly deconstructionist approach.' The back cover of the book also describes the incorporation of qualitative and quantitative methods as distinctly British. Editors Kitzinger and Coyle (2002) agree that the incorporation of positivist, essentialist contributions *and* qualitative, social constructionist contributions is evidence of both the vitality of the field and its utility for lesbian and gay politics. They point to Clarke's (2002) discourse analytic work in particular within their volume as exemplary of what social constructionism can offer British lesbian and gay psychology.

---

[1] By LGBTQ I mean, lesbian, gay, bisexual, trans and queer. This is not to say that my argument will contribute equally to all of these movements, draw equally on all of them, or assume their compatibility or complimentary.

Out in Psychology: Lesbian, gay, bisexual, trans and queer perspectives. Edited by Victoria Clarke and Elizabeth Peel.
© 2007 John Wiley & Sons, Ltd.

This chapter contests both the map of LGBTQ psychology that locates us within a field staked out by 'positivist' and 'social constructionist' flags, and the celebration of our representation of many points within this terrain. My argument is not with methodological or epistemological diversity in LGBTQ psychology. Rather, I suspect that measures of LGBTQ psychology's success that use yardsticks imported from psychology will under-estimate the areas that this map leaves uncharted. This chapter focuses in particular on the frontiers of social constructionism, which are often presented as radical, democratic or interdisciplinary. I hope to show that heteronormative assumptions can operate in social constructionist dialogues, can work to pen us in and can domesticate the animal that LGBTQ psychology might become.

I will first briefly situate my concerns with regard to the complex field of *queer theory*. This field – like discourse analysis – has complex roots, a commitment to post-structuralism, and an unease about being formulated as a single discipline or paradigm. Consequently my review of queer theory will be both partial and strategic. Next, I will review and critique a much-cited debate between 'critical discourse analysts' and 'con-versation analysts' regarding the proper objects and methods of qualitative inquiry. The debate in question makes reference to critical psychology, feminism and social construc-tionism. Yet, throughout there is a repeated erasure of the possibility that gendered people could be anything other than straight. This debate suggests that LGBTQ psychology ought to interrogate social constructionist paradigms rather than simply import or apply them. Finally, I conclude with some tentative ideas about forms of social construction that are lived out in sexual subcultures which provide resources and motivations for critiquing social constructionist assumptions.

QUEER THEORY AND THE 'DISCIPLINE' OF PSYCHOLOGY

In *Discipline and Punish*, Foucault (1975/1977) described a system of power called *dis-cipline* that involved the definition and inscription of a person's individuality, such that it could become an object of governmental power.[2] The double-meaning of 'discipline' as a professional standard of knowledge and as an exercise of power is not accidental. For Foucault, to have one's self written about, described, defined, measured or compared was to be in the grips of modern power. Psychology is pivotal to modern discipline, but does not have equal consequences for all:

> In a system of discipline, the child is more individualist than the adult, the patient more than the healthy man, the madman and the delinquent more than the normal and the non-delinquent . . . All the sciences, analyses of practices employing the root 'psycho-' have their origin in this historical reversal of the procedures of individual-ization. (Foucault, 1975/1977, p. 193)

Much critical psychology departs from this recognition that we are put-into-discourse, or subjected to it in the course of becoming subjects of psychological fields of documentation

---

[2] Lest there be any confusion, I want to make clear that I am not promoting 'Foucaultian discourse analysis' even though I am talking about Foucault and about discourse analysis. 'Foucaultian discourse analysis' has come to refer to a form of discourse analysis that examines relationships between large power structures (such as patriarchy) and local forms of talk. It has often been defined against conversation analysis which is considered to focus on microsociological concerns (see e.g. Potter & Wetherell, 1987, pp. 6–7; Wetherell, 1998). Like Hook (2001), I am deeply sceptical of the use of Foucault to sanction forms of discourse analysis that reduce 'discourse' to language, narrative and text, and that fail to historicize rela-tions between knowledge and power.

in exam marks, case histories, 'employability' profiles and so on (e.g. Henriques et al., 1984; Rose, 1989, 1996).

However, in *The History of Sexuality, Volume 1*, Foucault (1976/1978) ventured further that 'sexuality' is a privileged site where the goals of knowledge and the goals of power become interlaced. As with his account of disciplining practices and institutions, Foucault described the discourse of 'sexuality' as one that focused explicitly on abnormalities (see also Foucault, 2003). Pre-modern religious injunctions about sex were directed primarily at the sexual conduct of married couples. However, the edifice of modern 'sexuality' gained increased recognition in the late nineteenth century when it was used by psychiatrists and other experts to individualize such figures as hysterical women, masturbating children and sexual deviants. The resulting sexual typologies according to which we modern westerners live our lives are neither based on natural kinds nor internally consistent taxonomies – whether we consider the zoorasts, scopophiles and antipathic instincts of nineteenth-century sexology (e.g. Krafft-Ebbing, 1887/1931), or the contemporary paraphilias and personality disorders of today's Diagnostic and Statistical Manual (American Psychiatric Association, 1994; see Hagger-Johnson, Chapter 5). The term 'homosexuality' was used to describe abnormality several decades before its complement 'heterosexuality' came to be used to describe 'normal' people (Katz, 1995).[3]

In *The History of Sexuality*, Foucault also problematized the common sense notion that power works primarily through the political or psychological repression of what is natural. 'Sexuality' is not a system of understanding that is simply imposed on people top-down. Rather it is one that people reach for. Modern people often put their own sexualities into discourse through confessional practices (such as psychotherapy) quite freely, rather than under conditions of coercion. Foucault insisted that the production of knowledge about – or invention of – seemingly natural 'sexualities' was a more basic, pervasive and invidious extension of power than repression could ever be. Seemingly 'natural' sexualities with which people identified were historically recent inventions, and afforded a means of extending power over the individual. Indeed, if 'sexuality' is the means by which modern people are made subjects of power, then liberationist sexual politics only serve to inscribe power still further. As a result, Foucault considered it necessary to problematize both expert claims about the nature of sexual 'others' that came from above, and those that came 'from below' when people insisted upon the 'nature' of their repressed sexualities. As Rose (1989, 1996) explains, we live in a society where 'freedom of the individual' is not the opposite of power, but rather where power works by obliging us to be free.

Of course, many feminists have come to similar conclusions about the limits of identity-based political movements. Where women's bodies have been defined by biology, any politics based on 'women's nature' is vulnerable to reifying sexist biological discourses, and to limiting the scope of feminist politics as a result (Haraway, 1991). Kitzinger and Perkins (1993) described the power that operates between lesbian therapists and their clients as heavily reliant on the language of 'empowerment.' Their work also demonstrates the political limits of liberationist rhetoric that is allied with psychological essentialisms. In her critique of social science writings about lesbianism, Kitzinger (1987) described

---

[3] This dynamic of naming the exception prior to naming the norm is not unique to the homo/hetero binary, nor confined to the past. Many more people would recognize the meaning of 'bisexual' than 'monosexual', particularly those who are monosexual themselves. Similarly, bio males and bio females would be most likely to be more familiar with the terms 'trans men' and 'trans women' than the terms that define their own genders.

authors' rhetorical claims that expertise comes 'from above' through scientific objectivity and 'from below' through the experiential authority of lesbians' own experiences. Such 'insider accounts' in the social sciences promise 'special sensitivities, unusual skills, and privileged access to exclusive groups or exclusive information' (Kitzinger, 1987, p. 30). More recently, biological essentialist research on sexuality has been conducted by openly gay scientists, who use their sexual identities to present their work as gay-friendly, yet still traffic in biological discourses that are heteronormative and sexist (see e.g. Terry, 1997). In short, we are surrounded with reasons to question the ways that claims that are presented as self-evidently radical function to exclude critique of what our natures are and what they might become.

Sedgwick (1990) provided a further torque on Foucault's theory. While Foucault described sexuality as an 'especially tense transfer point' (1976/1978, p. 103) for the exchange of knowledge into power and back again, Sedgwick showed why *ignorance* must also be historicized and understood as a form of power. At its simplest, Sedgwick's argument is illustrated by the fact that the privilege of heterosexuality is best accomplished by silence. To insist on your straightness only raises the question of why you feel the need to insist. Sedgwick further described how disciplinary knowledge actively constructs ignorance in its formulation of knowledge. For example, she pointed to the terrifying ignorance within developmental psychology about how to care for effeminate boys who are likely to grow up gay (Sedgwick, 1993). Such ignorance as this is not simply a void that enlightenment has not yet illuminated. Rather it is historically produced, and can often be used as the means of exerting power. Thus Sedgwick and Foucault present a complicated schema about the relationship between visibility and power in modern sexual politics. On the one hand, normativity is both evidenced and extended by its remaining implicit and taken-for-granted within discourses such as psychiatric taxonomies. On the other hand, neither theorist denies that repression occurs, or that control over homosexuality can operate through discourses that work through denial, silence or deliberate ignorance.

As a counter-disciplinary impulse, queer work insists that disciplinary knowledge should remain open to critique, particularly with regard to the ways that knowledge disciplines and creates ignorance about sexual and gender minorities and subversive sexual and gender practices. British lesbian and gay psychology – described by Kitzinger and Coyle (2002) as occupying a space marked by the disciplines of positivist science and social constructionism – is no exception. It is easy to see how positivist science is a form of knowledge that is founded on ignorance. Empiricism was invented as a system of claims about 'matters of facts' that arise directly from nature in complete ignorance of the opinions or politics of those scientists who craft the experiments that reveal them. However, experiments have always relied on the testimony of witnesses to establish such matters of fact, such that the credibility of witnesses – and very rapidly that of scientific authors – became an indispensable resource in the process of establishing natural facts (Shapin & Schaeffer, 1985). Since the seventeenth century, scientific credibility has been anxiously gendered as masculine, and has produced heteronormative effects. Even seventeenth-century natural philosophers such as Robert Boyle enacted performances of masculinity in the course of reporting experiments (Haraway, 1997).[4] When psychologists adapted

---

[4] Haraway (1997) describes how the Fellows of the Royal Society enacted 'modest witnessing' as a new performance of masculinity that had an unstable grip on social acceptability. Modest witness invoked a gendered discourse in which proper science was conducted between male scientists and a female nature (see also Keller, 1985).

experimental methods to studying sexuality in the twentieth century these questions of trustworthiness were amplified still further. To present their work as science, psychologists with varying sexual identities have routinely erased the identities and the scientific work of lesbians, gays, bisexuals and sex worker collaborators (see e.g. Gathorne-Hardy, 1998; Hegarty, 2003a; Irvine, 1990; Minton, 2002; Terry, 1999).

However, it is not positivist science, but social constructionist epistemology, and discourse analytic methods in particular, which are held up as the sophisticated – and distinctively British – component of British lesbian and gay psychology. Keeping in mind Foucault's insistence that 'sexuality' comes from below as well as from above, I want to turn now to consider how ignorance about queerness is actively produced in a dialogue among social constructionists who consider themselves to have moved beyond positivist goals. In revisiting this debate, I am hoping to move away from discussions about the locations within the positivist-constructionist field from which LGBTQ psychology might strategically engage (see e.g. Bell et al., 2002; Coyle, 2000b; Kitzinger, 1997; Rivers, 2000). Perhaps we can instead locate these poles themselves, and push past the disciplinary boundaries that they mark?

WHEN IS A CONVERSATION GENDERED?

The debate in question centres on differences between conversation analysis's and critical discourse analysis's claims as to when social identities in general – and gender in particular – may be used as an analytic tool for interpreting conversational data. It began with Schegloff's (1997) restatement of conversational analytic principles. Conversation analysis (CA) is a sociological tradition that is derived from the ethnomethodological assumption that the rules of social order are not pre-given, but must be remade continuously in local social interactions through forms of social practice (see Garfinkel, 1967). Conversation analysts are particularly concerned with the reproduction of the rules of conversational 'turn-taking', through which people come to occupy and give up 'the floor' of a conversation (Sacks, Schegloff & Jefferson, 1974). Conversation analysis contextualizes causal processes and thus conversation analysts also query appeals to long-standing social identities – such as gender, age, etc. – as explanations of why any particular conversation proceeds as it does. Rather, participants' social identities may be used as analytic tools only if the participants themselves orient towards them (see Antaki & Widdicombe, 1998; Edwards, 1998, for similar accounts of this disciplinary standard).

Schegloff (1997) explained this position with reference to the category 'gender' through an analysis of two extracts of conversations involving men and women. The first conversation occurred between 'Tony' and 'Marsha' described as 'the parents – now separated or divorced – of the teenaged Joey, who lives with his father in Northern California, but has just spent a period of vacation from school with his mother in southern California' (p. 172). The second conversation occurred when 'Michael and Nancy are having dinner with Shane and Vivien.' Four pages of analysis are devoted to 14 lines of talk from the first extract. However, Schegloff, who repeatedly described his analysis as 'formal' and 'serious', also often signalled that he was reigning himself in with phrases such as 'it may be worth considering – though not now' (p. 175) and 'we haven't the time to work through the grounds for this assertion' (p. 178). In spite of their being male and female, Schegloff insisted that gender is not a useful category to bring to the analysis of what Tony and

Marsha are doing with their talk. However, gender *did* become relevant in the second conversation at the point where Shane levelled a gender-related insult at Vivian, an insult that is discussed below in greater detail.

Schegloff (1997) did not emphatically claim that gender only ever became relevant when people refer to it explicitly. But he gave little sustained attention to the thorny issue of when participants might be said to be orienting towards gender without mentioning it at all. He was emphatic, however, that several forms of 'critical discourse analysis' employed gender as a category of analysis prematurely and inappropriately. Such uses of gender imposed 'a kind of hegemony of the intellectuals' (p. 167), which CA's interpretive norms avoided. Thus, in contrast to positivist discourses, which establish a social scientist's legitimacy through objectivity performances or appeals to empirical truths, Schegloff's (1997) account of CA argued for a form of disciplined enquiry on the basis that it is consistent with the interests of the people we are enquiring about.

In defence of critical discourse analysis, Wetherell (1998) presented an analysis of an interview involving a male interviewer and a group of 'white, 17–18 year old male students' that centred on one of the participants' 'behaviour at a pub on the Friday night and at a party on the Saturday night and the nature of his involvement with four different young women' (p. 389). For Wetherell, this conversation was intelligible at more than one level. She first analysed the participants' talk conversational-turn-by-conversational-turn in the manner of a conversation analyst, and next described the *interpretative repertoires* used in the talk. This concept is a discourse analytic one; it refers to clusters of terms and metaphors used to characterize people and events (Potter & Wetherell, 1987, p. 138). In this context, Wetherell mentioned such repertoires as 'male sexuality as performance and achievement' and 'an ethics of sexuality as legitimated by relationships and responsibility'. She argued that attention to such repertoires provides a more complete, historically situated account of the participants' talk than the turn-by-turn analysis could accomplish on its own. Not surprisingly, Schegloff (1998) responded by applauding the first aspect of Wetherell's analysis and critiquing her use of repertoires on the grounds that it imposes Wetherell's own interests where they do not belong.

Billig (1999) offered a second response to Schegloff by arguing that the practice of CA was inconsistent with the desire to use only participants' own terms during analysis. Indeed, conversation analysts are centrally interested in turn-taking (Sacks et al., 1974), which is rarely the topic of anyone's conversation (apart, of course, from conversation analysts themselves). The shift from participants' own vernacular to the analytic terms of 'serious' or 'disciplined' CA represented for Billig 'not a pure empiricism, but an unexamined view of the social order' (p. 556). In particular, Billig (1999) noted that 'conversation' was often presented as a privileged object of study by virtue of being a 'natural' form of talk-in-interaction, in ignorance of the historicity of the concept. For Billig, positioning conversation as the default form of talk-in-interaction assumes that talk ordinarily occurs between equals in informal settings. However, informal settings are structured by systematic gender inequalities, suggesting that CA operates with a constructed account of talk which has the effect of obscuring such inequalities.

Billig described the naming of participants as one practice that constructs a problematic account of the social order. Sometimes participants are identified in CA as 'A', 'B' or with similar terms of anonymity. However, Schegloff used first names such as 'Tony' and 'Marsha' throughout, suggesting individuality, familiarity and – of course – gender. Here, Billig's argument took a questionable turn as he asked his readers to imagine how the identities of a male rapist and his female victim might be identified in CA. 'A' and 'B' would assume an interchangeability of roles that their genders would trouble. Yet, if roles such as 'rapist' and 'victim' are to be used in this case, why wouldn't roles be used to identify separated partners? Billig (1999, p. 555) argues 'if it is "rapist" and "victim" in the rape situation (or "bully" and "victim" / "racist" and "victim" etc.), then why should it be "Marsha" and "Tony", not "primary caretaker" and "secondary caretaker"?'. The point of this comparison was to question whether Schegloff's disciplinary standards operate more smoothly when violence and coercion between men and women are absent rather than present, and whether those standards do not privilege consensual conversations between equals as the normative form of talk-in-interaction as a result.

Schegloff's (1999) response did not engage with Billig's recognition that disciplinary norms set up certain kinds of identities and interactions as defaults and obscure others as deviant cases. In response to the claim that 'conversation' was naturalized as the default form of talk-in-interaction, Schegloff referred only to early conversation analytic work that stated how talk *could* be structured by varying degrees of inequality. In response to the point that CA runs aground when it approaches gendered violence, Schegloff referred to a study of 'recidivism among wife batterers' (1999, p. 561) but gave no indication of how such men were or ought to have been identified by name, role or capital letter. Unable to categorically defend any particular naming convention, Schegloff argued that the point was of minimal importance. He defended his particular identification of 'Tony' and 'Marsha' on the grounds that: 'first name is opaque except (as Billig points out) with respect to gender and (as he does not) sometimes age, given fashions in naming practices' (1999, p. 566). However, Schegloff asserted that attaching roles to participants would be wrong as it would presume too much in advance. Of course, this rejoinder only serves to confirm Billig's point that the assumption that men and women do *not* occupy unequal roles in modern society informs Schegloff's account of CA.

CONJOINED COUPLES: HETEROSEXISM BY COMMISSION

My recap of this debate may appear to have brought us very far from queer theory. However, this debate confirms Foucault's call for a critique of power that comes from below as well as from above is relevant here; the disciplinary perspectives put forward in this debate appeal to their humble origins in participants' own terms (Schegloff, 1997), non-positivist scholarship (Wetherell, 1998) and feminism (Billig, 1999). Nor have we strayed as far from 'sexuality' as it might at first seem. Heterosexuality is ever-present in this debate, but everywhere it goes without saying. The contributions to the debate are characterized by something akin to what Braun (2000) called 'heterosexism by commission'; the explicit use of heterosexual assumptions without marking their specificity or particularity. All of the interactions that are presented as real or fictional cases involve interactions between men and women whose relationships are structured by heterosexuality. These include the disputes of partnered and separated heterosexuals (Schegloff, 1997), the heterosexual exploits of one young man (Wetherell, 1998) and a heterosexual rape (Billig, 1999).

Argumentation, exploitation and violence are far from being normative or ideal enactments of heterosexuality. But only at one point in the debate was there any recognition that these conversations reflect badly on heterosexuality as a practice, or on heterosexuals as a group. It is difficult to imagine any reason – other than liberal trepidation about sexual difference – that would have made these same authors resist naming participants as 'gay' or 'lesbian' so consistently, or of avoiding the question of generalizing to all gay or lesbian people, had the participants involved been Toni and Marsha, or Tony and Mark. Further, the more obviously coercive forms of heterosexuality were imagined or reported rather than actually observed. The debate moved from actual arguments to first-person reports of students' 'gitty' actions, to the imagination of unambiguous violence. Both CA and critical discourse analysis are interested in talk as a form of action rather than as a form of representation. Both proscribe disinterest and heightened suspicion about the factual basis of what participants are actually reporting. As a result, there is an empirical focus on mild forms of problematic heterosexuality – such as verbal argument – but a relative ignorance about more problematic kinds of heterosexuality, such as heterosexual rape, which are more likely to be reported than observed.[5]

Morever, the internal logic of both Schegloff's position and Billig's critique of it would break apart if one remembered that not all people are straight or equally gender-conforming. Schegloff's account of CA holds that talk must be analysed *in context*. Yet, in his response to Billig, he argued that first names such as 'Tony' and 'Marsha' communicate only gender and age. Obviously, this latter claim is weak. If names communicate something about age because of changes in naming fashions (as Schegloff asserts) then they can also connote something about ethnicity, nationality, first language and much more. This simple fact is obscured by the use of the Anglo names 'Tony' and 'Marsha'. These pass without comment, much as English language use tends to do in Schegloff's country of residence (see Hill, 1999).

More to the point, if language use is to be interpreted *in context* as Schegloff insists, then surely these names should be understood as 'Tony and Marsha' rather than as 'Tony' and as 'Marsha'? Isn't the conjunction 'and' a vital part of these names' context that should appear inside the quotation marks? The 'and' suggested that Tony and Marsha are a heterosexual couple, and 'and' is only one of several ways that this pair were positioned as such.[6] We were told that they are married – a right that continues to be denied to same-sex couples in the USA. They are Joey's parents, a legal status that same-sex couples enjoy to variable degrees across the individual American states. Heterosexuality by commission abounds.

However, in Schegloff's second example, the conjunction of names on its own was sufficient to organize a party of four dinner guests into two heterosexual couples. Schegloff (1997, p. 180) introduced the participants as follows:

> In the following exchange Michael and Nancy are having dinner with Shane and Vivian. The occasion is being videotaped by Vivian for a course in which she has enrolled; the exchange occurs shortly after the start of the tape.

---

[5] This trend is far from arbitrary or isolated. In an argument for feminist conversation analysis, Kitzinger (2000) suggests that the approach would be well suited to the study of sexual harassment and sexual violence. However, she notes 'I am not aware of any examples of conversation analytic work on actual instances of (what analysts might gloss as) sexual harassment' (p. 168). Indeed, Billig's invention of the rape deserves further scrutiny in light of Hammersley's (2003) claim that critical discourse analysis and CA are insulated from other forms of social science, and Erlich's (2002) argument that feminist discourse analysis must engage with the realities of violence against women. If Billig had been interested in highlighting sexual coercion and inequality, why not interview the very real women that Wetherell's (1998) participants bragged about rather than invent a fictionalized idealized scenario?

[6] By 'heterosexual couple,' I mean a couple made up of two people who identify with different genders. I am mindful that either or both members of any such couples may not identify with the term 'heterosexual' for a range of reasons.

Schegloff insisted that a converation must be analysed in its own terms, and that the participants' social identities cannot be used as analytic resources until the participants themselves orient towards them. However, their talk might be analysed differently if their identities were not assumed to be heterosexual. This conversation was reported by Schegloff (1997, p. 181) as follows:

```
1      Shane:              [.hghh huh 'hhhh most wishful thinking

2                      → hey had me some a 'dat fuckin budder willyou?

3                (0.8)

4      ?Shane:      °°Oh::yeah°°

5                (1.1)

6      Nancy:  →   C'n I have some t[oo

7      Michael:                    [mm-hmm[hm:

8      Nancy:                            [hm-mm-^h[m    [^he-ha-]ha'hehh ]

9      Vivian:→                                   [Ye[h[I wa]nt]sometoo.]

10     Shane:                                      [N[o:. ]   [(  )-

11     Shane:            No.

12                (0.2)

13     Shane:  →   Ladies la:st.
```

According to Schegloff (1997, p. 182) Shane's last comment made gender relevant and was an ironic inversion of the politeness rule 'ladies first'. But the analysis of what Shane's comment does might proceed very differently if the dinner party guests had not already been constructed by Schegloff as heterosexual couples. What if Michael and Nancy are a bio man and bio woman respectively who are meeting Vivian, a trans woman, and Shane her bio female lesbian partner for the first time? Perhaps then, Shane was not making gender 'the relevant thing about her' (see Edwards, 1998), but was orienting to Michael's and Nancy's mutterings on lines 7–8, and constructing them as unfamiliarity with, or unease about, trans people. Alternatively, perhaps Shane is a butch dyke who is ironizing masculinity and performing for the video camera – perhaps with an eye to providing Vivian's sociology class with a quandary as to whether or not this is how queers really talk.

I am not claiming *any* realism for such alternatives to Schegloff's analysis. Indeed, Schegloff's (1997) norms are aimed not at distinguishing true from false accounts, but at distinguishing between equally true accounts of this conversation on the basis of their relevance to their participants' own concerns. My point is that in these examples 'the participants concerns' are not easily read from the data but depend on the assumptions that the analyst brings to them (as Stokoe & Smithson, 2001, have forcefully argued). These assumptions include, of course, the matter of the participants' sexual and gender identities. 'The participants' concerns' are as variable as the assumptions about their identities that we might make.

Thus, it makes sense to agree with Billig that conversation analysis is always more than CA and that analysts' descriptions of their methodological norms are not quite the same thing as their interpretive practices. However, Billig's (1999) critique of CA was as firmly grounded in heterosexism by commission as Schegloff's (1997) account. Billig (1999, p. 554) similarly conjoined individuals into implicitly heterosexual couples, beginning his discussion of a rape as follows: 'one might imagine that the talk, in the course of a rape . . .' Note that the genders of the rapist and the victim are not identified. When subsequently discussing the possible labels that could be used for these persons, Billig writes: 'perhaps they should be "man" and "woman" or "rapist" and "victim"' (p. 555). Setting up the conjoined pairs *man/woman* and *rapist/victim* as alternatives shows that it was to be assumed all along that the rapist was male and the victim female. Moreover, the lack of any explanation of the conjunction further instantiates the normativity of this arrangement of genders. Other possibilities are simply beyond this discussion (but see Davies, 2000). Again, the heterosexual couple goes without saying.

Billig's use of conjunctions also endows Tony and Marsha with gender roles that they may not recognize. Kitzinger (2000) described how Billig's (1999) use of feminism assumes rather rigid power differences between men and women, and as a result reproduces essentialist forms of feminist argument. However, she did not point out the obvious way that this occurs in Billig's use of the fictional rape to trouble Schegloff's naming conventions. Let me quote this passage once again.

> If it is 'rapist' and 'victim' in the rape situation (or 'bully' and 'victim'/'racist' and 'victim' etc.), then why should it be 'Marsha' and 'Tony', not 'primary caretaker' and 'secondary caretaker'? (p. 555)

Not only did Billig's mapping of *Marsha/Tony* onto *primary/secondary caretaker* assume that gender determines caregiving roles in some absolute essential sense, it was at odds with Schegloff's (1997) description of Joey as living primarily with Tony rather than Marsha. Indeed, it was at odds with Billig's (1999) own recognition that: '"Tony" and "Marsha" are that statistically less frequent couple where the father has primary care responsibility for the child' (pp. 553–554).

The error is not a trivial one. If gender did not determine childcare roles in an absolute sense (and Marsha and Tony's arrangements show that it did not) then Billig's argument that gendered power in the private sphere can be assumed in advance begins to falter. Ironically, while Billig insisted that conversation analysis is always more than CA, his own analysis failed to recognize how gender is always more than gendered roles. While he invented a 'deviant case' of a heterosexual rape to forward his argument, he overlooked the way that Marsha and Tony's deviation from gender roles problematizes his own account of feminism.

Yet, in a rejoinder, Schegloff (1999) cited the very passage in Billig's article that I have quoted twice, but did not refer to Billig's construction of Marsha and Tony's household arrangements. Thus both Schegloff and Billig ignored what they already knew about Marsha and Tony's lives (other than the snippet of conversation that is reported). This dis-attending to Marsha and Tony's lives is not idiosyncratic. Hammersley (2003) has critiqued the focus on language in both CA and critical discourse analysis as a form of 'methodological severity' that engenders disinterest in participants' lives, limits engagement with other forms of social science, and leads to 'ontological gerrymandering' between realist and constructionist claims.[7] Both approaches insist on the *constructed* nature of participants' claims about the world, while forwarding *realist* accounts of participants' lives, and of discursive objects such as 'conversational turns' or 'interpretive repertoires' not in terms of their functions, but as claims about real kinds of talk. As I have shown above, it is within these realist sections of their articles – such as Schegloff's description of Michael, Nancy, Shane and Vivian – that participants are constructed by commission to be heterosexual. How might we query these constructions?

GENDER? WHICH GENDER?

Toward the end of her article, Wetherell provides the only gesture toward a movement beyond heterosexism by commission:

> We should also be interested in the 'heteronormativity' (Kitzinger, personal communication) evident throughout the discussion which supplies a further taken for granted discursive back-cloth organizing these young men's participant orientations and their members' methods for making sense. (p. 404)

Here, Wetherell constructs 'heteronormativity' as a queer object indeed. She suggests that we *should* be interested in it, but she is not so interested in it except to mention it as anything but an afterthought to her lengthy analysis. The quotation marks around the term suggest it is unfamiliar to Wetherell, her readers, or to both. Yet there is no attempt to elaborate what this foreign term might mean. The citation leads to a *personal communication*, suggesting that it is known only through informal academic networks. Wetherell constructs heteronormativity as odd, at some distance from herself, and barely a proper object of academic knowledge at all. 'Heteronormativity' is quite unlike 'gender', which Schegloff, Wetherell and Billig all construct as a patently obvious topic for social scientists to debate.

   Wetherell's construction of 'heteronormativity' obscures the queer work of the previous decade (see e.g. Turner, 2000, for a review), which had taken it as a central analytic term, rather than an optional add-on, that could be included in debates about gender and discourse as an afterthought. Butler (1990, 1993) draws attention to the way that 'gender' functions as an oppositional term to 'sex'; the former being seen as constructed, social and volitional and the latter as real, material, or given.[8] Yet, the point where 'sex' ends

---

[7] 'Ontological gerrymandering' is a term used by Woolgar and Pawluch (1985) to describe the unprincipled and self-serving ways that scientists move between realist claims and constructionist ones to grant their own work a greater epistemological status than that of their opponents. Within social constructionist debate the term has particular force, as social constructionists imagine themselves to be working with epistemologies that supersede those of positivist science, not those that share its problematics.

[8] The meaning of the term 'gender' evidences Foucault's claim that 'sexuality' originates with discourses about abnormality first and normality only second. Originating with studies of intersex children, the term was used to craft a psychological basis for dividing the world into two types of people in the absence of physical evidence for a categorical distinction between males and females (see e.g. Dreger, 1998; Fausto-Sterling, 2000; Hausman, 1995). Similarly, attempts to study 'masculinity' and 'femininity' in psychology originate in the impulses to study and normalize gender transgression, not the impulse to study sex differences in personality (see Terry, 1999). This point is entirely absent from the Schegloff-Wetherell-Billig debate. Ironically, both CA and critical discourse analysis claim ethnomethodology as an influence, but all parties in the debate ignored Garfinkel's (1967) foundational work on ethnomethodology, which forcefully argued that sexed bodies were culturally constructed.

and 'gender' begins is inherently debatable. Multiple accounts of the boundary might be offered, and Butler (1993) insists that each account constructs a different form of material sex. In this sense, material 'sex' becomes understood not as the solid material bedrock on which gender is 'constructed' but rather as an effect of gendered discourse, perhaps that discourse's most forceful effect, as it no longer even appears to be an effect at all. Moreover, Butler argues that those accounts of 'sex' that have been conceded as being 'beyond construction' have been heteronormative. By ungrounding 'sex' we might not only live gender differently, but also queer the materiality of sex and allow for the recognition of material bodies that are currently obscured.

LGBTQ psychologists are used to thinking about the ways that contemporary essentialist accounts of gay and lesbian bodies proceed through discourses that presume the normative body to be straight (see e.g. British Psychological Society Lesbian and Gay Psychology Section, 2004; Hegarty, 2003b). However, we are less explicit about the heteronormativity of social constructionist assumptions, or about how they might limit our scholarship and politics. Butler's critique of the notion that there is a material 'sex' onto which 'gender' is constructed resonates with Hammersley's (2003) critique of CA and critical discourse analysts' practice of describing a 'real' context, within which participants socially construct the world. Both express dissatisfaction with forms of social constructionism that limit themselves to examining some objects (gender, participants talk) but remain realistic about others (physical sex, analysts' descriptions of context). Hess (1997) calls this 'conservative constructionism'. When heterosexism remains part of the real that is being conserved – as in Schegloff's description of the four dinner guests, or as in the version of 'gender' that is under debate – I am minded to use such disciplinary standards as objects of critique rather than guiding epistemologies.

CRUISING PAST SOCIAL CONSTRUCTIONS

I have focused on one specific, but highly influential, debate here to show how heteronormativity is routinely reproduced in social constructionist debates about both the 'formal' and the 'critical' ways of reading gender from conversations. In conclusion I want to raise a broader question about the relationship between LGBTQ psychology and social constructionist scholarship. Central to social constructionism, particularly discourse analysis, is the orientation to sociality as a form of *textuality*.[9] Yet, an increasing number of critical psychologists are recognizing that this orientation has its blind spots (e.g. Brown, 2001; Hook, 2001; Nightingale & Cromby, 1999). In the remainder of this chapter, I want to examine the possibility that LGBTQ psychology might contribute to the imagination of what social constructionism might become as we move past the rigid assumption that sociality can be represented by textuality.

---

[9] Discourse analysis has been defined as primarily if not exclusively concerned with language. For example, Potter and Wetherell (1987, p. 7) announced that '[w]e will use "discourse" in its most open sense . . . to cover all forms of spoken interaction, formal and informal, and written texts of any kind'. Parker (1992) allows some more latitude in allowing material non-textual objects into the definition of 'discourse' but still relies on the verbality of a social practice to define what is and what is not 'discourse'. In regard to a video game in which a figure chases ghosts with a crucifix, he writes 'this is a text. A Christian discourse inhabits this text, and it is the translation of this text into a written and spoken form that renders that discourse "visible" or, more accurately, in which the category "discourse" becomes appropriate' (p. 6).

It is extremely common for ethnographic accounts of sexual subcultures to point out the salience of non-verbal forms of communication. This point has been obvious since the very earliest work in LGBTQ psychology. For the sake of brevity I will refer to only one case:

> If one watches very carefully and knows what to watch for in a 'gay' bar, one observes that some individuals are apparently communicating with each other without exchanging words, simply by exchanging glances – but not the kind of quick glance that ordinarily passes between men. Homosexuals say that, if another man catches and holds the glance, one knows immediately that he is one of them. The psychological structure of that meeting of glances is a complex one, involving mutual recognition of social but not personal identity, sexual intent, and agreement; but we are far from being able to analyze that structure. Many men in a bar, then, are not engaged in conversation but are standing along a wall or by themselves at vantage points in the room, so that they may be seen as well as see, and are scanning faces and bodies. Occasionally, one may see a glance catch and hold another glance. Later, as if in an accidental meeting, the two holders-of-a-glance may be seen in brief conversation followed by their leaving together – or the conversation may be omitted . . . What I have described is one form of 'cruising'. (Hooker, 1965, pp. 96–97)

What does the cruising that Hooker observed tell us about social constructionism? First, let's consider how a 'methodologically severe' (Hammersley, 2003) discourse analyst might approach Hooker's work. Potter and Wetherell (1987, p. 30) insist that ethnographic accounts are less valid than verbatim transcripts of interaction, as the former rely on 'pre-packaged' talk rather than recordings of the social interaction in its full complexity. They would insist that Hooker's description be read as an *account* of social interactions rather than a literal description of them. This approach orients our attention towards the rhetorical construction of Hooker's account, towards the actions that her words perform, and it would suspend judgement or interest in the facticity of her claims. In short, it would orient our attention away from the gay men and their subculture towards the academic and her writing.

Ethnographic writing is certainly a genre that interprets events (see e.g. Pratt, 1986) and Hooker's writings are characterized by liberal assumptions (see Hegarty, 2003a; Warner, 2004). However, rather than develop a constructionist critique of Hooker's account of these practices, LGBTQ psychologists have the option of transgressing the methodological severity of social constructionist principles. Indeed, if we take Hooker's description at face value for a moment, it suggests that the central assumption of social constructionism – that the social can be understood as the textual – may be deeply flawed and can have heteronormative effects. These men appear to be deliberately avoiding verbal forms of communication, or at best to be using language as a secondary dispensable medium of social interaction. The methodological severity of discourse analysis ensures a state of ignorance about the forms of social construction with which they are engaged, as it orients our attention away from them. Hammersley (2003) has argued that the exclusive focus on language in CA and in discourse analysis insulates the field from critical engagement with other forms of social science. I would argue that it also insulates researchers from critical engagement with the people that they study, some of whom may be practicing social construction in ways that academic accounts of 'social construction' do not recognize.

I would further insist that these men most certainly are engaged in social construction. Cruising proceeds through mutual gaze, mutual flouting of implicit cultural rules about the length of eye gaze between men, and mutual recognition of the possibilities of sexual intentions and desires that the gaze might communicate. Cruising is much more social than discourse; it depends absolutely on the recognition of another to become 'cruising' rather than gazing. You cannot cruise alone as easily as you can talk, read or write alone. Cruising also constructs the meaning of individuals (e.g. as gay), their intentional states (e.g. as sexually interested) and desires (e.g. for particular partners or actions) and enables forms of practice (e.g. sex). But it does so, commonly, without language. More than discourse or text, cruising shows that personhood falls out from social interaction rather that precedes it. Yet, there is very little that cruising represents that it does not also construct.

In forwarding cruising as a model for social constructionism, I am not arguing that LGBTQ psychologists need to always consider social construction 'in their participants' own terms'. Nor am I arguing for a form of phenomenological analysis which assumes that language is a permeable medium for accessing a participants' phenomenological self (Reid, Flowers & Larkin, 2005). Rather, I am arguing that ordinary observations about sexual cultures routinely trouble academics' equations of social life with a narrow sense of 'discourse', or of communication with verbal communication. LGBTQ psychologists have choices about how to theorize these questions. Much as Butler (1993) has argued that sex/gender boundaries are omnipresent *and* contingent, I suspect that psychology all but inevitably engages in ontological gerrymandering between realist and constructionist claims. But LGBTQ psychologists also make informed collective and individual political epistemological choices about when to move against established cannons and theories, and when to regard our participants as theorists in their own right who are not simply 'data' for analysis, but critics of the forms of analysis which have been canonized as radical in contemporary psychology. In presenting cruising as an alternative model of social constructionism to 'text', I am insisting on a form of analysis that requires familiarity with and knowledge of sexual subcultures – rather than distance from and ignorance of them – as an epistemological requirement of analysis.

Foucault's (1976/1978) *History of Sexuality* has been considered by some to end with more of a whimper than a bang. Having rejected liberationist politics, Foucault was reluctant to erect a utopian alternative of his own. He was also mindful that any such vision could become a norm that would have the effects on people that he was trying to critique and contest. Instead, he gestured towards 'a different economy of bodies and pleasures' (Foucault, 1976/1978, p. 159) that we might recognize when he came to understand 'sexuality' as a modern imposition with which we had come to identify rather than a God-given part of our nature. In this chapter, I have critiqued the operations of heteronormativity in debates about the 'discipline' of CA and in 'critical' forms of discourse analysis. But my goal has not been to 'liberate' LGBTQ psychology from an oppressive methodological yoke, as much as to throw the impulse to create disciplinary knowledge about gender and discourse into question.

Perhaps the cruising that was going on in Hooker's gay bar has a final lesson by showing us that social construction can be performed for the sake of engendering pleasure rather than producing disciplinary knowledge. I am forwarding cruising not so much to return material bodies to social constructionism, as to query the way that disciplines can become evacuated of pleasure. Gay men learn how to cruise – which is to say they learn to analyse, enact and transform modes of social construction of self and other – in the service of engendering pleasure in themselves and others. Academics, by contrast, learn to conduct social constructionist analysis with the goal of contributing to a discipline, or of entering one. In contrast to the thrills – and disappointments – of cruising, learning to do discourse analysis has been described as a process that is devoid of pleasure, and consists only of repeated disappointments. Potter and Wetherell (1987) describe it as follows:

> Analysis involves a lot of careful reading and rereading. Often it is only after long hours struggling with the data and many false starts that a systematic patterning emerges. False starts occur as patterns appear, excitement grows, only to find that the pattern postulated leaves too much unaccounted, or results in an equally large file of exceptions. (p. 168)

LGBTQ psychologists need not look to such descriptions as this for models of how to feel our about academic work. Instead, we can look to LGBTQ communities for possibilities of how knowledge and pleasure might go together more easily. Yet, it should not come as a surprise that LGBTQ psychologies – which have not critically engaged with social constructionism and its denial of non-verbal communication and of pleasure in particular – have ironically had little to say about sex at all. To return to *Lesbian and Gay Psychology*, Kitzinger and Coyle (2002) write that: 'ironically, the psychology of lesbian and gay *sexuality* is only touched on in this book (although the psychology of gay male sexuality has been partly addressed in the substantial literature on HIV/AIDS)' (p. 18, original emphasis). British LGBTQ psychology has often been defined as occupying a space between positivism and social constructionism. But the field may become what it has not yet been. We might cruise past these poles to bring psychology in new directions, bringing new pleasures to research as we go.

REFERENCES

American Psychiatric Association (1994). *The Diagnostic and Statistical Manual of Mental Disorders* (4th edn). Washington, DC: American Psychiatric Association.

Antaki, C. & Widdicombe, S. (1998). Identity as an achievement and as a tool. In C. Antaki & S. Widdicombe (Eds), *Identities in Talk* (pp. 1–14). London: Sage.

Bell, S., Kitzinger, C., Hodges, I., Coyle, A. & Rivers, I. (2002). Reflections on 'science', 'objectivity' and personal investment in lesbian, gay and bisexual psychology. *Lesbian & Gay Psychology Review*, **3**(3), 91–95.

Billig, M. (1999). Whose terms? Whose ordinariness? Rhetoric and ideology in conversation analysis. *Discourse & Society*, **10**(4), 543–582.

British Psychological Society Lesbian and Gay Psychology Section (2004). A complex multidisciplinary issue [Letter]. *The Psychologist*, **17**(6), 320–321.

Braun, V. (2000). Heterosexism in focus group research: Collusion and challenge. *Feminism & Psychology*, **10**(1), 133–140.

Brown, S.D. (2001). Psychology and the art of living. *Theory & Psychology*, **11**(2), 171–192.

Butler, J. (1990). *Gender Trouble: Feminism and the subversion of identity*. New York, NY: Routledge.

Butler (1993). *Bodies that Matter: On the discursive limits of 'sex'*. New York, NY: Routledge.

Clarke, V. (2002). Resistance and normalization in the construction of lesbian and gay families: A discursive analysis. In A. Coyle & C. Kitzinger (Eds), *Lesbian & Gay Psychology: New perspectives* (pp. 98–116). Oxford: BPS Blackwell.

Coyle, A. (2000a). Discourse analysis. In G.M. Breakwell, S. Hammond & C. Fife-Schaw (Eds), *Research Methods in Psychology* (2nd edn) (pp. 243–258). London: Sage.

Coyle, A. (2000b). Qualitative research and lesbian and gay psychology in Britain. *Newsletter of the British Psychological Society Lesbian and Gay Section*, **Issue 4**, 2–5.

Davies, M. (2000). Male rape: The invisible victims. *Lesbian & Gay Psychology Review*, **1**(1), 11–15.

D'Augelli, A.R. (2002). The cutting edges of lesbian and gay psychology. In A. Coyle & C. Kitzinger (Eds), *Lesbian and Gay Psychology: New perspectives* (pp. xiii–xvi). Oxford: BPS Blackwell.

Dreger, A. D. (1998). *Hermaphrodites and the Medical Invention of Sex*. Cambridge, MA: Harvard University Press.

Edwards, D. (1998). The relevant thing about her: Social identity categories in use. In C. Antaki & S. Widdicombe (Eds), *Identities in Talk* (pp. 15–33). London: Sage.

Erlich, S. (2002). Discourse, gender and sexual violence. *Discourse & Society*, **13**(1), 5–7.

Fausto-Sterling, A. (2000). *Sexing the Body: Gender politics and the construction of Sexuality*. New York, NY: Basic Books.

Foucault, M. (1975/1977). *Discipline and Punish: The birth of the prison* (trans Alan Sheridan). New York, NY: Vintage Books.

Foucault, M. (1976/1978). *The History of Sexuality: An introduction, Volume 1* (trans Robert Hurley). New York, NY: Random House.

Foucault, M. (2003). *Abnormal: Lectures at the Collège de France 1974–1975* (trans Graham Burchell). London: Verso.

Garfinkel, H. (1967). *Studies in Ethnomethodology*. Engelwood Cliffs, NJ: Prentice-Hall.

Gathorne-Hardy, J. (1998). *Sex the Measure of all Things: A life of Alfred C. Kinsey*. London: Chatto & Windus.

Hammersley, M. (2003). Conversation analysis and discourse analysis: Methods or paradigms? *Discourse & Society*, **14**(6), 751–781.

Haraway, D. (1991). *Simians, Cyborgs, and Women*. New York, NY: Routledge.

Haraway, D. (1997). *Modest_Witness@Second_Millenium.FemaleMan©_Meets_Oncomouse*[TM]. New York, NY: Routledge.

Hausman, B.L. (1995). *Changing Sex: Transsexualism, technology, and the idea of Gender*. Durham, NC: Duke University Press.

Hegarty, P. (2003a). Homosexual signs and heterosexual silences: Rorschach studies of male homosexuality from 1921 to 1967. *Journal of the History of Sexuality*, **12**(3), 400–423.

Hegarty, P. (2003b). Pointing to a crisis: What finger-length ratios tell us about the construction of sexuality. *Radical Statistics*, **83**, 16–30.

Henriques, J., Hollway, W., Urwin, C., Venn, C. & Walkerdine, V. (1984). *Changing the Subject: Psychology, social regulation and subjectivity*. London: Methuen.

Hess, D. (1997). *Science Studies: An advanced introduction*. New York, NY: New York University Press.

Hill, J.H. (1999). Language, race and white public space. *American Anthropologist*, **100**, 680–689.

Hook, D. (2001). Discourse, knowledge, materiality, history: Foucault and discourse analysis. *Theory & Psychology*, **11**(4), 521–547.

Hooker, E. (1965). Male homosexuals and their worlds. In N. J. Marmor (Ed.), *Sexual Inversion: The multiple roots of homosexuality* (pp. 83–107). New York, NY: Basic Books.

Irvine, J. (1990). *Disorders of Desire: Sex and gender in modern American sexology*. Philadelphia, PA: Temple University Press.

Katz, J. (1995). *The Invention of Heterosexuality*. New York, NY: Dutton.

Keller, E.F. (1985). *Reflections on Gender and Science*. New Haven: Yale University Press.

Kitzinger, C. (1987). *The Social Construction of Lesbianism*. London: Sage.

Kitzinger, C. (1997). Lesbian and gay psychology: A critical analysis. In D. Fox & I. Prilleltensky (Eds), *Critical Psychology: An introduction* (pp. 202–216). London: Sage.

Kitzinger, C. (2000). Doing feminist conversation analysis. *Feminism & Psychology*, **10**(2), 163–193.

Kitzinger, C. & Coyle, A. (2002). Introducing lesbian and gay psychology. In A. Coyle & C. Kitzinger (Eds), *Lesbian & Gay Psychology: New perspectives* (pp. 1–29). Oxford: BPS Blackwell.

Kitzinger, C. & Perkins, R. (1993). *Changing our Minds: Lesbian feminism and Psychology*. New York, NY: New York University Press.

Krafft-Ebing, R. von (1887/1931). *Psychopathia Sexualis*. Brooklyn, NY: Physicians and Surgeons Book Company.

Minton, H. L. (2002). *Departing from Deviance: A history of homosexual rights and emancipatory science in America*. Chicago, IL: University of Chicago Press.

Nightingale, D.J. & Cromby, J. (Eds) (1999). *Social Constructionist Psychology: A critical analysis of theory and practice*. Milton Keynes: Open University Press.

Parker, I. (1992). *Discourse Dynamics: Critical analysis for social and individual Psychology*. London: Routledge.

Potter, J. & Wetherell, M. (1987). *Discourse and Social Psychology: Beyond attitudes and behaviour*. London: Sage.

Pratt, M.L. (1986). Fieldwork in common places. In J. Clifford & G. E. Marcus (Eds), *Writing Culture: The poetics and politics of ethnography* (pp. 27–50). Berkeley, CA: University of California Press.

Reid, K., Flowers, P. & Larkin, M. (2005). Exploring lived experience. *The Psychologist*, **18**(1), 20–24.

Rivers, I. (2000). Counting matters: Quantitative research in lesbian and gay Psychology. *Lesbian & Gay Psychology Review*, **1**, 28–31.

Rose, N. (1989). *Governing the Soul: The shaping of the private self*. London: Routledge.

Rose, N. (1996). *Inventing our Selves: Psychology, power, and personhood*. Cambridge, UK: Cambridge University Press.

Sacks, H., Schegloff, E.A. & Jefferson, G. (1974). A simplest systematics for the organization of turn-taking in conversation. *Language*, **50**(4), 696–735.

Schegloff, E.A. (1997). Whose text? Whose context? *Discourse & Society*, **8**(2), 165–187.

Schegloff, E.A. (1998). Reply to Wetherell. *Discourse & Society*, **8**(3), 165–187.

Schegloff, E.A. (1999). 'Schegloff's texts' as 'Billig's data': A critical reply. *Discourse & Society*, **10**(4), 558–572.

Sedgwick, E.K. (1990). *The Epistemology of the Closet*. Berkeley, CA: University of California Press.

Sedgwick, E.K. (1993). How to bring your kids up gay. In M. Warner (Ed.), *Fear of a Queer Planet: Queer politics and social theory* (pp. 69–81). Minneapolis, MI: University of Minnesota Press.

Shapin, S. & Schaffer, S. (1985). *Leviathan and the Air Pump: Hobbes, Boyle and the experimental life*. Princeton, NJ: Princeton University Press.

Stokoe, E.H. & Smithson, J. (2001). Making gender relevant: Conversation analysis and gender categories in interaction. *Discourse & Society*, **12**(2), 217–244.

Terry, J. (1997). The seductive power of science in the making of deviant Subjectivity. In V.A. Rosario (Ed.), *Science and Homosexualities* (pp. 271–295). New York, NY: Routledge.

Terry, J. (1999). *An American Obsession: Science, medicine and homosexuality in modern society*. Chicago, IL: University of Chicago Press.

Turner, W.B. (2000). *A Genealogy of Queer Theory*. Philadelphia, PA: Temple University Press.

Warner, D.N. (2004). Towards a queer research methodology. *Qualitative Research in Psychology*, **1**, 321–337.

Wetherell, M. (1998). Positioning and interpretive repertoires: Conversation analysis and post-structuralism in dialogue. *Discourse & Society*, **9**(3), 387–412.

Woolgar, S. & Pawluch, D. (1985). Ontological gerrymandering: The anatomy of social problems explanations. *Social Problems*, **32**, 214–227.

CHAPTER 4

Recognizing Race in LGBTQ Psychology: Power, Privilege and Complicity

Damien W. Riggs
University of Adelaide, Australia

INTRODUCTION

Recognize (def.)

1. to know again; perceive to be identical with something previously known
3. to perceive as existing or true
4. to acknowledge formally as existing or as entitled to consideration
7. to acknowledge acquaintance with

(*Macquarie Concise Dictionary*, 1998)

As psychological researchers and practitioners, the vast majority of our work is concerned with words. Most researchers spend considerable time elaborating the concepts and justifying the terms that inform their work, and a broad range of psychological therapies focus on language. In this spirit, I begin this chapter by providing definitions of three key terms I use throughout this chapter. First, I use the word 'recognize' to demonstrate some of the complex ways in which race works in LGBTQ psychology. More specifically, I seek to elaborate how whiteness and white race privilege are often ignored in LGBTQ psychological research due to it being predominantly based on the experiences of white, middle-class individuals. As the definition quoted above suggests, to 'recognize' race is to see something that is already there, and to acknowledge something that we already have a relation to – something that is in need of attention (in particular, from those of us who identify as white and who often do not 'see' our race).

The second word in need of definition is 'race'. Critical race and whiteness studies draw attention to the fact that even though race is no longer considered a 'biological truth', it persists in defining our experiences. Race continues to warrant attention from researchers and practitioners – it is not going to 'go away' simply because we recognize its oppressive histories. This suggests that race as a concept must be continually subjected to critical analyses. These analyses should consider how race structures subjectivities and legitimates

Out in Psychology: Lesbian, gay, bisexual, trans and queer perspectives. Edited by Victoria Clarke and Elizabeth Peel.
© 2007 John Wiley & Sons, Ltd.

categories of difference. Looking at how oppression and privilege are interconnected, and how they are played out within research on LGBTQ individuals is the best starting place for 'recognizing race in LGBTQ psychology'.

The final term to be defined is the acronym 'LGBTQ'. The term LGBTQ is widely used, but with little attendant focus on the experiences of bisexual people, transgendered people, or people who identify as queer (the present volume being a rare exception). The result is that their experiences remain marginalized, but this marginalization is disguised by the LGBTQ label. With this in mind, I use the acronym LGBTQ to highlight the need to widen our focus when researching the experiences of people marginalized on the basis of their sexual and gender identifications. At the same time, however, it would be glib to claim that this chapter adequately accounts for the experiences of all people marginalized in relation to race, sexuality and gender. Due to the limited nature of the data I analyse (as described below), this chapter focuses predominantly on the experiences of lesbians and gay men, with some focus on the experiences of bisexual people. No appropriate data were located on transgendered or queer identified individuals, but this is not to say that issues of race, privilege and oppression are not relevant to these groups. The issues raised in this chapter apply to the experiences of all individuals living in a society that privileges racialized differences, irrespective of sexual orientation (Riggs, 2004a, 2004b).

In order to more closely examine racialized practices in LGBTQ psychology, I provide an analysis of ten journal articles focusing on intersections of race, ethnicity, culture and sexuality. From these articles I draw out some of the dominant discourses that render invisible the race of white LGBTQ individuals. These discourses include the assumption that: (1) only 'racial minorities' are influenced by ethnicity/race; (2) 'ethnic minority' groups are 'all the same'; (3) ethnicity is a 'benign variable' that can be factored out in psychological research; and (4) a generic (white) model can be applied universally to all LGBTQ individuals, regardless of cultural differences. I suggest that these discourses together work to maintain a focus on the racialized other, the result being that white LGBTQ individuals are seen as not 'having race'. Although it is problematic to focus on people positioned as non-white, this is necessary in order to highlight the ways in which race is constructed in LGBTQ psychological research. As Wong (1994, p. 136) suggests, 'only by sketching out the silhouettes of "Blackness" situated at the perimeters will "whiteness" be dragged out into the foreground'. My purpose in this chapter is not to analyse the phenomenon of the 'token racial diversity chapter' (akin to Kitzinger's [1996] analysis of the 'token lesbian chapter'). While it may well be the case that many texts on LGBTQ individuals *do* provide an isolated chapter on the experiences of non-white LGBTQ individuals, it is nonetheless the case that all of the chapters in any such text are framed around race – whether the word 'race' appears or not.

In the final major section of this chapter, I outline some of the possibilities for change for research on LGBT individuals. I emphasize a need to engage more thoroughly with Indigenous/lesbian feminist/African American theorists (amongst others) who have challenged the ethnocentrism of psychological research. This work engenders a focus on the multiple interactions of privilege and oppression, rather than solely on the axis of sexuality. This is not to suggest that we should do away with 'LGBTQ studies', but rather that it is important to engage with the ways in which identities intersect with one another. White LGBTQ psychologists need to more adequately engage with and understand their privilege in order to contribute to social action and the destabilization of heteronormative practices.

SCIENCE/IMPERIALISM

In this first section I elaborate an understanding of psychological knowledge that emphasizes its location within ongoing histories of privilege and oppression. In particular, I draw
attention to the normative assumptions of race that inhere in psychological knowledge.
I also challenge white LGBTQ psychologists to examine the frameworks and implicit
assumptions that they bring to their work.

Traditionally, psychological knowledge has been organized through the broad framework of positivism. This approach assumes that we can directly know or understand the
world through the application of appropriate methodological tools (i.e. the scientific
method). Positivism provides a relatively benign account of knowledge formation that fails
to recognize how our perception of the world is influenced by the surrounding cultural
context (Waldegrave, 1998). Furthermore, it fails to appreciate the impact that particular
social locations (e.g. in relation to gender, sexuality or race) have on our ability to state
our knowledge claims and have them heard and accepted by other people. The discipline
of psychology has gradually incorporated qualitative and critical methodologies that challenge the status of positivism. However, positivist/quantitative research continues to hold
sway over the ways in which the discipline responds to issues of heterosexism and racism.
As I show below, a focus on single axes of oppression (e.g. sexuality), and the failure to
explicitly recognize race privilege, is a product not only of quantitative research, but is
also evident in qualitative research on the experiences of racially marginalized LGBTQ
individuals.

Within psychology, the failure to both recognize the implications of race privilege and
question the legitimacy of white forms of knowledge is evident in the desire of white psychologists to measure, describe and 'know' the 'other'. Historically, this has involved such
barbaric practices as measuring skull differences 'between races', and incarcerating, medi-
cating or silencing those people who do not conform to the white, heterosexual, male,
middle-class subject of psychological knowledge (Dudgeon, Garvey & Pickett 2000; Smith,
1999). Such practices continue today, for example, through the use of 'conversion therapies'
to 'correct' same-sex orientation (e.g. Nicolosi, 1991), or attempts to 'prove' racialized
differences in 'intelligence' (e.g. Herrnstein & Murray, 1996). Organizations such as the
American Psychological Association and British Psychological Society are critical of
racism and challenge racial discrimination in their publications. However, discourses of
race within psychology continue to provide those convinced of the deviancy of non-white
individuals with a means of pathologizing and stigmatizing difference (Terry, 1999).

In her Maori account of practices of oppression, Linda Tuhiwai Smith (1999) outlines
how we may understand 'psychological imperialism'. Smith suggests that one interpretation of the term 'imperialism' depicts it as referring to the:

> Enlightenment spirit which signalled the transformation of economic, political and
> cultural life in Europe. In this wider Enlightenment context, imperialism becomes an
> integral part of the development of the modern state, of science, of ideas and of the
> 'modern' human person. (p. 22)

Imperialism is a way of thinking about the world based on the values of white people.
This includes the assumption that it is possible to understand the world through perception,
and that white researchers have the right to do so, even at the expense of the groups under
investigation. Smith also suggested that one specific mode of imperialism is colonization:

the imposition of one set of beliefs onto another. Indeed, within a binary framework of self and other (where the former is considered superior to the latter), the colonization of those considered different works to position them as other and 'naturally' inferior (Johnson-Riordan, Conway Herron & Johnston, 2002).

The assumptions of imperialism have played out in psychology in the form of a number of methodological and theoretical positions, namely: quantification, universality, acontextualism and individualism. These four positions (amongst many others) are important influences on psychological research and practice, and evidence what Todd and Wade (1995) term 'psycolonization'. This term describes the ways in which white psychological knowledge has been asserted as truth through a number of different but related claims. The measuring, aggregating and reporting of 'individual differences' is thought to represent an ever-growing picture of human experience (what Kitzinger [1987] termed 'the up the mountain saga'). In premising this picture on white individuals it is presumed to somehow represent a 'universal picture', one that is unrelated to particular social or cultural contexts. Finally, this is all achieved through a focus on isolated individuals who are measured as such, rather than as members of complex social systems. This results in the psycolonization of people's life experiences, by inserting them into a model of humanity that privileges white (heterosexual, middle-class men's) worldviews (Riggs, 2004a).

This approach to understanding the world is also premised on the notion that the subjectivity of the researcher is irrelevant (Morawski, 1997). As a result, the predominance of white, heterosexual, middle-class researchers means that participants are often marked and labelled (and implicitly rendered 'problematic or normal', 'healthy or unhealthy'), whereas the privileges of white researchers are left unmarked. However, distinctions such as these have long been challenged by those marginalized within psychological research. This has occurred when those who have been positioned as objects of the scientific gaze have resisted this gaze, or have turned this gaze around to examine the researchers (Smith, 1997). It is also important to note that race has always been evident in psychological research; white researchers have just failed to recognize it. Race is an object of psychological knowledge either implicitly (in the unmarked status of white researchers or white subjects) or explicitly (in the measurement of those located as the racialized other). The normative status of whiteness in psychological research is often imported into LGBTQ research. As a result, the logic of positivism and the impact of psycolonization contribute to the marginalization of 'non-white' people in LGBT psychology.

DATA

The papers analysed in the following section were located through database searches (Academic Search Elite, Expanded Academic ASAP, Medline and PsycInfo) using combinations of key terms such as: race, culture, ethnicity, multiculturalism, white, black, African, Asian, Latin, Native, lesbian, gay, bisexual, transgendered, psychology. Relatively few matches were retrieved for any of these combinations (approximately 50 articles in total), and the vast majority of the matches retrieved did not appear in psychological journals or texts (10 psychology-related articles were found in total), and where thus not of relevance to the present research. Finally, using the 10 psychology-related articles that I had found via database searches I was able to identify five further articles from their reference lists – 10 of the 15 papers were selected for detailed analysis. I examined the ways in which these papers constructed race, and the mention they made of whiteness and white race privilege in particular, using insights from critical race and whiteness studies (e.g. Moreton-Robinson, 2000; Riggs & Selby, 2003; Wong, 1994). Four predominant themes emerged from repeated readings of the literature. These were:

1. A focus on non-white people as 'having race' (white people were often not racialized or even named as 'white').
2. The presumption that all non-white racial groups experience racism and other forms of oppression in the same way (this presumption effectively ignores how privilege and oppression operate differentially, and suggests that all people *within* any one racial group experience race in the same way).
3. The notion that race could be 'factored out'; that race could be treated as a benign variable with little explanatory power.
4. The assumption that a white model of subjectivity (in the form of psychological measures or theories) could be adequately used to understand the experiences of non-white LGBTQ individuals.

Of the literature surveyed, the 10 papers analysed here are representative of these four themes, and of the majority of research on the experiences of non-white LGBT individuals in the discipline of psychology. Table 4.1 provides a brief summary of the articles analysed. Only a few of the articles engaged with issues of race privilege and problematized whiteness. It is important to note that the vast majority of the research reviewed here (and the broader literature surveyed for the analysis) represents an important contribution to understanding the experiences of non-white LGBT individuals. The following analysis is not intended to undermine the research per se, but to explore some of the implications of the ways in which race is represented in the articles.

CONSTRUCTIONS OF RACE IN LGBT PSYCHOLOGY

Only 'Other People' Have Race

In this first theme, 'ethnicity/race'[1] is understood as an important factor in research on non-white people. The implication is that white people 'don't have race': that race is only of relevance when the group being researched are explicitly seen as 'having race'. Of course, all LGBTQ psychology research looks at race – those of us living in western societies are racialized in varying ways, and this is evident in what we write, the research we conduct and the lives we live. I am not being dismissive of the importance of looking at and listening to the experiences of racism and oppression experienced by those people positioned as racialized others. However, solely doing this ignores how race (and, more specifically, racism) works both *for* and *against*: it privileges and oppresses (Fine, 1997; Riggs & Selby, 2003).

An example of this theme appears in Dube and Savin-Williams's (1999) research on 'ethnic sexual minority male youths'. In their literature review they outline the factors

---

[1] I use the terms 'ethnicity/race' because they are used interchangeably in the papers examined here. This is problematic because the terms 'ethnicity' and 'race' are conceptually distinct, and their use achieves differing rhetorical outcomes (Jackson, 1998).

Table 4.1 Summary of the articles included in the analysis

Author	Summary
Consolacion, Russell & Sue (2004)	An examination of the associations between 'multiple minority status' (race/ethnicity and sexual attraction) and mental health. Focusing on the experiences of marginalized youth, this study compared the experiences of white adolescents with those of Hispanic/Latino and African American adolescents.
Dube & Savin-Williams (1999)	An examination of 'how ethnicity influences sexual identity development'. This research compared the experiences of young males who identified as both bisexual/gay and African American, Latino, Asian American/Pacific Islander or white.
Rosario, Schrimshaw & Hunter (2004)	This study focused on young lesbian, gay and bisexual people, and compared the coming-out experiences of 'white, black and Latino' youth.
Quadagno, Sly, Harrison, Eberstein & Soler (1998)	The study focused on sexual behaviour and decision making amongst Hispanic, white and African American women.
Whitam, Daskalos, Sobolewski & Padilla (1998)	This research examined the 'emergence of lesbian sexuality and identity cross-culturally' in Brazil, Peru, the Philippines and the United States of America.
Parks, Hughes & Matthews (2004)	An investigation of the differences in African American, Latina and white lesbians' choices to disclose their sexuality.
Siegel & Epstein (1996)	An examination of the 'psychological stressors in relation to gay lifestyle' among HIV positive African American, 'Caucasian' and Puerto Rican men.
Peterson, Folkman & Bakeman (1996)	An examination of the experiences of HIV positive African American gay men in regards to 'stress, coping and depressive mood'.
Mashburn, Peterson, Bakeman, Miller & Clark (2004)	A study exploring the 'influence of demographic characteristics on HIV testing among young African American MSM'.
Smith (1997)	An examination of the coming-out process in relation to 'cultural diversity'.

under examination in their research (e.g. 'adjustment to sexual identity', 'internalized homophobia' and 'integration of sexual and ethnic identities'). The discussion of each of the factors elaborates the 'factor' itself and then its impact on 'ethnic sexual minority youth'. The implication is that while all youth are affected by these factors, only 'ethnic sexual minority youths' are burdened by the added impact of ethnicity. This is evident in the statement that: 'ethnic minority youths face greater barriers in adjusting to their sexual identity because this identity must be integrated with and accepted in the context of an ethnic identity' (p. 1390). The suggestion is that only 'ethnic minority youths . . . adjust to their sexual identity . . . in the context of an ethnic identity'. Ethnicity is not seen to be a salient context for ethnic *majority* youths, nor is it something that must be 'integrated'. This statement discounts the fact that all youths 'have' an ethnic identity, and that this works in conjunction with other aspects of identity (such as gender or sexuality) to privilege or oppress the young person. A similar example is provided by Rosario, Schrimshaw and Hunter (2004) in their research on 'ethnic/racial differences in the coming out process of lesbian, gay and bisexual youths'. Much like Dube and Savin-Williams (1999), Rosario and her colleagues begin by outlining previous research on 'LGB sexual identity formation', and then state that: 'for ethnic/racial minority LGB individuals, the coming-out process may be complicated by cultural factors that operate to retard or arrest the process' (p. 216). This suggests that only 'ethnic/racial minority LGB individuals . . . [experience] cultural factors' (p. 216): White LGB individuals are free to enjoy a 'coming-out process' that is not 'retard[ed] or arrest[ed]'. As can be seen from this short extract, not only are 'ethnic/racial minority LGB individuals' positioned as solely affected by race, but race also works to potentially render their coming out experiences as pathological (i.e., 'retarded or arrested'). In contrast to this is the implicit statement that majority group (white) LGB individuals can experience a 'race-free' coming out process.

Rosario et al. also imply that 'only Other people have race' when discussing their results: 'once again, the ethnic/racial groups did not differ on the developmental milestones . . .' (p. 224). Here they are referring to the 'Black and Latino youths' in their study – those marked as being 'ethnic/racial groups' – effectively dismissing the race of their white participants. The focus on 'developmental milestones' also does little to challenge the ways in which white norms for development are used as a measure for non-white young people (Burman, 1994; Riggs, 2006a). The assumption of a normative white model of development imposes on marginalized young LGBTQ people an account of development that ignores their experiences of oppression.

In a similar way to that of Dube and Savin-Williams (1999) and Rosario et al. (2004), Smith (1997) proposed that 'culture' only impacts on non-white people in relation to the 'coming out process'. She suggested that:

> Another way to approach coming out and cultural diversity would be to focus on coming out and cultural identity as individual processes that a person moves through in his or her development. That is, the two would be treated as separate developmental processes, with sexual orientation apart from who a person is as a cultural being . . . [Previous research] specifies specific variables such as time and reason for immigration, language, acculturation, and assimilation as some of the relevant cultural factors in the lives of immigrant lesbians . . . These approaches suggest that many cultural variables affect the lives of lesbian, gay, and bisexual people of color. (p. 284)

It appears automatic for Smith to move from suggesting that 'coming out and cultural identity [are] individual processes' to an exploration of the experiences of 'immigrant lesbians'. This move is premised on the positioning of culture as an attribute primarily associated with 'lesbian, gay, and bisexual people of color'. This ignores the fact that all LGBTQ people 'have culture', and that white LGBTQ people may benefit from their membership of a particular cultural group. Also, this extract from Smith echoes the extract from Dube and Savin-Williams (1999), with regard to the presumption that culture and sexuality are usefully separable. This ignores the ways in which sexual identities are shaped in the context of particular cultures, and the inseparability of sexuality from culture.

Finally, the theme 'only Other people have race' was identified in the work of Mashburn et al. (2004), in which they explore some of the forces that impact on risk behaviours for African American men who have sex with men (MSM). They suggest that: 'Empowerment, sense of community, interpersonal attachments, resources, and culture are active forces that compel risk behaviors, and they especially may be useful for understanding risk behaviors of non-Caucasian MSM' (p. 49). The notion that 'active forces' such as 'culture, empowerment and sense of community' will be helpful for understanding the 'risk behaviors of non-Caucasian MSM' is premised on the notion that 'culture' primarily impacts on or is useful to non-white people. This draws on a set of cultural stereotypes (which I outline in the second theme) that depict non-white people as always already benefiting from 'community and culture'. Although community support is often central to combating oppression, this discursive practice minimizes the ways in which white people also benefit from the support provided by the 'resources, community and empowerment' that come from being a member of a dominant group.

The theme 'only Other people have race' maintains racialized hierarchies within LGBTQ psychology research. By focusing on race as the 'cage of the other' (Hage, 1998) such research effectively blames those positioned as racialized others for their experiences of racism. If race is understood to be intrinsic only to 'minority group members', the implication is that such groups are at fault for their racialized (and thus oppressed) status. By focusing on the racialized other, LGBTQ psychology reinforces the normative status of whiteness in psychological research and does little to challenge white hegemony. As I now show, this ignorance of white race privilege is also played out in constructions of 'ethnic minorities'[2] as homogenous others.

Ethnic Minority Groups Are 'All The Same'

The second theme relies on an assumption of out-group homogeneity – that all people who are not white experience race and racism in much the same way. It also presumes that non-white cultures are internally homogenous – that all people who identify with a particular culture are the same. The outcome of such assumptions is that little attention is paid to the specificities of racial oppression and the specificity of the concept of race itself. It is important to recognize the effects of racism, but it is not useful to categorize all people who are oppressed by racism as the same. One example of this is the vastly different experiences of racism between African American and Native American people. Each group (and the members within each group) experience racism differently because of a range of relationships to colonization, slavery and dispossession. To describe these experiences as all the same is to ignore how some groups may experience privilege at the expense of others' oppression.

Assumptions of homogeneity are played out in a number of ways in research on ethnicity/race and sexuality. In the first instance, one ethnic minority group is assumed to be substitutable for another. For example, Siegel and Epstein (1996) report in their research on HIV status and ethnicity that: 'We extended the findings [on HIV-infected Hispanic men] by showing that another minority group, African-American men, also reported higher ratings on cumulated severity of hassles than Caucasian men' (p. 310). By this logic, researchers who examine the experiences of one ethnic minority group may simplistically map their findings across to another 'similar' group, in order to compare them. (It is also worth nothing here that both groups [Hispanic and African-American men] are being compared to 'Caucasian' men – as I discuss below, this assumes that white people represent the norm from which other groups of people differ). This logic effectively dismisses the incommensurable differences that shape the lives of Hispanic and African-American men living in the USA. As a result, LGBTQ psychological research that employs

---

[2] Again, I use this term as it predominates in the literature analysed here.

this framework assumes a form of universality underpinning the experiences of people positioned as racialized others (Wong, 1994).

A second example of the assumed sameness of individuals from differing marginalized racial groups appears in the work of Parks, Hughes and Matthews (2004). Their research, which looks at intersections of racial and sexual identities, uses a reductive understanding of race, wherein it is considered to be useful to group together non-white people. They suggest that their: 'Analysis of data focused on two sets of comparisons: (a) African American with Latina women and (b) lesbians of color (African American and Latina) with White lesbians' (pp. 245–246). Here African and Latina women are grouped together under the heading 'lesbians of color'. Wong (1994) critiques the category 'lesbians of color' for ignoring the specificities of experience of African American and Latina women (for example), and, when used by (typically white) researchers, for ignoring the complex histories that inform the use of the term by African American and Latina women themselves. The use of 'lesbians of color' in 'cross-cultural research' is a form of appropriation, where the language used by non-white people is co-opted into the explanatory categories of white researchers.

LGBTQ psychological research also presumes that all people 'within' a culture experience the world in the same way. I have done this by suggesting that all white people are privileged, however, this suggestion achieves somewhat different rhetorical effects. The former suggestion uses 'culture' as a tool to stereotype and legitimate prejudice, whereas my suggestion makes generalizations in order to demonstrate a point about privilege and its relationship to oppression (see also Wong, 1994). Examples of overgeneralizations about marginalized cultures include 'all lesbians are man haters' or 'African-American culture is matriarchal'. Examples such as these promote a uniform depiction of these two cultures and communities that elides some of the reasons why aspects of these statements may well be true (e.g. that some lesbians may justifiably 'hate men', or that some African-American households may be matriarchal). These depictions also mask political underpinnings (e.g. that some lesbians may choose separatism in order to challenge or reject patriarchy, or that some African-American households may be shaped through matriarchy as a result of histories of slavery and oppression). Assumptions of homogeneity do little to examine the intersections of privilege and oppression, and instead reinforce the very stereotypes that warrant racialized (and sexualized) hierarchies.

An example of this is evident in the research of Quadagno et al. (1998) on 'ethnic differences in sexual decision making'. Although they acknowledge in their results section that the 'Hispanic' women in their study were a heterogeneous group, they devote considerable space in their introduction to outlining Hispanic culture (in the singular form). For example, 'Hispanic culture reinforces gender roles and promotes male dominance in a relationship . . . Sex is considered a private issue in Hispanic culture, and sexual topics are not usually discussed' (p. 58). My argument is not that these claims are untrue *in general*; rather, I query making such statements, particularly if they do not pertain per se to the experiences of the women in the study. These generalizations are used as a form of 'stick culture' against which to contrast more clearly the heterogeneous experiences of the women reported in the study. This may be a relatively common rhetorical ploy in writing up research reports (indeed, in this chapter I have used the most obvious examples of the four themes identified in order to make my point), but in papers on marginalized ethnic groups broad sweeping statements that reinforce stereotypical views held about non-white cultures are not useful (Walker, 2003). As Wong (1994, p. 141) suggests, 'by limiting culture within such clean coherent groups, it is difficult to analyze the zones of difference within and between cultures'.

The theme 'ethnic minority groups are all the same' elides the differences that shape experiences of culture and race, according to a person's location within particular social and historical contexts. It does so by promoting the view that non-white people are uniformly oppressed. Constructions of self and other are reliant on the imposition of one particular worldview onto a wide range of people: Assumptions of across (and within) culture homogeneity are another form of psycolonization. Additionally, as Carby (1992) suggests, a focus on difference as a matter of individual identity fails to adequately recognize how categories of difference work to legitimate unequal social relations. Research on the experiences of LGBTQ people classified as non-white can therefore serve to normalize the dominance of white LGBTQ experiences. The effects of assuming homogeneity are also played out in the analytic presumption that ethnicity/race is a variable that can be controlled for, as I elaborate in the following section.

Ethnicity/Race As A 'Benign Variable'

The construction of ethnicity/race as a variable that can be controlled for in order to account for individual differences forms the basis of the third theme. This construction assumes a form of universality, where 'ethnicity' is thought to affect people in a general way. The treatment of ethnicity/race as a variable in psychological research dehistoricizes the effects of ethnicity/race and reduces the visibility of the race of white people. If ethnicity is seen as a 'benign variable' – as something that can be 'objectively measured' and accounted for – then the violence that is often enacted in the name of ethnic/racial difference becomes sidelined to the main work of psychological research: accounting for difference. As a result, the experiences of people as they relate to ethnicity/race are in effect equalized. Claims to a 'level playing field' have been used to counter claims of discrimination and calls for affirmative action strategies (Riggs, 2004a).

In their work on 'sexual identity formation', Quadagno and colleagues (1998) suggest that: 'when a limited number of factors are controlled, ethnic differences diminish to a large degree' (p. 74). This claim is premised on an earlier statement that: 'Numerous factors other than ethnicity, including marital status, age, and education, have been shown to influence sexual activities' (p. 59). Together, these two statements demonstrate the assumption that ethnicity is a 'factor' that can be isolated and accounted for, rather than something that influences experiences in multiple ways. To suggest that 'factors other than ethnicity . . . influence sexual activities' is to promote the idea that ethnicity only influences sexual activities *as ethnicity*, rather than as a more generalized effect that influences how people may have differential access to (for example) marital status and education, *as a result of their ethnicity*. This is not to suggest a hierarchical ranking of subject positions, in which ethnicity is 'more influential' than other aspects of a person's subjectivity. Rather, the point is that subjectivity cannot be separated into individual factors. Ethnicity is always present in the 'limited number of factors' (p. 74) and there is little use in claiming to be able to 'diminish' ethnic differences. The fact that controlling for these variables reduces the effect of ethnicity in the statistical sense is not problematic, but the interpretation that 'factors other than ethnicity . . . influence sexual activities' (p. 59) is.

Rosario and her colleagues (2004) make this claim more strongly in their suggestion that: 'These nonsignificant findings suggest that sexual identity formation is not significantly influenced by cultural factors' (p. 225). To claim that 'sexual identity formation is not significantly influenced by cultural factors' is to take a very narrow reading of culture. Indeed, it dismisses entirely the fact that non-heterosexually identified people form a range of specific cultures of our own – 'sexual identities' that are done in a context of lesbian, gay, bisexual, transgendered or queer communities are intimately related to that particular community/culture. By extension, all sexual identities are formed in a relationship to a wide range of cultures, none of which can be accounted for by attempting to control for cultural differences.

The assumption that ethnicity is a benign variable that can be isolated in LGBTQ research promotes a positivist interpretation of the experiences of LGBTQ individuals. The assumptions of universality, acontextualism, individualism and quantification all discount the wide range of influences that constructions of ethnicity have. Such assumptions encourage people to 'choose which oppression is the greatest', rather than looking at the interplays between differing subject positions. This essentialist model of identity politics fractures the experiences of people who experience multiple oppressions. As Harris (1995, p. 255) suggests:

> The result of essentialism is to reduce the lives of people who experience multiple forms of oppression to addition problems: 'racism + sexism = straight black women's experience', or 'racism + sexism + homophobia = black lesbian experience'. Thus, in an essentialist world, black women's experiences will always be forcibly fragmented before being subjected to analysis, as those who are 'only interested in race' and those who are 'only interested in gender' take their separate slices of our lives.

Employing ethnicity/race as a variable in psychological research holds the potential for enacting considerable violence on the experience of non-white people. Attempting to account for ethnic/racial difference masks the effects of privilege based on ethnicity/race. As I show in the final section, accounting for ethnic/racial difference through a model of 'individual identity' normalizes a white model of subjectivity by promoting the belief that sameness equals whiteness.

Generic Models of Subjectivity

As the title suggests, this final theme draws attention to the belief that a 'one size fits all' model can be used to understand the experiences of all LGBTQ individuals, regardless of ethnicity/race. This model takes a number of different (but related) forms in research on sexuality and race. The first is the use of measures normed on white populations to understand the experiences of people from non-white cultures. For example, Dube and Savin-Williams (1999) use the Kinsey, Pomeroy and Martin (1948) sexual orientation scale to assess the experiences of the 'ethnic sexual-minority youths' in their study. Similarly, Consolacion, Russell and Sue (2004) use the Rosenberg self-esteem scale (1965) to measure the mental health status of the 'multiple minority youths' in their study, and Rosario et al. (2004) use the Marlowe-Crowne (1960) social desirability scale to look at 'ethnic/racial difference in the coming-out process'. None of these measures were adapted specifically to cater for the experiences of 'ethnic minority individuals', nor do the articles mention the cultural specificity of the measures. This use of a generic model of subjectivity supposes that non-white individuals can (and should) be measured against a white norm (cf, Howitt & Owusu-Bempah, 1994).

Peterson, Folkman and Bakeman (1996) *do* acknowledge the cultural specificity of their measure for 'coping', but persist in using the measure as the basis for their research (because it has been validated elsewhere). They suggest that:

> Differences in appraisal and coping may be associated with cultural difference in value beliefs and life experiences. With respect to validity, it is possible that the Ways of Coping, which was developed with a white, middle-class suburban sample, is not valid for use with an urban African American sample . . . However, a recent study of the validity of the Ways of Coping in an urban socioeconomically diverse African American samples provides support for the use of this measure in the current study (p. 475).

This fails to recognize that many psychological measures have been normed on specific populations (before being applied to other populations). The outcome is that a semblance of validity is achieved (Dudgeon et al., 2000). Such measures reflect participants' knowledge of the dominant culture, rather than their 'fit' with the norms of the dominant group. The use of such measures does little to challenge the normative status of particular forms of knowledge, or to recognize the experiences and theories of marginalized group members.

Assumptions of a generic model were also evident in the use of terms that may be specific to white cultures. For example, in their research on 'lesbian sexuality', Whitam, Daskalos, Sobolewski and Padilla (1998) use the term 'lesbian' to describe women from four different cultural groups (Brazilian, Peruvian, Phillipina and 'American'), even though they acknowledge that the word 'lesbian' (or a translation of it) was not typically used by the women from countries other than the USA who identified as same-sex attracted. This is explicit both in the use of the word 'lesbian' in the title of their paper, and in the statement that: 'lesbians are not a unique creation of Western European societies, but probably a universal aspect of human sexual orientational arrangements' (p. 32). This claim to universality supposes not simply that same-sex attraction is something experienced across cultures, but that 'lesbians' exist across cultures. This term has a wide range of meaning within white cultures. To think that it would have the same set of meanings (or any meaning at all) across cultures is to impose a white interpretation of subjectivity onto the experiences of all same-sex attracted women.

The words that we use carry sets of meanings that implicate us in practices and histories of oppression and privilege (cf, Brauner, 2000). The assumption of a generic term serves the interests of the white majority, rather than paying attention to non-white people's experiences of sexuality. Obviously this is a result of a desire to make 'cross-cultural comparisons'. My question here is: how do such comparisons contribute to meaningful interventions into practices of privilege and oppression, and on whose terms is such research conducted? In the following section I elaborate some of these concerns by looking at research that has been conducted by Indigenous/lesbian feminist/African American theorists who have sought to challenge the hegemony of whiteness within academic research.

INTERPLAYS OF PRIVILEGE AND OPPRESSION

In this final section of the chapter I draw together some of the ways in which LGBTQ psychologists may more adequately engage with issues of privilege and oppression. I draw on the theoretical and personal insights that have been elaborated by groups of people oppressed by white heteropatriarchy. This extremely rich literature has often been given limited attention in psychological research. However, its capacity to demonstrate issues of racism, sexism and other forms of discrimination is an essential tool for challenging interplays of privilege and oppression, particularly in colonial nations. From this literature I take two main foci: the complexities and multiplicities of privilege and oppression, and the need to reconceptualize subjectivity in the face of these complexities. These two foci may help to engender a more reflexive engagement with race and sexuality in LGBTQ psychological research.

Examining the interplays of privilege and oppression requires a willingness to understand how people who experience oppression primarily as a result of sexual orientation (for example) may well in turn be involved in practices of oppression in relation to groups of people who differ from them in regards to race, gender, ethnicity or class (hooks, 1981). This may be as implicit as the privilege that white LGBTQ individuals experience, or as explicit as knowingly refusing to address race privilege or to support the rights of groups other than our own. Looking at experiences of oppression should entail looking at experiences of privilege – how are they overlaid, and how may our privileges outweigh our experiences of oppression (and vice versa)?

Croteau, Talbot, Lance and Evans (2002) suggest that oppression and privilege are often mediated by visibility: a person's ability to 'pass', or to not mention their 'difference' from the white, heterosexual, middle-class norm is a form of privilege. This is not to discount the fact that being forced to 'pass' as a heterosexual person (for example) is oppressive. Rather, issues of oppression and privilege are intimately related to power and choice – the ability to choose particular framings of ourselves (albeit from a limited range of options) that allow us to access privilege. The 'visibility' of non-white people (in contrast to the presumed invisibility of white people, for white people) effectively denies this choice.

This point about visibility draws attention to the problematic notion that 'experiences of oppression are universal'. Simply because some of us may experience oppression as a result of sexual orientation only does not mean that these experiences are anything like those of someone who experiences racialized oppression (or perhaps racialized *and* sexualized oppression, to name but two). Privilege is a social fact that changes in degrees: as Carla Trujillo (1997) suggests (writing as someone who identifies as Latina), 'the fact that I can be an out lesbian and not formally persecuted by the U.S. government is a privilege' (p. 271). Privilege is relative. Though it is true that lesbians experience forms of persecution within the USA (i.e. little access to adoption rights, marriage rights, maternity payment for supporting partners, etc.), this is a radically different experience from those women who identify as same-sex attracted in countries outside the USA, who experience far more extreme forms of persecution or disavowal. Rather than aggregating experiences and reporting them *en masse*, it may instead be more important to look at the ways in which oppressions work both independently from *and* simultaneously with one another (hooks, 1981). This brings me to the second focus of this section: the need to reconceptualize subjectivity in order to better understand the operations of privilege and oppression.

My starting point for this reconceptualization is the suggestion that white LGBTQ psychology researchers need to engage more adequately on a theoretical level with those researchers who have challenged our epistemic authority (hooks, 1981). It is far too easy (and unthreatening) to simply employ the research of non-white scholars as a form of moral authority in order to demonstrate our claim to be 'engaging with our privilege' (Moreton-Robinson, pers comm, September 2004). Instead, what is required is a critical engagement with the theories of those scholars who challenge white models of subjectivity, and create a space to elaborate understandings of privilege and oppression grounded in the multiplicities of everyday life.

bel hooks (1989) is one such scholar who has confronted white women's feminism (for example) with its complicity in racist practices. hooks suggests that the use of concepts such as 'identity politics' to gain access to rights may do very little to challenge the individualistic and essentialist understandings of subjectivity that have been used to justify the oppression of marginalized racial, sexual and gender minority groups (cf, Riggs & Riggs, 2004). Such concepts rely on an understanding of subjectivity that reifies these points of difference as a priori facts, rather than as socially constructed markers of difference that are used to legitimate the status quo. hooks suggests that slogans such as 'the personal is political' only serve to reduce issues of inequality and oppression to the personal – to internalized difference rather than challenging it and its connections to privilege (see also Kitzinger & Perkins, 1993, for a white lesbian feminist analysis of how such individualism serves to blame lesbians for their experiences of discrimination).

In contrast to this, we may understand subjectivity as an *inter*subjective practice that is shaped through our ever-changing relations to multiple subject positions, dependent on our context. Rather than reducing experience down to one particular point, or expecting people to choose 'which subject position oppresses them most', we should examine the interplays between the subject positions that we inhabit, and through which we are located in a relationship to privilege and oppression (Mama, 1995). By looking at how we came to be who we are through our relationships to other people (oppressive or otherwise), it may be possible to examine more thoroughly sites of dominance and how they actively attempt to produce their other (e.g. heterosexuality and the production of the deviant other). (See Kitzinger & Wilkinson, 1993, for more on this, and Wong, 1994, in relation to whiteness and racism.)

This need to examine sites of dominance is particularly compelling for white researchers examining issues of race and sexuality within LGBTQ psychology. This calls for not a focus on white people per se (as in yet more research that examines the lives of white people), but a critical examination of how white subjectivities are constituted through networks of power that bestow unearned privilege at the expense (or oppression) of non-white groups (Moreton-Robinson, 2000). This approach refuses to legitimate the hegemony of whiteness, and instead examines exactly how this hegemony came about, and how it implicates all white people (regardless of sexuality) in practices of privilege and oppression (Riggs, 2006b). This entails analysing how power works to both limit and make possible various subject positions, and the implications of this for researching the lives of LGBTQ individuals. It is not sufficient to simply look at how heterosexual hegemony shapes our lives as LGBTQ individuals, regardless of race. We must also look at how heterosexual hegemony is shaped in a relationship with other modes of dominance, for example, racism, classism and imperialism more broadly (what Aileen Moreton-Robinson, 2004, has referred to as 'the possessive logic of patriarchal white sovereignty').

CONCLUSIONS

Throughout this chapter I have argued that LGBTQ psychologists need to look at how race is done, rather than simply measuring racialized differences (a practice that, in effect, reifies racialized categories without concurrently examining their relationship to privilege and oppression). By looking at four examples of how issues of race are managed within LGBTQ psychological research, I have demonstrated that such research identifies race as it pertains to those who are raced-as-other – it does not pay sufficient attention to the race of the white people, nor to white people's unearned privileges.

Those of us who identify as white need to ask questions such as: 'who is our research useful to?' and 'whose purposes does it serve?' (Smith, 1999). We need to consider how our research justifies practices of oppression and how the psychological method itself – particularly, universalism, acontextualism, individualism and quantification – is implicated in practices of oppression. This is often also the result of the presumption that 'objective research' can be moral and value free. Yet, researchers bring a range of cultural assumptions to their work. There is a need to be more transparent about the moral assumptions that we make in our work and to privilege accounts of morality that challenge the norms of white heteropatriarchy (cf, Kitzinger & Perkins, 1993). As such, LGBTQ psychology will become more than a simple 'add-on' to the discipline of psychology: it will become a field that takes as central the experiences of LGBTQ individuals, and which challenges the normative assumptions of all forms of psychology, LGBTQ or otherwise (Kitzinger & Coyle, 2002).

There is a direct contradiction between a desire to challenge racism and race privilege and the tenets of psychological research. While it is of course possible to examine racism (or heterosexism) within the context of psychology, such examinations are often limited by their reliance on particular white understandings of subjectivity and science. This does not mean abandoning psychology altogether. Although it has and continues to be deployed as a means of oppression, it also wields considerable rhetorical power in regards to rights. As Clarke (2001, p. 157) suggests, what is required is a '"multiplicity of perspectives" on LGBT psychology, rather than a hegemony of positivist-empiricism'. An approach that values a 'multiplicity of perspectives' requires us to question which 'perspectives' are valued over others in the context of western cultures, and the ways in which the voices of marginalized racial groups are often depicted as 'mere perspectives' (Nicoll, 2000).

Finally, I draw attention to the potential that LGBTQ psychology may hold for challenging the self/other binaries that underpin constructions of racialized and sexualized difference. The normative status of white people in LGBTQ psychological research leads to the exclusion of non-white people. The invisibility of whiteness (to white people) is dependent on the visibility of those raced as other, whether through stereotypical depictions or the presumption of a 'natural difference' between the two. I am not suggesting that we should aim towards a utopian vision of 'racelessness' – this would only serve to deny the ongoing histories of oppression based on racialized differences and the fallacy of white invisibility. Rather, by looking at the interplays of privilege and oppression, we can more closely examine how whiteness is always already implicated in the networks of power that inform racialized practices. As a consequence, we may challenge the a priori status of white privilege as a site always under contestation.

ACKNOWLEDGEMENTS

I would first like to acknowledge the sovereignty of the Kaurna people, upon whose land I live in Adelaide, South Australia. In doing so I seek to recognize the ongoing relationship that white people in Australia have to indigenous sovereignty, and the implications for this when attempting to critically analyse issues of race and whiteness. I would like to thank Victoria and Liz for suggesting that I write this particular chapter, and to Jane, my honours supervisor, who originally suggested this means of examining whiteness in psychologists' writings on race. And, as always, I would like to thank Greg for support and proof reading, and our foster child, Gary, just for being himself.

REFERENCES

Brauner, R. (2000). Embracing difference: Addressing race, culture and sexuality. In C. Neal (Ed.), *Issues in Therapy with Lesbian, Gay, Bisexual and Transgendered Clients* (pp. 7–22). New York, NY: McGraw Hill.

Burman, E. (1994). *Deconstructing Developmental Psychology*. London: Routledge.

Carby, H. (1992). The multicultural wars. *Radical History Review*, **54**(7), 7–18.

Clarke, V. (2001). The psychology and politics of lesbian and gay parenting: Having our cake and eating it? *Lesbian & Gay Psychology Review*, **2**(2), 36–42.

Consolacion, T. B., Russell, S. T. & Sue, S. (2004). Sex, race/ethnicity, and romantic attractions: Multiple minority status adolescents and mental health. *Cultural Diversity and Ethnic Minority Psychology*, **10**(3), 200–214.

Croteau, J. M., Talbot, D. M., Lance, T. S. & Evans, N. J. (2002). A qualitative study of the interplay between privilege and oppression. *Journal of Multicultural Counseling and Development*, **30**(2), 239–258.

Crowne, D. & Marlowe, D. (1960). A new scale of social desirability of psychopathology. *Journal of Consulting Psychology*, **24**(4), 329–354.

Dube, E. M. & Savin-Williams, R. C. (1999). Sexual identity development among ethnic sexual-minority male youths. *Developmental Psychology*, **35**(6), 1389–1398.

Dudgeon, P., Garvey, D. & Pickett, H. (2000). *Working with Indigenous Australians: A handbook for psychologists*. Perth: Gunada Press.

Fine, M. (1997). Witnessing whiteness. In M. Fine, L. Weis, L. C. Powell & L. Mun Wong (Eds) *Off White: Readings on race, power and society* (pp. 57–65). New York, NY: Routledge.

Hage, G. (1998). *White Nation: Fantasies of white supremacy in a multicultural nation*. Annandale, NSW: Pluto Press.

Harris, A. P. (1995). Race and essentialism in feminist legal theory. In R. Delago (Ed.), *Critical Race Theory: The cutting edge* (pp. 220–241). Philadelphia, PA: Temple University Press.

Herrnstein, R. J. & Murray, C. (1996). *Bell Curve: Intelligence and class structure in American life*. New York, NY: The Free Press.

hooks, b. (1981). *Ain't I a Woman: Black women and feminism*. Boston, MA: South End Press.

hooks, b. (1989). *Talking Back: Thinking feminist, thinking black*. Boston, MA: South End Press.

Howitt, D. & Owusu-Bempah, J. (1994). *The Racism of Psychology: Time for change*. New York, NY: Harvester Wheatsheaf.

Jackson, R. L. (1998). Tracing the evolution of 'race', 'ethnicity', and 'culture' in communication studies. *Howard Journal of Communications*, **9**(1), 41–55.

Johnson-Riordan, L., Conway Herron, J. & Johnston, P. (2002). Decolonising the 'white' nation: 'White' psychology. *International Journal of Critical Psychology*, **6**, 10–51.

Kinsey, A. C., Pomeroy, W. B. & Martin, C. E. (1948). *Sexual behavior in the human male*. Philadelphia, PA: W. B. Saunders.

Kitzinger, C. (1987). *The Social Construction of Lesbianism*. London: Sage.

Kitzinger, C. (1996). The token lesbian chapter. In S. Wilkinson (Ed.), *Feminist Social Psychologies: International perspectives* (pp. 119–144). Buckingham: Open University Press.

Kitzinger, C. & Coyle, A. (2002). Introducing lesbian and gay psychology. In A. Coyle & C. Kitzinger (Eds), *Lesbian and Gay Psychology: New perspectives* (pp. 1–29). Oxford: BPS Blackwell.

Kitzinger, C. & Perkins, R. (1993). *Changing our Minds: Lesbian feminism and psychology.* New York, NY: New York University Press.

Kitzinger, C. & Wilkinson, S. (1993). Theorizing heterosexuality. In S. Wilkinson & C. Kitzinger (Eds), *Heterosexuality: A feminism & psychology reader* (pp. 1–32). London: Sage.

Macquarie Concise Dictionary (1998). 3rd edn. Sydney, Australia: Macquarie Library.

Mama, A. (1995). *Beyond the Masks: Race, gender and subjectivity.* London: Routledge.

Mashburn, A. J., Peterson, J. L., Bakeman, R., Miller, R. L. & Clark, L. F. (2004). Influences on HIV testing among young African-American men who have sex with men and the moderating effect of the geographic setting. *Journal of Community Psychology,* **32,** 45–60.

Morawski, J. G. (1997). White experimenters, white blood, and other white conditions: Locating the psychologist's race. In M. Fine, L. Weis, L. C. Powell & L. M. Wong (Eds), *Off white: Readings on race, power, and society* (pp. 13–27). New York, NY: Routledge.

Moreton-Robinson, A. (2000). *Talkin' up to the White Woman: Indigenous women and feminism.* St Lucia: UQ Press.

Moreton Robinson, A. (2004). The Possessive logic of patriarchal white sovereignty: The High Court and the Yorta Yorta decision. *Borderlands e-journal 3.* Retrieved 15 May 2005, from http://www.borderlandsejournal.adelaide.edu.au/vol3no2_2004/moreton_possessive.htm

Nicoll, F. (2000). Indigenous sovereignty and the violence of perspective: A white woman's coming out story. *Australian Feminist Studies,* **15,** 369–386.

Nicolosi, J. (1991). *Reparative Therapy of Male Homosexuality: A new clinical approach.* Northvale, NJ: Jason Aronson.

Parks, C., Hughes, T. L. & Matthews, A. K. (2004). Race/ethnicity and sexual orientation: Intersecting identities. *Cultural Diversity and Ethnic Minority Psychology,* **10**(3), 241–254.

Peterson, J., Folkman, S. & Bakeman, R. (1996). Stress, coping, social support, and depressive mood in African-American gay, bisexual, and heterosexual men. *American Journal of Community Psychology,* **24**(4), 461–487.

Quadagno, D., Sly, D. F., Harrison, D. F., Eberstein, I. W. & Soler, H. R. (1998). Ethnic differences in sexual decisions and sexual behavior. *Archives of Sexual Behavior,* **27**(1), 57–75.

Riggs, D. W. (2004a). Challenging the monoculturalism of psychology: Towards a more socially accountable pedagogy and practice. *Australian Psychologist,* **39**(2), 118–126.

Riggs, D. W. (2004b). 'We don't talk about race anymore': Privilege, power and critical whiteness studies. *Borderlands-ejournal, 3.* Retrieved 15 May 2005, from http://www.borderlandsejournal.adelaide.edu.au/vol3no2_2004/riggs_intro.htm

Riggs, D. W. (2006a). Developmentalism and the rhetoric of 'best interests of the child': Challenging heteronormative constructions of families and parenting in foster care. *Journal of GLBT Family Studies,* **2**(2), 57–73.

Riggs, D. W. (2006b). *Priscilla, (White) Queen of the Desert: Queer rights/race privilege.* New York, NY: Peter Lang.

Riggs, D. W. & Selby, J. M. (2003). Setting the seen: Whiteness as unmarked category in psychologists' writing on race in Australia. In M. Katsikitis (Ed.), *Proceedings of the 38th APS Annual Conference* (pp. 190–195). Melbourne: Australian Psychological Society.

Riggs, D. W. & Riggs, L. D. (2004). Talking about heterosexism: Politics, complicity and identification. In D. W. Riggs & G. A. Walker (Eds), *Out in the Antipodes: Australian and New Zealand perspectives on gay and lesbian issues in psychology* (pp. 416–434). Perth: Brightfire Press.

Rosario, M., Schrimshaw, E. W. & Hunter, J. (2004). Ethnic/racial differences in the coming-out process of lesbian, gay, and bisexual youths: A comparison of sexual identity development over time. *Cultural Diversity and Ethnic Minority Psychology,* **10**(3), 215–228.

Rosenberg, M. (1965). *Society and the Adolescent Self-image.* Princeton, NJ: Princeton University Press.

Siegel, K. & Epstein, J. A. (1996). Ethnic-racial differences in psychological stress related to gay lifestyle among HIV-positive men. *Psychological Reports,* **79**(1), 303–312.

Smith, A. (1997). Cultural diversity and the coming out process: Implications for clinical practice. In B. Greene (Ed.), *Ethnic and Cultural Diversity Among Lesbians and Gay Men* (pp. 279–300). London: Sage.

Smith, L. T. (1999). *Decolonizing Methodologies*. London: Zed Books.

Terry, J. (1999). *An American Obsession: Science, medicine and homosexuality in modern society.* Chicago, IL: University of Chicago Press.

Todd, N. & Wade, A. (1995). Domination, deficiency, and psychotherapy, part I. *The Calgary Participator,* **Fall**, 3–9.

Trujillo, C. M. (1997). Sexual identity and the discontents of difference. In B. Greene (Ed.) *Ethnic and Cultural Diversity Among Lesbians and Gay Men* (pp. 266–278). Thousand Oaks, CA: Sage.

Waldegrave, C. (1998). The challenges of culture to psychology and postmodern thinking. In M. McGoldrick (Ed.), *Re-visioning Family Therapy: Race, culture, and gender in clinical practice* (pp. 404–413). New York, NY: The Guilford Press.

Walker, P. (2003). Colonising research: Academia's structural violence towards Indigenous peoples. *Social Alternatives,* **22**(3), 37–40.

Whitam, F. L., Daskalos, C., Sobolewski, C. G. & Padilla, P. (1998). The emergence of lesbian sexuality and identity cross culturally: Brazil, Peru, the Phillipines, and the United States. *Archives of Sexual Behavior,* **27**(1), 31–57.

Wong, L. M. (1994). Di(s)-secting and dis(s)-closing 'whiteness': Two tales about psychology. In K. K. Bhavnani & A. Pheonix (Eds), *Shifting Identities, Shifting Racisms: A feminism & psychology reader* (pp. 133–154). London: Sage.

CHAPTER 5

Personality, Individual Differences and LGB Psychology

Gareth Hagger-Johnson
University of Edinburgh, UK

INTRODUCTION

This chapter calls for a collaborative research agenda between personality and individual differences (PAID) research and lesbian, gay, bisexual (LGB)[1] psychology. The chapter is divided into five sections, two historical and three contemporary. The first section demonstrates that early LGB psychology (pre-affirmative and affirmative) placed an important emphasis on personality. The second section continues this discussion with a focus on psychological testing. The third and fourth sections review recent developments in the areas of personality disorders and in sexual risk-taking. High rates of borderline personality disorder diagnoses in LGB people and issues surrounding personality approaches to sexual risk-taking are used to demonstrate that LGB and PAID psychology share concerns relevant to LGB people's lives. Finally, criticisms of PAID research by socially oriented LGB psychologists are discussed and I conclude by proposing an LGB PAID research agenda for the future. I now begin by defining the four areas of work key to this chapter – LGB psychology, social psychology, critical social psychology and PAID research – and my central argument.

LGB psychology is one of the newest recognized sub-disciplines of psychology and is concerned with the psychological aspects of LGB people's lives and experiences. Researchers in this sub-discipline share a diverse range of concerns including documenting and challenging homophobia and heterosexism, understanding LGB identity development and maintenance, and exploring same-sex relationships and parenting (see Kitzinger & Coyle, 2002). LGB psychology is also committed to a positive social change for non-heterosexually identified people. Wilkinson and Coyle (2002) argue that LGB psychologi-

---

[1] Personality research in relation to transgender populations is not included in this chapter because it generally focuses on 'gender related traits' which have been reviewed elsewhere (see Lothstein, 2002, for a review of psychological testing with transsexual people and cf. Hegarty, 2002, for a critical perspective on the notion of gender related traits).

Out in Psychology: Lesbian, gay, bisexual, trans and queer perspectives. Edited by Victoria Clarke and Elizabeth Peel.
© 2007 John Wiley & Sons, Ltd.

cal research in Europe (and, I would add, Australasia) looks epistemologically and methodologically much like social psychology, and could loosely be described as social psychological in nature. Furthermore, LGB psychology in Europe and Australasia tends to prioritize qualitative methods (Kitzinger & Coyle, 2002) and critical social psychological approaches. Critical social psychology is a developing area of research, theory and therapeutic practice and a generic term for a wide variety of radical perspectives on the discipline of psychology. The perspectives are considered radical because they question the very foundations of psychological knowledge (and the role played by psychological knowledge in the maintenance of inequality and oppression) and explicitly stress the socially 'constructed' nature of experience (Gough & McFadden, 2001).

Personality and individual differences (PAID) research, sometimes called differential psychology, is often placed under the umbrella of social psychology. For example, each issue of the *Journal of Personality and Social Psychology* (JPSP) has included a specific section devoted to PAID research since 1980 (Swann & Seyle, 2005). PAID researchers generally focus on individual differences in personality traits, mental abilities and personality disorders. Personality is an umbrella term for the way in which we appear to others, deriving from the Greek word *persona* (mask). Personality traits refer specifically to the stable or enduring elements of a person's character, the portion resistant to change or consistently present across many situations (Butt, 2003). The declining popularity of personality measures in social psychology since the 1970s has recently been reversed, with more than 50% of research studies published in contemporary issues of JPSP including some measure of personality (Swann & Seyle, 2005). Widespread criticism of PAID research spurred improvements in the reliability and validity of PAID measures and motivated PAID researchers to show that personality moderates the influence of situations and social factors on behaviour. Contemporary personality trait research suggests that the following five concepts adequately describe the main dimensions on which people vary – extraversion, neuroticism, openness to experience, agreeableness and conscientiousness (the 'big five'). Because trait theorists describe dimensions (e.g. extroversion, neuroticism), this replaces the notion of types or categories to which people can be assigned (e.g. extravert, neurotic). The trait theorists' approach to personality is called *idiographic*, whereas the type theorists' is called *nomothetic*. To support their claims, PAID researchers use instruments such as questionnaires or interviews that are evaluated according to the criteria of reliability (the internal consistency of a measure), stability (across times, different languages and cultures) and validity (the questionnaire measures what it claims to measure and is associated with external 'real-life' outcomes, for example, health, career success or mortality) (see Matthews, Deary & Whiteman, 2003). At the time of writing, 'personality disorders', discussed later in this chapter, are defined categorically and nomothetically. They are 'enduring patterns of inner experience and behavior that deviates markedly from the expectations of the individual's culture' (American Psychiatric Association, 2000, p. 689). Personality disorders are described as being pervasive and inflexible, starting in adolescence or early adulthood, stable over time and leading to distress and impairment.

Although PAID research is considered part of social psychology, it foregrounds individual rather than social factors, and its methods and epistemological assumptions are sometimes incompatible with qualitative and critical social psychology. Indeed, this difference in emphasis has led to some antagonism between PAID research and LGB psychology. For example, Fish (2002) has argued that PAID researchers fail to acknowledge the socio-political forces at work in their research. Conversely, Rahman and Wilson (2003) have described qualitative, critical and constructionist approaches to sexual orientation as 'incoherent' with a 'poor intellectual framework' (p. 1338). Further examples of antagonism are reviewed in the last section of this chapter.

My argument in this chapter is that since LGB and PAID psychology share important concerns, they can potentially work together and such a collaboration will benefit both fields. A collaborative agenda stands in opposition to the argument that one particular theoretical framework or set of epistemological assumptions represents *the* way forward for LGB psychology. For example, Kitzinger (1997, 1999), whose work is synonymous with the constructionist 'turn' in LGB psychology, argued that the field is best served by a philosophy of methodological, theoretical and epistemological plurality. She critiqued the assumption that qualitative and critical LGB psychological theories and methods and positive social change are necessarily related. She maintained that mainstream theories and methods, such as those associated with the PAID research tradition, have been used effectively by LGB psychologists to aid positive social change for LGB people. In contrast, alternative approaches, such as discourse analysis, have so far not delivered on this promise. My argument in this chapter builds on Hegarty's call (Chapter 3) for LGBTQ psychologists to be suspicious of claims about any inherent radicalness in qualitative approaches such as discourse analysis – and indeed any approach that presents itself as representing the totality of the critical inclination in psychology or its sub-disciplines.

PERSONALITY RESEARCH AND LGB PEOPLE: HISTORICAL REVIEW

In this first section, I consider the history of the relationship between LGB psychology and PAID research. As Peel (2002, p. 53) notes, 'the social-cultural context shapes the possibilities for psychological enquiry'. Historical events and processes inevitably impact on the type and quantity of PAID research. This is particularly apparent for LGB PAID research, which has been conducted in parallel with, and in response to, key events in modern LGB history. When reviewing LGB personality research, it is important to bear in mind an important distinction between testing *for* and testing *about* homosexuality (Reiss, 1980). Researchers or clinicians tested for homosexuality when they attempted to discover whether an individual was lesbian, gay or bisexual. For example, Rorschach inkblot tests were used during the Second World War[2] to test *for* homosexuality (discussed below). Testing *about* homosexuality involves the correlation or association of an LGB sexual orientation with other psychological or health variables. Studies that compare LGB people and heterosexuals on psychological measures fall into this category (Reiss, 1980). The assumption that homosexuality is psychopathological or abnormal has often underpinned PAID research, particularly in earlier studies that tested *for* homosexuality. More recent studies are likely to discuss personality or other differences as correlated *with* or reflecting inequalities in mental or physical health (e.g. Sandfort, de Graaf,

---

[2] Inkblot tests remain in use today in several countries.

Bijl & Schnabel, 2001), although some still adopt a psychopathological view. For example, Zanarini et al. (2003, p. 479) describe 'nonheterosexual orientation as a manifestation of the identity problems that plague many borderline patients'. Similarly, van den Aardweg (1985, p. 85) argued that homosexuality 'springs from some kind of psychic pathology . . . I, for one, have always been convinced of the disturbance character of this condition'.

Homosexuality and the Diagnostic and Statistical Manual of Mental Disorders (DSM)

The American Psychiatric Association (APA) is a professional organization representing psychiatrists in the USA and it publishes the *Diagnostic and Statistical Manual of Mental Disorders* (DSM). The DSM is used by psychiatrists, and a variety of other professionals, to describe and classify mental disorders. It is not only used in clinical settings, but also in research, education, administration, insurance and in court. There have been four major revisions of the DSM since the first edition (APA, 1952). These are DSM-II (APA, 1968), DSM-III (APA, 1980), DSM-III-R (APA, 1987) and DSM-IV (APA, 1994). A minor text revision to DSM-IV formed the current edition, DSM-IV-TR (APA, 2000). At the time of writing, the revision process for DSM-V has begun, with publication scheduled for approximately 2011.

Freud's influence is clear in the organization of the three types of diagnoses included in DSM-I: psychoses, neurosis and personality disorders (Kutchings & Kirk, 1997, p. 57). Personality disorders included a category called 'Sexual Deviation', the diagnosis used for homosexuality. A separate diagnosis of homosexuality was added in DSM-II. The DSM has always been a compromise between many theoretical perspectives in psychiatry (Coid, 2003). Matthews et al. (2003, pp. 298–299) describe the text as 'a raft on which many heterogeneous concepts have climbed'. In its later editions, the manual became a compromise between psychiatry, the wider public, political groups and other professional organizations, such as the American Psychological Association (Kutchings & Kirk, 1997). Taking the example of personality disorders, for instance (see below for further discussion of personality disorders), the origins of the categories include psychoanalysis (narcissistic and borderline personality disorder), empirical longitudinal research (antisocial personality disorder), and clinical observations by influential early twentieth-century German clinicians (dependent, obsessive-compulsive and paranoid disorders). Each of these categories has developed over time as a result of changes in clinical opinion, new research and negotiations preceding each new edition (Coid, 2003).

There were at least two forces that resulted in the removal of homosexuality (as a separate diagnosis) from the DSM. First, the APA underwent an internal struggle to develop a more satisfactory definition of 'mental disorder', one which removed psychoanalytic concepts from the DSM. Kutchings and Kirk (1997) describe how the psychoanalytic approach had become vulnerable due to limited success of psychoanalytic treatments and the paucity of scientific data to support psychodynamic explanations of behaviour. The APA sought to adopt a medical model and use empirically determined scientific definitions of mental illness. Homosexuality was one psychoanalytic category that many psychiatrists found problematic, precisely because of its psychoanalytic roots. Once mental illness was defined as a source of 'present distress or disability or with a significantly increased risk of suffering death, pain, disability, or an important loss of freedom' (APA, 2000, p. xxxi), it then became difficult to interpret homosexuality as a mental illness. The desire to expunge psychoanalytic constructs from the DSM is one reason why the diagnosis of 'Ego Dystonic Homosexuality' (EDH), distress about a homosexual orientation, added to DSM-III, was unpopular with psychiatrists. Kutchings & Kirk (1997, pp. 77–86) discuss how, for many, the reference to 'ego' felt like a retrograde step and was a compromise between psychiatry and the second force, which was external: LGB activism. LGB activist groups began to form shortly after the publication of the Kinsey reports (Kinsey, Pomeroy & Martin, 1948; Kinsey, Pomeroy, Martin & Gebhard, 1953). Gay community organizations, such as the Mattachine Society, campaigned for the removal of homosexuality from DSM and protested aspects of the psychiatric treatment of homosexuality. Between 1970 and 1973, demonstrations staged at the annual APA convention led to the inclusion of gay speakers in the debate about homosexuality (see Kutchings & Kirk, 1997, pp. 65–77).

The removal of homosexuality, as a separate diagnosis, from the DSM shows a point of connection between LGB psychology and PAID research: both are concerned with improving the validity of personality disorder descriptions in the DSM. It also shows how historical events and processes can bring LGB psychology into contact with other disciplines.

The Second World War and Military Bans on Homosexuality

PAID research, like any research, can be used for positive social change or for objectionable purposes. This section provides one example of how personality assessment has supported discrimination against LGB people. LGB historians have documented the persecution of LGB people during and after the Second World War (Mondimore, 1996; Plant, 1986). Bans on homosexuality in the US military were introduced during the Second World War on the grounds that homosexuals (and anyone who engaged in homosexual behaviour) were not psychologically fit for duty (Hegarty, 2003a; Herek, 1993). Service men and women were encouraged to report homosexual desires to psychiatrists. Psychiatrists performed a twin role, as therapist and as informant, often reporting servicemen to military officials. Rorschach inkblot personality tests, among other tests, were used by psychiatrists and psychologists to test for homosexuality; however, the emphasis was on detecting heterosexual men who were pretending to be homosexual in order to get discharged from the armed forces. Rorschach inkblots are ambiguous shapes printed on cards and presented to individuals, who interpret and describe them. It was (and often still is) claimed that people 'project' their psychology or personality onto them. Hegarty (2003a) describes how the developers of the Rorschach believed that it provided a 'royal road' or path to the homosexual unconscious. The researchers claimed expertise in the test's interpretation, but 'were careful to describe that path as unfamiliar' (Hegarty 2003a, p. 410). Wheeler (1949) generated 20 'homosexual signs' from Rorschach analyses, which became known as 'Wheeler signs'. Since 85% of people produced at least one

Wheeler sign, the number needed to indicate homosexuality was arbitrarily set at three. It is important for LGB and PAID researchers to be aware of the potential for such negative consequences of their research.

Affirmative LGB Personality Research

The removal of a diagnostic category of homosexuality from the DSM sparred a third historical epoch: the LGB affirmative era. Affirmative LGB psychology is defined by LGB psychologists as research that contributes to positive social change for LGB people. The ten criteria for LGB affirmative research (modified from Oberstone & Sukoneck, 1976; Hegarty, 2003b) are:

1. The study examines homosexuality in its social context, with sensitivity to the possible individual differences in LGB people.
2. The study presents a clear definition of sexual orientation.
3. The study samples from non-clinical and non-institutionalized participants and does not reply solely on LGB organizations.
4. Appropriate controls are used if group-level comparisons are made (for example, if comparing single LGB people, then single heterosexuals rather than heterosexuals in relationships form the comparison group).
5. Reliable and valid measures are used.
6. Current behaviour and feelings are studied.
7. The variety of sexual identities and behaviours are emphasized in relation to everyone, not just in relation to LGB people.
8. Stereotypes are challenged.
9. If collaborating with LGB organizations or voluntary sector agencies, these are acknowledged in the research publications (Hegarty, 2003b).
10. The study does not make heterosexist claims.

As noted earlier, there was a strong emphasis on personality testing in early affirmative research and a large number of early studies focused on comparing the personalities and psychologies of LGB people and heterosexuals. These studies generally revealed few or no differences between the two groups (e.g. Gonsiorek, 1982; Oberstone & Sukoneck, 1976).

Evelyn Hooker (1957), a US-based clinical psychologist, conducted one of the first gay-affirmative personality studies. She tested 30 gay men with three projective tests: the Rorschach, the Thematic Appreciation Test and the Make a Picture Story test (all of these are tests where an ambiguous stimulus is described and the interpretation is thought to reflect the underlying personality). Hooker asked two experts to guess each man's sexual orientation based on their Rorschach response alone. A third expert was asked to guess each man's sexual orientation based on his responses to the other two tests. None of the three experts could guess the sexual orientation of the men better than chance. Hegarty (2003b, p. 4) describes this as a 'foundational moment' in LGB psychology. Using measures of personality, Hooker simultaneously challenged the traditional psychodynamic and clinical approach to testing for homosexuality and the psychopathological assumption that had been present in much pre-affirmative research.

However, Hegarty (2003b) argues that it was Hooker's personal contact with gay men, not her training as a psychologist, which led her to challenge the view that homosexuality was pathological. Because Hooker's links with gay organizations were not mentioned in the research paper, Hegarty argues that the study was not truly affirmative because affirmative research studies acknowledge the contribution that gay community groups make in the recruitment process (this has been added to the criteria in the list above).

Twelve years after the publication of Hooker's ground-breaking study, an equally ground-breaking study of the lesbian personality was published by a British-based clinical psychologist, June Hopkins (1969; see also Clarke & Hopkins, 2002; Clarke and Peel, 2007). Hopkins (1969) found that lesbian women scored higher than heterosexual women on the 16PF personality inventory measures of reserved, detached, critical, cool, dominant, assertive and progressive. Their scores indicated that they were more careless of practical matters, bohemian and self-sufficient. Prior to this study, lesbianism was considered a symptom of neurosis or a personality disorder in and of itself. While Hooker's (1969) work is typically celebrated as a ground-breaking affirmative study because it showed no differences between gay and heterosexual men, in a recent reappraisal, Hopkins's (1969) work was celebrated precisely because it emphasized differences between lesbians and heterosexual women. Hopkins said, 'there were differences and all of the differences, I felt, were healthy and were *good* ones' (Clarke & Hopkins, 2002, p. 44, my emphasis). Peel (2002, p. 53) suggests that in this context, 'difference does not necessarily encode deviance'. The notion that some personality traits are considered to be more desirable than others can be problematic, and Peel (2002) notes that 'dominant' may not have been considered a 'good' trait for women in the context of 1969. The aim of contemporary PAID research is usually to describe individual differences, not to describe averaged differences of entire social groups (e.g. of all lesbian women). Contemporary PAID research is less likely to state that some traits are better per se than others.

Personality research had become less popular in LGB psychology by the mid-1970s when researchers turned their attention towards LGB people's experiences of homophobia and heterosexism, and away from LGB people's personalities and psychological adjustment. However, personality research continues to have important implications for LGB people's lives. In the USA, justification for the exclusion of lesbians and gay men from the military, law enforcement and government security was, until the mid-1990s, based partly on beliefs about personality traits. For example, it was argued that gay men possessed an inordinate amount of psychopathology and character flaws such as instability, illegal conduct, dishonesty, untrustworthiness, poor teamwork and relationship formation skills. Gay men were described as being highly strung and neurotic as a result of leading double lives (see Herek, 1990, 1993). Sexual orientation differences on psychological measures can be used to argue that homosexuality is indicative of psychopathology (van den Aardweg, 1985; Zubenko, George, Soloff & Schulz, 1987), or alternatively to argue for a positive agenda for social change, by revealing differences and inequalities.

The next section moves our discussion into the present day, where LGB people are being studied in relation to sexual risk-taking and personality disorders. These are two important areas researched by LGB and PAID psychologists, but currently without much collaboration.

PERSONALITY RESEARCH AND LGB PEOPLE: CONTEMPORARY REVIEW

In this section I argue that LGB psychology could help improve personality researcher's measurement of sexual risk-taking. Sexual risk-taking and its relationship to personality traits is a good example of an area where social factors combine with individual ones to impact on LGB people's lives, but where the phenomenon is difficult to understand without some knowledge of LGB psychological research into sexual behaviour.

Personality and Sexual Risk-Taking in Gay/Bisexual Men

A large amount of PAID research using gay and bisexual men as participants has been conducted in relation to HIV and sexual risk-taking, since the advent of the HIV epidemic in the 1980s. A recent review of personality and sexual risk-taking studies conducted by Hoyle, Fejfar & Miller (2000) showed that the personality trait 'sensation-seeking' is strongly related to sexual risk (defined either in terms of the number of sexual partners or rates of condom use). Sensation-seeking, a measure used in 64% of the studies reviewed, refers to the pursuit of novel, intense and complex sensations and experiences, and the willingness to take risks for the sake of these experiences. The defintion of 'sexual risk', like many concepts in psychology, is controversial. Flowers et al. (Flowers, Smith, Sheeran & Beail, 1997; Flowers, Duncan & Knussen, 2003) and Coxon (2003) are examples of LGB oriented researchers who have offered suggestions on how to improve definitions of sexual risk-taking in psychology, although few personality and sexual risk-taking studies have adopted their recommendations.

Hoyle et al. (2000) presented 'limiting sexual activity to a single, uninfected partner' as a recommended HIV reduction strategy. This definition of sexual risk-taking, in terms of numbers of casual sexual partners, does not acknowledge the fact that the HIV status of the single partner needs to be known. Low rates of HIV testing in some countries mean that many HIV+ gay/bisexual men are unaware of their HIV status, and therefore are not offered treatments (Flowers et al., 2003). Another limitation of the assumption that 'promiscuity' puts men at risk for HIV transmission is that many transmissions occur between 'main' sexual partners, rather than between casual partners (Flowers et al., 1997; Xiridou et al., 2004). LGB psychological research has raised awareness of HIV testing and relationship factors as dimensions of sexual risk and opened up new avenues for collaboration between LGB and PAID researchers, using more valid definitions of the sexual risk-taking outcome. One possible avenue of research is determining the individual and social factors that influence decisions to undergo HIV testing and discontinue condom use.

Coxon (2003) has made important contributions to our understanding of gay/bisexual men's sexual behaviour and, therefore, to LGB psychology. Under the umbrella project 'Socio-sexual Investigations of Gay Men and AIDS' (SIGMA), Coxon conducted research that challenged widely held assumptions about gay men's sexual practices and the rates of HIV infection among gay men. He challenged the notion that gay men are inherently 'promiscuous', that gay men universally practice anal intercourse and that these factors lead to high rates of HIV transmission among gay men. Coxon and his collaborators undermined these assumptions by using an individual differences paradigm and measuring individual sexual behaviour rather than those of defined groups such as 'gay men'. SIGMA researchers also introduced the concept of 'penetrative sexual partner' (PSP) as distinct from 'sexual partner'. In one study, Hunt et al. (1991) found that HIV status correlated with PSPs but not 'number of partners' alone. It is important to acknowledge that men with a higher number of casual partners can often use condoms to reduce the risk of HIV transmission. Although many studies in the Hoyle et al. (2000) review measured condom use, many referred solely to 'number of partners' without taking condom use into account. Xiridou et al. (2004) showed that the relative infrequency of unprotected anal intercourse in casual encounters explained the high rate of HIV transmissions from main partners. Understanding individual differences in sexual behaviour has therefore proved essential to generating an accurate definition of the outcome under investigation. PAID researchers interested in sexual risk-taking could improve their research by drawing on insights from LGB research with regard to measures of relationship status, HIV testing behaviour and penetrative versus non-penetrative sex.

Personality Disorders

In this section I discuss the current position of homosexuality in DSM-IV-TR (APA, 2000) and argue that DSM-IV-TR still allows the diagnosis of mental illness in relation to homosexuality (although not as directly as in the past). As noted above, the category 'Ego Dystonic Homosexuality' does not appear in DSM-IV-TR as a separate category because it was unpopular with psychiatrists seeking a switch from a psychodynamic to a medical model. However, one DSM-IV-TR criterion for the diagnosis of 'Sexual Disorder Not Otherwise Specified' is conceptually similar to EDH. A diagnosis relating to homosexuality can still be made if the patient shows 'persistent and marked distress about sexual orientation' (APA, 2000, p. 582). Egodystonic Sexual Orientation is currently listed in the International Classification of Diseases (ICD)-10 Classification of Mental Disorders (World Health Organisation [WHO], 1993, p. 222) and is defined as follows: 'the gender identity or sexual preference is not in doubt but the individual wishes it were different because of associated psychological and behavioural disorders and may seek treatment in order to change it'. Homosexuality also appears indirectly in the instruments used to assess borderline personality disorder.

Personality disorders are defined and listed in the WHO's ICD (WHO, 1993) and the DSM-IV-TR (APA, 2000). The definitions refer to the existence of symptoms or behaviour that cause distress to the sufferer or interfere with personal functions, in particular those that are enduring (stable) 'patterns of inner experience' and differ from cultural expectations (APA, 2000, p. 689). Personality disorders are relevant to a discussion of LGB personality research for two reasons. First, there is the possibility that LGB people are more likely to receive a diagnosis of personality disorder. Second, the criteria for borderline personality disorder refer to sexual risk-taking and identity disturbance, which have implications for gay and bisexual men in particular. Avoiding false positive diagnoses, where a diagnosis is given but no disorder is present, is important for clinicians because unnecessary treatment and care is expensive (Coid, 2003), and because personality disorders are stigmatized (Lewis & Appleby, 1988).

There is evidence that gay and bisexual men are more likely to receive a diagnosis of borderline personality disorder, although the reasons for this are not currently known.

Table 5.1   Proportions of LGB people in borderline personality disorder samples

Study	% gay or lesbian	% bisexual
Zubenko et al. (1987) (1) males	57	–
Zubenko et al. (1987) (2) males	53	5
Zubenko et al. (1987) (2) males	11	5
Dulit et al. (1993) males	22	26
Dulit et al. (1993) females	3	11
Stone (1987) males	9.8	–
Stone (1987) females	1.4	–
Paris, Zweigfrank & Guzder (1995) males	16.7	–
Ramos, Perera, Urdaniz & Iglesias (2002) males and females	5	12.5

Note: If the proportion of gay/lesbian people with borderline personality disorder were equal to heterosexuals, we would expect that 1–5% (depending on estimates used e.g. Johnson et al., 2001) of borderline personality disorder patients would be to be lesbian or gay.

Borderline personality disorder is described as a pervasive pattern of instability of inter-personal relationships, negative self-image, identity disturbance, negative affectivity and poor impulse control that begins in early adulthood and is present in a variety of contexts (e.g. substance misuse, sexual risk-taking, manipulative threats). In Table 5.1, I have listed the small number of published studies of borderline patients where the sexual orientation was reported. Most published studies of personality disorders do not break statistics down by sexual orientation so we cannot assess the extent of the problem. In contrast, studies reporting prevalence of Axis I diagnoses, such as mood, anxiety and substance misuse, broken down by sexual orientation, are available. For example, Sandfort et al. (2001) reported higher rates of mood and anxiety disorders in gay men and higher rates of substance use disorder diagnoses in lesbian women, compared to heterosexuals.

Table 5.1 shows a general trend towards a larger proportion of gay and bisexual men (and to a lesser extent, lesbian women) being found in samples of patients given a border-line personality disorder diagnosis. The borderline disorder has attracted much criticism, and many clinicians recognize its definition as problematic. It has been described as a 'wastebasket' diagnosis of exclusion, made only after other diagnoses and treatments have failed (Kutchings & Kirk, 1997). There is evidence that women (Widiger, 1998; Widiger & Spitzer, 1991) and ethnic minorities (Widiger & Axelrod, 1995) are also more likely to receive a borderline diagnosis. There are at least three possible explanations for the high number of gay and bisexual men in the samples of borderline patients. First, there is the possibility that the instruments used to assess the disorder are biased. Second, there is the possibility that confounding psycho-social stressors caused apparent association between sexual orientation and the disorder. Finally, there is the possibility of the presence of confounding Axis I disorders (anxiety, mood and substance misuse).

Biased Instruments

The bias that might exist in personality disorder diagnostic systems could come from several sources or emerge at several points in the diagnostic process. In response to criticism that more females than males receive borderline, dependent and histrionic personality disorder diagnoses, Widiger (1998) reviewed several possible sources of sex bias, which may also apply to sexual orientation bias. He concluded that we should distinguish between sources of bias that relate to diagnostic constructs, the thresholds for disorders (cut-off points), the instruments used to measure disorders (such as questionnaires or clinical interviews), how people with disorders are sampled, and, finally, how clinicians apply criteria. If we suspect bias in terms of sexual orientation, it is important to first clarify which of these sources is under scrutiny. Concerns that instruments used to assess borderline personality disorder are heterosexist were raised by Zucker (1996). One item in the Diagnostic Interview for Borderline Patients (DIBP) (Gunderson, Kolb & Austin, 1981) refers to 'a pattern of promiscuity, homosexuality or repetitive sexually deviant practices', which 'is explicitly heterosexist because it equates homosexuality per se with a feature of the borderline personality disorder (Zucker, 1996, p. 966). This is explicitly heterosexist because it equates homosexuality per se with a feature of the disorder (Zucker, 1996). This increases the number of LGB people reaching the diagnostic threshold, and increases the number of false positive diagnoses. Zucker (1996) requested that the item be reworded to include heterosexual and homosexual risk-taking behaviour. In my view, the criteria would benefit from a redefinition that explicitly refers to condom use and HIV testing in addition to numbers of sexual partners. The DIBP was revised by Zanarini et al. (1989, 2003) and now refers to 'sexual deviance'. It is not clear from the published revisions how sexual deviance is defined by clinicians.

The Structured Clinical Interview for DSM-IV-TR (SCID, First, Spitzer, Miriam & Williams, 1997) is a semi-structured diagnostic interview used by clinicians, researchers and trainees in making DSM-IV-TR personality disorder diagnoses. I have listed three of the 13 items for borderline personality disorder below that have the potential to introduce biases against LGB people into the diagnostic process. The guidelines given to the clinician are shown in italics:

> (90) You've said you've often done things impulsively. What kinds of things? How about . . . having sex with people you hardly knew, or 'unsafe sex'? *Impulsivity in at least two areas that are potentially self-damaging.*

> (96) You've said you are different with different people or in different situations so that you sometimes don't know who you really are. Give me some examples of this. *Marked and persistent identity disturbance manifested by uncertainty about at least two of the following: self-image, sexual orientation, long-term goals or career choice, type of friends desired, preferred values. Note: Do not include normal adolescent uncertainty about these issues.*

> (98) You've said that you often change your mind about the types of friends or lovers you want. Tell me more about that. Do you ever feel confused about whether you're gay or straight? *Often uncertain about identity and is not limited to a circumscribed period of time.*

Egan, Nathan and Lumley (2003) argue that clinical interviews are highly susceptible to idiosyncrasies, inaccurate assumptions, or gender, cultural and ethnic biases (see also Widiger & Axelrod, 1995). They attribute this to heuristics – the shortcuts people use when problem-solving, which are known to evoke social stereotypes. For example, information available in the clinical interview about identity disturbance, distress about sexual orientation, substance misuse, self-harm, sexual risk-taking (or clinicians' inaccurate assumptions about sexual risk) in LGB patients might stand out as a salient piece of information to the clinician, encouraging a borderline personality disorder diagnoses over other diagnoses with less salient criteria, such as avoidance of social situations. It is plausible that these three questions alter the diagnostic threshold for LGB people and create false positive diagnoses. LGB people are likely to feel uncertain or distressed about their sexual orientation at some point in their lives, gay and bisexual men typically have a higher than average number of sexual partners (Johnson et al., 2001), and clinicians may assume that 'unsafe sex' equates to a high number of casual partners (they may not take condom use, relationships and HIV testing into account). These are examples of confounding factors which could lower the reliability of borderline diagnostic instruments. Questionnaire items or interview questions should not be affected by external variables such as gender or sexual orientation. If LGB people respond in a different way to the questions, by virtue of their sexual orientation, this violates the psychometric assumption that the instrument measures borderline symptoms equally well in LGB and heterosexual populations. An interview of 12 questions, where three are confounded by sexual orientation, has questionable reliability and may increase the likelihood of LGB people receiving false positive borderline diagnoses, via their differing interpretation of, and responses to, these questions. LGB and PAID researchers might collaborate to ensure that the reliability and validity, important concerns for many researchers, of measures used to assess borderline personality disorder are improved.

Confounding Psychosocial Stressors and Axis I Disorders

A second set of hypotheses that may explain the high proportion of LGB individuals in Table 5.1 is that LGB people experience different psychological or social stressors, and it is these stressors that manifest themselves as personality disorder symptoms or traits. These stressors may confound an LGB orientation and personality disorder association. LGB psychology is well placed to evidence the existence of these stressors, which include stigma, prejudice, discrimination, victimization and intolerance (Frable, Wortman & Joseph, 1997). These stressors are associated with higher rates of anxiety, depression, substance use disorders and suicidal behaviour in LGB people (King et al., 2003). The coming out process is a major stressor, with a strong temporal component. Crucially, coming out most often occurs in adolescence and early adulthood, the same time period in which the personality disorders are most likely to develop. If professional help were sought during this time, Egan et al.'s (2003) concern that the availability of certain information can bias the clinical interview is worthy of attention. It is possible that experimentation with new identities, substance use, sexual behaviour and instability are related to the coming out process rather than to the onset personality disorder.

Confounding and co-morbidity from Axis I disorders (anxiety, mood and substance misuse) is also an important factor to consider in relation to findings such as those from Table 5.1. Migration in search of social support, insufficient legal and social support for developing relationships, and different norms and values regarding sexuality and personal relationships could all influence the presence of Axis I disorders (King et al., 2003;

Sandfort et al., 2001). Axis I disorders frequently overlap with the personality disorders of Axis II (Krueger, 1999), a problem that DSM-V will need to address.

In summary, there are many variables and confounding factors that may confuse the apparent association between sexual orientation and personality disorder. These factors should be included in future research to ensure that LGB and PAID psychologists can obtain a measure of true, unconfounded prevalence of diagnosed disorders in LGB populations. The apparent association between sexual orientation and borderline personality disorder is most likely caused by something else, such as psychosocial stressors. This cannot be investigated until statistics on personality disorder prevalence are broken down by sexual orientation as a matter of routine, as they currently are for gender.

CRITICISMS OF PAID RESEARCH

Several concerns have been raised in LGB psychology about PAID research and these discussions mirror broader debates between social psychologists and PAID researchers.In discussing the development of a social psychological agenda for personality trait research, Matthews et al. (2003, pp. 209–210) suggested that 'we are hindered by the traditional antagonism of the two fields of enquiry and the reluctance of researchers to engage with the constructs of the "enemy" camp'. The suggestion is that contact between PAID research and social psychology, and by extension, PAID research and LGB psychology, would help each to engage with the constructs and concerns of the other. In this section, I provide two examples of criticisms of PAID research and suggest some ways in which these might be addressed, so that a collaborative research agenda can be formed.

The first criticism made of PAID research is that it neglects social and situational factors in favour of individual factors, such as personality traits. Some social psychologists adopting a social constructionist or critical perspective go further, suggesting that personality traits do not exist, or exist only in the eye of the beholder (Butt, 2003). To Sloan (1997, p. 101), personality is in fact a 'congealed moment' or social process whereby 'my "shyness" and your "confidence" are manifestations of a complex intertwining of social class, ethnicity, socialization, life experience, identity development, and so forth'. Sloan argued that PAID researchers 'see the person as not only the container but also the origin of enduring characteristics'. Similarly, the neglect of situations in favour of personality traits, when explaining behaviour, has been criticized. This is the long running 'person-situation' debate, which has been reviewed elsewhere (see Matthews et al., 2003; Swann & Seyle, 2005). It is worth noting that contemporary personality trait theories do acknowledge situational factors, but situational factors alone do not explain why traits correlate with external variables, why people make similar judgements about an individual's traits, why the same dimensions are found in questionnaire or lexical studies of adjectives in many of the world's languages, and why personality trait measures show stability across the lifespan (Swann & Seyle, 2005). As Butt (2003, p. 12) argues, radical constructionism is dangerous in that it can 'evaporate' the person entirely. Social psychological research that does not recognize individual differences is not compatible with PAID research and presents what Matthews et al. (2003, p. 206) called a 'dead end' for personality trait research. However, social psychology has a second set of epistemologies that are compatible with PAID research, namely social cognitive ones. In contrast to social constructionist approaches, social cognitive approaches propose the existence of stable cognitive structures within individuals, which interact with social factors to produce behaviour (Matthews et al., 2003). Collaboration is possible if we support at least one of the two assumptions of the social cognitive approach: (1) social knowledge is built at least partially by nomothetic dimensions; (2) social knowledge is supported at least partially by cognitive structures within the individual, which vary from person to person. Rejecting both these assumptions, to Matthews et al., is a form of radical constructionism, which is not compatible with PAID research.

In a second set of criticisms, commentators have argued that PAID psychology fails to appreciate political factors and the potential for objectionable applications of its findings (as in the use of Rorschach testing in the military). Psychiatrists and feminists disagreed over the proposed inclusion of three new diagnoses for DSM-III-R: Masochistic Personality Disorder, Paraphilic Rapism and Premenstrual Dysphoric Disorder (Kutchings & Kirk, 1997). Kitzinger (1996) questioned why hegemonic masculinity is absent from the DSM scheme despite meeting the criteria for being a personality disorder. Although not the focus of this chapter, PAID research has also focused on the possible *causes* (as opposed to *correlates*) of homosexuality and bisexuality (see Rahman & Wilson, 2003, for a review). This has attracted criticism from many commentators concerned that such research is unnecessary (e.g. Allen, 1997; Hegarty, 1999). Clearly, PAID and LGB psychologists should be aware of the history of personality research and the continued potential for misuse of findings. Separating research findings from the possible ways in which they might be used is delicate matter for all researchers, with no easy solution. However, individual differences is a broad field, which can include research into, for example, inequalities in mental health, personality disorder diagnoses, psychological distress, substance use, anxiety and depression. PAID research is not limited to investigating the possible origins of homosexuality and bisexuality and PAID research should not be rejected *in toto* because some of the research conducted in this area is potentially objectionable. Using PAID and LGB psychology, researchers and policymakers can first describe, and then address, inequalities in life outcomes for LGB people.

CONCLUSION

I have reviewed the history of LGB and PAID psychology, areas of research that were once closely related. Indeed, two of the founding moments of LGB psychology were personality studies (Hooker, 1957; Hopkins, 1969). I then described how two areas of PAID research have begun to show points of connection with LGB psychology: personality traits and sexual risk-taking, and borderline personality disorder diagnoses. Having reviewed the two main criticisms of PAID research, its individual focus and neglect of political consequences, I conclude the chapter by proposing a five point collaborative LGB-PAID research agenda:

1. Improve the reliability and validity of PAID measures, with the ultimate aim of reducing the number of false positive diagnoses of personality disorder.
2. Establish the ways in which individual and social factors interact and influence life outcomes for LGB people.
3. Summarize and break down PAID research data by sexual orientation, to avoid rendering important group differences invisible (this is particularly pressing in relation to personality disorder prevalence and sexual orientation).

4. Assess the contribution of confounding factors to the association between sexual orientation and personality disorders.
5. Develop PAID research to gain a better understanding of LGB inequalities (e.g. in mental or physical health).

In conclusion, there are two overarching, basic questions that (some) LGB and PAID researchers are concerned with. First, how do individual and social (psychosocial) factors interact to create psychologically important outcomes for people? Second, how can we improve the reliability and validity of individual differences measures? Swann and Seyle (2005) observed that we can characterize 'person vs situation' debates as 'person x situation' interactions, given that neither personality nor situational nor social factors are best at predicting important life outcomes. Reviews of research show that interactions usually 'win': points of contention 'melt away' and we are left with 'two subdisciplines united by their commitment to finding answers to the same basic questions' (p. 162). It may be possible for LGB and PAID researchers to cast research questions in a 'single voice', combining insights from their different theories, methods and assumptions. Although LGB psychology and PAID research appear to have fundamentally different agendas, theories, methods and approaches, it is time to bridge the divide that currently separates these two fields. There is great potential here for collaboration.

ACKNOWLEDGEMENTS

I would like to thank the following people for their comments on earlier versions of this book chapter: Christopher Hewitt, Peter Hegarty, Darren Langdridge, Roshan das Nair and Gillian Proctor. I would also like to thank Victoria Clarke and Elizabeth Peel for their editorial support and input.

REFERENCES

Allen, G. E. (1997). The double-edged sword of genetic determinism: Social and political agendas in genetic studies of homosexuality, 1940–1994. In V. A. Rosario (Ed.), *Science and Homosexualities* (pp. 242–271). New York, NY: Routledge.
American Psychiatric Association (1952). *Diagnostic and Statistical Manual of Mental Disorders: DSM*. Washington, DC: American Psychiatric Association.
American Psychiatric Association (1968). *Diagnostic and Statistical Manual of Mental Disorders: DSM* (2nd edn). Washington, DC: American Psychiatric Association.
American Psychiatric Association (1980). *Diagnostic and Statistical Manual of Mental Disorders: DSM* (3rd edn). Washington, DC: American Psychiatric Association.
American Psychiatric Association (1987). *Diagnostic and Statistical Manual of Mental Disorders: DSM* (3rd edn, text revision). Washington, DC: American Psychiatric Association.
American Psychiatric Association (1994). *Diagnostic and Statistical Manual of Mental Disorders: DSM* (4th edn). Washington, DC: American Psychiatric Association.
American Psychiatric Association (2000). *Diagnostic and Statistical Manual of Mental Disorders: DSM* (4th edn, text revision) Washington, DC: American Psychiatric Association.
Butt, T. (2003). *Understanding People*. Basingstoke: Palgrave Macmillian.
Clarke, V. & Hopkins, J. H. (2002). Victoria Clarke in conversation with June Hopkins. *Lesbian & Gay Psychology Review*, **3**(2), 44–47.

Clarke, V. & Peel, E. (2007). LGB psychosocial theory and practice in the UK: A review of key contributions and current developments. *Journal of Gay & Lesbian Psychotherapy*, **11**(1–2).

Coid, J. (2003). Epidemiology, public health and the problem of personality disorder. *British Journal of Psychiatry*, **182**, S3–S10.

Coxon, A. P. M. (2003). Gay men and AIDS: Project SIGMA's approach and method. *Radical Statistics*, **83**, 58–70.

Dulit, R. A., Fyer, M. R., Miller, F. T., Sacks, M. H. & Frances, A. J. (1993). Gender differences in sexual preference and substance-abuse of inpatients with borderline personality-disorder. *Journal of Personality Disorders*, **7**(2), 182–185.

Egan, S., Nathan, P. & Lumley, M. (2003). Diagnostic concordance of ICD-10 personality and comorbid disorders: A comparison of standard clinical assessment and structured interviews in a clinical setting. *Australian & New Zealand Journal of Psychiatry*, **37**(4), 484–491.

First, M. B., Spitzer, R. L., Miriam, G. & Williams, J. B. W. (1997). *Structured Clinical Interview for DSM-IV Personality Disorders (SCID-II)*. Washington, DC: American Psychiatric Press.

Fish, J. (2002). Personality differences research: A feminist perspective. *Lesbian & Gay Psychology Review*, **3**(2), 56–59.

Flowers, P., Smith, J. A., Sheeran, P. & Beail, N. (1997). Health and romance: Understanding unprotected sex in relationships between gay men. *British Journal of Health Psychology*, **2**(1), 73–86.

Flowers, P., Duncan, B. & Knussen, C. (2003). Re-appraising HIV testing: An exploration of the psychosocial costs and benefits associated with learning one's HIV status in a purposive sample of Scottish gay men. *British Journal of Health Psychology*, **8**(2), 179–194.

Frable, D. E. S., Wortman, C. & Joseph, J. (1997). Predicting self-esteem, well-being, and distress in a cohort of gay men: The importance of cultural stigma, personal visibility, community networks, and positive identity. *Journal of Personality*, **65**(3), 599–624.

Gonsiorek, J. C. (1982). Results of psychological-testing on homosexual populations. *American Behavioral Scientist*, **25**(4), 385–396.

Gough, B. & McFadden, M. (2001). *Critical Social Psychology: An introduction*. Basingstoke: Palgrave Macmillian.

Gunderson, J. G., Kolb, J. E. & Austin, V. (1981). The diagnostic interview for borderline patients. *American Journal of Psychiatry*, **138**(7), 896–903.

Hegarty, P. (1999). Opening the black box: A reply to Rahman. *Lesbian & Gay Psychology Section Newsletter*, **Issue 2**, 11–14.

Hegarty, P. (2002). More feminine than 999 men out of 1,000: Measuring sex roles and gender nonconformity in psychology. In T. Lester (Ed.), *Gender Nonconformity, Race, and Sexuality: Charting the connection*. (pp. 62–83). Madison, WI: University of Wisconsin Press.

Hegarty, P. (2003a). Homosexual signs and heterosexual silences: Rorschach research on male homosexuality from 1921 to 1969. *Journal of the History of Sexuality*, **12**(3), 400–423.

Hegarty, P. (2003b). Contingent differences: An historical note on Evelyn Hooker's use of significance testing. *Lesbian & Gay Psychology Review*, **4**(1), 3–7.

Herek, G. M. (1990). Gay people and government security clearances – A social science perspective. *American Psychologist*, **45**(9), 1035–1042.

Herek, G. M. (1993). Sexual orientation and military service – A social science perspective. *American Psychologist*, **48**(5), 538–549.

Hooker, E. (1957). The adjustment of the male overt homosexual, *Journal of Projective Techniques & Personality Assessment*, **21**(1), 18–31.

Hopkins, J. H. (1969). The lesbian personality. *British Journal of Psychiatry*, **115**(529), 1433–1436.

Hoyle, R. H., Fejfar, M. C. & Miller, J. D. (2000). Personality and sexual risk taking: A quantitative review. *Journal of Personality*, **68**(6), 1203–1231.

Hunt, A. J., Davies, P. M., Weatherburn, P., Coxon, A. P. & McManus, T. J. (1991). Sexual partners, penetrative sexual partners and HIV risk. *AIDS*, **5**(6), 723–728.

Johnson, A. M., Mercer, C. H., Erens, B., Copas, A. J., McManus, S., Wellings, K., Fenton, K. A., Korovessis, C., Macdowall, W., Nanchahal, K., Purdon, S. & Field, H. (2001). Sexual behaviour in Britain: Partnerships, practices, and HIV risk behaviours. *Lancet*, **358**(9296), 1835–1842.

King, M., McKeown, E., Warner, J., Ramsay, A., Johnson, K., Cort, C., Wright, L., Blizard, R. & Davidson, O. (2003). Mental health and quality of life of gay men and lesbians in England and Wales – Controlled, cross-sectional study. *British Journal of Psychiatry*, **183**, 552–558.

Kinsey, A. C., Pomeroy, W. B., & Martin, C. E. (1948). *Sexual Behavior in the Human Male*. Philadelphia, PA: Saunders.

Kinsey, A. C., Pomeroy, W. B., Martin, C. E. & Gebhard, P. H. (1953). *Sexual Behavior in the Human Female*. Philadelphia, PA: Saunders.

Kitzinger, C. (1996). Speaking of oppression: Psychology, politics, and the language of power. In E. D. Rothblum & L. A. Bond (Eds), *Preventing Heterosexism and Homophobia* (pp. 3–19). Thousand Oaks, CA: Sage.

Kitzinger, C. (1997). Lesbian and gay psychology: A critical analysis. In D. Fox & I. Prilleltensky (Eds), *Critical Psychology: An introduction* (pp. 202–216). London: Sage.

Kitzinger, C. (1999). Lesbian and gay psychology: Is it critical? *Annual Review of Critical Psychology*, **1**(1), 50–66.

Kitzinger, C. & Coyle, A. (2002). Introducing lesbian and gay psychology. In A. Coyle & C. Kitzinger (Eds), *Lesbian & Gay Psychology: New perspectives* (pp. 1–29). Oxford: BPS Blackwell.

Krueger, R. F. (1999). The structure of common mental disorders. *Archives of General Psychiatry*, **6**(10), 921–926.

Kutchings, H. & Kirk, S. A. (1997). The fall and rise of homosexuality. In H. Kutchings (Ed.), *Making us Crazy: DSM – The psychiatric bible and the creation of mental disorders* (pp. 55–99). London: Constable.

Lewis, G. & Appleby, L. (1988). Personality-disorder – the patients' psychiatrists dislike. *British Journal of Psychiatry*, **153**, 44–49.

Lothstein, L. M. (1984). Psychological-Testing with Transsexuals – A 30-Year Review. *Journal of Personality Assessment*, **48**(5), 500–507.

Matthews, G., Deary, I. J. & Whiteman, M. C. (2003). *Personality Traits* (2nd edn). Cambridge: Cambridge University Press.

Mondimore, F. (1996). *A Natural History of Homosexuality*. London: The Johns Hopkins University Press.

Oberstone, A. K. & Sukoneck, H. (1976). Psychological adjustment and life-style of single lesbians and single heterosexual women. *Psychology of Women Quarterly*, **1**(2), 172–188.

Paris, J., Zweigfrank, H. & Guzder, J. (1995). Psychological-factors associated with homosexuality in males with borderline personality-disorder. *Journal of Personality Disorders*, **9**(1), 56–61.

Peel, E. (2002). 'The lesbian personality' three decades on. *Lesbian & Gay Psychology Review*, **3**(2), 52–54.

Plant, R. (1986). *The Pink Triangle: Nazi war against homosexuals*. New York, NY: Henry Holt & Company.

Rahman, Q. & Wilson, G. D. (2003). Born gay? The psychobiology of human sexual orientation. *Personality and Individual Differences*, **34**(8), 1337–1382.

Ramos, R. M., Perera, J. L. C., Urdaniz, A. P. & Iglesias, S. S.(2002). Factors associated to the diagnoses of borderline personality disorder in psychiatric out-patients. *Actas Espanolas de Psiquiatria*, **30**(3), 153–159.

Reiss, B. F. (1980). Psychological tests in homosexuality. In J. Marmor (Ed.), *Homosexual Behavior: A modern reappraisal*. New York, NY: Basic Books.

Sandfort, T. G. M., de Graaf, R., Bijl, R. V. & Schnabel, P. (2001). Same-sex sexual behavior and psychiatric disorders – Findings from the Netherlands Mental Health Survey and Incidence Study (NEMESIS). *Archives of General Psychiatry*, **58**(1), 85–91.

Sloan, T. (1997). Theories of personality: Ideology and beyond. In D. Fox & I. Prilleltensky (Eds), *Critical Psychology: An introduction* (pp. 87–103). London: Sage.

Stone, M. H. (1987). Homosexuality in patients with borderline personality-disorder. *American Journal of Psychiatry*, **144**(12), 1622–1623.

Swann, W. B. & Seyle, C. (2005). Personality psychology's comeback and its emerging symbiosis with social psychology. *Personality and Social Psychology Bulletin*, **31**(2), 155–165.

van den Aardweg, G. J. (1985). Male homosexuality and the neuroticism factor. *Dynamic Psychotherapy*, **3**(1), 79–87.

Widiger, T. A. (1998). Invited essay: Sex biases in the diagnosis of personality disorders. *Journal of Personality Disorders*, **12**(2), 95–118.

Widiger, T. A. & Axelrod, S. R. (1995). Recent developments in the clinical assessment of personality disorders. *European Journal of Psychological Assessment*, **11**(3), 213–221.

Widiger, T. A. & Spitzer, R. L. (1991). Sex bias in the diagnosis of personality-disorders: Conceptual and methodological issues. *Clinical Psychology Review*, **11**(1), 1–22.

Wheeler, W. M. (1949). An analysis of Rorschach indices of male homosexuality. *Rorschach Research Exchange*, **13**, 97–126.

Wilkinson, S. & Coyle, A. (2002). Social psychological perspectives on lesbian and gay issues in Europe: The state of the art. *Journal of Community & Applied Social Psychology*, **12**(3), 147–152.

World Health Organization (1993). *The ICD-10 classification of mental and behavioural disorders: Diagnostic criteria for research*. Geneva: World Health Organization.

Xiridou, M., Geskus, R., de Wit, J., Coutinho, R. & Kretzschmar, M. (2004). Primary HIV infection as source of HIV transmission within steady and casual partnerships among homosexual men. *AIDS*, **18**(9), 1311–1320.

Zanarini, M. C., Franckenburg, F. R., Chauncey, D. L. & Gunderson, J. G. (1989). The revised diagnostic interview for borderlines: Discriminating BPD from others axis II disorders. *Journal of Personality Disorders*, **3**, 10–18.

Zanarini, M. C., Parachini, E. A., Frankenburg, F. R., Holman, J. B., Hennen, J., Reich, D. B. & Silk, K. R. (2003). Sexual relationship difficulties among borderline patients and axis II comparison subjects. *Journal of Nervous and Mental Disease*, **191**(7), 479–482.

Zubenko, G. S., George, A. W., Soloff, P. H. & Schulz, P. (1987). Sexual practices among patients with borderline personality disorder. *American Journal of Psychiatry*, **144**(6), 748–752.

Zucker, K. J. (1996). Sexism and heterosexism in the diagnostic interview for borderline patients? *American Journal of Psychiatry*, **153**(7), 966.

CHAPTER 6

Heteronormativity and The Exclusion of Bisexuality in Psychology

Meg Barker

London South Bank University, UK

INTRODUCTION

Higher education is a site of 'thundering heteronormativity', where lesbian, gay and bisexual (LGB) sexualities continue to be silenced (Epstein, O'Flynn & Telford, 2003, p. 102). While curricula at liberal institutions occasionally add on LGB-relevant material, a heterosexual norm is still perpetuated in the hidden curriculum (Epstein, 1995) through overt harassment of staff and students, structural impediments to those who identify as LGB, and only tokenistic course coverage that gives a clear message that LGB sexualities are different and strange (Eyre, 1993). This chapter updates Simoni's (2000) research to display the ways in which such heteronormativity is reproduced within psychology textbooks.

As with research and theory in the discipline, the history of psychology teaching has been marked by prejudice and discrimination, failing to represent minorities or to include relevant new scholarship on minority groups (Bronstein & Quina, 1988). Higher education is a time during which many people negotiate issues of personal and sexual identity, and psychology students in particular tend to apply course material to their own lives (Whitbourne & Hulicka, 1990). If certain groups are omitted or presented as deviant in course material, this could close off opportunities for some and exacerbate feelings of exclusion for others. Kitzinger (1990) and Snyder and Broadway (2004) link the lack of coverage of lesbian and gay sexualities in psychology curricula to isolation, marginalization and even depression and suicide amongst lesbian and gay students, as well as the continued acceptance of homophobic abuse within educational settings. Epstein et al.'s (2003) longitudinal study of gay male undergraduates revealed several examples of homophobic abuse from both staff and students, including innuendos about anal sex, the word 'gay' being used an insult, and comments in seminars that gay sexuality might 'die out' because of AIDS. There were very few examples of staff trying to prevent or challenge this, and some students had been forced to leave university accommodation because of constant

Out in Psychology: Lesbian, gay, bisexual, trans and queer perspectives. Edited by Victoria Clarke and Elizabeth Peel.
© 2007 John Wiley & Sons, Ltd.

taunts and abuse, or to hide their sexuality from peers who responded to lesbians and gay men with physical violence. Students particularly reported being very surprised by the lack of coverage of lesbian and gay issues on psychology programmes.

Psychology degrees are second only to law in popularity in the UK, and the students who complete these courses are one of the routes via which mainstream psychological research and theories filter through into popular understanding. Therefore, it is of serious concern if what is taught on psychology degrees is heterosexist or if homophobic assumptions are not challenged. An absence of LGB content in curricula also affects students' future professional abilities (Epstein et al., 2003). It is particularly vital that those psychology students who go on to work in applied arenas (e.g. counselling, clinical, occupational and educational psychology) have been well educated in issues of sexuality since their work is likely to inform therapeutic treatments, organizational equality and diversity strategies, sex education, legal policy-making, and so on (British Psychological Society, 2005b).

Kitzinger's influential (1990) paper reported that heterosexist and pathological depictions of lesbians and gay men were still prevalent in psychology and that this was reflected in textbook coverage. Textbooks are vital in shaping both curricula and the views and conceptual frameworks of students. Yanowitz and Weathers (2004) report that they often drive the content and presentation of undergraduate programmes, and that the majority of students see them as the most important sources of information on their courses. Whitbourne and Hulicka (1990) argued that textbooks both reflect and help shape the 'zeitgeist' of the academic discipline (p. 1127), and McDonald (1981) stated that it is widely understood that 'textbooks function as agents of socialization by reflecting cultural values, articulating prevailing social norms, and conveying appropriate or socially acceptable standards of behaviour' (p. 46).

Higher education textbooks in other social sciences and humanities subjects have been analysed for their constructions of sexuality (e.g. Phillips, 1991; Zimmerman, 1982), but examinations of psychology textbooks have tended to focus more on gender (e.g. Gray, 1977; Yanowitz & Weathers, 2004), with some research addressing the portrayal of lesbians in psychology of women textbooks (Fontaine, 1982; Peel, 2001). The key study on the representation of sexuality in psychology textbooks is McDonald's (1981) content analysis of 48 US and Canadian introductory books. McDonald found that lesbian and gay relevant material was generally included in chapters on sexual 'deviation', 'dysfunction' or 'abnormality'. Gay male sexuality was often only mentioned in passing, while lesbians were omitted altogether or assumed to be similar to gay men. For every source of relevant or accurate information there were five sources of inaccurate, misrepresentative and/or heterosexist data, and 75% of textbooks contained five or more sources of misrepresentative information than relevant information. McDonald also found little improvement in content between 1975 and 1979.

There appears to be no systematic analysis of the coverage of lesbian and gay male sexualities in psychology textbooks between McDonald's (1981) study and Simoni's (2000) research on books published in the 1990s. However, King (1988) gave a feel for the way lesbian and gay male sexualities were covered in US texts published in the 1980s, reporting that lesbian and gay psychology was still either not mentioned at all, or considered in chapters on abnormal psychology or psychopathology. Such chapters discussed the removal of homosexuality per se from the American Psychiatric Association (APA)'s *Diagnostic and Statistical Manual of Mental Disorders* (DSM) in 1973, but continued to discuss what 'causes homosexuality' and/or therapies that may 'cure' people of it. Like McDonald,

King called for lesbian and gay issues to be considered under a number of 'normal' psychology topic areas such as lifespan development, the health psychology of HIV and AIDS, and the social psychology of prejudice, minority groups, social movements, and interpersonal attraction and relationships. McDonald also argued that textbooks should acknowledge continued discrimination against lesbians and gay men with regard to, for example, parenthood, legal recognition and homophobic attacks.

Simoni's (2000) survey of 24 introductory, developmental, social and abnormal psychology textbooks suggested some positive movement forward along the lines recommended by McDonald and King. Slightly fewer of the texts she analysed failed to mention lesbian and gay sexuality at all (13% compared with McDonald's 16%), and, while introductory textbooks tended to restrict relevant material to sections on sexual orientation, some social and developmental textbooks included material in several places, particularly in sections on prejudice, AIDS and the declassification of homosexuality as a mental illness. However, Simoni also found an excessive focus on the origins of homosexuality with no consideration of the origins of heterosexuality, and a lack of presentation of anyone other than heterosexuals in sections on attraction, love relationships and parenting. She argued that the continued absence of lesbians and gay men in some texts, coupled with the tendency of many to consider lesbians and gay men only in contexts relevant to their sexual orientation, implies that they are 'deviant, less important, and less natural' (p. 83) than heterosexual people.

Bisexuality

The current research, reported in this chapter, revisits Simoni's analysis and focuses on textbooks published in both the USA and the UK in the 2000s. In addition to Simoni, it also considers an area that has been neglected in the literature so far: the coverage of 'non-heterosexual' sexualities other than lesbian and gay sexualities, particularly bisexuality. Thus it will provide a somewhat fuller picture of heteronormativity within psychology textbooks. Heteronormativity is 'the hegemonic discursive and non-discursive normative idealization of heterosexuality' (Hird, 2004, p. 27). In other words, it relates to the ways in which heterosexuality is explicitly or implicitly presented as the normal and/or ideal way of being and relating in textual accounts and elsewhere – for example, in images and cultural practices.

Petford (2003) states that bisexuality is almost completely disregarded in the psychological literature as a whole, and Angelides (2001) reports that if bisexuality is mentioned, it tends to be named once and omitted subsequently. This is in spite of research demonstrating bisexual identities and behaviour in significant numbers of individuals (Fox, 2000), in some estimates exceeding the extent of lesbian and gay sexualities (Klein, 1993). There is growing acknowledgement of bisexuality in social science disciplines. Collections of current research and theory on bisexuality have been published by cultural theorists (Hall & Pramaggiore, 1996), sociologists (Storr, 1999) and psychologists (Fox, 2004), and there is an international *Journal of Bisexuality* published by Haworth Press. The American Psychological Association's Division 44 have incorporated bisexuality into their name: 'The Society for the Psychological Study of Lesbian, Gay and Bisexual issues', and there are moves in the British Psychological Society Lesbian and Gay Psychology Section to follow suit. The current analysis will examine whether the research and theory on bisexuality has filtered through into psychology textbooks, and the ways in which such texts do, or do not, represent bisexuality and bisexual people.[1]

METHODOLOGY

Previous research on the representation of homosexuality in textbooks has ranged from an in-depth analysis of one particular aspect of a small number of textbooks (such as images, Whatley, 1992) to content analysis of the entire coverage of representations of certain groups in a large number of textbooks (e.g. over 100 textbooks in Whitbourne & Hulicka's [1990] study on ageism). This analysis follows Simoni (2000) by sampling just over 20 textbooks from a number of relevant areas of psychology and conducting both a quantitative analysis of the overall coverage and an in-depth analysis of the presentation of specific material. It is important to combine quantitative and qualitative techniques in this way because questions of quantity and structure are telling. For example, the number of pages devoted to LGB sexualities gives an idea of how much importance is placed on students having an understanding of them. If information is included in 'add on' boxes or sections, rather than being integrated into the main text, this suggests that LGB people are perceived as different or abnormal (Eyre, 1993). The inclusion or exclusion of bisexuality as an index term may be seen as indicative of whether bisexuality is viewed as a legitimate sexual identity. A more in-depth qualitative analysis is necessary to examine, for example, whether homosexuality and bisexuality are presented as requiring explanation, which explanations are privileged, or what images are used to illustrate same-sex relationships.

Textbook Sample

I reviewed 22 undergraduate textbooks, including seven in the area of introductory psychology, and five in each of the following areas: biological psychology, developmental psychology and social psychology (see Table 6.1 below). The aim was to cover key areas of the psychology curriculum that all students study internationally (e.g. American Psychological Association, 2002; British Psychological Society, 2005a) and where issues of sexual identity and relationships are relevant.[2] All were published between 2000 and 2005 with the exception of Malim and Birch (1998), a popular UK text which has not yet been updated in the 2000s.

Textbooks were selected from the lists of bestsellers on the US and UK Amazon websites (amazon.com and amazon.co.uk), as these stood in the early Autumn of 2005, in an

---

[1] I use the term 'bisexual' throughout this chapter because it is probably the most widely used and clearly understood term. However, as with 'homosexual', it is a word that necessitates ongoing scrutiny in terms of its implications and the history of its usage, as will become apparent in the analysis.

[2] There is no analysis of specifically gender, sexuality or 'critical psychology' textbooks here because courses in these areas are offered on few psychology degrees and tend to be optional rather than part of the core curriculum. I also chose not to include abnormal or clinical psychology textbooks (as Simoni did) because, at least in the UK, these are often optional areas of the psychology curriculum. Instead I analysed biological psychology textbooks as this is a core component.

Table 6.1 Textbooks analysed

Area	Textbooks
Introductory Psychology	Gross, R. (2005). *Psychology: The science of mind and behaviour.* London: Hodder Arnold.
	Hayes, N. (2000). *Foundations of Psychology: An Introductory Text.* London: Thomson Learning.
	Kosslyn, S. M. & Rosenberg, R. S. (2004) *Fundamentals of Psychology: The brain, the person, the world.* Boston, MA: Allyn & Bacon.
	Malim, T. & Birch, A. (1998). *Introductory Psychology.* Basingstoke: Palgrave MacMillan.
	Myers, D. G. (2003). *Psychology.* New York: Worth Publishers.
	Passer, M. W. & Smith, R. E. (2003). *Psychology: The science of mind and behavior.* Burr Ridge, IL: McGraw Hill.
	Smith, E., Nolen-Hoeksema, S. & Fredrickson, B. (2002). *Atkinson and Hilgard's Introduction to Psychology.* Belmont, CA: Wadsworth/Thompson Learning.
Biological Psychology	Kalat, J. W. (2003). *Biological Psychology.* Belmont, CA: Wadsworth/Thompson Learning.
	Martin, G. N. (2003). *Essential Biological Psychology.* London: Hodder Arnold.
	Pinel, J. P. J. (2005). *Biopsychology.* Boston, MA: Allyn & Bacon.
	Rosenzweig, M. R., Breedlove, S. M. & Watson, N. V. (2004). *Biological Psychology: An introduction to behavioral and cognitive neuroscience.* Sunderland, MA: Sinauer Associates.
	Toates, F. (2001). *Biological Psychology: An integrative approach.* Hove: Pearson Education.
Developmental Psychology	Berger, K. S. (2004). *The Developing Person Through the Life Span.* New York: Worth Publishers.
	Berk, L. E. (2003). *Development Through the Lifespan.* Boston, MA: Allyn & Bacon.
	Boyd, D. & Bee, H. (2005). *Lifespan Development.* Boston, MA: Allyn & Bacon.
	Harris, M. & Butterworth, G. (2002). *Developmental Psychology: A student's handbook.* Hove: Psychology Press.
	Santrock, J. W. (2005). *Life-span Development.* Burr Ridge, IL: McGraw Hill.
Social Psychology	Aronson, E., Wilson, T. D. & Akert, R. M. (2004). *Social Psychology.* Upper Saddle River, NJ: Prentice Hall.
	Baron, R. A., Byrne, D. & Branscombe, N. R. (2005). *Social Psychology.* Boston, MA: Allyn & Bacon.
	Brehm, S. S., Kassin, S. M. & Fein, S. (2002). *Social Psychology.* Boston, MA: Houghton Mifflin Co.
	Hewstone, M. & Stroebe, W. (Eds) (2001). *Introduction to Social Psychology: A European perspective.* Oxford: Blackwell Publishers.
	Hogg, M. A. & Vaughan, G. (2004). *Social psychology.* Upper Saddle River, NJ: Prentice Hall.

attempt to focus on the most popular and widely used books.[3] I chose texts from the top 10 in each category including the number one bestseller plus a range of others from a variety of publishers and authors. The market is dominated by US published texts, but I attempted to include at least one European book in each category as a point of comparison.[4]

Like Simoni, I must raise a note of caution about generalizing from what is clearly a small and not statistically representative sample of textbooks. However, I would concur with her suggestion that 'the striking similarity among recently published textbooks in each area argues for the generalizability of the findings' (p. 78). Certainly, there is marked similarity in the areas of these books that cover sexual orientation and relationships (see Table 6.2), the theories and research which are, and are not, included, and the ways in which these are presented.

Quantitative Analysis

For the quantitative component of the analysis I updated Simoni's (2000) study by tallying, as she did, the number of index headings/subheadings and pages devoted to relevant terms. Like Simoni, I focused on the terms *lesbian, gay, homosexual, heterosexual* and *sexual orientation* (and derivatives of these such as *lesbian relationships* and *gay male*). However, I also included the term *bisexual* (and derivatives) in this analysis. Following Simoni, I also scanned all the sections likely to include relevant passages in order to avoid missing anything. Two books, one biological (Martin, 2003) and one introductory (Kosslyn & Rosenberg, 2004) failed to include index references to their sections on *sexual orientation*. As in Simoni's (2000) analysis, the general thematic content of the coverage was noted, as was the context of the chapters/sections it was presented in. I constructed a slightly amended version of her table summarizing this quantitative analysis and also including a separate section on the coverage of bisexuality. Simoni's tally of the number of relevant glossary terms was left out because very few of the textbooks I analysed included any of these. Instead, glossary definitions were incorporated into the qualitative analysis where relevant.

Qualitative Analysis

McDonald (1981) and Simoni (2000) rated the quality of the coverage in their textbooks using scoring systems. Rather than emulating this, I describe the ways in which sexual orientation and relationships were presented so that readers can make up their own minds about the quality of this coverage in relation to LGB people. A simple scoring system was not viable because some textbooks thoroughly engaged with one aspect of representation (e.g. including images of gay parenting, considering the biases involved in searching for the 'cause of homosexuality'), but were relatively poor at another aspects (e.g.

---

[3] It is difficult to find measures of the sales of individual textbooks, therefore the Amazon websites were used because Amazon is the most popular bookseller worldwide (http://www.woopidoo.com/biography/jeff-bezos/)

[4] The US texts I examined were generally the 'international' versions (marked 'not for publication in the US') because I was accessing them from UK bookshops and libraries. However, these do not differ by and large in content from the original US versions.

Table 6.2 Coverage of LGB sexualities and relationships in 22 undergraduate psychology textbooks

Evaluation criteria	Textbook subject area				All Total
	Introductory	Biological	Developmental	Social	
Quantity of coverage					
Index citations (range/mean)	0–9/3.4	1–5/3.6	0–17/8.8	0–5/2.4	**0–17/4.6**
Pages (range/mean)	0–5.5/2.1	1.5–4.5/2.5	0–4/2.2	0.25–4.5/1.25	**0–5.5/2.0**
Context of coverage (chapter)	*n*	*n*	*n*	*n*	***n***
Not mentioned at all	1	0	1	0	**2**
Sexual orientation section (motivations/gender)	4	5	2	0	**11**
Same-sex relationships (early adult development)	1	0	3	0	**4**
Same-sex relationships (interpersonal relationships)	2	0	0	4	**6**
Same-sex parenting (early adult development)	1	0	4	0	**5**
Identity formation/coming out (adolescent development)	1	0	4	0	**5**
Homophobia/prejudice (social psychology)	1	0	0	2	**3**

Table 6.2 (Continued)

Evaluation criteria	Textbook subject area				All Total
	Introductory	Biological	Developmental	Social	
DSM declassification (abnormal psychology)	3	0	0	0	3
HIV/AIDS (in any section)	1	0	2	0	3
Sexual violence in same-sex relationships (in any section)	0	0	3	0	3
Heterosexism in psychology (theories/methods)	2	0	0	0	2
Older adulthood/bereavement (older adult development)	0	0	1	0	1
Suicide/anorexia nervosa (adolescent mental health)	0	0	1	0	1
Gay men being promiscuous (evolutionary psychology)	1	0	0	0	1
Bisexuality					
Not mentioned at all	3	3	3	5	14
Mentioned just at one or two points in relevant sections	4	2	2	0	8
Mentioned throughout relevant sections	0	0	0	0	0

incorporating bisexuality, lesbian sexuality, or alternative relationship structures). Also, readers of this chapter may disagree with my conclusions about whether an emphasis on biological explanations classifies the texts as 'good', 'fair' or 'poor'.

For the qualitative component of my analysis, I drew on both critical psychological and queer theory perspectives, particularly the techniques employed by Anderson and Accomando (2002) in their discourse analysis of popular psychology texts and Snyder and Broadway (2004) in their queer analysis of high school biology textbooks. Snyder and Broadway recommend asking questions throughout the analysis, such as: in which content areas is sexuality outside the heterosexual norm represented and how is it represented? Which groups and explanations are privileged in the text? Which are silent/absent? I also tried to consider the potential implications of the representations. In addition to approaching my analysis with these questions in mind, like Anderson and Accomando, I considered how authors presented material in ways that appear to *describe* reality rather than *constructing* only one possible version of it. I share their sense that 'beneath a veneer of objectivity certain issues are foregrounded and others are ignored' (p. 493).

RESULTS OF QUANTITATVE ANALYSIS

A comparison of the quantity of coverage displayed in Table 6.2 with Simoni's (2000) equivalent table reveals very little change since her analysis. Simoni found three textbooks that did not mention LGB sexualities at all, I found two (one introductory, one developmental), and the range and mean number of index citations and pages were extremely similar. Overall, I found an average of 4.6 citations compared with Simoni's 3.5[5] and 2.0 pages of material compared with her 2.8. The longest and most extensive sections covering LGB sexualities were those on sexual orientation within the US introductory textbooks, the biological textbooks, and three of the developmental textbooks (Santrock, 2005; Berger, 2004; Boyd & Bee, 2005). Therefore, it is these sections that the qualitative analysis will focus on in depth, following a brief overview of the coverage of LGB sexualities in other sections.

Although clearly there are not enough texts in the analysis for any generalizable comparison between the US and UK publications, it was the case that the eight UK books reviewed contained, overall, much less coverage of LGB sexualities and relationships than the other books. The three introductory texts (Gross, 2005; Hayes, 2000; Malim & Birch, 1998) did not cover theories or research on sexual orientation at all, and none mentioned bisexuality. Despite the very small amount of LGB relevant material in these UK texts (there is none at all in Hayes), it could be argued that what was included was good. The lack of coverage of explanations of sexual orientation may not be entirely a negative thing, as I will go on to discuss. Indeed, Malim and Birch, and Gross both made explicit references to heterosexism as a potential bias in psychology research. The single UK developmental text (Harris & Butterworth, 2002) made no mention of lesbian and gay sexualities at all. This was partly because, like many UK developmental texts, it did not go beyond adolescence to include adult development. However, the US texts all mentioned lesbians and gay men in sections on adolescent development and parenting of children in early

---

[5] My inclusion of *bisexuality* as an index term as well as Simoni's terms made very little difference since only three books indexed this.

childhood. The two social psychology texts (Hewstone & Stroebe, 2001; Hogg & Vaughan, 2004) were more similar to the US texts, although with somewhat less mention of lesbian and gay sexualities. Hogg and Vaughan was the only text to mention critical psychological work on homophobia. The UK biological psychology texts (Martin, 2003; Toates, 2001) were very similar in coverage to the equivalent US books.

RESULTS OF QUALITATIVE ANALYSIS

Overall Coverage of LGB Sexualities

Simoni (2000) critiqued the textbooks she analysed for failing to systematically incorporate references to lesbians and gay men in contexts that were not related specifically to their sexual orientation. My analysis suggests that things have improved since then: the majority of the developmental psychology textbooks considered lesbians and gay men in their sections on adolescent identity and early adult relationships and parenting, and the majority of social psychology textbooks mentioned same-sex relationships in their chapters on attraction and love. Introductory textbooks were generally not as good at integrating LGB psychology into sections other than those on sexual orientation: they tended to avoid mention at all in sections on relationships, or made very brief comments that the findings discussed also applied to lesbians and gay men (e.g. with regard to benefits of relationships for well-being [Myers, 2003]). Malim and Birch (1998) acknowledge the heterosexual bias in their coverage, stating: 'we have tended to ignore the gender of lovers in this discussion. While heterosexual love has been the major focus (the research is very much greater here), love experiences do not appear to be very different for people with different sexual orientations' (p. 605). Gross (2005) makes similar points about lesbian and gay parenting.

While social and developmental textbooks do now mention lesbian and gay sexualities, it is mostly in a separate tokenistic section (Kitzinger, 1996) rather than throughout their coverage of interpersonal relationships. Relationships are presented in the textbooks in heteronormative ways, with the vast majority of images, examples and reported studies being about heterosexual couples. However, none of the textbooks in the current analysis went quite as far as one of the textbooks analysed by Simoni (2000), which clearly positions the reader as heterosexual, and presents them with a heteronormative pathway to follow: 'chances are that one day the "right" person will come along, you will fall in love with that person, get married, and perhaps have children' (Carlson & Buskist, 1996, p. 518).

Coverage of early adult social development is very similar across all the introductory and developmental textbooks examined. Those that include this tend to locate early adulthood on Erikson's (1959) life stage model and Levinson's (1978) theory of the 'seasons of a man's life' before focusing on marriage and parenting in depth. Both Erikson and Levinson's theories are clearly heteronormative. Erikson's states that, in early adulthood 'the adult seeks deep and lasting personal relationships, particularly with a partner of the opposite sex' (Malim & Birch, 1998, p. 545), and Levinson's focuses on the need to achieve a new life structure following the transition of marriage (Boyd & Bee, 2005). Same-sex relationships, where covered, tend to be mentioned after the sections on marriage as one of the 'diversity of adult lifestyles' (Berk, 2003; Santrock, 2005) along with being single, co-habiting, and remarrying following divorce. Most books emphasize that 'homosexual couples have the same relationship issues as heterosexual couples' (Berger, 2004, p. 472). Some challenge 'misconceptions', such as same-sex relationships being shorter-lived, or involving more sex or the adoption of masculine and feminine roles, and several mention the fight for legalization of same-sex marriage in various countries (e.g. Santrock, 2005). Sections on same-sex parenting emphasize the similarity between lesbians and gay men and heterosexual parents, and challenge myths that lesbian and gay parents are less adequate or more likely to have lesbian and gay children (e.g. Berk, 2003). Developmental textbooks also sometimes mentioned 'homosexual families' in sections on child development and LGB identities in sections on adolescence (e.g. Berger, 2004; Boyd & Bee, 2005). Berk (2003) was the only text to cover same-sex relationships in late adulthood and aging as recommended by Kimmel (2000).

As with developmental texts, social psychological chapters and sections on attraction and close relationships mostly covered theories and research concerning who heterosexual men and women are attracted to and form relationships with (on the basis of physical attraction, similarity, proximity, etc.). All those I analysed – except Hogg and Vaughan (2004) – included evolutionary theories of what men look for in women and vice versa. Some began with vignettes about heterosexual couples (e.g. Greg and Linda – Baron et al., 2005, p. 294; or Mark and Karen – Hogg & Vaughan, 2004, p. 515). Lesbian and gay relationships are sometimes covered within sections on marriage: Baron, Byrne and Branscombe (2005) include a two-page segment on the campaign for same-sex marriage, while the rest of their 10-page long section on marriage considers the formation, maintenance and break-up of heterosexual relationships. Other textbooks make sporadic references to research that includes lesbian and gay couples: for example Kurdek's (1992, cited in Aronson, Wilson & Akert, 2004, p. 363) research supporting exchange theory in lesbian and gay relationships and Schreurs and Buunk's (1996, cited in Hewstone & Stroebe, 2001, p. 395) research on the importance of equity in lesbian relationships. Occasionally they specify that the majority of the research reviewed in the textbook is based on heterosexual couples, but generally this is left implicit. Brehm, Kassin and Fein (2002), for instance, state in a brief paragraph that research on married couples focuses on men and women, but that same-sex couples are now able to have civil unions in some countries. However, they title their whole section on intimate relationships 'Relationship issues: the male-female "connection"' (p. 334), and only mention 'homosexual couples' once to say that they are just as likely as heterosexual couples to break up due to problems in communication.

The focus of developmental and social textbooks on couple relationships and marriage also clearly presents monogamy as the norm. Blumstein and Schwartz (1983) found that 29% of US lesbian couples and 65% of gay male couples had some kind of non-monogamous arrangement, compared with 15–28% of heterosexual couples. However, this appears to be almost completely excluded from psychology textbooks, which have no images of anything other than couple relationships and present monogamy as 'natural' and 'normal' despite evidence of non-monogamy in the majority of non-western societies (Goodwin, 1999) and the emergence of polyamorous communities in the US and UK (Barker, 2004). Only two of the textbooks I analysed briefly mentioned the existence of open relationships in gay men (Boyd & Bee, 2005; Santrock, 2005) and none in other groups.

Whatley (1992) argued that the photographic images of lesbians and gay men in textbooks are very important because they are assumed by the reader to be 'objective and unable to "lie" ' (p. 197). Moreover, because images depicting lesbians and gay men are so rare in textbooks they are likely to be interpreted by the reader as representative. None of the biological and few of the introductory textbooks included images at all, probably due to their emphasis on lesbians and gay men only in the context of sexual orientation (which did not tend to be illustrated with images of people). Photographs and cartoons of couples in developmental and social textbooks were overwhelmingly opposite-sex. General questions, such as 'why do we fall in love?', and discussions of different kinds of love were invariably illustrated with an opposite-sex couple in close physical contact, kissing or holding one another (e.g. Hewstone & Stroebe, 2001, p. 373; Hogg & Vaughan, 2004, p. 519). I only found eight images of same-sex couples in total, generally illustrating sections on lesbian and gay relationships or parenting, and very rarely in any closer proximity than holding hands. My analysis certainly concurs with Whatley's (1992) observation that visual representations of lesbians and gay men are 'isolated and ghettoized' in textbooks (p. 208). However, whereas Whatley found that images of lesbians and gay men in the health and sexuality textbooks she examined were predominantly of white, young people, who were rarely depicted with children, half the images I found portrayed culturally mixed relationships, half were at least in their 40s, and a third showed couples with children. One of the most interesting images was Aronson, Wilson and Akert's (2004) photograph of a middle-aged black woman and a white woman walking in the woods (p. 372). It seems from the context (love relationships) and the caption (including the word 'partners') that they were representing a same-sex couple. This is a rare example of a same-sex relationship being used to illustrate a general point about relationships, as recommended by Whatley (1992).

There was very little mention of bisexual people in any of the sections described above. This omission will be discussed in detail below, however it is worth pointing out here that developmental and social textbooks generally only mention 'homosexual' or 'lesbian and gay' relationships and there are no images that could easily be read as bisexual.[6] Only Berk (2003) and Santrock (2005) occasionally tag the word 'bisexual' onto 'lesbian and gay' or 'homosexual', but there is slippage in this, and the sections in which they do so are titled 'homosexual' and 'lesbian and gay' respectively. Similarly, bisexuality is excluded from other areas of the textbooks that cover lesbian and gay issues. Sections on homophobia fail to mention the existence of biphobia. Petford (2003) reports that bisexuals often experience the same prejudice as lesbians and gay men, but that this can be coupled with a lack of acceptance or support within lesbian and gay communities and general stereotypes that bisexuality is unreal or a phase on the way to heterosexuality or homosexuality. Biphobia has been linked to relatively high levels of mental health problems within bisexual communities (e.g. Jorm et al., 2002). While many textbooks mention the removal of homosexuality from the DSM, no textbook considered the impact of this on perceptions of bisexuality. Fox (2000) argues that, although this event helped build a more affirmative approach to homosexuality within psychology and psychiatry, the APA retained a dichotomous model of sexual orientation (that people can only be heterosexual or homosexual), which 'supported the belief that bisexuals were psychologically maladjusted' (p. 180).

---

[6] Examples of visibly bisexual images would be bisexual activists on pride marches or at bi conferences, holding banners or wearing bi T-shirts. Images taken from bisexual newsletters and websites could also be used. Alternatively, images could be presented of the same person at different points in time with partners of more than one gender, and/or of non-monogamous bisexual people with multiple differently gendered partners (although this latter should be used cautiously so as not to imply that all bisexual people are non-monogamous).

Sexual Orientation

Context and Content of Coverage

The introductory textbooks that cover sexual orientation include this in their chapters on motivation – generally towards the end of a longer section which examines the drives behind animal and human sexual behaviour. By 'sexual behaviour' it is apparent that the books mean 'heterosexual behaviour' since the topics covered all relate to arousal and preference for 'the opposite sex'. A fairly representative exemplar, Kosslyn and Rosenberg's (2004) section on sexual behaviour, begins with a vignette of a heterosexual date and reports research findings about 'mating preferences' (the kinds of men women prefer and vice versa) and women's responses to pictures of nude men at the time of ovulation. Their section 'sexual orientation: more than a choice' then presents research on various biological differences between 'heterosexual and homosexual people' (p. 428), prior to the final section of the chapter covering 'sexual dysfunction' and 'atypical sexual behaviour' (fetishism, androgen insensitivity syndrome and transvestism).

Like introductory textbooks, biological psychology textbooks tend to include sections on sexual orientation within chapters on sexual, or even 'reproductive', behaviour (Kalat, 2004). The sexual orientation section in Pinel (2005) starts by saying 'so far, this chapter has avoided the issue of sexual orientation' (p. 347), suggesting an awareness of the underlying assumption in the previous section that 'sexual' equals 'heterosexual'. In the two developmental textbooks that cover sexual orientation, Boyd and Bee (2005) consider it in a separate section on 'homosexuality' at the end of their section on relationships in adolescence. Santrock (2005) gives equal space to 'heterosexual attitudes and behavior' and 'attitudes and behavior of lesbians and gay males' (pp. 445–446) in an early adulthood chapter. However, it is the latter section, not the former, which includes a three-paragraph consideration of biological bases of sexual orientation. This implies that the cause of sexual orientation is an issue for lesbians and gay men and not for heterosexuals. The general coverage of homosexuality and bisexuality within separate sections on sexual orientation seems tokenistic (Kitzinger, 1996; Peel, 2001) and suggests that these sexualities constitute problems for overall theories of sexual behaviour and therefore require explanation.

Within the sections on sexual orientation it is clear that heterosexual norms frame the questions posed by both textbook authors and the researchers whose work they cite. Some textbooks minimally acknowledge the heterosexism implicit in searching for explanations and causes of homosexuality rather than heterosexuality, something Simoni (2000) reported was lacking in the books she analysed. For example, Smith, Nolen-Hoeksema and Fredrickson (2002) begin their section on 'causes of sexual orientation' with this statement 'the common question "what causes homosexuality" is scientifically misconceived because it implicitly assumes either that heterosexuality needs no explanation or that its causes are self-evident' (p. 380). However, all textbooks then go on to present biological research that searches for ways in which lesbian and gay, and occasionally bisexual, people differ from heterosexuals. It seems likely that this common rhetorical strategy serves to construct subsequently reported studies as 'good science' as well as protecting the authors from any accusation of heterosexism.

Hegarty and Pratto's (2004) research found that people were generally more likely to focus on lesbian/gay than heterosexual people in their explanations of differences on the basis of sexual orientation, thus constructing heterosexuality as the neutral standard and anything else as a deviation from it. Such 'norming' is prevalent in textbook sections on sexual orientation which generally report findings in this format, for example:

- 'response to a click [in the ear] is less frequent and weaker for homosexual and bisexual women than for heterosexual women' (Kosslyn & Rosenberg, 2004, p. 428)
- 'gay men and lesbians were . . . more likely than their heterosexual counterparts to report that they had not been masculine (for men) or feminine (for women) as children' (Smith et al., 2002, p. 380)
- 'long bones in the legs and arms of school-aged children who grow up to be homosexual do not grow as rapidly as those of children who eventually become heterosexual' (Boyd & Bee, 2005, p. 334)
- 'gay more than straight men express interest in occupations such as decorator, florist and flight attendant that attract many women' (Myers, 2003, p. 479).

Percentages are given for the proportion of 'homosexual' people, not heterosexual people, in the population (generally reporting that the common statistic of 10% is an overestimate). In relation to such research on sexual orientation, Tavris (1993) argues that 'the study of "difference" is not the problem; of course people differ. The problem occurs when one group is considered the norm with others differing from it, thereby failing to 'measure up' to the ideal, superior, dominant standard' (p. 151). As King (1988) writes 'questions of causality . . . are no more or less pertinent to the study of gays and lesbians than to the study of their heterosexual counterparts' (p. 168). Although some textbooks pay lip-service to this perspective, it is clearly not embedded in their subsequent presentation of research.

Focus on Biological Explanations

The explanations of sexual orientation given in textbooks are overwhelmingly essentialist and biological. The possibility of a choosing one's sexuality is consistently denied. For example, Kalat (2003) states that 'sexual orientation, like left- or right-handedness, is not something that people choose or that they can change easily' (p. 346). While this is generally presented as an argument against homophobia and for equal rights (e.g. Myers, 2003), it denies the possibility of, for example, lesbianism as a politically chosen identity (Rich, 1978) and any role for personal agency in sexual identity or behaviour. Further, Hegarty (2002) found that the belief that sexual orientation is immutable is not necessarily correlated with more tolerant attitudes amongst heterosexual people.[7] Textbooks frequently equate and reduce social theories of the origins of sexuality with sexual orientation being 'chosen'. Myers states that sexual orientation is 'biological influenced – an enduring identity, not a choice' (p. 480), as if these are the only two possibilities. But neither social essentialist nor social constructionist understandings of sexuality imply that sexuality is something that is 'freely chosen' by individuals, rather that it is learnt or shaped by social forces.

---

[7] Hegarty found that such a correlation was only apparent with people who thought that immutability beliefs would be expressed by more tolerant people.

Very few textbooks cover social theories of sexual orientation at all, except to dismiss previous problematic myths such as the link between homosexuality and relationships with parents, or seduction by an 'adult homosexual' as children (e.g. Myers, 2003; Santrock, 2005). Some textbooks argue that environmental factors are involved in sexual orientation but that what these are is unknown, explaining that this is why they give little space to their consideration (e.g. Boyd & Bee, 2005). Myers (2003, p. 477) makes an unusual (for these textbooks) shift from the third to the first person in his statement:

> the bottom line from a half-century's theory and research: if there are environmental factors that influence sexual orientation, we do not yet know what they are. If someone were to ask me, 'what can I do to influence my child's sexual orientation?' my answer would have to be 'I haven't a clue'.

This invites the reader to conclude that 'environmental factors' are not involved, if 50 years of research has failed to reveal them and even an expert like the author is forced to admit his ignorance. Arguably, it also suggests that the question of influencing one's child's sexual orientation might be a reasonable one, or at least leaves this unchallenged.

Smith et al. (2002) include two pages claiming to present 'both sides' of the argument over whether sexual orientation is 'innate or socially determined' (pp. 382–383). This involves J. Michael Bailey summarizing his theory that child gender non-conformity (CGN) and adult homosexuality are intrinsically linked and have genetic origins. Following this, Daryl J. Bem presents the 'social' side of the argument with his 'exotic becomes erotic' theory, which agrees that genes and hormones cause CGN but argues that this places children in the company of the 'other sex' who are thus seen as more similar to themselves and therefore, later on, as less sexually attractive. This positioning of Bailey and Bem as the two sides of the debate over the origins of sexual orientation excludes the possibility of more social understandings of sexuality. The social constructionist theories that dominate most of the other social sciences when it comes to understanding sexuality (Weeks, 2003) are not represented at all, and there is very little consideration of the vast historical and cultural variation in sexual behaviour and understandings of sexuality. Indeed, authors avoid the issue and use universalizing statements like 'as far as we know, all cultures in all times have been predominantly heterosexual' (Myers 2003, p. 475).

Along with Bailey and Bem's theories of genetic involvement, many books present studies on the influence of maternal hormones and/or stress levels on sexual orientation during gestation. As Hegarty (2003) points out, the construction of the maternal body as altering the infant's body in this way implicitly shifts responsibility for gay men's sexuality onto their mothers, perhaps echoing old stereotypes of mothers causing gayness in their sons. Textbooks also present Simon LeVay's (1991) finding that the brains of heterosexual men have a larger third interstitial nucleus of the anterior hypothalamus than those of women or homosexual men. This is generally followed by a summary of the problems with LeVay's research: the lack of replication; the small sample size; the fact that the men had died of AIDS-related illnesses and that their sexual orientation was assumed on the basis of whether they contracted HIV through intravenous drug use or not; and the fact that experience could affect the brain rather than the other way round (e.g. Rosenzweig et al., 2004). Despite these recognized flaws, LeVay's study is still reported in all the sections on sexual orientation. Indeed, Pinel (2005) concludes that although LeVay's research is controversial: 'it has been widely publicized and has stimulated a major effort to identify neural correlates of sexual orientation' (p. 348) – implying that this is good reason to give it so much page space.

Many of the biological studies reported in the texts are presented as finding that lesbian women are more masculine than heterosexual women and gay men more feminine than heterosexual men (in terms of hormones, brain size, childhood behaviour, etc.), while some present gay men as 'even more "male-like" than the average male' (who, presumably, is heterosexual) (e.g. Kalat, 2003, p. 347). The ways in which conclusions are drawn from the former studies seem to support persistent myths that confuse gender identity and sexual orientation, seeing lesbians as 'masculine' women and gay men as 'feminine' men (Gainor, 2000). These conclusions are often based on the spurious and overly simplistic notion that certain hormones and behaviours are 'female' and others are 'male' (Hird, 2004). There is generally no reflection on the conflicting nature of the findings that gay men are 'more male', and these still manage to present gay men as deviating from 'the usual male pattern' (Kalat, 2003, p. 347).

Bisexuality and Dichotomous Theories

Roughly half of the textbooks covering sexual orientation failed to mention bisexuality at all as a possible sexual orientation. Kalat (2003, p. 345) asks 'why do some people prefer partners of the other sex and some prefer partners of their own sex?', failing to mention those who do not prefer one or the other. Boyd and Bee (2005, p. 334) chart the pathway of the 'great majority of teens' from unisexual groups to heterosexual groups and then heterosexual pairs, stating that the process is different for 'the subgroup of homosexual teens'. Toates (2001) and Myers (2003) both define sexual orientation as whether a person is heterosexual or homosexual, indicating that these are the only possibilities. Of all the textbooks analysed, only one introductory (Smith et al., 2002) and two developmental texts (Berk, 2003; Santrock, 2005) included index terms for bisexuality. In 1979, Newton argued that the complete omission of homosexual content in textbooks was an implied antihomosexual statement to students, and the equivalent could be said of this omission of bisexuality.

Pinel (2005) and Toates (2001) were the only biological psychology textbooks analysed to mention bisexuality. Pinel follows the pattern of all the introductory psychology books which cover bisexuality by mentioning and/or defining it briefly at the start but then focusing on differences between 'homosexuals and heterosexuals' (p. 347). Some books only mention bisexuality briefly in order to downplay its existence, for example, Myers (2003, p. 476) reports low frequencies of bisexuality, and continues the analogy between sexual orientation and handedness to state that 'most people are one way, some the other. A very few are truly ambidextrous'. This conceptualization of bisexuality corresponds with current arguments in popular psychological sources (e.g. Dickins et al., 2005) and the media (Borno, 2006) about bisexuality. Wilson and Rahman (2005) shed some light on why there might be an agenda amongst some biological psychologists to prove the non-existence of bisexuality. They argue that a dichotomous understanding 'implies that sexual orientation is set from an early age, whereas a prevalence of intermediate sexualities fits better with the argument that later learning experiences, "chance" factors or lifestyle choices are influential' (p. 16). Putting to one side the problematic construction of sexuality as *either* biologically *or* socially determined, this argument is not consistent with much current biological and evolutionary thinking that emphasizes variation and diversity, finds widespread bisexuality amongst animal species and humans, and critiques dichotomous understandings of sexuality (Hird, 2004).

Some textbooks do present the possibility of non-dichotomous sexual orientation, however my feeling is this is generally done in a way that would be quite confusing to students, because the authors then go on to focus almost entirely on differences between homosexual and heterosexual people. Smith et al. (2002) define an individual's sexual orientation as 'the degree to which he or she is sexually attracted to persons of the other sex and/or to persons of the same sex' (p. 379) and begin their section with a summary of Kinsey et al.'s (Kinsey, Pomeroy & Martin, 1948; Kinsey, Pomeroy, Martin & Gebhard, 1953) famous research, arguing – like Kinsey et al. – that: 'most behavioural scientists conceptualize sexual orientation as a continuum, ranging from exclusive heterosexuality to exclusive homosexuality' (p. 379). This statement is not reflected in the overall tone and content of the textbooks, as I will explain shortly. Smith et al. go on to define bisexuals as those who score 2–4 on the six-point Kinsey scale. Like Passer and Smith (2003) – the other introductory textbook that considers non-dichotomous theories – they then point out that sexual orientation comprises different components (e.g. attraction, behaviour, self-identity) and that people may be at different points on the scale for different elements. They also state that 'individuals may shift over time on one or more of the components' (p. 379), suggesting that sexual orientation is mutable – a possibility that would seem to be denied by most of the biological research they go on to present. The words 'bisexual' and 'bisexuality' are mentioned three times in the first two paragraphs but then never mentioned again in the three pages on sexual orientation that follow.

There is some similar confusion in the literature on sexuality in general over whether continuum or dichotomous theories are accepted within psychology. King (1988) reports that sexuality 'is viewed as a continuum along which an individual's identity and sexual activities may move at different stages of life' (p. 168) and Fox (2000) states that there is 'a greater acknowledgement of bisexuality as a valid sexual orientation and sexual identity' within psychology, following 'a critical reexamination of the dichotomous model of sexual orientation' (p. 161). However, Rust (2000a) reports that both popular understandings and scientific research on sexuality collapse bisexuality into dichotomous either/or enquiry. The research investigating genetic, hormonal and brain differences presented in the textbooks is clearly based on a dichotomous framework that 'erases bisexuality as an epistemological category' (Petford, 2003, p. 7). The coverage in the textbooks suggests that bisexuals are sometimes excluded from research completely and at other times lumped in with lesbians or gay men (Tavris, 1993). Garber (1995) notes that much genetic and physiological research fails to make clear the criteria on which sexual orientation is judged (e.g. behaviour, identity, attraction) and that the changeability of these across a lifetime makes such research problematic. Also, as Rust (2000b) points out, both dichotomous and continuum-based theories define sexual orientation in terms of dichotomous sex/gender because they present sexuality as attraction to men and/or to women. This understanding of 'opposite sexes' underpins heteronormativity as evidenced by Kessler's (1998) finding that, in western cultures, those people (up to 5% of the population) who are born ambiguously sexed are assigned a gender according to criteria that categorizes 'male' as having an appendage of a certain length which is capable of becoming erect and penetrating a vagina, and 'female' as having a vagina capable of being penetrated (see Hird, 2004, for a full discussion of non-dichotomous sex and gender diversity in both non-human and human animals). Petford

(2003) found – in contrast to textbook definitions of bisexuality as attraction 'to both sexes' (Kosslyn & Rosenberg, 2004) – that the preferred definition of bisexuality from the bisexual communities she studied was 'mutable sexual and emotional attraction to people of any sex, where gender may not be a defining factor' (p. 6).

Only one textbook showed some recognition of the problems that acknowledging the existence of bisexuality posed for the dichotomous explanations presented. Toates (2001) queried dichotomous explanations (genes *or* environment) and went on to say 'also we should not dichotomise into neat categories of gay or heterosexual and we need to recognize overlap' (p. 465). However, as with all textbooks that mentioned bisexuality, there was a great deal of slippage in wording, and bisexuality was not consistently included when 'non-heterosexual' sexual orientations were being written about. McDonald (1981) found that gay men were more frequently mentioned than lesbians in writing on sexual orientation. In my analysis it seemed that most of the time people of 'non-heterosexual' sexual orientations were referred to as either 'gay and lesbian' (in that order) or 'homosexual'. Sometimes 'lesbian' would be missed off, and sometimes 'bisexual' would be added to the end ('gay, lesbian and bisexual'), but this inclusion of bisexual was inconsistent.

Dichotomous understandings of sexuality erase bisexuality as a category and this may well contribute to discrimination experienced by many bisexuals and the myth that bisexuality is only ever 'a phase' en route to a mature heterosexual or homosexual identity. Textbooks would do well to draw on Tavris's (1993) consideration of research on sexual orientation. As she highlights, studies on brain differences are small and inconclusive, the meanings of terms keep changing, there is far more evidence of similarity than difference, brain differences do not prove innateness and 'there are many sexualities which do not divide up neatly into heterosexuality and homosexuality' (pp. 157–158). Some of the textbooks analysed include awareness of the impact of homophobia on the lives and experiences of lesbians and gay men within their sections on sexual orientation, which seems a positive move forward. Myers (2003, p. 475) poses the question 'what does it feel like to be homosexual in a heterosexual culture?' and considers various examples of heterosexism and homophobia. However, when I read this question my immediate response was 'probably rather similar to the way it feels to be bisexual reading these textbooks'.

CONCLUSIONS

It is clear from my analysis that the coverage of lesbian and gay sexualities in textbooks has improved since the studies of McDonald (1981) and King (1988). Texts may still make brief reference to the removal of homosexuality per se from the DSM in sections on 'abnormal psychology', but most of the coverage takes place in chapters on aspects of 'normal' psychology, and few social or developmental psychology textbooks completely exclude lesbian and gay relationships from their coverage of intimate relationships. As Simoni (2000) found, there is still excessive focus on the origins of homosexuality, although some textbooks now acknowledge the flaws in searching for causes of homosexuality and not heterosexuality. Coverage of lifespan development, intimate relationships and sexual behaviour is still largely heteronormative, as are the images and examples used to illustrate them. Most mention of LGB sexualities is in tokenistic boxes or subsections. However, a minority of textbooks have made progress by illustrating general points about relationships with images of same-sex couples, by considering lesbian and gay relationships throughout the lifespan, or by referencing heterosexist biases in mainstream psychology and the existence of lesbian and gay psychology.

Sexual orientation is generally constructed as rooted in biology, unchangeable and dichotomous. Bisexuality is rarely mentioned and, when it is, it is only included sporadically and not theorized in any depth. None of the recent psychological research on bisexual identities, experiences or behaviour (e.g. Fox, 2004) seems to have filtered through into psychological textbooks. I share Petford's (2003) concern that this marginalization and exclusion of bisexuality and reliance on dichotomous models of sexual orientation risks perpetuating biphobia and models of mental health and psychotherapy that regard bisexuality as deviant or disordered.

Further research in this area should continue to chart changes in the representation of LGB sexualities in psychology textbooks and to check the generalizability of the conclusions drawn here by conducting larger scale content analyses of both textbooks and curricula. There are also important areas for in-depth qualitative analysis that were beyond the scope of this study, for example in relation to the depictions of transgender and/or intersex people. As previously mentioned, dichotomous understandings of sex and gender, as well as sexual orientation, are inherent within heteronormativity. However, most coverage of sex and gender in mainstream textbooks constructs male and female, man and woman, as 'opposites'. Many introductory and biological textbooks consider intersex people in sections on gender identity but they are often portrayed as deviations or abnormalities and only understood within the two-gender model. For example, Kosslyn and Rosenberg (2004, p. 432) write about people with androgen insensitivity syndrome who 'should have been boys' and who can, in most cases, have 'normal female sex lives'. There is very little coverage of transgender in textbooks outside the pathologizing language of 'gender identity disorder' (Gainor, 2000), and no consideration of sex and gender diversity or the challenges intersex and transgender might pose to mainstream understandings of sex/gender (Hird, 2004). Despite the fact that abnormal psychology texts no longer include homosexuality as a disorder, it would be useful to examine them for the ways in which they present homosexuality's removal from the DSM, for their depiction of transgendered people, and for their continued construction of deviance around same-sex and non-monogamous relationships. Also, the continued pathologization of certain sexual practices, like sadomasochism, as paraphilias is of relevance to many in LGB communities (see Barker, 2005). There is scope for a more detailed analysis of the coverage of LGB parenting in psychology textbooks (see Clarke, 2000) and of issues of ethnicity and (dis)ability, which are rarely considered in relation to sexuality (Simoni, 2000).

Snyder and Broadway (2004) in their textbook analysis argue that 'the pervasive acceptance of heteronormative behaviour privileges students that fit the heterosexual norm, and oppresses through omission and silence those who do not' (p. 617). I would suggest that this is largely the case in psychology texts and that bisexuals especially are excluded from these books. As mentioned earlier, this is damaging for LGB students who could understandably feel that they are not part of human behaviour or normal development on the basis of these texts. It is also problematic on a much wider societal level because these (mostly) heteronormative textbooks are one of the main sources of knowledge and understanding for many future therapists, clinical psychologists, educators, occupational psychologists, law-makers and so on, and because the theories and research presented in them tend to filter through into popular understanding.

I would support Greene and Croom's (2000) call for a more lesbian and gay affirmative psychology to pervade textbooks where 'lesbians and gay men are acknowledged to be equal to heterosexuals in their psychological adjustment and in their capacity to love, relate, and contribute to society' (Simoni, 2000, p. 76). However, I would argue strongly for the addition of bisexuals and transgender people to 'lesbians and gay men' and for a continued critical consideration within LGBTQ psychology of the dichotomous under-standings of sexuality, sex and gender that underlie heteronormativity and much psycho-logical theory and research. Until textbooks reflect these aims, I would call on psychology teachers to actively choose the most inclusive textbooks to recommend on their courses and to embed LGBTQ relevant material throughout their courses, particularly that which encourages students to reflect on their existing assumptions (see Barker, 2005).

ACKNOWLEDGEMENTS

Huge thanks to Liz Peel and Victoria Clarke for their kind patience and clear advice during the researching and writing of this chapter, and for helping me to produce something of which I'm proud. Thanks also to members of the Lesbian and Gay Psychology Section Committee for giving me a home within psychology and to Peter Hegarty in particular for introducing me to research on explanations of sexual orientation. Thanks to the UK bisexual communities for useful discussions and much enthusiasm, and thanks to Erich Schultz and Ani Ritchie for feedback on chapter drafts and for their invaluable support during the project.

REFERENCES

American Psychological Association (2002). *Report on undergraduate psychology major learning goals and outcomes*. Retrieved 15 December 2005 from http://www.apa.org/ed/pcue/reports.html

Anderson, K. J. & Accomando, C. (2002). 'Real' boys? Manufacturing masculinity and erasing privilege in popular books on raising boys. *Feminism & Psychology*, **12**(4), 491–516.

Angelides, S. (2001). *A History of Bisexuality*. Chicago, IL: University of Chicago Press.

Aronson, E., Wilson, T. D. & Akert, R. M. (2004). *Social Psychology*. Upper Saddle River, NJ: Prentice Hall.

Barker, M. (2004). This is my partner, and this is my . . . partner's partner: Constructing a polyamorous identity in a monogamous world. *Journal of Constructivist Psychology*, **18**, 75–88.

Barker, M. (2005). Developing an SM awareness tool. In M. Barker & D. Landridge (Eds), Special Issue: Contemporary perspectives on sadomasochism (S/M). *Lesbian & Gay Psychology Review*, **6**(3), 268–273.

Baron, R. A., Byrne, D. & Branscombe, N. R. (2005). *Social Psychology*. Boston, MA: Allyn & Bacon.

Berger, K. S. (2004). *The Developing Person Through the Life Span*. New York, NY: Worth Publishers.

Berk, L. E. (2003). *Development Through the Lifespan*. Boston, MA: Allyn & Bacon.

Blumstein, P. & Schwartz, P. (1983). *American Couples: Money, work, sex*. New York, NY: William Morrow & Co.

Borno, H. (2006). Why we're all bisexual. *Psychologies Magazine*, **January**, 41–43.

Boyd, D. & Bee, H. (2005). *Lifespan Development*. Boston, MA: Allyn & Bacon.

Brehm, S. S., Kassin, S. M. & Fein, S. (2002). *Social Psychology*. Boston, MA: Houghton Mifflin Co.

British Psychological Society (2005a). *Qualifying Exam*. Retrieved 15 December 2005 from http://www.bps.org.uk/membership/grades/gbr.cfm

British Psychological Society (2005b). *So You Want to be a Psychologist*. Retrieved 15 December 2005 from http://www.bps.org.uk/careers/careers_home.cfm

Bronstein, P. & Quina, K. (Eds) (1988). *Teaching a Psychology of People: Resources for gender and sociocultural awareness*. Washington DC: American Psychological Association.

Carlson, N. R. & Buskist, W. (1996). *Psychology: The science of behaviour*. Boston, MA: Allyn & Bacon.

Clarke, V. (2000). 'Stereotype, attack and stigmatize those who disagree': Employing scientific rhetoric in debates about lesbian and gay parenting. *Feminism & Psychology*, **10**(1), 152–159.

Dickins, T., Hardman, D. & Sergeant, M. (2005). Nothing to be sniffy about. [letter] *The Psychologist*, **18**(9), 532.

Erickson, E. (1959). *Identity and the Life Cycle: Psychological issues, Vol 1(1) Monograph 1 (Selected papers by Erik H. Erickson)*. New York, NY: International Universities Press.

Epstein, D. (1995). In our (new) right minds: The hidden curriculum in higher education. In L. Morley & V. Walsh (Eds), *Feminist Academics: Creative agents for change* (pp. 56–72). London: Taylor & Francis.

Epstein, D., O'Flynn, S. & Telford, D. (2003). *Silenced Sexualities in Schools and Universities*. Stoke on Trent: Trentham Books.

Eyre, L. (1993). Compulsory heterosexuality in a university classroom. *Canadian Journal of Education*, **18**(3), 273–284.

Fontaine, C. (1982). Teaching the psychology of women: A lesbian feminist perspective. In M. Cruikshank (Ed.), *Lesbian Studies: Present and future* (pp. 70–80). Old Westbury, NY: Feminist Press.

Fox, R. (2000). Bisexuality in perspective. In B. Greene & G. Croom, (Eds), *Education, Research, and Practice in Lesbian, Gay, Bisexual, and Transgendered Psychology: A resource manual* (pp. 161–206). Thousand Oaks, CA: Sage.

Fox, R. (Ed.) (2004). *Current Research on Bisexuality*. Binghamton, NY: Haworth Press.

Gainor, K. A. (2000). Including transgender issues in lesbian, gay and bisexual psychology. In B. Greene & G. Croom (Eds), *Education, Research, and Practice in Lesbian, Gay, Bisexual, and Transgendered Psychology: A resource manual*. (pp. 131–160) Thousand Oaks, CA: Sage.

Garber, M. (1995). *Vice Versa: Bisexuality and the eroticism of everyday life*. London: Penguin.

Goodwin, R. (1999). *Personal Relationships Across Cultures*. London: Routledge.

Gray, V. (1977). The image of women in psychology textbooks. *Canadian Psychological Review*, **18**, 46–55.

Greene, B. & Croom, G. (Eds) (2000). *Education, Research, and Practice in Lesbian, Gay, Bisexual, and Transgendered Psychology: A resource manual*. Thousand Oaks, CA: Sage.

Gross, R. (2005). *Psychology: The science of mind and behaviour*. London: Hodder Arnold.

Hall, D. E. & Pramaggiore, M. (Eds) (1996). *RePresenting Bisexualities*. New York, NY: New York University Press.

Harris, M. & Butterworth, G. (2002). *Developmental Psychology: A student's handbook*. Hove: Psychology Press.

Hayes, N. (2000). *Foundations of Psychology: An introductory text*. London: Thomson Learning.

Hegarty, P. (2002). 'It's not a choice, it's the way we're built': Symbolic beliefs about sexual orientation in the US and Britain. *Journal of Community & Applied Social Psychology*, **12**(3), 153–166.

Hegarty, P. (2003). Pointing to a crisis? What finger-length ratios tell us about the construction of sexuality. *Radical Statistics*, **83**, 16–30.

Hegarty, P. & Pratto, F. (2004). The difference that norms make: Empiricism, social constructionism, and the interpretation of group differences. *Sex Roles*, **50**(7/8), 445–453.

Hewstone, M. & Stroebe, W. (Eds) (2001). *Introduction to Social Psychology: A European perspective*. Oxford: Blackwell Publishers.

Hird, M. (2004). *Sex, Gender and Science*. Basingstoke: Palgrave MacMillan.

Hogg, M. A. & Vaughan, G. (2004). *Social Psychology*. Upper Saddle River, NJ: Prentice Hall.

Jorm, A., Korten, A., Rodgers, B., Jacomb, P. & Christensen, H. (2002). Sexual orientation and mental health: Results from a community survey of young and middle-aged adults. *British Journal of Psychiatry*, **180**, 423–427.

Kalat, J. W. (2003). *Biological Psychology*. Belmont, CA: Wadsworth/Thompson Learning.

Kessler, S. J. (1998). *Lessons from the Intersexed*. New Runswick, NJ: Rutgers University Press.

Kimmel, D. C. (2000). Including sexual orientation in life span psychology. In B. Greene & G. Croom (Eds), *Education, Research, and Practice in Lesbian, Gay, Bisexual, and Transgendered Psychology: A resource manual* (pp. 59–73). Thousand Oaks, CA: Sage.

King, N. (1988). Teaching about lesbians and gays in the psychology curriculum. In P. Bronstein & K. Quina (Eds), *Teaching a Psychology of People: Resources for gender and sociocultural awareness* (pp. 168–174). Washington DC: American Psychological Association.

Kinsey, A. C., Pomeroy, W. B. & Martin, C. E. (1948). *Sexual Behavior in the Human Male*. Philadelphia, PA: Saunders.

Kinsey, A. C., Pomeroy, W. B., Martin, C.E. & Gebhard, P.H. (1953). *Sexual Behavior in the Human Female*. Philadelphia, PA: Saunders.

Kitzinger, C. (1990). Heterosexism in psychology. *The Psychologist*, **3**(9), 391–392.

Kitzinger, C. (1996). The token lesbian chapter. In S. Wilkinson (Ed.), *Feminist Social Psychologies: International perspectives* (pp. 119–144). Buckingham: Open University Press.

Klein, F. (1993). *The Bisexual Option*. New York: Harrington Park Press.

Kosslyn, S. M. & Rosenberg, R. S. (2004). *Fundamentals of Psychology: The brain, the person, the world*. Boston, MA: Allyn & Bacon.

LeVay, S. (1991). A difference in hypothalamic structure between heterosexual and homosexual men. *Science*, **253**, 1034–1037.

Levinson, (1978). *Seasons of a Man's Life*. New York: Alfred Knopf.

Malim, T. & Birch, A. (1998). *Introductory Psychology*. Basingstoke: Palgrave MacMillan.

Martin, G. N. (2003). *Essential Biological Psychology*. London: Hodder Arnold.

McDonald, G. (1981). Misrepresentation, liberalism, and heterosexual bias in introductory psychology textbooks. *Journal of Homosexuality*, **6**(3), 45–59.

Myers, D. G. (2003). *Psychology*. New York, NY: Worth Publishers.

Newton, D. E. (1979). Representations of homosexuality in health science textbooks. *Journal of Homosexuality*, **4**(3), 247–253.

Passer, M. W. & Smith, R. E. (2003). *Psychology: The science of mind and behavior*. Burr Ridge, IL: McGraw Hill.

Peel, E. (2001). Neglect and tokenism: Representations of violence against lesbians in textbooks. *Psychology of Women Section Review*, **3**(1), 14–19.

Petford, B. (2003). Power in the darkness: Some thoughts on the marginalisation of bisexuality in psychological literature. *Lesbian & Gay Psychology Review*, **4**(2), 5–13.

Phillips, S. R. (1991). The hegemony of heterosexuality: A study of introductory texts. *Teaching Sociology*, **19**(4), 454–463.

Pinel, J. P. J. (2005). *Biopsychology*. Boston, MA: Allyn & Bacon.

Rich, A. (1978). Compulsory heterosexuality and lesbian existence. *Signs: Journal of Women in Culture and Society*, **5**(4), 631–660.

Rosenzweig, M. R., Breedlove, S. M. & Watson, N. V. (2004). *Biological Psychology: An introduction to behavioral and cognitive neuroscience*. Sunderland, MA: Sinauer Associates.

Rust, P. (2000a). Criticisms of the scholarly literature on sexuality for its neglect of bisexuality. In P. Rust (Ed.), *Bisexuality in the United States* (pp. 5–10). New York, NY: Columbia University Press.

Rust, P. C. R. (2000b). Bisexuality: A contemporary paradox for women. *Journal of Social Issues*, **56**(2), 205–221.

Santrock, J. W. (2005). *Life-span Development*. Burr Ridge, IL: McGraw Hill.

Simoni, J. M. (2000). Confronting heterosexism in the teaching of psychology. In B. Greene & G. Croom (Eds), *Education, Research, and Practice in Lesbian, Gay, Bisexual, and Transgendered Psychology: A resource manual* (pp. 74–90). Thousand Oaks, CA: Sage.

Smith, E., Nolen-Hoeksema, S. & Fredrickson, B. (2002). *Atkinson and Hilgard's Introduction to Psychology*. Belmont, CA: Wadsworth/Thompson Learning.

Storr, M. (Ed.) (1999). *Bisexuality: A critical reader.* London: Routledge.

Snyder, V. K. & Broadway, F. S. (2004). Queering high school biology textbooks. *Journal of Research into Science Teaching,* **41**(6), 617–636.

Tavris, C. (1993). The mismeasure of woman. *Feminism & Psychology,* **3**(2), 149–168.

Toates, F. (2001). *Biological Psychology: An integrative approach.* Hove: Pearson Education.

Weeks, J. (2003). *Sexuality.* London: Routledge.

Whatley, M. H. (1992). Images of gays and lesbians in sexuality and health textbooks. *Journal of Homosexuality,* **22**(3/4), 197–211.

Whitbourne, S. K. & Hulicka, I. M. (1990). Ageism in undergraduate psychology texts. *American Psychologist,* **45**(10), 1127–1136.

Wilson, G. & Rahman, Q. (2005). *Born Gay: The psychobiology of sex orientation.* London: Peter Owen.

Yanowitz, K. L. & Weathers, K. J. (2004). Do boys and girls act differently in the classroom? A content analysis of student characters in educational psychology textbooks. *Sex Roles,* **51**(1/2), 101–107.

Zimmerman, B. (1982). One out of thirty: Lesbianism in women's studies textbooks In M. Cruikshank (Ed.), *Lesbian Studies: Present and future* (pp. 128–131). Old Westbury, NY: Feminist Press.

PART II

Lives and Experiences

The Challenge of Understanding LGBTQ Lives and Experiences

Becky J. Liddle

University of Toronto, Canada

In the mid-twentieth century, psychological research seemed to be mostly the study of white male (presumably) heterosexual introductory psychology students. The results of these studies were assumed to be generalizeable to all of humanity. In the late-twentieth century, as members of other demographic groups elbowed their way into academia, the point was finally accepted that this practice of studying one convenient group and assuming findings would apply to other groups was not acceptable science. Yet when we finally began studying non-heterosexual people, history repeated itself. Early studies of LGBTQ people (conducted in the early 1970s) were typically studies of gay or lesbian urban residents of California or New York City. Although certainly important and ground-breaking, these studies were no more applicable to all LGBTQ people than the studies of white male psychology students were of all of humanity.

In the 1970s and 1980s, researchers attempted to describe the 'gay experience' in a general way. One of the common attempts during this period involved constructing gay and lesbian identity development models (e.g. Cass, 1979; Coleman, 1982; Troiden, 1979), however such models have been criticized for glossing over individual differences (e.g. McCarn & Fassinger, 1996) and cultural differences (e.g. Liddle, 2006), and for being steeped in a particular historical time (Rust, 2003). Even the basic assumption of a final, static, sexual orientation simply does not fit the data. For example, it is not uncommon for sexual minority women to experience significant fluctuations in both sexual attractions and identities over time, even long after initially coming out as lesbian or bisexual (Diamond, 2006; Rust, 1993). Although some LGBTQ researchers have attempted to construct more complex theories to try to encompass the great variety in individual experience (e.g. McCarn & Fassinger, 1996; Rosario et al., 2001), most researchers have abandoned the quest for overarching theories of LGBTQ experience. Nationality, religion, ethnic group, class, disability and a multitude of other social and identity variables shape LGBTQ lives. Experiences vary so widely and are so culture-bound that to attempt to make generalizations across countries and cultures is unrealistic. For this reason, recent

Out in Psychology: Lesbian, gay, bisexual, trans and queer perspectives. Edited by Victoria Clarke and Elizabeth Peel.
© 2007 John Wiley & Sons, Ltd.

research typically focuses in on a smaller subgroup of LGBTQ people, for example those of a particular ethnicity, religion or nationality.

Even within one country LGBTQ experiences can vary dramatically. For example, in the USA, where I have done most of my research, the proportion of LGB respondents who have come out to their parents has been found to be nearly twice as high in one geographic region compared to another (cited in Herek, 2003). Level of outness also varies by age and ethnicity (Bradford et al., 1994). Certain variables under study may not even make sense within some cultural contexts. For example, in some cultural groups the coming-out process of LGBTQ members is considered successfully completed when family members treat a same-sex partner with the same respect as they treat the heterosexual partners of other family members (Smith, 1997). This goal may be reached without sexual orientation ever being explicitly discussed or acknowledged. If a researcher then measures outness using a definition that does not make sense within this cultural context, the portrait of these participants' experience may be clouded by the researcher's inability to discern cultural subtleties. Examination of the lives and experiences of a particular cultural group (especially qualitative examination by a researcher already familiar with that group) is thus more likely to acquire results that are true to the participants' lived experience.

Even the central importance of LGBTQ community in providing primary social support to its members (e.g. Bradford, et al., 1994; Kurdek & Schmidt, 1987; Oswald, 2000) turns out to be culture-specific, as so many findings about LGBTQ people are. In contrast to white US LGBTQ people who typically report getting most of their social support from LGBTQ friends rather than blood family (e.g. Bradford, et al., 1994; Kurdek & Schmidt, 1987), Cochran and Mays (1986, cited in Ritter & Terndrup, 2002) found that African American lesbians were more likely to seek instrumental help from heterosexual members of the African American community than from White lesbians. US LGB people of color often maintain a sexual orientation identity quite separate from other identities (Fukuyama & Ferguson, 2000), and typically report experiencing conflicts in allegiances to their ethnic and sexual orientation communities (e.g. Chan, 1997; Greene, 1994; Loiacano, 1989; Walters, 1997). LGB members of some spiritual communities may experience similar conflicts between communities as do LGB people of colour (e.g. Dworkin, 1997; Fygetakis, 1997; Schuck & Liddle, 2001). National and ethnic cultures as well as various religions and sects differ widely in their acceptance of LGBTQ people. Thus, the level of integration or separation of sexual orientation identities with other aspects of identity (e.g. ethnic or religious identity) will vary greatly across cultures and religious groups.

Finally, it should be noted that LGBTQ people's lives are not all about explicitly LGBTQ issues. LGBTQ people have the same life demands as everyone else: achievement, work stress, family, etc., and thus in some ways their lives are as mundane as anyone's. But being LGBTQ adds a wrinkle (at the very least) to every other identity, life task, or life circumstance. Understanding how these variables come together and interact is the central business of modern day research on LGBTQ lives.

The chapters in this section are part of the continuing effort of researchers to understand the intricate complexities of LGBTQ lives. Each chapter alone, like most contemporary research on LGBTQ lives, provides a glimpse of only a tiny fragment of all LGBTQ experience. But as more and more of such research is conducted, and as these individual snapshots are painstakingly pieced together, what begins to take shape is a more accurate representation of the intricately complex mosaic that is LGBTQ life and experience.

REFERENCES

Bradford, J., Ryan, C. & Rothblum, E. D. (1994). National lesbian health care survey: Implications for mental health care. *Journal of Consulting and Clinical Psychology,* **62**(2), 228–242.

Cass, V. C. (1979). Homosexual identity formation: A theoretical model. *Journal of Homosexuality,* **4**(3), 219–235.

Chan, C. S. (1997). Don't ask, don't tell, don't know: The formation of a homosexual identity and sexual expression among Asian American lesbians. In B. Greene (Ed.), *Ethnic and Cultural Diversity among Lesbians and Gay Men* (pp. 240–248). Thousand Oaks, CA: Sage.

Coleman, E. (1982). Developmental stages of the coming-out process. *Journal of Homosexuality,* **7**(2/3), 31–43.

Diamond, L. M. (2006). What we got wrong about sexual identity development: Unexpected findings from a longitudinal study of young women. In A. M. Omoto & H. S. Kurtzman (Eds), *Sexual Orientation and Mental Health: Examining identity and development in lesbian, gay, and bisexual people.* (pp. 73–94). Washington, DC: American Psychological Association.

Dworkin, S. H. (1997). Female, lesbian, and Jewish: Complex and invisible. In B. Greene (Ed.), *Ethnic and Cultural Diversity among Lesbians and Gay Men* (pp. 63–87). Thousand Oaks, CA: Sage.

Fukuyama, M. A. & Ferguson, A. D. (2000). Lesbian, gay, and bisexual people of color: Understanding cultural complexity and managing multiple oppressions. In K. J. Bieschke, R. M. Perez & K. A. DeBord (Eds), *Handbook of Counseling and Psychotherapy with Lesbian, Gay, and Bisexual Clients* (pp. 81–105). Washington, DC: American Psychological Association.

Fygetakis, L. M. (1997). Greek American lesbians: Identity odysseys of honorable good girls. In B. Greene (Ed.), *Ethnic and Cultural Diversity among Lesbians and Gay Men* (pp. 152–190). Thousand Oaks, CA: Sage.

Greene, B. (1994). Ethnic-minority lesbians and gay men: Mental health and treatment issues. *Journal of Consulting and Clinical Psychology,* **62**(2), 243–251.

Herek, G. M. (2003). Why tell if you're not asked? Self-disclosure, intergroup contact, and heterosexuals' attitudes toward lesbians and gay men. In L. D. Garnets & D. C. Kimmel (Eds) *Psychological Perspectives on Lesbian, Gay, and Bisexual Experiences* (2nd edn) (pp. 270–298). New York, NY: Columbia.

Kurdek, L. A. & Schmidt, J. P. (1987). Perceived emotional support from family and friends in members of homosexual, married, and heterosexual cohabiting couples. *Journal of Homosexuality,* **14**(3/4), 57–68.

Liddle, B. J. (2006). Mutual Bonds: Lesbian Women's Lives and Communities. In K. J. Bieschke, R. M. Perez, K. A. DeBord (Eds), *Handbook of Counseling and Psychotherapy with Lesbian, Gay, Bisexual, and Transgender Clients* (2nd edn). Washington, DC: American Psychological Association.

Loiacano, D. K. (1989). Gay identity issues among black Americans: Racism, homophobia, and the need for validation. *Journal of Counseling & Development,* **68**(2), 21–25.

McCarn, S. R. & Fassinger, R. E. (1996). Revisioning sexual minority identity formation: A new model of lesbian identity and its implications for counseling and research. *The Counseling Psychologist,* **24**(3), 508–534.

Oswald, R. F. (2000). Family and friendship relationships after young women come out as bisexual or lesbian. *Journal of Homosexuality,* **38**(3), 65–83.

Oswald, R. F. & Culton, L. S. (2003). Under the rainbow: Rural gay life and its relevance for family providers. *Family Relations: Journal of Applied Family & Child Studies,* **52**(1), 72–81.

Rosario, M., Hunter, J., Maguen, S., Gwadz, M. & Smith, R. (2001). The coming-out process and its adaptational and health-related associations among gay, lesbian, and bisexual youths: Stipulations and exploration of a model. *American Journal of Community Psychology,* **29**, 133–160.

Ritter, K. Y. & Terndrup, A. I. (2002). *Handbook of Affirmative Psychotherapy with Lesbians and Gay Men.* New York: Guilford.

Rust, P. C. (1993). Coming out in the age of social constructionism: Sexual identity formation among lesbians and bisexual women. *Gender & Society,* **7**, 50–77.

Rust, P. C. (2003). Finding a sexual identity and community: Therapeutic implications and cultural assumptions in scientific models of coming out. In L. D. Garnets & D. C. Kimmel (Eds),

Psychological Perspectives on Lesbian, Gay, and Bisexual Experiences (2nd edn) (pp. 227–269). New York, NY: Columbia.

Schuck, K. D. & Liddle, B. J. (2001). Religious conflicts experienced by lesbian, gay, and bisexual individuals. *Journal of Gay & Lesbian Psychotherapy,* **5**(2), 63–82.

Smith, A. (1997). Cultural diversity and the coming-out process: Implications for clinical practice. In B. Greene (Ed.), *Ethnic and Cultural Diversity among Lesbians and Gay Men* (pp. 279–300). Thousand Oaks, CA: Sage.

Troiden, R. R. (1979). Becoming homosexual: A model of gay identity acquisition. *Psychiatry: Journal for the Study of Interpersonal Processes,* **42**, 362–373.

Walters, K. L. (1997). Urban lesbian and gay American Indian identity: Implications for mental health service delivery. In L. B. Brown (Ed.), *Two Spirit People: American Indian lesbian women and gay men* (pp. 43–65). Binghamton, NY: Haworth Press.

CHAPTER 7

A Minority Within a Minority: Experiences of Gay Men with Intellectual Disabilities

Christopher Bennett
Hertfordshire Partnership NHS Trust, UK
and
Adrian Coyle
University of Surrey, UK

INTRODUCTION

People with intellectual disabilities[1] have long been viewed as belonging to a socially devalued minority group and consequently have to manage the stigma attached to such a position. But what of people with intellectual disabilities who also occupy another socially devalued position by having a lesbian, gay or bisexual identity? Such people could be considered to be a minority within a minority. To date, there has been little research exploring how lesbians, gay men and bisexual men and women with intellectual disabilities manage the processes of sexual identity, particularly within the context of care services. This chapter presents a qualitative study which investigated the experiences of 10 men with intellectual disabilities, who identified as gay or who *thought* they might be gay but did not want to self-identify as such at the time of the study.[2] The research was particularly interested in how these men represented and/or developed a gay identity and, where relevant, how they managed any threats to identity that arose from their

---

[1] In the study presented in this chapter, 'intellectual disability' was defined as a full-scale IQ score of 70 or below, existing concurrently with limitations in social and adaptive functioning. This is the most commonly-used definition within the intellectual disability field. Different terms are applied to this condition in different countries (for example, 'learning disability' is most commonly used in the UK). As this book is directed at an international audience, we have decided to employ the most commonly-used international term.

[2] The study reported here did not include women with intellectual disabilities who identified as lesbian as we did not feel that we could do justice to the complexities of gay *and* lesbian identity in this context within a small-scale qualitative study. Some of our findings may apply to lesbian women with an intellectual disability but some may be specific to (the) gay men (whom we studied); there may also be issues specific to lesbian identity that could only be unearthed by a separate study. Also, we cannot apply our findings to bisexual people with intellectual disabilities with any confidence or to transgendered people: further research is required to explore these groups' perspectives and experiences.

Out in Psychology: Lesbian, gay, bisexual, trans and queer perspectives. Edited by Victoria Clarke and Elizabeth Peel.
© 2007 John Wiley & Sons, Ltd.

marginalized social positions. The findings from this study highlight a number of salient issues, both for the men themselves and for the organizations responsible for the care contexts in which they lived. These will be elaborated in the chapter and illustrated with relevant quotations drawn from the data set.

The Historical Perspective

In recent decades, there has been a dramatic change in the way people with intellectual disabilities have been cared for in the UK. Large long-stay hospitals have been closed and people have been resettled into smaller residential care homes within local communities. Along with the change of setting has come a change of beliefs and values about the way people with intellectual disabilities should be enabled to lead their lives. Services for people with intellectual disabilities now operate within a framework of 'normalization' (Wolfensberger, 1972) or 'ordinary living' (King's Fund, 1980). This framework holds that people with intellectual disabilities should be afforded the right to an 'ordinary life' in the community, making use of local community facilities and participating in community activities. This view was further developed by the UK Government White Paper[3] entitled *Valuing People* (Department of Health, 2001), which had as its guiding principle the belief that individuals with intellectual disabilities should be placed at the centre of service planning: 'The Government's objective is to enable people with learning disabilities to have as much choice and control as possible over their lives and the services and support they receive' (p. 4). *Valuing People*, however, was not just concerned with where people with intellectual disabilities live and the type of facilities they use. It was also concerned with fundamental quality-of-life issues, such as life scope and meaning: 'Our objective is to enable people with learning disabilities to lead full and purposeful lives in their communities and develop a range of activities including interests, friendships and relationships' (p. 7).

Implicit in the principles of 'ordinary living' and explicit in *Valuing People* is the belief that individuals with an intellectual disability have the same value, the same needs and the same human rights as any other group in society, including the right to sexual self-expression. But what of the rights and needs of lesbians, gay men and bisexual men and women with intellectual disabilities? Much that has been written on the sexual needs and rights of people with intellectual disabilities has been from a heterocentric perspective (for example, Craft, 1983, 1994), with homosexuality and bisexuality, until very recently, being seen as deviant and/or dangerous forms of sexual expression. Research pertaining to men with intellectual disabilities who have same-sex relationships has tended to focus on the issues of safer sex, HIV prevention and sexual abuse (McCarthy & Thompson, 1994; Murray, MacDonald & Minnes, 1995; Sobsey, 1994). Lesbian, gay and bisexual identity among people with intellectual disabilities has so far been a subject that few researchers – either in the area of intellectual disabilities or in lesbian, gay and bisexual psychology – have been willing or able to address. One possible reason for this relates to the myths that surround the sexuality of people with intellectual disabilities. Thompson, Bryson and De Castell (2001) point out that there are two persistent myths about the sexuality of people with intellectual disabilities, namely that disability implies asexuality and

---

[3] A White Paper is a document issued by a UK government department containing detailed proposals for legislation.

that, if sexuality *is* present, it is heterosexual. As they state, 'persons with disabilities report they are rarely asked about their sexual needs by health care workers, even by those workers with whom they are in daily contact' (p. 57). This can make the recruitment of lesbian, gay or bisexual research participants with intellectual disabilities extremely difficult as the process relies heavily on co-operation from the health care workers and services supporting them. It is also possible that researchers may fear that any attempt to recruit participants for research on lesbian, gay and/or bisexual sexuality may be seen as opening up undesirable possibilities for sexual expression amongst people with intellectual disabilities and increasing their vulnerability.

For men without intellectual disabilities, the process of gay identity formation can have a deleterious effect on self-esteem and psychological well-being (Grossman & Kerner, 1998; Meyer, 1995; Rotheram-Borus, Hunter & Rosario, 1994). Therefore, a case can be made that men with intellectual disabilities are doubly disadvantaged when it comes to gay identity formation. Not only do they have to manage the possible threat to self-esteem and psychological well-being posed by constructing and maintaining a sexual identity that is socially devalued in many contexts, but they also have to manage threats to self-esteem and psychological well-being that arise from their membership of an already devalued group within society. Although a detailed exploration of this theme is beyond the scope of this chapter, it is discussed at some length by Kruse (2007).

Previous Research on Men with Intellectual Disabilities who Identify as Gay

Research on men with intellectual disabilities who have same-sex relationships has tended to focus on the men's vulnerability and the possibility of exploitation (that is, being sexually abused or coerced into sexual activities by more able men). Little research has been conducted on the experiences (positive or negative) of men with intellectual disabilities who are trying to construct and maintain a gay identity; little work has been done that portrays a gay identity, gay relationships and a gay 'lifestyle' for men with intellectual disabilities in a positive or at least a non-pathologizing light. Moreover, several researchers (for example, Dowsett & Davis, 1992; Thompson, 1994) have argued that sexual identity concepts for men with intellectual disabilities are largely irrelevant. This is based on their findings that men with intellectual disabilities who have sex with men refuse, on the whole, to self-identify as gay. A reason cited for this is the men's awareness of the societal stigma and prejudice associated with labels such as 'homosexual' and 'gay'. They are consequently unwilling to take on such negatively valued labels for themselves. However, by adopting such a strategy, men with intellectual disabilities who may wish to self-identify as gay may be denied opportunities to develop a more positive perception of their sexuality.

One study that has investigated the experiences of men with intellectual disabilities who identified as gay and who were exploring their gay identity was carried out by Davidson-Paine and Corbett (1995). They interviewed two young men about their feelings and perceptions related to being gay and their experiences of social acceptance, both generally and within gay social contexts. There appeared to be little support available for these men from family, carers or even from gay contexts. A reason given for this is that, within gay social contexts, a high value is often placed on style, fashion and aesthetics – ideals that few men with intellectual disabilities are able to embody. Therefore, as Thompson (1994) noted, 'it must be recognised that [men with intellectual disabilities] would not be easily absorbed into a gay community' (p. 260). One solution to this difficulty proposed by Thompson, Bryson and De Castell (2001) is to create gay 'community' contexts specifically for people with intellectual disabilities in the form of support groups. Such groups, in their words, 'would allow people to process their experiences, know they are not alone and access information concretely' (p. 63).

Although Davidson-Paine and Corbett (1995) acknowledged that people with intellectual disabilities are more vulnerable and open to exploitation from others, they argue that they can be helped to become more assertive and well informed with regard to their sexuality. They suggested that the process of normalization for gay men with intellectual disabilities needs to include an induction into gay social contexts and networks in the hope that they will then be able to take a more active role in the forming of their own sexual identities. Similar views are shared by Edmunds and Collins (1999) who, based on their work with a 21-year-old gay man with intellectual disabilities, argued that carers and professionals should help gay clients integrate into gay contexts and networks as a way of assisting them in the development of their sexual identity. However, the problem remains that men with intellectual disabilities may be seen by other gay men as having a socially undesirable difference and consequently may experience rejection. Of course, gay men with intellectual disabilities are not alone in their need for supportive gay contexts. Ellis (2007) draws attention to the lack of and need for 'safe' non-sexualized spaces for all lesbians and gay men where they can meet socially and obtain information and support. Perhaps attitudinal change within lesbian and gay social contexts towards an acceptance of diverse differences may set the scene for more inclusive lesbian and gay spaces.

Attitudes of Professionals and Care Staff towards Sexuality

Gay men with intellectual disabilities may not only experience a lack of support from carers in terms of sexual identity development but may also have to contend with care staff's negative attitudes and beliefs about homosexuality.[4] As Craft and Brown (1994) suggest, the attitudes and beliefs of care staff can have a strong influence on the attitudes, feelings and beliefs of their clients: 'Whether staff members like it or not, whether they acknowledge it or not, they are enormously powerful in the lives of people with learning disabilities' (p. 1). In this respect, carers become important role models for their clients. If care staff hold and express anti-gay attitudes and beliefs or overlook (either intentionally or unintentionally) the fact that their clients may be gay, it can feel extremely unsafe for people in their care who are gay or who think they may be gay to discuss this issue with them openly. In such cases, people with intellectual disabilities may be given the message that homosexuality is not something to be spoken about. This can have serious consequences for gay identity development. Furthermore, care staff's negative attitudes towards homosexuality are likely to lead to their clients internalizing these negative attitudes themselves. Findings from a study carried out by McCabe and Schreck (1992) support this contention. They found that 86% of people with intellectual disabilities thought that homosexuality was

---

[4] In this context, 'care staff' refers to people who work in residential care homes and who are paid to provide care to people with intellectual disabilities. 'Day service staff' (a related term that will be used later) refers to people employed within day centres that provide daytime activities and occupations for people with intellectual disabilities.

wrong, compared with 31% who viewed heterosexual intercourse as wrong. This closely mirrors findings from studies examining care staff's attitudes and beliefs. Hingsberger (1993) explored US care staff's attitudes and beliefs about the acceptability of certain sexual activities for people with intellectual disabilities. He found that, whereas 77% of respondents approved of heterosexual 'petting' and 72% approved of heterosexual sexual intercourse, only 26% approved of homosexual behaviour between men with intellectual disabilities. Based on anecdotal evidence, he states that these attitudes were also being mirrored in practice with homosexual behaviour between clients being stopped or even punished. Similar results were found by Jones (1995) who explored the attitudes and beliefs of 150 British care staff and day service staff. She found that barely one-third of her respondents had discussed homosexuality with their clients compared with two-thirds who had talked about heterosexual sex. Of greater concern was the finding that, even when staff knew or suspected that a client might be gay, only 31% stated that they had actually discussed the issue of homosexuality with their clients. Reasons given for this reluctance to discuss homosexuality with clients ranged from a lack of training/experience and lack of support from senior managers to a fear of possible recriminations.

This raises important issues for gay men with intellectual disabilities who are trying to develop and manage a gay identity within the context of care services and who are likely to be dependent on care staff for their day-to-day existence. Disclosing their sexual identity in such circumstances may feel extremely unsafe, especially if to do so is to jeopardize essential relationships. Furthermore, the internalization of negative attitudes can have a deleterious effect on self-esteem and emotional well-being and further complicate the process of constructing and maintaining a gay identity.

GAY MEN WITH INTELLECTUAL DISABILITIES SPEAK OF THEIR EXPERIENCES: THE CURRENT STUDY

The study reported in this chapter aimed to build on the work carried out by Davidson-Paine and Corbett (1995) by exploring in-depth the experiences of men with intellectual disabilities who were exploring/constructing or who had constructed a gay identity. The process of gay identity formation can have detrimental effects on mental health, with the majority of gay men experiencing some form of psychological distress related to their sexuality at some point in their lives (see Coyle, 1993; Robertson, 1998). In extreme cases, this has resulted in suicide and attempted suicide (D'Augelli & Hershberger, 1993; Rotheram-Borus, Hunter & Rosario 1994). Internalized homophobia and minority status can both contribute to the stigma and emotional distress experienced by gay men. This study, therefore, aimed to look at how gay men with intellectual disabilities perceived and interpreted their status as both gay men and men with intellectual disabilities and to consider the effects this may have on their well-being. In addition, it explored the experiences gay men with intellectual disabilities have had of societal and institutional responses to their sexuality and the effects this may have had on their identity and well-being.

Identity process theory (Breakwell, 1986, 1996) was used as a framework within which to consider the identity experiences of gay men with intellectual disabilities and to explore how they manage threats to identity. Although this theory was developed to shed light on situations of identity threat, its ideas about identity structure and about identity processes and principles can be applied to diverse situations of identity change. When faced with a situation of identity threat that is difficult to manage through the operation of identity processes, Breakwell (1986) claims that the individual may turn to three types of coping strategy. Intra-psychic strategies operate at the level of cognitions and emotions (for example, denial); interpersonal strategies focus on action to remove aspects of the social environment which generate threat (for example, isolation from or conflict with anyone who challenges the existing identity); and intergroup strategies involve seeking support from others in a similar situation in order to avoid social isolation and/or to share information relevant to coping. Identity process theory has been used to shed psychological light on identity issues in a range of contexts, including sexual identity (Coyle & Rafalin, 2000; Markowe, 1996). However, in this study, it was used very 'lightly' so as not to violate the phenomenological commitment of the study and of the analytic approach.

METHOD

Approaches were made to a support group for gay men with intellectual disabilities in the London area (the facilitator of which was known to the researchers) and to London-based community learning disability teams within the health service and voluntary agencies. As difficulties in recruitment were anticipated, it was decided to focus recruitment efforts on the London area where there was a wide variety of services for people with intellectual disabilities. When potential participants had been identified, they were sent an information sheet (written in suitable language) outlining the aims of the study and explaining what participation would involve. Individuals were identified within the various recruitment settings who could support potential participants in reading the information and answer any questions they had about the content of the information sheet.

Ten men (mean age 37.3 years; range 27–54 years; standard deviation 9.0) participated in the study. Four men were recruited from the support group for gay men with intellectual disabilities and six from the other contexts. All participants had been deemed to have mild intellectual disabilities. All either self-identified as gay or thought they might be gay but did not want to self-identify as gay at the time of the study. Thus, the study could not satisfactorily explore *whether* sexual identity concepts are relevant to men with intellectual disabilities. Five participants had been in a same-sex relationship in the past; one of these men was in a relationship at the time of the interview. Six of the men lived in a staffed residential care home, two lived within their family home and two lived independently in the community. All but one had at some point in their lives resided in residential or hospital care. Eight participants were in paid employment (either full-time or part-time), one attended college and one had a part-time job and also attended college.

Participants were interviewed face-to-face by the same researcher at a place of their choosing. Interviews were conducted in private (but see the extract from Peter's interview within the analysis) and lasted between one and two hours. The interviews examined a range of issues relevant to the research focus, including participants' experiences of gay identity development, their experiences of gay social contexts and care staff's reactions to their sexuality. To provide an indication of the nature of the questions, the initial question which explored the development of gay identity was 'Can you tell me about when you first thought you were gay?'; this was followed by questions about the age at which this occurred, where the participant was living at the time, whether they knew any other gay men at the time and, if so, what they thought of them, how they felt when they first thought they were gay and what they did (if anything). All interviews were audio-taped and transcribed verbatim.

The transcripts were analysed using interpretative phenomenological analysis (IPA) (Smith, 1996; Smith, Flowers & Osborn, 1997; Smith, Osborn & Jarman, 1999; Smith & Osborn, 2003). This approach has been used to analyse qualitative data on a range of topics in health psychology (for example, Reynolds & Prior, 2003; Senior, Smith, Michie & Marteau, 2002; Smith, Michie, Stephenson & Quarrell, 2002), in clinical and counselling psychology (for example, Golsworthy & Coyle, 2001; Macran, Stiles & Smith, 1999) and in social psychological work on identity in various contexts (for example, Clare, 2003; Turner & Coyle, 2000), including sexual identity (Coyle & Rafalin, 2000). IPA aims to understand lived experience and how research participants make sense of their experiences. It is concerned with the meanings that those experiences hold for research participants. IPA is characterized by both phenomenological and interpretative commitments. Its phenomenological commitment is seen in its aim to explore an individual's personal perception or account of an experience rather than trying to produce an objective record of the experience. At the same time, it is recognized that a researcher cannot access a participant's world directly or completely. Instead, access to that world is regarded as dependent on the researcher's own conceptions, which are used to make sense of the participant's world through a process of interpretative activity.

The first step in the analytic process involved repeated reading of the transcripts, which resulted in notes being made on each transcript regarding key phrases and processes. These notes included summaries of content, connections between different aspects of the transcript and initial interpretations. Within each transcript, these notes were condensed to produce initial themes, with care being taken to ensure that these themes were consistent with and could be illustrated by the data. When this process had been repeated with each transcript, the resulting sets of initial themes were examined to identify recurrent patterns across the transcripts, producing a final set of superordinate themes. The links between these themes and the data set were checked again at this stage. Themes were then ordered in such a way as to produce a logical and coherent research narrative. While the themes and sub-themes arose from the analysis of the data, inevitably some also reflected the content of the interview schedule, with general topics on the interview schedule being elaborated into more specific themes and sub-themes through the analysis. For more detailed accounts of the analytic process in IPA, see Smith et al. (1999) and Smith and Osborn (2003).

In the following sections, extracts from the interviews are used whenever possible to illustrate interpretations.[5] In these quotations, empty brackets indicate where material has been omitted; information appearing in square brackets has been added for purposes of clarification and ellipsis points (. . .) indicate a pause in the flow of the participants' speech.

DEVELOPING A GAY IDENTITY

As the issue of gay identity development has been considered at length elsewhere (for example, see Cass, 1979; Coyle, 1992; McDonald, 1982; Minton & McDonald, 1984;

---

[5] Pseudonyms have been used to protect participants' confidentiality.

Troiden, 1979; Weinberg, 1983), it will not be examined in depth here. In many respects, the accounts given by the men in this study are consistent with previous research on gay identity, which has been conducted with non-intellectually disabled gay men.

In common with many gay men, the majority of participants in the current study acknowledged an awareness of their sexuality from an early age on the basis of attraction and/or behaviour:

> Um, I remember when I was about 12 or 13, um, I was sort of like, I knew I was gay straight away cos I used to, um, have like all these posters from *Smash Hits* [a pop music magazine] and they used to be like men posters and I used to put them up on my wall. I knew straight away that I was gay. (Ray)

> I think, I think [I first realised I was gay when I was] 14. Then I start to kiss a bloke. (Stuart)

Although both Ray and Stuart appear to have developed a strong, almost unequivocal sense of their sexuality from an early age, others, such as John, reported going through a period of uncertainty akin to what Cass (1979) termed 'identity confusion':

> Um, that's when I decided if I wanted to be married and have children. The next day I'm gay. The next day I want to get married and have children [ ] Um, I been confused from about 12 years old. (John)

One area worthy of further discussion – and something that does not always appear in other studies – is the sense that some participants tried to make of the origins of their sexuality. As mentioned earlier, people with learning disabilities, because of their inherent vulnerability and reliance on others for care, can be susceptible to sexual abuse. Several participants thought that the sexual abuse they reported having experienced in their lives was formative in the development of their gay identity. For example, John, having been sexually abused as a child while in residential care, traced his gay identity back to an 'unhappy childhood':

> Um, some people, um, cannot help themselves being gay because of their childhood and all that. Um, they may have had an unhappy childhood like myself.

For others, like Jason and Graham, sexually abusive experiences later in life have for them become linked with the origins of their gay identity:

> Interviewer: How old would you say you were, Jason, when you first found yourself attracted to men?
> Jason: When I got hurt by them. [ ] They abused me so I thought I'd be gay.
>
> Interviewer: Can you tell me about the time when you first thought you might be gay?
> Graham: Well at the time my mates, you know, my mates at that time, my mates pushed me into it. They just gave me a cup of coffee at their place. It was drugged with sleeping tablets. [ ] They were too strong for me, you know, one holding my legs down, one holding my arms down and they just whipped my clothes off.

In these accounts, gay identity has been construed by the participants as being the result of the negative experiences they had had earlier in their lives. In so doing, there is a sense in which they are trying to develop a narrative that explains and makes sense of but does not blame them for their sexuality. It could be argued that the participants are trying to protect themselves from the potential stigma or identity threat associated with being gay.

This could be seen as an example of the intrapsychic coping strategy described by Break-well (1986) as 'reconstrual' or 're-attribution'. By employing this strategy, the individual exonerates themselves from any responsibility for being in the identity-threatening situa-tion, as they attribute their position to external forces beyond their control. However, in this case, by employing such a strategy, gay identity may become negatively evaluated by the individual through its association with experiences of abuse. An alternative explana-tion of the link that participants made between sexual abuse and gay sexuality is that this link could have been suggested to these participants by others, such as care staff; the men might have accepted this suggested link in the absence of other ways of making sense of the origins of their sexuality. However, there are no data that permit one of these inter-pretations to be favoured over the other.

Although not explored as a main theme within the current study, it is worth noting that the majority of participants reported experiences of being sexually exploited or abused by non-intellectually disabled men. Limited problem solving skills (related to level of cogni-tive impairment) often meant that the men did not have the strategies for avoiding or extricating themselves from positions of vulnerability. For others, the importance attached to having a sexual partner meant they tolerated what might be viewed as 'abusive' situa-tions for fear of losing their sexual partner.

STIGMA AND INTELLECTUAL DISABILITY/GAY IDENTITY

One of the principal aims of the current study was to explore whether men who identify as gay and who have an intellectual disability experience a 'double discrimination' on account of occupying two stigmatized positions. The majority of participants in this study reported experiencing a form of prejudice or discrimination related to their intellectual disability at one or more points in their lives. For some participants, this took the form of overt verbal abuse:

> Children took the mickey out of you [ ] Keep calling 'spastic' and that, 'cripple' and that sort of thing. (Jonathan)

> They used to call me 'moron' and 'divvy' and all that. (Mark)

This raises an important issue within identity process theory (Breakwell, 1986, 1996) and one that is particularly pertinent to people with intellectual disabilities. For something to pose a threat to identity, there needs to be awareness that the identity element is relevant to them and also carries a negative social evaluation. Studies in this area (see Davies & Jenkins, 1997; Finlay & Lyons, 1998; Jahoda, Markova & Cattermole, 1988) disagree over the issue of whether people with intellectual disabilities understand the terminology used to refer to them, understand the stigma that has been attached to these labels and conse-quently internalize this stigma. The comments above and elsewhere imply that some men are not only aware of the negative evaluations made by others about intellectual disability but are also aware that these evaluations are being made of them. This in turn can then lead to an awareness of 'difference' from the mainstream and can reinforce the individual's minority status. This is highlighted in the following comments made by John:

> Interviewer: Why do you think they were looking at you?
> John: The way I act.

Interviewer: How were you acting?
John: Um, I think the clothes I was wearing yeah. [ ] Well not clothes but I
             think the way I acted really was different.

In this extract, John was talking about the way he was treated by gay men in a gay club
he frequented – a club to which he had initially been unsuccessful in gaining entry because
of his lack of conformity to what could be termed 'gay social norms' (that is, accepted
ways of dressing and behaving within gay social contexts). This quotation highlights
John's awareness of his difference from those around him.

Awareness of difference is an issue that several other participants commented on and
highlighted through the use of words such as 'normal':

Interviewer: What would be different if you didn't have a learning disability?
Mark: I would be more like normal other men.
Interviewer: Do you perhaps feel that you're not like normal other men?
Mark: No, I feel different.

When I lived here now with my carers I thought to myself that I don't really like
having this learning difficulty. I just wish I was a normal, young human being and not
have all these learning difficulties bothering me all the time. (Ray)

It is widely held (Breakwell, 1986; Mest, 1988) that being aware of stigma alone is not
enough to place an individual in a position of identity threat. Rather, it is the experiences
that people have which mediate threats to their identity. From the above comments, it can
be seen that these men have not only been made aware of others' negative evaluations of
intellectual disabilities; they have also had direct experience of this and, to a certain
degree, have experienced these as threats to identity.

In addition to others' negative evaluations of intellectual disabilities, the majority of
participants in this study expressed an awareness of others' negative evaluations of homosexuality. These were said to have been experienced through the media, especially through
television, but also through first-hand experience. For example, Jason was exposed to
anti-gay prejudice directly from a group of friends who wanted him to join them in assault-
ing gay men:

My friends outside, gay bashers, they said do I want to go gay bashing and I said 'I
don't want to do it'.

The majority of men in the study had experienced some form of anti-gay prejudice or
verbal abuse directly. For some like Jack, anti-gay verbal abuse came from strangers:

Yeah because sometimes I walk down the street and they say 'You're a fucking
queer'.

For others, the experience of prejudice came from closer to home. For Ray, this came from
a close friend who suspected him of being gay after he tried to defend gay men:

And he said to me, 'Well are you gay? Is that why you're trying to stick up for them?
Because if you are, I don't want you in my house.'

The above quotations indicate that gay men with intellectual disabilities are not only aware
of, but are also the victims of, anti-gay prejudice. Moreover, this takes the same form as
prejudice directed towards other gay men and is at all three levels of prejudice described
by Davies (1996) – verbal rejection, discrimination and physical attack.

As would be expected, participants' reactions to this prejudice encompassed feelings of sadness, hurt, fear and anger. Some participants responded by taking direct action. For Peter, this meant informing his employment officer of anti-gay remarks made by his manager. For Ray, strategies for dealing with anti-gay comments included directly confronting others about their prejudice. In the following quotation, Ray is responding to a friend who had just told him that he attacked a gay man after being winked at by him:

> I felt really upset because it's not really for people to make judgement on them. It's sort of for guys who are gay to go out and not for people who are straight beating them up for the hell of it because they think gays give people AIDS because of it. I mean I said to him 'What about women?' And he said, 'Oh women are alright. If one woman gets off with another woman that's OK', he said. I said 'What about men getting off with other men?' And he said, 'That's wrong. Men are supposed to be on this earth to go out with women.' I said, 'Not necessarily – if they want to be like that.'

It would appear then that, from this data set, gay men with intellectual disabilities can indeed be considered a minority within a minority and, as such, are aware of and experience the double discrimination arising from occupying two negatively evaluated identity positions.

SOCIAL ISOLATION/DESIRE FOR AFFILIATION WITH GAY 'COMMUNITY' CONTEXTS

An important factor in the development of lesbian or gay identity cited in several studies (see Garnets & Kimmel, 1993, for a review of these; for a more recent example, see Ellis, 2007) is contact with lesbian and gay social contexts or 'communities'.[6] Indeed, in her study of lesbian identity, Markowe (1996) discovered that a need for affiliation (with other lesbians) was so strong that she designated it a basic identity principle within identity process theory. It is contended that contact with lesbian and gay communities helps to foster a sense of group identity, provides role models and diminishes feelings of isolation and difference. Frable, Wortman and Joseph (1997) found that having strong gay community networks and visibility was correlated with higher levels of self-esteem and lower levels of psychological distress.

All participants in the current study were aware of the existence of gay venues such as pubs and clubs and spoke of wanting to be able to access them. As Graham stated when asked if he ever went to gay venues, 'No, [ ] but I wouldn't mind'. Those who had already accessed some gay community contexts spoke of wanting to be able to access a wider range of venues. However, one issue that arose for many participants was knowing where to find them:

> Interviewer: Would you like to be going to more gay pubs?
> Paul: Yes, can you find out for us, can you find out? [ ] To start with you can help me, help me find out, find out for us where they are and let me know.

---

[6] We have placed the term lesbian and gay 'community'/'communities' within inverted commas here to signal that the 'community' nature of lesbian and gay social groupings and contexts is open to debate.

In response to Paul's direct request for help, the interviewer advised him to discuss this at the support group for gay men with intellectual disabilities that he attended.

Other participants used a variety of methods to try and find out about gay venues for themselves. Mark adopted the strategy of going out and asking passers-by where to find a gay pub:

> Interviewer: How did you find out where the gay pubs were?
> Mark: I just had a look around and asked people.
> Interviewer: Which people did you ask?
> Mark: Just people on the street [laughs]

Mark's laughter perhaps indicates his awareness that such a strategy carries risks, particularly if he had approached the wrong people. Jonathan decided he would telephone directory enquiries to find out about gay venues and, although this proved to be partially successful, he was only told about one pub in central London, which was too far away for him to access alone. Other participants telephoned a lesbian and gay switchboard service and were given details of pubs and, in John's case, information about a group for gay men and lesbians who were 'coming out'. Jason reported having found out about gay venues through reading the gay press. Although this was a successful strategy for Jason, other participants highlighted difficulties with this, such as not being able to buy gay magazines in their local shops, finding the magazines too expensive to buy or not having the reading skills necessary to understand the magazines. Even when participants knew where gay venues were, they often experienced difficulties in accessing them. For some, difficulties arose because the venues were located some distance from where they lived and their intellectual disability impeded their ability to travel independently:

> I, I haven't been to any pubs (. . .) I haven't been anywhere because like it's too far for me, too far from my, too far from where I live. (Paul)

> No, there are some up London but I couldn't travel up there [ ] in case I get lost. (Graham)

Even when participants were able to travel independently to gay venues, they still experienced difficulties accessing the venues alone. Several participants mentioned feeling nervous or fearful of going into a pub alone for the first time, a feeling that many non-intellectually disabled gay men would share. Some, however, were able to overcome their fear:

> It was a bit scary really and I was a bit nervous (. . .) but after a bit I got used to it. (Mark)

But for others, such as Ray, the fear was so great that even after he had arrived at a gay pub, he still could not go in:

> I sort of just had this feeling as soon as I got to the doors. I thought 'Should I go in?' And I just set foot in one door and then there was another door but I just couldn't go through with it. I was just too scared.

For Ray, as with some other participants, this fear appeared to be linked to not knowing what to expect when he entered a gay pub:

> I kept thinking if I go to the West End they'll probably be taking drugs and all that and I got a bit scared about that for going in the first time.

The inability to access a gay venue appeared to have a significant impact on Ray's emotional well-being and on his self-perception at that time:

> It felt a bit like I was lost and all that but I couldn't sort of figure out which way to turn. And I felt sort of like lonely, because I felt stupid as well, because I knew that if I had gone in it would have changed my life and it would have helped me. But I knew I couldn't do it. I just felt sort of um, scared and stupid, really silly.

This highlights the importance placed by almost all participants on being part of a gay social context, whether this is to combat feelings of isolation and loneliness or to meet the type of affiliation need that Markowe (1996) identified amongst lesbian women. What is evident from the above accounts, though, is the support and help needed by many of the men to access gay venues and to feel part of gay 'community' contexts. However, there is a difference between being able to access venues and having a sense of belonging or a feeling of membership.

SENSE OF BELONGING

As discussed above, all participants spoke of their desire to be part of a gay social context or gay community. Yet, as many of the participants experienced, feeling part of a gay community or having a sense of affiliation involved more than just accessing gay venues. Awareness of difference and issues such as other gay men's reactions to them played a big part in how accepted or welcome participants felt. As John experienced, being different and not conforming to others' expectations about gay men initially led to him being excluded from a gay club that he wanted to enter:

> John: Yeah because at first they turn me away and that's the reason why I went
>   back every week and then they knew my face and let me in.
> Interviewer: That's interesting. When you first went they turned you away?
> John: A couple of times yeah.
> Interviewer: How did they turn you away?
> John: [They said] 'Can you move to the side?' [ ] They asked me to leave.
> Interviewer: What did you think about that?
> John: Awful.
> Interviewer: And why do you think they wouldn't let you in, John?
> John: Like before, the way I act (. . .) the way I walk, the way I talk.

John's persistence eventually paid off but he clearly sensed that his initial exclusion was related to being unacceptably different. This experience also had lasting implications for John as it made him wary of trying to access other gay venues:

> John: I think I would like to go to more but I think I'm worried they won't let
>   me in [ ] because of the way I look, the way I act towards people.
> Interviewer: So that stops you from going to other places?
> John: Yeah. But if someone could come with me, then I would be happy.

Such experiences and concerns can only add to the anxiety of entering a new gay venue for the first time. However, even when participants had negotiated entry to gay venues, they reported experiencing a mixed reception from the other gay men there. For some participants, the reception they received was neither welcoming nor hostile and in this respect would probably be no different to the reception given to any gay man without an intellectual disability. For other participants, such as John, the responses received could be described as overtly hostile and threatening:

John: Someone came up to me and said 'Why are you here?' and all that.
Interviewer: Did that feel uncomfortable?
John: Yeah.

In this case, it would seem that John's right to be in the club was being questioned by another gay man. Participants' experiences of neutral or hostile reactions from other gay men are consistent with Davidson-Paine and Corbett's (1995) findings that the gay community offered little support to the men with intellectual disabilities in that study, perhaps because of the particular difficulties that these men have in living up to ideals of style, fashion and physical aesthetics. This sense of not 'measuring up' and of being unacceptably different was highlighted by John in his comments on the way he looks, acts and talks. Peter was also aware of the difficulties he had of fitting in with what he saw as the expectations of gay venues. This appeared to be linked to his uncertainty about how to behave and what to say to other gay men:

I just feel like, um, I'm stuck in some sort of corner somewhere. Yeah, I don't feel I know where to put myself. [ ] I don't feel shy with gay men. No, it's just, er, I don't know how to start a conversation off with people, how to speak to people, other gay men – no.

Peter's reported difficulties may reflect a lack of shared experiences and interests with non-intellectually disabled gay men, making it difficult to find common experiential and conversational ground. Again, the lack of access to gay venues, gay press and the internet means that men with intellectual disabilities are perhaps less well informed about the nature and norms of gay social contexts and about gay-related interests than most other gay men.

Despite the difficulties experienced by some of the participants in feeling accepted and welcomed by other gay men and the concerns raised about fitting in, other participants also spoke of their enjoyment in being part of a gay social context and of the positive experiences they had had. For example:

I was going out every night and I was happy because I was going out every night enjoying myself. [ ] I'm happy, yeah, because if you go to the pub what's gay they're nice to you – 'Hello darling, what would you like?' But if you go to a normal pub, they say 'Half a lager – that will be 52p' because they're not nice to you. When you go to a gay pub, they're more nice to you. (Jack)

Although a number of the participants were regularly going to gay venues, they tended to do so on their own. Very few of the men had a network of gay friends whom they could call on or with whom they could socialize. The opportunities for gay men with intellectual disabilities to meet other gay men and to develop friendships are somewhat limited. There are few established support groups and organizations for gay men with intellectual disabilities (Thompson et al., 2001) and, as highlighted by the participants here, several factors make accessing gay venues difficult.

A lack of meaningful contact with other gay men, especially other gay men with intellectual disabilities, can lead to a sense of frustration and a feeling of isolation, as the following quotations illustrate:

I'm sick and tired of going to a club on my own, all on my own, and I need someone to come with me. (John)

I'm lonely. I'm lonely. (Stuart)

All of the men in the study spoke of wanting to have a wider network of gay friends. Issues such as having more in common with other gay men, being able to talk openly about sex and relationships, obtaining support in accessing gay venues and having a shared understanding of what it is like to be gay were all cited by participants as reasons why they considered it important to have gay friendships. These reasons for wanting to be part of a gay social network overlap with those cited by non-intellectually disabled gay men (and lesbians) in other studies. For example, in her study of 32 lesbians and gay men, Ellis (2007) found that participants talked about wanting a context in which others shared their understandings, values and experiences. Ray summed up his reasons for wanting gay friends in the following way:

Well sort of like being friends with a group of gay men, sort of going like, sort of having, like and we could sort of be the same, you know, like people have the same personality and they sort of like, if you talk about gay stuff they'll understand about it because they're like the same as you and all that. And they would sort of be understanding, what it's like to be gay or homosexual. [ ] It will be really exciting to be friends with other homosexuals and gays. If I went to clubs and all that and I met them and we told each other our roots and all that. [ ] We could sort of go out to places that we've never done before and sort of go to lots of different areas where we could sort of, er, not get started on – where people will accept us for who we are.

What Ray seems to be invoking here is Breakwell's (1986) idea that obtaining group support can be an important intergroup strategy for managing threatened identities. She holds that the formation of a group of people sharing the same type of threat (in this case, being both gay and intellectually disabled) can alleviate isolation and provide social and informational networks.

RESTRICTIONS OF BEING IN CARE

In common with the majority of people with intellectual disabilities, all but one of the participants in this study were either living in residential homes with paid carers or had previous experience of living in a care setting. All of the men who had experience of care settings stated that this had adversely affected the possibility of living as openly gay men. One factor mentioned by almost all participants was the lack of privacy that comes from living in communal housing. For Paul, this meant the constant feeling that others knew his business and that it was impossible to keep things private from either staff or other residents – something that he found frustrating and upsetting:

All the Cedars [name of care home] know. The Cedars knows everything, everyone knows. I tell you the whole of the staff at the Cedars knows everything. [ ] All the other people, the residents know everything about where I go, who I go out with, this and that. It just drives me mad – I don't like it. It's very embarrassing for me, it really is. I wish people would just leave me alone for five minutes and give me space. [ ] It's none of their business at all – it's private.

In addition to the emotional consequences of having little or no privacy, living in a care setting can also affect the individual's ability to develop relationships. Several participants mentioned that they did not or would not feel comfortable taking partners back to where they lived because of the lack of privacy. For example:

Interviewer: Would you be able to bring people back here?
Peter: If I wanted to.
Interviewer: Have you ever done that?
Peter: No.
Interviewer: What's stopped you, do you think?
Peter: (. . .) Nothing's stopped me. I'd just feel uncomfortable doing it I suppose.
Interviewer: What would feel uncomfortable about doing that?
Peter: Um (. . .) [the interview was interrupted at this point by someone coming into the room without knocking] I don't know. It's just not as private as I would like.
Interviewer: That demonstrates it really [referring to the interruption] – was that what you meant?
Peter: Yeah.

The interview with Peter took place within the care home in which he lived and demonstrated that even having the space within his home to talk to someone in private and without interruption was clearly difficult. One can only imagine how much harder it would be to have privacy with a partner, especially for sex. For most people, the only private space they had was their bedrooms. Even if participants wanted to be alone in their bedrooms with a partner, care services often have strict policies about clients having guests (especially overnight guests) in their bedrooms.

As stated earlier, the lack of gay role models and gay support networks means that gay men with learning disabilities are often strongly influenced by their carers' attitudes and beliefs about same-sex relationships. These can be far from conducive to the development of a positively-evaluated gay identity (see Hingsberger, 1993; Jones, 1995). This is demonstrated in the following extract from the interview with Jonathan, who had been reprimanded by care staff for engaging in consensual sexual behaviour in a day centre:

Interviewer: So you got told off for having sex with Derek?
Jonathan: Yeah. But I don't do it any more now.
Interviewer: Why is that?
Jonathan: Don't know, probably got fed up with it.
Interviewer: What made you fed up with it?
Jonathan: Not very clean and nice.
Interviewer: It's not very clean and nice? Who said that?
Jonathan: The staff [ ] Don't do it any more. If you want to come to the centre, you got to be good. I learned my lesson now. [ ] Keep out, keep out of those sort of things.

As can be seen from this extract, reported comments from his carers have led Jonathan to construe his sexual behaviour as something that is 'not very clean and nice' and as something that is not 'good', which he says led him to stop having sexual relationships with other men.

For many of the participants, living in care settings meant having to answer to care staff on a day-to-day basis. There was also the expectation that participants would live by the rules and regulations of the care services. For Jonathan, this affected his ability to access gay venues as there was an expectation that he would be home by a certain time:

> The only problem in here is that the staff like me back before it gets too late. They go to bed about eleven. Some staff go [to bed] about ten they do.

Although other participants were expected to comply with carers' requests and wishes, not all did so. For Jack, this meant defying carers and doing his own thing:

> And then one day I was going out. It was the day they were doing the party. [They said] 'Jack, are you going out on the party? Can you get back here for seven o'clock?' and I went 'OK, seven o'clock. I'll be here for seven.' [ ] I was in the pub, right, and I thought half past five, six o'clock, six fifteen and then I thought I'll go to King's Cross and book into a B and B [bed and breakfast]. [ ] It was not a gay hotel. I did not know no nice discos to go to so I just went dancing here and then the day after I went back to the hospital. They told me off and said, 'You're not allowed to go out for the day' and then when it got to about lunchtime, I went back into London for the day.

As the above extracts demonstrate, living in a care setting can and does affect participants' ability to develop a positively evaluated gay identity. It can also restrict access to gay venues and opportunities for developing both friendships and relationships with other gay men.

CONCLUSIONS

All participants in the current study who acknowledged both their gay identity and their identity as intellectually disabled were able to articulate something of the difficulties they had encountered when trying to hold both identities and function as gay men with intellectual disabilities. In many respects the issues raised by the participants in this study are similar to those raised by non-intellectually disabled gay men, especially in relation to the desire for affiliation. However, unlike most gay men in the general population, the men in this study also had to manage the prejudice and stigma that arise from having an intellectual disability. All participants were aware of the negative societal attitudes directed towards both gay men and people with intellectual disabilities. In common with gay men from ethnic and cultural minority backgrounds, the participants in this study can be seen as a minority within a minority. As such, they are exposed to multiple oppressions and potentially multiple threats to identity. However, further levels of discrimination were highlighted in the current study – discrimination from carers and discrimination in gay contexts. These findings are accord with those of Davidson-Paine and Corbett (1995) and Thompson (1994).

The majority of participants spoke of feeling isolated and cut off from gay social contexts and networks. For some, this reflected a lack of knowledge about the location of gay venues. For others, there was a reluctance to enter gay venues alone as they were unsure what to expect or how to behave. All participants, though, expressed the desire to access gay social contexts and acknowledged the importance of having friendships with other gay men – factors that researchers have consistently linked to higher levels of self-esteem and lower levels of psychological distress in gay men (for example, see Frable et al., 1997; Weinberg & Williams, 1974). However, living in and being dependent on care services that fail to attend to the needs of gay clients mean that gay men with intellectual disabilities can be denied the opportunity and support needed to develop a gay identity within a safe and nurturing environment. So, mindful of this, what can care services and professionals do to support their gay clients (and also their lesbian and bisexual clients, to the extent that the findings from this study might also reflect their experiences)?

Services need to be fully aware of the impact that care staff's attitudes and beliefs about homosexuality can have on clients who are gay or who are exploring a gay identity. Within a context where homosexuality is at best not discussed (as found by Jones, 1995) and at worst pathologized, clients are not going to feel safe raising issues pertaining to their sexuality. This is perhaps an issue best addressed through staff training, where an opportunity can be provided for care staff to explore and acknowledge their beliefs about homosexuality and same-sex relationships. If this process is handled with sufficient sensitivity and skill, it may help to foster a non-judgemental and accepting culture within which (lesbian, gay and bisexual) sexuality can be openly discussed. This may also go some way to mitigate the negative societal attitudes that gay clients may encounter. Such a culture may also enable gay-identified care staff to be more open about their own sexuality and, in so doing, provide much needed role models for gay clients.

Gay-identified staff should also be given the full backing of their services (following appropriate discussions and risk assessments) to support gay clients, whenever possible, in accessing gay social contexts. In services where there are no (openly) gay care workers, gay advocates or befrienders could be recruited to work with gay clients. If this is not possible, clients could be supported in accessing local support groups for people wishing to explore a gay identity. In certain situations, it may be appropriate for informed and accepting heterosexual care staff to accompany gay clients to gay venues.

This study highlights a number of implications for clinical and counselling psychologists (and other psychotherapeutic professionals) working with gay men with intellectual disabilities. As discussed, the process of gay identity development, especially for those already occupying a stigmatized position, can be extremely stressful and may give rise to a range of psychological difficulties. Therefore, within the context of psychological therapy, the issue of gay identity formation and the mechanisms employed for managing/avoiding identity threat may need to be explored and addressed (Kruse, 2007). However, as in psychotherapeutic work with non-intellectually disabled gay men (Milton & Coyle, 1998), it is also important for psychologists not to assume that sexual identity is at the root of psychological distress amongst their gay intellectually disabled clients.

Clinical and counselling psychologists might also take a lead role in the setting up and facilitation of training programmes for care staff around attitudes to and beliefs about homosexuality and other related matters. Through training programmes, psychologists can model and encourage a non-judgemental and de-stigmatizing approach to gay clients. Given the lack of resources for gay men with intellectual disabilities, psychologists could, perhaps in conjunction with gay voluntary organizations, take the lead in setting up and facilitating support groups aimed specifically at men with intellectual disabilities who identify as gay or who are exploring a gay identity. This would provide much needed informational and social networks and help to alleviate feelings of isolation.

In addition, the early experiences of sexual exploitation/abuse reported by several men and the fact that the majority of participants reported experiences of sexual exploitation or abuse at some time in their lives reveal that the sexual abuse focus of some previous research is legitimate (but not as an *exclusive* focus). These findings emphasize a need for psychologists and care services to ensure that gay men with intellectual disabilities are equipped to negotiate sexual situations in ways that minimize the possibility of exploitation. Such interventions need to be properly informed and non-pathologizing.

Finally, this study highlighted issues for gay communities in general. There is a responsibility on the part of these communities to face up to their possible non-acceptance of intellectually disabled men in order to ensure that truly safe and inclusive spaces are created in which gay men with intellectual disabilities and all individuals who are exploring sexual identity issues are supported, regardless of the extent to which they conform to gay social 'norms' concerning looks, fashion or articulacy. It is only when the problematic issues highlighted in this study have been addressed that the objectives set out in government legislation for people with intellectual disabilities can be achieved for *all* people with intellectual disabilities regardless of their sexuality.

REFERENCES

Breakwell, G. M. (1986). *Coping with Threatened Identities.* London: Methuen.

Breakwell, G. M. (1996). Identity processes and social changes. In G. M. Breakwell & E. Lyons (Eds), *Changing European Identities: Social psychological analyses of social change* (pp. 13–27). Oxford: Butterworth Heinemann.

Cass, V. C. (1979). Homosexual identity formation: A theoretical model. *Journal of Homosexuality,* **4**(3), 219–235.

Clare, L. (2003). Managing threats to self: Awareness in early stage Alzheimer's disease. *Social Science & Medicine,* **57**, 1017–1029.

Coyle, A. (1992). 'My own special creation'? The construction of gay identity. In G. M. Breakwell (Ed.), *Social Psychology of Identity and the Self Concept* (pp.187–220). London: Surrey University Press/Academic Press.

Coyle, A. (1993). A study of psychological well-being among gay men using the GHQ-30. *British Journal of Clinical Psychology,* **32**, 218–220.

Coyle, A. & Rafalin, D. (2000). Jewish gay men's accounts of negotiating cultural, religious, and sexual identity: A qualitative study. *Journal of Psychology & Human Sexuality,* **12**(4), 21–48

Craft, A. (Ed.) (1983). *Sex Education and Counselling for Mentally Handicapped People.* London: Costello.

Craft, A. (Ed.) (1994). *Practice Issues in Sexuality and Learning Disabilities.* London: Routledge.

Craft, A. & Brown, H. (1994). Personal relationships and sexuality: The staff role. In A. Craft (Ed.), *Practice Issues in Sexuality and Learning Disabilities* (pp. 1–22). London: Routledge.

D'Augelli, A. R. & Hershberger, S. L. (1993). Lesbian, gay, and bisexual youth in community settings: Personal challenges and mental health problems. *American Journal of Community Psychology,* **21**, 421–448.

Davidson-Paine C. & Corbett, J. (1995). A double coming out: Gay men with learning disabilities. *British Journal of Learning Disabilities,* **23**, 147–151.

Davies, D. (1996). Homophobia and heterosexism. In D. Davies & C. Neal (Eds), *Pink Therapy: A guide for counsellors and therapists working with lesbian, gay and bisexual clients* (pp. 41–65). Buckingham: Open University Press.

Davies, D. A. & Jenkins, R. (1997). 'She has different fits to me': How people with learning difficulties see themselves. *Disability and Society,* **12**, 95–109.

Department of Health (2001). *Valuing People: A new strategy for learning disability for the 21ˢᵗ Century.* London: HMSO.

Dowsett, G. W. & Davis, M. P. (1992). *Transgressions and Intervention: Homosexually active men and beats.* Sydney: National Centre for HIV Social Research.

Edmunds, C. & Collins, A. (1999). Using social and educational approaches to enable a man with learning disabilities to develop his sexual identity and orientation. *British Journal of Learning Disabilities,* **27**(4), 127–131.

Ellis, S. J. (2007). Community in the 21ˢᵗ century: Issues arising from a study of British lesbians and gay men. *Journal of Gay & Lesbian Psychotherapy,* **11**(1–2).

Finlay, W. M. L. & Lyons, E. (1998). Social identity and people with learning difficulties: Implications for self advocacy groups. *Disability and Society,* **13**(1), 37–51.

Frable, D. E. S., Wortman, C. & Joseph, J. (1997). Predicting self esteem, well-being, and distress in a cohort of gay men: The importance of cultural stigma, personal visibility, community networks, and positive identity. *Journal of Personality,* **65**, 599–624.

Garnets L. & Kimmel, D. (1993). Lesbian and gay male dimensions in the psychological study of human diversity. In L. Garnets & D. Kimmell (Eds), *Psychological Perspectives on Lesbian and Gay Male Experience* (pp. 1–51). New York, NY: Columbia University Press.

Golsworthy, R. & Coyle, A. (2001). Practitioners' accounts of religious and spiritual dimensions in bereavement therapy. *Counselling Psychology Quarterly,* **14**, 183–202.

Grossman, A. H. & Kerner, M. S. (1998). Self esteem and supportiveness as predictors of emotional distress in gay male and lesbian youth. *Journal of Homosexuality,* **35**(2), 25–39.

Hingsberger, D. (1993). Staff attitudes, homosexuality and developmental disability: A minority within a minority. *Canadian Journal of Human Sexuality,* **2**(1), 19–22.

Jahoda, A., Markova, I. & Cattermole, C. (1988). Stigma and the self concept of people with a mild mental handicap. *Journal of Mental Deficiency Research,* **32**, 103–115.

Jones, V. (1995). *Heterosexism and homosexual oppression in the provision of services to support the sexuality of people who have a learning difficulty.* Unpublished thesis: King Alfred's College, Winchester.

King's Fund. (1980). *An Ordinary Life: Comprehensive locally based residential services for mentally handicapped people.* London: King's Fund.

Kruse, S. (2007). Gay men with learning disabilities: UK service provision. *Journal of Gay & Lesbian Psychotherapy,* **11**(1–2).

Macran, S., Stiles, W. B. & Smith, J. A. (1999). How does personal therapy affect therapists' practice? *Journal of Counseling Psychology,* **46**, 419–431.

Markowe, L. A. (1996). *Redefining the Self: Coming out as lesbian.* Cambridge: Polity Press.

McCabe, M. & Schreck, A. (1992). Before sex education: An evaluation of the sexual knowledge, experience, feelings and needs of people with mild intellectual disabilities. *Australia and New Zealand Journal of Developmental Disabilities,* **16**, 75–82.

McCarthy, M. & Thompson, D. (1994). HIV/AIDS and safer sex work with people with learning disabilities. In A. Craft. (Ed.), *Practice Issues in Sexuality and Learning Disabilities* (pp. 186–201). London: Routledge.

McDonald, G. J. (1982). Individual differences in the coming out process of gay men: Implications and theoretical models. *Journal of Homosexuality,* **8**(1), 47–60.

Mest, G. (1988). With a little help from their friends. *Journal of Social Issues,* **44**, 117–126.

Meyer, I. H. (1995). Minority stress and mental health in gay men. *Journal of Health and Social Behavior,* **36**, 38–56.

Milton, M. & Coyle, A. (1998). Psychotherapy with lesbian and gay clients. *The Psychologist,* **11**, 73–76.

Minton, H. & McDonald, G. (1984). Homosexual identity formation as a development process. *Journal of Homosexuality,* **9**(2–3), 91–104.

Murray, J. L., MacDonald, R. A. R. & Minnes, P. (1995). Staff attitudes towards individuals with learning disabilities and AIDS: The role of attitudes towards client sexuality and the issue of mandatory testing for HIV infection. *Mental Handicap Research,* **8**, 321–332.

Reynolds, F. & Prior, S. (2003). 'Sticking jewels in your life': Exploring women's strategies for negotiating an acceptable quality of life with multiple sclerosis. *Qualitative Health Research,* **13**, 1225–1251.

Robertson, A. E. (1998). The mental health experiences of gay men: A research study exploring gay men's health needs. *Journal of Psychiatric and Mental Health Nursing, 5*, 33–40.

Rotheram-Borus, M. J., Hunter, J. & Rosario, M. (1994). Suicidal behavior and gay related stress among gay and bisexual male adolescents. *Journal of Adolescent Research, 9*, 498–508.

Senior, V., Smith, J. A., Michie, S. & Marteau, T. (2002). Making sense of risk: An interpretative phenomenological analysis of vulnerability to heart disease. *Journal of Health Psychology, 7*, 157–168.

Smith, J. A. (1996). Beyond the divide between cognition and discourse: Using interpretative phenomenological analysis in health psychology. *Psychology and Health, 11*, 261–271.

Smith, J. A., Flowers, P. & Osborn, M. (1997). Interpretative phenomenological analysis and the psychology of health and illness. In L. Yardley (Ed.), *Material Discourses of Health and Illness* (pp. 68–91). London: Routledge.

Smith, J. A., Michie, S., Stephenson, M. & Quarrell, O. (2002). Risk perception and decision-making processes in candidates for genetic testing for Huntington's Disease: An interpretative phenomenological analysis. *Journal of Health Psychology, 7*, 131–144.

Smith, J. A. & Osborn, M. (2003). Interpretative phenomenological analysis. In J. A. Smith (Ed.), *Qualitative Psychology: A practical guide to research methods* (pp. 51–80). London: Sage.

Smith, J. A., Osborn, M. & Jarman, M. (1999). Doing interpretative phenomenological analysis. In M. Murray & K Chamberlain (Eds), *Qualitative Health Psychology: Theories and methods* (pp. 218–240). London: Sage.

Sobsey, D. (1994). Sexual abuse of individuals with intellectual disability. In A. Craft (Ed.), *Practice Issues in Sexuality and Learning Disabilities* (pp. 93–115). London: Routledge.

Thompson, D. (1994). Sexual experience and sexual identity for men with learning disabilities who have sex with men. *Changes: An International Journal of Psychology & Psychotherapy, 12*, 254–263.

Thompson, S. A., Bryson, B. & De Castell, S. (2001). Prospects for identity formation for lesbian, gay, or bisexual persons with developmental disabilties. *International Journal of Disability, Development and Education, 48*, 53–65.

Troiden, R. R. (1979). Becoming a homosexual: A model of gay identity acquisition. *Psychiatry, 42*, 362–373.

Turner, A. J. & Coyle, A. (2000). What does it mean to be a donor offspring? The identity experiences of adults conceived by donor insemination and the implications for counselling and therapy. *Human Reproduction, 15*, 2041–2051.

Weinberg, M. S. & Williams, C. J. (1974). *Male Homosexuals: Their problems and adaptations.* New York, NY: Oxford University Press.

Weinberg, T. S. (1983). *Gay Men, Gay Selves: The social construction of homosexual identities.* New York, NY: Irvington.

Wolfensberger, W. (1972). *The Principle of Normalization in Human Services.* Toronto, ON: Toronto National Institute on Mental Retardation.

CHAPTER 8

Closet Talk: The Contemporary Relevance of the Closet in Lesbian and Gay Interaction

Victoria Land
University of Surrey, UK
and
Celia Kitzinger
University of York, UK

```
[Land:YU24] Making Babies the Gay Way

01   Chl:   .hhh uhm Now an' another thing is did you see that

02          #uh# (0.2) programme Making Babies the Ga:y #Wa:y.#

03   Mum:   O:h Go:d.=I didn't see it.

//

56   Mum:   ... But Oh:: all round the to:wn

57   Chl:   (Yeah/Mm)

58   Mum:   Everybody was talking about it.

59   Chl:   (Yeah/Mm)

60   Mum:   So I had to decide which ones to come out

61          t[o:]
```

Making Babies the Gay Way was a two-part documentary shown (to high viewing figures) on British national television in January 2004 and described by one reviewer as 'tawdry tiresome tabloid crap which reinforced stereotypes [. . .] cheap and nasty stuff of which Channel 4 should be ashamed' (Mclean, 2004). In the fragment of conversation reproduced above, Chloe (a 20-something lesbian) is in conversation with her (heterosexual) mother, and she launches the topic of the programme (lines 1–2) in order – as we will see

---

Out in Psychology: Lesbian, gay, bisexual, trans and queer perspectives. Edited by Victoria Clarke and Elizabeth Peel.
© 2007 John Wiley & Sons, Ltd.

later (see p. 157) – to complain about its 'bad representation' of lesbians and gay men. For her Mum (who, as it happens, did not see the programme) the import of the programme is different: she reports that, because it was widely discussed, she found herself having to make decisions about whether, and to whom, to 'come out' (lines 56–61). Mum uses the phrase 'come out' (in line 60 and twice more during the course of this conversation) to mean letting people know that she has a lesbian daughter. For Mum – as we will see – this becomes relevant for her when other people, in the course of her interactions with them, make negative or judgemental statements about gay people – something which apparently happened repeatedly after the airing of this programme. As she says 'Nobody seems to think that gay people have pa:rents' (lines 148–9).

Coming out (and passing) are recurrent events in lesbian and gay people's lives – and, sometimes, in the lives of their families and friends who have 'courtesy stigmas' (Goffman, 1963) by virtue of their association with lesbian and gay people:

> Family members are likely to become aware that, even as heterosexuals, they are vulnerable to the homophobia and anti-gay sentiments that permeate the society . . . Marginalization may cause the family member, like the gay or lesbian person, to wrestle with the issue of passing as normal versus coming out (Crosbie-Burnett et al., 1996, p. 399).

The significance of coming out, both for lesbian and gay people and for our families, is reflected in the extensive self-help literature (Borhek, 1983; Eichberg, 1990; Owens, 1998; Signorile, 1996) and in research generated both by human rights campaigns (e.g. Amnesty International 1999, 2001) and by psychological research (Cass, 1979; Fields, 2001; Herek, Cogan, Gillis & Glunt, 1998; Markowe, 2002; Meyer, 2003; Morris, Waldo & Rothman 2001). Much of it focuses on the serious detrimental consequences of coming out for lesbian and gay people internationally. For instance, in many countries, lesbian, gay, bisexual and transgender (LGBT) people continue to be executed, imprisoned, tortured, raped and forced to undergo so-called medical or psychiatric 'treatment' in state institutions because of their sexual identities (Amnesty International, 1999, 2001). Historically, in the west, coming out of the closet has meant psychiatric labels and attempts at cures or criminal proceedings (Kitzinger & Coyle, 2002). In the UK, treatments for homosexuality were provided by National Health Service (NHS) hospitals in the 1960s and 1970s (Smith, Bartlett & King, 2004). Although these official interventions no longer routinely take place, organizations such as Exodus International (see www.exodus-international.org) that condemn homosexuality and purport to convert lesbian and gay people to heterosexual lifestyles continue to thrive globally. Lesbian and gay people are routinely denied rights, such as access to marriage, that are enshrined in law for heterosexual people (Kitzinger & Wilkinson, 2004; Wilkinson & Kitzinger, 2005). Indeed, despite the lip-service paid to greater 'tolerance' and acceptance of diversity (e.g. Seidman et al., 1999), derogatory comments, jokes and gossip about non-heterosexual sexual identity persist (Markowe, 2002) and the effects of heteronormativity (Kitzinger, 2005a) and heterosexism (Peel, 2001) continue.

Leaving aside the external consequences of coming out (or not), research has recognized and explored the psychological cost associated with a stigmatized social identity (Meyer, 2003) including the daily hassles and stressors associated with managing identity concealment and disclosure. On the one hand, '[h]iding takes its toll!' (Powers & Ellis, 1996, p. 2): '[c]loseted gays pay a psychological price for passing' (Cruikshank, 1992,

p. 3) and 'being exposed' as homosexual against our will (Lewis et al., 2001) is an ever-present risk, requiring constant vigilance so that there is a cost of hiding one's stigma in terms of the resultant cognitive burden involved in the constant preoccupation with hiding (Smart & Wegner, 2000). On the other hand, coming out is also stressful: even when it does not result in violence or hostility from others, it frequently requires accounts, explanations and topicalization of homosexuality such that the otherwise ongoing business of the interaction is derailed (Land & Kitzinger, 2005).

Recent research has commented on 'the declining significance of the closet' (Seidman, Meeks & Traschen 1999, p. 440) in contemporary lesbian and gay lives, pointing to the increasing 'normalization' and 'routinization' of homosexuality, and suggesting that many lesbian and gay people today live 'beyond the closet' (Seidman et al., 1999). The research reported in this chapter explores the significance of the closet in the lives of lesbian and gay people today through the analysis of naturalistic data in which lesbian and gay people (and their friends and family) talk about coming out and passing as an ordinary issue in the course of their everyday lives. We show the continuing significance of the closet in the lives of 'out' lesbian and gay people, and how it extends in time and significance beyond the actual occasion of coming out or concealing one's lesbian and gay identity. In talk about coming out and concealment, identity management issues affect not only the people who were participants in the original coming out (or closet) episodes, but also those to whom they recount these experiences and with whom they negotiate their mean-ings and implications. These interactions in which coming out experiences are reported and discussed can – and often do – involve a whole new set of stressors and hassles in lesbian and gay lives. In the first section of this chapter, we show three interactional epi-sodes in which participants' talk about the closet and coming out, and we focus especially on the interactional hassles generated in this talk. In the second section, we draw on these same three episodes to consider what kind of world lesbian and gay people and their allies take for granted – and reproduce – in talk about the closet. This chapter contributes then, both to research about coming out and the closet and to our understanding of the role of the closet in the stressors and hassles of lesbian and gay lives.

DATA AND METHOD OF ANALYSIS

The data used in this chapter are drawn from a collection of naturalistic recorded telephone conversations involving lesbians and gay men. We use conversation analysis to understand the moment-by-moment construction of these conversational interactions (see also Speer, Chapter 16 and Hegarty, Chapter 3) and we use our analysis of these data to reflect on the role of 'the closet' in contemporary lesbian and gay lives, and to explore what kind of world talk about 'the closet' takes for granted.

The Land data corpus (collected by the first author as part of her doctoral research under the supervision of the second author) consists of over 150 telephone conversations, ranging in length from about 10 seconds to over 40 minutes, comprising the incoming and outgoing calls from five lesbian households in England.[1] Participants were recruited

---

[1] The intention had been to collect conversations from people who identified as anything other than heterosexual; however, it turned out that only lesbians volunteered to record their calls for this research. The corpus does include conversations between our lesbian volunteers and gay male co-conversationalists (see Fragment 1) as well as heterosexual co-conversa-tionalists and many whose sexuality never becomes apparent over the course of the calls.

through advertisements placed in lesbian, gay, bisexual and transgender (LGBT) publications and meeting places. Each of the five volunteers completed an informed consent form for herself and undertook to obtain informed consent from everyone she recorded. The recording equipment was set up and operated by the volunteers who were free to choose which of their conversations to record and also which, if any, to delete before mailing the tapes to the first author. All identifying names (of people and places), and other personal details have been changed. The resulting corpus includes conversations between these five volunteers (and, in three cases, their co-resident partners) and their friends, family members, and institutional contacts.[2] The calls have been transcribed (using the method developed by Gail Jefferson[3]) so as to preserve many of the features of their delivery (see Appendix on p. 168 for the transcription key).

Our analysis in this chapter is based on extracts from just three conversations in which issues relevant to 'the closet' come to the fore. These episodes were selected because they are explicit and extensive examples of closet-talk. We are not claiming that they are necessarily 'typical' or 'representative' instances of talk about coming out in general – indeed, our own experience as lesbians is that talk about coming out is very variable, and some of this variety is captured here. The conversations are between a lesbian and a gay man who are friends (Fragment 1, p. 153), between a heterosexual mother and her lesbian daughter (Fragment 2, p. 158) and between the two partners of a lesbian couple (Fragment 3, p. 162). Two of the conversations deal with past episodes in which a speaker did not come out – one told as a funny story (Fragment 1), the other is reported as having been stressful and difficult (Fragment 2) – while the third conversation is concerned with a possible future risk of being outed (Fragment 3). The episodes discussed involve not coming out to the parents of a lover (Fragment 1), a hairdresser (Fragment 2) and the members of the Youth Hostel Association (Fragment 3). In these three episodes, the speaker engaged in closet-talk is designing his/her talk for just this recipient (a friend, a daughter, a partner) on just this occasion, in just this context – each is, in that sense, representative only of itself: the very same story will be told differently in different contexts to different people.

As conversation analysts, our concern with representativeness takes a rather different form from the statistical version commonly deployed in psychology: what is crucial for us is the fact that these episodes of closet talk actually happened, unsolicited by a researcher, in spontaneous interaction. The overwhelming majority of social science research bases claims about the declining relevance of the concept of the closet (and other aspects of LGBT lives) on *interviews* with lesbians and gay men about (for example) when, where, why, how and to whom they reveal or conceal their gay identities. However many hundred such interviews are collected and reported, from however carefully randomized or stratified a sample, they are representative only of what lesbians and gay men say in interviews, when asked questions by a researcher. They are not, and cannot be, representative of how lesbians and gay men talk about revealing or concealing their gay identities when this arises in ordinary conversation not elicited by researchers. They can tell us nothing (except at second hand) about how talk about coming out and being closeted is

---

[2] Calls in the Land data corpus are tagged with mnemonics identifying from which of the five households each is taken. Calls collected by Karen are tagged NE; Nicola, OC; Rebecca (and her partner Julie), SW; Chloe (and her partner Katy), YU; and Sylvia (and her partner, Janice), SC. Calls from each household were numbered consecutively – so, for example, SW21 refers to the twenty-first call on the tapes returned by Rebecca.

[3] For further information about a CA approach to transcription see Jefferson (2004).

imbricated into everyday interactions. The data presented here, by contrast, consist of just such everyday interactions. They are not second-hand reports of closet-talk but the thing itself, 'live', happening outside of a research interview. For what we wanted to study (how closet-talk is done in the course of people's everyday lives), these are the ideal data. Of course it is possible that the 18 hours (approximately) of recordings of lesbian and gay conversation that constitutes the Land corpus is wildly atypical of the billions of hours of conversation that lesbians and gay men in UK engage in every day. But at least those 18 hours of lesbian and gay conversation actually happened – we didn't invent it, or reconstruct it, or ask research respondents to report to us what kind of conversations they have. Whereas talk in research interviews is not representative of *any* naturally occurring interactions, we at least have three such interactions – to our knowledge, the first ever captured on tape – and we present and analyse them in detail here.

Conversation analysis (CA) is a theoretically and methodologically distinctive approach to the study of social life and was developed in the late 1960s and early 1970s by Harvey Sacks, in collaboration with Emanuel Schegloff and Gail Jefferson, from intellectual roots in the sociological tradition of ethnomethodology (Sacks, Schegloff & Jefferson, 1974 – see also Speer, Chapter 16). CA is defined by a cumulative body of empirical research that describes the basic characteristics of talk-in-interaction. It develops technical specifications of the recurrent patterns, structures and practices that constitute key interactional phenomena, including: sequence organization and preference structure (e.g. Schegloff, 2007); turn-taking and turn-design (e.g. Sacks et al., 1974); repair and error correction (e.g. Schegloff, Jefferson & Sacks, 1977); storytelling (e.g. Sacks, 1972); word selection, person reference and membership categorization (e.g. Sacks & Schegloff, 1979); and the overall structural organization of interaction (e.g. Jefferson, 1980). Analysis begins with transcription of the recorded data, preserving fine-grained details such as in-breaths, sound stretches and (timed) pauses – all of which, research has shown, are oriented to by the participants in the conversation. If, as analysts, we want to understand how people do things in and through talk, then we need to attend to their talk at the same level of detail as they do. Feminist and other politically-engaged researchers are increasingly turning to CA to understanding how sexist, heterosexist, racist, etc. presumptions are threaded through the ordinary practices of talk and interaction that, cumulatively, reflect and constitute an oppressive social order (Kitzinger, 2000, 2005a; Kitzinger & Peel, 2005; Land & Kitzinger, 2005; Wilkinson & Kitzinger, 2007). Conversation analysis offers a powerful and rigorous method for exposing the mundane oppressions of everyday life.

Let us turn now to the data from which the three episodes to be analysed here are drawn. The speakers in the Land corpus (not surprisingly, perhaps, given that they were willing to participate in this research) may be considered to be living lives 'beyond the closet'. For example, the research participants include: Chloe (see Fragment 2) and Sylvia who talk about lesbian issues with their mothers; Paul (in the conversation from which Fragment 1 is taken) who mentions having invited his partner to his parental home for Christmas; and Karen who talks to and about her many LGBT friends, regularly attends 'gay nights' at local clubs (e.g. NE4) and is 'out' at university where she is the mature student representative on the LGBT committee. Participants also sometimes make their sexual identity available to strangers in institutional contexts (to dentist receptionists, medical advice helplines, car insurance salespeople) (Land & Kitzinger, 2005). This is clearly very different from the furtive, secretive, closeted worlds described in earlier research (Goffman, 1963; Ponse, 1978), and the lesbian identities mobilized in these interactions depart radically from the lesbian identities researched by the second author during the 1980s, which included a woman who treated her lesbianism as 'a cross to bear' and another who saw lesbianism as 'a slightly retarded state' (Kitzinger, 1987, p. 119). As we will see, however, concerns about when and how to reveal a lesbian or gay identity and interactional stress and hassles related to those concerns remain live issues for even these 'out' lesbian and gay participants. In their closet-talk, these speakers reflect a taken-for-granted heterosexist world.

We begin with a summary of each of the three extracts to be analysed in this chapter:

1. In Fragment 1, 'Meeting the parents', Paul[4] (a gay man) is telling his friend Chloe (a lesbian) about his new partner, Ashraf, and Chloe asks where Ashraf's parents live. This provides space for Paul to launch his telling about meeting Ashraf's parents. Ashraf is not out to his father and he and Paul had decided that Paul should pass as Ashraf's heterosexual friend. Chloe is an active and supportive recipient throughout most of the telling.
2. Fragment 2, 'Making babies the gay way', also features Chloe – this time in conversation with her mother. Mum tells Chloe about occasions where talk about a recent television programme, *Making Babies the Gay Way*, made relevant decisions about whether or not to come out as the mother of a lesbian daughter. She refers to one occasion where she *did* come out; one where it was not necessary because the other person already knew; and one where she did *not* come out. We will focus on the last of these in which Mum did not come out as the mother of a lesbian when her hairdresser attempted to dissuade her from a particular hairstyle on the grounds of its apparent similarity to those of the lesbians who appeared on the previous evening's television programme. Chloe responds to Mum's telling by engaging with the issue of whether the people featured in the television programme had 'stereotypical hair'.
3. In Fragment 3, 'The Feathers', Lucy mentions to her partner, Karen, that Ben (a mutual friend) has passed on Karen's warning that it's 'YHA night down at the Feathers' (a gay pub that both Lucy and Karen go to). It turns out that Lucy and Karen have been Youth Hostel Association (YHA) members in the past but they were apparently not out as lesbians in that context. The warning is prompted by Karen's concern that Lucy might find her lesbianism inadvertently exposed to the YHA members should she decide to go to the Feathers that night.

These conversations clearly display the continuing significance of the closet in the lives of these speakers. They are 'closeted' to a partner's father (1), to a hairdresser (2), and to the YHA members (3), and in the conversations analysed here they negotiate (in each case with a lesbian or gay person) the relevance of that closeting. As we will see, these negotiations, in turn, involve a new set of hassles in the interactions currently underway – the challenges and disagreements of a co-conversationalist. We are analysing here then, not the problems that arose in the original context of coming out (or not) – although undoubtedly there were hassles and stressors there too – but in the secondary context of talk *about* these coming out episodes. Our research shows, for these people on these three occasions, the closet is still relevant and exerts a negative influence in interactions *between lesbian*

---

[4] Although all of the participants recording their calls were lesbian, people of other gender and sexuality groups (e.g. Paul) are included in these data as co-conversationalists of the participants.

and gay people and between them and their LGBT-positive family members. Finally, we consider what kind of world is taken for granted in these conversations. We hope that this research also demonstrates the value of conversation analysis and naturalistic data for lesbian and gay research.

INTERACTIONAL HASSLES IN CLOSET TALK

Meeting the Parents

In 'Meeting the Parents' (Fragment 1), Paul is telling his friend Chloe about an instance in which the concealment of his sexuality has been pre-planned and his telling focuses on how successfully the plan was implemented. Paul's utterance 'it was really funny' (lines 9–10) frames his telling and indicates how Chloe should understand it and respond to it (as humorous). He details the extensive preparations that were necessary before he met Ashraf's father for the first time in order to maintain the closet: the couple agreed to tell Ashraf's father that Paul was a friend rather than his partner (lines 25–26); they fabricated plans for the evening (lines 31–35); they worked out how Paul's presence could be justified (i.e. they pretended that Paul was a student on the same course as Ashraf, lines 39–42); and they devised a plan to respond to any questions that Ashraf's father might ask (lines 44–46). Chloe does not challenge any of this: she simply receipts it (lines 27, 36, and 43), thereby showing her understanding and acceptance of the necessity for Paul and Ashraf to conceal their relationship from Ashraf's father.

```
Fragment 1

[Land:YU9]  Meeting the parents

01  Chl:    Where does his (.) parents live.

02          (.)

03  Pau:    Northwood. °North London°

04  Chl:    Right=

05  Pau:    =I got to meet them on- last Saturday 'cause I

06          I drove 'im to the air[port >on Sunday morning<]

07  Chl:                          [ But    I    thought    ]

08          he wasn't- (.) [ his  dad  didn't  know ]

09  Pau:                   [Well that's the thing I-] huh it

10          was really funny 'cause .hhhh he like said to me

11          "well d'you-" 'cause I said "well I'll drive you to

12          the airport" I said "what I'll do is pick you up

13          Saturday evening uhm [and ] and the:n c- you can
```

```
14  Chl:                    [Yeah]

15  Pau:  stay at mine 'cause it was- and then we'll get up at

16        half four to drive you to the air[port] in the

17  Chl:                                    [Mm. ]

18  Pau:  morning" .hhhh uhm so he was like "okay" an' he

19        was like .hhh an' I said "y'know obviously I can

20        just wait for you outside an' an' he said "no my

21        mum wants you to come m- m- wants to meet you

22        anyway so we could like" an' I said "well this is

23        a way of n- not making it formal uh[m:  ]

24  Chl:                                      [Yeah]

25  Pau:  "Got to pick you up anyway and obviously we can

26        just say to your dad I'm a friend of yours."

27  Chl:  Yeah

28         (.)

29  Pau:  (So I said "Yeah that's great") He phoned me up

30        just before I arrived just when I'd left my house

31        so an' he went "Look I told y- m- my dad that we're

32        all going out for a meal toni:ght y- your- I'm

33        staying at yours and you're picking up-= we're

34        gonna pick up some other people from East London

35        in the morning"

36  Chl:  Yeah

37  Pau:  U:hm

38         (0.2)

39  Pau:  Uhm "an' that's all I've- y'know an' that's all

40        I've said to him an' that you're actually coming

41        to Madrid and you're a history of art student

42        as well"

43  Chl:  Yeah

44  Pau:  And I was like "fine" >he said< "But don't worry

45        he won't talk to you:" uhm "an' you answer any
```

```
46            questions with "fine""

47   Chl:     Yea:::h? Huh huh huh

48   Pau:     So I s[aid (    )]

49   Chl:          [ Famous ] last words

50   Pau:     Uhm and then we went upstairs to his room 'cause

51            he wanted to show me his room 'cause he'd done it

52            out in Ottoman Empire sort'v front room of an

53            Ottoma- It's amazing anyway his bed- He's got like

54            a four thousand pound (.) Persian carpet it's

55            beautiful his parents bought for him. .hh[hh ]

56   Chl:                                              [Go:d]

57   Pau:     And uhm an' then we went back downstairs and he

58            was getting all his bags together and his Mum's

59            like (.) (    ) talking to me and obviously his

60            mum knows who I a:m=

61   Chl:     =Yeah=

62   Pau:     =Uhm (.) an' she's like "why don't y-" "Don't

63            stand in the hall come into the front room"

64            where his dad was sitting watching Tee Vee.=An'

65            I thou[ght °"Oh] God"°

66   Chl:           [ Yeah ]

67   Chl:     Yeah=

68   Pau:     =Well I went an' sat down an' then Ashraf's like

69            "I'm just going to go to the loo"

70            [>an' I thought< [°"Don't leave me"°]

71   Chl:     [ .h h h        [ But    also is  ]

72              (.)

73   Chl:     Is he screaming? 'Cause you are.

74              (0.8)

75   Pau:     Pardon?

76   Chl:     Is he screaming? Because you are. Like won't yih

77            dad 'ave known.
```

```
78              (.)

79   Chl:   Won't his dad have known that you're gay?

80   Pau:   No:. Well yeah well (   ) that's what I always

81          thought.

82              (.)

83   Pau:   Uhm

84   Chl:   Huhuh huh huh .hhh

85   Pau:   An' so but I think that when it's your own kids

86          you can tell 'cause you're quite biased not

87          [really  [(                        )]

88   Chl:   [Yea::h. [But he'll have seen with] you wun 'e?

89   Pau:   Yea:h. But

90              (.)

91   Pau:   So an [('e's like)] "so are you this friend that

92   Chl:           [ But  yeah ]

93   Pau:   lives in Stanstead"

94   Chl:   Right?
```

Paul's telling embodies a range of judgements: that meeting his partner's father would be an occasion when coming out might be deemed relevant (hence the elaborate arrangements for concealment); that they could *not* come out; and that inadvertent disclosure in this context would have had serious detrimental consequences. However, we will focus here on Paul's judgement that he (and Ashraf) can easily pass as heterosexual – at least on this occasion. His whole story is premised on his assessment that he can conceal his sexual identity and successfully pass as heterosexual unless or until he explicitly comes out as gay. This is the judgement that Chloe challenges at line 73.

Up until Paul gets to the point in the story where his partner, Ashraf, has left him alone with his (Ashraf's) father ('then Ashraf's like "I'm just going to the loo"', lines 68–69), Chloe is supportive of Paul's telling (receipts and continuers[5], lines 14, 17, 24, 27, 36, 43, 61, 66 and 67, and appreciations[6], lines 49 and 56). But at line 71 she interrupts Paul to ask the question she redoes after the overlap ('Is he screaming? 'Cause you are', line 73). This temporarily derails the progressivity of the telling. It is obviously not fitted to the part of the telling Paul was delivering immediately prior to Chloe's question; it may also be difficult for Paul to work out exactly why this question is relevant at this point. Furthermore, it is possible that the choice of language employed by Chloe might be unfamiliar to Paul ('screaming' is sometimes applied to gay men who are readable as gay through

---

[5] See Gardner (1987) for further discussion of receipts and continuers.
[6] See Drew (2003, p. 143) for further examples of appreciations.

their camp or effeminate mannerisms). Both of these factors may account for the 0.8 second gap (line 74) before Paul responds. With this question Chloe – who, it seems, has not met Ashraf – is seeking to ascertain how easy it might be to discern that Ashraf is gay merely from his appearance and mannerisms. She is also displaying her perception of Paul as someone who *is* readable as gay on first encounters. She reissues this turn (lines 76–77) after Paul's repair initiation[7] (line 75) and adds by way of clarification, 'won't his dad have known that you're gay' (line 79).

Chloe's question presents a challenge to Paul's telling. If Paul confirms that Ashraf's appearance indicates to others that he is in fact gay, then the credibility of Paul's telling is potentially undermined. The possibility of both the speaker (Paul) and his partner (Ashraf) passing as heterosexual is the basic premise to the telling. The telling is built from the assumption that both, but specifically Paul, can pass as heterosexual and the interest in the telling comes from whether Paul did or did not manage to pass himself off as heterosexual in the company of Ashraf's father. Therefore, if it were obvious that both Paul and Ashraf are gay merely from interacting with them then the point of the telling is lost. Moreover, if Paul believes himself able to pass as heterosexual (as is here implied), Chloe's question undermines that belief and potentially challenges Paul's sense of his own appearance and his personal safety in a heterosexist world.

Not surprisingly then, Paul disagrees with Chloe's claim that Ashraf's father would have known he was gay ('No', line 80). He does however concede that he, too, would have thought his homosexuality was obvious (lines 80–81) – perhaps a concession prompted by the fact that Chloe is in a position to judge Paul as 'screaming' since she knows him. In continuing, Paul avoids engaging with these issues by employing an account based on the 'bias' that parents have about their children which makes them unlikely to suspect that their own children are gay (lines 85–87). Chloe agrees with this explanation but then points out that it does not apply to Paul (line 88), as he is not related to Ashraf's parents. Paul's 'Yea:h. But' (line 89) acknowledges Chloe's turn, but it does not engage with (or resolve) the potential problem to the telling that Chloe has presented. Rather, Paul leaves the problem unresolved and continues with his story. In sum, this naturally arising talk between a lesbian and a gay man about the closet involves interactional difficulties and interpersonal hassle in relation to the extent to which Paul is *able* to conceal his sexual identity.

Making Babies the Gay Way

In Fragment 2 (which is taken from later in the same conversation as that which is presented at the beginning of this chapter), Mum is talking about the conversations generated by the television programme, which necessitated her having to decide whether or not to come out as the mother of a lesbian daughter. She starts (lines 105–121) by describing the environment in which it was necessary to decide whether or not to come out (i.e. the talk about the programme). She then goes on to detail three incidents: one where she did come out (to Ethel, lines 126–149); one where there was no need to come out (since Ralph already knew, lines 154–156); and one where she chose not to come out (in the hairdresser's, lines 158–166). In each of the three episodes she presents coming out as relevant. In

---

[7] Paul's 'pardon?' (line 77) targets Chloe's prior utterance and marks it as problematic. It is this turn ('pardon'?) that suggests that the prior turn requires repairing, therefore, it is a repair initiation. See Schegloff et al. (1977) for further information about repair.

the hairdresser's coming out became relevant because the hairdresser advised her to avoid having her hair cut too short as she might be labelled (lines 159–161) – and the label implied here is 'lesbian' as inferred from the insertion 'according to that programme last night' (i.e. in the programme *Making Babies the Gay Way*). Given that Mum treats coming out as relevant but reports that she did not come out, this is potentially a difficult telling in a conversation with her lesbian daughter. She is presenting the hairdresser's perspective as inaccurate and prejudiced and – as someone who is the mother of a lesbian daughter – she is here treating not coming out as a possible failing on her part.

Fragment 2

[Land:YU24] Making Babies the Gay Way

105   Mum: [W]ell I got lo:ts of people

106   telling m- talking to me about it and I- some

107   people I did come out to and some people I ↓did↑n't

108   Chl: M[m]

109   Mum: [huh] huh huh

110   Chl: So what did- who was- people you knew were

111   talking to you or not.

112   Mum: Yeah. Well e- everybody I came upon.

113   Chl: Ri:gh'

114   Mum: Uh:m

115   Chl: What were they saying then.

116   Mum: All sort'ov uhm saying "Did you see that

117   programme last night. #I# don't think it's

118   right" and all that [sort] of stuff

119   Chl: [Yeah]

120   Chl: Yeah

121   Mum: Uh:m Oh well my daughter's (gay)

122   (1.0)

123   Chl: (Mm/Uh)

124   (.)

125   Chl: What did they say

126   Mum: Well Ethel was quite funny 'cause (.) she lives at

127   the bott'm of the road the one at the very end

128   (who had a break in) uhm and uhm (.) she said

```
129           "Oh well I do- I don't think females should (j-)

130           y'know have children (in wha-)" I have to admit

131           that I haven't seen the programme anyway

132   Chl:    #Yeah#

133   Mum:    But it was quite interesting 'cause (.) she's

134           just had a new hip an' she's out walking I could

135           see she was struggling on the way back I was going-

136           trying to y'know (giving her a chance to have) a

137           breather. But at the end of it she said "Are you

138           gonna come f- round for coffee on your way back

139           from shopping" (an') I said "Oh:" Just the usual

140   Chl:    [Yeah]

141   Mum:    [ Y']know. So it didn't make any difference

142   Chl:    Yeah

143   Mum:    Quite an outspoken woman.=But (.) she she didn't

144           y'know kind'ov sort'ov it didn't affect he[r

145   Chl:                                              [Y]eah

146   Mum:    Uhm (.) she looked a bit nonplussed really=

147   Chl:    =Yeah=

148   Mum:    =Uhm nobody seemed to think that gay people

149           have pa:rents

150   Chl:    Huh huh huh huh .hhh Yeah

151   Mum:    U[h:m ]

152   Chl:     [Yeah]

153          (.)

154   Mum:    An' Ralph of course already knows anyway so it

155           didn't come up with him. It would 'ave done if

156           (h) he (h) ha(huh)dn't of (I thin[k ) huh huh huh

157   Chl:                                     [Yeah.   Yeah

158   Mum:    But in the hai:rdressers (.) (              hair)

159           "Well you don't want your hair too short 'cause

160           y'know that (.) uh according to that programme
```

```
161          last night looks (like that) labels you" an' I

162          thought ["(        )"]

163   Chl:              [ .h h h   ] They did have shocking

164          stereotypical hair

165   Mum:   An' I thought "Oh I'm not going to get into the

166          (the whole)

167   Chl:   But it's true:! I mean the thing is that some

168          stereotypes are true.

169          (.)

170   Chl:   Uhm (.) the thing is is that when you agree

171          that y'know there's lots of stereotypes about

172          (.) it's easy to think "Oh that's really bad"

173          but it's more likely that you just think the

174          reason people have stereotypes is that a lot of

175          'em are true

176          (.)

177   Mum:   Well that [is   th]:at is the point isn't i[t]

178   Chl:             [Alrigh']                          [Y]eah

179          An' an' I mean .hh it (.) it's actual- but it's

180          shocking ho:w how much it's (.) is the case

181          y'know .hh but (.) there is a lot of really bad

182          hair.

183          (.)

184   Chl:   .hhhh Yea:h

185   Mum:   Anyway uhm (0.2) we've just been talking about

186          holidays
```

In this interaction, then, Mum displays a judgement that it was relevant for her to come out as the mother of a lesbian. As previous research has suggested 'at the same time that their identities as straight parents of gay men and lesbian women jeopardize their moral standing, these identities also lend authority' (Fields, 2001, p. 165) and Mum treats herself as having the knowledge and expertise (about lesbians) to challenge her hairdresser's views. However, Chloe challenges her mother's judgement and supports the hairdresser's point of view. There are potentially many ways in which Chloe could have responded to the report of the hairdresser's words: she could have expressed some kind of appreciation of the position that Mum had found herself in and sympathised with her dilemma, or she could have reassured her that it wasn't necessary to come out in this situation. However, Chloe does not engage with Mum's concerns about coming out at all. Instead she interrupts Mum to assert that 'they did have shocking stereotypical hair' (lines 163–4) – an assessment of lesbians on the television programme and not a comment on Mum's coming out dilemma. The alternative course of action for Chloe would be for her to align with Mum, which would mean acknowledging and accepting the existence of the anti-lesbian views reported by Mum. Chloe's lack of alignment, then, is potentially a strategy for enabling her to avoid having to confront such prejudice.

Mum, apparently undeterred by Chloe's confrontational response, continues (lines 165–6) with the talk that was underway before Chloe's turn (thereby sequentially deleting Chloe's talk). She prefaces her talk with a repeat of 'an' I thought' (line 165), which marks this as a redone version of what came before, and she uses reported thought to illustrate her response to the hairdresser's talk: 'Oh I'm not going to get into the (the whole)' (lines 165–6). Mum's turn displays that she did not come out to the hairdresser; however, she does not complete her turn so it is not clear exactly what she didn't 'get into' (line 165). That the hairdresser's turn might have made relevant something that Mum didn't want to 'get into' demonstrates that Mum did not agree with the views expressed by the hairdresser. By not completing her turn (line 166), Mum avoids saying what she is claiming that she thought (but didn't say) at the time. By not making explicit what this was exactly, she relies on Chloe knowing what sort of thing she (Mum) might have said to challenge the hairdresser's expressed opinion. Mum also conveys to Chloe, that even though she didn't challenge the stereotypical views of the hairdresser, she does not endorse such views herself.

In the face of Mum's displayed disagreement with the hairdresser's opinion, Chloe responds by aligning with the hairdresser ('But it's true!', line 167). What Mum has displayed herself as knowing to be false (the implication that lesbians have short hair), Chloe is emphatically treating as true. She then generalizes her claim: it is not just that this particular stereotype is true, but that many stereotypes have a basis in fact. After a micro-gap (line 169) (with no uptake from Mum), Chloe accounts for her view that stereotypes are true by displaying an awareness that believing stereotypes can easily be judged as 'bad' behaviour, but she then explains why stereotypes might be nonetheless accurate. Whereas Mum has positioned herself as having more authority on the subject of lesbian stereotypes than the hairdresser, in challenging Mum, Chloe presents *herself* as the authority on stereotypes and (at line 177) Mum concedes authority to Chloe. In sum, during this episode there is a struggle between Mum and Chloe in which Chloe challenges Mum by aligning with the views attributed to the hairdresser, asserting herself as the authority on what lesbians are like. This interactional difficulty erupts in naturally occurring talk between a lesbian and her (generally supportive) mother.

The Feathers

In Fragment 3, a lesbian couple (Karen and Lucy) are discussing the news (and its implications) that the local Youth Hostel Association (YHA) members are to hold a meeting in a gay pub (the Feathers) they frequent. Lucy introduces the topic by reporting that their mutual friend Ben has told her that it's YHA night in the Feathers (lines 1–2). In so doing

she is referring to Karen's warning (conveyed via Ben) that Lucy may be outed if she is
seen by the YHA members in the gay pub. This conversation is about the relevance of the
YHA meeting for the exposure of Lucy's lesbian identity. On the surface, this is a fairly
'light-hearted' and good-humoured conversation, but, underpinning it, there is a fundamental disagreement about the level of threat posed by the YHA meeting, the appropriateness of Karen's warning, and their dissonant views of oppression in this world. For Karen
the world is a more dangerous place than Lucy is prepared to acknowledge.

```
Fragment 3

[Land:NE3]  The Feathers

01  Luc:   Ben was saying that u:m (0.2) tcht u:h th't it's

02          the YH↑A: (.) ni:gh[t in the Fea:ther[s.]

03  Kar:                     [ .h h h h   [ Y]eah I told 'im

04          tuh mention it to yuh. hhh uhm >I d'kn[ow<]

05  Luc:                                        [ >I] thought

06          they w- I thought they met up↑stairs in the little

07          room.= But (.) d'they m-=actually meet in the pu:b?=

08  Kar:   =mcht .hhhh [>They do-]=

09  Luc:              [ ↑A:::w! ]=

10  Kar:   =They do both I belie:ve. hh

11          Th[ey end up down in the pub.   ]

12  Luc:     [They meet in a gay pub D'they] know it's a gay

13          pu(h)b. huh [huh ]

14  Kar:               [Yeah] I kno:w. I-[Int'restin'  ]=

15  Luc:                                [Really fu↑nny]=

16  Kar:   =((sniff)) [I don't know that they know it-]

17  Luc:             Ou[t of all of the pubs they pick ] that

18          one!

19  Kar:   Hm?

20  Luc:   Out of all of the pubs that they pi£(huh)£ck that one.

21          [ huh  ]

22  Kar:   [Well I] dunno if they know it tuh be honest.=

23  Kar:   =hu[h huh huh huh huh mhm hm ]

24  Luc:      [ hoh  hoh  hoh  hoh  hoh ]
```

```
25  Kar:  Kay Pee p'raps picks up on stuff like tha:t =atch'ly I

26        think.= which- which makes me al- has always made me

27        wonder about Kay Pee huh huh huh .hhh

28  Luc:  Well yea:::h.

29  Kar:  >I m-< 'E does pick up on it I [think]

30  Luc:                                 [ A b ]solutely.

31           (.)

32  Kar:  But he just follows real ale. ((cough))

33        He just follows ['is nose 'n 'is taste] buds=

34  Luc:                  [ O::::H  YE:::::ah.  ]

//

50  Luc:  Don't care whe:re they go if th- if the real ale's

51        there they're not bo(h)th(huh)ered. huh huh

52          (0.5)

53  Luc:  >C'd be< .hhhhh gay transgender(ed) pub they'd still be

54        [('uite 'appy with the) ale w'ld'nt] th(h)e:y=

55  Kar:  [  HUH     HUH     HUH      HUH    ]

56  Luc:  =[  H u h u h  ]  ((laughter while exhaling))

57  Kar:  =[To be honest ac]tually if 'alf of them- most of

58        them knew it'd frighten th'crap outta them I'm sure it

59        woul[d. ]

60  Luc:      [huh] huh [huh huh]

61  Kar:                [hah hah] .hhhh (If they knew they'd bin

62        sat round)

63          (.)

64  Luc:  Yeah [Well I-] I [don't know any-]▪ I mean I don't

65  Kar:       [(    )]   [ h h h h ]

66  Luc:  think (.) Kay Pee would recognise me = I don't know

67        anyone from- .hhhh yeah I don't think.= I mean 'e must

68        by thee- one of thuh few- oh 'part from Don but I dunno

69        if he goes >.hhh< must be one of thuh fe:w still go:ing

70        'cause th'must be a whole load of new people no:w.
```

```
71  Kar:   Oh yeah. Mmm. [ .h h h h]hhh=

72  Luc:                 [°(going)°]

73  Kar:   =YEAH You might w- .hhhhhh er I mean I just said put

74         you- to put you in t'picture in case- so you had a

75         choice really.

76  Luc:   O:h >yeah<= Oh no >I sh'll be fi:ne< I mean it's a big

77         enough pub anyway >isn't it.< ku- [.hhhh]

78  Kar:                                     [ Mmh ] hhh=

79  Luc:   =Last time you were sat in t'corner weren't you hhhh

80         try(h)in' t'blend in [with the (            ).]

81  Kar:                        [huh  huh  huh  huh  .hhh] huh huh

82         .hhhhh

83         (Oh) yea:hhhh. [.hhhhhhh]

84  Luc:                  [ I hadda] uhm really good morning at

85         work actually cos uhm it's really odd you know I was

86         saying all that stuff about (0.2) about wor- er what
```

Despite Karen's deliberately 'casual' reference to the YHA meeting as something she'd 'mention[ed]' (line 4), the status of this information as a warning, and the possible threat posed by the YHA meeting in Lucy's local gay pub is clear. The women discuss the exact location of the meeting: if it is upstairs in the little room (lines 6–7) above the pub itself then the YHA members may not see Lucy, whereas if – as in fact turns out to be the case – the YHA members 'end up down in the pub' (line 11) Lucy risks exposure. They discuss whether or not the YHA group *knows* that the Feathers is a gay pub (lines 12–13, 16 and 22) and whether individual members of the group have the capacity to 'pick up on' clues to a lesbian or gay identity (lines 25–30). Their discussion both of the location of the meeting and of the knowledge status of the YHA meeting is oriented precisely to the possible threat of Lucy being outed to this group.

Lucy has treated the YHA's choice of venue for their meeting as a coincidence or puzzle (see lines 17–18 and 20). After jokingly speculating about KP's sexuality as a possible explanation, Karen offers 'real ale' as a possible factor in their choice of pub (lines 32–33). Lucy's uptake (line 34) treats this explanation as solving her puzzle. The two women agree, then, that the YHA members are meeting in a gay pub – possibly in ignorance that it is such – because it is (also) a real ale pub. Karen treats being outed to the YHA group as a risk that Lucy will confront if she goes to the Feathers that night, and she is judging the consequences of this as something that will be negative for Lucy.

Lucy explicitly orients to the possible threat of being outed to the YHA group in the course of denying it. According to Lucy the YHA group 'don't care where they go if th- if the real ale's there they're not bothered' (lines 50–51). Lucy, therefore, is dismissing

Karen's warning as unnecessary. Being seen by the YHA members when they emerge from the little room upstairs for their pints of real ale will not matter. For Lucy then, Karen is being over-protective, excessively cautious, and seeing oppression where none exists.

The half second silence that follows Lucy's dismissal of Karen's warning is dispreference-implicative[8] (line 52) and Lucy hears it as indicating that Karen might be going to disagree with her. In response, she upgrades her claim: it is not just that the YHA are 'not bothered' (line 51) by being in a gay pub – even in a 'transgendered pub' they'd be 'quite happy' (lines 53–54) as long as the real ale is there! At line 57 Karen produces the disagreement that Lucy has been expecting since the silence at line 52. Far from not 'being bothered' or being 'quite happy', Karen claims 'it'd fr<u>i</u>ghten th'cr<u>ap</u> outta them I'm <u>su</u>re it would' (lines 58–59). Karen assumes that the YHA group do not know that it is a gay pub and that their meeting at the Feathers is evidence of this ignorance: the implication being that they would avoid it if they knew. Karen assumes high levels of prejudice from the YHA members, thereby justifying her warning to Lucy. Lucy, by contrast, treats the YHA members as more tolerant and open-minded; they 'don't care whe:re they go' (line 50) (i.e. even a gay pub) as long as the ale is good – and, if this is the case, Karen's warning is unnecessary. It is not until line 66 that Lucy orients explicitly to Karen's reiterated concern of the threat to Lucy posed by the YHA meeting and then it is to argue that the threat of being outed is not as great as Karen might otherwise have perceived. She addresses the possibility that even if KP were to be 'bothered' he would not recognize her (line 66). It has evidently been a while since Lucy was a YHA member and the membership is likely to have changed in the interim (line 70). Finally, even if KP (or any other person Lucy knows who might still be attending the YHA) is there then they might not spot her since it is a big pub (lines 76–77).

In sum, Karen is displaying her judgement that it is unsafe for Lucy to go to the gay pub where the YHA are meeting since her presence there would be sufficient for her to be outed. Lucy, on the other hand, is challenging Karen by claiming, both that going to the Feathers may be insufficient to out her (the YHA group might not see her or none of the members might know her) and also by claiming that Karen has misjudged the level of hostility that she would encounter from the YHA group should she actually be outed. A lesbian couple here find themselves struggling to reconcile their discrepant views of the world.

In each of these three tellings, then, there is some problem of mismatched expectations and understanding between the teller of the 'coming out'-relevant experience and his or her recipient. In Fragment 1, Chloe's interruption, 'Is he screaming? 'Cause you are' (line 73), substantially disrupts Paul's telling (lines 71–90 are occupied with this disruption). In Fragment 2, Chloe disaffiliates from Mum's concerns – perhaps because she is the lesbian daughter whose very existence put Mum in the difficult position she is describing – and vies for the position of authority on the topic of lesbians and stereotypes. In Fragment 3 (perhaps the most difficult interaction for the participants), Lucy denies the relevance of Karen's warning and – when Karen pursues it – she downplays its necessity. The members of this couple are displaying incompatible views here: Karen has gone out of her way to ensure that Lucy receives the warning, and, instead of appreciating this, Lucy is treating it as unnecessary. Karen is insisting on the YHA meeting as

---

[8] Silences after initiating actions (such as first assessments) often indicate that the action will not be forwarded by the next speaker. See Pomerantz (1984) for further details of the features of dispreferred second actions.

a potential threat, continuing to treat it *as* a threat even after Lucy has displayed that this is not how she has interpreted it (or at least this is not the way that she wants to treat it).

These three episodes reflect the cost of oppression for lesbian and gay relationships, in each case resulting in interactional hassles in the ongoing interaction. These kinds of interactional issues are personally costly. They constitute the hassles and stressors that damage our interactions with our lovers, friends and family, since it is, in part, through talk that our relationships with others are defined and reconstituted. These interactional difficulties do not occur in a social vacuum but in the everyday interactions between lesbians, gay men and their families and friends, and they impact on those personal relationships.

INVOKING AND REPRODUCING A HETEROSEXIST WORLD

Despite the interactional difficulties experienced by the speakers, the participants in these interactions often align over what they take for granted. By examining what the speakers treat as unproblematic we can see speakers' shared understandings of the world. Four features are common across the interactions:

Participants Orient to the Continuing Relevance of the Closet and Coming Out as Significant Issues

These episodes arose spontaneously in everyday conversations rather than in researcher-generated data and in them we see participants treating coming out issues as significant and newsworthy in their lives. Making available a lesbian or gay identity to interlocutors is treated quite differently from making a heterosexual identity available. Nowhere – either in the Land data set or in the classic CA data sets – are there any comparable data in which making available one's heterosexuality is treated as an event or a tellable in its self (Kitzinger, 2005b). The continuing relevance of the closet and coming out in psychology is displayed here through participants' own treatment of it as newsworthy and important.

Participants Treat 'Lesbian' and 'Gay' as Identities to be 'Closeted' or 'Out' About (Whereas 'Heterosexual' is Not)

Speakers treat having a lesbian or gay identity as 'marked' in a way that having a heterosexual identity is not. In Fragment 1, the basic premise of Paul's telling is that *not* coming out will be sufficient for Paul to pass as heterosexual (it is this foundation that Chloe undermines by pointing out that Paul's appearance and behaviour are sufficient to indicate or 'give away' his gay identity). The participants take for granted that as long as someone is not marked 'gay' (although Chloe suggests that Paul *is* so marked) it normally will be sufficient for them to be assumed heterosexual. In Fragment 3, the speakers seek to account for the YHA's presence in a gay pub by reference to one of the group's members, KP, who they intimate might be gay (lines 25–30). By singling out KP in this way they treat the other members of the group as presumptively heterosexual (without explicitly labelling them as such), thereby taking for granted the group's heterosexuality (although – on the basis of prior interactions with them – they may also know or have evidence on the basis of which to infer that these people are heterosexual).

In these extracts, then, the closet is relevant for lesbian and gay people in a way that it is not for heterosexuals: their talk reflects and reproduces a world in which, in the absence of contrary indications it is acceptable and reasonable to assume that everyone is heterosexual. This reifies heterosexuality as the unmarked norm or default.

Participants do not Anticipate Explicitly Positive Responses to Coming Out of the Closet

Actual or projected possible responses to coming out of the closet are never fully positive in these episodes. In Fragment 2, Mum presents Ethel's reaction as positive given Ethel's anti-lesbian views ('Oh well I do- I don't think females should (j-) y'know have children' (lines 129–130) where 'females' here must be a euphemism for 'lesbians' or more specifically lesbian couples raising children since it is unlikely that Ethel disagrees with all women having children!). Nonetheless, despite learning that Mum has a lesbian daughter, Ethel still invites Mum 'round for coffee' (line 138) – a return to the usual *in spite of* their discussion, 'So it didn't make any difference' (line 141). It does not need to be articulated that the difference it *could* have made would have been a negative one, and neither speaker considers making a difference in a positive way as a possible reaction. Not making 'any difference' (line 141) and 'just the usual' (line 139) are used here by Mum to present a *good* response to coming out. Chloe does not challenge this presentation and in so doing it is treated by both participants as understandable. In Fragment 3, both speakers take for granted that Lucy's presence in a gay pub could 'discredit' her in the eyes of the YHA membership by outing her as a lesbian. They take for granted that this would have negative implications: at best they wouldn't be 'bothered' (line 51) and at worst it would 'frighten th' crap outta them' (line 58): there is no suggestion that this could be viewed positively.

Participants Assume that a Lesbian or Gay Identity has to be Managed in Relation to the Closet

Being lesbian or gay is treated as something that has to be managed in a way that being heterosexual does not. These speakers take for granted that preparations have to be made regarding revealing or concealing their sexual identities (or, in Mum's case, that of her daughter). In Fragment 1, Paul describes the extensive preparations that were necessary to conceal his relationship with his partner from his partner's parents and Chloe is aligned throughout most of this telling. They both treat a significant degree of planning as required and expectable (although Chloe demonstrates that she is willing to challenge Paul's story, she does not challenge this aspect). This is consonant with research that has demonstrated that only a small minority of lesbian and gay people never take any precautions to monitor their outness for the sake of their safety (D'Augelli & Grossman, 2001; Stonewall, 1996).

There is some resistance to this from Lucy in Fragment 3. However, ultimately she accepts Karen's presentation of the problem *as* a warning by offering reasons for why the warning is unnecessary.

We have shown, then, that despite the interactional hassles that resonate throughout these episodes of talk about the closet, participants are aligned about features of the heterosexist world they share in common. It is one in which the closet has continuing significance for lesbian and gay people.

CONCLUSION

Our use of naturalistic data – the ordinary conversations of lesbian and gay people and their co-interactants from the Land corpus – has enabled us to recognize and to explore the continuing relevance of the closet in the lives of lesbian and gay people. As we outlined at the outset of this chapter, conventional psychological research has identified stressors and hassles associated with coming out, concealment and fear of being outed. The interactions we have analysed here include reports that are consistent with the existing research. We have added to previous research by giving empirical evidence that when lesbian and gay people and their (supportive) family members talk about hassles and stressors associated with the closet, these interactions can themselves be stressful. These conversations about coming out can themselves sometimes constitute *secondary* stressors in lesbian and gay lives. We have used conversation analysis to identify moments of interactional difficulty (made manifest through the absence of relevant next turns, delayed responses and so on). It is through this fine-grained analysis that we have shown how the harmful effects of the closet extend beyond the moment of concealment or coming out and permeate our relationships with our friends, lovers and families.

The lesbian and gay people (and their family members) in our data set are 'out' about their sexuality (or the sexuality of their family members) across a broad range of social contexts. They do not live in the world of shame and secrecy that characterized the lives of many of their (recent) historical counterparts. However, our analysis here shows the continuing significance of the closet in their everyday lives.

ACKNOWLEDGEMENTS

With thanks to Sue Wilkinson for her helpful feedback on an earlier version of this chapter.

APPENDIX: TRANSCRIPTION KEY

.	closing intonation
,	continuing intonation
?	rising intonation
↑	rise in pitch immediately after the arrow
↓	fall in pitch immediately after the arrow
!	animated expression

.hhh	inbreath
hhh	outbreath
<u>underlining</u>	word or syllable produced with emphasis
[ ]	overlapping talk between two or more speakers
=	no discernable beat of silence between turns
(0.5)	silence (the number represents length of the silence in seconds)
(.)	a discernable gap or pause that is too short to measure
::::	stretch on the preceding sound (the number of colons used represents the relative length of the sound stretch)
huh/hah	laughter
(h)	laughter particles but less that a full laugh
£	'smile voice'
#	'creaky voice'
° °	talk within symbols is quieter than the surrounding talk
CAPITALS	talk is louder than the surrounding talk
> <	talk within symbols is faster than the surrounding talk
–	an abrupt cut off on the immediately prior sound
( )	talk inaudible to the transcriber
(word)	possible hearing
(( ))	additional information or sounds provided by transcriber

REFERENCES

Amnesty International (1999). *'The Louder We will Sing': Campaigning for lesbian and gay human rights*. London: Amnesty International Publications.

Amnesty International (2001). *Crimes of Hate, Conspiracy of Silence*. London: Amnesty International Publications.

Borhek, M. V. (1983). *Coming Out to Parents: A two-way survival guide for lesbians and gay men and their parents*. Cleveland, OH: The Pilgrim Press.

Cass, V. (1979). Homosexual identity formation: A theoretical model. *Journal of Homosexuality*, **4**(3), 219–235.

Crosbie-Burnett, M., Foster, T. L., Murray, C. I. & Bowen, G. L. (1996). 'Gays' and lesbians' families-of-origin: A social-cognitive-behavioral model of adjustment. *Family Relations*, **45**(4), 397–403.

Cruikshank, M. (1992). *The Lesbian and Gay Movement*. London: Routledge.

D'Augelli, A. R. & Grossman, A. H. (2001). Disclosure of sexual orientation, victimization, and mental health among lesbian, gay, and bisexual older adults. *Journal of Interpersonal Violence*, **16**(10), 1008–1027.

Drew, P. (2003). Conversation analysis. In J. A. Smith (Ed.), *Qualitative Psychology: A practical guide to research* (pp. 132–158). London: Sage.

Eichberg, R. (1990). *Coming Out: An act of love*. London: Penguin.

Fields, J. (2001). Normal queers: Straight parents respond to their children's 'coming out'. *Symbolic Interaction*, **24**(2), 165–187.

Gardner, R. (1987). The conversation object "mm": A weak and variable acknowledging token. *Research on Language and Social Interaction*, **30**(2), 131–156.

Goffman, E. (1963). *Stigma: Notes on the management of spoiled identity*. New Jersey, NJ: Prentice-Hall.

Herek, G. M., Cogan, J. C., Gillis, J. R. & Glunt, E. K. (1998). Correlates of internalised homophobia in a community sample of lesbians and gay men. *Journal of the Gay and Lesbian Medical Association*, **2**(1), 17–25.

Jefferson, G. (1980). On 'trouble-premonitory' response to inquiry. *Sociological Inquiry*, **50**(3–4), 153–185.

Jefferson, G. (2004). Glossary of transcript symbols with an introduction. In G. Lerner (Ed.), *Conversation Analysis: Studies from the first generation*, (pp. 13–31). Philadelphia, PA: John Benjamins.

Kitzinger, C. (1987). *The Social Construction of Lesbianism*. London: Sage.

Kitzinger, C. (2000). Doing feminist conversation analysis. *Feminism & Psychology*, **10**(2), 163–193.

Kitzinger, C. (2005a). Heteronormativity in action: Reproducing the heterosexual nuclear family in 'after hours' medical calls. *Social Problems*, **52**(4), 477–498.

Kitzinger, C. (2005b). Speaking as a heterosexual: (How) does sexuality matter for talk-in-interaction? *Research on Language and Social Interaction*, **38**(3), 221–265.

Kitzinger, C. & Coyle, A. (2002). Introducing lesbian and gay psychology. In A. Coyle & C. Kitzinger (Eds), *Lesbian and Gay Psychology: New perspectives* (pp. 63–80). Oxford: BPS Blackwell.

Kitzinger, C. & Peel, E. (2005). The de-gaying and re-gaying of AIDS: Contested homophobias in lesbian and gay awareness training. *Discourse & Society*, **16**(2), 173–197.

Kitzinger, C. & Wilkinson, S. (2004). Social advocacy for equal marriage: The politics of 'rights' and the psychology of 'mental health'. *Analyses of Social Issues and Public Policy*, **4**(1), 173–194.

Land, V. & Kitzinger, C. (2005). Speaking as a lesbian: Correcting the heterosexist presumption. *Research on Language and Social Interaction*, **38**(4), 371–416.

Lewis, R. J., Derlega, V. J., Berndt, A., Morris, L. M. & Rose, S. (2001). An empirical analysis of stressors for gay men and lesbians. *Journal of Homosexuality*, **42**(1), 63–88.

Markowe, L. A. (2002). Coming out as lesbian. In A. Coyle & C. Kitzinger (Eds), *Lesbian and gay psychology: New perspectives* (pp. 63–80). Oxford: BPS Blackwell.

Mclean, G. (2004). Children of the revolution. Review of *Making Babies the Gay Way* published in *The Guardian* 22 January 2004. Retreived 8 July 2004, from www.pinkparents.org.uk

Meyer, I. H. (2003). Prejudice, social stress, and mental health in lesbian, gay, and bisexual populations: Conceptual issues and research evidence. *Psychological Bulletin*, **129**(5), 674–697.

Morris, J. F., Waldo, C. R. & Rothman, E. D. (2001). A model of predictors and outcomes of outness among lesbian and bisexual women. *Journal of Orthopsychiatry*, **71**(1), 61–71.

Owens, R. E. (1998). *Queer Kids: The challenges and promise for lesbian, gay, and bisexual youth*. London: The Haworth Press.

Peel, E. (2001). Mundane heterosexism: Understanding incidents of the everyday. *Women's Studies International Forum*, **24**(5), 541–554.

Pomerantz, A. (1984). Agreeing and disagreeing with assessments: Some features of preferred/dispreferred turn shapes. In J. M. Atkinson & J. C. Heritage (Eds), *Structures in Social Action: Studies for conversation analysis* (pp. 57–101). Cambridge: Cambridge University Press.

Ponse, B. (1978). *Identities in the Lesbian World: The social construction of self*. Westport, CT: Greenwood Press.

Powers, B. & Ellis, A. (1996). *A Family and Friend's Guide to Sexual Orientation*. London: Routledge.

Sacks, H. (1972). On the analyzability of stories by children. In J. J. Gumperz & D. Hymes (Eds), *Directions in Sociolinguistics: The ethnography of communication* (pp. 329–345). New York, NY: Holt, Rinehart and Winston.

Sacks, H. & Schegloff, E. A. (1979). Two preferences in the organization of reference to persons in conversation and their interaction. In G. Psathas (Ed.), *Everyday Language: Studies in ethnomethodology* (pp. 15–21). New York, NY: Irvington.

Sacks, H., Schegloff, E. A. & Jefferson, G. (1974). A simplest systematics for the organization of turn-taking in conversation. *Language*, **50**(4), 696–735.

Schegloff, E. A. (2007). *Sequence Organization: A primer in conversation analysis*. Cambridge: Cambridge University Press.

Schegloff, E. A., Jefferson, G. & Sacks, H. (1977). The preference for self-correction in the prganization of repair in conversation. *Language*, **53**(2), 361–382.

Seidman, S., Meeks, C. & Traschen, F. (1999). Beyond the closet? The changing social meaning of homosexuality in the United States. *Sexualities*, **2**(1), 9–34.

Signorile, M. (1996). *Outing Yourself: How to come out as lesbian or gay to your family, friends, and coworkers*. New York, NY: Fireside.

Smart, L. & Wegner, D. M. (2000). The hidden costs of hidden stigma. In T. F. Heatherton, R. E. Kleck, M. R. Hebl & J. G. Hull (Eds), *The Social Psychology of Stigma* (pp. 220–242). New York, NY: Guilford Press.

Smith, G., Bartlett, A. & King, M. (2004). Treatments of homosexuality in Britain since the 1950s – an oral history: The experience of patients. *British Medical Journal*, **328**(7437), 427–429.

Stonewall (1996). *Queer bashing*. Retrieved 6 June 2004, from www.stonewall.org.uk/stonewall/information_bank/violent_hate_crime/resources/queer_bashing.html

Wilkinson, S. & Kitzinger, C. (2005). Same-sex marriage and equality. *The Psychologist*, **18**(5), 290–293.

Wilkinson, S. & Kitzinger, C. (2007). Conversation analysis, gender and sexuality: A feminist perspective. In A. Weatherall, B. Watson & C. Gallois (Eds), *Language, Discourse and Social Psychology*. London: Palgrave Macmillan.

CHAPTER 9

Romance, Rights, Recognition, Responsibilities and Radicalism: Same-Sex Couples' Views on Civil Partnership and Marriage

Victoria Clarke
University of the West of England, Bristol, UK
Carole Burgoyne
University of Exeter, UK
and
Maree Burns
Eating Difficulties Education Network, Auckland, NZ

INTRODUCTION

Partnership recognition and same-sex marriage are very firmly at the top of the global LGB political agenda. Radical gay and lesbian feminist demands that marriage be dismantled seem now whispers from a distant past (but see Auchmuty, 2004; Jeffreys, 2004). The editors of a recent exploration of the same-sex marriage debate within LGB communities note that it is often polarized around two distinct and competing positions: first, that marriage represents the gold standard of relationship recognition and the key to lesbian and gay equality. Second, that same-sex marriage represents accommodation to heterosexual standards and the loss of distinctively lesbian and gay cultural and relational practices (Clarke & Finlay, 2004). Clarke and Finlay (2004) argue that the same-sex marriage debate, as well as being polarized and lacking nuance, has tended to be academic and abstract. Explorations of the lived experiences of same-sex couples are largely confined to popular celebratory texts about same-sex relationships and commitment ceremonies (e.g. Marcus, 1998; Martinac, 1998). They further argue that current debates are in danger of only recycling positions that were established in the 1980s (e.g. Ettelbrick, 1997/89; Stoddard, 1997/89), and failing to take account of the substantial changes in the political and legislative climate since then. Clarke and Finlay call for a reinvigoration of the same-sex marriage debate that addresses these changes and that is grounded in the

Out in Psychology: Lesbian, gay, bisexual, trans and queer perspectives. Edited by Victoria Clarke and Elizabeth Peel.
© 2007 John Wiley & Sons, Ltd.

personal (and political) experience of same-sex partners. Harding and Peel (2006) also point to important differences between academic debates and the views of members of the broader LGBT community. They note that most advocates of marriage in academic discussions are men, which has led to the assumption that it is only men who support marriage. However, their survey demonstrated that lesbians are as positive about legal recognition as gay men, suggesting that a gender-divide is limited to academic discussions and is not reflective of the views of the wider LGBT community (see also Solomon, Rothblum & Balsam, 2004, 2005). We respond to Clarke and Finlay's (2004) call for a reinvigoration of the same-sex marriage debate in this chapter by exploring the perspectives on marriage and partnership recognition of 22 same-sex couples living in the UK. The data are drawn from the qualitative phase of a larger study of same-sex[1] couples, money management, and relationship recognition and celebration (see also Clarke, Burgoyne & Burns, 2005, 2006a, 2006b).

SAME-SEX MARRIAGE: NO LONGER A FAIRY TALE?

The first legally recognized civil partnership (CP) registrations in the UK took place in December 2005. The CP legislation, which was initially proposed by the Government in the form of a consultation document in June 2003, offers same-sex relationships most of the rights and responsibilities of marriage and represents a path to equality (of sorts) for same-sex couples in the UK. The successful passage of the CP legislation forms a backdrop to this research: the interviews started about two months after the consultation document was published and were completed around three months after the Bill was passed into law. Although the legislation is widely referred to and understood – both in the mainstream press and in the gay press – as 'gay marriage', it is not marriage (see Clarke et al., 2006a). The UK is one of a growing number of jurisdictions that offer some form of recognition to same-sex partnerships (at the time of writing jurisdictions that permit same-sex marriages include Belgium, the Netherlands, Spain, Canada and the US state of Massachusetts).

The quest for rights as partners and as families is at the forefront of LGB political activism. Taking place alongside political action is debate, discussion and dialogue about the meaning of marriage for lesbian and gay couples, and about the implications of same-sex marriage for heterosexuals – particularly women – and for the institution and practice of marriage itself. Typical questions include: will same-sex marriages transform the institution of marriage? That is, will it divest marriage of its patriarchal origins and turn it into something new and inclusive – something that no longer contributes to the oppression of LGB people, *and* heterosexual women? Is marriage the best route to equality for non-heterosexuals? Will marriage bestow significant benefits (including financial benefits) (see Stoddard, 1997/89)? Or, to consider the other side of the debate, will marriage succeed only in normalizing LGB people? Will marriage dispossess non-heterosexuals of their difference? Will it confer advantages only on the most privileged LGB people and increase

---

[1] Our primary concern in this chapter is with the legal recognition of same-sex relationships. The definition of 'same-sex relationships' in the broader study was inclusive of all those people involved in non-heterosexual relationships including those who do not identify with the labels 'lesbian', 'gay' and 'bisexual'. Discussions of same-sex marriage and relationships are typically confined to people who identify with the labels 'lesbian' and 'gay' (and on occasion 'bisexual') – our usage of 'lesbian and gay' or 'LGB' reflects this. The emphasis within trans politics – at least in the UK – has been on securing rights to heterosexual marriage. This chapter is inclusive of trans people to the extent that the broader study intended to be inclusive of all those involved in 'same-sex' relationships. It is important to note however that all but one of the participants identified as either lesbian or gay (see below).

the gap between the socially acceptable 'good gays' and the 'dangerous queers' who refuse to 'settle down' and to 'fit in' (see Ettelbrick, 1997/89)?

Such questions are underpinned by and point to broader debates within LGB communities about the goal of LGB politics: is the goal to seek acceptance and inclusion in the wider society (and in seeking membership to emphasize fundamental similarities to heterosexuals)? Or is it to seek social transformation, and the overthrow of institutions, such as marriage, which are founded on inequality and replace them with something radically different and better? These two positions are associated with liberal and radical gay/lesbian feminist politics respectively.

In recent years, a third position had emerged that emphasizes the importance of choice and equality, and the necessity of suspending (abstract) ideological arguments about sameness and difference, assimilation and transformation until after some semblance of equality has been achieved. These authors argue that marriage may well be normalizing, but any discussion about the ideological effects of marriage should only take place after lesbians and gay men have gained equal relationship rights (e.g. Bevacque, 2004). Bevacque (2004), drawing on Cagan (1999), uses the example of the exclusion of lesbians and gay men from the military to explain her argument. Opposing war and the use of military force does not prevent us from viewing lesbians and gay men's exclusion from the military as an infringement of their civil rights. The same can be said of marriage: we may not agree with it in principle, but in practice access to marriage is an important part of what it means to be a citizen in the current political context, and as such is an issue of social justice. Such arguments are used to support campaigns for full marriage rights in the UK and elsewhere (see Kitzinger & Wilkinson, 2004).

The Literature

There are numerous popular polls examining the views of the LGB community on same-sex marriage and a significant body of (mainly sociological) research on lesbian and gay relationships (for examples of the latter see Dunne, 1997; Kurdek, 1993). However, there is a dearth of empirical research on the meaning of marriage and partnership recognition for the non-heterosexual community (Harding, 2006; Harding & Peel, 2006). The little research there is consists of a handful of (mostly sociological and social anthropological) studies exploring the multiple meanings of lesbian and gay relationship celebrations (e.g. Clarke et al., 2006b; Lewin, 1996, 1998, 1999; Liddle & Liddle, 2004; Mandori, 1998; McQueeney, 2003; Steirs, 1999). And, an equally small handful of studies exploring non-heterosexuals' perspectives on partnership recognition (e.g. Clarke et al., 2006a; Harding, 2006; Harding & Peel, 2006; Lannutti, 2005; Weeks, Heaphy & Donovan, 2001; Yip, 2004). The only published study solely focused on legally recognised same-sex relationships is Solomon et al. (2004, 2005).

Solomon et al. (2004) compared 212 lesbians and 123 gay men who had had civil unions in the US state of Vermont during the first year that the legislation was made available, with 166 lesbians and 72 gay men in their friendship networks who had not had civil unions, and with their married heterosexual siblings (219 women and 193 men). The authors' aim was to compile a demographic and relationship profile of couples who had civil unions in Vermont. They found that married heterosexual couples had been together longer and had more traditional divisions of labour and childcare then did lesbian and gay couples. A second analysis of the same data, focused on (among other things) the division of finances and household tasks and relationship maintenance behaviours (Solomon et al., 2005), again found that married heterosexuals exhibited more traditional (gendered) divisions and behaviours than same-sex couples. This supports the broader finding that domestic/relational practices in same-sex relationships are more equal than those in heterosexual relationships (e.g. Chan et al., 1998; Kurdek, 1993).

This kind of study continues the comparative tradition evident in much lesbian and gay psychological (and sociological) work on lesbian and gay relationships and families (for a critique see Clarke, 2002a). Although it provides useful information on the similarities and differences between lesbian, gay and heterosexual relational/familial lives and practices (and legally recognized and non-legally recognized lesbian and gay relationships), it tells us little about the underlying meaning and significance of the identified patterns for the participants. It also does not tap into the more subtle and nuanced (and potentially less 'egalitarian') negotiations that take place between partners. Moreover, whether or not the comparisons favour lesbians and gay men (as they appear to in this study), such studies invoke heterosexuality as the baseline against which lesbian and gay lives are compared (Clarke, 2002a).

Solomon et al. (2005) also documented the main reasons why lesbians and gay men had a civil union (using a range of forced choice options). A majority (93.7%) of the 336 participants who were members of civil union couples listed love and commitment as a reason for having a civil union, legal relationship status was the second most popular reason (91.6%), followed by a desire for society to know about lesbian and gay relationships (59.7%) and factors related to children (10.4%). Other factors that were mentioned by less than 10% of the participants included property, finances, health benefits and inheritance.

Studies exploring non-heterosexuals' perspectives on relationship recognition highlight the multiple and competing meanings that marriage and other forms of recognition hold and the interplay of accommodation and resistance to heteronormative relationship norms and wider cultural values in respondents' accounts. Lannutti (2005) conducted a web-based survey of 288 LGBT people in order to assess the impact of same-sex marriage on the LGBT community. The data were collected in the USA after the Massachusetts Supreme Judicial Court ruled that the ban on same-sex marriage in the state should be lifted. Nearly every participant mentioned that the legal recognition of same sex marriage represented an element of legal equality for LGBT people, affecting the LGBT community for the better. The theme of legal recognition had three sub-themes: first-class citizenship (same-sex marriage marks the end of different legal treatment), financial benefits and increased security for families in crisis and families with children. Lannutti described legal equality as a surface theme that was underpinned by deeper dialectical tensions. These tensions highlighted the potential for same-sex marriage to strengthen *and* weaken same-sex relationships, to create unity *and* division within the LGBT community, and to improve *and* worsen the relationship between the LGBT community and mainstream America, and to reduce *and* increase homophobia.

Yip (2004) surveyed 565 LGB christians' views on partnership recognition. Although Yip's research focused on the views of a specific group of non-heterosexuals, his findings are similar to those of Weeks et al. (2001), based on interviews with 98 non-heterosexuals. Most participants in both studies wanted equal treatment and recognition for their relationships, and supported the individual's right to choose to have access to legal recognition. Most participants in both studies were also critical of marriage, arguing that it is heteronormative, oppressive, restrictive and dysfunctional institution. These participants viewed heterosexual and same-sex relationships as qualitatively different and thought that marriage would assimilate lesbians and gay men into the mainstream. A small number of participants in both studies expressed a desire for marriage (in Weeks et al.'s study, a few participants also argued against any kind of legal recognition). In Yip's study, participants who supported marriage did not see it as heterosexist and their support for marriage was based on religious and practical considerations.

Harding and Peel (2006) conducted the first international (web-based) survey assessing 1538 LGBT and heterosexual people's views about the legal recognition of same-sex relationships. A majority (98%) of the respondents agreed that same-sex couples should be treated the same as heterosexual couples in law, and the vast majority agreed that same-sex couples should be allowed to marry (94.5%). Two-thirds of respondents would marry their partner if they could. More support was evident for marriage than for civil union/partnership (particularly among participants residing in North America). Civil union/partnership was perceived as inferior to marriage because of the lack of international recognition and because of differences in rights. Separate but equal laws were perceived as unequal and discriminatory on religious grounds (and civil union/partnership as second class); respondents argued that everyone should have the same choices. Harding (2006) provided an analysis of qualitative data from the same online survey, focusing on the views of a subset of 173 lesbians and 144 gay men. She identified five themes related to perceptions of legal recognition: formal equality (and an emphasis on the similarities between LGB and heterosexual people), the relationship between legal and social change (the law produces or is a reflection of social change), the naming of legally recognized same-sex relationships (civil partnership is not enough), human rights and citizenship claims.

Elsewhere, we have documented whether the participants in our broader study were for or against civil partnership and organized their accounts into five underlying themes (Clarke et al., 2006b). These themes attempt to capture the complexity of the data and the ways in which they are underpinned by ambivalence, contradiction and different ways of conceptualizing CP, marriage, relationship recognition and celebration. See Table 9.1 for a summary of the participants' views on civil partnership.

Table 9.1 Views on legal recognition

View on CP/legal recognition	N	Sample views
Yes to civil partnership (more or less)	27	'I suspect if it was available to us we probably would get civil partnerised' (Martha F12b) 'We will certainly register' (Bruce M18b) 'I'd be pleased to have that bit of paper' (Sally F04a)
Undecided, ambivalent about, not ready for civil partnership/ legal recognition	10	'I'm a little bit hesitant' (Marnie F01a) 'I don't feel ready for that' (Luke M16b)
No to civil partnership/ and legal recognition	6	'I just feel personally that it's not for me' (Ben M09a)
No codeable data	1	

Source: From Clarke et al., 2006b.

Across these different studies some similarities and differences are apparent: there is strong support for access to legal recognition but disagreement about the precise form that it should ideally take. In the Harding and Peel study (Harding, 2006; Harding & Peel, 2006), some or most participants presented marriage as the (optimum) path to equality. In other studies, most of the participants were either highly critical of marriage (Clarke et al., 2006a; Weeks et al., 2001; Yip, 2004), and/or identified multiple meanings of marriage (Clarke et al., 2006a; Lannutti, 2005). There is a strong emphasis on rights and equality in most of the studies, only Solomon et al. (2005) foregrounds love and commitment as the paramount reason for entering into a legally recognized relationship.

CURRENT STUDY

Aims

Our qualitative interview study is different from those of Yip (2004) and Weeks et al. (2001) because – like Lanutti (2005), and Harding and Peel (2006) – we conducted our interviews at a time when some form of legal recognition was either a genuine prospect or a concrete (future) reality for the participants. This means that this is one of the first UK studies to explore same-sex couples' accounts of a specific form of relationship recognition and how they made meaning of relationship recognition at a time when it was firmly on the Government's agenda. We were interested in how the participants understood CP and whether their accounts were informed by debates about same-sex marriage within LGB communities, and in particular, liberal, feminist and radical perspectives on marriage, and conventional heteronormative discourses of love and romance (see Peel & Harding, 2004).

The Participants

The only recruitment criterion for participation was that informants were involved in a long term/'committed' same-sex relationship. Participants were recruited mainly in the South West of England (some were recruited in the Midlands), using a range of techniques (such as contacting local LGB groups, advertising in the gay press and snowball sampling). The sample consisted of 22 couples: 12 lesbian couples and 10 gay male couples. See Table 9.2 for further details of the sample (see Clarke et al., 2006b, for further information on recruitment).

The Interviews

A team of four female researchers conducted the interviews: partners were interviewed separately, most concurrently and most in their homes. Each interview lasted between 40 and 70 minutes. The interview schedule was developed on the basis of a review of the relevant literature. This schedule was revised after the first eight interviews to take account

Table 9.2 Characteristics of the sample (N = 44)

Sexuality	Lesbian (24)
	Gay male (19)
	Bisexual male (1)
Race/ethnicity	White UK (37), white other, (5) Pakistani (2)
Disabled/able-bodied	Able-bodied (43) Disabled (1)
Age (range)	22–62 (mean: 36)
Qualifications	No legible data (1)
	No qualifications (2)
	Secondary level qualifications (6)
	Tertiary level qualifications (35)
Children	Children (4 participants), foster children (2 couples)
Length of relationship (range)	6 months–33 years (15 couples 1–9 years; 7 couples 10+ years)
Cohabiting	Cohabiting full-time (20 couples)
	Cohabiting part-time (1 couple)
	Not cohabiting (1 couple)
Rented/owned home	Renting (4 couples)
	Owner-occupiers (16 couples)
	One partner rents/one partner owns (2 couples)
Employment	Full-time (33): £10,000–£63,000 (mean approx. £29,000)
	Part-time (10): £2,000–£18,000 (mean approx. £9,000)
	No data (1)

of some of the unanticipated issues that emerged in these interviews. Participants were asked to discuss a range of topics including CP and marriage, weddings and relationship celebration, money management and financial decision making. Our approach to conducting the interviews was to address each of the major areas of interest, but not to conform rigidly to the schedule – to allow both scope for the participants to discuss what was important to them and scope for comparison across the data. In outlining the aims and purpose of the research to the participants, we discussed with them the CP legislation, and all of them had at least some awareness of it.

The interviews were audio-tape recorded and transcribed verbatim by one of the authors (MB) and by a research assistant. Identifying information was modified or removed and the participants were given pseudonyms. The transcripts were searched to identify all data relevant to partnership recognition, which were compiled into a separate file and then read and re-read to identify recurring themes (Braun & Clarke, 2006). Our analytical approach is inductive thematic analysis and the aim is to present and describe the participants' accounts. Although these are treated as 'real', they are not viewed as (unique) individual perspectives; rather, the assumption is that the participants' accounts are individual representations of the social/cultural discourses that weave through wider discussions of same-sex relationship recognition and celebration. As such, the data were read through a critical realist lens (Willig, 1999). We have organized the participants' conceptualizations into the following five discursive themes: romance, rights, recognition, responsibilities and radicalism (see also Ellis, Chapter 14). We map the terrain of each of the themes, as well as comment on their political/rhetorical costs and benefits, and effects and implications.

ANALYSIS

Romance

Heteronormative themes of love and romance dominate broader discourse on marriage, but less than a quarter of the participants made meaning of civil partnership and marriage in this way. In these participants' accounts, there was an emphasis on 'marrying' for love – 'we love each other' (Pete, M21a) – because your partner is 'the one' (Marnie, F01a). Marriage was conceptualized as a 'lifetime commitment' (Mike, M16a) and a public declaration: 'telling all your friends and family this is the person you love and you want to spend the rest of your life with, and you want to share everything with' (Janet F15b). Informing these accounts was the (heteronormative) notion of the 'natural' progression of relationships: marriage is the 'final step' (Laurel F01b) in the romantic journey. This notion was also reflected in accounts of being 'not ready' (Luke M16a) to formalize a relationship and in accounts of wanting to 'get married and settle down' (Fran F02a).

Themes of love and romance were evident in some participants' attempts to explain the pull of relationship recognition and celebration and their conceptualizations of the ('real') meanings of marriage. For instance, Dan (M22a) was ambivalent about CP but his 'old romantic' side wanted to 'let everybody else know the feelings that I've got for Rick'. Some participants – like Marnie (F01a) – cited the material and practical advantages of CP but would want to register their relationship for reasons of love: 'I can see the advantages from a sort of legal point of view, but I don't want that to be my reason for going into it'. Janet (F15b) was critical of some of her lesbian and gay friends for planning to register their relationship just because they could by saying: 'you should do it because you want to do it with the person you love, not because it's suddenly become legal'. Janet suggested that their actions were ultimately unhelpful to the 'gay community' because they conveyed the message that same-sex couples do not take marriage (and relationships more generally) seriously: 'whereas I would really want to do it, and I'd wanna make sure it's right with the person'. For Janet, marriage represented the supreme expression of love and commitment and should be treated with respect. Participants in Lannutti's (2005) study similarly expressed the concern that the excitement of having access to relationship recognition would render marriage a fad for the LGBT community.

For the participants who drew on discourses of love and romance, legal recognition was meaningful because it represented a way of creating and formalizing the ultimate relational commitment. Laurel (F01b) said:

> you can sort of tell someone you love them, you can live with them, you can, you know, share your finances and life with them, but I think making a final sort of legal commitment with them if you like, I think probably you're going that one stage further.

Note Laurel's use of the notion of the romantic journey, of which marriage is the destination. A conceptualization of marriage as the 'gold standard' of relationships underpins this account; it suggests that one of the consequences of the ban on same-sex marriage is that it prevents non-heterosexual relationships from being fully realized.

At first sight, the minimal emphasis on love and romance in participants' accounts was surprising (cf. Solomon et al., 2005). Some commentators argue that in the absence of fixed reference points, talk about love has become a way of warranting same-sex relationships and calls for same-sex marriage (Lewin, 1998; Weeks et al., 2001). In discussions of lesbian and gay parenting (both in lesbian and gay, and in mainstream contexts), there is frequently a strong emphasis on love, and lesbian and gay families are validated with the claim that 'love makes a family' (see Clarke, 2002b; Clarke & Kitzinger, 2004). However, we did not require participants to defend their partnerships and the focus on finances in the broader study may have directed attention towards more practical and material concerns.

Emphasizing love and romance does, as Lewin (1998) and others argue, authenticate lesbian and gay relationships, presenting them as meaningful (and as essentially the same as heterosexual ones), and serve as a rhetorically potent way of arguing for same-sex marriage. This account also moves the debate onto (unthreatening) terrain that is recognizable to the wider (heterosexual) society. Bourassa (2004), for instance, argues that same-sex marriage is 'a simple and visible extension' (p. 61) of the romantic ideal of marriage for love that emerged in the Victorian era. At the same time, discourses of love and romance shore up the dominance of heteronormative conceptions of relationships. Peel and Harding (2004) argue that heteronormative discourses of love and romance obscure the legal and social meanings of marriage. In their view, appropriating the superficial and consumerist discourses and symbolism of heterosexual romance leads ultimately to the commodification of same-sex relationships and divesting LGB people of their difference. Ingraham's (1999) notion of the 'wedding industry complex' is important here. Bevacqua (2004) raises the question of what lesbians and gay men will do once they obtain the right to marry: 'Will we march ourselves quickly to the trendiest department stores to register for expensive gifts and get fitted for Vera Wang designer gowns, in preparation for queen-for-a-day nuptials?' (p. 38). She argues that lesbians and gay men who have commitment ceremonies do just that, which suggests that the wedding industry complex will not dissolve once lesbians and gay men gain admission to marriage (see also Peel & Jowett, 2006).

We Don't Need CP to Validate Our Love and Commitment

Just over a third of the participants drew on contrasting discourses that functioned to de-emphasize romance and commitment, and did not use love to justify entering into a CP. Some were dismissive of (the legal dimensions of) CP and marriage, conceptualizing legal recognition as 'just a piece of paper' (Ellen F02b) and not necessary to create or formalize their commitment to their partner: 'it's never needed a state sanction to be real' (Paula F03b). Ellen said: 'I don't have to write that on a piece of paper [. . .] I think we're living like a married couple [. . .] and so just a piece of paper is not going to make any difference'. A number of these participants, like Ellen, stated that entering into a CP would not make any substantial difference to their relationships. These accounts contrasted with the rights theme that emphasized the important practical and material advantages associated with CP and the recognition theme that emphasized the social validation afforded by CP (see below). A few participants cited these advantages, but felt that the length or nature of their relationship and commitment voided any of the ritualistic or romantic dimensions of CP: 'I think after 30 years or nearly 30 I don't feel an emotional need to do something not after all this time' (Steve M05b). Will (M18a) and his partner had had a commitment ceremony. Although they were keen to register their relationship: 'it doesn't feel so important in some ways 'cos we've already made the commitment to each other that we wanted to make, so it won't fulfil that kind of bond of love stuff'. In contrast to accounts of marriage as the ultimate loving commitment, these accounts emphasized the already realized fullness and completeness of same-sex relationships:

> we've been together so long now, that sounds quite negative doesn't it? It's not a negative thing at all, like our families accept us completely and our friends accept us as we are as well, and so on one hand it feels like 'well, why does it need to be different?' (Liv F08b).

Others commented that legal recognition removes choice, a private chosen commitment becomes a (state regulated) obligation: 'it forces people together, whereas if you naturally always want to be together then there's no particular force trying to keep you together, then that to me is a deeper measure of love and commitment' (Bert M06a). For Bert, his commitment to his partner did not require CP to be validated, therefore, CP was not about romance and love. Thelma (F08a) described her commitment to her partner as qualitatively different from the one she made when she got married: 'we didn't have to say "I will love you forever and I will be here forever and we will be together forever, and ever, and ever" [. . .] we said things like, you know, "we really want to be together for as long as we want"'. Thelma's marriage vows 'weighed very heavily and [. . .] felt terribly restrictive' whereas her commitment to Liv 'felt slightly freer, it felt more fluid'. In Thelma's view, marriage enforces a heteronormative model of relational commitment – her concern was that if relationship recognition for same-sex couples was presented as, or as akin to, marriage, it would threaten the freedom and creativity same-sex couples currently experience in negotiating their relationships.

There is perhaps some indication of participants attending to wider concerns about lesbian and gay relationships in accounts that present CP as not necessary for validating their love and commitment. One argument in favour of same-sex marriages circulating in LGB communities and in wider debates in favour of same-sex marriage is that a ban on equal marriage rights prevents lesbian and gay relationships from being fully realized (see Lannutti, 2005). The argument goes that without access to affirming and legally binding rituals and commitments, it is a lot easier to enter into and exit relationships and for relationships to be less than optimally stable and enduring. Other contributors to the same-sex marriage debate are unwilling to concede that lesbian and gay relationships are less meaningful and successful than heterosexual ones. In this study, arguing that CP is not needed to validate love and commitment presented lesbian and gay relationships as meaningful independent of legal recognition. Many of the participants who made this argument highlighted another justification for legal recognition – that of rights and equality.

In sum, a number of participants aligned with heteronormative conceptions of marriage as the ultimate form of relational achievement, and the supreme expression of love and commitment. Others indicated that CP would, at best, affirm an already realized commitment, and others still felt that legal recognition threatened the creativity and counternormativity of same-sex relational practices. Some participants juxtaposed the theme of romance with that of rights, and it is to the latter theme that we now turn.

Rights

Almost all of the participants drew on the theme of rights and equality, citing the 'equality issues' (Bert M06a), 'legal stuff' (Rick M22b) and 'civil rights' (Brenda F11b) associated with CP. Many participants mentioned specific rights (or the denial of these rights) or the general principle of rights and equality as a reason for supporting legal recognition in general and CP in particular. For instance, 'you can't visit somebody in the hospital because you're not family, you can't say whether you want to switch the ventilation machine off [. . .] I pay into a pension that partners aren't recognized [. . .] I'd be pleased to have that bit of paper' (Sally F04a). Here, the CP certificate becomes more than a mere 'piece of paper', it becomes a legal contract between the partners, and between the couple and the state. As noted above, for a minority of participants – those who drew on the theme of love and romance in their interviews – rights were perceived as an additional benefit, secondary to the importance of having their commitment publicly acknowledged and celebrated. For most, however, rights were paramount.

Specific and Packaged Rights, Fairness and Equality, Protection and Stability

The rights associated with legal recognition most frequently mentioned by participants (both rights that participants wanted and/or rights that they expected the CP legislation to incorporate) included those in the areas of 'next of kin' (including medical decision-making and hospital visiting) (mentioned by 18 participants), inheritance (17) and pensions (15). Other rights less frequently mentioned included registering the death of a partner, tenancy rights, power of attorney and the entitlement to joint assets.[2] There was an emphasis in participants' accounts (either explicitly or implicitly) on equality with heterosexuals: 'you get exactly the same rights as would a married couple' (Bert M06a). David (M17b) was adamant that legal recognition 'must happen on an equal footing with heterosexual relationships'. For Luke (M16b) legal recognition was a route to integration and acceptance for same-sex couples: 'it makes everyone feel equal and [. . .] we're not like zoned into different areas, like all straight people can get married and then you can't [. . .] I don't agree that that should be the divide'. A few participants presented LGB and heterosexual peoples' common humanity as a reason for legal recognition: 'we're all human beings, that's how it should be' (Bert M06a) (see Harding, 2006, for an analysis of citizenship and human rights rhetoric).

Many participants commented on the unfairness of the lack of legal recognition for same-sex relationships: 'it seems so unfair' (Marcus M05a); 'this is discriminatory' (Liv F08b); 'it's completely inequitable' (Eddie M06b). Perhaps unsurprisingly, there was a strong emotional dimension in some participants' articulation of this discourse, they expressed anger over the denial of equality: 'it's totally outrageous' (Alice F07b); 'that's disgusting' (Mike M16a); 'that really hacks me off' (Sally F04a). Paula (F03b) commented that 'if Erica dies and I couldn't register her death because I'm not a blood relative you know that would be absolutely devastating, outrageous'. Bert (M06a) discussed the 'horror stories' of lesbians and gay men being prevented from attending their partner's funeral.

---

[2] As Heath (M19h) pointed out 'next of kin doesn't formally exist in legal terms but there's a perception that a husband and a wife have certain rights [. . .] if one of them were to be incapacitated or in hospital'. In fact, hospital visiting is governed by hospital policy and marriage law does not regulate medical decision-making on behalf of another person. Pensions will be covered by the CP legislation (but were not at the time of writing); tenancy rights and power of attorney are covered by different legislation. The other areas mentioned by participants are covered by the CP legislation.

There was also an emphasis on 'protection' (Laurel F01b), 'security' (Debra F04b), '[not] having to worry' (John M19a), and 'peace of mind' (Marcus M05a) (see also Lannutti, 2005). A few participants discussed the importance of being (financially/legally) protected in relation to having children: 'I would like for the sort of legal stuff to do with our family to be sorted before then [having children]' (Una F12a). Stef (F14a) noted that 'if you've got children you need to have that provision, you need to have that extra security'. Participants emphasized the material advantages of legal recognition: there were frequent mentions of the 'financial benefits' (Laurel F01b), 'financial stability' (John M19a) and 'financial implications' (Brenda F11b) of CP (see also Lannutti, 2005). Brenda (F11b) discussed death duties: 'it's actually quite a big dob of money that the State gets if you don't take up this civil partnership'. Una (F12b) talked about the transfer of assets between partners, this 'can be exempt from capital gains tax, which could be useful for us in the future'.

A few participants highlighted the importance of access to a package of rights, such as that associated with CP (see Kitzinger & Wilkinson, 2004). A package is less costly and provides more security and coverage than a fragmentary approach to securing rights: 'there are some things that can't happen with the package with, you know, if you haven't got civil partnership' (Brenda F11b). Martha (F12b) commented that 'the problem with the piecemeal approach to getting protections [. . .] is that they can be contested [. . .] and it's expensive'. By contrast, some participants suggested that rights could be (easily) secured outside of a framework of relationship recognition: 'if there's anything I've forgotten, you know, that might sort of push me towards some sort of official celebration (laughs) [. . .] but I think we're fairly covered' (Thelma F08a). Eddie (M06b) commented that: 'I mean it is that they [same sex relationships] are [legally recognized] already to some extent, but indirectly, you know, like a joint mortgage'. Underpinning these competing accounts were different conceptions of what counts as equality and legal recognition.

'Exactly the Same' or Tailored Rights?

The notion of sameness was evident in most of the participants' accounts of rights and equality in terms of being essentially the same as heterosexuals, wanting the same rights as heterosexuals, and seeking inclusion in mainstream institutions and practices. However, a number of participants *combined* notions of equality with notions of difference, arguing for – in legal terms – substantive rather than formal equality. Substantive equality refers to the process of applying the law differently to different groups in order to achieve an equal outcome for the groups (see Harding & Peel, 2006, and Chapter 12). These participants argued that same-sex relationships are essentially different from heterosexual relationships and the law should acknowledge this: 'I mean you have to tailor and think through the implications of being in a same-sex relationship, which is different to being in an opposite sex relationships' (Martha F12b). Di (F15a) described lesbians and gay men as 'always going to be different' from heterosexuals and asked whether 'we should have exactly the same [rights] or if we should have something different to replicate our needs'. The CP legislation includes a 'pregnancy clause', which dictates that a CP is potentially rendered void if one of the parties is pregnant by somebody else when the relationship is registered. For Una (F12a) this was a prime example of 'taking a model and trying to make it fit to a situation that doesn't work, that is different'. A few participants' support for legal recognition, and CP in particular, was purely pragmatic: Martha (F12b) emphasized the 'practicalities' and 'the realities of day-to-day life' as a reason for entering into a CP even though 'politically, ideologically, I'm not for it at all, in fact I'm against it'.

Discourses of rights and equality are at the forefront of many LGB political campaigns (see, for example, Ellis & Kitzinger, 2002). Lannutti (2005, p. 9) argues that 'the themes of legal equality should not be surprising given that same-sex marriage has been promoted by LGBT advocacy groups . . . as a necessary means to ending the discrimination experienced by LGBT people'. Intersecting the theme of rights and equality in these data were assimilationist (formal equality) conceptions of rights and pragmatic conceptions of rights. Liberal assimilationist conceptions assume fundamental similarities between same-sex and heterosexual relationships and posit heterosexual modes of relating and kinship as the norm. By contrast, pragmatic rights accounts assume differences between same-sex and heterosexual relationships but nonetheless demand access to the broad framework of rights conferred on heterosexual relationships (see Bevacque, 2004). A number of participants intended to enter into a civil partnership because that is what is available to them, in an ideal world they would prefer an alternative form of relationship recognition or route to rights.

Rights (particularly human rights) rhetoric is acquiring an increasingly 'bottom-line' and self-justifying status in the contemporary western world (Harding, 2006). Many commentators have suggested that the most effective way forward for LGB politics is to focus on obtaining equal legal treatment, particular relationship rights and recognition (Eskridge, 2002). Other commentators have queried the limitations of liberal equality politics and have sought a revitalization of radical gay and lesbian feminist programmes of political liberation and social transformation (Clarke, 2002a).

In sum, most participants drew on notions of rights and equality and most saw rights as paramount and as superseding other dimensions of CP such as romance and political and ideological objections to legal recognition (particularly in the form of marriage – see below).

Recognition

Linked to the theme of rights and equality was a theme of recognition that emphasized the importance of CP for securing social and cultural affirmation and acknowledgement of same-sex relationships. Just under a quarter of participants drew on this theme. Marcus (M05a) commented that: 'there is the acknowledgement that we are a couple and legally I suppose that that is as important as the financial aspect, that we do have something worth acknowledging'. According to Liv (F08b) her relationship 'is as important as the heterosexual couple next door I think, and we should have the benefits and the acknowledgement that goes with that'. A few participants felt that an additional benefit of CP is assisting same-sex couples in dealing with the daily onslaught of homophobia and heterosexism that is part and parcel of the lives of most non-heterosexuals. For instance, Liv (F08b) talked about the problem she and her partner encountered when attempting to secure a 'family' membership of their local health club: 'for very kind of everyday things, you know, like if you're trying to join a gym say, you have to join as two single members [. . .] it's like everyday issues that heterosexuals probably don't even consider, that it just happens for them'. Wilma (F11a) talked about the difficulties she encountered when her partner, Brenda, was off sick from work and she went to collect a sick note from their general practice (family) clinic:

> I said [to the clinic receptionist] 'can't you tell me?' 'Oh no that would breach confi-
> dentiality'. I said 'I'm her partner' and she said – and it was, you know, real kind of
> like huffiness and unhelpfulness, and I came away absolutely bloody furious and
> subsequently had a go at the doctor about it, and then rang up the practice manager
> [. . .] 'cos they wouldn't have done that kind of had I been Brenda's husband . . .

Brenda's view was that legal recognition provides non-heterosexuals with a sense of enti-tlement – 'the right to exist' – that helps them to negotiate such pervasive discrimination. According to Paul (M21b) registering his relationship was both a product of, and a con-tribution to, social change: 'I think for me this is about not just me, it's about other people and the future, growing up as a young gay man, I'm very pleased now I can do this for people coming in the future'. Lannutti (2005) similarly reported that same-sex marriage is perceived as healing rifts between the LGBT community and mainstream society by reducing homophobia and ignorance.

This theme highlighted the more diffuse benefits that legal recognition of relationships brings and is perhaps an indication of the way CP functions as a (broader) path to equality for non-heterosexuals (see Harding, 2006). The suggestion was that the benefits of CP may be felt much further than the individual couples who choose to register their relation-ships. As Bourassa (2004) argues 'the intangible goods and goals of marriage' such as social recognition 'do not find expression in the laws or contracts that support the institu-tion; yet they are equally vital' (p. 57). Like rights rhetoric, recognition rhetoric provides a potent bottom-line argument for CP, and other forms of legal recognition, that highlights the privileges that heterosexuals take-for-granted, beyond the obvious rights associated with marriage, and the importance of CP for challenging both discrimination and preju-dice. However, such social validation is arguably secured by conforming to dominant expectations of being coupled, monogamous and cohabiting; in essence by being a 'good gay', and leaving 'bad gays' (feminists, separatists, radicals, queers, bisexuals, and uncou-pled or non-monogamous non-heterosexuals) to bear the brunt of social derision and marginalization.

Responsibilities

The theme of 'responsibilities' consisted of a range of perspectives on the financial and relational obligations and dependencies potentially associated with CP, and was articulated by just under half of the participants. The themes of romance, rights and recognition was primarily used to construct arguments in support of CP (and/or the general principle of legal recognition). By contrast, this theme centred on the potential limitations (and bene-fits) of the precise form of recognition offered by CP. As indicated above, many partici-pants highlighted the financial gains that CP would offer, some also indicated possible financial losses. These participants said that because the CP legislation obligates partners to support each other financially and to be assessed as a couple for state benefits they would be worse off (see Ettelbrick, 1997/89). Erica (F03a) noted – in relation to pensions – 'it would mean you'd have to then share your pension whereas, you know, at the moment you'd have independent pensions, which would end up as more of an income'. Dec (M20b) was disabled and receiving housing benefit: 'it would just alter the money coming in, but wouldn't cause us a problem'. Most participants thought they could cope with such losses (an indication perhaps of the relative material privilege of most of the participants in our sample). A number of participants indicated that the financial provisions of the legislation do not reflect their current money management practices. Paula (F03b) felt that the CP legislation represents financial dis-empowerment and state regulation of same-sex relationships: 'if one of us had to sign on we would have to declare that we're living with a partner and the partner would be expected to support us which is not how we do it [. . .] so I'm a bit wary about that stuff'. Eddie (M06b) noted that 'it would be less easy to worm out of that financial responsibility'. Some participants could identify material costs *and* benefits to CP, but the benefits outweighed the costs: 'I think there are more benefits to it than not' (Pete M21b).

Others saw no (personal) costs associated with financial dependency, and indicated that entering into a CP would simply formalize their existing arrangements: 'I think we regard ourselves as being that anyway so it would just formalize it' (Marcus M05a). For Dec (M20b) 'support[ing] each other' financially (and emotionally) was part and parcel of being a couple: 'we're a couple, we're together, and that's what happens, we just take it as it comes'. Financial obligation was part of 'seeing yourselves as an entity, as a couple, as a mutually supportive duo, rather than as two individuals who happen to inhabit the same space' (Heath M19b). Rick (M22a) thought that if couples are registering their relationship 'then they should be of the opinion that "what's mine is theirs and what's theirs is mine", so they shouldn't really be feeling that they're losing out at all'.

A number of participants argued that the financial benefits of CP are not universal, the package of rights and responsibilities associated with the legislation strongly favour the interests of middle-class same-sex couples. The least privileged couples would benefit little from certain provisions (for example, those in the areas of inheritance and tax) and would be disadvantaged by others (such as joint assessment for state benefits). Una (F12a) felt that: 'there will be same-sex couples who will lose out financially and unfortunately it will be those of the lowest end of the socio-economic scale who will lose out most from civil partnership'.

Equality of rights meant equality of responsibilities for some of our participants; they had to accept the duties and obligations associated with CP if they desired the material and practical advantages. Mike (M16a), for instance, argued that: 'if you're gonna want the same rights then [. . .] you have to be the same right the way through I think'. Una (F12a) similarly commented that: 'I think that the obligation to support one another financially no matter what is an important part of joining together legally and becoming sort of one legal entity'. In general, participants did not entertain the possibility of resisting the assumptions embedded in the CP legislation in relation to financial practices. Alice (F07b) was critical of a 'pick and mix' or tailoring approach to obtaining rights: 'if you have true equality then you should have everything that goes with it, I mean, the good bits and the bad bits [. . .] so you can't tailor it by saying "oh well, we just don't fancy having that bit, but we'll have all the rest." '

The other dimension of responsibility that participants discussed was being legally obliged to commit to, and care for, their partner. Not all welcomed this obligation. For example, James (M09b) expressed concern about being legally committed to his partner: 'it would then be a duty rather than a desire [. . .] I think it could detract from the relationship [. . .] I'm being a better person by choosing to put up with it rather than being forced to put up with it'. Dan (M22a) was of the view that a legally binding commitment 'can cause a lot of stress on the relationship, even if you're not going to walk out tomorrow, there's that thing in the back of your mind that's saying, you can't because, you know, if you do there's legal repercussions'. In contrast, many participants welcomed the responsibilities associated with what they referred to as 'next of kin rights' such as making medical decisions on behalf of their partner. Peter (M21a) commented that: 'the fact that we are responsible for each other [. . .] we can actually have that responsibility, so if either of us was in hospital or something the other one could make a decision for the other one'. Steve (M05b) wanted to have 'next of kin relations' with his partner – 'the right to see each other and to make decisions and so on, if necessary, in the same way that a married couple would'.

These accounts highlight the complexity of legal recognition and the multiple conceptions of same-sex relationships that exist in LGBT communities. A few participants described their relationship in ways that closely conform to dominant notions of heterosexual relationships, invoking concepts such as mutual dependency. Others described their relationships in ways that confounded those notions, emphasizing the importance of what Weeks et al. (2001) dub 'co-independent' ways of relating.

Radicalism

Alongside the theme of rights and equality, the other prominent theme was radicalism. About two-thirds of participants were critical of marriage (and CP to the extent that it is modelled on marriage) for a number of different reasons. It is important to note that this radicalism was, by and large, articulated within a broader framework of support for relationship recognition. Most participants were – like the participants in existing research – pro choice (see Weeks et al., 2001; Yip, 2004). None rejected partnership recognition outright. A few of the participants who were critical of marriage (and relationship recognition more generally) were suspicious of state regulation: 'I'm a bit wary about those sort of legal institutions because of the fact that once you've signed a piece of paper and the state knows you're a couple, you're probably penalised in other ways' (Paula F03b).

Many participants highlighted the 'baggage' (Marcus M05a) and 'negative connotations' (Sarah F13a) associated with marriage. Rick (M22b) thought 'marriage is archaic and it's lost its purpose' and 'I don't really like the institution full stop'. Criticisms of marriage were framed in terms of a number of different themes. Some dismissed marriage as religious and specifically 'a church thing' (Steve M05b). 'The religious side' of relationship recognition and celebration was something that Andi (F14b) did not want to 'have anything to do with'. Marcus (M05a) discussed the conservative christian associations of marriage: 'it's got the aura of happy families and a lot of, I was going to say right-wing prejudice, especially in the church, where people have fought tooth and nail to stop gays having anything like marriage'. Some conceptualized marriage as a heteronormative institution and practice, marked by proscriptive gender roles and power imbalances, and as irrelevant to their lives and relationships. Sally (F04a) 'wouldn't really want it [CP] to be seen as a gay marriage, (sighs) I just don't agree with marriage, it's just the whole heterosexual image'. Similarly, John (M19a) did not 'believe in marriage for gay people'. Ben (M09a) rejected relationship recognition and celebration because: 'I don't want to follow the traditional heterosexual lifestyle, I mean, I quite enjoy my lifestyle and it's not important'. Related to this critique of the heteronormativity of marriage, some participants argued that marriage was fundamentally bad for women:

> I tend to think within marriage women don't always have a very good time [. . .] that is about the stereotypes of what women will do and what the woman's role in the marriage might be, and that women actually end up with little choice often within the marriage (Liv F08b).

Some of the lesbian participants explicitly identified as feminists and a number of participants articulated opposition to marriage on the grounds that it is an oppressive, patriarchal institution. Sarah (F13a) was 'quite against same-sex marriage because I'm just too feminist about it (laughs)'. She thought that marriage was a 'heterosexual problematic institution'. Heath (M19b) said that marriage is 'historically tied up with woman's position in society where she was a good and a chattel that was handed over and it was [. . .] blessed by the church, you know, for the union to encourage the production of heirs'. However, some participants argued that that the meaning of marriage is not fixed and opening it up to LGB people would change its meaning. Brenda (F11b) commented: 'I'm a '70s feminist, (laughs) I'm opposed to marriage, you know, as an institution, although the institution does change if non-heterosexual people can marry, it actually changes the nature of the institution'. Like some of the participants in Weeks et al.'s (2001) study, some of our lesbian participants' critique of marriage was informed by their own experiences of marriage. Thelma (F08a) indicated that she did not like it when legal recognition of same-sex relationships is termed 'marriage' because 'I s'pose it smacks of the, you know, the heterosexual norms of marriage and that's something that I don't particularly want to necessarily bring into our relationship'.

Another theme related to the critique of marriage as heteronormative was that marriage was 'very normalizing' (Jen F13b) – in the words of Mike (M16a), 'you're conforming to society by accepting marriage rather than being gay'. Martha (F12b) expressed concern that access to CP and legal recognition more generally would create a hierarchy within the lesbian and gay community: 'you've got your [. . .] straight acting lesbian couple at the top because they can access the same sorts of things as heterosexuals, and then you've got this kind of sliding scale, which would be problematic, you know, politically and in all sorts of different ways'. The final theme evident in critiques of marriage was that marriage is bad for relationships: 'sometimes relationships can turn completely on their heads, especially when you get married' (James M09b). James proceeded to give the example of a friend who got married and divorced within six months: 'of course there were things going wrong before he actually got married and he thought that, as I would do, it would get better. Of course it's the other way around isn't it? (laughs) Things get a million times worse'. Martha (F12b) made the following barbed, tongue-in-cheek observation about some heterosexual couples' motives for getting married: 'I'm convinced that some straight couples get married because they've run out of things to talk about'.

These criticisms led some participants to suggest abolishing marriage as the norm: 'everybody should have to have a civil partnership and then they can have a marriage as a matter of choice [. . .] let's de-privilege marriage' (Brenda F11b). For Brenda and others, marriage should be reconstituted as something akin to a religious blessing, an optional extra for those who desire it. Similarly, Harding and Peel (2006) reported that a small number (18) of their respondents suggested that all state recognition should be civil and marriage should become an exclusively religious practice divested of its legal status.

Few participants (personally) rejected legal recognition wholesale; however, most offered some kind of critique of marriage and of the ways in which CP replicates some of – what they perceived as – the negatives aspects of marriage. Underpinning many of these critiques was the assumption that non-heterosexual lives and relationships are different in important ways from heterosexual ones. Many participants were torn between a desire for social justice and a desire to retain choice and creativity in their relational practices.

SUMMARY AND CONCLUSIONS

We have outlined five themes informing our participants' conceptualizations of CP and same-sex marriage. A minority of participants emphasized the importance of marrying or entering into a CP for reasons of love, and others downplayed or dismissed the role of legal recognition in solidifying or constituting a relational commitment. Most participants highlighted the practical and material benefits attached to relationship recognition (whether or not they wanted to access these benefits for their relationship) and the potential for CP to secure equality for same-sex relationships in the UK. A smaller number of participants emphasized the more diffuse and less tangible benefits of CP, such as social validation and the potential for reducing mundane heterosexism (Peel, 2001). These three themes all provided powerful support for the 'rightness' of legal recognition. Some participants highlighted potential losses associated with CP, such as a shrinking income and the replacement of freedom, choice and creativity with regulation and obligation. Others welcomed the mutual dependency associated with CP and saw it as part of the equality package. Finally, a significant number of participants raised objections to marriage and the ways in which CP mirrored marriage, and some suggested the possibility of reforming or replacing marriage. The last two themes highlight the complexities of legal recognition and disagreement over the precise form it should take.

The accounts of the participants certainly were less dichotomized and were more 'messy' than scholarly debates about same-sex marriage. Few participants were unambiguously pro or anti marriage, or CP or legal recognition of relationships in general. This said, most participants – like those in existing research – supported the principle of legal recognition of same-sex relationships. What this analysis suggests is that polarized debates about same-sex marriage and tick box responses to simple yes/no, either/or questions about same-sex marriage in popular polls and in (some) quantitative research (although important for a number of reasons) possibly conceal a great deal of complexity.

Across the small number of empirical studies, including the current study, exploring non-heterosexuals' views on partnership recognition, some patterns emerge. There is a great deal of support for choice and the general principle of access to legal recognition, although disagreement about what form recognition should take. Views on the latter hinge on how marriage is viewed, and how same-sex relationships are viewed (in relation to heterosexual ones). It seems that people are more likely to support same-sex marriage if they view marriage as the gold standard of relationship recognition and path to equality for non-heterosexuals, and same-sex relationships as largely the same as heterosexual ones. Those who are more likely to endorse alternative forms of recognition tend to view marriage as a conventional (heteronormative, religious) and flawed institution and emphasize the differences between same-sex and heterosexual relationships, cultures and communities. It is likely that other studies have identified similar views because the same arguments are endlessly recycled in public debates and discussions within LGBT communities (see Smith & Windes, 2000). Harding and Peel (2006) argued that the greater understanding and acceptance of liberal formal equality arguments (compared with substantive equality or radical arguments) in their data is reflective of wider public discourse on the legal recognition of same-sex relationships. Certainly, many of the positions adopted by the participants in this study echo those found in public discussions. One theme apparent in our data and in broader discussions is the notion of the 'good gay/ dangerous queer' binary (Ettelbrick, 1997/1989; Smith, 1994) and the potential for legal recognition to reinforce the operation of this binary. The dichotomy is evident both in pro-LGBT discourse and heterosexist discourse. A distinction is made between acceptable and unacceptable forms of homosexuality, and the potential for dangerous queers (such as single lesbian mothers, bisexuals, lesbian feminists, radical gays, working-class and non-white LGBT people and non-monogamous couples) to give good gays (white, middle-class, monogamous, cohabiting lesbian and gay couples) a 'bad name'. Because CP is modelled on marriage, it evokes explicitly and implicitly the norms of marriage such as monogamy, cohabitation, interdependency and public avowals of commitment. Some participants highlighted the potential for CP to contribute to positive social change only for the most privileged and heteronormative of homosexuals.

It is important to note, however, that this study (and LGBT research more generally) is limited by the use of a homogeneous and privileged sample of lesbians and gay men. It could be that the views reported in research to date are not reflective of the views of LGBT communities *in toto*, and further research is needed before we can claim to speak for these communities on matters of same-sex marriage and partnership recognition.

Some of the complexity and ambivalence in our participants' accounts is perhaps indicative of their attempts to navigate through the polarized, 'either/or' nature of the discursive field surrounding and constituting same-sex marriage. A number sought to carve out a 'both/and' position on CP and legal recognition. Following Peel and Harding (2004), our analysis highlights the need to get beyond 'either/or' debates and to appreciate the ways in which discourses of romance, rights, recognition and responsibilities and radicalism both diverge and intersect to produce multiple accounts of the meaning of legal recognition. With the advent of CP, new challenges await LGB communities and politics in the UK – perhaps seeking marriage rights or attempting to resist the (potentially) normalizing effects of CP. The latter path could be achieved by living CP in transgressive ways, thereby troubling the assumptions on which the legislation is based, or by refusing to enter into the institution. Whichever path (or paths) are travelled, these are truly exciting times both for LGB communities and politics and for LGBTQ psychological theory, research and practice on same-sex relationships.

ACKNOWLEDGEMENTS

Thanks to our participants and everyone who helped us to recruit them. Thanks to Rosie Harding and Liz Peel for their comments on an earlier version of this chapter. Special thanks go to Katherine Ashby and Eileen Goodall for their help with interviewing and transcription. This research was funded by an ESRC grant (award no.: RES-000-22-0588).

REFERENCES

Auchmuty, R. (2004). Same-sex marriage revived: Feminist critique and legal strategy. *Feminism & Psychology*, **14**(1), 101–126.

Bevaque, M. (2004). Feminist theory and the question of lesbian and gay marriage. *Feminism & Psychology*, **14**(1), 36–40.

Bourassa, K. (2004). Love and the lexicon of marriage. *Feminism & Psychology*, **14**(1), 57–62.

Braun, V. & Clarke, V. (2006). Using thematic analysis in psychology. *Qualitative Research in Psychology*, **3**.

Cagan, L. (1999). This dyke's a leftie – this leftie is a dyke. In K. Kleindienst (Ed.), *This is What a Lesbian Looks Like: Dyke activists take on the 21ˢᵗ century* (pp. 47–61). Ithaca, NY: Firebrand.

Carrington, C. (1999). *No Place Like Home: Relationships and family life among lesbians and gay men*. Chicago, IL: University of Chicago Press.

Chan, R. W., Brooks, R. C., Raboy, B. & Patterson, C. J. (1998). Division of labour among lesbian and heterosexual parents: Associations with children's adjustment. *Journal of Family Psychology*, **12**(3), 402–419.

Clarke, V. (2002a). Sameness and difference in research on lesbian parenting. *Journal of Community & Applied Social Psychology*, **12**(3), 210–222.

Clarke, V. (2002b). Resistance and normalisation in the construction of lesbian and gay families: A discursive analysis. In A. Coyle & C. Kitzinger (Eds), *Lesbian and Gay Psychology: New perspectives* (pp. 98–118). Oxford: BPS Blackwell.

Clarke, V. & Finlay, S. J. (2004). Lesbian and gay marriage: Personal, political and theoretical perspectives. *Feminism & Psychology*, **14**(1), 17–23.

Clarke, V. & Kitzinger, C. (2004). Lesbian and gay parents on talk shows: Resistance or collusion in heterosexism. *Qualitative Research in Psychology*, **1**(3), 195–217.

Clarke, V., Burgoyne, C. & Burns, M. (2005). For love or money? Comparing lesbian and gay, and heterosexual relationships. *The Psychologist*, **18**(6), 356–358.

Clarke, V., Burgoyne, C. & Burns, M. (2006a). Just a piece of paper?: A qualitative exploration of same-sex couples' multiple conceptions of civil partnership and marriage. *Lesbian & Gay Psychology Review*, **7**(2).

Clarke, V., Burgoyne, C. & Burns, M. (2006b). *Darling, dearest, queerest: Same-sex couples' accounts of relationship celebration*. Paper presented at the Society for Australasian Social Psychologists 35ᵗʰ Annual Conference, 20–23 April, The Australian National University, Canberra, Australia.

Dunne, G. A. (1997). *Lesbian Lifestyles: Women's work and the politics of sexuality*. London: Macmillan.

Ellis, S. J. & Kitzinger, C. (2002). Denying equality: An analysis of arguments against lowering the age of consent for sex between men. *Journal of Community & Applied Social Psychology*, **12**(3), 1–14.

Eskridge, W. (2002). *Equality Practice: Civil unions and the future of gay rights*. New York, NY: Routledge.

Ettelbrick, P. L. (1997[1989]). Since when is marriage a path to liberation? In M. Blasius & S. Phelan (Eds), *We are Everywhere: A historical sourcebook of gay and lesbian politics* (pp. 757–761). New York, NY: Routledge.

Harding, R. (2006). 'Dogs are "registered", people shouldn't be': Legal consciousness and lesbian and gay rights. *Social & Legal Studies*, **15**(4), 513–535.

Harding, R. & Peel, E. (2006). 'We do?' International perspectives on equality, legality and same-sex relationships. *Lesbian & Gay Psychology Review*, **7**(2), 123–140.

Ingraham, C. (1999). *White Weddings: Romancing heterosexuality in popular culture*. New York, NY: Routledge.

Jeffreys, S. (2004). The need to abolish marriage. *Feminism & Psychology*, **14**(2), 327–331.

Kitzinger, C. & Wilkinson, S. (2004). The re-branding of marriage. *Feminism & Psychology*, **14**(1), 127–150.

Kurdek, L. A. (1993). The allocation of household labor in gay, lesbian, and heterosexual married couples. *Journal of Social Issues*, **49**(3), 127–139.

Lannutti, P. J. (2005). For better or worse: Exploring the meanings of same-sex marriage within the lesbian, gay, bisexual and transgendered community. *Journal of Social & Personal Relationships*, **22**(1), 5–18.

Lewin, E. (1996). 'Why in the world would you want to do that?' Claiming community in lesbian commitment ceremonies. In E. Lewin (Ed.), *Inventing Lesbian Cultures in America* (pp. 105–130). Boston, MA: Beacon Press.

Lewin, E. (1998). Weddings without marriage: Making sense of lesbian and gay commitment rituals. In M. Bernstein & R. Reimann (Eds), *Queer Families, Queer Politics: Challenging culture and the state* (pp. 44–52). New York, NY: Columbia University Press.

Lewin, E. (1999). *Recognising Ourselves: Lesbian and gay ceremonies of commitment*. New York, NY: Columbia University Press.

Liddle, K. & Liddle, B. J. (2004). In the meantime: Same-sex ceremonies in the absence of legal recognition. *Feminism & Psychology*, **14**(1), 52–56.

Manodori, C. (1998). This powerful opening of the heart: How ritual affirms lesbian identity. *Journal of Homosexuality*, **36**(2), 41–58.

Marcus, E. (1998). *Together Forever: Gay and lesbian marriage*. New York, NY: Anchor Books.

Martinac, P. (1998). *The Lesbian and Gay Book of Love and Marriage: Creating the stories of our lives*. New York, NY: Broadway Books.

McQueeney, K. B. (2003). The new religious rite: A symbolic interactionist case study of lesbian commitment rituals. *Journal of Lesbian Studies*, **7**(2), 49–70.

Peel, E. (2001). Mundane heterosexism: Understanding incidents of the everyday. *Women's Studies International Forum*, **24**(5), 541–554.

Peel, E. & Harding, R. (2004). Divorcing romance, rights, and radicalism: Beyond pro and anti in the lesbian and gay marriage debate. *Feminism & Psychology*, **14**(4), 584–595.

Peel, E. & Jowett, A. (2006). *'Pride and groom': Media representations of civil partnership*. Paper presented at the British Psychological Society Annual Conference, 30 March–1 April, University of Cardiff, Cardiff, UK.

Smith, A. M. (1994). *New Right Discourse on Race and Sexuality: Britain, 1968–1990*. Cambridge: Cambridge University Press.

Smith, R. R. & Windes, R. R. (2000). *Progay/antigay: The rhetorical war over sexuality*. Thousand Oaks, CA: Sage.

Solomon, S. E., Rothblum, E. D. & Balsam, K. F. (2004). Pioneers in partnership: Lesbian and gay male couples in civil unions compared with those not in civil unions and married heterosexual siblings. *Journal of Family Psychology*, **18**(2), 275–286.

Solomon, S. E., Rothblum, E. D. & Balsam, K. F. (2005). Money, housework, sex, and conflict: Same-sex couples in civil unions, those not in civil unions, and heterosexual married siblings. *Sex Roles*, **52**(9/10), 561–575.

Steirs, G. A. (1999). *From this Day Forward: Commitment, marriage, and family in lesbian and gay relationships*. London: Macmillan.

Stoddard, T. B. (1997[1989]). Why gay people should seek the right to marry. In M. Blasius & S. Phelan (Eds), *We are Everywhere: A historical sourcebook of gay and lesbian politics* (pp. 753–757). New York, NY: Routledge.

Weeks, J., Heaphy, B. & Donovan, C. (2001). *Same-sex Intimacies: Families of choice and other life experiments*. London: Routledge.

Willig, C. (1999). Beyond appearances: A critical realist approach to social constructionism. In D. J. Nightingale & J. Cromby (Eds), *Social Constructionist Psychology: A critical analysis of theory and practice* (pp. 37–51). Buckingham: Open University Press.

Yip, A. K. T. (2004). Same-sex marriage: Contrasting perspectives among lesbian, gay and bisexual Christians. *Feminism & Psychology*, **14**(1), 173–180.

CHAPTER 10

The Experience of Social Power in the Lives of Trans People

Clair Clifford

University of Birmingham, UK

and

Jim Orford

University of Birmingham, UK

This chapter presents a qualitative exploration of the experience of social power in the lives of trans people. The theoretical perspective employed derives from social and community models of clinical psychology, which locate 'pathology' at a societal and contextual level, but acknowledge individual experiences of distress (Smail, 1995). Despite a large body of psychological data on trans, professional understanding of the phenomenon remains limited. The aim of this chapter is to contribute to our knowledge of trans in the field of LGBTQ psychology and the broader (multidisciplinary) field of trans research, particularly in relation to the lived and embodied experience of trans in western contexts such as the UK.

RESEARCHING TRANS[1]

Transsexualism was first documented in the medical literature in 1853 (Hoenig, 1982) and was subsequently categorized as a medical phenomenon about a century later (Benjamin, 1966). The most recent epidemiological data for the UK are from 1966–1968 (Hoenig & Kenna, 1974) when the prevalence for male-to-female transsexuals was 1/34000 and for female-to-male transsexuals was 1/108000, giving a male/female ratio of approximately 3 : 1. A recent survey of transsexualism and gender dysphoria in Scotland (Scottish Needs Assessment Programme, 2001) reported comparable rates. The DSM-IV-TR defines trans-

---

[1] The term 'trans' is used in this chapter as this was the expressed preference of the majority of participants, over 'transgender' or 'transsexual'. It is also the term favoured by UK organizations such as Press for Change, and it incorporates the experiences of people who opt for no or 'partial' medical interventions (Zandvliet, 2000). No doubt this term, like so many before it, will become an artefact of this particular era in time. In some ways this is a positive sign of the rapid development of the trans community.

Out in Psychology: Lesbian, gay, bisexual, trans and queer perspectives. Edited by Victoria Clarke and Elizabeth Peel.
© 2007 John Wiley & Sons, Ltd.

sexualism as a psychiatric illness through the diagnosis of 'Gender Identity Disorder' (American Psychiatric Association, 2000). Criteria for diagnosis are: 'a strong and persistent cross-gender identification; a persistent discomfort with his/her sex, or sense of inappropriateness in the gender role of that sex; and clinically significant distress or impairment in social, occupational, or other important areas of functioning' (First & Tasman, 2004, p.1080).

There have been three main approaches to researching trans within psychology and related disciplines. First, biomedically oriented research into the causes of trans and possible treatments. Studies have searched for genetic (Cryan & O'Donahue, 1992), neurophysiological (Zhou et al., 1995) and hormonal (Walinder, 1967) factors, attachment difficulties (Person & Ovesey, 1974), dysfunctional family environments (Fajkowska-Stanik, pers comm) and pathological personality factors (Bodlund & Armelius 1994) as a basis for transsexualism. A single causal factor has not been identified. Because of the expense and irreversibility of sex reassignment surgery, there have been investigations into which factors predict or preclude a positive outcome (Walinder, Lundström & Thuwe, 1978). Other studies have examined the implications of psychotherapy (Kirkpatrick & Friedmann, 1976), or no treatment (Meyer & Reter, 1979) as responses to gender dysphoria. No firm conclusions can be drawn from biomedical research, in part because of methodological and theoretical weaknesses (see Clifford, 2003, for a review). Lothstein's (1984, p. 505) observation about the state of psychological research on trans over two decades ago still holds true today in relation both to psychological and to biomedical research: 'masses of psychological data have been accumulated without significantly increasing our understanding of the phenomena'.

Second, there is a growing body of constructionist and discursive research on the social/historical phenomenon of trans and the socio-cultural production of trans identities (see Johnson, Chapter 21 and Speer, Chapter 16). Much of this work draws on postmodern, feminist and queer theories. For instance, in a key paper, Mason-Schrock (1996) discussed how trans identities are constructed through storytelling and modelling other trans people's narratives. His work identifies central themes in trans narratives using constructionist and narrative theories of identity, such as identity commitment, identity salience and the social organization of human experience. Parsons (2005) adopts a discourse analytic approach to trans, which locates the production of trans identities at the level of language and interaction. Notions of 'self' and 'identity' – central to the narratives of her participants – are viewed as the product of dominant discourses. In considering the limitations of a social constructionist approach to trans experience, Fortado (2002) argues that social interpretation has become excessively valued over bodily experience, and that gender identity is more than a social product and also involves internally mediated experiences. Constructionist analyses of trans are in some ways reminiscent of Raymond's (1979) problematic radical feminist analysis of trans women as parodying a stereotype of patriarchal womanhood.

Finally, research has explored the phenomenon of trans from an experiential standpoint, examining the lived experiences of people from the trans community. The most comprehensive of these pieces of work is Tully's (1992) grounded theory exploration of the life stories of over 200 people petitioning for gender reassignment. He concluded that the psychiatric syndrome does not fit well with the reality of the experience. He discussed how gender dysphoria is a consequence of a socialization process, the impact of experiencing oneself as a 'faulted person', and the resulting social stigma. Although Tully's emphasis was not on the operation of social power forces, his analysis acknowledges the importance of social influences (such as social support and gender socialization) in the lives of trans people. There is clearly a need for more experiential research – community psychological models and social power research provide a useful framework for such research. The study reported in this chapter seeks to develop knowledge of social power influences in relation to trans people's lived experience.

THE PRESENT STUDY

Social Power

The current study draws on a social power perspective that views individual lives and contexts as the outcome of social processes that exist outside of our control and often also our perception (Hagan & Smail, 1997a, 1997b; Smail, 1993). In undertaking our analysis, we assumed that trans people, like other people who occupy a marginal position in society, would experience powerlessness of various forms, such as prejudice, oppression and discrimination, and 'transphobia' – akin to homophobia. It has been argued that the psy-professions, such as psychiatry and psychology, contribute to the powerlessness of marginal groups by privileging individualistic explanations of distress, rather than helping people develop a consciousness of the sources of power in society that act to limit or constrain them (Smail, 1995). Empowerment is an important concept in social power research. For instance, individuals may be empowered by being members of organizations or communities that promote esteem and connection (Zimmerman, 2000). However, some ways of thinking about empowerment have been criticised for being too individualistic – as in the notion of a 'psychological sense of empowerment' (e.g. Riger, 1993). A social power analysis requires a more social and politicized account of empowerment and the notion of critical consciousness (or 'conscientization', Freire, 1972) is useful here. Critical consciousness captures the process of understanding how dominant ways of thinking and feeling serve to perpetuate rigid understandings of gender, sexuality and other forms of social categorization, which in turn maintain existing structures of inequality and oppression (Burton & Kagan, 2005; Watts, Williams & Jagers, 2003).

The concept of social power has been developed by community psychologists during the 1990s (see Hagan & Smail, 1997a, 1997b). The concept highlights people's access to resources of various kinds, including personal, interpersonal, institutional, legal and material resources, which provide people with the means to control their life chances. It overlaps with the concept of 'social support' (from family, friends and others), but the two concepts are not identical since social power focuses on a wider range of resources that confer control. Social power overlaps, also, with notions such as 'quality of life' and 'positive mental health' since elements of those concepts (e.g. having a well-paid job or having a good level of self-confidence – elements of quality of life and positive mental health respectively) are amongst the factors contributing to social power. The present study is designed to identify the social influences on trans people's experiences, and their role in individual psychological distress. The approach taken assumes that participants are the experts on the 'reality' of life as a trans person.

Experiential Qualitative Research

There are a number of well-established approaches to qualitative research including grounded theory (GT) (Glaser & Strauss, 1967; Strauss & Corbin, 1998), interpretative phenomenological analysis (Smith 1996), and discourse analysis (Willig, 2001). The approach used in the present research is similar to GT, of which there are a variety of different approaches. Glaser (1992) defended what he saw as the original aims of GT: to explore a phenomenon in depth and to produce a 'dense' descriptive model, against the more analytic, hypothesis-generating and testing direction taken by Strauss and Corbin (1998). Henwood and Pidgeon (1994) have distinguished between a 'realist' approach to GT where a tangible 'reality' exists and the aim is to define and explore it, and a 'constructivist' approach where reality is viewed as constructed by the researcher and participants through their interaction with the data. Examples of the use of GT within LGBTQ psychology include Milton, Coyle and Legg's (2002) study of therapists who described themselves as practising lesbian and gay affirmative therapy and clients who had received such therapy; and Gough's (2002) study of the way male students talked about masculinity, using a combination of constructionist GT and discourse analysis. The approach adopted in the present research contains elements of each of the different varieties of GT, however, we favour Glaser's approach and a realist (or experiential) framework. Although we recognize the subjective element of all qualitative analysis, and hence the way in which the product is inevitably a joint construction of the participants and the researchers, we aim to give voice to trans people by recording their lived experience.

Process of the Study

A model of the process of identifying as trans was developed from data collected from 28 trans women and men living in the UK, recruited through trans and LGBTQ networks (see Tables 10.1–10.3 for details of the participants). Participants could choose to be involved in one of the three stages: developing, refining or validating the model. The methods of advertising the project, and the opportunity to participate via email and the internet, facilitated the generation of an unusually large sample size (for a small-scale, qualitative study of the experiences of trans people). Many qualitative researchers advocate a process of respondent validation or member checking, where preliminary findings are taken back to participants for feedback and commentary (e.g. Reason & Rowan, 1981). The three-stage process was used in order to refine and validate the model. It is important to note that neither author identifies as a trans person – both authors have academic and clinical interests in community psychological models, and the first author has academic and clinical interests in trans people's experiences.

Stage One: Developing the Model

In-depth semi-structured interviews with eight participants were used to elicit comprehensive accounts of experiences of being trans and experiences of social power. Semi-structured interviews allow for comparison across the data set and the opportunity for participants to raise topics that are important to them, and are widely used in GT research

Table 10.1 Characteristics of participants at stage one

Name	Age	Gender status	Stage	Method
Rich	23	FTM	Complete as far as desired at present (RLT, hormones and bilateral mastectomy). Will consider phalloplasty if methods improve. Will require hysterectomy and bilateral oophorectomy in the future	Private
Jon	25	FTM	Complete as far as desired at present (RLT, hormones and bilateral mastectomy). Will consider phalloplasty if methods improve	Private
Lauren	39	MTF	Completed SRS (RLT, hormones and full SRS – bilateral orchidectomy, penectomy, clitoroplasty, vaginoplasty)	Private
Natalie	38	MTF	Full-time RLT and taking hormones. SRS on hold until can finance privately	Previously NHS now private
Lisa	62	MTF	Full-time RLT and taking hormones. SRS on hold until children are older	Private
Karen	43	MTF	Waiting for GIC appointment	NHS
Dan	19	FTM	Waiting for GIC appointment	NHS
Sarah	59	MTF	Completed SRS (RLT, hormones and full SRS – bilateral orchidectomy, penectomy, clitoroplasty, vaginoplasty)	Private

Key: FTM – female to male; MTF – male to female; RLT – Real Life Test; SRS – sex reassignment surgery; GIC – Gender Identity Clinic.
Phalloplasty – construction of a penis; Bilateral Orchidectomy – removal of testes; Penectomy – removal of penis; Clitoroplasty – construction of a clitoris; Vaginoplasty – construction of a vagina; Bilateral Oophrectomy – removal of ovaries; Bilateral Mastectomy – removal of breasts; Hysterectomy – removal of uterus.
Real Life Test (RLT) – historically up to two years living in role before commencing treatment, however, some clinics advocate as little as three months in this stage.

(Charmaz, 1995). The interview began with a broad question designed to elicit a summary of each participant's experiences and a sense of their current situation. The next question was designed to facilitate a chronological account of their earlier life experiences. A number of prompts were employed to remind the interviewer to explore certain aspects of the participants' experiences, to follow the trans journey, and to elicit what the participants felt were significant aspects of their experiences. The interview concluded by asking participants for the most and least helpful aspects of their experiences, and for their understanding of and reflections on social power and empowerment. New themes suggested by participants were added to the schedule in the course of the research (e.g. the notion of puberty as a trigger to crisis, relationships as a form of 'denial').

Stage Two: Refining the Model

A second cohort of 12 participants was involved at Stage two. These participants were presented with a preliminary version of a three-phase biographical, developmental model of the process of becoming trans. The presentation included a diagram of the preliminary model, a description of each of the three phases in the model and a list of questions to

Table 10.2 Characteristics of the participants at stage two

Name	Age	Gender status	Stage	Method
Helen	50	MTF	Full-time RLT and taking hormones. Awaiting SRS on NHS	NHS
Isobel	55	MTF	Completed SRS (RLT, hormones and full SRS – bilateral orchidectomy, penectomy, clitoroplasty, vaginoplasty)	Private
Paul	42	FTM	Completed RLT, hormones and bilateral mastectomy. Currently awaiting phalloplasty, hysterectomy and bilateral oophorectomy	NHS
Will	33	FTM	Complete as far as desired at present (RLT, hormones and bilateral mastectomy). Would consider phalloplasty if methods improve	Private
Marie	45	MTF	Part-time RLT (this is as far as she wishes to go)	N/a
Anne	50	MTF	Completed SRS (RLT, hormones and full SRS – bilateral orchidectomy, penectomy, clitoroplasty, vaginoplasty)	Private
Judith	52	MTF	Completed SRS (RLT, hormones and full SRS – bilateral orchidectomy, penectomy, clitoroplasty, vaginoplasty)	Private
Nichola	45	MTF	Part-time RLT and may consider hormones/surgery in the future	N/a
Abbey	35	MTF	Full-time RLT and taking hormones. Awaiting SRS on NHS	NHS
Georgia	42	MTF	Completed SRS (RLT, hormones and full SRS – bilateral orchidectomy, penectomy, clitoroplasty, vaginoplasty)	NHS
Mike	36	FTM	Full-time RLT and taking hormones. Awaiting SRS on NHS	NHS
Peter	41	FTM	Complete as far as desired at present (RLT, hormones and bilateral mastectomy). Will consider phalloplasty if methods improve	Private

consider. They were invited to reflect on the relevance of the model to their own experience, and to identify aspects of the model that were either unclear or did not fit with their experience. As a result of the feedback received from this group of participants, some categories in the preliminary model were collapsed and combined, others were split into two or more categories, and feedback loops were added to the model, thus producing a more refined model.

Stage Three: Validating the Model

A number of qualitative researchers have suggested that the process of research should be empowering for participants, and participatory forms of research and processes such as

Table 10.3 Characteristics of the participants at stage three

Name	Age	Gender status	Stage	Method
David	28	FTM	Complete as far as desired at present (RLT, hormones and bilateral mastectomy). Will consider phalloplasty if methods improve	Private
Karen	35	MTF	Completed SRS (RLT, hormones and full SRS – bilateral orchidectomy, penectomy, clitoroplasty, vaginoplasty)	Private
Paul	38	FTM	Complete as far as desired (RLT, hormones and bilateral mastectomy)	NHS
Faye	55	MTF	Completed SRS (RLT, hormones and full SRS – bilateral orchidectomy, penectomy, clitoroplasty, vaginoplasty)	Private
Catherine	58	MTF	RLT and taking hormones, awaiting SRS	NHS
Teresa	43	MTF	Waiting for GIC appointment	NHS
Louise	20	MTF	Completed SRS (RLT, hormones and full SRS – bilateral orchidectomy, penectomy, clitoroplasty, vaginoplasty)	Private
Deborah	32	MTF	RLT, taking hormones and preparing for surgery	Private

'member checking' are increasingly advocated in order to achieve this (e.g. Balcazar et al., 2004; Travers, 1997). The final stage of consultation consisted of inviting a further group of eight participants to comment on the refined model (including a detailed discussion of each of the three phases). Participants were asked to provide broad comments on the overall model. Their comments are summarized at the end of the analysis section. At Stage two, when the model still required further development, participants were asked to provide detailed feedback. In contrast, the process of respondent validation at Stage three consisted of a final check of the explanatory power of the model and an opportunity to identify any further material for negative case analysis. Negative case analysis refers to the identification of 'cases' (one person's biography or a phase or event that was part of a biography) that do not fit with the overall model/analysis of the data. Undertaking negative case analysis could mean reporting additional data not explained by the model, but ideally the opportunity is taken to revise and improve the model in such a way that it can embrace a larger amount of the data under analysis.

THE MODEL: POWER CONFLICTS IN THE EXPERIENCE OF BECOMING TRANS

The model that emerged from interviews and consultation with participants across the three stages is a three-phase biographical, developmental model of the process of identifying as trans (see Table 10.4 for an overview of the different phases). The influence of social power is felt throughout the three phases in terms of the distress associated with the participants' conflicted feelings about their 'true' gender and their embodied and visual appearance. The model shows that social power assumes heightened importance at

Table 10.4   Summary of the model

Phase One: Developing an awareness of being different	Phase Two: Starting the process	Phase Three: Acclimatizing to a new life
People see me as different and I'm different to others Coping strategies Trigger Crisis Awareness	Telling someone else Acceptance Adaptation Rejection Starting the ball rolling – seeing the doctor Diagnosis The decision and transition options Living in role Hormone treatment Surgical treatment Financial resources Effect on others Informal support networks	Immediate relief and acclimatizing Wishes and regrets

specific stages, including: developing an awareness of being different to other people, experiences of social support (from friends, family, trans networks, professionals), and in relation to access to financial resources. The model will be illustrated with participants' comments[2] to highlight the conflicts encountered at different stages of the process of becoming trans.

Phase One: Developing an Awareness of Being Different

The first phase focused on the participants' developing awareness of being different and managing these feelings internally, until the point when the experience is externalized by telling someone else.

'People See Me as Different' and 'I'm Different to Others'

These two categories are interlinked and operate together. The initial category was entitled 'the experience of being different', but this was separated into two categories in order to capture the external origins of the developing awareness of being different, and to clarify the interaction between external perceptions and internal experience. Participants became aware of how their behaviour was perceived as different to the 'norm' mainly through subtle feedback: for example, a look shared between adults, or gradual rather than explicit exclusion from a social group. All of the participants described feeling different from their contemporaries, and being acutely aware of this difference from a young age. They

---

[2] Participants' pseudonyms and basic demographic information (MtF – male to female, and FtM – female to male, and their age) are provided in brackets following any quotations.

described becoming aware of it at school, in relation to their peers – 'it was partly being at school . . . that's when I noticed that there was something wrong with who I was' (Lauren, MtF, 39); feedback from parents – 'My father noticed too, I felt I was a huge disappointment to him' (Abbey, MtF, 35); and teachers – 'they thought I was probably quite eccentric, curious' (Jon, FtM, 25); and even strangers – 'I often got taken for a boy, most of the time' (Dan, FtM, 19).

Some participants reported that others did not see them as different, which they attributed to their skill at hiding their feelings. However, these participants remained highly sensitive of gender-related expectations, particularly regarding dress, hairstyle and activities. They developed an awareness that their own preferred behaviours were not considered appropriate to their biological sex. Lisa (MtF, 62) said: 'when I was about nine . . . there was a romp going on with another lad, my reactions to that were . . . significantly non-butch'. Their difference was evidenced by having different interests from same sex peers, but also through a realization that they were not able to be part of the opposite sex group. Lauren (MtF, 39) reported that: 'I liked the girls and wanted to be part of their group, but I didn't fit in there either, and I remember feeling that I didn't fit in with either'. Some participants mentioned becoming aware that other people did not feel the same in respect of being in the 'wrong' gender, and as a result became secretive about these feelings. Natalie (MtF, 38) said: 'No one else ever expressed a similar desire in that direction, so I sort of kept it to myself'. Lauren (MtF, 39) was caught trying on his sister's clothes as a young child: 'I remember thinking "I had better not let anyone know if I do this again" '.

Most participants expressed a growing feeling that there was something wrong with them, and some participants talked about trying to find an alternative explanation for their feelings. Marie (MtF, 45) said: 'I knew that the other boys had no interest in women's clothes and so assumed I was gay, however, as I did not find boys sexually attractive, I concluded that could not be the case either'. Paul (FtM, 42) said 'I sought refuge in trying to convince myself I was neither male nor female'. In the participants' accounts, there were consistent themes of perceiving oneself as different to others, and the notion of the self as incongruent with others' perceptions and expectations. These uncomfortable feelings were managed by a range of coping strategies.

Coping Strategies

Participants described a range of coping strategies to manage their feelings of being different. Some were designed to help them fit in, such as enthusiastically participating in activities considered appropriate to their biological sex (such strategies were now understood as examples of 'denial'). Others were designed to negate the importance of their not fitting in, by, for example, making other aspects of their character more noticeable (e.g. their sense of humour, academic achievements and helpfulness). These strategies may be seen as ways of trying to balance the social power deficit that was experienced as a result of feeling that they did not belong to the 'group'. Most people reported hoping that their gender dysphoric feelings would go away in time, and several participants recounted using potentially harmful methods of avoiding their difficult feelings, such as alcohol, drugs or food. Dan (FtM, 19) said 'well, it did mess me up for a while. I mean I started doing this [shows interviewer scarred forearms from self-harming behaviours]'.

Trigger

Feedback on the first presentation of the model resulted in the suggestion by several participants of the category 'trigger', as a prelude to 'crisis'. We had found it difficult to explain why certain events caused a crisis for some people and not others. So when the participants in the second stage suggested the addition of the category 'trigger', we felt that this significantly enhanced the explanatory power of the model. This category emphasizes the individual nature of triggers to a crisis (such as the gender of a newborn child, a health scare, a bereavement or retirement). It also allows the inclusion of a feedback loop to 'coping strategies', which explains why some people do not go into crisis in response to the first trigger encountered. Many people reported being moved to act on their feelings by media coverage of another trans person's experience. Rich (FtM, 23) said: 'it was only when I watched the TV programme *The Decision*[3] and I was in tears'. Jon (FtM, 25) reported watching the same television programme: 'I saw *The Decision* on Channel 4, and I was just at the point where I really needed to see it'. Most participants noted increased difficulties in managing their feelings about their gender at puberty, and for some this was a trigger to crisis. The rapidity and finality of the physical changes associated with puberty (such as beginning to menstruate) caused a sudden increase in the differences felt between their external presence and internal experience, which in turn facilitated the crisis. A large number of participants also described their triggers to crisis in terms of relationship breakdown – whether the cause of the breakdown was related to their gender feelings or not. Lauren (MtF, 39) said that: 'it was after another relationship breakdown, she found out about my dressing and it seemed like my relationships always went down the same old path'. Social power is implicated in these trigger events because of the change in the participants' 'balance of resources'. For example, the removal of an obstacle, such as ending a relationship with a partner or retirement, can make transition suddenly more possible. By contrast, experiences that increase the distance between the external appearance and the internally experienced self (such as puberty) can make transition seem less likely. This explains how both experiences that draw the individual closer to their ideal self and those that distance them from their ideal self can serve as a trigger to crisis.

Crisis

This category refers to the trans person no longer being able to contain or manage their feelings alone. In coping with a trigger, a person may rely on their existing coping strategy repertoire, or be prompted to develop new strategies. Several triggers may be endured before the eventual trigger to crisis happens and their gender difficulties are expressed to others. The crisis seems to be the culmination of the developing internal distress, which becomes too much for the individual to contain anymore. It can occur at any point in the individual's life – participants reported experiencing a crisis as young as 10 and beyond retirement age.

---

[3] *The Decision* was a documentary broadcast on British television (on Channel 4) in 1996, which followed the personal and medical experiences of several trans people.

Awareness

Awareness emerged from the process of managing the conflicts between internal feelings and the expectations of the broader environment. This stage represents a consolidation of feelings of being different and the triggers and crises that develop over time. It may surface and be repressed by denial and the use of coping strategies. A number of participants described how finding out that sex reassignment surgery was available was a key moment in their awareness of their gender difficulties because it presented a way to resolve them. Natalie (MtF, 38) said: 'one of the kids . . . said that did you know you can have operations to make you a woman and straightaway I knew that was what I wanted, it just crystallized'.

In summary, phase one concerns the developing realization that one feels different from other people in regard to gender, and culminates in the full awareness of feeling that one's internal and psychological gender is different from the physical body.

Phase Two: Starting the Process

Phase two captures the start of the process of externalizing the distress experienced as a result of feelings of gender confusion. A severe crisis – one that cannot be managed by means of existing coping strategies or the development of additional ones – will result in the disclosure of the individual's distress to another person. This may progress to accessing professional assistance and making decisions regarding treatment.

Telling Someone Else: Acceptance, Adaptation and Rejection

There was universal agreement among the participants that this was a very difficult stage to negotiate, and many participants agonized over how to manage it. Others disclosed their feelings of gender confusion suddenly during a moment of extreme distress, and sometimes to people they had not planned to disclose to. Lisa (MtF, 62) reported that: 'I had been passing the church, and I saw a friend there . . . we were talking and then I just blurted it out, I told her all of it'. This category interacts with another phase two category – 'effects on others' – that also impacts on the process of disclosure. The majority of participants stated that their disclosure was mediated by anticipated responses from significant others in their lives.

Participants received a range of responses to their disclosures, captured by the subcategories: acceptance, adaptation and rejection. Some participants felt that their disclosure was treated with understanding, acceptance and sympathy and that support and help were offered. Jon (FtM, 25) reported that: 'My mother rang up the help-line for me and finally persuaded me to talk to them'. Dan (FtM, 19) said: 'Well, my dad . . . it's strange, he just talked very seriously to me about it, it was almost more frightening because he didn't just laugh it off'. Other participants described receiving a mixed response to their disclosure – they felt this was because their disclosure would have a significant impact on the people they told. In these instances, after an initially shocked response, the confidantes adapted and were eventually able to offer support and acceptance: 'She [sister] had a time of bereavement for who I was . . . but we are close again now' (Lauren, MtF, 39). Finally, some participants described on-going negative responses to their disclosure, which had not improved with time. These participants did not receive support or understanding and felt guilty about their disclosure. Sometimes the confidante refused to hear anymore about the feelings of gender confusion, which created an ongoing difficulty in the participant's relationship with them. Natalie (MtF, 38) said: 'They know I'm transsexual and seeking a sex change, but they refuse to talk about it. I feel I have betrayed my parents and it's very hard to bear'. Some people had 'lost' family because of their transition and lived in hope of their family members 'coming around'. Lauren (MtF, 39) said of her children: 'I hope it will be different in the future and that they will want to get in touch'.

Starting the Ball Rolling: Seeing the Doctor

This stage focuses on disclosing feelings of gender distress to a 'professional' who may or may not be familiar with gender identity issues (see Speer, Chapter 16). In the majority of cases, the first contact was with the participants' General Practitioner (GP) (family doctor) or a non-specialist counsellor. In addition, a small number of participants reported making their initial contact with a private Gender Identity Clinic (GIC). A range of experiences emerged as a result of accessing professional assistance and these were generally positive when the professional was familiar with trans treatment. Karen (MtF, 43) reported: 'He's [GP] seen a couple of people who were transsexual before he said, so at least he was aware of what to do about making a referral and that'. The participants valued professionals who were sympathetic and understanding: 'he [GP] understood it was a gender thing, not just that I liked dressing in women's clothes. . .he was very sympathetic and knew the process' (Lauren, MtF, 39). Many participants described difficulties accessing National Health Service (NHS) support for treatment from primary care medical services such as GP clinics. Several participants felt that their negative encounter was the result of their GP's lack of experience in relating to trans patients:

> The problem was, and he didn't even admit this . . . he was quite young and inexperienced. If he had just said to us 'this is too big for me, I can't deal with this, I think you should find another doctor' but he didn't, he just said 'Oh, I'll make some phone-calls'. (Rich, FtM, 23)

Similarly Dan (FtM, 19) reported that:

> The first one [GP] was just like 'well you know there's no point referring you whilst you're taking antidepressants, so you might as well forget about it'. I think she thought it was about my sexuality . . . which of course it isn't.

In relation to referrals to a GIC, some doctors had a reputation in the transgender community for being 'difficult': 'He has a reputation for unethical behaviour' (Natalie, MtF, 38). Some participants felt that they had to wait unnecessary periods of time to fit in with the doctor's and/or the clinic's model of trans treatment. For example, participants described having to undertake the 'Real Life Test' (RLT) for between 12–24 months, followed by taking hormones for a further 12 months, before they were referred for sex reassignment surgery. Rich (FtM, 23) reported that his doctor had commented:

> 'well you have obviously done everything but you haven't done two years of coming to [hospital]'. And because I had spent so much time waiting to get an appointment, and he said it didn't count – the hardest time in my life and he said it didn't count.

In the participants' experiences there did not appear to be any scope for flexibility in this treatment framework. Some female-to-male trans people questioned the usefulness of this model: 'That's the way the NHS forces you to do it. And that's because they have based it upon the MTF model' (Jon, FtM, 25). It was widely acknowledged by the participants that waiting for NHS treatment could be a frustrating process. Several participants were financially able to seek a private consultation: 'I was able to pay and by this time I just wanted to get moving' (Lauren, MtF, 39). When people were able to fund their own treatment, a considerably higher degree of flexibility was reported: 'I went as a private patient and had been in role for three months altogether before surgery' (Lauren, MtF, 39). Lisa (MtF, 62) indicated that: 'It was a private clinic . . . let's say their selection procedure was very simple to get through'.

Diagnosis

Although the majority of participants described 'awareness' developing through phase one, it was nevertheless significant to receive a formal diagnosis. Receiving a diagnosis was often experienced as empowering. Jon (FtM, 25) said: 'It was fantastic, I felt like I was given my life back'. Trans people have usually developed an understanding of their difficulties and what they would like to do about them in terms of gender dysphoria, so a diagnosis is viewed as a passport to treatment. As Lauren (MtF, 39) stated: 'He [GIC Psychiatrist] was good, I saw him for about an hour and he prescribed me hormones and I started living in role part-time, straight away'.

The Decision and Transition Options: Living in Role, Hormone Treatment, Surgical Treatment and Financial Resources

Making the decision about how to and how far to make the transition is highly individual: some people choose to live in role (on a part- or full-time basis), but not to have any hormonal or surgical treatment. Some take hormones and defer a decision about surgery until later because of their life circumstances, and some choose to have surgery as soon as possible. Depending on the 'direction' the person is transitioning (male-to-female or female-to-male), they may face several operations. Both individual circumstances (such as confidence in their ability to 'pass' as their chosen gender, their level of conviction about the decision) and/or life circumstances (such as their family commitments, health, support and financial resources) inform participants' experiences of social power at this stage. Marie (MtF, 45), who was living in role on a part-time basis, captures the social power based concerns of risk and vulnerability, as consequences of medical intervention:

> Would I ever be accepted truly as a member of the opposite sex? Or would I be regarded as a 'trans-'person? Or even worse a freak? Will surgery give me a female body without medical complications? Will hormones screw up my head? Will I ever be passable? Will I ever be able to earn a penny again? Will I have to spend the rest of my life alone?

Some participants choose to live in role on a part-time basis – Marie (MtF, 45) described this as 'living a dual existence'. As we noted above, the initial phase of medical treatment involves undertaking the RLT (living in role) and then taking hormones. Participants had varied experiences of the RLT. Rich (FtM, 23) felt he was already perceived as male during his RLT (so hormones were hardly necessary): '99% of the people on my course, when I wasn't taking the hormones, they all saw me as male anyway'. Some participants reported preferring to take hormone treatment, and postpone any decision regarding surgery. One participant opted to take this course to allow her son to recover from her divorce, another had her NHS treatment halted, so was saving for private surgery. Abbey (MtF, 35) was also waiting for surgery: 'I seriously underestimated the difficulties ahead of me. I thought I would get the medical help that I needed without too much trouble. I was very naïve'. Some participants had complicating medical conditions, which necessitated extra caution. Mike (FtM, 36), for example, had to be monitored closely: 'I've been given testosterone patches rather than injections, as a safer alternative because of my diabetes'. Participants were overwhelmingly positive about taking hormones and many described gains in 'confidence' (Rich, FtM, 23; Jon, FtM, 25; Sarah, MtF, 59; Isobel, MtF, 55; Paul, FtM, 42) and the opportunity to experience: 'a whole range of emotions' (Natalie, MtF, 38). Of the female-to-male participants, several expressed a desire for phalloplasty but were dissatisfied with the current methods available, and therefore preferred to wait for surgical improvements. Only one intended to have phalloplasty shortly, and he commented: 'I have no fears really – as long as the operation is successful' (Paul, FtM, 42). More of the male-to-female participants had completed full sex reassignment surgery including vaginoplasty. Lauren (MtF, 38) described the feeling after having this surgery as 'a major milestone, it meant I had arrived'. Most of the participants raised the issue of 'financial resources' – such resources clearly impacted on the participants' ability to pursue transition (and in particular to pursue it at their desired pace). Some participants described advantages of being able to pay privately for treatment: 'I found out from the help-line that if you can't get funding on the NHS, there is a private psychiatrist you can go and see who can book you in fairly quickly' (Jon, FtM, 25). Rich (FtM, 23) reported that: 'I did it privately because my dad had the money'. Finances appeared to be a highly empowering proximal resource for the participants.

Effects on Others

This category relates to the people important to the trans person: family, friends, spouse/ partner, children, employer and members of their church. Depending on the point at which the crisis is reached and action taken, different people may be affected. For Rich (FtM, 23): 'I spoke to my parents, and said something has to change'. Participants' feared adverse responses from their significant others. Jon (FtM, 25): 'A lot of shame went with it and I wasn't sure about sharing it with anyone really'. Significant others were also implicated directly in any decision made about whether and when to transition. Sarah (MtF, 59) said: 'I mean if we're thinking about social power, you ought to talk to wives and partners of people going through this – they are the ones who lose everything with no real warning of what's impending'. Many participants described postponing their transition until their children were older, or they had retired. The need to consider the responses of others was experienced as disempowering by some of the participants.

Informal Support Networks

The informal support networks reported by participants included national, regional and local support groups, internet networks and telephone helplines. Jon (FtM, 25) indicated that such forums reassured him that he was not alone: 'I went along to the meeting, and I was absolutely amazed that there were these ordinary looking guys here, with jobs and families, and they were just ordinary guys, and I thought "God, it is possible"'. Access to information was also important: 'I have used [national organization] and the web, I have found that a very useful source of information and I think it has brought people closer together when we are all so far spread' (Sarah, MtF, 59). Lauren (MtF, 39) mentioned web-based forms of support: 'the most useful resource was the internet – it has so much information and you can take it at your own pace. I emailed with a few people going through the same thing and it was a fantastic support'. Generally, participants found informal support networks empowering sources of solidarity and a sense of belonging.

Phase Three: Acclimatizing to a New Life

This final phase concerns the participants' psychological adjustments to the decisions they have made regarding their gender identity and any subsequent lifestyle changes, and their reflections on this process.

Immediate Relief and Acclimatizing

These categories reflect the participants' experiences of empowerment as a consequence of new-found 'integrity or congruence of inner and outer' (Paul, FtM, 42). 'Immediate relief' captured the participants' internal feelings after transition (whether that was living in role, taking hormones or having surgery) – feelings of 'rightness', relief at never going back, and 'no longer forced to be an impostor' (Paul, MtF, 42). Participants also described the feeling of being accepted by the outside world in the gender they had always experienced themselves to be. As Judith (FtM, 52) said: 'I now feel "at peace" with my body and myself'. Nichola (MtF, 45) said: 'it's like suddenly being "in synch", like a car that has been going but wasn't properly in gear until now, suddenly the ride is smooth and beautiful'. Paul (FtM, 42) said he felt: 'a huge sense of integrity'. Rich (FtM, 23) described relief at knowing: 'it wouldn't be hard, it would never be as hard again'. One participant (Isobel, MtF, 55) suggested that each step of the transitional process is followed by settling in, a key element of the 'acclimatizing' process: 'There is a settling in period after each step . . . you have to get used to yourself and how you deal with others and how they deal with you . . . it takes time for things to settle down'. Several participants described feeling that their gender confusion no longer 'ruled their lives': 'Before I think it ruled my life, but maybe not for a year now. I'd been trying to control myself so much beforehand, how I hold myself, how I act, who knows and who doesn't, the way I looked and how they perceived me' (Rich, FtM, 23). Many participants reported experiencing a belated 'adolescence': 'A bio guy of 35 has been socialized into a male role for 35 years – I've been doing it for three with the added disadvantage that no-one is actively trying to help you fit in as they do when you are a child, young adult' (Will, FtM, 33). Isobel (MtF, 55) described a time of getting into: '"mischief" most trans people at some stage go through a "live dangerously" and "show off" stage, which is part of growing up'. Rich (FtM, 23) mentioned a feeling of pride: 'sometimes . . . it comes across that I've moved on . . . it's something that I'm really proud of, it's not something I just want to put away and never ever think about'. Others reported increasing confidence within themselves: Paul (FtM, 42) felt 'more self-confident, relaxed and at ease in myself'. Similarly, Isobel (MtF, 55) indicated that: 'I have the confidence, I can tackle anything: a formidable female is, I think, the expression'. Most participants commented that they just wanted to get on living their lives, the same as anybody else: 'we just would like to live as people with rights' (Helen, MtF, 50). Isobel (MtF, 55) said: 'I got on with my life as a woman'.

Most participants were significantly concerned about finding a partner who would accept them sexually (this was a concern both pre- and post-transition). For some, this was felt to be the last remaining hurdle to overcome. Rich (FtM, 23) said: 'but I'm still just getting to terms with my body, and I actually need someone to accept my body, and then I think I will accept it a lot more'. According to Sarah (MtF, 59): 'one of my fears now [is] that I won't find someone with whom I can enjoy a full relationship, somebody who would be able to accept the transgender situation'.

'Acclimatizing' also included getting used to the negative implications of one's transitioned gender and becoming aware of what had been lost. Some of the negative implications were anticipated by the participants, others only became apparent after time. For Isobel (MtF, 55) there was the realization of her 'vulnerability and consequent need to ensure personal safety'. For Paul (FtM, 42), 'I had to remember to act in a way as to minimize seeming a threat'. This experience was shared by Jon (FtM, 25): 'I was shocked the first time I was walking down the street and this woman crossed the road to avoid me. I'm only five foot four inches and I thought I wasn't that scary, but then she must have been scared of me, and that made me quite sad really'. Paul (FtM, 42) also found 'women generalizing about men in a derogatory way' to be difficult. Lauren (MtF, 39) commented that: 'I've noticed that it is harder to get airtime since I have transitioned and it seems to be harder to be taken seriously as a woman [in business]'. Following the decision, people re-enter the outside world with a new internal–external congruence in relation to gender, and ideally had this re-affirmed by the external feedback they received from others. Heightened sensitivity to feedback is a characteristic of this stage because the participants were keen to evaluate whether they were 'passing' successfully. Abbey (MtF, 35) said: 'the biggest (worry) is still "passing". I can spend all day shopping, being referred to as Miss, her, she, lady, et cetera, and it only needs one stranger to look at me for a moment longer than necessary and I'm worried I have been "read"'. Peter (FtM, 41) also found life post-transition difficult because of 'fear of being found out, watching what you say in conversations, so that you are not found out'.

Wishes and Regrets

Several participants spoke about wishing they had transitioned sooner and some expressed regret about not having been born in the correct gender and therefore missing out on what they perceived as 'milestone' events associated with being male or female. As Judith (MtF, 52) said:

I get depressed over the things I missed by not being a genetic female from the start . . . slumber parties . . . the prom . . . never get to wear a formal gown . . . never get engaged, married and have a family. Never experience menstrual cycles or pregnancy. These things may seem trivial to any genetic woman who has taken it for granted but it pains me deeply.

Abbey (MtF, 35) expressed sadness at having to be a trans woman: 'I know I will never be a bio-woman, I will always be a trans-woman'. Some people expressed concern about the possible effects of the treatment, for example: 'the long-term effects of the hormones, which are unknown' (Will, FtM, 33). UK law did not recognise trans persons in their chosen gender at the time of conducting the interviews (this has now changed with the Gender Recognition Act 2004), as a result some participants were concerned about their uncertain legal status. For example, Abbey (MtF, 35) was worried about the following issues: 'legal status, birth certificates, post-op male-to-females being sent to male prisons, employment discrimination, feminist discrimination, lack of NHS funding, the incredibly high suicide rate among transsexuals'. Will (FtM, 33) articulated how political issues translate into personal concerns: 'What will happen to me when I'm old and maybe in a home – will I be respected? There are many countries, places I wouldn't go because of the reaction if my trans status were discovered, for example if I had an accident'. There was also a strong commitment among the participants to give something back to the trans community, to use their experiences to empower others experiencing similar difficulties. Isobel (MtF, 55) reported that: 'I remain involved with transsexuals'. Mike (FtM, 36) said: 'I wish to keep publicly helping the "cause"'. Rich (FtM, 23) mentioned involvement with a young person's support organization: 'it's always going to be with me and I can't run away from it . . . I know what my community is'.

Respondent Validation

The final stage of consultation with participants produced the following remarks. Karen (MtF, 35) commented on the universality of the model: 'I think the model and process itself should – meaning: does/will – hold irrespective of the age of the individual'. Karen also commented on the emphasis on the social in the model, noting that it demonstrated how 'many of the problems we face/endure are socially rather than medically driven'. One respondent (David, FtM, 28) said: 'I would . . . like my father to read it, and it may well make him understand that I am not the only one to be like this, and that my feelings and way of expressing them are not unique!' Catherine (MtF, 58) noted that: 'It should help many others to understand the thoughts and processes that we are up against in our quest to find and become ourselves'.

Negative Case Analysis

The use of negative case analysis is advocated as good practice in GT (Henwood & Pidgeon, 1992; Willig, 2001). Negative case analysis is the examination of those participants' reports that do not fit the proposed model or analysis in order to enable the elaboration of the theory to capture the full complexity of the data. In terms of phase one of the model, one participant's experiences varied because his 'difference' was not perceived negatively by his parents or teachers when he was a child. He attributed this to growing up in a very liberal and strongly feminist environment. However, he did report experiences of not belonging and knowing that there was something 'wrong' with him. His experiences also departed from the model in relation to his reasons for not wanting to disclose his gender difficulties. He felt that his desire to be a man would be regarded as an offence to the feminist values of his immediate environment. However, like the other participants, he was inhibited from externalizing his feelings of gender confusion. Few participants diverged from the model at phase two because it was significantly developed in the second part of the research process to account for the dramatic variations in the point at which participants chose to disclose their feelings and seek help. A profound influence on participants' experiences at phase two was age – it would appear that in the current era society has become more tolerant of diversity (Ekins, 1997), and trans people from previous generations now feel more able to 'come out'. In terms of phase three of the model, the majority of participants who had fully transitioned described positive surgical outcomes and satisfaction at having transitioned. One participant (Jon, MtF, 25) felt that although his chest surgery had left unsightly keloid[4] scarring, he was nonetheless positive about his transition. Faye (MtF, 55) made contact with us during the write up of the study and was invited to be part of the respondent validation. She described her surgery as 'a mistake . . . a total failure . . . and I am left as a eunuch more or less'. She felt that it was too easy to access private surgery and she simply gave textbook responses in her psychiatric assessment. However, we are unsure how far her experiences might be applicable in the UK because her treatment was undertaken in Denmark.

DISCUSSION

The model acknowledges interaction between social, political and environmental influences and the impact of these on the intrapsychic experience of trans people. We have termed this external–internal incongruence (conflict between internal experience and external presentation and the expectations others have based on the external presentation), which impacts considerably on the coping, choices and psychological functioning of trans people. The model emphasizes the continuous influence of the individual's social context.

There are no previous models of trans experience in the literature with which to compare these results, although this model has some interesting parallels with Cass's (1979, 1984) six-stage model of homosexual identity development. The stages are: (1) identity awareness, when one is conscious of being different; (2) identity comparison, when one may feel differently but tries to act heterosexually; (3) identity tolerance, when one acknowledges homosexuality; (4) identity acceptance, when one begins to explore the homosexual community; (5) identity pride, becoming active in the gay community; and (6) identity synthesis, accepting oneself and others. In developing her model, Cass drew on social interaction theory, which posits that stability and change in behaviour are governed by interaction between the individual and society. She drew in particular on Secord and Backman's (1961) concept of interpersonal congruence within personality, behaviour and perception by the outside world, to explain how growth occurs when incongruence

---

[4] A keloid is an overgrowth of dense fibrous tissue that usually develops after healing of a skin injury.

between these elements becomes unmanageable. Her model corresponds closely with how the participants in this study described their psychological distress and conflict. Cass's model has been criticized for not considering the importance of social interaction and for being too linear (Troiden, 1988). Recent stage models of homosexuality have sought to remedy the prescriptive nature of earlier models such as Cass's and accommodate the alternate routes through which individuals may come to identify their sexuality (Coleman, 1981; D'Augelli, 1994; Troiden, 1988). The present model of trans experience attempted to integrate social interaction with personal experience, through the employment of a social power perspective. It also attempted to integrate the retrospective nature of self-identification and move away from a linear model to reflect the myriad experiences reported by the trans people participating in the study.

The present findings reveal a number of ways in which trans people can be perceived as a disempowered group. The feeling of being an outsider was dominant in the participants' early life experiences, and is a common experience for members of socially marginalized groups (Foster, 2004). There are similarities between the experiences of trans people and, for example, immigrants. Immigrants are conscious of their difference from the majority, find it difficult to fit in, may experience an 'identity vacuum' on arrival in a new country, and may feel pressure to conform, assimilate or 'pass' as fully fledged citizens of the new country (Colic-Peisker & Walker, 2003; Onishi & Murphy-Shigematsu, 2003). Although participants in the present research were all well advanced in the process of making a transition to their chosen gender, like immigrants to a new country, they remained sensitive to feedback about how well they fitted their new identities. The participants' biographies gave ample evidence of the uncertain and fragile ways in which their informal and formal social networks might be empowering or disempowering as a result of support given or withheld. The same is true for members of many other marginalized and stigmatized groups, whose social networks include both individuals and groups who provide empowering positive support and those who fail to do so. It is perhaps unsurprising that members of marginalized groups are likely to come together to provide each other with help and support. Research shows that successful mutual support groups are empowering of their members because they provide, amongst other things, emotional support, a powerful belief system that gives members a positive identity and encourages them to recognize their strengths, information and opportunities to achieve a sense of mastery (Katz & Hermalin, 1987; Maton & Salem, 1995). The participants in the present study felt empowered by media coverage of the trans experience and by acceptance from significant others. Professionals (especially doctors) had the power to raise or lower barriers in the way of participants' journey to their new lives. Participants experienced the knowledge that they were not alone and feelings of solidarity with other trans people as empowering. A lack of finances and an awareness of discrimination, including legal discrimination, impacted negatively on the participants' experiences of social power.

In the wider social power literature, there is a strong emphasis on the experiences of marginalized groups, including non-white groups (Fatimilehin & Coleman, 1999), the working class/poor (Hagan & Smail, 1997a, 1997b) and women (Holland, 1997). The application of a social power analysis to a group that possesses varied material resources, as in the present study, is a new venture. This has enabled a consideration of wider distal factors, such as the effects of prevailing politics and policies – for example, the availability of free healthcare – and the current cultural climate, which may affect how well gender ambiguity is tolerated (Zandvliet, 2000). Social power research remains in its infancy within clinical and counselling psychology. It is therefore important to note that in this study, social power did not have a universal and predictable effect: what may be an asset for one person may be a liability for another. This study has also demonstrated that social power research is not only useful in highlighting the socio-economic disadvantages of particular groups in society, but that it is also a meaningful concept at the emotional and interpersonal level. For example, a close family may preclude one person from contemplating transition, or it may be a buffer that facilitates transition for another person. Such examples demonstrate the need to develop the breadth of the definition of social power, and draw attention to the necessity for the researcher or clinician to explore carefully the personal meaning of a particular resource with individual participants and clients.

Finally, we note the very marginal position of trans studies in psychology, reflecting the marginal and misunderstood position of trans people in society. There was a significant struggle to establish lesbian and gay psychology as a recognizable part of the broader discipline of psychology (Milton et al., 2002), and there is now a struggle to move away from 'lesbian and gay psychology' to the more inclusive label and field of 'LGBTQ psychology'. This volume, and the inclusion of this chapter and other chapters on trans, is a welcome sign of the recognition of trans people as a group whose voice needs to be heard.

ACKNOWLEDGEMENTS

We are grateful to the many research participants who have kindly voiced their experiences and offered insights. The first author would also like to thank Mike Drayton for many stimulating discussions over the years, and to Victoria Clarke and Liz Peel for their excellent editorial guidance on this project.

REFERENCES

American Psychiatric Association (2000). *Diagnostic & Statistical Manual of Mental Disorders* (4th edn, text rev). Washington DC: American Psychiatric Association.

Balcazar, F. E., Taylor, R. R., Kielhofner, G. W., Tamley, K., Benziger, T., Carlin, N. & Johnson, S. (2004). Participatory action research: General principles and a study with a chronic health condition. In L. A. Jason, C. B. Keys, Y. Suarez-Balcazar, R. R. Taylor & M. I. Davis (Eds), *Participatory Community Research: Theories and methods in action* (pp. 17–36). Washington DC: American Psychological Association.

Benjamin, H. (1966). *The Transsexual Phenomenon*. New York, NY: Julian Press.

Bodlund, O. & Armelius, K. (1994). Self-image & personality traits in gender identity disorders: An empirical study. *Journal of Sex & Marital Therapy*, **20**(4), 303–317.

Burton, M. & Kagan, C. (2005). Liberation social psychology: Learning from Latin America. *Journal of Community and Applied Social Psychology*, **15**(1), 63–78.

Cass, V. C. (1979). Homosexual identity formation: A theoretical model. *Journal of Homosexuality*, **4**(3), 219–235.

Cass, V. C. (1984). Homosexual identity: A concept in need of definition. *Journal of Homosexuality*, **9**(2/3), 105–126.

Charmaz, K. (1995). Grounded theory. In J. Smith, R. Harré & L. van Langenhove (Eds), *Rethinking Methods in Psychology* (pp. 27–49). London: Sage.

Clifford, C. (2003). A critical review of the psychological literature relating to transsexualism. *Lesbian & Gay Psychology Review*, **4**(1), 8–18.

Coleman, E. (1981). Developmental stages of the coming out process. *Journal of Homosexuality*, **7**(2/3), 31–43.

Colic-Peisker, V. & Walker, I. (2003). Human capital, acculturation and social identity: Bosnian refugees in Australia. *Journal of Community & Applied Social Psychology*, **13**(5), 337–360.

Coyle, A. & Wilkinson, S. (2002). Social psychological perspectives on lesbian and gay issues in Europe: The state of the art. *Journal of Community & Applied Social Psychology*, **12**(3), 147–152.

Cryan, E. & O'Donoghue, F. (1992). Transsexualism in a Klinefelter male – a case report. *Irish Journal of Psychological Medicine*, **9**, 45–46.

D'Augelli, A. R. (1994). Identity development and sexual orientation: Toward a model of lesbian, gay and bisexual development. In E. J. Trickett, R. J. Watts & D. Birman (Eds), *Human Diversity: Perspectives on people in context* (pp. 312–333). San Francisco, CA: Jossey-Bass.

Ekins, R. (1997). *Male Femaling: A grounded theory approach to cross-dressing & sex-changing.* London: Routledge.

Fatimilehin, I. A. & Coleman, P. G. (1999). 'You've got to have a Chinese chef to cook Chinese food!' Issues of power and control in the provision of mental health services. *Journal of Community & Applied Social Psychology*, **9**(2), 101–117.

First, M. B. & Tasman, A. (2004). *DSM-IV-TR Diagnosis, Etiology and Treatment.* Chichester: Wiley.

Foster, D. (2004). Liberation psychology. In D. Hook (Ed.), *Introduction to Critical Psychology* (pp. 559–602). Capetown, South Africa: University of Capetown Press.

Fortado, J. L. (2002). Boundaries of Gender: Framing transgender, transsexual and intersex indentities. Paper presented at the Annual American Sociological Association Conference, Atlanta, Georgia, August.

Freire, P. (1972). *Pedagogy of the oppressed.* Harmondsworth: Penguin.

Glaser, B. G. (1992). *Emergence vs Forcing: Basics of grounded theory analysis.* Mill Valley, CA: The Sociology Press.

Glaser, B. G. & Strauss, A. L. (1967). *The Discovery of Grounded Theory: Strategies for qualitative research.* New York, NY: Aldine.

Gough, B. (2002). 'I've always tolerated it but . . .': Heterosexual masculinity and the discursive reproduction of homophobia. In A. Coyle & C. Kitzinger (Eds), *Lesbian and Gay Psychology: New perspectives* (pp. 219–238). Oxford: BPS Blackwell.

Hagan, T. & Smail, D. (1997a). Power-mapping I: Background and basic methodology. *Journal of Community & Applied Psychology*, **7**, 257–267.

Hagan, T. & Smail, D. (1997b). Power-mapping II: Practical application: The example of child sexual abuse. *Journal of Community & Applied Psychology*, **7**, 269–284.

Henwood, K. L. & Pidgeon, N. F. (1992) Qualitative research and psychological theorising. *British Journal of Psychology*, **83**(1), 97–112.

Henwood, K. & Pidgeon, N. (1994). Beyond the qualitative paradigm: A framework for introducing diversity within qualitative psychology, *Journal of Community & Applied Social Psychology*, **4**(4), 225–238.

Hoenig, J. (1982). Transsexualism. In K. Gransville-Grossman (Ed.), *Recent Advances in Clinical Psychiatry Vol. 4* (pp. 181–190). London: Churchill Livingstone.

Hoenig, J. & Kenna, J. (1974). The prevalence of transsexualism in England and Wales. *British Journal of Psychiatry*, **124**, 181–190.

Holland, S. (1997). Woman and urban mental health: 20 years on. *Clinical Psychology Forum*, **100**, 45–48.

Katz, A. & Hermalin, J. (1987). Self-help and prevention. In J. Hermalin & J. Morell (Eds), *Prevention Planning in Mental Health* (pp. 151–190). Newbury Park, CA: Sage.

Kirkpatrick, M. & Friedmann, C. (1976). Treatment of requests for sex-change surgery with psychotherapy. *American Journal of Psychiatry*, **133**(10), 1194–1196.

Lothstein, L. (1984). Psychological testing with transsexuals: A 30-year study. *Journal of Personality Assessment*, **48**(5), 500–507.

Mason-Schrock, D. (1996). Transsexuals' narrative construction of the 'true self'. *Social Psychology Quarterly*, **59**(3), 176–192.

Maton, K. I. & Salem, D. A. (1995). Organizational characteristics of empowering community settings: A multiple case study approach, *American Journal of Community Psychology*, **23**(5), 631–656.

Meyer, J. & Reter, D. (1979). Sex reassignment. *Archives of General Psychiatry*, **36**(9), 1010–1015.

Milton, M., Coyle, A. & Legg, C. (2002). Lesbian and gay affirmative psychotherapy: Defining the domain. In A. Coyle & C. Kitzinger (Eds), *Lesbian and Gay Psychology: New perspectives* (pp. 175–197). Oxford: BPS Blackwell.

Onishi, A. & Murphy-Shigematsu, S. (2003). Identity narratives of Muslim foreign workers in Japan. *Journal of Community & Applied Social Psychology*, **13**(3), 224–239.

Parsons, C. (2005). Exploring transsexual narratives of identity (trans)formation: A search for identity. *Psychology of Women Section Review*, **7**(2), 60–70.

Person, E. & Ovesey, L. (1974). The transsexual syndrome in males: 1: Primary transsexualism. *American Journal of Psychotherapy*, **28**, 4–20.

Raymond, J.G (1979). *The Transsexual Empire*. Aylesbury, Bucks: The Women's Press.

Reason, P. & Rowan, J. (Eds) (1981). *Human Inquiry: A sourcebook of new paradigm research*. Chichester: Wiley.

Riger, S. (1993). What's wrong with empowerment. *American Journal of Community Psychology*, **21**(3), 279–292.

Scottish Needs Assessment Programme (2001). *Transsexualism and Gender Dysphoria in Scotland*. Glasgow: University of Glasgow.

Secord, P. F. & Backman, C. W. (1961). Personality theory and the problems of stability and change in individual behaviour: an interpersonal approach. *Psychological Review*, **68**(1), 21–32.

Smail, D. (1993). *The Origins of Unhappiness*. London: Harper Collins.

Smail, D. (1995). Power and the origins of unhappiness: working with individuals. *Journal of Community & Applied Social Psychology*, **5**(5), 347–356.

Smith, J. A. (1996). Beyond the divide between cognition and discourse: Using interpretative phenomenological analysis in health psychology. *Psychology & Health*, **11**, 261–271.

Strauss, A. & Corbin, J. (1998). *Basics of Qualitative Research: Techniques and procedures for developing grounded theory* (2nd edn). London: Sage Publications.

Travers, K. D. (1997). Reducing inequities through participatory research and community empowerment. *Health Education & Behavior*, **24**(3), 344–356.

Troiden, R. (1988). *Gay and Lesbian Identity*. New York, NY: General Hall.

Tully, B. (1992). *Accounting for Transsexualism and Transhomosexuality*. London: Whiting & Birch.

Walinder, J. (1967). Transsexualism: A study of forty-three cases. *International Journal of Transgender*. Retrieved 29 December, 2006, from http://www.symposium.com/ijt/walinder/index.htm

Walinder, J., Lundström, B. & Thuwe, I. (1978). Prognostic factors in the assessment of male treanssexuals for sex reassignment. *British Journal of Psychiatry*, **132**, 16–20.

Watts, R. J., Williams, N. C. & Jagers, R. J. (2003). Sociopolitical development. *American Journal of Community Psychology*, **31**(1/2), 185–194.

Willig, C. (2001). *Introducing Qualitative Research in Psychology: Adventures in theory and practice*. Buckingham: Open University Press.

Zandvliet, T. (2000). Transgender issues in therapy. In Neal, C. & Davies, D. (Eds), *Issues in Therapy with Lesbian, Gay, Bisexual and Transgender Clients* (pp 176–189). Buckingham: Open University Press.

Zhou, J.-N., Hofman, M., Gooren, L. & Swaab, D. (1995). A sex difference in the human brain and its relation to transsexuality. *Nature*, **378**(6552), 68–70.

Zimmerman, M. A. (2000). Empowerment theory: Psychological, organizational and community levels of analysis. In J. Rappaport & E. Seidman (Eds), *Handbook of Community Psychology* (pp. 43–63). New York, NY: Plenum Press.

CHAPTER 11

'What Do They Look Like and Are They among Us?': Bisexuality, (Dis)closure and (Un)viability

Maria Gurevich
Ryerson University, Canada
Jo Bower
Independent Research Consultant, Canada
Cynthia M. Mathieson
University of British Columbia, Canada
and
Bramilee Dhayanandhan
Center for Addiction and Mental Health, Canada

INTRODUCTION

> At the women's dance, my friend . . . was in the bathroom and . . . everybody had seen your signs and stuff, and bisexuals, there aren't any of those here. And it's like we're still foreign creatures and it's like what do they look like, you know, they could be among us. (P2)

This excerpt is taken from a Canadian study of 22 women who self-identify, with varying degrees of (dis)comfort, as bisexual (Bower, Gurevich & Mathieson, 2002). As this quote illustrates, bisexuals are simultaneously constructed as 'non-existent', 'foreign', 'unrecognizable' and 'interlopers' within the lesbian, gay, bisexual and transgendered (LGBT) community. The 'bisexual' lingers uncomfortably in this growing list of awkward identity markers, which now includes the even more elusive 'questioning'. Although this extensive inventory is intended to expand our thinking about the multiplicity of sexual repertoires, it also serves to homogenize the socio-historic and psycho-social specificity of these complex identities. The seemingly expansive catalogue begins to resemble a grab-bag of sexual and social (mis)fits, rather than a descriptively meaningful designation of inexhaustible sexual possibilities. In part, this is a result of a well-meaning attempt to include

Out in Psychology: Lesbian, gay, bisexual, trans and queer perspectives. Edited by Victoria Clarke and Elizabeth Peel.
© 2007 John Wiley & Sons, Ltd.

'all the girls [and boys] in the team' (Eagleton, 1996, p. 14), wherein the chain of identity markers is continually extended (lesbian, gay, bisexual, transgendered, questioning, etc.). Residing in this ceaseless propagation is the inevitable *supplément* (Derrida, 1997).[1] The *supplément* denotes an 'excluded "other"', which is forever subordinate, but which, paradoxically, also complements that which it augments' (Kaloski Naylor, 1999, p. 53). Thus, bisexuality, along with other 'sexual outlaws', highlights the limits of the 'original' inclusions (lesbian and gay), while simultaneously remaining an 'embarrassed "etc." at the end of' (Butler, 1990, p. 143) an inexhaustible enumeration of identities. This trailing 'etc.' of 'elaborate predicates'[2] is instructive, underscoring as it does 'that the effort to "encompass a situated subject" is invariably incomplete, and thus a tacit reminder not only of the possibilities of exclusions, but more productively, of the impossibly of fixing and exhausting identity categories' (Bower, 1999, p. 58).

Bisexuality, in particular, is misleading in its labelling and positioning within this roll call, framed as it is as comprising 'one part gay, one part straight, and mix' (Weasel, 1996, p. 8). This well-intentioned insertion of bisexuality in the evolving list of sexual identities paradoxically points to 'a curious disappearing of bisexuality, at once accepting and dismissive' (Kaloski Naylor, 1999, p. 56). Although bisexuality is invited to the proliferating identity party, it remains submerged in sexual categories that have achieved greater sociopolitical primacy, namely lesbian and gay identities: 'bisexual women (as bisexual women) are rarely in anyone's team' (Kaloski Naylor, 1999, p. 54). Bisexuality occupies a precarious cultural location; it is both unseen and ubiquitous (Esterberg, 2002). On the one hand, it is often subsumed under the categories of lesbian and gay within both popular and social scientific discourse, leaving little social, theoretical or political space for considering it as a sexual identity in its own right (Yoshino, 2000), and delimiting the possibilities for community building and political action (Fox, 1995; Rust, 2001). On the other hand, images of bisexuality are alternately and paradoxically positioned as natural (i.e. the default if society left us to our own devices), confused, hyper-sexualized, predatory, subversive, privileged and menacing (Esterberg, 2002). In this way, bisexuality appears to be simultaneously 'everywhere and nowhere' (Esterberg, 2002, p. 215, see also Barker, Chapter 6).

The recent trend of 'marketing bisexuality as "a la mode"' to both women who identify as lesbian and as heterosexual (Wilkinson, 1996, p. 293) as a fashionable (and fetishized) transient alternative both to what is positioned as 'stale and sanitized' lesbian sex and to 'rough and phallocentric' heterosex further oversimplifies and depoliticizes bisexuality. For lesbians, sex with men is presented as an 'exciting', 'forbidden', leisure-time activity, an uncomplicated 'sport fuck'; for heterosexual women, sex with women is touted as 'soft', 'sensuous', 'safe' and 'carefree' (Wilkinson, 1996). Both types of border-crossing sex emphasize the liberatory, entertaining and recreational potential associated with having sex outside one's sexual identity straightjacket. Thus, a viable cultural space for intelligible bisexual desires, practices and identities is quashed in favour of catering to disconnected, decontextualized pleasure and stylistic imperatives (Wilkinson, 1996). Paradoxically, the exalted status of this new brand of 'bisexuality a la mode' simultaneously:

---

[1] Derrida borrowed the term *supplément* from Jean Jacques Rousseau's (1755) *Essay on the Origin of Languages*. Rousseau defined it as 'an inessential extra, added to something complete in itself' (Culler, 1989, p. 103). The term contains within it an inherent contradiction – if something is complete in itself, it should not need or benefit from a supplement; if it can be supplemented, an originary lack becomes apparent (Derrida, 1997).

[2] Although Butler uses 'elaborates' as a verb in the original quote, our transposition is intended to emphasize the unwieldy reach of such endless identity lists.

reinforces the old idea that there are 'essentially' two sexual identities: lesbian and straight. If a lesbian having heterosex is 'transgressive', there must be some basic, underlying sexual identity that *can* be transgressed. Lesbians who have sex with men once in a while can be reassured that such practice does not mean they have to renounce a 'fundamental lesbian' sexual identity. Likewise, the notion of 'essential' sexual orientations provides a safety-net for heterosexual women who occasionally have sex with women: They remain certain that they are 'heterosexual really', returning securely to the arms of their men after a little lesbian 'fun' (Wilkinson, 1996, p. 294).

Importantly, this essentialism permits 'safe' sexual exploration, without destabilizing the ostensible solidity and politics of identity anchors. In this way, bisexuality's simultaneous 'uniquely conceivable and uniquely inconceivable' status is retained (Rust, 2000a, p. 205). Such behaviourally anchored formulations of bisexuality, by eliding issues of identity, community and politics, ensure its erasure (Yoshino, 2000).

The mainstream film (Jenkins, 2005; Stewart, 2002), television (Kachgal, 2004; McKenna, 2002) and music industries (Diamond, 2005; Mistry, 2000), in particular, have capitalized on the 'bisexual chic'/'lesbian chic' with a steady production of appropriated images of queer sexuality. Among the more well-known filmic examples of bisexual themes, of one kind or another, are: *Chasing Amy* (1997), *The Object of My Affection* (1998), *Bedrooms and Hallways* (1998), *Wild Things* (1998), *Girl, Interrupted* (1999), *Cruel Intentions* (1999), *Just One Time* (2000), *A Girl Thing* (2001), *Not Another Teen Movie* (2001), *American Pie 2* (2001), *Kissing Jessica Stein* (2002), *Frida* (2002), and *Kinsey* (2004).

Incidentally, even the ostensibly independent film makers are also cashing in on the feverish fascination with clichéd images of 'girl on girl' sexuality. *My Summer of Love* (2004), which originally premiered at The Edinburgh International Film Festival in 2004 and with a recent North American debut at The Inside Out Lesbian and Gay Film Festival (Canada, 2005) is one such recent example. The film has won numerous awards (including British Independent Film Award, Best New British Feature, Directors Guild of Great Britain) for its decidedly cinematically beautiful depiction of teenage first love. Although there is certainly much to recommend the film, what is surprising is that critics have almost unanimously lauded it for its ostensibly unusual and non-salacious depiction of sexuality between women. As one critic states, 'that such a compelling vision of teen-girl love could be created by a middle-age Polish man is slightly surprising' (Anderson, 2005, p. 3). The director himself, Pawel Pawlikowski, is quoted as asserting that 'what's more important than the homosexual element is that these girls are totally different types' (Anderson, 2005, p. 6). However laudable the film is on many levels, there is no denying that at times the male gaze (Mulvey, 1989) lurks luridly and conspicuously, and that not an insignificant part of the overwhelming appeal of the film can be attributed to what has been repeatedly referred to as the striking 'physical allure' of the female leads (Anderson, 2005, p. 7).

Television versions that have contained (occasional) instances of bisexual content have included: *Roseanne*, *Will and Grace*, *Ally McBeal*, *Friends*, *Sex and the City*, *Buffy the Vampire Slayer* and *The Real World*. The music industry is likewise relying on numerous 'girly action' images to peddle its wares.[3] Numerous sexually suggestive poses and

---

[3] The role of bisexuality in the music world is given more sustained attention in the 'fictional biopic' (Kelly, 1998), *Velvet Goldmine* (1998). Although on the surface purporting to tell the tale of glam rock, the film documents bisexuality in this domain. The gay American film director, Todd Haynes, has in fact explicitly stated that he would 'like to see questions about identity and sexuality ignited by *Velvet Goldmine*' (Haynes in interview with Kelly, 1998).

provocative kisses of this genre populate the music videos; among the more famous posing 'couples' are Madonna and Britney Spears, Madonna and Christina Aguilera, and Julia Volkova and Lena Katina of t.A.Tu. Although images of 'bi-boys' (Bledsoe, 2004) are increasingly infiltrating these domains, the stage is more often than not occupied by 'girl-on-girl action'.[4] Taken together, such imagery is part of a broader increasing rise in the commodification of same-sex desire (Ingebretsen, 1999), wherein queer sexuality and a 'queer aesthetic' (Gamman & Makinen, 1994) has been appropriated as a marketing ploy (Janes, 2004; Mistry, 2000). Apparently queer sells. Notably, bisexuality is rarely explicitly named within these popularized representations, much less explored as a viable identity (Diamond, 2005; Wilkinson, 1996). The focus is on transient (and titillating) experimentation, fantasies (expressed or enacted) – frequently for the amusement of a male consumer – and very occasionally on lives lived but left very much unarticulated. And above all, depictions of heterosexualized 'luscious lesbianism' predominate (Ciasullo, 2001; Jenkins, 2005). In this way, the project of dismantling heteronormativity remains a fractured, apolitical enterprise that continues to reinforce simplistic dichotomous notions of sexuality and reinstalls heterosexuality as the norm, all the while claiming that it is all a matter of 'personal choice' rather than the outgrowth of specific socio-political dictates (Diamond, 2005).

The proliferation of these images continue to be the target of mainstream news fascination, speculation and even occasional attempts at critique, with such headlines as 'Women who "switch teams" – Drifting sexual orientation is in the pop culture spotlight' (Takahama, 2001), 'How Britney gets her satisfaction' (Adams, 2000), 'As times go bi' (*The Toronto Star*, 2000), 'Manufacturing lesbianism for CD sales' (Richler, 2003), 'Breaking down taboos: Hollywood coming out of the closet on bisexuality' (Portman, 2005). The growing popularity among teens, girls in particular, of exploring the bisexual option, is also the subject of numerous headlines: 'Hello, good bi' (*The Toronto Star*, 2001), 'Teen girls exploring "bisexual chic" trend: Debate rises over whether a kiss is just a kiss' (Malernee, 2003), 'Wave of "bisexual chic" sweeping American high schools' (*The Guardian*, 2004), 'Partway gay? For some teen girls, sexual preferences is a shifting concept' (Stepp, 2004).

The phenomenon is now sufficiently pervasive to become the target of frantic warnings by the religious right. *The Council on Biblical Manhood and Womanhood*, which claims to be in the business of 'helping the church deal biblically with gender issues' recently ran a story lamenting the rise of bisexuality's popularity, while cleverly appropriating the *argo* of popular culture, as well as of cultural and media studies critics: 'The newest teen girl fad: Bisexual chic' (Mohler, 2004). Rev Jerry Falwell, the infamous Christian evangelist TV star, has also weighed in on the issue, condemning bisexual experimentation: 'Teens commit to chastity until marriage' (Falwell, 2004).

Thus, bisexuality remains simultaneously invisible, by virtue of its status as a non-legitimate category and highly conspicuous, owing to its status as a 'spoiled identity' (Goffman, 1963), that is a discredited, socially alienated location that is disqualified from access to 'normal' identity status. Although bisexuality may be 'everywhere' in form (i.e. the deluge of bisexual chic images), the content continues to largely elude the cultural

---

[4] While these images proliferate, on-screen critiques of these representations are virtually absent. A notable exception is *Off the Straight & Narrow* (1998), which is the first in-depth critical documentary featuring media scholars who address the pros and cons of the steady rise of queer televised images.

frame (i.e. the dearth of well-articulated, non-sensationalized portrayals). Bisexuals continue to be largely positioned as frivolous, exotic creatures at best, and as contaminating interlopers at worst. This paradoxical positioning is clearly illustrated in the opening quote of the chapter: there is both a negation of its viability ('there aren't any of those here') and a terror that its presence is always lurking ('they could be among us'). This dread is amplified by an uncertainly about locating markers of recognition ('what do they look like').

Bisexuality continues to be under-theorized, relative to the increasingly substantial literature on lesbian and gay identity, although significant exceptions that attempt to articulate a theory and a politics of bisexuality are emerging (e.g. Atkins, 2002; Bi Academic Intervention, 1997; Esterberg, 2002; Firestein, 1996; Fox, 1995, 2000; Garber, 1995; Hemmings, 2002; Rust, 1995; 2000b; Storr, 1999; Tucker, 1995). For a summary of the theoretical and empirical status of bisexuality in psychology, the reader is referred to these works and our companion piece to this chapter (Bower et al., 2002). In this chapter, we hope to add to these efforts by drawing on women's account of bisexual lives, identities, and politics to examine what it means to (dis)close bisexual identities. What sets of openings and foreclosures follow such revelations? As Däumer (1999) asserts, bisexuality presents a problem that extends beyond issues of visibility: 'the problems of bisexuals are social and political ones' (p. 159) and, therefore, require an epistemological shift that destabilizes and reconfigures gender and sexuality. As long as our socio-political systems benefit from keeping two ostensibly different sexual cultures (straight and non-straight) and gender cultures (male and female) in a divided and antagonistic relation to each other, then owning or displaying a bisexual identity is not necessarily a radical response to heterosexism and sexism. In other words, we need to be more than merely visible or tolerable to represent a subversive force. As Foucault says (1990), sexuality is not a 'natural given which power tries to hold in check, or an obscure domain which knowledge tries gradually to uncover' (p. 105). Rather, it is a historically constructed matrix of variously inflected bodies, pleasures, discourses, knowledges and power. Therefore, it is through the deployment of sexuality that knowledge/power takes effect in bodies, pleasures and identities. As the women in our study attest, 'living' bisexual identities is difficult because they are always already submerged in the service of displaying and revealing identities that are more recognizable and more viable (i.e. heterosexual and lesbian and gay) within the existing social and political context. The aim of this chapter is to articulate an epistemology and politics of (dis)closure in relation to bisexual identities.

PARTICIPANTS AND METHOD

The description of the methodological, theoretical and analytic approach is extracted from the original study (Bower et al., 2002). Twenty-two open-ended interviews were conducted during the summer of 1999 with women living in Nova Scotia, Canada who self-identified as bisexual. These participants were recruited via posters and brief introductory letters publicized at selected and appropriate community and university organizations and events (e.g. university women's centres; women's dances; bookstores). Given the constraints of accessing an invisible population, snowball sampling (wherein participants solicit likely participants via their own social networks) was also used to increase recruitment.

The average age was 26, with a range of 19–41. Thirteen participants were cohabiting with a partner, four were dating and five were single. Of those who were dating or cohabiting, 15 were involved in a primary relationship with a man and of these, nine identified as non-monogamous, either in theory or in practice. Two participants were in primary relationships with women and both identified as monogamous. Although we advertised widely in order to obtain a heterogeneous sample, the majority were white, and 82% had, or were in the process of obtaining, university (including graduate) degrees. Eight participants were full-time students, eight were in full-time employment and six were in part-time employment or were unemployed.

The interviewer was a post-doctoral research fellow who identifies as a bisexual woman. The interview schedule was comprised of two parts: (1) general background and demographic questions; and (2) questions pertaining to sexual identity. The second part consisted of open-ended questions, followed by prompts, addressing four broad domains: sexual identity and meaning; coming out; community/social resources; key issues and unique concerns. For instance, within the category of sexual identity and meaning, we asked participants to tell us how they currently self-identify. This was followed by prompts that pertained to the meaning of this label and the circumstances under which they use it (e.g. How do you currently identify yourself sexually? What does this label mean to you? Have you always used this label?). Under the category coming out, questions included the following: When did you first begin to identify as bisexual (or whatever label they used) (publicly/privately)? What were the circumstances? Under the category community/social resources, questions included the following: Do you know other women who identify as bisexual? Are there places where you can socialize or obtain information about your sexuality? Under the category of key issues and unique concerns, questions included the following: What is most important for us to understand about your life? How much acceptance do you think there is of bisexuality?

To preserve anonymity, details that might identify participants were omitted. Participants are distinguished by the notation P#, appended at the end of each excerpt. A standard grammatical convention is used in the presentation of excerpts in order to enhance readability and clarity; speech features, such as intonation or length of pauses are not highlighted (see also Malson, 1998). Participants were paid an honorarium of $20. The interviews ranged from one to two hours, with and average of 1.5 hours. All of the interviews were audio-taped and transcribed.

THEORETICAL AND ANALYTIC APPROACH

The analysis of the interview material was guided by following questions: What does it mean for a woman to claim a bisexual identity? How do bisexual women construct their identities? What are some of the component parts of the bisexual narrative that allow us to theorize bisexual identity? With these questions as the central focus, thematic decomposition analysis (Stenner, 1993; Woollett, Marshall & Stenner, 1998) was adopted to explicate dominant themes. This analytic technique combines discursive approaches with thematic analysis. The term 'themes' here refers to coherent patterns identified in participants' talk (Stenner, 1993). We also use 'themes' here to emphasize that the patterns were not simply extracted from the interviews; rather, they emerged partly in response to the kinds of questions posed and the researchers' specific interests. These interests focused on the ways in which participants negotiated the contradictions that arose as they worked with the core questions indicated above. The themes here are also constituted by a variety of discourses. 'Discourse' here is defined in the Foucauldian sense, as not only referring to language, as in the 'general domain of all statements,' but also to regulated social practices (Foucault 1972). In this respect, Foucault suggests that discourses can be defined as 'practices that systematically form the objects of which they speak' (Foucault, 1972, p. 49). Thus, these 'objects' (identities, events and experiences) are not anterior to discourse and awaiting discovery, definition and classification, but rather are brought into existence thought their entry into discourse. As Prior (1989, p. 3) succinctly notes, these objects 'are not referents about which there are discourses but objects constructed by discourse'. In this sense, discourses are fundamentally productive. That is, they produce 'things' (e.g. objects, social institutions, individual subjectivities and subjects) and they have real effects. In so doing, discourses also have a fundamentally material dimension; they productively constitute objects, individuals and social realities in particular ways. For example, arguably identity politics and monosexism regulate the 'discursive field' within which sexuality is currently constructed. Identity politics comprise a complex array of political and theoretical leanings, largely organized around membership in specific marginalized groups; affiliation with a given political movement is centred on combating oppression, reclaiming previously stigmatized identities and working towards self-determination (Heyes, 2002). Monosexuality refers to the assumption that sexual 'object choice' must either be exclusively heterosexual or homosexual (Fox, 1995). Minimally, therefore, bisexual subjects constitute their specific identities and realities against, and within, this discursive backdrop. Thus, although participants echo similar 'themes', these can be understood as being negotiated within a broader 'discursive field', which both produces individual and social meanings and relays meaning through culture.

The women in our study construct bisexuality as a matrix of ongoing interpersonal and socio-cultural negotiations. These centre on: issues pertaining to the limits and possibilities of labelling; questions about the viability (and desirability) of rendering bisexuality a coherent, visible and culturally intelligible identity; and the necessity for and struggles over formulating bisexual epistemologies and politics. A pervasive tension in these accounts pivots on the desire to achieve cultural intelligibility and social acceptance, while simultaneously wanting to retain bisexuality's transformative possibilities, such that this acceptance does not risk entrenching yet another fixed identity category.

(Re)Drawing Sexual Boundaries

A central pre-occupation in these accounts pertains to definitional issues (see Bower et al., 2002 for a comprehensive discussion). Questions about the (in)adequacies of labels, (ir)relevant identificatory criteria, and struggles over meaning predominate:

> It's hard because usually once you define yourself as bisexual, you end up going one way or the other at some point. Or you try to put a label somewhere, and I learned early on you don't have to have a label as long as you're comfortable with what you're doing . . . And, now that I'm in a relationship with a woman, I look back and I say it's

difficult being bisexual because when people ask you, 'What is your preference?' And you say, 'I don't have one'. 'Well, what do you mean you don't have one?' I have a preference of a person, not a preference of gender. And I think that's the hardest thing for people trying to understand bisexuality is that it's not a gender preference. It's a preference of a person. (P6)

I've been struggling with labels recently, in the past few years . . . At the moment I guess politically and in attitude I'm a dyke. That's how I would describe myself. But I'm also bisexual and polyamorous, so that would also be included in that . . . I think, the term bisexual is . . . so limited because really I just fall in love with . . . or like I'm attracted to people. It's secondary, whether they're male or female really . . . it frustrates me sometimes because it's the word that people understand the most but it really doesn't describe my sexuality at all. It's very superficial in terms of labels. (P2)

Although the necessity and accuracy of labels is questioned and resisted, the socio-cultural injunction to tag (in its noun and verb forms) preferences, genders and identities is never far away. The women move back and forth between questioning the usefulness of fixed categories and resorting to these groupings (or inventing new ones) when trying to convey accurately their own identities and lives:

It's really hard to just even divide things into gay, lesbian, bisexual or heterosexual, I mean there's just a trillion different combinations of all of those words and any other words you feel like throwing in there . . . But I suppose, for all intents and purposes, my label would be bisexual. (P8)

It's a very broad spectrum of people and because it's so broad, it's almost impossible to group us into one group . . . The only thing that we have in common is that we're bisexual . . . but hetero-flexible, I think that's probably my new identity. (P18)

The inadequacy of the bisexual descriptor in capturing the vagaries, vicissitudes, and fissures of identity landscapes is reiterated throughout as a desire 'for a language differentiated enough to capture the wealth of contradictions that pervades the efforts of individual men and women to subvert or modify dominant constructions of gender and sexuality' (Däumer, 1999, p. 158). This struggle over the 'startling dearth of currently available options (hetero, homo, bi)' (Däumer, 1999, p. 157) echoes Däumer's (1999) cautionary reminder that 'the effort to disambiguate bisexuality and elevate it into a sign of integration might counteract the subversive potential of bisexuality as a moral and epistemological force' (p. 159). That is, it is the very status of bisexuality as an ambiguous identity within the binary logic of monosexism, that gives it the potential to reveal (and even revel in) the inevitable inconsistencies and discontinuities within all identities. There is another tension at work here – between what is seen as a totalizing impingement of the bisexual signpost (i.e. the bisexual label runs the risk of fixing identities, in much the same way as the labels straight or gay) and a woefully persistent cultural incomprehensibility of bisexuality. The resolute desire to dismantle the limits of existing signs stands alongside the equally insistent demand to be understood, or at least admitted as an ontological possibility:

Oh, valid options. I think that the most important thing for researchers to do or for society to know rather is that bisexuality is a valid option, that it can be. I mean I'm sure some people play, I mean people play. But I'd like to see more evidence and more told that allows bisexuality to be respected as real, it's real, people aren't faking. (P4)

(Un)Viable Identities

Bisexuality threatens to contaminate the ostensibly stable boundaries of, among others, heterosexual and homosexual, male and female (Eadie, 1999):

> I think that the most important thing anyone should understand about bisexual women is that it's not just bisexual in terms of what you like, it's also bisexual in terms of who you are. Sometimes I feel like a boy, sometimes I feel like a girl. And I can't describe it any more than that. Sometimes I feel really macho and sometimes I feel as feminine as Scarlet O'Hara. You know, it just changes from day to day and maybe it's partly a mood swing can affect it, but honestly, like I mean sometimes I'll be dressed in combat fatigues, the next day I'll be wearing like a mini-dress and high heels. (P1)

The resistance to being fixed within a gendered or a sexual prototype works in tandem with the claim that sexuality represents a 'way of being' (Eadie, 1997). Although the women in this study want to retain the terms of this 'beingness' perpetually open, they are equally adamant that bisexuality is a real (and radical) identity:

> So that makes me quite angry in fact that, that because I've decided that I'm attracted to men and women, I feel that attraction, I'm not pretending, I'm not making it up, and I don't want to walk down the street holding some guy's hand just for heterosexual privilege, because I know what it's like to be discriminated against on other bases and for other reasons, so, that makes me, I think, more upset than anything. That I'm just going to adopt this [label] because that's the safest thing to do. I don't live my life in that safe a manner, actually I consider myself kind of a radical person. (P11)

As Eadie (1999) asserts, 'by being non-prescriptive around sexual desires, practices, relationships and identities, bisexual collectivities undermine the very ground on which they gather' (p. 123). Declaring a bisexual identity paradoxically works against the claim of its indeterminacy. In other words, if owing a bisexual identity implies a way of being that resists fixedness, explicitly adopting this identity (as individuals or as groups) to convey a complex and shifting trajectory of emotional, physical, epistemological and political navigations also runs the risk of rendering it less flexible:

> I have to admit, I have to commit, to say that that's what I think I am. And part of it again is not feeling legitimate. I mean even before we started [the interview] I was sitting here thinking I don't have, I don't know the answers, like I don't have all the short answers to explain how and everything that I am. It's still a process that I'm going through . . . I feel like my friends are all wondering, what's the next gender I'm going to bring home, so to speak . . . I think I have a tendency to go from one to the other almost like to balance anything so that I don't get labelled one way or the other. And then maybe people will get more used to the idea that, that I'm not a lesbian, and maybe I'm not straight, and maybe it doesn't matter. (P21)

The imperative to 'admit a commitment' reveals 'bi discourse' as functioning as both 'an "instrument and effect" of power, marked as it is by the binary structures and sexually conservative features of the dominant discourse' (Ault, 1999, p. 184). As Foucault (1990, p. 100) argues, the 'tactical polyvalence of discourses' operates such that, although discourse can be a catalyst for strategic resistance, it can also be 'both an instrument and an effect of power' (p. 101). The project of instantiating a bisexual identity in order to 'undermine and expose' (Foucault, 1990) the fragility and permeability of sexed and gendered borders not only becomes a moment 'when women marked by the sign of the bisexual begin to establish the terms of legitimate bi identity', it also marks the very point at which they simultaneously 'participate in the discursive reinforcement of the sex/gender structure. The construction and definition of categories is an exercise in imposing order, not an exercise in disrupting it' (Ault, 1999, p. 184).

Bisexuality's intractably tainted standing relegates it to an 'unviable (un)subject position' (Butler, 1991, p. 306). That is, within the domain of the normative, and therefore, intelligible, bisexuals are 'unthinkable' and, thus, outside the contours of viable subjects:

> Sometimes I do feel, in certain contexts and in certain situations, I feel like it's simpler to just say that I'm a dyke or I'm a lesbian. It's more understood, it's more intelligible to people and unless I have time to go into why I say I'm bisexual or how I'm bisexual, I don't always feel comfortable saying that. Especially, actually, in the lesbian community. (P16)

As Butler (1993) asserts, subjects are constituted through forces of exclusion and disavowal:

> This exclusionary matrix by which subjects are formed thus requires the simultaneous production of a domain of abject beings, those who are not yet 'subjects', but who form the constitutive outside to the domain of the subject. The abject designates here precisely those 'unlivable' and 'uninhabitable' zones of social life which are nevertheless densely populated by those who do not enjoy the status of the subject, but whose living under the sign of the 'unlivable' is required to circumscribe the domain of the subject. (p. 3)

Bisexuality is this 'constitutive outside', which is both menacing and mandatory in the regulation of identificatory and sexual practices. In as much as lesbian and gay identities have attained the status of viable subjects within the LGBT communities, the dreaded disclosure of a bisexual domain jeopardizes this thinkable, inhabitable location. At the same time, the possibility of a bisexual identity underscores the 'actuality' and greater legitimacy of lesbian and gay identity (i.e. the 'true queers'):

> I still have a feeling that bisexuality doesn't really exist. That it's not defined, or even seen as something meaning laden, rather it's just something 'other' and not defined and maybe defined negatively . . . it's like well, that is not gay and that is not straight and therefore it doesn't mean anything to me and it just gets pushed away. (P17)

> I might perhaps feel that bisexuality is not legitimate whereas being a lesbian, I'd see that as being legitimate . . . I can never be legitimate and so I feel like a little lost soul, like, that I'm floating in between two sides that are very, very sure of what they are. (P2)

> I think we're pretty invisible. I don't think you can talk about a bisexual culture, except as part of a larger, gay and lesbian and bi culture . . . I don't think there is a separate bisexual culture. (P22)

In these accounts, bisexuality as an identity marker is positioned as impossible, incredible, illegitimate and meaningless. Inhabiting a viable bisexual identity is forestalled by the predominant cultural assertion that bisexuality is provisional, posing and pretence, that is, non-existent (Rust, 2000a).

(In)Visibly Contagious

Paradoxically, bisexuals are situated as both unviable and as (in)visible potential contaminants, in some cases in very literal ways:

> A lot of the lesbians and gay men will say, how can you say that you're bisexual? That doesn't make any sense. Does that mean that you're not going to settle down, or you're not a monogamous person? What are you? You're going around spreading AIDS, what's your problem? Make a decision. So it's kind of like we're stuck in the middle. (P18)

Their 'polluting' force also stems from bisexuality's defiance of 'forms of separation and demarcation which serve particular social interests' (Eadie, 1999, p. 130):

> I've heard a lot of really negative comments about bisexual people . . . Like I'd hear 'Oh well, bisexual people, it's just like a cop-out because they don't want to choose or it's just like if they can't get a male, then they'll go with a female. If they can't get a female, they'll go with a male'. (P5)

> I feel like, like bisexuals are disappeared in the queer community. I think it's . . . you're gay or you're lesbian or you're, oh, yeah, bi. Hmm? Just, it doesn't seem like . . . it still seems like bisexuality is a fringe, a fringe non-option. (P4)

> I find a lot of time there's an expectation that it's the gay and lesbian community. A lot of men and women who are bi, who are working to talk about the gay and lesbian community, who don't talk about being bi. Like, you know, a group will put out a lot of literature that never, ever mentions being bi . . . there's a certain stigma that's attached to being bi that . . . or a certain status that's attached to not being bi, like people are more willing to listen to you talk about like your position as a lesbian then they are willing to listen to you talk about your position as being bi, I think. (P20)

Although bisexuals appear to be an afterthought, a 'copout,' a 'fringe non-option,' that cannot be located on equal footing with other sexualities, they loom as a threat to both homo- and hetero-sexualities:

> I think also that bisexuality threatens to invalidate the claims of people in the hetero and the homo side and that might, might make them hold off from accepting that as a viable option . . . However, having, just having a third option which says, you can kind of, as they say, go between the two, that makes it, that makes those two seem fluid and a lot of people feel threatened I think by that, that they don't want to see their own identity as fluid. I don't necessarily agree with it actually being that way. Like I'm sure there are people who are really straight and really gay. Why not? And I don't think that bisexuality invalidates those, but I can see why it would be perceived as a threat. (P4)

> We don't seem to belong to the straight community, and we don't seem to belong to the gay community, but most of us don't want to belong to the bisexual community either. Most of us just want to be us. Or just me. We're not deviant. We're not experimenting for the rest of our lives. It's not, for a lot of people it's not a phase. It's not something that they just get into and just toss out later on when they settle down with someone. (P18)

> The two camps of homosexuality and heterosexuality, neither one wants any bisexual people around because it's just not good for their image, for either one. So, we're left in the middle. (P21)

Because disclosure of stigmatized identities constitutes a confessional moment, as much as a declaration (albeit unintentionally), the one who receives the utterance has the power to legitimate or invalidate. Thus, disclosure can have both a constructive and constrictive function in the constitution of subjectivity. Non-normative and stigmatized self-ascriptions, in particular, risk (in)jurious consequences owing to their position as sites of contagion. That is, their articulation is not merely a communication but a production that threatens to contaminate the listener by transmitting the referent's disposition or practice. In this sense, such utterances not only perform a constitutive function in configuring the subjectivity of the speaker but they also take effect in the listener. This effect can engender acceptance and facilitation *or* contamination and judgement. So, statements that are intended as 'reflexive, that attribute a status only to oneself, [are] taken to be solicitous, that is, a claim that announces . . . the intention to act, the act itself' (Butler, 1997, p. 113). Hearing the utterance (here, a declaration of a bisexual identity) is equated with 'contracting' the act/identity to which it refers. In these accounts, public avowals of a bisexual identity (i.e. saying one is bisexual) are frequently met with fears of contamination, and relatedly, accusations of betrayal.

> I talk to a lot of the gay women. And there are certain gay women that don't like bisexual women at all. There's a sort of almost a heterosexual fear, the opposite of the homophobic thing. (P10)

> Sometimes I go into circumstances and I don't even mention being bi. I just say I'm a dyke and let people make all those assumptions . . . Because then, once I've talked enough and then once I've got people's respect and people's attention, then I can say I'm bi and I won't lose their attention. But if I go into a situation and I say I'm bi, then I don't get their attention in the first place. (P20)

> I find that in the lesbian and gay community, there's like an out-casting of bisexuals, or bisexual people, which is such hypocrisy and such contradictions . . . Because of the gay and lesbian community and their opinions on your bisexuality, it makes it hard for certain people to sort of stand up, stand their ground and even admit, so they'll just say they're either gay or lesbian and not bisexual, which is you know, the case. 'Cause there's a lot of anger in that community towards bisexuality. So it's not nearly as open as it could or should be. (P7)

Most of the women who identified strongly socially and politically with the lesbian community also experienced a pervasively painful disjuncture between such socio-political commitments and displacement from the 'insider group':

> At times I felt not good enough because I knew I had a boyfriend and I knew that many of the women I was meeting were lesbians or appeared to be or seemed to be or whatever. And at times I kind of felt, not like I didn't belong, like that I was not quite as valid because I wasn't supporting the cause by being with women. (P21)

> I also wanted to say something in terms of the sort of the betrayal or the lack of trust. The issue of culture I think is also something that makes it tricky to identify as bisexual versus gay or lesbian because there is a very strong queer culture or lesbian culture that I feel a part of. Through movies, through singers, through music, all kinds of figures in popular culture, and even sayings and certain ways of talking, those are all part of my culture. And so the bisexuality part is tricky because it's like, well if that is my culture and I'm not allowed to have complete claim on that culture somehow because it's a lesbian culture and if I identify as a bisexual woman, then I'm kind of not exactly one hundred percent part of that culture or supposed to have the membership . . . There's always this feeling of having to negotiate this straight looking relationship and my queer community or queer culture. But then if I'm with a woman, it's like well, I'm a dyke and there's a complete like negation of any kind of opposite sex relationships that I've had in the past. So, I feel like either way, I kind of lose in terms of bisexual kind of positive identification, or existence. (P16)

Acknowledgment of the legitimacy of bisexuality by others is equated with ontological validity. Central here are appeals to the importance of visibility and public avowals.

Incitement to Reveal and Conceal

Given the risks of disclosure, decisions about the costs and benefits of revealing and concealing were cited as a key struggle for many of the participants. In contrast to allegations of bisexual women's ability 'to pass', most of the women asserted that passing was neither a desirable nor a viable option in either the straight or the gay world. Not only was discovery always an imminent risk in many social contexts, in a significant way, being able to voice or display their bisexual identities was positioned as integral to rendering their identities as bisexual women viable. Foucault (1990) has argued that western societies routinely rely on confession as a central mechanism for the production of truth, among which truth about the individuation and authenticity of the 'self' is central: 'the individual. . . . [is] authenticated by the discourse of truth he [sic] [is] able or obliged to pronounce concerning himself [sic]. The truth confession [is] inscribed at the heart of the procedures of individualization by power' (pp. 58–59). Sexuality in particular, holds a key place in this domain of discursive imperatives:

> sex became something to say, and to say exhaustively in accordance with deployments that were varied, but all, in their own way compelling . . . sex has not ceased to provoke a kind of generalized discursive erethism . . . that compels everyone to transform their sexuality into a perpetual discourse (Foucault, 1990, pp. 32–33).

As part of the 'will to knowledge regarding sex' (Foucault, 1990, p. 65), incitement to confess the truth of one's 'sexual peculiarity' has been codified not only scientifically (i.e. in the form of *scientia sexualis*, the development of a science of sex that systematically classifies sexual types and establishes norms for regulating desire) and socially, but also intrapsychically, as part of the formation of subjectivity.

Importantly, this 'obligation to confess' is so thoroughly installed that it is not viewed as an impingement of power but rather barriers to revealing 'our most secret nature' are now positioned as the 'violence of power' that constrain the emergence of truth (Foucault, 1990, p. 60). And sexuality, owing to its peculiar status as a sentinel of an 'individual and fundamental secret', has become firmly entrenched not only in the 'economy of pleasure but in an ordered system of knowledge' (Foucault, 1990, p. 69). Knowledge and pleasure are now yoked. That is, individual subjectivity is now so thoroughly caught up in the interplay among confession, truth, and power that the individual is not merely an object of study by scientific methods, but has also become an object of knowledge to oneself. The pleasure is in knowing, being known, discovering the truth about self, and effecting change in the self. The proliferation of pleasures in the 'production of the truth about sex' are inexhaustively manifold:

> pleasure in the truth of pleasure, the pleasure of knowing that truth, of discovering and exposing it, the fascination of seeing it and telling it, of captivating and capturing others by it, of confiding it in secret of luring it out in the open – the specific pleasure of the true discourse on pleasure (Foucault, 1990, p. 71).

The regulatory force of confessional discourses is affected in large measure by the real or virtual presence of the listener:

> who is not simply the interlocutor but the authority who requires the confession, prescribes and appreciates it, and intervenes in order to judge, punish, forgive, console, and reconcile; a ritual in which the truth is corroborated by the obstacles and resistances it has had to surmount in order to be formulated; and finally a ritual in which

the expression alone, independently of its external consequences, produces intrinsic modifications in the person who articulates it: it exonerates, redeems, and purifies him; it unburdens him of his wrongs, liberates him, and promises him salvation (Foucault, 1990, p. 62, sic).

Thus, speaking the 'truth' about the self is a requirement for producing an individuated selfhood. Such proclamations, however, are in turn regulated by 'normalizing surveillance procedures' (Foucault, 1995) that assess, categorize and discipline subjects in relation to particular social norms. The potency of these 'techniques of subjection' does not lie in an exteriorized imposition, but rather in the internalization of 'disciplinary power,' such that self-monitoring and self-constraining subjects and subjectivities are produced (Foucault, 1995). In this way, 'discipline "makes" individuals; it is the specific technique of a power that regards individuals as both objects and as instruments of its exercise' (Foucault, 1995, p. 170). This form of power functions through 'humble modalities' rather than grand sovereign gestures by exerting a sustained but 'calculated economy' (Foucault, 1995). In other words, power is affected not by coercive external legal or social forces but by the more subtle, less visible but much more efficient mechanism of ongoing self scrutiny and self management.

The norm of monosexuality that governs both straight and lesbian communities functions in precisely this way as a 'disciplinary regulator' (Foucault, 1995) in producing self-governing and self-containing subjects. Negotiating 'fields of visibility' (Foucault, 1995) that construct and constrain gendered, sexed and sexualized subject positions and subjectivities is a precarious enterprise that eludes balance. Although the women in this study are insistent on retaining the flexibility of bisexuality, in its naming and enactment, as these accounts also attest, occupying the 'ambiguous' bisexual position 'creates painful contradictions, incoherences, and impracticalities in the lives of those who adopt it' (Däumer, 1999, p. 159). Marginalized to some extent by both the straight and lesbian communities and caught, in many respects much like 'queer', in the unstable 'gap of disidentification' (e.g. Nguyen, 1999), bisexual women confront a series of difficult negotiations in relation to disclosure issues:

> I guess the worst is the mistrust and the feeling that I'm going to betray someone or that I've already betrayed. I've betrayed a lesbian community because I can become a het, because I can walk down the street with a guy. And mistrust on behalf of straight women who think I can either make a pass at them or their boyfriend, because I have twice as many to choose from, I immediately go after everyone. (P11)

> I seem to remember a very uncomfortable situation with somebody I worked with who was saying 'it's fine for gay, it's fine for straight, it's this bisexual thing, that's just children who haven't grown up', blah, blah, blah. I remember fighting tooth and nail with her over that for a few hours after work one day and being so upset and so angry when I went home but never being able to say, never feeling I could say, you know, but I am bisexual. (P9)

Accusations of betrayal, predatory impulses and maturational inadequacy are presented as evidence of the impossibility (and inadvisability) of bisexuality. Both self-declarations of bisexuality and the perpetual possibility of being 'discovered' put the women at risk of being ascribed diminished psychological, moral *and* social status:

> I had one bad experience, it was kind of like my first lesbian party and I was with my partner and we were still closeted because of her and a woman at the party basically just kind of leaned forward and said, 'So are you a lesbian or what?' I was

dumbfounded, I didn't know what to say cause I was never expected to be asked out-right like that. I just didn't think it would be really good to say no, and I didn't want to say, well, no, but you know what, I'm sleeping with this woman sitting next to you. (P21)

I mean, having to out myself as bisexual at the store, even with customers when they ask, when it comes up that I live with a man, if it ever does come up. Where I live on [street name] next to the Woman's Co-op, so it does come up actually. That's been sort of difficult. I felt uneasy, felt other people were uneasy with that . . . People aren't out and out asking or anything but you do get the double take if I meet up with people at the market or something Saturday morning. You're shopping with your lover, it's pretty obvious that you know, you're shopping together for home. You know, it's like, 'Is this your brother?' (P9)

The explicit political identifications with the lesbian community run counter to the 'indict-ment of bisexuality as apolitical' (Hemmings, 1999, p. 197):

I appreciate the point that there are a lot of lesbian and gay men that have worked really hard, that had a really hard time of it, that are really adamant about their stand-ing. And there is sort of that community for lesbians and for gay men I think more so than there is for bisexuals, so they sort of have a bit more of a cohesive unit . . . so I think that just gets pushed to the top more . . . I mean I feel like bisexual women, like I feel I experience that from both sides, so I get a lot of negative feedback or whatever you call it from the lesbian community. And not even negative, just pressure . . . Things like 'I'm just not interested at all in hearing about any relationship that you have with a man, well not completely disinterested but very not interested.' It usually comes with some snide remark and I understand that, whatever, people, animosity or something but like it's just tiring . . . But I would probably shrivel up and die if I didn't know at least some lesbians. (P12)

If I walk into a queer environment, I'm still married to a man, with the ring and the marriage certificate and the whole bit and that can cause some rejection from the queer groups I've found. And I'm cautious about that as a result. (P4)

Resulting from the 'nested' power differentials of 'hierarchized surveillance' (Foucault, 1995), many of the participants experience greater freedom to proclaim a bisexual identity in the straight world, given a much diminished concern about approval by this community. That is, although being subject to scrutiny is an ever-present possibility, the scrutinizing forces (i.e. the lesbian and gay community vs the straight community vs the self) have different impacts, depending on shifting socio-political realities:

In the straight world of school [university], which is mainly straight and I'm the only out, queer person in my class of 50 as far as I know, yet I felt that it was easier to come out as a bisexual woman in that context and be queer and talk about my attrac-tions to men and my attractions and relationships to women. Just because there's this feeling that if they don't accept me, screw them. Like, I don't care. I don't need their approval or need their acceptance. I think it's because I don't look for acceptance from straight people in the same way that I do from lesbians, from like the lesbian com-munity. (P16)

The rhetorical, social and political primacy of 'gay' and 'lesbian' within these commu-nities ensures that bisexuality, along with its other 'abject' associates (Butler, 1993) (e.g. transgendered, questioning), retains its repudiated status:

I was perceived as being a lesbian or a dyke and it was assumed that I was because of the way I look. And I just let that assumption carry forward. I thought that was safer for me and that's still true today. It's still true. (P11)

> I should say that when I was playing along and just being queer and letting other people identify me as lesbian that it was great . . . but now I look back on it and it seems very hollow. It all seems leading up to the time when I was sort of ostracized . . . I just know that I only had those experiences because I knuckled under, that if I stood up and insisted, I'm bisexual and that's different from you, you know, that I would have been . . . ostracized. (P17)

Rejection (and ejection) by the lesbian community is the cost of publicly avowing a bisexual identity. 'Passing' becomes a handy mode of avoiding 'normalizing judgement' (Foucault, 1995), albeit simultaneously constraining the possibility of mutually pleasurable recognition:

> Simply being able to assert your identity, have it recognized by people around you, and finding a community of similarly identified people is easier [for lesbians]. I mean it's still hard for lesbian women but it's easier for them than bisexual women. Because as soon as you're with a man, it's like suddenly everything that you struggled to gain in terms of recognition is gone . . . at work you don't say, 'I'm married, but I'm bisexual too' . . . just if people could know that it's a real thing. That it's like as concrete in a way as other identities . . . and yet concrete is sort of the wrong word because it's almost more like that you can live your whole life, your whole lifespan in what seems to be a sort of flux and that flux can be a wholeness. That a wholeness doesn't have to be a singularity as well. (P17)

The struggle here centres on whether it is possible to achieve 'any sense of belonging on the basis of temporary identifications and alliances. The burning question is how one can become a *subject of dislocation* that is able to recognize other such subjects' (Hemmings, 1999, p. 199, original emphasis).

This raises the issue of whether 'sexual identity must be continuously performed to be proven' (Whitney, 2002, p. 116). If, as Butler (1999) contends, the subject is constituted by 'certain rule-governed discourses that govern the intelligible invocation of identity' and if this operates through a '*regulated process of repetition* that both conceals itself and enforces its rules precisely through the production of substantializing effects' (p. 185, original emphasis), what is the status of repetition and performance for dissident identities? Butler (1999) enjoins such outsiders to 'enter into the repetitive practices of this terrain of signification' (p. 189) because 'it is only *within* the practices of repetitive signifying that subversion of identity becomes possible' (p. 185 original emphasis). The status of lesbian and gay as privileged signifiers within the economy of dissident sexualities makes 'qualify[ing] as a substantive identity an arduous task' (Butler, 1999, p. 184):

> I mean, I think it's really important to do stuff like this because, I mean, I have been feeling less and less bisexual, if that makes any sense. Like in the sense that it's just so much easier to say I'm a dyke and to be, to simplify things that way, especially when I had a girlfriend and I guess if anything that this interview has done is renewed my hope that a bisexual identity can be, can be okay. (P16)

The precariousness of maintaining both 'being' and 'being legitimate' is a reminder of the 'constitutive failure of all gender enactments for the very reason that these ontological locales are fundamentally uninhabitable' (Butler, 1999, p. 186). And we would add to this the 'constitutive failure' of all sexualities. More specifically:

> when the disorganization and disaggregation of the field of bodies disrupt the regulatory fiction of coherence . . . that regulatory ideal is then exposed as norm and a fiction

> that disguises itself as a developmental law regulating the sexual field that it purports
> to describe. (Butler, 1999, p. 173)

The flimsiness of these fictive masquerades underscores the importance of sustaining a politics of 'radical difference' (Eadie, 1999). As Haraway (1990, p. 223) argues, the goal here is 'not of [creating] a common language, but of a powerful infidel heteroglossia', wherein the matrices of resistance need not require coherence but rather maintain their 'productively conflictual' force (Eadie, 1999).

(Im)Possible Bisexual Epistemologies and Politics

The primacy of the 'Big G's' – gender and genitals – is particularly entrenched in both lay and theoretical discourses about sexual varieties. Although these biological and social markers are not inherently or inevitably linked to sexuality, they typically take centre stage in our sexual understandings and enactments (Rust, 2000a). The women in our study attempt to de-couple this insistent link between sexuality and the gender/genitals dyad:

> Even bisexual is hard for me to adapt to because my definition which I would think is the general consensus of bisexual is where your sexual orientation is and mine isn't necessarily sexual. It's an emotional, mental bond with somebody and, like I said, that could be any one person . . . So it's just, it's clearly for me just a person. So I usually say I'm bi, not necessarily bisexual because I have no sexual desire to be with a man, but if I was in love, it probably would come back . . . I fell in love with my partner before ever laying eyes on her. I talked to her on the computer for two hours before I actually knew she was a woman . . . (P6)

> Just a person, who identifies, wants to connect sexually but with both men and women . . . I guess when I talk about connecting sexually with someone I'm not necessarily just talking about physical connections. I mean if I'm in a heterosexual relationship for the rest of my life, does that mean I'm not bisexual anymore? So, I guess I figure that I still will always be bisexual as long as . . . I still feel interested. (P14)

Like our participants, Sedgwick (1990) muses over this puzzling conflation of sexuality and gender/genitals and the neglect of other, potentially more relevant, characteristics in decisions about sexual object options:

> of the very many dimensions along which the genital activity of one person can be differentiated from that of another . . . precisely one, the gender of object choice, emerged from the turn of the century, and has remained, as *the* dimension denoted by the ubiquitous category of 'sexual orientation' (p. 8, original emphasis).

Notably, although 'gender is not a deal breaker' for bisexuals, 'conceptualized with a gender-based dichotomous sexual classification system, . . . *bi*sexuality is constructed in terms of the one characteristic that does *not* define it: gender' (Rust, 2000a, p. 209, original emphasis). The women in our study work against this negation of non-gendered/non-genital features in ascribing partner attractions and choices. Instead, they rely on other explanations for these leanings, as indicated throughout this chapter such as an 'emotional, mental bond', the desire for 'just a person', feeling 'interested' in principle in the absence of physical enactments, 'who you meet', experiencing 'intimacy', being 'in love', the transition from love to 'sexual expression', and 'inner beauty':

> Usually I say bi-sexual. It's the most simple way of saying it. Except for, usually I say I'm in love with one person now, so that is my sexuality, is this one person. (P15)

> When I settled down with my current partner, who is male, as the relationship progressed I discovered that I probably would be staying with him and I love him more as a person, not necessarily as a man so it's not really a matter of gender in our relationship, he just happens to be male . . . It's just a matter of this person is a nice person, I could grow to love this person. And if I love this person, I can express it to them sexually. (P18)

> Essentially I'm just gender inspecific. I don't have a preference. I don't have a preference for height or for body size or other than that I'm not particularly concerned. I care a lot about a person's mind, and I know that's very cliché to say about the inner beauty . . . I'm attracted to the beauty and I discovered that when I was young, like very young that I was attracted to people and not to sexes . . . I don't see gender anymore, I just see faces. I see a beautiful face, I see a beautiful body and I see a beautiful person inside. (P19)

Gender is positioned as largely irrelevant by these participants, to the extent of being equated with the preferential status of other subjective social markers such as 'height or body size' (see P19 above). Paradoxically, in de-emphasizing the genital and the gendered in describing a bisexual identity, anxieties about being found 'insufficiently bisexual' emerge. Although a fixed identity may not be desirable or possible, 'in the absence of a coherent (which would also mean policed) bisexual identity, [bisexuals'] expression of sexuality is [found] wanting' (Eadie, 1999, p. 123). This issue of whether one 'counts as bisexual' in the presence or absence of specific (sexual) enactments was expressed by most of the women, as indicated in the preceding (P6 and P14) and the following excerpts:

> If I said bi-sexual, people expect me to go 50% with guys and 50% with girls, you know. I think it's more who you meet and you know, like the person rather than their sex . . . if you meet somebody and you really like them and you become intimate with them, you don't necessarily have to have sex with them to be intimate but, so it depends on, if the intimacy is there. (P3)

> And to me, you don't have to be in a lover's relationship with someone to be out. That's going back to it's not all about sex, that's only part of it. I mean I consider myself a single person. I'm not interested in pursuing anyone right now, I'm not looking for a partner in particular, but I'm still bi. That hasn't changed. That hasn't changed at all. (P11)

> I think that when people say bisexual, because you're saying bi, people see it as half and half. So either people identify I think, or understand that you're half, half of you is attracted to men and half to women . . . I mean what happens if I'm attracted to a transgendered person? Then you know, my bisexual, how can you be bisexual then? (P9)

The criteria for a 'true bisexual' are indeterminate, shifting and murky, but closure is a perpetual possibility. At any moment, unspecifiable, unruly attractions, desires and practices may disqualify one as 'truly bisexual'. The cultural expectation of equalizing sexual or gender proportions ('half and half') runs counter to the way in which most bisexual people view their identities. Most bisexuals do not report having both male and female partners simultaneously (Rust, 2000b), nor do most require both male and female partners, or experience equal or the same kinds of attractions to men and women (Rust 2000c). Identifying as bisexual often reflects attractions or capacities for attractions or actions, rather than their enactments.

This re-mapping of bisexuality outside the contours of the gendered/genital is also firmly anchored in epistemological and political imperatives (Rust, 2000c):

> I hesitate to identify being bisexual as being action or intention or ethic or mentality or what have you because I've been through stages covering the gamut of that so I wouldn't want to exclude anybody . . . I think that choosing you know, to identify as bisexual or identifying as bisexual is as much political as sexual and emotional. (P4)

This resistance to being consigned to an easily understood and identifiable category stands alongside concerns about the absence of a political handle that could render bisexuality visible and viable:

> I think there's a lack of a movement, politically because I think bisexuals can be really invisible . . . Lots of people don't like it when you don't make a choice apparently and frankly this is how I am and it's the choice that I have made, that's how I've chosen to label myself and I'm not going to choose to be something I'm not. (P2)

Allegations invoking undecided 'fence-sitters,' or 'switch hitters'[5] (Yuen Thompson, 2000) are defended against by appeals to deliberate choice, on the one hand, and remaining true to one's essence, on the other. The disordering of classificatory regimes is seen as a potent political force that confronts society's 'very real fear of the collapse of a symbolic system: the heterosexual/homosexual dyad' (Eadie, 1999, p. 131):

> I think it's significant not to be taken as straight because a lot of our society is based on assuming that everyone is straight. So it's important to me politically not to be taken that way, just because I'm sleeping with a man because I'm in love with somebody who's of the opposite sex as I am. It just feels more important to wrestle with that than to just be pigeonholed. (P9)

Attempts to locate themselves simultaneously within and outside of erected sexual borders, the women call for 'models of a non-devouring relationship to difference' (Eadie, 1997, p. 131). While declaring relative 'comfort in other people's discomfort' (Yuen Thompson, 2000), they continue to ask 'who will be loyal to me? Which group/community/movement(s) will claim me as their member and comrade?' (p. 178):

> And I think that needs to be challenged, that people in particular in the gay and lesbian community aren't as accepting of bisexual people as they could be, or even should be . . . People who are marginalized because of their sexual orientation shouldn't immediately turn around and say, 'Oh, you're not bi, you just haven't made up your mind.' That's not validating what my choices are or what my orientation is at all. But trying to deny it, in fact, it's not validating anything. It's a rejection of what my choice is and what my orientation is. And that's quite wrong, and I'm not going to take it. So, for myself, being more and more out, I plan on challenging that more, challenging those assumptions. And without having to justify that I'm bisexual, I shouldn't have to explain that. (P11)

While the identity of bisexuality is adopted as an epistemological and a socio-political necessity, the women are equally adamant about the project of interrogating, re-defining and expanding the boundaries of the term. These accounts highlight the tension between 'the desire for bisexuality to be accepted as a coherent and stable sexual identity, but also

---

[5] The term 'switch hitter' is taken from baseball, where a batter who can switch-hit, or hit the ball from either the right or left side of the plate, is in a better position to get to first base, which is the initial object of the game (Garber, 1995).

(ambivalently!) a recognition of the necessity and pleasure of such wavering' (Kaloski Naylor, 1999, p. 58). For Kaloski Naylor, wavering here refers to the ways in which the bisexual female subject is left suspended in feminist lesbian texts, unsure if it pertains to her. We are extending this concept here to describe the ways in which, in these accounts, there is a sustained (and alternately pleasurable and painful) ambivalence about simultaneously being counted (as part of the non-heterosexual category) and not being counted.

DISCUSSION

The women in this study exhort us to consider the pleasures and pains of bisexuality 'coming out of the "etc.," if only for brief and strategic moments' (Kaloski Naylor, 1999, p. 55). Their accounts can be understood as strivings to establish an alternative discourse around bisexuality. The bisexual label is alternately strategically adopted, resisted, questioned and modified. Neither the exclusivity of 'lesbian' nor the inclusivity of 'queer' capture the specificities of these bisexual women's identities, lives and experiences. The difficulties associated with producing such a discourse must be considered, and we outline three of these here. First, any such discourse is both potentiated and constrained by the organization of existing discourses. The organization of the discursive field around the politics of sexual identities is characterized by mutually exclusive either/or binaries. Thus, any alternative discourse, for coherence, must first establish itself to some extent in terms borrowed from the dominant order and, in so doing, risks reifying precisely those binary structures it seeks to undermine. As Hemmings (1999) powerfully asserts:

> To maintain a sense of my (privileged) outsider position, I must invest heavily in reproducing those binarisms, particularly as having 'nothing to do with me'. So I rail against the dualisms that I claim are 'keeping me down', preventing an adequate theory of my own *marvellous fluidity* from emerging triumphant. But of course, those 'dreadful binaries' are scarcely somewhere 'out there,' they inform and produce my identity as much as anyone else's. The conversations I have with myself, the operation of binaries within my psyche, the way I see the world, etc., all reconstruct what I claim to deconstruct. (p. 197)

The second difficulty in formulating an alternative discourse of bisexual identity is that rendering bisexuality 'visible' also risks fixing its meaning. The danger here is that it sets up its own regulatory regime, similar to the construction of lesbianism (or heterosexuality). That is, achieving an 'identity' through labelling and definition establishes it as oppositional (i.e. always already in opposition to something else), and thus risks simply reversing existing hierarchies and re-inscribing the very power relations it seeks to undermine (Bower, 1999). Not surprisingly, 'heteronormativity' (Wilton, 1996) may be transposed into another version of normativity, in this case 'binormativity'.

The third difficulty arises because accessing alternative discourses depends on changes in real conditions outside of the texts (Parker, 1992). Although often presented in this chapter as the hetero/homo oppositional binary, there are continuing clear social and material inequities between the two sides of this divide. That is, being allocated to, or identifying with, non-heterosexual categories is not the same as identifying as heterosexual. Heterosexism, as an ideologically rooted set of structures and practices, operates through negation, disparagement and oppression of non-heterosexual acts, relationship identities and communities (Herek, 1995). The manifold persistence of heterosexism can

be seen in continuing derogatory public attitudes, discriminatory social and legal practices, harassment and physical violence. Thus, there remains a pressing requirement for
these marginalized others to continue to assert the legitimacy of their identities, albeit
often at the expense of other sexual identities, including bisexuality. Accordingly, although
both 'bisexuality' and 'queer' promise to transgress the categories of both gender and
sexuality, the lesbian and gay communities remain invested in maintaining a significant
discursive distance from heterosexuality, a distance that is not always or preserved (or
served) by 'bisexuality'.

The predominant assertions about the utility and significance of a bisexual identity
centre, in varying degrees, on one of three positions:

> (i) bisexuals have (potentially) a viable identity, and should seek to make themselves
> more distinct; or (ii) bisexuals are (primarily) either heterosexual or homosexual: there
> is no such things as bisexual identity; or (iii) bisexuals have neither a consistent and
> distinct identity, nor are they either straight or gay – instead bisexuality can be best
> understood as a perspective, though also containing within it the possibility and indeed
> necessity for a strategic and non-essential identity. (Kaloski Naylor, 1999, p. 54)

In our study, the accounts gesture towards the latter stance: 'critical heterogeneity' (Kaloski
Naylor, 1999). This pivots on a desire to retain the 'fluidity' of bisexuality and its definitional uncertainties, while simultaneously retrieving bisexuality from invisibility and
cultural invalidation. As one of our participants states:

> I think that bisexuality is the broadest possible, or it is a very broad identity, so I think
> that there is a possibility within bisexuality . . . if the visibility is increased with
> bisexual people, there is a possibility to expand that even further. And so I think there
> is a real chance to just break open that box that sex is kept in and to give it a wider
> definition and to make it a more, a wider context within the world that we live. So I
> think that bisexual people are probably identified with that idea, that sexuality is quite
> fluid and that can be experimented with and can be played with and that it just means
> sort of a wider space within our society. (P13)

Notably, 'fluidity' frequently appears as a 'metaphor for bisexuality,' although its meaning
is not as apparent as its ubiquitous usage suggests (Herdt, 1999). Although bisexuality is
figured 'as fluid presence in a landscape of monoliths' (Eadie, 1997, p. 9), 'routinized and
elaborated, fluidity is itself a discourse, whose origins are firmly within the ambit of
thought about the sexual' (Eadie, 1997, p. 10), the social, the gendered and the self. Eadie
(1997) reminds us that the centrality of 'fluidity' in contemporary bisexual discourse is
situated within a broader move in modernity towards 'relentless progress through time
towards absolute self-realization' (p. 7). Thus, bisexuality as a specific socio-cultural
iteration may not so much represent the 'epitome of "unrepressed" sexuality' (Eadie, 1997,
p. 8), but rather, its valorization of 'fluidity' is consistent with modernity's rush to progressive propulsion. If 'change' and 'flux' are the currently exalted commodities, a politically
radical reading of bisexuality requires that we do

> not stop with its celebration, but [that we] go on to ask exactly what conceptions of
> bisexuality are being celebrated, and whether they dislodge, or merely consolidate,
> other assumptions that perpetuate the dominant social order. (Eadie, 1997, p. 8)

The women in this study call for an epistemology and a politics of might be termed *pragmatic (in)coherence*. Bisexuality's resistance to definition, its refusal to assimilate into
invisibility and its cultural incoherence within the binaries of contemporary sexualities,

all signal its potential to question sexual politics and hetero-/homo-normativity. At the same time, 'bi discourse' (Ault, 1999) threatens to re-instantiate the very binaries it is intended to dismantle. As Ault (1999) reminds us:

> At the present, a great deal of tension exists between the emergence of a visible but ambiguous space in our sexual culture and the impetus for the construction of a well-bounded, highly defined structure as an easily identifiable hybrid between the familiar oppositional categories. (p. 185)

In our study, the *provisional* adoption of identity labels and their continued, judicious use is positioned as inevitable, albeit ultimately unsatisfying. The tension is this: On the one hand, such identity signs may enable marginal identities (including those as-yet-unnamed) to become or remain visible and *dis*order normative categories (Butler, 1991; Dollimore, 1991; Doty, 1993; Phelan, 1993). On the other hand, the challenge, as Phelan (1993) argues, is to explicitly resist characterizing such identities as *re*ordered, foundational or essential and instead recognize them as impermanent, perpetually in the process of 'becoming', and subject to questioning and disruption. The women in our study assert that the disruptive and denaturalizing potential of a bisexual identity is neither obvious nor guaranteed:

> In the contested space of the bisexual body, the ultimate conflict is not *between* categories but *about* them, and the move to define and defend the bisexual subject paradoxically seems the move most likely to undermine the radical, transformative potential of its indeterminacy (Ault, 1999, p. 185, our emphasis)

Importantly, these accounts remind us that the troubles and triumphs of bisexuality may be irreconcilable, as transformative moves that potentiate culturally intelligible identities simultaneously risk becoming epistemologically truncated. In other words, as Ault (1999) reminds us, while the adoption and use of specific categories (e.g. bisexual) and definable category markers (e.g. sexually attracted to both men and women) may render bisexuality more culturally comprehensible and viable (e.g. enabling the constitution of bisexual communities), retaining category borders (even permeable ones) does little to dismantle the dualistic and simplistic logic of hetero/homo and male/female.

ACKNOWLEDGEMENTS

The data collection was supported by a Social Sciences and Humanities Research Council of Canada grant awarded to the third author. The preparation of this manuscript was supported by a Ryerson University New Faculty SRC Fund (Social Sciences and Humanities Research Council of Canada) and a Ryerson Internal SSHRC grant awarded to the first author. The authors would also like to thank Piera Defina for her energetic and resourceful detective work in locating key (and sometimes obscure) references, and Andrew Hunter for thoughtful and insightful reading and commentary.

REFERENCES

Adams, J. (2000). How Britney gets her satisfaction – Whatever Jagger was singing about all those years ago, some things are best when lost in translation. *The Globe and Mail*, 12 June, p. R03.

Atkins, D. (Ed.) (2002). *Bisexual Women in the Twenty-first Century*. New York, NY: Harrington Park Press.

Ault, A. (1999). Ambiguous identity in an unambiguous sex/gender structure: The case of bisexual women. In M. Storr (Ed.), *Bisexuality: A critical reader* (pp. 167–185). New York, NY: Routledge.

Anderson, J. (2005). Young love goes wild in Pawel Pawlikowski's swoony British drama. *Eye Weekly Magazine*, 30 June, pp. 2–7.

Bi Academic Intervention (1997). *The Bisexual Imaginary: Representation, identity and desire.* London: Cassell.

Bledsoe, E. (2004). Bi-boys, fly girls: Bisex for Gen X. In *Interface* (pp. 32–34). Sydney: Vibewire Youth Services.

Bower, J. (1999). *(Im)possible Women: Gender, sexuality and the British army*. Unpublished doctoral thesis, University of London.

Bower, J., Gurevich, M., & Mathieson, C. (2002). (Con)tested identities: Bisexual women reorient sexuality. *Journal of Bisexuality*, **2**(2/3), 23–52.

Butler, J. (1990). *Gender Trouble: Feminism and the subversion of identity*. London: Routledge.

Butler, J. (1991). Imitation and gender insubordination. In D. Fuss (Ed.), *Inside/Out: Lesbian theories, gay theories* (pp. 13–31). New York, NY: Routledge.

Butler, J. (1993). *Bodies that Matter: On the discursive limits of 'sex'*. New York, NY: Routledge.

Butler, J. (1997). *Excitable Speech: A politics of the performative*. New York, NY: Routledge.

Butler, J. (1999). *Gender Trouble: Feminism and the subversion of identity* (10th edn). London: Routledge.

Ciasullo, A. (2001). Making her (in)visible: Cultural representation of lesbianism and the lesbian body in the 1990s. *Feminist Studies*, **27**(3), 577–608.

Culler, J. (1989). *On Deconstruction: Theory and criticism after structuralism*. London: Routledge.

Däumer, E. D. (1999). Queer ethics; or, the challenge of bisexuality to lesbian ethics. In M. Storr (Ed.), *Bisexuality: A critical reader* (pp. 152–161). New York, NY: Routledge.

Derrida, J. (1997). *Of Grammatology* (trans G. C. Spivak). Baltimore, MD: John Hopkins University Press.

Diamond, L. M. (2005). 'I'm straight, but I kissed a girl': The trouble with American media representations of female-female sexuality. *Feminism & Psychology*, **15**(1), 104–110.

Dollimore, J. (1991). *Sexual Dissidence*. Oxford: Oxford University Press.

Doty, A. (1993). *Making Things Perfectly Queer: Interpreting mass culture*. Minneapolis, MN: University of Minnesota Press.

Eadie, J. (1997). Living in the past: *Savage Nights*, bisexual times. *Journal of Gay, Lesbian and Bisexual Identity*, **2**(1), 7–26.

Eadie, J. (1999). Activating bisexuality: Towards a bi/sexual politics. In M. Storr (Ed.), *Bisexuality: A critical reader* (pp. 119–137). New York, NY: Routledge.

Eagleton, M. (1996). Who's who and where's where: Constructing feminist literary studies. *Feminist Review*, **53**(Summer), 1–23.

Esterberg, K. G. (2002). The bisexual menace. Or, will the real bisexual please stand up? In S. Seidman & D. Richardson (Eds), *The Handbook of Lesbian and Gay Studies* (pp. 215–227). London: Sage.

Falwell, Rev. J. (2004). Teens commit to chastity until marriage. WorldNetDaily, 17 January. Retrieved 11 July 2005, from http://www.worldnetdaily.com/news/article.asp?ARTICLE_ID=36642

Firestein, B. (Ed.) (1996). *Bisexuality: The psychology and politics of an invisible minority*. Thousand Oaks, CA: Sage.

Foucault, M. (1972). *The Archaeology of Knowledge*. New York, NY: Harper and Row.

Foucault, M. (1990). *The History of Sexuality: Volume I an Introduction* (trans R. Hurley). New York, NY: Vintage Books.

Foucault, M. (1995). *Discipline and Punish: The birth of the prison* (trans A. Sheridan). New York, NY: Vintage Books.

Fox, R. C. (1995). Bisexual identities. In A. R. D'Augelli & C. J. Patterson (Eds), *Lesbian, Gay, and Bisexual Identities over the Lifespan: Psychological perspectives* (pp. 48–86). Oxford: Oxford University Press.

Fox, R. C. (2000). Bisexuality in perspective: A review of theory and research. In B. Greene & G. Croom (Eds), *Education, Research, and Practice in Lesbian, Gay, Transgendered Psychology: A resource manual* (pp. 161–206). Thousand Oaks, CA: Sage.

Gamman, L. & Makinen, M. (1994). *Female Fetishism: A new look*. London: Lawrence & Wishart.

Garber, M. (1995). *Vice Versa: Bisexuality and the eroticism of everyday life*. New York, NY: Simon and Schuster.

Goffman, E. (1963). *Stigma: Notes on the management of spoiled identity*. Englewood Cliffs, NJ: Prentice-Hall.

The Guardian (2004). Wave of 'bisexual chic' sweeping American high schools. 5 January, p. 7.

Haraway, D. (1990). A manifesto for cyborgs: Science, technology and socialist feminism in the 1980s. In L. J. Nicholson (Ed.), *Feminism/Postmodernism* (pp. 190–233). London: Routledge.

Hemmings, C. (1999). Locating bisexual identities: Discourses of bisexuality and contemporary feminist theory. In M. Storr (Ed.), *Bisexuality: A critical reader* (pp. 193–200). New York, NY: Routledge.

Hemmings, C. (2002). *Bisexual Spaces: A geography of sexuality and gender*. New York, NY: Routledge.

Herdt, G. H. (1999). A comment on cultural attributes and fluidity of bisexuality. In M. Storr (Ed.), *Bisexuality: A critical reader* (pp. 162–166). New York, NY: Routledge.

Herek, G. M. (1995). Psychological heterosexism in the United States. In A. R. D'Augelli & C. J. Patterson (Eds), *Lesbian, Gay, and Bisexual Identities over the Lifespan: Psychological perspectives* (pp. 321–346). Oxford: Oxford University Press.

Heyes, C. (2002). Identity Politics. The Stanford Encyclopedia of Philosophy (Fall 2002 Edition), Edward N. Zalta (Ed.). Available from <http://plato.stanford.edu/archives/fall2002/entries/identity-politics/>

Ingebretsen, E. (1999).Gone shopping: The commercialization of same-sex desire. *Journal of Gay, Lesbian, and Bisexual Identity*, **4**, 125–148.

Janes, W. E. (2004). Commercial homosexuality: Selling lesbianism. *The Edwardsville Journal of Sociology*, **4**(Spring), 1–12. Available from http://www.siue.edu/SOCIOLOGY/journal/v4.htm.

Jenkins, T. (2005). 'Potential lesbians at two o'clock': The heterosexualization of lesbianism in the recent teen film. *Journal of Popular Culture*, **38**(3), 491–504.

Kachgal, T. (2004). 'Look at the *The Real World*. There's always a gay teen on there': Sexual citizenship and youth-targeted reality television. *Feminist Media Studies*, **4**(3), 361–364.

Kaloski Naylor, A. (1999). 'Gone are the days': Bisexual perspectives on lesbian/feminist literary theory. *Feminist Review*, **61**(Spring), 51–66.

Kelly, D. (1998). Glam, bam, shazam! *The Globe and Mail*, 7 November, p C22.

Malson, H. (1998). *The Thin Woman: Feminism, post-structuralism and the social psychology of anorexia nervosa*. London: Routledge.

Malernee, J. (2003). Teen girls exploring 'bisexual chic' trend: Debate rises over whether a kiss is just a kiss. *South Florida Sun – Sentinel*, 30 December, p. 1.A.

McKenna, S. E. (2002). The queer insistence of Ally McBeal: Lesbian chic, postfeminism, and lesbian reception. *The Communications Review*, **5**, 285–314.

Mistry, R. (2000). From 'hearth and home' to a queer chic: A critical analysis of progressive depictions of gender in advertising. Unpublished 'Communications Long Essay,' Institute of Communications Studies, University of Leeds, UK. Available from http://www.theory.org.uk/mistry.htm

Mohler, R. A. (2004). The newest teen girl fad – Bisexual chic. The Council on Biblical Manhod and Womanhood, 27 January. Retrieved 11 July 2005, from http://www.cbmw.org/news/ram270104.php

Mulvey, L. (1989). Visual pleasure and narrative cinema. In L. Mulvey (Ed.), *Visual and Other Pleasures* (pp. 14–27). Bloomington, IN: Indiana University Press.

Nguyen, M. (1999). Why queer theory? Available from http://www.theory.org.uk/

Parker, I. (1992). *Discourse Dynamics: Critical analysis for social and individual psychology*. London: Routledge.

Phelan, S. (1993). (Be)coming out: Lesbian identity and politics, *Signs*, **18**(4), 765–790.

Portman, J. (2005). Breaking down taboos – Hollywood coming out of the closet on bisexuality. *The Daily News (Halifax)*, 6 January, p. 13.

Prior, L. (1989). *The Social Organisation of Death: Medical discourse and social practice in Belfast*. Basingstoke: Macmillan.

Richler, C. (2003). Manufacturing lesbianism for CD sales. *The Chronicle~Herald*, 3 April, p. A8.

Rust, P. C. (1995). *Bisexuality and the Challenge to Lesbian Politics: Sex, loyalty and revolution*. New York, NY: New York University Press.

Rust, P. C. (2000a). Bisexuality: A contemporary paradox for women. *Journal of Social Issues*, **56**(2), 205–221.

Rust, P. C. (Ed.) (2000b). *Bisexuality in the United States: A social science reader*. New York, NY: Columbia University Press.

Rust, P. C. (2000c). Too many and not enough: The meaning of bisexual identities. *Journal of Bisexuality*, **1**(1), 33–70.

Rust, P. C. (2001). Make me a map: Bisexual men's images of bisexual community. *Journal of Bisexuality*, **1**(2/3), 47–108.

Sedgwick, E. K. (1990). *Epistemology of the Closet*. Berkley, CA: University of California Press.

Stenner, P. (1993). Discoursing jealousy. In E. Burman & I. Parker (Eds), *Discourse Analytic Research: Repertoires and readings of texts in action* (pp. 114–142). London: Routledge.

Stepp, L. S. (2004). Partway gay? For some teen girls, sexual preference is a shifting concept. *Washington Post*, 4 January, p. D01.

Stewart, S. (2002). Bisexual chic at the bijou. *The Gay and Lesbian Review Worldwide*, **9**(5), 50.

Storr, M. (Ed.) (1999). *Bisexuality: A critical reader*. New York, NY: Routledge.

Takahama, V. (2001). Women who 'switch teams' – Drifting sexual orientation is in the pop culture spotlight. *The Toronto Star*, 14 July, p. M9.

The Toronto Star (2000). As times go bi. 14 June, p. J3.

The Toronto Star (2001). Hello, good bi. 19 June, p. E1, E4.

Tucker, N. (Ed.) (1995). *Bisexual Politics: Theories, queries, and visions*. New York, NY: Haworth Press.

Weasel, L. H. (1996). Seeing between the lines: Bisexual women and therapy. *Women & Therapy*, **19**(2), 5–16.

Whitney, E. (2002). Cyborgs among us: Performing liminal states of sexuality. *Journal of Bisexuality*, **2**(2/3), 109–128.

Wilkinson, S. (1996). Bisexuality 'a la mode'. *Women's Studies International Forum*, **19**(3), 293–301.

Wilton, T. (1996). Which one's the man? The heterosexualisation of lesbian sex. In D. Richardson (Ed.), *Theorising Heterosexuality: Telling it straight* (pp. 125–142). Buckingham: Open University Press.

Woollett, A., Marshall, H. & Stenner, P. (1998). Young women's accounts of sexual activity and sexual/reproductive health, *Journal of Health Psychology*, **3**(3), 369–381.

Yoshino, K. (2000). The epistemic contract of bisexual erasure. *Stanford Law Review*, **52**(2), 353–461.

Yuen Thompson, B. (2000). Fence sitters, switch hitters, and bi-bi girls: An exploration of *Hapa* and bisexual identities. *Frontiers*, **21**(1/2), 171–180.

PART III

Work and Leisure

LGBTQ Psychologies
Go To Work

Suzanna M. Rose
Florida International University, Miami, USA

It has been said that 'it is easier to smash an atom than a prejudice' (Allport, 1954). Diagnosis, treatment and research aimed at lesbians, gay men, bisexual, trans and queer people (LGBTQ) during the past several decades have provided much evidence in support of this truism. Psychiatric views of homosexuality as abnormal were in effect until recently and the high prevalence of hate crime victimization suggests that prejudice against LGBTQ people continues relatively unabated. The experience of lesbians and gay men in the workplace, however, is one important area of life affected by prejudice that has been sorely understudied. Stress in the workplace has been long regarded as an important component of both psychological and physical health among the general heterosexual population, but scarcely a mention has been given to issues related to marginal status, stress or coping (e.g. Nelson & Burke, 2002). Thus, the light shown on this topic by the authors of the chapters in this section is most illuminating and timely.

Rosie Harding and Elizabeth Peel's ground-breaking chapter (Chapter 12) on hetero-sexism at work lays the foundation for conceptualizing the impact of legal advances, organizational intervention and the combination of the two on LGB people. Their analysis of anti-discrimination law in the United Kingdom and European Union provides room for both optimism and caution concerning the effectiveness of laws as catalysts for social change. Although progressive legislation is in place in the UK that outlaws sexual orientation discrimination in the workplace, some specific categories of discriminatory behaviour, such as direct and indirect discrimination, would be quite difficult to prove. In fact, the only cases of discrimination that have succeeded in the UK have been those that have contended there was harassment (e.g. name calling) based on sexual orientation. Harding and Peel rightly conclude that the importance of such legislation may be to change the discourse concerning what is normative at work, rather than provide recourse for lesbians and gay men who have experienced discrimination.

Out in Psychology: Lesbian, gay, bisexual, trans and queer perspectives. Edited by Victoria Clarke and Elizabeth Peel.
© 2007 John Wiley & Sons, Ltd.

Similarly, organizational interventions such as diversity training have significant, if limited, effects in terms of changing attitudes. At present, a combination of both legal and educational approaches clearly is required to confront homophobia and heterosexism at work.

The next three chapters on lesbians in sport (Krane & Kauer, Chapter 13), contemporary issues in the lives of lesbians and gay men in the UK (Ellis, Chapter 14), and successful lesbian professionals (Rostad & Long, Chapter 15) illustrate the need for in-depth analysis concerning workplace issues, as well as the fruitfulness of work as a research area. Sonja Ellis provides an excellent brief recent history of legal changes and their effect on workplace policy and practice as a backdrop for her investigation of LGB peoples' lives. Her innovative interview study focuses on a range of topics concerning LGB peoples' experiences and identifies three significant 'sites of oppression', including the workplace, relationships and the LGB(T) community. Responses concerning the workplace are particularly interesting in terms of revealing the broad scope of issues lesbians and gay men face concerning their sexual orientation, including casual 'joking', silencing, censoring and differential employment conditions and treatment (e.g. for lesbian parents versus heterosexual ones).

Both the chapters by Krane and Kauer, and Ellis are significant for their focus on lesbians, an understudied group even within sexual orientation research. Vikki Krane and Kerrie Kauer in their work on lesbians in sport demonstrate the consequences of the interaction of discrimination based on both sexual orientation and gender – an effect that is often ignored or not acknowledged in lesbian and gay research. Sport provides a unique context in that it represents a male domain into which girls and women have recently made some inroads, at least at the non-professional level. However, lesbian-baiting has been part of the territory of women's sports since the 1950s (Pierman, 2005). Krane and Kauer's findings emphasize the psychological resiliency lesbians must exhibit in order to achieve in this arena. The pressures on lesbians to remain silent about their sexual orientation are enormous, yet lesbian athletes and coaches found ways to cope and sometimes challenge the status quo. Many managed by accepting a bicultural divide in their lives, that is, by keeping the worlds of sport and lesbian life separate.

The successful lesbian professionals described by Faith Rostad and Bonita Long provide an upbeat ending for this section. Rostad and Long examine the social and political barriers that lesbians face at work compared to heterosexual women and other marginalized groups, as well as what accounts for the achievement of the 15 women they interviewed. Participants noted various obstacles they had encountered in their careers, including lack of mentors or role models, having to be in the closet, or keeping a social distance from colleagues. However, a process of 'striving for holistic integration' was also identified as a coping mechanism that arose under certain circumstances such as changing social times, having love and support for being a lesbian, and/or being in a LGBT friendly work environment, amongst others.

In conclusion, work and leisure are major sources of identity, self-esteem, and well-being that have long been neglected in LGBTQ research. This section of *Out in Psychology*, however, reveals that new developments in law and society have paved the way for LGBTQ researchers to be more proactive in terms of selecting what is important to study. It has become less necessary to show heterosexuals that lesbians and gay men are 'normal' and more relevant to understand LGBTQ lives as a whole. The chapters in 'work and leisure' take a big step onto this new path.

REFERENCES

Allport, G. W. (1954). *The Nature of Prejudice*. Cambridge, MA: Addison-Wesley.
Nelson, D. L. & Burke, R. J. (Eds) (2002). *Gender, Work Stress, and Health*. Washington, DC: American Psychological Association.
Pierman, C. J. (2005). Baseball, conduct and true womanhood. In C. J. Pierman (Ed.), Women and sports, Special issue of *Women's Studies Quarterly*, **33**, 68–85.

CHAPTER 12

Heterosexism at Work: Diversity Training, Discrimination Law and the Limits of Liberal Individualism

Rosie Harding
University of Kent, UK
and
Elizabeth Peel
Aston University, UK

INTRODUCTION

Heteronormativity and heterosexism infiltrate working environments in various ways and 'combating heterosexism in (and beyond) the workplace is the responsibility of each and every person' (Kitzinger, 1991, p. 236). We spend most of our adult lives working. According to recent Department of Trade and Industry estimates, there are between 1.5 million and 2 million lesbians, gay men and bisexuals in the UK workforce (Govan, 2005). Yet there is a dearth of LGBTQ psychological literature focusing on the work environment (see Ellis, Chapter 14) and a pervasive assumption that 'sexuality has no legitimate place at work' (Martin & Collinson, 1999, p. 295). Gore (2000) suggests that the mere presence of visible or 'out' lesbians, gay men and bisexual people[1] at work 'is transformative' (p. 282). This may well be the case in some contexts (Herek & Capitanio, 1996), but transforming public and private sector organizations beyond their overwhelmingly heteronormative frameworks and practices requires much more than individuals choosing to be out or visible. Challenging heterosexism at work requires complex

---

[1] LGBTQ psychology is the acronym encompassing the field which is increasingly being used in the UK and elsewhere. However, we have chosen to use LGB when referring to either the law or education/training about sexualities because both these areas tend to focus on LGB people. Discrimination on the basis of gender identity is covered through sex discrimination laws (see Whittle, 2002 for a detailed discussion of trans rights) and therefore trans issues are likely to be best addressed in sex/gender awareness diversity training.

Out in Psychology: Lesbian, gay, bisexual, trans and queer perspectives. Edited by Victoria Clarke and Elizabeth Peel.
© 2007 John Wiley & Sons, Ltd.

and multi-layered strategies and thoroughgoing challenge at structural, inter-group and individual levels.

It is clear that sexualities in the workplace have been an overlooked issue in LGBTQ psychology and the literature that addresses lesbians and gay men's experiences in the workplace is drawn from disparate fields and is often unpublished (see also Ellis, Chapter 14, and Rostad and Long, Chapter 15). Levine (1995) pointed out with regard to gay men that 'no one knows exactly how often gay men are victimized in the workplace' (p. 220) but cited four studies which collectively found that 30% of a total of 1874 gay men perceived that their sexuality had adverse consequences on their careers and that 13% had experienced employment discrimination. Croteau's (1996) review of nine studies examining the workplace experiences of LGB people undertaken between 1983 and 1995 concluded that 'discrimination is pervasive in the experiences of this population' (p. 198). Three of the reviewed studies asked participants directly whether they had experienced discrimination in employment and found that 25–66% reported that they had experienced discrimination. Ryan-Flood (2004) examined the workplace experiences of lesbians and gay men in Brighton and Hove (UK). On the basis of an opportunistic sample of LGB workers in the area (45 questionnaire respondents and 15 interviewees), Ryan-Flood suggests that one strategy LGB employees use is to choose workplaces that they perceive to be open-minded and tolerant of their sexuality, therefore actively managing the potential for experiencing discrimination at work prior to entering particular work environments. Moreover, once LGB people are within particular workplaces a key aspect of employment that they face is negotiating their level of 'outness' which, because of the heterosexual assumption, results in LGB invisibility in the workplace and a rift between the supposed 'private' (LGB) self and the 'public' employee self (Kitzinger, 1991). The advent of legal protection in the UK against discrimination on the basis of sexual orientation may facilitate the dissolution of the distinction between 'private' non-heterosexual sexualities and 'public' assumed-to-be-heterosexual sexualities, because workplace legislation including sexual orientation makes sexuality visible within the workplace at a group level.

In this chapter we address the topic of overcoming heterosexism at work by making the argument that affecting positive change in organizational cultures and individual 'attitudes' is a difficult task that may benefit from a two-pronged approach involving legal and educational interventions. An anti-discrimination legal framework provides a 'top-down' structural steer against heterosexism, on the one hand, and education about LGB issues, on the other hand, provides a 'bottom-up' individual or inter-group challenge to heterosexism. We claim that this two-pronged approach provides a way forward in creating positive social change for LGB people at work and beyond. Effective legal prohibition of discrimination, when coupled with more creative approaches to combating heterosexism through sexualities awareness training and education, may provide a meaningful contribution to solving problems associated with heteronormativity.

We begin with a discussion of the creation and implementation of employment anti-discrimination legislation, focusing on the impact that the new Employment Equality (Sexual Orientation) Regulations (EE(SO)R) have had in the UK, as well as exploring the limitations of anti-discrimination law and the liberal diversity model that it embodies. We then shift our focus to diversity training about sexualities, critically evaluating the aims and objectives of such training, through a qualitative analysis of the perceived effectiveness of training via interview data with 16 people who had experienced LGB awareness training.[2] These accounts form part of a broader analysis of LGB awareness training, other aspects of which have been published elsewhere (see Kitzinger & Peel 2005; Peel 2001a, 2001b; Peel 2002a, 2002b; Peel 2005). Finally, we conclude with a discussion of the limitations of both of these frameworks for tackling heterosexism at work. We highlight problematic issues of liberal sameness, diversity and the difficulties of essentialist constructions of lesbian, gay or bisexual sexualities.

OUTLAWING DISCRIMINATION IN THE WORKPLACE

The Anti-Discrimination Framework

Despite being a relatively recent addition to employment law, anti-discrimination legislation has become the hegemonic legal approach to combating discrimination in the workplace. The basic tenet of anti-discrimination law is that a person has a right to be treated equally in employment, throughout their employment, from hiring to the end of an employment relationship. The earliest examples of anti-discrimination law in the UK were the Race Relations Acts of 1965 and 1968, followed by the Equal Pay Act in 1970 and the Sex Discrimination Act 1975. The statutory form of this body of legislation borrowed heavily from the US Civil Rights Act of 1964, which had been the US Federal Government's response to the civil rights movements of the 1950s and 1960s (Deakin & Morris, 1998). The UK's membership of the European Union (EU) has also had a direct influence on the body of legislation surrounding equal treatment in the workplace, through the Equal Pay Directive (1975 – covering equal pay for equal work), the Equal Treatment Directive (1976 – covering sex discrimination), the Race Directive (2000 – covering 'race' discrimination) and the Framework Directive (2000 – covering religion or belief, disability, age and sexual orientation).[3] These pieces of European legislation lay down the framework for anti-discrimination provision in the workplace for all 25 EU member states. Similar forms of anti-discrimination also exist in a number of other countries worldwide, for example, 10 US states outlaw employment discrimination based on sexual orientation (Gore, 2000, p. 289). However, as the legal specifics of anti-discrimination provision vary considerably around the world,[4] this chapter will focus on the situation in the UK and Europe.

Most European anti-discrimination protection on the basis of sexual orientation is very new. The current UK legislation outlawing discrimination on the basis of sexual orientation in the workplace is the Employment Equality (Sexual Orientation) Regulations 2003. These regulations were implemented as a direct result of the EU Framework Directive 2000, and have adopted the same definitions of discrimination and limitations on protection as laid out in the EU legislation. In the EE(SO)R, 'sexual orientation' means a sexual orientation towards – (1) persons of the same sex; (2) persons of the opposite sex; or (3)

---

[2] It is of note that these interview data were collected prior to the EE(SO)R coming into force. To our knowledge no similar data has been collected or analysed since the advent of legal workplace sexual orientation protection in the UK.

[3] This is not an exhaustive list of EU discrimination law – for a more comprehensive account, see Fredman (2001).

[4] A list of international sexual orientation anti-discrimination laws compiled by Robert Wintemute (as of September 2002) can be found on the International Lesbian and Gay Association website at: http://www.ilga.info/Information/Legal_survey/list_of_international_treaties.htm.

persons of the same and opposite sex (Regulation 2). So, the EE(SO)R technically apply as much to heterosexual workers as they do to lesbian, gay or bisexual workers. Broadly speaking, the EE(SO)R protect workers from discrimination based on their sexual orientation in relation to 'direct discrimination', 'indirect discrimination,' 'victimization' and 'harassment'. There are a number of important points that need to be made concerning the definitions of discrimination within the EE(SO)R, and the limitations that these definitions impose.

Direct Discrimination

The first form of discrimination outlawed by the EE(SO)R is 'direct discrimination'. Direct discrimination (Regulation 3(1)(a)), only occurs when one person is treated less favourably than another would be, as a *direct result* of their sexual orientation. This means that in order to claim direct discrimination, the person bringing the claim must be able to compare the way they were treated with they way another person of a different sexual orientation (a comparator) was or would be treated. An example of direct discrimination would be when a person is sacked for being gay and this is the explicit reason given for the termination of employment. Where there is no comparator available, it is generally very difficult to prove that direct discrimination has occurred.

Direct discrimination is the 'common sense' version of discrimination, in that it would seem to be the most easily understood. This does not mean that direct discrimination is either the most common or the easiest to prove form of discrimination. The concept of direct discrimination could, however, be argued to have discursive power, in that the introduction of laws prohibiting discrimination on the basis of sexual orientation sends out a powerful message that this form of disparate treatment is not acceptable. But, even in instances where sexual orientation is a salient factor in the way an employee is treated, the conduct will not necessarily be found to be discrimination. Take this case as an example:

> A UK designer who was dismissed for using a company computer to send explicit e-mails to her lesbian lover won her claim for unfair dismissal yesterday. A Nottingham employment tribunal had heard that Helen Brearley was fired from shop fitting company Timber Tailors because she had let her standard of work slip because of her 'excessive' email use, which the company said constituted gross misconduct. Brearley claimed that she was unfairly dismissed. 'I was not aware the content was in any way against company policy, as they were personal emails,' Brearley said. The tribunal awarded Brearley £26,245 for unfair dismissal and said that the firm had 'grossly overstated' the problem and that they should have warned her instead of sacking her. (Stonewall, 2005a)

Although this case could be described as an instance of direct discrimination, the sexual orientation aspect of the case was sidelined and it was instead foregrounded as an instance of unfair dismissal. As noted above, direct discrimination requires that the treatment received must be comparable to that of another person from another group – so in the case of sex discrimination, a woman needs a male comparator. Interestingly, as the definition of sexual orientation distinguishes between orientation towards 'persons of the same sex' and 'persons of the same and opposite sex', this opens up more potential comparators in sexual orientation cases. So, in the case of discrimination on the basis of sexual orientation, this would mean that a lesbian or gay man could use a bisexual or heterosexual person as a comparator; and vice versa. In practice it is likely that 'heterosexual' people will be used as the comparator for any instance of discrimination against LGB people, as heterosexuality is still the norm against which all other sexual orientations are compared. As yet, no successful case of direct discrimination under the EE(SO)R has been reported, either in official law reports or by the media.

Indirect Discrimination

The second form of discrimination outlawed by the regulations is indirect discrimination. Indirect discrimination (Regulation 3(1)(b)), covers instances where a person is disadvantaged as a result of their sexual orientation by an apparently neutral criterion or provision. This form of discrimination is defined in a fairly restrictive manner. For example, the person disadvantaged by a neutral practice would have to prove not only that the particular provision is likely to disadvantage people who have the 'same sexual orientation' as them, but also that the provision did actually disadvantage them. At the same time the employer would have the opportunity to claim that the provision was 'a proportionate means of achieving a legitimate aim', which has the capacity to prioritise discriminatory business practices (as long as they are 'proportionate' and have a 'legitimate aim') over an individual's employment rights. Again, no cases of indirect discrimination under the EE(SO)R have yet been reported.

Victimization

The third type of discrimination prohibited by the EE(SO)R is 'victimization' (Regulation 4). This is an unusual species of discrimination protection, as it is concerned with instances where a person is treated less favourably *as a result of making a claim of discrimination* under the regulations, or providing evidence on behalf of a colleague under the regulations. But there is only limited protection against this form of discrimination in the regulations – if the allegation or evidence was 'false and not made . . . in good faith' there is no protection. Given the difficulties of proving discrimination (as discussed above), it is unlikely that claims of victimization will be a common form of discrimination claim under the EE(SO)R. Unsurprisingly, no cases of victimization have been reported.

Harassment

The final type of discrimination outlawed by the EE(SO)R is 'harassment'. Harassment (Regulation 5) means unwanted conduct (in relation to sexual orientation), which has the 'purpose or effect' of 'violating a person's dignity', or 'creating an intimidating, hostile, degrading, humiliating or offensive environment'. Harassment is, perhaps, the most common (and least difficult to evidence) form of discrimination in the workplace, as it not only has a relatively broad definition, but also because the effect of such conduct is as important as the purpose or intent behind it.

Of the cases under the EE(SO)R that have been reported in the media, the form of discrimination alleged was usually harassment, taking the form of name calling and bullying. For example, the first successful case under the EE(SO)R was that of a manager in an international waste disposal firm, whose line manager and colleagues nicknamed him 'Sebastian' after the camp political aide in the British TV comedy show *Little Britain*[5] and called him 'a queen', 'queer' and accused him of liking 'poofy drinks and handbags' (Wainwright, 2005). In another case, the language used was much more explicit, with the term 'fucking chutney ferret' being used by a senior manager to describe a gay male employee. In this case, the tribunal held that the term used was 'exceptionally offensive' and, even though the comments were not said directly to the employee in question, that this one instance of the use of homophobic language was enough to constitute constructive unfair dismissal. The employee, who resigned after being told about the comment by another colleague, was awarded nearly £10 000 in compensation (Personnel Today, 2005). A third example of a successful claim of harassment on the basis of sexual orientation was that of a theatre worker at Durham's Gala Theatre, who was repeatedly called 'gay boy' by his manager (BBC News, 2005).

So, these three cases were all predominantly concerned with the problematic use of homophobic and heterosexist language in the workplace, and the duty of employers to take action to protect employees from this form of verbal abuse. Although other types of cases have undoubtedly been brought and resolved, this type of case has been most commonly reported by the media, perhaps because of the commonplace nature of homophobic or heterosexist slights in everyday life (Peel, 2001b). It is worth noting that, although the eventual outcome of these cases was positive for the individuals concerned, they each had to resign from their jobs and claim constructive dismissal.

As the above discussion shows, in spite of a handful of high-profile cases, the EE(SO)R have not had wide-reaching effects. In the first 15 months of the regulations being in force in the UK, 410 claims of discrimination on grounds of sexual orientation were registered with Employment Tribunals (Employment Tribunals Service (ETS), 2005). Of these 410 complaints, 260 had also been completed within the first 15 months, with just 12 (4.6%) being successful at a tribunal hearing (Richard Walker, pers comm 3 August 2005). Of the remaining 248 claims, over half (133, 51.1%) reached a conciliated settlement through Acas, a publicly funded industrial relations mediation service; 73 (28.1%) were either withdrawn or came to a private settlement; 20 (7.7%) were unsuccessful at an employment tribunal hearing and the outcome of the remaining 22 (8.5%) is unknown or other. These statistics about claims that are successful at tribunal are broadly in line with the success rates of other discrimination claims (ETS, 2005).[6]

The Limits of Anti-Discrimination Law

As will be evident from the discussion above of the cases of discrimination on the basis of sexual orientation, legal prohibition of discrimination can, and does, give indi-

---

[5] *Little Britain* is a popular BBC comedy series that contains a number of gay and trans characters.
[6] In 2004–2005, 2% of sex discrimination, 3% of race discrimination, 5% of disability discrimination and 4% of religion or belief discrimination claims were successful at tribunal.

viduals a form of redress for the treatment they have received. There are limits to anti-discrimination law, however, which make this a problematic solution to the realities of heterosexism in the workplace for LGB people. The limits can be split into two broad categories: (1) the way equality is defined; and (2) the hierarchy of inequalities.

Defining Equality

The most common way of defining equality is concerned with treating everyone the same. This is generally referred to as 'formal equality'. Discrimination law is a paramount example of legal approaches to formal equality, as it works on the principle that 'but for' the group characteristic that is the reason for discrimination, all people are the same, and therefore should be treated alike. There are limits to formal equality, as this framework can do nothing to address the situation where, for example, everyone is treated equally badly, nor can it address the differential situations that people find themselves in as a result of the structural causes of inequality. An alternative formulation of equality, which focuses on the structural causes of inequality, is substantive equality. Substantive approaches to equality take the structural basis of inequalities as their focus, and attempt to create equality through positive interventions. Examples would include positive action or affirmative action programmes, which move away from the meritocratic approach of formal equality (see Peel & Harding 2004, for a discussion of formal and substantive equality with respect to the legal recognition of same sex relationships).

Equality and equal treatment are foundational principles in many western legal systems and most justifications for the equal treatment of all individuals are premised on the assumption that all individuals are (in some way) the same, and as such are entitled to equal rights before and under the law and equal opportunities to achieve their goals in life (Wallerstein, 2003). This approach to equality is consistent with the liberal tradition, which aims to allow everyone the freedom to live their lives according to their own conception of the 'good life', free from the constraints of the state (Dworkin, 1977). The focus on the individual within liberal equality has been the subject of much criticism with many writers dismissing the effectiveness of concentrating on the fundamental sameness of individuals (Young, 1990). Cynthia Ward (1997) argued that liberalism can include difference, by expounding the liberal conception of diversity:

> Because liberalism posits normatively that all people have equal moral worth, the empirical fact of human difference mandates respect for each person's 'right to be different' and to have his [sic] differences tolerated by others. (p. 69)

There are several problems with this liberal conception of difference. The first is that it reduces difference to an 'empirical fact' devoid of any social or historical constraints, and therefore ignores the effect of oppression on those subjected to inequalities. This reduction of difference to an empirical fact is based in the liberal assumption that all adult human beings have a level of autonomy (Ward, 1997, p. 69), which ignores the constraints of differing levels of autonomy caused by privilege and oppression. Second, Ward implies that there is some class of person who is capable of 'tolerating' (p. 69) another, rather than all people being equal irrespective of difference. A third problem with liberal diversity is that it serves as its own limitation: 'One's right to pursue one's own vision of life, which derives from the liberal's equal respect for all people, is simultaneously limited by the equal right of everyone else to do the same' (Ward, 1997, p. 70). Contrary to Ward's thesis that this is an unquestionable good in liberal diversity, it serves to position the views of the 'moral majority' over those of whom they disapprove, through the balancing of rights. In essence, the liberal standard of toleration assumes that there is one group (the norm) who have the power to tolerate those who are different, thus creating a hierarchy.

There are, however, benefits to taking the individual as the subject of equality, first, an individual focus can circumvent the problems which arise through underlying or implicit assumptions that 'groups' constitute homogenous communities, where everyone is the same. Second, an individual focus allows for the different facets of identities to be considered in relation to equality and inequality, and the ways in which different group positions intersect and interlock within individuals. Finally, an individual focus allows for the possibility that individuals can change identities, and prioritize different aspects of their identities at different times.

The way that the UK government advertised the introduction of protection against discrimination on the basis of sexual orientation is a useful example of the ways that discrimination law – and indeed 'awareness raising' – is rooted in these liberal conceptions of sameness. The Department for Trade and Industry published two 'adverts' for the new regulations. The first, (Figure 12.1) is aimed at white collar workers and was published in February 2004 (three months after the EE(SO)R came into force); the second (Figure 12.2), is aimed at manual workers, and was published in March 2004.[7]

There are a number of significant points to be made about these adverts. First, they are both depictions of four identical images, in the first advert a pen, in the second advert a car wheel, therefore encoding the liberal notion of the inherent sameness of individuals. Second, the large type at the top of the page on both adverts refers to 'lesbians', 'gay men', 'bisexuals' and 'heterosexuals', invoking essentialist identity categories. Thus, implying that such identity categories are fixed and immutable, rather than acknowledging the potential fluidity of sexual orientation, or any other forms of sexual identity (such as queer).

In both adverts, the construction of the image itself is salient. In particular it is notable that there are lines linking lesbians and gay men, lesbians and bisexuals, and bisexuals and heterosexuals, but no line linking either lesbians or gay men to heterosexuals, therefore portraying a physical gap or space between heterosexuality and lesbians and gay men. This lack of visual connection between heterosexuality and homosexuality arguably (re)inscribes dichotomous and polarized notions of monosexualities. Moreover, the adverts construct bisexuality as in between lesbian/gay and heterosexual, as a hybrid rather than a 'real' or distinct identity category. Also, the adverts have been constructed so as to avoid depicting stereotypes of LGB people. The images focus on the work undertaken: 'a tyre fitted by a lesbian' or 'a tyre fitted by a bisexual'; rather than on the ways in which sexuality is manifest in the work place. The 'pen' advert is especially interesting in this respect, as rather than captioning the pictures as 'a lesbian's pen' or 'a gay man's pen', the images are simply captioned 'a lesbian', 'a gay man', 'a bisexual' and 'a heterosexual',

---

[7] The DTI also published similar posters to advertise the Employment Equality (Religion or Belief) Regulations, which also came into force in December 2003. These posters can be found on the DTI website at http://www.dti.gov.uk/er/equality/index.htm. We have not been able to ascertain where the DTI advertised their 'religion or belief' and 'sexual orientation' posters. However, we saw the religion and belief poster on trains and in generic public contexts, but we only saw the sexual orientation posters advertised in the gay press.

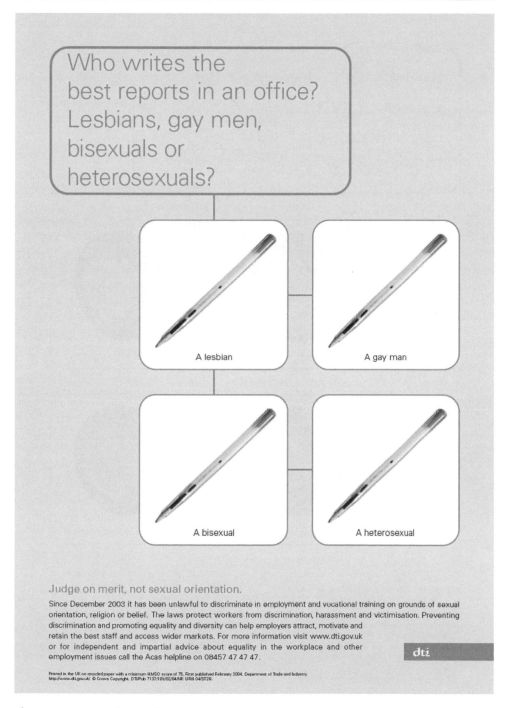

Figure 12.1 DTI white-collar worker poster
Crown Copyinght: Reproduced by permission of the Controller of Her Majesty's Stationery Office.

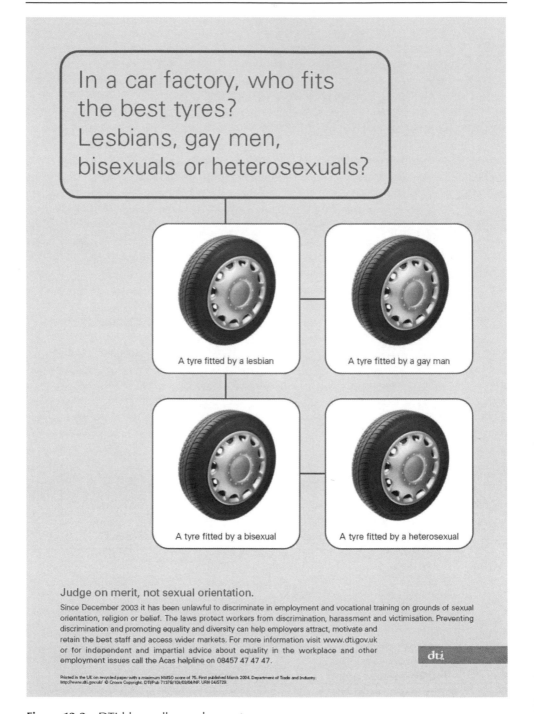

Figure 12.2 DTI blue-collar worker poster
Crown Copyright: Reproduced by permission of the Controller of Her Majesty's Stationery Office.

emphasizing the sameness, not of the work done by people of difference sexual orientations, but of people of different sexual orientations themselves. A final obvious reference
to the ideology of liberal sameness derives from the text 'judge on merit not sexual orientation', clearly signalling an overarching meritocratic framework – a level playing field
blind to societal/structural constraints surrounding different sexualities.

A Hierarchy of Inequalities

A second facet of the limitations of the discrimination law framework is the way in which
it results in a hierarchy of inequalities. Although the particular group which is most
strongly protected by anti-discrimination law does change over time, the current European
hierarchy has 'race' at its pinnacle, followed by gender, disability, religion, sexual orientation and finally age (Fredman, 2001; Day & Davidson, 2003). There are currently publicly
funded equality bodies established to assist those who experience inequality and discrimination on the basis of gender, 'race' and disability,[8] each with wide ranging powers. There
is currently no centrally-funded equality body specifically concerned with religion, sexual
orientation or age discrimination. Prior to the introduction of the EE(SO)R, there was a
small London-based charitable organization, Lesbian and Gay Employment Rights
(LAGER), who advised lesbians and gay men on employment rights. This organization
unfortunately had to close shortly after the regulations came into force due to a lack of
funding. The 'new' discriminations are to be covered by the ambit of a new single equality
body, the Commission for Equality and Human Rights, which should come into existence
in 2007. One of the reasons behind the creation of a single equality body is to attempt to
break down the possibility of the 'old' discriminations being seen as more important than
the 'new' discriminations (Day & Davidson, 2003, p. 17). This will not remove the distinctions in the anti-discrimination protections offered to each group.[9]

Emphasis on the differences between groups, as created by the hierarchy of protections
offered, can also operate to make differences within groups invisible and therefore to
marginalize particular individuals (Fredman, 2001). Also, a focus on group identity can
marginalize the individual through the reinforcement of stereotypes and can lead to claims
of 'special treatment' (Brickell, 2001). The hierarchy of inequality not only constructs
some groups as more deserving of equality than others, but also causes problems for those
who find themselves members of more than one 'minority group'. Black women, for
example may have to choose between fighting for 'racial' equality *or* gender equality;
lesbians may have to choose whether to align themselves with the struggle for gender
equality *or* equal rights for lesbians and gay men (Fraser, 1997).

In summary then, anti-discrimination legislation has a number of problematic aspects
which are inherent in its focus on the liberal individual, as well as the categorization of
individuals into 'groups' which form the ontological basis for their experience of discrimination. The complex nature of heterosexism in the workplace is, therefore, unable to be

---

[8] Equal Opportunities Commission, Commission for Racial Equality, Disability Rights Commission.
[9] For example, whereas protection is offered to the 'old' discriminations in the provision of goods, facilities, and services as
well as employment and education, the legislation dealing with the 'new' discriminations is currently limited to employment
and vocational training. In the case of sexual orientation, the regulations even allow for discrimination on the basis of sexual
orientation where the employer is a religious body (EE(SO)R). This is set to change in the near future, as provision to
outlaw discrimination in the provision of goods and services was introduced by the Equality Act 2005.

challenged solely through recourse to liberal anti-discrimination law, and other approaches to combating disparate treatment are necessary. In the following section, we shift our focus away from legal approaches to more creative forms of tackling prejudice in the workplace through diversity training. We begin with a brief overview of diversity training, before providing an analysis of whether training 'works' through a qualitative analysis of in-depth interviews with diversity trainees.

DIVERSITY TRAINING ABOUT SEXUALITIES

Diversity training is seen as a 'growing innovation' (McCauley, Wright & Harris, 2000, p. 113) in the workplace. Historically, equal opportunities training or diversity training has taken issues of race, gender and disability discrimination as its focus, while sexuality and LGB issues have been a neglected aspect of training (Hill, 1995; Trotter & Gilchrist, 1996). However, the implementation of the sexual orientation regulations means that sexual orientation has been placed more firmly on the workplace agenda. For example, Stonewall has produced a Corporate Equality Index (CEI) that indicates the top 100 employers for LGB people in the UK. In 2005 they invited 630 of the largest employers to participate in the scheme that assesses employers along a number of criteria including work-related benefits applied to same sex and different sex couples and the provision of diversity training covering sexual orientation. Ninety-three of their top 100 employers provided training covering 'sexual discrimination' and of those, 53 organizations had made training compulsory for all staff (Stonewall, 2005b). According to Stonewall, employers are 'ever mindful of the need to attract and retain a diverse workforce [and] are utilizing resources such as sexual orientation-specific diversity training' (Lorenzo Di Silvio, pers comm 9 December 2005), and since the implementation of the EE(SO)R 'there has definitely been an increase in training' (Jenn Bonito, pers comm 31 January 2006).

Within the literature on sexualities diversity training, there are three main (interconnecting) approaches to educating heterosexuals. All three of these approaches are premised on cognitivist assumptions of 'stereotypes', 'misperceptions' and 'ignorance' about LGB issues on the part of heterosexual employers and employees. First, the provision of 'facts' about LGB people is conceptualized as an antidote to the 'myths' that heterosexual people hold (van de Ven, 1995). 'Learning the facts' (Messing, Schoenberg & Stephens, 1984, p. 69) and proving 'accurate and valued information' (Schreier, 1995, p. 21) is seen as crucial in fostering the replacement of 'stereotypes' with supposedly more realistic images. The second approach foregrounds 'getting to know' LGB people as 'human beings . . . not just gay men or lesbians' (Cotton-Huston & Waite, 2000, p. 128), and so provides an 'emotional component' (Schreier, 1995, p. 21) to training as well as an application of the contact hypothesis[10]. Notions of the 'ethnic homosexual' (Altman, 1980) undergird a final approach that entails claiming that LGB people are similar to other

---

[10] The 'contact hypothesis' is well used in social psychology; the assumption is that 'positive contact and interaction' (Nelson & Krieger, 1997, p. 67) between heterosexuals and LGB people will improve negative attitudes toward LGB people (Herek & Glunt, 1993). Empirically this seems to be the case (Tropp & Pettigrew, 2005) although such researchers advocate LGBs should 'create a target out-group member who is the optimal blend of typicality and likableness' (Simon, 1998, p. 75).

'minority groups' – the assumption being that this will encourage heterosexuals to take LGB concerns more seriously (Henley & Pincus, 1978; McClintock, 1992).

In sum, the three prevalent approaches for educating heterosexuals involve the provision of 'facts' about LGB people, providing contact with individual LGB people, and parallels being drawn between LGB people as a group and other marginalized groups (the implicit assumption here being that LGB people are white, able-bodied and so on, see also Riggs, Chapter 4). It has been highlighted in previous work (e.g. Peel 2002a, 2002b) that evaluations of training show that it can be an effective tool for reducing 'homophobia' yet questions remain about how training works and how it translates into practice.

What Happens in Training?

Engagement with the specifics of LGB diversity training – concrete, practical guidance about its nature and content – is predominantly found in training manuals (e.g. Stewart, 1999), which encode liberal humanist, individualistic assumptions. For instance, Zuckerman and Simons (1996, p. ix) wrote: 'this book does not ask people to change who they are, but it does ask them to do their part to create smoothly working relationships with others'. Valuing a diverse workforce and embracing LGB colleagues – the message goes – results in a richer working environment for all. Indeed, we saw this message communicated to employers in the DTI posters through the phrase 'promoting equality and diversity can help employers attract, motivate and retain the best staff and access wider markets' (see Figures 12.1 and 12.2 above). Manuals impress on the presumed-to-be-heterosexual reader that everyone is 'on the same side', does not want to offend colleagues and shares the goal of 'smooth' working relations. Authors write of the dangers of blaming the 'SWUMs' (straight, white, US-born, men) for anti-LGB prejudice (McNaught, 1997, p. 411), and caution against trainers providing 'a stream of dour facts about antigay and antilesbian violence' and opening a training course with 'an attack against heterosexist oppression' (Crouteau & Kusak, 1992, p. 397).

As is common with the workshop format of diversity training sessions,[11] exercises conducted with trainees are the main constituent of 'what happens' in diversity training. In brief, two popular exercises are a 'language exercise' that explores the meanings and implications of language used to describe 'lesbians', 'gay men', 'bisexuals' (and 'heterosexuals', see Peel, 2005). A 'life stories' exercise involves trainees recreating the self-censorship and concealment that LGB people can experience in interactions with others by talking about themselves (in pairs) and omitting mention of personal information (e.g. about partners, home-life, etc.). Exercises are especially important as they are designed and managed by trainers (Chesler & Zuniga, 1991; Walters & Philips, 1994). Trainers have control over which tasks trainees are asked to engage in, at what point in the session, and what pedagogic messages are to be learned from them. Thus, exercises are crucial if we accept the claim that 'those who have the power to establish the language of public debate will have tremendous advantage in determining the debate's outcome'

---

[11] 'Speaker panels' wherein LGB people are invited into organisations to be asked questions by the (heterosexual) audience have also been evaluated as an approach to LGB diversity training (see Geasler, Croteau, Heineman & Edlund, 1995), but this format is far less prevalent than workshops.

(Hunter, 1994, p. 66, quoted in Smith & Windes, 2000, p. 37). A wide variety of exercises are used in training (e.g. see Stewart, 1999) and have been applied to various professional contexts (e.g. clinical psychology [Butler, 2004]; social work [Logan et al., 1996]; schools [Morjaria, 1999]; and the police [Windibank, 1995]).

Collecting the 'views' of those attending training is a popular way of evaluating the 'success' of a training program (Lai & Kleiner, 2001), although only a few studies report assessing training using some form of qualitative evaluation (Ben-Ari, 1998; Geasler et al., 1995; Imich, Bayley & Farley, 2001; Schneider & Tremble, 1986). In the next section, we contribute to this literature by analysing trainees' perspectives, and advance our argument regarding the liberalism embedded in training and more general challenges to discrimination.

Evaluating Diversity Training: Trainees' Perspectives

This analysis is based on interviews with 16 people who had experienced an LGB diversity training session.[12] Trainees talked about what they felt 'worked' and did not 'work' in the training they had experienced, their attitudes and behaviour towards lesbians and gay men, and how these had or had not changed following training. On the one hand, they were generally clear that 'we've got to be educated and we've got to be trained' (Donna), but this was tempered by comments along the lines of 'I don't think you should force people to go to training' (Tom). The themes in these data focus on trainees' talk about their 'attitudes', 'thoughts' and 'beliefs' about training and LGB people: (1) that training provided a space for reflection; (2) trainees' ideas changed as a result of training; (3) that training was, in fact, 'preaching to the converted'; and (4) trainees' admissions of (slight) homophobia.

Space for Reflection

Interviewees' accounts suggested that diversity training had been the first, or only, point in their professional lives that they had discussed, or thought about, issues pertaining to LGB people, heterosexism and homophobia: 'I have not had the opportunity before' (Sharon). Most expressed finding the opportunity to think about LGB issues 'interesting' (Ann) because 'it is something that isn't talked about [. . .] it's really good to talk about it' (Geraldine). Typically trainees made no explicit comparison between their attitudes before and after training, but made generic positive comments about the training experience being 'thought provoking' (James), 'open[ing] my eyes' (Lauren), and being 'useful'

---

[12] These interviews were conducted by EP during the period May 1999 to August 2000. The interviews were conducted within a few weeks of the trainees attending a workshop. Ten interviewees were members of university staff, four were youth workers, one was a clinical psychologist and one was a residential social worker. Nine of the interviewees were women, seven were men, 15 were white, Lauren was the only black interviewee, and all of the interviewees were able-bodied. Six interviewees were in their 20s, four were in their 30s, two were in their 40s, and four were in their 50s. All identified their sexuality as heterosexual, except Rachel who identified as bisexual. All names are pseudonyms. In this empirical section we take a broadly constructionist approach to the data, in that individual accounts are seen as expressions of socio-cultural discourses. Our analysis also incorporates an appreciation of the rhetorical and interactional features and functions of these data (Potter & Wetherell, 1987).

(Geraldine). James described the experience as one that 'just sort of stirred the grey matter a little'; and one which had acted as 'a catalyst' which 'got me thinking about how I thought about things, which I probably wouldn't have done unless something had triggered it'. Geraldine 'left the day thinking about that [sexuality] more, and in my work since thinking about that more'. Therefore, trainees' talk indicated that training functioned to carve out a space to enable them to 'consciously reflect' (James) on their perspectives about LGB issues.

Changed Ideas

There were, however, a number of accounts where interviewees suggested that training had changed their views. Trainees did not, in general, discuss experiencing dramatic shifts in 'attitudes' – as would be expected on the basis of a short training course – but they often made reference to some form of alteration: 'it maybe changed a bit my opinion' (Ann), and they felt they had become 'perhaps a little more accepting than I was' (Matthew). Heightened clarity and awareness was a frequent way interviewees communicated that training had impacted on their views: 'it's made me much more aware [. . .] It's made me a lot clearer on things, whereas before I was probably a little bit confused over certain issues and now things are much more clearer for me' (Donna).

There were occasions where interviewees recounted a *particular* change related to a localized aspect of training. For instance, Janine recounted the impact that statistics the trainer had presented about the higher number of LGB youth suicides had had on her. She found that such factual information 'gave me a lot more, sympathy's not the right word, but I can't think of a better one at the minute, sort of [to] really think these, particularly young men, you know, need help'. Lauren mentioned that training had made her realize 'that there are people getting beat up aren't there, and things are happening to people'. Lynn – in the extract below – recounted a change in her attitudes as they were expressed on a pre- and post-training homophobia scale[13] with regard to specific statements ('a woman's homosexuality should *not* be a cause for job discrimination in any situation' and 'male homosexuals should *not* be allowed to teach in school').

> When I originally filled in the survey I put – the question about erm er should there be some jobs that gay men shouldn't do or lesbians shouldn't do. Most things were one extreme or the other but that I put in the middle. And then I thought about it afterwards cos I was thinking of erm say a lesbian woman say being in a position where you're in charge of a house where erm runaway girls – young girls go to, or whatever, I thought 'that could be awkward' and then I thought 'no'. Cos you get – you get heterosexual male school teachers erm abusing kids anyway, you get homosexual y'know – and all this that and the other, and if you're a professional whatever you do then it shouldn't matter, and so that changed at the end. (Lynn)

The most striking feature of Lynn's account of change is that it is based on now viewing lesbians and gay men as 'professional whatever you do', and although she does not make explicit reference to holding the view prior to training that lesbians and gay men molest

---

[13] An adapted version of the Attitudes to Lesbians and Gay Men scale (ATLG, Herek, 1994) was the homophobia scale used (see also Peel 2002b).

children, she alludes to this when referring to heterosexual males 'abusing kids'. She narrates as her re-evaluation of her position the liberal notion that 'it [someone's sexuality] shouldn't matter', which conveys a newly acquired level of acceptance on her part. Therefore, though the majority of interviewees discussed not 'think[ing] any different than I did' (Lauren) in a global sense, they did mention *some* changes in their views resulting from training. The changes that trainees discussed were, on the whole, circumspect, and as the quotes demonstrate, were attributed to an aspect of training – for instance the acquisition of new knowledge. Interestingly, the account that stands out as the most extensive shift in 'attitude' hinged on seeing the gay male trainer as 'a decent bloke'. Donna described how she had previously thought that gay men were 'sick', because her ex-husband had allegedly had an affair with another man while she was pregnant, before continuing:

> to actually hear him talking it was like 'Oh my god, you are a decent bloke' [. . .] He seemed like a straight-forward kind of a guy and the only difference was he'd got a different sexuality from the majority of men [. . .] it changed my mind, it changed my whole opinion really, which was a good thing. (Donna)

The watershed in her perception of gay men ('oh my god' formulates this *as* a sudden realization, Frith & Kitzinger, 2001) was something she attributed to the trainer per se, through contact with individuals, rather than because of pedagogic elements of training or because of collective engagement or action.

'Preaching to the Converted'

The notion that training was 'preaching to the converted' was closely tied to accounts of attitude change in 10 of these interviews. Even though trainees typically discussed having undergone some form of change due to training, this was mitigated by reference to their 'attitude' prior to training – for instance 'it's made me much more aware' (Donna) implies already having the 'right' attitude towards LGB people. Further, such 'change' was immediately qualified through the statement 'not that I've not been equal towards gay people before' (Donna). Trainees were concurrently presenting themselves as having changed, or having learned something from training, while maintaining that they had not changed *too much*, thus avoiding the risk of being construed (by EP, a-known-to-be-lesbian, during the interview) as previously 'homophobic'. Interviewees worked to present the types of people who would attend training as those with a 'relatively liberal attitude' (Bill) and they often remarked that: 'the ones that you really want to go to these things are the ones that will never go to them' (Lynn); or 'I think if you were wanting to change attitudes you'd need to talk to perhaps to a different group' (Beryl). Consider the examples below:

> [It's] the converted talking to the converted a bit. (Beryl)

> You're certainly preaching to those people that have got an enlightened attitude, or a relatively liberal attitude. I can't imagine a homophobic turning up [. . .] I think predominantly you're preaching to the converted. (Bill)

> It suffers from the problem that you run the risk of slightly preaching to the converted. (James)

> I think one of the difficulties with things like that is it's always a bit like to an extent preaching to the converted [. . .] I couldn't remember what I had said the first time, what number I had given [on the homophobia scale], and I suppose it's important to try and get it right because it might influence, you know, your research if I put the wrong number down and I have gone and regressed when I don't mean to regress[14]. (Ian)

These examples unambiguously categorize those who attend training as 'enlightened' or 'converted' before training rather than holding 'traditional and conservative attitudes' (Bill). We are not suggesting that trainees are wrongly or inaccurately categorizing themselves, but by describing those who attend training in *this way* they are managing the stigma of the (hypothetical) allegation that they *themselves* are – or were – prejudiced towards LGB people. By classifying the characteristics of trainees as a group as 'converted' they circumvented directly saying *I* am enlightened, but at the same time portraying trainees in this way indirectly puts them personally in this category.

However, there was also a sense in some interviewees' accounts that training 'repressed' the expression of homophobia, and that people were conforming to 'politically correct' conventions about what they could and could not say on the topic. For instance, Rachel commented that there were men in her workplace who used 'gay' as a term of abuse, but during training would know that it 'wouldn't be a good idea' to talk in that way, thus training provides a context where '[I] wouldn't expect anyone to come out with something that was, I don't know, homophobic or anything like that' (Rachel). One interviewee characterized this as a 'missed opportunity':

> We're a bunch of psychologists and we're supposed to all be right on and everything. I feel like it was a missed opportunity in a way because I do feel like not everybody's honest, and people are too scared to say what they want, and everybody's worried about being erm anti-gay really and I think there is that feeling no matter how nice everybody is about it. (Geraldine)

Here Geraldine describes the group as not being 'honest' and how being 'nice' and 'right on' in training is a façade for underlying 'anti-gay' views. Interviewees described such 'dishonesty' as either a group characteristic or specific to certain group members (e.g. older members [Matthew] or male colleagues [Rachel]). Only Sharon directly described the 'fear of saying the wrong thing, and the fear of saying something that's not a p.c. thing to say'. Following on from this comment she announced that: 'I would like to think that I am quite aware, and quite informed, and quite erm open and, you know, I wouldn't be prejudiced'. Therefore, Sharon draws a distinction between 'saying the wrong thing' yet 'thinking the right thing'. Whereas others reversed this behaviour/cognition relationship by suggesting that their colleagues semantically present themselves as non-prejudiced, but underneath their talk resides discomfort about LGB sexualities.

---

[14] In the latter portion of this extract Ian raises an interesting issue about engagement in psychological research which uses scales and questionnaires. Clearly Ian is not a 'cultural dope' and here he is attending to the 'attitude' he represented on the homophobia scale and his related concern that he may have inadvertently 'regressed'. What is especially nice about this reflection about his completion of the pre- and post-training scale is the weight that he places on such measures to 'influence' the research findings.

Admitting (Slight) Homophobia

A fourth way that interviewees discussed their own and others' attitudes was by 'confessing' some issue or difficulty they had or have with LGB people. As we have seen, this was alluded to in their talk about the training context 'repressing' trainees' expression of their real views. Not all of the interviewees talked about their attitudes in this way (n = 6), because – we would argue – this is a risky strategy to 'pull off' without damaging personal investment in liberal individualism. Interviewees who claimed they were slightly homophobic pulled this off carefully, in various ways, for example:

> [training] makes me think back, it makes me feel a bit uncomfortable to tell you the truth [. . .] what my attitudes have been to people who've I've considered to be different, queer is the word I would have used years ago, always be queer and er I'm not terribly proud actually of my attitudes. (Bernie)

Similarly, Tom discussed taunting an 'odd boy' at school 'we'd get in a group and go "bumboy, bumboy" and we'd turn round and we'd leg it, you see'. Training had 'reminded' him about his behaviour as 'a lad' and he recounted in interview how now as an adult it was 'a bit embarrassing to think how you behaved as a boy'. Consider another example:

> If I was perfectly honest the answer is erm erm slightly uncomfortable (laughs) and I don't know quite how to describe it. I don't have an issue or problem with people who are gay. I– I have good friends who are openly gay and it is not an issue. Occasionally I find myself running into a social situation in which, if I am perfectly honest, I do feel slightly uncomfortable, and I– I– I am sort of thinking that I shouldn't and I– I do, and I think that the way I feel about that has actually changed over the years. (James)

In these extracts the interviewees are mainly talking about their attitudes in *the past* which creates temporal distance between their previous ('homophobic') and their current ('liberal unprejudiced') views. This way of talking about attitudes suggests improvement over time (often implicitly attributed to the simple passage of time); feelings 'change over the years' (James) and 'views have changed radically over the years' (Bernie). Admissions of holding heterosexist views *in the present* were manifest in very 'mild' forms, in phrases such as being 'a bit untolerant' (Ann), or finding LGB topics ones they didn't 'discuss very easily' (Bernie). Bernie discussed still having 'reservations' including 'gays in the army erm same sex couples bringing up children 'cos again I think in terms of the best way to bring a child up is in a family'. Thus, he manages presenting rather serious anti-lesbian and anti-gay views by formulating them rather benignly as 'reservations'. Similarly James, above, described himself as 'occasionally' 'feel[ing] slightly uncomfortable'. Consider the confessional quality of the extract below:

> I feel a bit ashamed to say but sitting with [the] person, my partner, and erm and she did not know many of the terms[15], or many famous people, or anything like that who were gay or whatever, and I was feeling she might think I am gay, do you know what I mean, I know too much. (Ian)

Ian begins with 'I feel a bit ashamed to say . . .', with 'ashamed' implying both sheepishness and contrition. He presents himself in a way reminiscent of therapeutic endeavours

---

[15] Ian is referring here to the language exercise which EP has described elsewhere (see Peel, 2005).

wherein a commitment to dealing with a particular 'problem' is initiated by the acknowl-edgement that there is a problem in the first place. However, having 'too much' knowledge about LGB issues suggests that he is an aware, informed person. Therefore, the negative connotation that could be attributed to his ashamed 'feeling' of being perceived as a gay man is tempered by its basis in knowledge. It is, of course, positive in the local context of the interview – and more broadly – that he displays that he is knowledgeable about LGB issues. He constructs his knowledge as the basis for the contention that he may be gay which functions to take the 'sting' out of his 'confession' of shame-by-association.

So, to summarize, although trainees' who were interviewed expressed satisfaction with the diversity training they had experienced, they used various strategies to convey an ideological investment in liberal individualism and manage the potential for being posi-tioned as 'prejudiced'. As is evident from this discussion of diversity training, while it can be useful in raising awareness of heterosexism and homophobia in the workplace, it does not offer any immediate remedy to those LGB people who actually experience heterosex-ism at work. We argue that only by combining the individualistic, remedy-based approach of discrimination law with the group-based educational approach of sexuality diversity training, can we even begin to challenge the realities of heterosexism at work. We will now move on to discuss the possibilities and limitations offered by both diversity training and discrimination law, in the context of three short vignettes outlining experiences of heterosexism at work.

TACKLING HETEROSEXISM AT WORK: COMBINING LEGAL AND EDUCATIONAL APPROACHES

In this section we synthesize the critical legal and critical psychological approaches explored above by applying them to case studies of heterosexism at work. We examine three examples of heterosexism at work, and discuss the possibilities (and pitfalls) that are raised by both discrimination law and diversity training in tackling the issues. In so doing, we underscore some of the limitations of liberal individualism that permeate law and education.

Example 1: Hiding structural inequality

> *During a formal meeting, a manager talks about his relationship with his wife and then asks a female employee whether she is married. She replies 'no' but mentions that she has a female partner. He physically recoils, folds his arms and responds 'I don't want to know any more' – the employee feels obliged to change the topic and powerless to challenge his overt heterosexism.*

This example highlights one of the issues often raised in diversity training exercises (see discussion of the 'life stories' exercise above). While it is commonplace for heterosexual people to discuss their partner or family life in the workplace, same-sex relationships are seen either as not worthy of mention in everyday interactions, or if they are mentioned they are construed as 'flaunting it' (Kitzinger, 2005; Land & Kitzinger, 2005). This is an example of the potentially adverse affects of coming out at work, and the ways in which sexual orientation is an integral part of workplace conversation. A second element to this

example is the imbalance of power between the individuals involved – the married heterosexual man is in a position of power by virtue of being the lesbian employee's manager
– thus limiting the potential for her to challenge his heterosexist behaviour. But even if
the roles were reversed, with the lesbian in the position of seniority, the effects of such
obvious disgust or distaste would still be present.

It is possible that under these circumstances, the female employee would have a claim
under the EE(SO)R for harassment, as this legal 'offence' includes conduct that has the
effect of creating 'an intimidating, hostile, degrading, humiliating or offensive environment'. Understandably, however, it is extremely unlikely that any LGB person would initiate a claim with an employment tribunal purely on the basis of an episode such as this.
There are a number of reasons for this, the most obvious being that, as a rule, individuals
do not wish to jeopardise their employment relationship by challenging the behaviour of
their employers, particularly when it is an isolated incident. Also, as discussed above, only
about four per cent of claims of discrimination actually succeed at tribunal, and if the
claim were unsuccessful the employee would leave herself open to victimization. It is
likely that if the manager in question had experienced diversity training on sexuality that
this episode would not have happened. As discussed in the previous section, individuals
who have experienced diversity training tend to say that they are more careful about being
'politically correct' when talking about issues related to sexuality in the workplace.
However, diversity training is generally not compulsory, and it is unlikely that anyone
who holds 'homophobic' views would volunteer themselves for this sort of professional
development training.

Example 2: Burdening those discriminated against

> *A proactive employee makes an appointment with her workplace Equal Opportunities
> Officer to ask how the organization is applying the new Sexual Orientation employ-
> ment regulations. The Equal Opportunities Officer informs her that 'certain sections'
> of senior management are 'resistant' to applying the legislation and that they feel
> that sexual orientation 'isn't a workplace issue' but a 'private matter.'*

This second example highlights the limitations of the introduction of legal protection
for LGB people in the absence of any requirement for employers to 'do' anything to
ensure that their staff do not experience discrimination on the basis of their sexual orientation at work. In this example, the legal anti-discrimination framework, in spite of being
the main reason why the interaction took place, is singularly unhelpful. There has been
no instance of discrimination, and so there would be no legal solution to this employee's
experience.

Diversity training, on the other hand, could be effective in combating the assumption
held by 'certain sections of senior management' that sexual orientation is not relevant in
the workplace. Many of the exercises used in diversity training seek to dispel exactly this
myth. The problem, of course, lies in the lack of compulsion on employers to introduce
any form of equal opportunities training for their staff. Paradoxically, it seems almost
impossible to challenge the views of these senior managers through diversity training, as
it is senior management who make the decision to introduce diversity training in the
workplace.

Example 3: Limitations of the workplace model

A University lecturer distributes a questionnaire to a large class of students. She is shocked, upset and angry when she discovers that on one of the returned questionnaires the student has scrawled 'FUCK OFF YOU UGLY DYKE!' Although her line manager takes positive action, and colleagues are outraged and supportive, she still feels emotionally vulnerable when on campus.

As this third example shows, even where line managers take action to combat homophobia and colleagues are supportive, there are instances where homophobia and heterosexism cannot be challenged through either discrimination law or diversity training. In many instances, LGB workers could be subjected to heterosexist or homophobic comments from people who are unrelated to the employment relationship. Although this example relates to a university lecturer who experienced homophobic abuse at the pen of a student, similar situations could arise in any number of occupations. For example, where LGB people work with young people in any setting (schools, youth clubs, social work, etc.), or in the provision of any form of service (such as waiting staff, shop assistants, on public transport, etc.), the actions of the service user would be outside of the remit of both workplace discrimination law and diversity training. If the abuse outlined above had been verbal abuse, or even if it had not been written anonymously, there would have been potential for some form of challenge to the overt homophobia expressed. But as this was an anonymous incident there was no real mechanism for challenging the perpetrator's behaviour. Although the person who experienced this abuse reported that her colleagues were 'outraged' and 'supportive' it is important to note that empathic and sympathetic behaviour, in and of itself, is not sufficient to mediate her very real experience of emotional vulnerability.

We would like to make clear that these three vignettes are not hypothetical; they are recent examples of actual experiences of heterosexism at work. Two of these examples were experienced by one of the authors of this chapter (EP), the third by the other editor of this book. These examples are, therefore, very real indicators of the sorts of difficulties that continue to face lesbians, gay men and bisexual people in the work environment. Difficulties that neither current discrimination law frameworks or voluntary diversity training within the workplace context can fully solve.

CONCLUDING REMARKS

We have argued that combining legal (top-down) and educational (bottom-up) approaches to challenging homophobia and heterosexism at work is a worthwhile endeavour. Both law and education typify 'the time-honored, non-violent means of social change, the alternative to revolution' (Gilligan, 1993, p. 162). Supporting the persuasive power and practical limitations of discrimination law with the potential for wide attitudinal change through diversity training can open up a more rounded strategy for confronting the realities of heterosexism at work. As our analysis has shown, the legal prohibition of discrimination on the basis of sexual orientation is not, on its own, as effective as the rhetorical force ascribed to law may suggest. Rather, legal forms for tackling discrimination are complex and subtle, and only offer very limited potential of success for individuals who have experienced discrimination. Combating heterosexism at work through diversity training also has its limitations, most notably the liberal framework of educating people about difference. While diversity training can challenge beliefs and bring about changes in the words people use, its founda-tion within liberalism enables people 'to sit on the fence, avoid taking sides, to denounce polarization, confrontation and the use of force. It is the perfect tool for the oppressor's use' (Sarachild, 1974, cited in Kramarae & Treichler, 1992, p. 231).

Our analysis has also highlighted the very real importance of language in both diversity training and discrimination law. The majority of successful sexual orientation discrimina-tion cases (at least, those that have been reported) have had harassment and the use of offensive, homophobic or heterosexist language at their very core. Our discussion of the effectiveness of diversity training has highlighted the ways in which this form of peda-gogical intervention can change the language people use in the workplace. Diversity training teaches people to be aware of how they speak, to know what is appropriate and what is not, and therefore it reduces the likelihood of 'offensive' language being used in the workplace. Diversity training, therefore, has the potential to improve the working lives of LGBs, lessen the need for employers to be drawn into costly and reputation-damaging discrimination claims, and reduce both the expression and experience of heterosexism at work and beyond.

In conclusion then, while both diversity training and discrimination law offer some potential for addressing heterosexism at work, there is still much to be done. The liberal, individualistic nature of each of these frameworks does little to challenge heterosexism and homophobia in society at large, and its more multifarious and insidious manifestations in the workplace are probably the most common. Yet we would not advocate the abandon-ment of either strategies, but rather that these diverse frameworks can be used to support and reinforce each other's strengths. By providing this synthesis of critical psychological and critical legal disciplinary lens, we have demonstrated that this sort of hybrid, inter-disciplinary approach can be theoretically and practically applied in LGBTQ research.

ACKNOWLEDGEMENTS

With thanks to Victoria Clarke and Peter Hegarty for their incisive comments on an earlier version.

REFERENCES

Altman, D. (1980). What changed in the seventies. In Gay Left Collective (Ed.), *Homosexuality: Power and politics* (pp. 52–63). London: Allison and Busby.
BBC News (2005). 'Gay jibe theatre worker wins case' *BBC News website* 4 May 2005. Retrieved 28 October 2005, from http://news.bbc.co.uk/1/hi/england/wear/4514485.stm.
Ben-Ari, A. T. (1998). An experiential attitude change: Social work students and homosexuality. *Journal of Homosexuality*, **36**(2), 59–71.
Brickell, C. (2001). Whose 'special treatment'? Heterosexism and the problems with liberalism. *Sexualities*, **4**(2), 211–235.
Butler, C. (2004). An awareness-raising tool addressing lesbian and gay lives. *Clinical Psychology*, **36**, 15–17.
Chesler, M. & Zuniga, X. (1991). Dealing with prejudice and conflict in the classroom: The pink triangle exercise. *Teaching Sociology*, **19**, 173–181.
Cotton-Huston, A. & Waite, B. (2000). Anti-homosexual attitudes in college students: Predictors and classroom interventions. *Journal of Homosexuality*, **38**(3), 117–133.

Croteau, J. M. (1996). Research on the work experiences of lesbian, gay, and bisexual people: An integrative review of methodology and findings. *Journal of Vocational Behavior*, **48**, 195–209.

Croteau, J. & Kusak, M. (1992). Gay and lesbian speaker panels: Implementation and research. *Journal of Counseling & Development*, **70**, 396–401.

Day, N. & Davidson, S. (2003). *'Equality and Diversity – Making it happen': Report on the consultation exercise*. London: Department for Trade and Industry.

Deakin, S. & Morris, G. S. (1998). *Labour Law* (2nd edn.). London: Butterworths.

Dworkin, R. (1977). *Taking Rights Seriously*. London: Harvard University Press.

Employment Tribunals Service (2005). *The Employment Tribunals Service Annual Report & Accounts 2004–05*. Norwich: TSO.

Fraser, N. (1997). *Justice Interruptus: Critical reflections of the 'postsocialist' condition*. New York, NY: Routledge.

Fredman, S. (2001). Equality: A new generation? *Industrial Law Review*, **30**(2), 145 168.

Frith, H. & Kitzinger, C. (2001). Reformulating sexual script theory: Developing a discursive psychology of sexual negotiation. *Theory & Psychology*, **11**(2), 209–232.

Geasler, M., Croteau, J., Heineman, C. & Edlund, C. (1995). A qualitative study of students' expression of change after attending panel presentations by lesbian, gay and bisexual speakers. *Journal of College Student Development*, **36**(5), 483–492.

Gilligan, C. (1993). Joining the resistance: Psychology, politics, girls, and women. In L. Weis & M. Fine (Eds), *Beyond Silenced Voices: Class, race, and gender in United States schools* (pp. 143–168). Albany, NY: State University of New York Press.

Gore, S. (2000). The lesbian and gay workplace: An employee's guide to advancing equity. In B. Greene & G. L. Croom (Eds), *Education, Research, and Practice in Lesbian, Gay, Bisexual, and Transgendered Psychology: A resource manual* (pp. 282–302). Thousand Oaks, CA: Sage.

Govan, F. (2005). Six per cent of population are gay or lesbian, according to Whitehall figures. *Telegraph Newspaper Online*. Retrieved 9 March 2006, from http://www.telegraph.co.uk/news/main.jhtml?xml=/news/2005/12/12/ngay12.xml.

Henley, N. & Pincus, F. (1978). Interrelationship of sexist, racist, and antihomosexual attitudes. *Psychological Reports*, **42**, 83–90.

Herek, G. M. (1994). Assessing heterosexuals' attitudes toward lesbians and gay men: A review of empirical research with the ATLG scale. In B. Greene & G. M. Herek (Eds), *Lesbian and Gay Psychology: Theory, research and clinical applications* (pp. 206–228). Thousand Oaks, CA: Sage.

Herek, G. M. & Capitanio, J. (1996). 'Some of my best friends': Intergroup contact, concealable stigma, and heterosexuals' attitudes toward gay men and lesbians. *Personal and Social Psychology Bulletin*, **22**(4), 412–424.

Herek, G. M. & Glunt, E. (1993). Interpersonal contact and heterosexuals' attitudes toward gay men: Results from a national survey. *Journal of Sex Research*, **30**(3), 239–244.

Hill, R. J. (1995). Gay discourse in adult education: A critical view. *Adult Education Quarterly*, **45**(3), 142–158.

Imich, A., Bayley, S. & Farley, K. (2001). Equalities and gay and lesbian young people: Implications for educational psychologists. *Educational Psychology in Practice*, **17**(4), 375–384.

Kitzinger, C. (1991). Lesbians and gay men in the workplace: Psychosocial issues. In M. Davidson & J. Earnshaw (Eds), *Vulnerable Workers: Psychosocial and legal issues* (pp. 224–240). London: Wiley.

Kitzinger, C. (2005). Speaking as a heterosexual: (How) does sexuality matter for talk-in-interaction? *Research on Language and Social Interaction*, **38**(3), 221–265.

Kitzinger, C. & Peel, E. (2005). The de-gaying and re-gaying of AIDS: Contested homophobias in lesbian and gay awareness training. *Discourse & Society*, **16**(2), 173–197.

Kramarae, C. & Treichler, P. (Eds), (1992). *Amazons, Bluestockings and Crones: A feminist dictionary*. London: Pandora Press.

Levine, M. P. (1995). The status of gay men in the workplace. In M. S. Kimmel & M. A. Messer (Eds), *Men's Lives* (3rd edn) (pp. 212–224). Boston, MA: Allyn & Bacon.

Lai, Y. & Kleiner, B. H. (2001). How to conduct diversity training effectively. *Equal Opportunities International*, **20**, 14–18.

Land, V. & Kitzinger, C. (2005). Speaking as a lesbian: Correcting the heterosexist presumption. *Research on Language and Social Interaction*, **38**(4), 371–416.

Logan, J., Kershaw, S., Karban, K., Mills, S., Trotter, J. & Sinclair, M. (1996). *Confronting Prejudice: Lesbian and gay issues in social work education*. Aldershot: Arena.

Martin, P. Y. & Collinson, D. L. (1999). Gender and sexuality in organizations. In M. M. Feree, J. Lorber & B. Hess (Eds), *Revisioning Gender* (pp. 285–310). Thousand Oaks, CA: Sage.

McCauley, C., Wright, M. & Harris, M. (2000). Diversity workshops on campus: A survey of current practice at U.S. colleges and universities. *College Student Journal*, **34**(1), 100–114.

McClintock, M. (1992). Sharing lesbian, gay, and bisexual life experiences face to face. *Journal of Experiential Education*, **15**(3), 51–55.

McNaught, B. (1997). Making allies of co-workers: Educating the corporate world. In J. T. Sears & W. L. Walters (Eds), *Overcoming Heterosexism and Homophobia: Strategies that work* (pp. 402–415). New York, NY: Columbia University Press.

Messing, A., Schoenberg, R. & Stephens, R. (1984). Confronting homophobia in health care settings: Guidelines for social work practice. In R. Schoenberg & R. Goldberg (Eds), *Homosexuality and Social Work* (pp. 46–79). New York, NY: Haworth Press.

Morjaria, D. (1999). *'Beyond a Phase': A practical guide to challenging homophobia in schools*. Bristol: Health Promotion Service Avon.

Nelson, E. & Krieger, S. (1997). Changes in attitudes toward homosexuality in college students: Implementation of a gay men and lesbian peer panel. *Journal of Homosexuality*, **33**(2), 63–81.

Peel, E. (2001a). 'I am what I am?' Using stereotypes in anti-heterosexism training. *Lesbian & Gay Psychology Review*, **2**(2), 50–56.

Peel, E. (2001b). Mundane heterosexism: Understanding incidents of the everyday. *Women's Studies International Forum*, **24**(5), 541–554.

Peel, E. (2002a). Lesbian and gay awareness training: Homophobia, liberalism, and managing stereotypes. In A. Coyle & C. Kitzinger (Eds), *Lesbian and Gay Psychology: New perspectives* (pp. 255–274) Oxford: BPS Blackwell.

Peel, E. (2002b). Challenging homophobic attitudes: Is lesbian and gay affirmative education effective? Paper presented at the British Psychological Society Annual Conference, 14–16 March 2002, Blackpool, UK. [Abstract published in Proceedings of The British Psychological Society, **10**(2), 92–93.]

Peel, E. (2005). Effeminate 'fudge nudgers' and tomboyish 'lettuce lickers': Language and the construction of sexualities in diversity training. *Psychology of Women Section Review*, **7**(2), 22–34.

Peel, E. & Harding, R. (2004). Divorcing romance, rights, and radicalism: Beyond pro and anti in the lesbian and gay marriage debate. *Feminism & Psychology*, **14**(4), 584–595.

Personnel Today (2005). 'Landmark case on homophobic words at work' *Personnel Today website* 31 May 2005. Retrieved 28 October 2005, from http://www.personneltoday.com/Articles/2005/05/31/30112/Landmark+case+on+homophobic+words+at+work.htm.

Potter, J. & Wetherell, M. (1987). *Discourse and Social Psychology: Beyond attitudes and behaviour*. London: Sage.

Ryan-Flood, R. (2004). *Beyond Recognition and Redistribution: A case study of lesbian and gay workers in a local labour market in Britain*. Issue 12 New Working Paper Series. London: LSE Gender Institute.

Schneider, M. & Tremble, B. (1986). Training service providers to work with gay or lesbian adolescents: A workshop. *Journal of Counseling and Development*, **65**, 98–99.

Schreier, B. (1995). Moving beyond tolerance: A new paradigm for programming about homophobia/biphobia and heterosexism. *Journal of College Student Development*, **36**(1), 19–26.

Simon, A. (1998). The relationship between stereotypes of and attitudes toward lesbians and gays. In G. M. Herek (Ed.), *Stigma and Sexual Orientation: Understanding prejudice against lesbians, gay men and bisexuals* (pp. 62–81). Thousand Oaks, CA: Sage.

Smith, R. & Windes, R. (2000). *Progay/antigay: The rhetorical war over sexuality*. Thousand Oaks, CA: Sage.

Stewart, C. (1999). *Sexually Stigmatized Communities: Reducing heterosexism and homophobia – an awareness training manual*. Thousand Oaks, CA: Sage.

Stonewall (2005a). *Court battles*. Retrieved 27 July 2005, from http://www.stonewall.org.uk/
information_bank/employment/73.asp.

Stonewall (2005b). *Stonewall corporate equality index 2005: The top 100 employers for gay people
in Britain*. Retrieved 9 December 2005, from http://www.stonewall.org.uk/documents/corpora-
teequityindex.pdf.

Tropp, L. R. & Pettigrew, T. F. (2005). Relationships between intergroup contact and prejudice
among minority and majority status groups. *Psychological Science*, **16**(12), 951–957.

Trotter, J. & Gilchrist, J. (1996). Assessing DipSW students: Anti-discriminatory practice in relation to lesbian and gay issues. *Social Work Education*, **15**(1), 75–82.

van de Ven, P. (1995). A comparison of two teaching modules for reducing homophobia in young
offenders. *Journal of Applied Social Psychology*, **25**(7), 632–649.

Wainwright, M. (2005). 'Landmark ruling on homophobic taunts' *The Guardian* January 29 2005.
Retrieved 28 October, from http://www.guardian.co.uk/gayrights/story/0,12592,1401332,00.
html.

Wallerstein, I. (2003). Citizens all? Citizens some!: The making of the citizen. *Comparative Studies
in Society and History*, **45**(4), 650–679.

Walters, A. S. & Phillips, C. (1994). Hurdles: An activity for homosexuality education. *Journal of
Sex Education and Therapy*, **20**(3), 198–203.

Ward, C. (1997). On difference and equality. *Legal Theory*, **3**, 65–99.

Whittle, S. (2002). *Respect and Equality: Transsexual and transgender rights*. London:
Cavendish.

Windibank, M. (1995). *Straight Talking: A training manual for police officers*. Kingston: M.W.
Security Services.

Young, I. M. (1990). *Justice and the Politics of Difference*. Princeton, NJ: Princeton University
Press.

Zuckerman, A. J. & Simons, G. F. (1996). *Sexual Orientation in the Workplace: Gay men, lesbians,
bisexuals & heterosexuals working together*. Thousand Oaks, CA: Sage.

CHAPTER 13

Out On The Ball Fields: Lesbians In Sport

Vikki Krane
Bowling Green State University, USA
and
Kerrie J. Kauer
University of Tennessee, USA

INTRODUCTION

No longer is sport solely the domain of boys and men. Young girls now have opportunities to learn the same life lessons through sport that boys have had access to for generations. Both girls and boys now discover the joys of competition and teamwork, acquire the self-esteem that comes from becoming skilled, and gain insight about how to be good winners and good losers. Girls who participate in sport reap a myriad of mental and physical health benefits. Compared with their non-sporting peers, athletic girls have a more positive body image, are less likely to experience depression, have higher self-esteem and more positive self-worth (Sabo, Miller, Melnick & Heywood, 2004). They also have better academic achievement and are less likely to become sexually active or engage in risky sexual behaviors, smoke cigarettes and use illicit drugs (Sabo et al., 2004). However, heterosexism and homonegativism can nullify many of these benefits and possibly lead to unhealthy outcomes such as poor self-esteem, isolation, self-injurious behaviour, substance abuse or poor body image (Krane, Surface & Alexander, 2005). To ensure that female athletes gain the mental and physical health benefits of sport participation, it is important to understand and eradicate prejudice based on sexual identity.

Before examining these issues, it is important to clarify the terminology used in this chapter. We use the term *homonegativism* to refer to purposeful 'negative stereotypes, prejudice, and discrimination against nonheterosexuals' (Krane, 1997, p. 145) whereas *heterosexism* denotes a belief system that privileges heterosexuality as the dominant, normal and natural sexual orientation (Herek, 1992). Heterosexism often is ubiquitous yet indiscernible, lesbian individuals are marginalized through omission rather than overt intolerance (Braun, 2000). While our worldview is to be inclusive and write about all sportswomen, including bisexual, transgender and intersexed women, the empirical

Out in Psychology: Lesbian, gay, bisexual, trans and queer perspectives. Edited by Victoria Clarke and Elizabeth Peel.
© 2007 John Wiley & Sons, Ltd.

literature is rather limited. Worldwide, few studies have been conducted that overtly identify bisexual, transgender and intersexed identities. Overall, when examining the atmosphere of women's sport, researchers have not identified the sexual orientations or identities of participants and instead focused on the athletes' and coaches' perceptions of the sport climate devoid of their particular standpoint. The studies that have acknowledged participants sexual identity, included predominantly lesbian athletes or coaches. Very few studies have examined bisexual and transgender experiences in sport. Therefore, our primary focus in this chapter is lesbian athletes' and coaches' experiences; when possible we include information about other sexual minorities (for an analysis regarding gay male athletes, see Anderson, 2005; Gough, 2007).

It has long been assumed that there are many lesbian women in sport (Cahn, 1993). This presumption is unavoidable because of the way gender and sexuality are inextricably linked in our culture. Because sport traditionally values characteristics associated with men and masculinity (e.g. aggression, confidence, strength), the sexuality of successful sportswomen who possess such characteristics have been questioned and they are presumed lesbian (e.g. Clarke, 2002). This (hetero)normative perception of gender and sexuality and the accompanying stereotypes shape the experiences of all sportswomen, lesbian and heterosexual. Thus, it seems that researching heterosexism, homonegativism and sexual identities in sport would be an imperative of sport psychologists. Yet, as a whole, sport psychology and its national and international organizations have been remiss in doing so and few scholars have tackled these issues. In fact, most 'diversity' presentations are still on the margins at regional, national and international sport psychology conferences and very few articles appear in mainstream sport psychology journals on these issues (Ram, Starek & Johnson, 2004). Many people in the field believe that cultural and social issues are not within the domain of sport psychology; rather, they are considered the purview of sport sociology. Much anecdotal evidence necessitates that change is needed to ensure that positive, unbiased, safe and healthy sport climates are available for lesbian, bisexual and transgender women in sport. Despite that, dismantling the prejudiced climate of sport is not viewed as an important sport psychological concern.

Sport psychology consultants, and the coaches and athletes with whom they work, do not exist in a vacuum, exempt from socio-cultural issues. Discrimination based on sexual identity is a widely cited problem in women's sport (e.g. Griffin, 1998), which negatively affects the mental and physical health of athletes and impedes athletic performances (Krane et al., 2005). Rather than considering social differences and diverse identities as an integral piece to performance enhancement in sport psychology, the minority experience in sport often is marginalized and devalued. Kontos and Breland-Noble (2002) emphasized the importance of being culturally sensitive in sport psychology practice. As they described, 'applied sport psychology practice has traditionally been practiced from an ethnocentric, White male perspective' (p. 297). We would add that it also is grounded in a heterosexual stance. It is essential to step outside of this perspective and integrate a more sophisticated understanding of the social context of sport into sport psychology practice.

The socio-cultural context of sport greatly influences sport participation as well as one's ability to learn and implement psychological skills. In a heteronormative environment, routine practices implemented by sport psychology consultants become difficult, if not impossible for lesbian, bisexual and transgender sportswomen. Teaching performance enhancement techniques to manage anxiety, motivation or confidence, for example, will not be effective when individuals are fearful due to prejudice and discrimination. Thus, it is essential that consultants be aware of the cultural context of sport and the constraints it imposes into the practice of applied sport psychology. Failure to do so will negate our ability to meet the needs of athletes and coaches in the quest for performance enhancement.

Many conventional practices implemented by sport psychology consultants can be useful toward diminishing homonegativism in sport. Sport psychologists often discuss the importance of team climate, coach credibility, effective leadership and the coach–athlete relationship. Such topics easily could be focused toward minimizing homonegativism and heterosexism (Barber & Krane, 2005). Further, sport psychology consultants have access to the whole hierarchy of sport participants (i.e. administrators, coaches, athletes) and are well placed in the sport culture to enact change (Barber & Krane, 2005).

Interestingly, this edited collection in LGBTQ psychology is one of the first to include a chapter on sport. This is an important addition because of the role of sport in our culture and its impact on LGBTQ people. As a dominant industry, from local youth sport communities to global competition, its influence on LGBTQ people can be considerable. As women have become more visible in international sport, more girls also began participating. Thus, it is quite likely that LGBTQ psychologists will have clients to whom sport is an important aspect of their lives, necessitating an understanding of this context. If we further consider the numbers of girls and women involved in exercise, an understanding of sport and exercise psychology becomes more essential, especially if sport or exercise lead to mental health issues (e.g. body image problems) in LGBTQ populations. Bridging the gap between scholars in sport and scholars in LGBTQ psychology can provide a strong foundation for meeting the varied needs of LGBTQ sportswomen and creating healthy athletic climates.

A beginning point for addressing heteronormative sport climates is confronting stereotypes about female athletes. A myriad of research documents that all girls and women in sport are affect by the 'lesbian label'; that is, whether they are tagged tomboy, butch, masculine or dyke, the assumption is that female athletes are lesbians (e.g. Burroughs, Ashburn & Seebohm, 1995; Clarke, 1998; Young, 1997). Some athletes ignore the contention whereas other athletes get angry and frustrated with this label (Kauer & Krane, 2006). Still, others are lesbian, bisexual and transgender competitors. As such, the institution of women's sport is struggling to balance negative social perceptions with lived reality. In some situations, there is no conflict – all girls and women simply participate in unbiased climates. Other contexts range from a 'don't ask, don't tell' climate (Griffin, 1998; Krane & Barber, 2005) to an overtly prejudicial and intolerant atmosphere (Baks & Malecek, 2004; Griffin, 1998; Krane, 1997). We seem to be in a period of transition – today's young people have been exposed to media attempting to normalize lesbians (e.g. television shows like *Will & Grace*, *Ellen* and *The L Word* [in the USA]) juxtaposed with social rhetoric condemning 'amoral lifestyles'. In sport, there has been gradual movement from intolerance to grudging acknowledgement, and in some settings, to complete acceptance of sexual diversity. It is this movement, or lack thereof, that we will explore in this paper.

In a summary of the research on sexual orientation and sport in Europe, Baks and Malecek (2004) concluded 'sport is an extremely heterosexual dominated social context where discrimination and homophobia seem to be structurally embedded' (p. 6). Many scholars have established the heterosexist and homonegative climate in women's sport and its detrimental effect on female athletes, lesbian and heterosexual (e.g. Veri, 1999; Wright, & Clarke, 1999). Yet, little work specifically has explored how these women cope within such settings, maintain productivity, and resist strong social pressure to maintain the heterosexual and male hegemony in sport. To remedy this gulf in the literature, we will review the literature on lesbian athletes and coaches using social identity perspective to guide our interpretations of these previous findings. First, we will explore social norms supporting heterosexist bias and the consequences of heterosexism and homonegativism on lesbian sportswomen. Then we will examine their resiliency in the face of prejudice and efforts towards social change attempts. We frame our analysis within a social identity perspective (Krane & Barber, 2003) and situate current knowledge about the experiences of lesbian sportswomen within this framework.

SOCIAL IDENTITY PERSPECTIVE

To provide a comprehensive framework for understanding the experiences of lesbian sportswomen, and the concomitant social response, Krane and Barber (2003) have employed a social identity (SI) perspective. This framework combines social identity (Tajfel & Turner, 1979) and social categorization theories (Turner et al., 1987). It is a particularly effective perspective for understanding the experiences of marginalized individuals because it illustrates the development of discrimination, stereotypes and oppression that surround marginalized groups in society. It also emphasizes the psychological processes underlying resiliency, which leads to high-level performance within intolerant situations. As research on lesbian coaches has revealed (Barber & Krane, 2001; Iannotta & Kane, 2002; Krane & Barber, 2005), these women are incredibly resilient and very productive within discriminatory and sometimes hostile work settings. Similarly, lesbian athletes have attained very elite levels in sport, revealing their resilience in spite of largely homonegative and heterosexist sport climates (Baks & Malecek, 2004).

As SI perspective describes, individuals notice the various social groups around them and cognitively organize people based on collective similarities and differences (Hogg, 2001). During this process of social categorization, individuals self-categorize or place themselves within a particular social group (Hogg, 2001). An outcome of self-categorization is the development of one's social identity or acknowledgement of social group membership. Ultimately, depersonalization occurs in which individuals redefine themselves as group members, downplay individuality, and adopt the group norms for behaviour, values and attitudes (Hogg, 2001). Ideally, social identities and depersonalization enhance feelings of self-worth and self-esteem.

Society is composed of a myriad of social categories (e.g. based on race, sexual orientation or employment) and, accordingly, individuals belong to multiple social groups. Individuals also may have conflicting social identities. Negotiation amongst various social identities, especially if one or more are marginalized identities, is necessary. Lesbians in sport, for example, learn to negotiate identities such as coach/athlete, lesbian, feminine and student/professional (Krane & Barber, 2005; Krane et al., 2004). Additionally, through the process of social comparison, individuals recognize the unequal social status and privilege amongst groups (Hogg & Abrams, 1988). Individuals with marginalized social identities must balance social bias with self-worth. While high-status social group membership is related to high self-esteem (Hogg & Abrams, 1988), social oppression does not automatically result in poor self-esteem or self-worth. Instead, marginalized people engage in a variety of self-protective behaviours that increase self-esteem, maintain productivity or enhance the status of the group (Crocker & Major, 1989, 1994).

For example, when individuals in marginalized groups experience discrimination, such acts may be attributed to prejudice against their social group rather than be perceived to reflect negatively against them personally (Crocker & Major, 1994). Additionally, oppressed individuals may emphasize different values than members of the dominant group (Crocker & Major, 1989). Female basketball players, for instance, recognize that they do not use the same power moves as male basketball players, instead they value and emphasize their strong fundamental skills and teamwork. Collective esteem, the self-worth derived from the collective aspects of the self and group membership, acts as a buffer against the potential negative effects of prejudice (Crocker & Luhtenan, 1990). Individuals with high collective esteem are most likely to confront and transgress restrictive social expectations. SI perspective proposes two avenues for addressing one's marginalized status: social mobility and social change (Hogg & Abrams, 1988).

Social mobility refers to 'passing' as a member of a high-status social group, whereas social change involves overt confrontation of social injustice. The use of passing strategies commonly has been described in the literature on lesbian sportswomen (e.g. Baks & Malecek, 2004; Griffin, 1998; Krane, 1997; Kauer & Krane, 2006). Social mobility strategies are predicted to lead to increased self-esteem, enhanced social status and avoidance of discrimination. However, this type of behavior poses no threat to, and often reinforces, the dominance of the high-status group (Abrams & Hogg, 1990). As Krane and Barber (2005) described, lesbian sportswomen may unwittingly be complicit in maintaining hegemonic, heterosexist sport environments. People who use social mobility strategies adopt the salient characteristics of the dominant group, reinforcing their high social status. The position of the subordinate group is unchanged, the status quo remains unchallenged and the dominant group maintains high social status (Abrams & Hogg, 1990). Conversely, social change occurs through overt actions to increase power, status and resources of a marginalized social group. Such action leads to broad based social change, improving the social conditions for all members of the marginalized social group. All women in sport struggle with their obvious marginalized status and the potential repercussions of fighting for greater resources. Lesbian athletes and coaches contend with additional constraints and bias.

THE EXPERIENCES OF LESBIAN SPORTSWOMEN

Social Norms and the Climate of Women's Sport

The limited research on sexual identity in sport likely reflects the primary social norm that has surrounded lesbian sportswomen for decades: silence. This pervasive norm has been discussed and supported in almost every study about lesbians in sport. Simply, issues about sexual identity and sexual orientation are not discussed in sport settings, and lesbian sportswomen conceal their sexual identities so their presence continues to be veiled and disregarded. As Baks and Malecek (2004) stated about European sport: 'The problem is twofold. Athletes do not come out of the closet and therefore homosexuality is not a topic in mainstream sports clubs and sports clubs are often not aware about the heteronormativity that exists in their club' (p. 6). Nelson (1991) referred to this omission as 'a silence so loud it screams'. If this silence can be more palpable, bisexual and transgender athletes are especially obscured. Even in gay sport settings such as the Gay Games, bisexual and transgender athletes are on the margins (Krane & Waldron, 2000).

Consistently, interviews with lesbian athletes and coaches reveal silence as a dominant theme when they describe their athletic climates. As one university coach stated, 'it's amazing how silent it is' (Krane & Barber, 2005, p. 72). Lesbian sportswomen understand that they should not call attention to their sexual identities (Baks & Malecek, 2004; Griffin, 1998; Krane, 1997). The climate of women's sport also has been described as 'don't ask, don't tell' (Griffin, 1998), or more aptly, as stated by a lesbian coach interviewed by Krane and Barber (2005), 'don't ask, don't tell, don't make waves' (p. 72). This description refers to the marginal acceptance of lesbians in sport, assuming they don't 'flaunt' or 'make an issue' of their sexual identity (i.e. overtly reveal or talk about it) (Griffin, 1998). Further, when lesbian athletes remain silent, the mundane, taken-for-granted language surrounding heterosexuality becomes increasingly more normalized, therefore renouncing lesbian experiences without saying a word. In other words, as long as lesbians remained silent about their sexual identity, they could be 'accepted' in mainstream sport (Baks & Malecek, 2004; Clarke, 1995; Griffin, 1998).

Silencing lesbian athletes and making them invisible is reinforced through the media. Consistently, studies show that media coverage evades athletes who do not have appropriate 'heterosexual credentials' or who appear masculine. For example, Pirinen (1997) revealed that lesbian and 'masculine-appearing' elite female athletes were rendered invisible in the Finnish press whereas athletes who were noticeably heterosexual (via visibility of husbands and children) were privileged and highlighted by the media. Likewise, boyfriends, husbands and children often were mentioned along with commentary about women rugby union players in the UK and Australian press (Wright & Clarke, 1999). As Wright and Clarke expressed, due to this writing bias, 'the existence of lesbian rugby union players is denied and obliterated' (p. 240). That the media privileges feminine, heterosexual women is consistent across media studies in the USA (Andrews, 1998), UK (George et al., 2001), Sweden (Koivula, 1999), and Australia (Lenskyj, 1998). Interestingly, elite Swedish and Norwegian football players believed that the media also perpetuated the stereotype that many elite female athletes are lesbian (Fasting, 1997). In Australia, a similar perception was developed by the media coverage of the national cricket team (Burroughs et al., 1995).

Interpreted through SI perspective, the silence surrounding lesbian athletes is so pervasive that it has become a social norm. That is, not only is silence a characteristic of sport climates, it is an expected behaviour of lesbian sporting women (Krane & Barber, 2005). For example, a lesbian athlete described that she was told by her lesbian assistant coach that it was essential that she remain closeted (i.e. silent) about her lesbian identity if she wanted to become a university coach (Krane, 1994). Even when not directly told to sustain the silence, young athletes and coaches recognize the behaviours of experienced athletes and coaches and adopt this perceived social norm. Most research on lesbians in sport confirms that the majority conceal their lesbian identity from coaches, team-mates or fans (e.g. Baks & Malecek, 2004; Clarke, 1995; Krane & Barber, 2005). The little that is known about transgender athletes also corroborates that concealing their identity is a tactic used to avoid alienation or exclusion (Semerjian & Cohen, 2006).

Disconcertingly, many sportswomen are complicit in the heterosexist climate in women's sport, both intentionally and unintentionally. Through the process of social comparison, sportswomen recognize that heterosexually attractive women in sport are privileged over other women. The status given to these feminine sportswomen creates an atmosphere in which femininity become a commodity. Sportswomen fitting feminine social expectations receive greater fan approval, publicity, media attention and endorsements compared with other athletes (e.g. Festle, 1996; Kolnes, 1995). Because lesbians are stereotyped as 'butch' or masculine-looking, it is assumed that their presence will hurt the status of women's sport. For example, a female football player in the UK stated 'I am not homophobic in the slightest. I have many lesbian friends. However, I feel [visible lesbian] players do give "the sport a bad name"' (Caudwell, 1999, p. 396). Norwegian and Swedish football players expressed the same sentiment; as one player stated, 'I like many lesbians as football buddies as long as they don't flaunt their homosexuality to much' (Fasting, 1997). In 2003, Jan Stephenson, a golfer in the US Ladies Professional Golf Association (LPGA), said, 'society is more open now about gay relationships, but it does hurt the tour. It hurts with sponsors' (Blauvelt, 2003).

In some situations, the concern for the 'image' of one's sport has led some heterosexual women to become discriminatory toward lesbians to sustain the resources and privilege afforded heterosexually attractive sportswomen (Barber & Krane, 2005). In such cases, they will be exclusionary and attempt to distance themselves from women perceived as lesbians. Similar actions may occur among lesbian athletes; 'closeted' lesbian team-mates may distance themselves from obvious lesbian team-mates to avert attention to themselves (Krane, 1997). Rather than all sportswomen coming together to counter sexist discrimination, some females in sport have become divided by sexual orientation (Griffin, 1998; Lenskyj, 1997). Fear of losing already scarce resources, along with negative societal stereotypes about lesbians, perpetuates heterosexist and homonegative sport climates and sustains the silence about lesbian sportswomen. However, research outside of sport consistently supports that individuals who know someone who is lesbian, gay, bisexual, or transgender tend to be more open-minded toward these minorities (Herek, 1997). Yet in women's sport, there are few openly lesbian athletes, coaches and administrators. Thus, the silence surrounding these women does not allow for personal knowledge and overt contact with a known lesbian person and negative perceptions are reinforced. Paradoxically, female athletes are labelled lesbian, yet their presence is hidden, decreasing the likelihood of discouraging negative stereotypes and beliefs.

Consequences of Heterosexism and Homonegativism

Coaches and athletes who defy the social norm of silence, often face social repercussions, further decreasing the probability of breaking the silence. Athletes have been threatened with dismissal, passed over or cut from teams, and coaches have lost their jobs when their lesbian identities were revealed or assumed (Baks & Malecek, 2004; Fasting, 1997; Griffin, 1998; Hargreaves, 2000; Robinson, 2002). A university basketball player described that her coach:

> cleaned out the program, literally cleaned [it] out. He cut five people, four of them were gay, two of them were starters from the year before . . . [Coach] called me into his office and made the comment about 'Did you notice anything about the other people I cut?' My internal response was 'You cut all my friends.' He never said the particular reason why. He just said 'There was no place for that on his team, too disruptive.' (Krane, 1997, p. 152)

Other research documented that some coaches will not allow athletes whom they assume or know are lesbians to participate on their teams (Griffin, 1998; Hargreaves, 2000; Krane, 1997; Robinson, 2002).

Knowledge of the reprisals that materialize to presumed, 'outed,' or openly lesbian sportswomen leads to another common social norm amongst sportswomen: fear (Krane & Barber, 2005). While it may seem odd to consider fear a social norm, it is so pervasive that young lesbians in sport are socialized to be fearful of being labelled or identified lesbian (Krane, 1997). In fact, all women in sport, regardless of sexual identity, learn of the detrimental effects of being labelled lesbian (Fasting, 1997; Kauer & Krane, 2006). Even when they could not identify examples of individuals being treated negatively, lesbian university athletes clearly expressed that something bad would happen if their coaches and team-mates learned of their lesbian identities (Krane, 1997). Generally, their fears were related to not knowing how others may react and that coaches or team-mates would treat them unfairly or callously. Fusco (1998) interviewed Canadian university and elite team sport athletes who expressed that it was 'risky' to be out; they could lose their status on the team, the respect of others, and be rejected by team-mates. These athletes were 'hypersensitive' and 'paranoid' about team-mates and coaches learning of their lesbian identity (Fusco, 1998, p. 99).

Lesbian university coaches have described concerns centred on the consequences of being fired and not being able to recruit top athletes to their programme (e.g. Griffin, 1998; Krane & Barber, 2005). University coaches are often privy to prejudiced statements about women perceived to be lesbians during employment searches (Krane & Barber, 2005). From these experiences emanated the deeply entrenched perception that to be revealed as a lesbian would put their job at risk and minimize mobility within coaching. Most of the lesbian coaches, across US studies, felt that being open about their sexual orientation would impede their ability to effectively recruit athletes into their programme (Griffin, 1998; Krane & Barber, 2005). Additionally, coaches have referred to the potential concerns of parents should parents learn that a coach or players are lesbian (Krane & Barber, 2005). This sentiment has also been expressed by Nordic football players; as one player described,

> What may hurt the sport is if the rumor is spread about lesbians in the club, and if one makes that to be an important point. Then we get more 'mothers' who will not permit their children to play soccer. (Fasting, 1997)

Another elite football player interviewed by Fasting described:

> one year the whole junior team left the club, because parents were afraid that their daughters would become lesbians when they were playing among the seniors. Parents think that one can be infected by it as if it were a virus. Therefore they don't want their daughters to play on the highest level, where the big girls would harass them. In this way it is a problem. It's from outside, but the problem for us as a sport club is that the better players don't dare to move up among the best, which is a huge problem for us.

Stereotypes about lesbians may lead parents to be suspicious of lesbian coaches. Parents may be concerned that lesbian coaches will be poor role models, may influence their daughter to become a lesbian, or may seduce their daughter. Although parents have much more reason to be concerned about heterosexual male coaches acting inappropriately toward female athletes (Brackenridge, 1997), society perpetuates prejudices against lesbians. Coaches may be highly susceptible to these unfounded concerns because of the amount of time they spend with athletes, they are likely to have physical contact with athletes (e.g. when helping learn a new skill), they are in an emotional setting with athletes, and they may be in the locker room when athletes are showering or changing their clothes. Many lesbian coaches feel compelled to submit to these stereotypes. For example, some coaches described not going into a locker room while athletes are changing or being very careful to avoid touching athletes in ways that may be misinterpreted (Krane & Barber, 2005).

In women's university, elite and professional sport environments, lesbian athletes and coaches often feel compelled to remain silent regarding their sexual orientation. These sportswomen fear the negative repercussions of being labelled lesbian and, therefore, believe that hiding one's sexual identity will protect their careers. Young lesbians involved in sport as athletes or coaches adopt the perceived norms of this social group. Therefore, lesbians learn to conceal their identity to protect themselves from the perceived negative outcomes of being identified as a lesbian.

Social Mobility and Negotiation of Lesbian Identities

SI perspective posits that individuals in devalued social groups who face discrimination and stereotypes may use social mobility strategies and attempt to pass into groups that have high social status to increase self-esteem and social status (Hogg & Abrams, 1988). As we noted earlier, heterosexual and lesbian women in sport often engage in social mobility strategies to avoid stigma and as a form of self-protection from discrimination (Fusco, 1998; Griffin, 1998; Krane & Barber, 2003, 2005; Krane et al., 2004). While SI perspective would propose that an individual who moved between social groups will dis-identify with the socially inferior group, this may not be the case in sport. Rather, lesbian sportswomen may attempt to pass and avoid discrimination in sport settings, yet embrace their lesbian identity in social settings where social support is more abundant (Krane & Barber, 2005).

Research on lesbians in sport documents the wide range of strategies used to conceal lesbian identities. Lesbian athletes described dating men, using gender neutral pronouns when discussing their partner, laughing at 'gay jokes,' 'creative planning' to avoid being seen with their partner too often, and avoiding situations where their sexuality might be exposed (Fusco, 1998; Griffin, 1998; Kauer & Krane, 2006; Krane, 1997). Lesbian athletes often construct a feminine appearance by wearing make-up, doing their hair and wearing feminine clothing (Krane, 1997; Griffin, 1998). A transgender athlete, born a female and competing as a male, described being very attentive to not displaying too much of his body in the showers and locker room (Semerjian & Cohen, 2006). The goal of these social mobility behaviours was to sustain the support of their coaches and team-mates and minimize stigmatization.

Lesbian coaches described attempting to keep their coach identity separate from their lesbian identity; as they explained, there was continuous negotiation between their identities as 'coach' and 'lesbian' (Barber & Krane, 2001; Krane & Barber, 2005). For example, lesbian high school coaches often lived outside of their school district so they would not encounter athletes and parents when coaches were with their partners (Barber & Krane, 2001). Coaches also described maintaining an aloofness between them and their colleagues (Krane & Barber, 2005). Their colleagues typically responded to this perceived unfriendliness by continuing to keep this distance.

Lesbian coaches and athletes continuously negotiate identity performance (Iannotta & Kane, 2002; Krane & Barber, 2005); they must learn to balance their social identities as females, sportswomen and lesbians within social environments that privilege silence and heterosexuality. Further, that few visible lesbian coaches or athletes are out perpetuates the idea that being open about one's sexual identity in sport is not safe and will lead to discrimination (Hargreaves, 2000; Krane & Barber, 2003). Being closeted appears to be a self-protective mechanism to minimize intolerance, and somehow enables coaches and athletes to remain productive.

Empowerment, Collective Esteem and Resiliency

Athletes and coaches have discussed the difficulty of coping with heterosexist and homo-negative sport climates; it may be distracting, frustrating, stressful and difficult (Fasting, 1997; Fusco, 1998; Griffin, 1998; Krane & Barber, 2005), all of which potentially could impair athletic performances. Additionally, Krane et al. (2005) detailed a myriad of mental and physical health issues that may arise when faced with hostile sport climates: low self-esteem, anxiety, depression, isolation, body image concerns and unhealthy eating or exercise patterns. Lesbian athletes and coaches also may experience harassment from teammates, coaches or administrators. Yet, in spite of such obstacles, many lesbian sports-women are incredibly resilient and very successful. Explained within the SI perspective, marginalization does not necessarily lead to poor self-perceptions and impaired abilities. Instead, strong collective esteem appears to buffer such potential negative outcomes. For example, lesbian and bisexual Gay Games participants recognized their marginalized social status, yet also identified positive aspects of, and strength gained from, being a member of the lesbian community (Krane, Barber & McClung, 2002).

Through sport, female athletes acquire qualities such as assertiveness, independence, strength and competence (Blinde, Taub & Han, 1994). Thus, sport participation is empow-ering (Cox & Thompson, 2000; Krane et al., 2004; Theberge, 2000) and female athletes develop qualities that may provide lesbians in sport the means to counter negative percep-tions and discrimination. For example, female athletes often describe struggles while negotiating the conflict between being perceived in a socially desirable manner and excel-ling in their sport (Cox & Thompson, 2000; Krane et al., 2004; Russell, 2004). Yet, ath-letes also recognized the important role their large, muscular bodies played in their sport success and were proud of the dedication and effort that went into developing their muscles and size. Importantly, these athletes also expressed self-assurance, inner strength and independence that generalized across life situations (Cox & Thompson, 2000; Krane et al., 2004). Similarly, after discussing the stereotyping and discrimination they encoun-tered, university athletes in Kauer and Krane's (2006) study also expressed the benefits of sport participation that extended beyond sport: developing mental strength and a strong work ethic, and learning to be disciplined, responsible and able to overcome obstacles.

In spite of the stereotypes and homonegativism aimed at lesbian sportswomen, over-whelmingly they describe their sport experiences as 'an opportunity of a lifetime' (Kauer & Krane, 2006, p. 52) and rewarding (Krane & Barber, 2005). Although lesbian athletes and coaches perceived homonegativism as an inevitable, and even accepted, aspect of women's sport, some of them not only coped with it, but were motivated by it. Lesbian coaches explained that a strong form of protection against discrimination was to become highly successful (Krane & Barber, 2005). As expressed by one coach, 'I need to be better than other people around me, more ethical, harder working, more successful' (p. 73). Some lesbian athletes also recognized that exceptionally talented lesbian athletes would be tolerated within otherwise hostile climates (Krane, 1997). Other lesbian sportswomen became motivated by homonegativism and noted that it compelled them to attempt to change unreceptive sport climates (Ianotta & Kane, 2002; Krane & Barber, 2005; Krane et al., 2002).

When members of marginalized social groups are in oppressive settings, they may engage in one of several courses of action: individual action, social change or inaction (Wright, 2001). Social mobility, or passing, is a form of individual action that benefits the person who is able to be perceived as a member of a higher status group. In sport, passing or downplaying one's lesbian identity allows that individual access to the privilege bestowed heterosexual, feminine sportswomen and averts potential prejudice and discrimination. Social change actions in sport are aimed at increasing the circumstances of all lesbian, bisexual and transgender sportswomen and include collective action. An alternative reaction to individual and social change actions is inaction in which group members do not attempt to change their individual or social group status. On the surface, it appears that inaction is much more common among lesbian sportswomen than social change actions (Krane & Barber, 2005). Yet this appearance is deceiving and social change is occurring (Iannotta & Kane, 2002).

An intriguing question is, why do some sportswomen acquiesce to the homonegative social conditions of women's sport while others attempt social change. Wright (2001) described a number of conditions that affect individuals' responses to oppressive circumstances. When a lesbian identity is not salient or is not considered an essential component of one's identity, inaction will occur. Some athletes and coaches have expressed that being lesbian was 'not an issue', or was a part of their 'private lives' (Fasting, 1997; Krane & Barber, 2005). In essence, these women inferred that their sexual identity was not a significant social identity in sport settings. When a social identity is not relevant to one's goals, its importance will be reduced (Wright, 2001). For some lesbians in sport, such an identity is perceived as incompatible with potential success, thus they silence that identity and inaction results.

Women in sport also assess the legitimacy and stability of their social standing (Wright, 2001). One outcome of the masculine and heterosexual hegemony in sport is submission to the status quo. That is, sportswomen are socialized within an environment that reinforces the prominence of boys' and men's sport, reminding girls and women that they are less important. Women's sport has fewer fans, makes less money and receives less publicity; therefore, the social rhetoric continues, they are less deserving. The prominence of this message leads to compliant acceptance that girls' and women's sport does not deserve the same resources as boys' and men's sport. Even if sportswomen do not believe that girls and women are less deserving, they may believe that their status will not change and that 'rocking the boat' (e.g. confronting heterosexism) will result in reduced resources. Additionally, because of the vast changes in women's sport, some coaches and athletes feel that things are improving and, with time, their status will continue to improve.

Tokenism further leads toward acquiescence (Wright, 2001). As long as a small number of closeted lesbians achieve prominent positions, the perceived need to conceal sexual identities is reinforced: 'The token closeted lesbians become models of "appropriate" behavior that can lead to a successful athletic career' (Krane & Barber, 2003, p. 9). The visibility of these few high status women perpetuates the belief that it is possible to gain such success only if you don't 'make waves' and you 'play the game' (Krane & Barber, 2005). As long as openly lesbian sportswomen are not visible, coaches and athletes will continue to believe that compliance is the only way towards acceptance and success. Such a belief system leads other lesbians in sport to fervently sustain the social norm of silence and it may create dissonance within the lesbian social group when someone becomes too outspoken. Therefore, concern that one's lesbian peers will reject them can be a powerful barrier to social change.

Another perceived obstacle to social change action is the belief that one must reveal her lesbian identity to do so. And even if they do not intentionally come out, outspoken coaches and athletes will be labelled lesbian. Fear of further discrimination or potential retribution keeps many sportswomen closeted and inactive. Concern for additional loss of status or overt retaliation fuels this inaction. However, it is important to point out that coming out is not a prerequisite to social change (Barber & Krane, 2001; Iannotta & Kane, 2002; Krane & Barber, 2005). There are many actions coaches put into practice without openly revealing their own sexual identity. Simply speaking out about heterosexism and homonegativism is an important challenge to heteronormative sport settings (Hargreaves, 2000).

As the SI perspective explains, individuals with high collective esteem, who believe their social group is deserving of greater status, and who believe that change is possible will be motivated to attempt social change (Hogg & Abrams, 1988; Wright, 2001). Additionally, to engage social change, these women need to be willing to accept some risk of retribution yet also believe that the potential gains are worth the risk. Even though in many sport settings it is not perceived as safe to be open about one's lesbian identity, women in these settings still engage in social change actions. Lesbian coaches described creating team climates of tolerance (Barber & Krane, 2001; Iannotta & Kane, 2002; Krane & Barber, 2005). Often they emphasized to their athletes the importance of respecting team-mates regardless of race, ethnicity, religion, etc. In these discussions, some coaches overtly mentioned lesbian identities and homonegativism. Coaches also described confronting homonegative incidents as teachable moments, and openly discussing issues related to sexual orientation with athletes (Krane & Barber, 2005).

Coming out has been described as a form of social change because visibility creates greater social acceptance (Hargreaves, 2000; Krane et al., 2002). Iannotta and Kane (2002) described a process of 'radical normalization – a concept we define as the accumulated effect of various strategies of coming and being out that, in turn, help create a cultural space which normalizes lesbian sexualities and undermines heteronormativity' (p. 364). While these coaches did not verbally state they were lesbian, they communicated this identity through, for example, the visibility of their partners at competitions, openly talking on the telephone with their partners in front of athletes, and having athletes to their home for team gatherings. By routinely acting naturally about their relationships, these coaches sent the message that their relationships were 'normal' in that they interacted with their partners in a similar way to any other couple. Athletes accepted this normal behaviour, which further created a safe team climate.

Kauer (2005) interviewed 'out' lesbian coaches, revealing how they disrupted, challenged and transgressed heteronormativity in sport. These coaches encouraged social

change while upholding effective leadership and developing strong coach–athlete relationships. For example, one coach came out to her team when she and her partner were pregnant and subsequently introduced her partner and her child to recruits, parents and fans.
Another coach advocated for more inclusive language in her athletic department's policy
on taking 'spouses' to tournaments (i.e. include the term 'partner' or 'significant other').
These openly lesbian coaches described themselves as role models and showed how being
open normalized their lesbian identity and led to social change. They expressed that being
candid about their sexuality created an atmosphere of honesty and trust. Some of the
coaches in Kauer's study reported that their athletes became members of gay/straight
alliances, advocated for gay and lesbian rights, and spoke out against homonegativism in
part because of their strong relationships with their lesbian coaches.

Some studies have found open and accepting climates among the athletes within sport
teams; some lesbian athletes are out to their heterosexual team-mates without negative
consequence (Fasting, 1997; Kauer & Krane, 2006; Mennesson & Clément, 2003). When
referring to Norwegian and Swedish football players, Fasting (1997) described:

> Independent of sexual identity the players express friendship, acceptance and solidar-
> ity in relation to each other. The four teams which the interviewees represented have
> all had or have one or a few more lesbian players. The degree of openness had varied.
> All players expressed verbally that homosexuality is accepted. . . . Many express that
> it does not matter what kind of sexual identity a player has.

In their study with university athletes, Kauer and Krane (2006) uncovered that as heterosexual, lesbian and bisexual athletes interacted, they grew and learned from each other.
As they described:

> a circular relationship emerged in which the LB [lesbian and bisexual] athletes were
> open about their sexual orientation with their teammates, their heterosexual team-
> mates learned to accept them, which increased the LBs self-acceptance and created
> an environment in which LBs felt comfortable being open about their sexual identity.
> (p. 52)

Several athletes stated that as first year players they had not previously known anyone
who was lesbian, and that they had prejudicial attitudes about them. However, getting to
know their lesbian and bisexual team-mates changed their outlook and was an important
educational experience. Interviews with French professional soccer players revealed a
similar situation (Mennesson & Clément, 2003). Within these elite soccer teams, players
discussed lesbian life and lesbian and heterosexual athletes became familiar and comfortable with each other.

Coaches and athletes on a highly competitive Canadian ice hockey team, the Blades,
initially described apprehension about having lesbian players on the team (Theberge,
2000). In fact, the coach previously had avoided selecting lesbian players for the team.
Yet, both players and coaches changed their attitudes. As the heterosexual and lesbian
athletes spent time together on the ice and while travelling, their concerns dissipated.
Heterosexual players described the experience as a learning process that occurred as they
came to know the lesbian players. Younger players who joined the team also came to be
comfortable around lesbian players. As Theberge explained, 'competitive interests provided motivation for the Blades to abandon their exclusionary policies. At the same time,
social change, which influenced the views of management and players, facilitated the shift
in policy' (p. 95). Cohen and Semerjian (2003) presented a case study where a player was

disqualified at USA Hockey's women's national championships because of her transgendered status. This athlete had not hidden her transgender identity and was supported by her team-mates, as well as coaches and players on other teams in the league. (Eventually she also was reinstated by USA Hockey.)

For some athletes, sport is a refuge from heterosexism and homonegativism experienced in other contexts. A transgender figure skater expressed that when skating, his ability was valued, he was accepted and that skating provided a place free from the harassment he experienced at school (Semerjian & Cohen, 2006). A male-to-female transgender ice hockey player stated,

> For me it's not just hockey, it's about being accepted as a person . . . just somewhere where I can fit and I don't feel like I have to hold back. It's [hockey] like affirmation for me...I do not feel male skating on the ice. I just feel like normal, just like everybody else. (Cohen & Semerjian, 2003)

Palzkill (1990) interviewed elite lesbian athletes in Germany. These athletes described sport as a place where they could transgress gender-role expectations, create personal meanings associated with being lesbian athletes and interact with women similar to themselves.

Participation in 'gay sport' seems to be particularly empowering (Hargreaves, 2000). Lesbians desiring to compete devoid of discrimination may turn to events such as the Gay Games, EuroGames and Outgames. Engagement in such inclusive and affirming environments are empowering for the participants, yet also provides visibility for lesbian and gay athletes, in turn promoting greater social acceptance (Hargreaves, 2000; Krane & Waldron, 2000). Further benefits are accrued by gay sport participants who become more politically inspired. For example, lesbian and bisexual athletes who participated in the Gay Games, who were not out in other contexts, expressed the desire to become more open about their sexual identities (Krane et al., 2002). Engagement in such an empowering and affirming sport setting appeared to enhance collective esteem about lesbians and compelled desire for social change. Many of these athletes also spoke of wanting to become more politically active concerning gay rights and causes.

Sport can be empowering and lesbian athletes are proud of their sporting successes and athletic status. These feelings apparently bolster their ability to contend with prejudice and discrimination, encourage resiliency and fuel action to counter bigotry. Simply being strong, successful female athletes is transgressive. Yet many sportswomen are engaged in more overt actions to improve the climate of women's sport. Expressing sexual identities with team-mates normalizes the multiplicity of identities; heterosexuals identify with lesbian sportswomen as individuals and come to understand their collective struggles. Speaking out against discrimination creates alliances among all sportswomen and limits intolerance. Ultimately, such actions will free all sportswomen to focus their energy towards enhanced performance.

CONCLUSION

Much as been written about the detrimental effects of the lesbian stereotype, heterosexism, and homonegativism in women's sport. In particular, girls and women in sport with variant gender and sexuality identities have to negotiate a multitude of social norms and expectations. Yet, amid much speculation, stereotyping, and outright prejudice and discrimination, lesbian sportswomen exhibit incredible resiliency. Sport is a tremendous source of self- and collective esteem. Women gain mental and physical strength; being athletic they transgress many social norms and constraints. Through sport, girls and women gain robust self-assurance that underlie attempts at social change. Whether or not lesbian athletes and coaches explicitly communicate their sexual identities, they often encourage tolerance and improve the climate of sport for lesbian girls and women in sport.

Findings from the limited research with lesbian sportswomen, explained through a social identity interpretation, help us understand the forces perpetuating prejudice as well as the resilience of many lesbian sportswomen. Still, much more research is necessary, especially that which is inclusive of other queer identities. Minimal attention has been paid to transgender women, while virtually no studies focus on bisexual women in sport. Additionally, sport psychologists need to recognize the limitations placed on many sportswomen due to heterosexism and homonegativism. It is imperative they consider how the field as a whole is complicit in this unfairness. Consultants routinely need to counter heterosexism within women's sport. Until such action is commonplace, sportswomen's attempts to achieve their full potential will remain compromised.

REFERENCES

Abrams, D. & Hogg, M. A. (1990). An introduction to the social identity approach. In D. Abrams & M. Hogg (Eds), *Social Identity Theory: Constructive and critical advances* (pp. 1–9). New York, NY: Springer-Verlag.

Anderson, E. (2005). *In the Game: Gay athletes and the cult of masculinity.* Albany, NY: State University of New York Press.

Andrews, D. L. (1998). Feminizing Olympic reality: Preliminary dispatches from Baudrillard's Atlanta. *International Review for the Sociology of Sport,* **33**(1), 5–18.

Baks, B. & Malecek, S. (2004). *Synopsis on homophobia and discrimination on sexual orientation in sport.* Retrieved 9 July 2005, from European Gay and Lesbian Sport Foundation web site: http://www.gaysport.info/eglsf/publications/EGLSF_synopsis_on_homophobia_2003pr.pdf

Barber, H. & Krane, V. (2001). *Examining Lesbian High School Coaches' Experiences: A social identity perspective.* Poster presentation at the 10th World Congress of Sport Psychology, Skiathos, Greece, June.

Barber, H. & Krane, V. (2005). The elephant in the lockerroom: Opening the dialogue about sexual orientation on women's sport teams. In M. Andersen (Ed.), *Sport Psychology in Practice* (pp. 259–279). Champaign, IL: Human Kinetics.

Blauvelt, B. (2003). Stephenson to play with seniors, says Asians hurt LPGA. *USA Today.* Retrieved 8 January 2005, from http://www.usatoday.com/sports/golf/champions/2003-10-09-stephenson-champions_x.htm

Blinde, E. M., Taub, D. E. & Han, L. (1994). Sport as a site for women's group and societal empowerment: Perspectives from the college athlete. *Sociology of Sport Journal,* **11**(1), 51–59.

Brackenridge, C. H. (1997) *Spoilsports: Understanding and preventing sexual exploitation in sport.* New York, NY: Routledge.

Braun, V. (2000). Heterosexism in focus group research: Collusion and challenge. *Feminism & Psychology,* **10**(1), 133–140.

Burroughs, A., Ashburn, L. & Seebohm, L. (1995). 'Add sex and stir': Homophobic coverage of women's cricket in Australia. *Journal of Sport & Social Issues,* **19**(3), 266–284.

Cahn, S. K. (1993). *Coming on Strong: Gender and sexuality in twentieth-century women's sport.* New York, NY: Free Press.

Caudwell, J. (1999). Women's football in the United Kingdom: Theorizing gender and unpacking the butch lesbian image. *Journal of Sport & Social Issues*, **23**(4), 390–402.

Clarke, G. (1995). Outlaws in sport and education? Exploring the sporting and education experiences of lesbian physical education teachers. In L. Lawrence, L. Murdoch & S.R. Parker (Eds), *Professional and Development Issues in Leisure, Sport and Education* (pp. 45–58). Eastbourne: Leisure Studies Association.

Clarke, G. (1998). Queering the pitch and coming out to play: Lesbians in physical education and sport, *Sport, Education and Society*, **3**(2), 145–160.

Clarke, G. (2002). Difference matters: Sexuality and physical education. In D. Penney (Ed.), *Gender and Physical Education: Contemporary issues and future directions* (pp. 41–56). London: Routledge.

Cohen, J. H. & Semerjian, T. Z. (2003). *The Collision of Trans-experience and the Politics of Women's Sports*. Paper presented at the North American Society for the Sociology of Sport, Montreal, Canada, October.

Cox, B. & Thompson, S. (2000). Multiple bodies: Sportswomen, soccer and sexuality. *International Review for the Sociology of Sport*, **35**(1), 5–20.

Crocker, J. & Luhtanen, R. (1990). Collective self-esteem and ingroup bias. *Journal of Personality and Social Psychology*, **58**, 60–67.

Crocker, J. & Major, B. (1989). Social stigma and self-esteem: The self-protective properties of stigma. *Psychological Review*, **96**(4), 608–630.

Crocker, J. & Major, B. (1994). Reactions to stigma: The moderating role of justifications. In M. P. Zanna & J. M. Olson (Eds), *The Psychology of Prejudice: The Ontario Symposium, Volume 7* (pp. 289–314). Hillsdale, NJ: Lawrence Erlbaum.

Fasting, K. (1997). Sexual stereotypes in sport – Experiences of female soccer players. *Sport, Media, and Civil Society*. Retrieved 9 July 2005, from http://www.playthegame.org/Knowledge%20bank/Articles/Sexual%20Stereotypes%20in%20Sport%20-%20Experiences%20of%20Female%20Soccer%20Players.aspx.

Festle, M. J. (1996). *Playing Nice: Politics and apologies in women's sports*. New York: Columbia Press.

Fusco, C. (1998) Lesbians and locker rooms: The subjective experiences of lesbians in sport. In G. Rail (Ed.), *Sport and Postmodern Times* (pp. 87–116). Albany, NY: State University of New York Press.

George, C., Hartley, A. & Paris, J. (2001). The representation of female athletes in textual and visual media *Corporate Communications: An International Journal*, **6**(2), 94–101.

Gough, B. (2007). Coming out in the heterosexist world of sport: A qualitative analysis of web postings by gay athletes. In E. Peel, V. Clarke & J. Drescher (Eds), *British LGB Psychologies: Theory, research and practice*. New York, NY: Harrington Park Press.

Griffin, P. (1998). *Strong Women, Deep Closets: Lesbians and homophobia in women's sport*. Champaign, IL: Human Kinetics.

Hargreaves, J. (2000). *Heroines of Sport: The politics of difference and identity*. New York, NY: Routledge.

Herek, G. M. (1992). The social context of hate crimes: Notes on cultural heterosexism. In G. M. Herek & K. T. Berrill (Eds), *Hate Crimes: Confronting violence against lesbians and gay men* (pp. 89–104). Newbury Park, CA: Sage.

Herek, G. M. (1997). Heterosexuals' attitudes toward lesbians and gay men: Does coming out make a difference? In M. Duberman (Ed.), *A Queer World: The center for lesbian and gay studies reader* (pp. 331–344). New York, NY: New York University Press.

Hogg, M. A. (2001). Social categorization, depersonalization, and group behavior. In M. A. Hogg & R.S. Tinsdale (Eds), *Blackwell Handbook of Social Psychology: Group processes* (pp. 56–85). Malden, MA: Blackwell.

Hogg, M. A. & Abrams, D. (1988). *Social Identifications: A social psychology of intergroup relations and group processes*. New York, NY: Routledge.

Iannotta, J. G. & Kane, M. J. (2002). Sexual stories as resistance narratives in women's sports: Reconceptualizing identity performance. *Sociology of Sport Journal*, **19**(4), 347–369.

Kauer, K. (2005). *Transgressing the closets: Female coaches' negotiations of heteronormativity in sport*. Unpublished doctoral dissertation, University of Tennessee, Knoxville.

Kauer, K. & Krane, V. (2006). 'Scary dykes and feminine queens': Stereotypes and female athletes. *Women in Sport and Physical Activity Journal*, **15**(1), 43–56.

Koivula, N. (1999). Gender stereotyping in televised media sport coverage. *Sex Roles*, **41**, 589–604.

Kolnes, L. J. (1995). Heterosexuality as an organizing principle in women's sport. *International Review for Sociology of Sport*, **30**(1), 61–79.

Kontos, A. P. & Breland-Noble, A. M. (2002). Racial/ethnic diversity in applied sport psychology: Multicultural introduction to working with athletes of color. *The Sport Psychologist*, **16**, 296–315.

Krane, V. (1994). *Speaking Out: Experiences of lesbian athletes*. Paper presented at the meeting of the Association for the Advancement of Applied Sport Psychology, Lake Tahoe, Nevada, October.

Krane, V. (1997). Homonegativism experienced by lesbian collegiate athletes. *Women in Sport and Physical Activity Journal*, **6**(2), 141–163.

Krane, V. & Barber, H. (2003). Lesbian experience in sport: A social identity theory perspective. *Quest*, **55**(4), 328–346

Krane, V. & Barber, H. (2005). Identity tensions in lesbian college coaches. *Research Quarterly for Exercise and Sport*, **76**(1), 67–81.

Krane, V. & Waldron, J. (2000). The Gay Games: Creating our own culture. In K. Schaffer & S. Smith (Eds), *The Olympics at the Millennium: Power, politics, and the Olympic Games* (pp. 147–164). Piscataway, NJ: Rutgers University Press.

Krane, V., Barber, H. & McClung, L. (2002). Social psychological benefits of Gay Games participation: A social identity theory explanation. *Journal of Applied Sport Psychology*, **14**(1), 27–42.

Krane, V., Choi, P. Y. L., Baird, S. M., Aimar, C. M. & Kauer, K. J. (2004). Living the paradox: Female athletes negotiate femininity and muscularity. *Sex Roles*, **50**(5/6), 315–329.

Krane, V., Surface, H. & Alexander, L. (2005). Health implications of heterosexism and homonegativism for girls and women in sport. In L. Ransdall & L. Petlichkoff (Eds), *Ensuring the Health of Active and Athletic Girls and Women* (pp. 327–346). Reston, VA: National Association for Girls and Women in Sport.

Lenskyj, H. J. (1997). No fear? Lesbians in sport and physical education. *Women in Sport and Physical Activity Journal*, **6**(2), 7–22.

Lenskyj, H. J. (1998). 'Inside sport' or 'on the margins'?: Australian women and the sport media. *International Review for the Sociology of Sport*, **33**(1), 19–32.

Mennesson, C. & Clément, J. P. (2003). Homosociability and homosexuality: The case of soccer played by women. *International Review for the Sociology of Sport*, **38**(3), 311–330

Nelson, M. B. (1991). *Are We Winning Yet? How women are changing sports and sports are changing women*. New York, NY: Random House.

Palzkill, B. (1990). Between gymshoes and high-heels – the development of a lesbian identity and existence in top class sport. *International Review for the Sociology of Sport*, **25**(3), 221–234.

Pirinen, R. M. (1997). The construction of women's positions in sport: A textual analysis of articles on female athletes in Finnish women's magazines. *Sociology of Sport Journal*, **14**(3), 290–301.

Ram, N., Starek, J. & Johnson, J. (2004). Race, ethnicity, and sexual orientation: Still a void in sport and exercise psychology? *Journal of Sport & Exercise Psychology*, **26**(2), 250–268.

Robinson, L. (2002). *Black Tights: Women, sport, and sexuality*. Toronto: HarperCollins.

Russell, K. M. (2004). On versus off the pitch: The transiency of body satisfaction among female rugby players, cricketers, and netballers. *Sex Roles*, **51**(9/10), 561–574.

Sabo, D., Miller, K. E., Melnick, M. J. & Heywood, L. (2004). *Her Life Depends on It: Sport, physical activity, and the health and well-being of American girls*. East Meadow, NY: Women's Sport Foundation. Retrieved 25 July 2005, from the Women's Sport foundation website: http://www.womenssportsfoundation.org/binary-data/WSF_ARTICLE/pdf_file/990.pdf].

Semerjian, T. Z. & Cohen, J. H. (2006). 'FTM means female to me': Transgender athletes performing gender. *Women in Sport & Physical Activity Journal*, **15**(2), 28–43.

Tajfel, H. & Turner, J. C. (1979). An integrative theory of intergroup conflict. In S. Worshel & W. G. Austin (Eds), *The Social Psychology of Intergroup Relations* (pp. 33–47). Monterey, CA: Brooks-Cole.

Theberge, N. (2000). *Higher Goals: Women's ice hockey and the politics of gender.* Albany, NY: State University of New York Press.

Turner, J. C., Hogg, M. A., Oakes, P. J., Reichter, S. D. & Wetherell, M. S. (1987). *Rediscovering the Social Group: A self-categorization theory.* Oxford: Basil Blackwell.

Veri, M. J. (1999). Homophobic discourse surrounding the female athlete. *Quest,* **51**, 355–368.

Wright, S. C. (2001). Strategic collective action: Social psychology and social change. In R. Brown & S. L. Gaertner (Eds), *Blackwell Handbook of Social Psychology: Intergroup processes* (pp. 410–430). Malden, MA: Blackwell.

Wright, J. & Clarke, G. (1999). Sport, the media, and the construction of compulsory heterosexuality. *International Review for the Sociology of Sport,* **34**(3), 227–243.

Young, K. (1997). Women, sport, & physicality. *International Review for the Sociology of Sport,* **32**(3), 297–305.

CHAPTER 14

Homophobia, Rights and Community: Contemporary Issues in the Lives of LGB People in the UK

Sonja J. Ellis

Sheffield Hallam University, UK

INTRODUCTION

The contemporary struggle to gain equal rights for lesbians and gay men[1] in the UK dates back to 1967 when the Sexual Offences Act (England and Wales) partially decriminalized consensual sexual practices between males (Ellis & Kitzinger, 2002; Waites, 1998, 2005). The struggle for equal rights was rekindled in Europe when, in 1993, Claudia Roth (a member of the European Parliament) submitted a landmark report on equality issues for lesbians and gay men (Sanders, Kickler & Croome, 1997). A year later, in response to the Roth Report, the European Parliament adopted a resolution calling for member states to abolish all laws criminalizing homosexuality; equalize all age of consent laws; end discrimination against homosexuals in housing, social security, adoption, inheritance and criminal laws; take measures to reduce violence against homosexuals and prosecute offenders; and combat social discrimination against homosexuals (IGLHRC, 1998; Sanders et al., 1997; Wilets, 1994). The resolution also requested that the UK repeal Section 28[2],

---

[1] As one participant in the study reported in this chapter defined herself as bisexual, I mostly use the acronym 'LGB'. My occasional use of the term 'lesbians and gay men' reflects the terminology employed in the policy/legislation or in the papers under discussion. No participants self-identified as transgender or transsexual, thus these terms (or the letter T) have only been used where issues directly relate to this group.

[2] In the UK, Section 28 of the Local Government Act 1988 stated that a local authority shall not 'intentionally promote homosexuality or publish material with the intention of promoting homosexuality' or 'promote the teaching in any maintained school of the acceptability of homosexuality as a pretended family relationship' (Trade Unionists Against Section 28, 1989, p. 27).

Out in Psychology: Lesbian, gay, bisexual, trans and queer perspectives. Edited by Victoria Clarke and Elizabeth Peel.
© 2007 John Wiley & Sons, Ltd.

and recommended that lesbians and gay men be guaranteed full and equal rights of marriage and parenting (IGLHRC, 1998). In 1997, this was followed by revisions to the Treaty of Amsterdam allowing the European Commission to act against member states that permit discrimination based on sexual orientation (IGLHRC, 1998).

Progress on Positive Social Change for Lesbians and Gay Men

As a direct result of this constitutional change, since the turn of the twenty-first century there have been a number of legal changes in the UK affording (relative) equality to lesbians and gay men across a range of areas of social life. This succession of changes began in January 2000 with the lifting of the ban on homosexuals in the military, and was followed in November the same year with the equalizing of the age of consent for sex between men at 16 (see Ellis & Kitzinger, 2002; Waites, 2005); the same as that for heterosexuals. Also in that year, Section 28 was repealed in Scotland, and then in 2003 in England and Wales. In 2002, the Adoption and Children Act was passed, which, for the first time, allowed unmarried couples (including same-sex couples) the right to apply for joint adoption; and in December 2003, the Employment Equality (Sexual Orientation) Regulations came into effect making it illegal to discriminate in employment and training on grounds of sexual orientation[3]. To cap it all off, in December 2005 the Civil Partnerships Act took effect making it legally possible for same-sex couples to 'marry' or to form legally recognized unions (see Kitzinger & Wilkinson, 2004; Wilkinson & Kitzinger, 2005; see also Peel & Harding, 2004 for an alternative view). Legislative change on this scale is unprecedented in relation to LGB issues and suggests that at least constitutionally; there is significantly increased inclusion of LGB people within society.

Although it is difficult to identify tangible evidence that society itself is more inclusive of LGB people, there is some (limited) evidence of this. In particular, positive representation in the popular media have become commonplace. In the UK today, there are a number of 'out' high-profile lesbian and gay TV presenters and broadcasters (e.g. Graham Norton, Dale Winton, Julian Clary, Paul O'Grady, Sue Perkins, Rhona Cameron) and 'out' LGBT individuals/couples have featured on reality TV shows (e.g. *Big Brother; Property Ladder*). LGB lives and lifestyles are also appearing with increasing frequency on mainstream British television. Currently, most British soaps/serials have LGBT characters (e.g. Naomi Julien in *Eastenders*; Zoe Tate in *Emmerdale*; Sean Tully and Haley Cropper in *Coronation Street*; Helen Stewart and Nikki Wade in *Bad Girls*); there have been several dramatizations of lesbian themed books of late (e.g. *Tipping the Velvet, Fingersmith, Sugar Rush*); as well as a number of LGBT-themed television advertisements for major multinational companies (e.g. Benetton; FCUK). In addition, since the mid-1990s, LGBT topics have increasingly been the subject of broadly positive coverage on television talk shows (see Clarke & Kitzinger, 2004; Gamson, 1998, for examples), and central to some mainstream cinema (e.g. *The Adventures of Priscilla,*

---

[3] This particular piece of legislation specifically includes bisexuals, but not trans people. Trans people are deemed to be protected from discrimination in the workplace by the Sex and Gender Discrimination Acts.

Queen of the Desert; Bound; Brokeback Mountain). Similarly, specifically lesbian/gay topics (especially civil partnerships) have been the subject of national radio programmes (e.g. 'The Long View' on Civil Partnerships, BBC Radio 4, 15/11/05); and of positive coverage on the television news, in most of the national broadsheet newspapers (e.g. *The Times*; *The Guardian*), and many local/regional newspapers (e.g. *The* [Sheffield] *Star*; *The Yorkshire Post*) as well. This level of representation is unprecedented, and has arguably significantly contributed to the normalization of LGBT lives and lifestyles (but see Ciasullo, 2001; see also Clarke, 2002b for a discussion of the political costs of normalizing strategies).

Considerable changes have also been made in the policies, and in some cases, practices of many organizations and workplaces. For example, even before the institution of the Employment Equality Regulations, many universities in the UK explicitly included sexual orientation as grounds for non-discrimination; and some service sector organizations (e.g. adoption agencies[4]) have demonstrated 'best practice' in relation to inclusiveness of LGB people. Furthermore, Stonewall, the primary LGB equality and justice campaigning group in the UK, has launched a 'Diversity Champions' programme that recognizes employers who are actively 'committed to tackling sexual orientation discrimination, and to sharing good practice, developing ideas and promoting diversity in the workplace' (http://www. Stonewall.org.uk). About 100 employers in England (including B&Q, British Airways, HSBC, Royal Mail, Sheffield City Council and Sainsburys), as well as some in Wales (e.g. The University of Cardiff), have been recognized as LGB-friendly employers under this scheme. Positive developments in workplace policy and practice – e.g. explicit protection in non-discrimination policies, LG(BT) awareness training, prohibition of discrimination – are also reported in the USA (see van Hoye & Lievens, 2003 for an overview). However, as others (e.g. Biaggio et al., 2003; Epstein, O'Flynn & Telford, 2003) remind us, these should be taken cautiously as indicators of social inclusion in that 'the presence of such statements does not necessarily translate into an affirming climate' (Biaggio et al., 2003, p. 549).

Changes in public views are much more difficult to assess. However, recent research suggests that, at least in principle, equal rights for lesbians and gay men are well supported (Ellis, 2002; Hegarty, Pratto & Lemieux, 2004). While there are obvious pockets of resistance to positive social change for LGB people (e.g. the anti-gay-marriage movement in the USA; the BNP[5] in the UK), and there is still ample evidence that institutionalized homophobia[6] and homophobic bigotry are still widespread, in Europe at least there is much evidence of a significant shift in the extent to which LGB issues and perspectives are incorporated into legislation, policy and practice. This makes it *feel* – at least on the surface – like society is more inclusive of LGB people.

As a direct result of this positive social change, the LGB community has increasingly become integrated into mainstream society. Historically, lesbians and gay men have organized socially because our marginalization within, and exclusion from, mainstream society has often rendered us invisible (Weinstock, 1998). The prevalence of hostility towards,

---

[4] For example, Waltham Forest Borough Council advertised the December 2005 issue of *Diva*.
[5] The BNP (British National Party) is an extreme right-wing political organization that promotes nationalist viewpoints on social issues, and which is opposed to the 'promotion' of gay rights.
[6] Although problematic (see Kitzinger, 1996) the term 'homophobia' has been used throughout this paper as this is widely used and understood in lay discourse to mean discrimination against lesbians and gay men.

and discrimination against, us meant that it was important to have networks, spaces and points of contact with a specifically LGB community. At the height of second-wave feminism and the gay liberation movement, 'the community' comprised a well-organized array of social networks (see Ellis, 2007) offering a 'safe space' to meet together, and when necessary seek support (Green, 1997; Harper & Schneider, 2003; Kitzinger & Perkins, 1993). Since the mid 1980s, however, services to LGB people have mostly been subsumed into mainstream organizations; and what was a distinct, diverse and vibrant community now comprises almost exclusively commercialized 'gay' venues that mirror the mainstream heterosexual (and sexually, rather than socially, focused) club culture.

Psychological Research on the Lives of Lesbian, Gay and Bisexual People

Since the institution of 'lesbian/gay-affirmative' psychology in the 1970s, the inclusion of lesbian and gay, and more recently bisexual and trans, perspectives within psychology has increased exponentially. There is now a well-established field that has contributed significantly to our understanding of LGB lives and lifestyles, particularly within social, developmental, health and psychotherapeutic psychology. However, despite this, there is a dearth of work exploring issues across the lifespan, with most studies focusing specifically on LGB youth, and a small number on lesbians in middle age (e.g. Adelman, 1990; Kitzinger & Wilkinson, 1995) and LGB people in old age (e.g. Grossman, D'Augelli & Hershberger, 2000; Heaphy, Yip & Thompson, 2004). There is, however, an absence of studies that explore issues which affect the lives of LGB people, largely independent of age.

Furthermore, although there is now a sizeable body of research about LGB issues, this has tended to focus on a limited range of topic areas. In the main, psychologists have typically researched identity development (e.g. D'Augelli, 1994; Kitzinger, 1987) and 'coming out' (e.g. Cowie & Rivers, 2000; Schneider, 2001); lesbian/gay parenting and families (e.g. Clarke, 2002a; Golombok & Tasker, 1994; van Reyk, 2004); and experiences of homophobia in school (e.g. Rivers, 1995; Warwick, Aggleton & Douglas, 2001) and university (e.g. Eliason, 1996; Taulke-Johnson & Rivers, 1999) settings. Attention to other aspects of the everyday lives of LGB people – for example, work life, community and social life, and relationships (including partner bereavement) – are very limited, while a more holistic approach is altogether absent from the psychological literature.

Rationale for a General Study on the Lives of Lesbian, Gay and Bisexual People

In light of the (relative) inclusivity of LGB lives and lifestyles within British society, there is a need to investigate current issues of concern for LGB people (collectively) in order to identify priorities for positive social change. For example, although there is much work on homophobia, this is based on the premise that homophobia is a significant issue in the lives of LGB people. In what may be seen as a more liberal socio-political climate, this may not be the only or even dominant issue facing LGB people today. However, it might underlie other significant issues, whatever they might be. Therefore, rather than focusing directly on homophobia, it is better to begin by researching the ordinary, everyday lives of LGB people and inducing the key issues from this.

The focus of the psychological literature on topical issues (e.g. parenting, homophobia in education settings, and more recently same-sex marriage) offers only a partial account. This is because these studies explore issues in the lives of LGB people only in relation to the topic under investigation. Therefore, they do not capture the extent to which issues of homophobia may pervade LGB people's lives as a whole. While there is a need for in-depth studies on specific issues (e.g. parenting, coming out) to assess the impact of changes in social climate on the lives of LGB people, there is also a need for work that explores a range of issues in order to re-evaluate what key issues for the LGB research agenda might be.

Taking a phenomenological approach, the purpose of this study was to generate narratives from LGB people about their experiences across a range of aspects of their lives, including work, relationships and social life. By simply asking LGB people to talk about these topics through semi-structured interviews, it was anticipated that participants would spontaneously raise issues pertinent to them, and that through these some insight into contemporary 'sites of oppression' for LGB people might be inferred.

ABOUT THE STUDY

The Participants

The data presented here was derived from interviews with women (N = 17) and men (N = 11) in the UK, aged 21–58. Participants for the study were initially recruited via an online network for professionals working in the area of LGBT psychology through which the request reached other related networks (e.g. health workers, clinicians). Further participants were recruited through letters to community-based organizations (e.g. youth organizations; student LGBT groups); community spaces likely to be frequented by LGB people (e.g. Women's Centres; LGB Centres); and LGB-centred organizations (e.g. The Metropolitan Community Church). Recruitment was undertaken across a wide geographical area predominantly comprising the Midlands and North of England, with 14 participants residing in or around Sheffield and Rotherham, 12 in or around one of seven other large metropolitan areas (Leeds, Leicester, Manchester, Liverpool, Newcastle, Coventry and Edinburgh) and two in semi-rural towns/localities (Lincolnshire; Lancashire).

While most participants defined themselves as 'lesbian' or 'gay', one woman self-defined as 'bisexual' because she had had sexual relationships with men in the past and felt that this label better defined her sexuality. Other women broadly accepted being referred to as lesbian, but indicated a preference not to label their sexual identity or provided alternative descriptions (e.g. 'my sexuality is called Penny'; 'sexually ambiguous'). In all cases, participants' sexual orientations and experiences at the time of interview were directed towards members of the same sex as themselves; and in recruiting and briefing participants, I made my own identity as lesbian explicit.

Although the sample is diverse in terms of the age, social background, life experiences and geographical location, it is not representative of the mix of racial and ethnic groups that comprise the UK LGB community. Apart from three participants (one self-identifying

Table 14.1 Breakdown of Participants

FEMALE PARTICIPANTS				MALE PARTICIPANTS			
Name	Age	Self-nominated sexual identity	Ethnic origin	Name	Age	Self-nominated sexual identity	Ethnic origin
Clare	42	bisexual	white	Brian	32	gay man	white
Donna	28	lesbian	white	Francis	49	gay man	white
Emily	38	lesbian	white	James	35	gay man	Irish
Karen	52	lesbian	white	Rajit	27	gay man	Indian
Leanne	39	lesbian	white	Wayne	21	gay man	white
Maria	23	lesbian	white	Zane	34	gay man	white
{ * Tina	53	lesbian	white	Chris	23	gay man	white
{ Vanessa	43	lesbian	white	David	30	gay man	white
Brenda	25	lesbian	white	Eddie	28	gay man	white
Gina	43	lesbian	white	Frank	35	gay man	white
{ Josie	50	lesbian	white	Howard	37	gay man	white
{ Kate	35	lesbian	white				
{ Lillian	58	lesbian	white				
{ Mary	56	lesbian	white				
Naomi	43	'I prefer not to use labels to describe my sexual identity'	Irish				
Penny	56	'My sexuality is called Penny'	white				
Steph	28	'sexually ambiguous'	white				

* Brackets denote participants who were interviewed together, two joint interviews were with couples, one joint interview was with work colleagues.

as 'Indian' and two as 'Irish') all others identified themselves as 'white'. A summary of participants can be found in Table 14.1, however, because some of the information collected (e.g. occupation, background, family composition and geographical location) could potentially make particular participants identifiable, the information reported in the table has been restricted to pseudonym, age, self-nominated sexual identity and ethnic origin only.

Carrying out the Study

Interviews were carried out to explore the social aspects of the lives of LGB people. This method was chosen to enable participants to talk about their lives and experiences in their own words and therefore to prioritize the issues and concerns that were important to them. Semi-structured (rather than unstructured) interviews fit with the aim of drawing comparisons across the data set and identifying common issues, and one-to-one (rather than group) interviews, afforded individuals the opportunity for their 'story' to be heard. In a small number of cases (six), participants requested to be interviewed in a pair (usually a couple) and this request was respected.[7]

Participants were asked a series of questions about a range of aspects of their lives including work/study, identity and coming out, relationships, family, community and growing older. Although a set of questions were prepared, in order to keep the interviews as fluid as possible, these were only used to help focus the interviews and participants were encouraged to set their own agenda in relation to the main topics. Depending on the age and life experiences of participants, interviews ranged from 40 to 90 minutes. The venue used for the interviews varied according to the wishes of the participants: some interviews were conducted in participants' workplaces or their own homes, some in university settings and others in public spaces.

Following interviewing, tapes were transcribed verbatim and the transcripts analysed using inductive thematic analysis (Braun & Clarke, 2006; Hayes, 2000) a 'transparent' analytical method involving the generation of 'themes' (key issues) from the data, rather than imposing predetermined categories on it. Because a phenomenological approach was employed in this study, participants were regarded as informants. So, in contrast with a discursive approach, the emphasis of the analysis focused on *what* was being said, as opposed to *why* it was being said. The transcripts were read and reread several times to identify recurring issues, which were then organized into clusters of similar issues, otherwise known as 'themes'.

ISSUES IN THE LIVES OF LESBIANS, GAY MEN AND BISEXUALS

Although a number of pertinent issues were raised in the interviews, many of these were idiosyncratic. For example, only one participant (Francis) had experienced a partner bereavement, and the narrative around his experience of that bereavement raised numerous personal and political issues about being both 'bereaved' and 'gay'. Similarly, although several interviewees were parents, only one participant (Leanne) was a custodial parent. Therefore, the issues raised by Leanne differed markedly from those of other participants (notably all gay men) who had lost custody of their children by coming out as gay. Furthermore, it was evident (as would be expected) that for older participants, growing old as an LGB person raised more issues than it did for younger participants. However, the analysis presented here focuses on issues that were common to most participants, irrespective of gender, class, age and life experience. The analysis revealed three main 'sites of oppression' for LGB people: the workplace, relationships and LGB community. Although these areas map onto subsections of the interview schedule, they were frequently spontaneously raised in other parts of the interviews and therefore are not simply a reflection of the questions asked.

The Workplace

As highlighted earlier in this chapter, the experiences of LGB people at work have too infrequently been a topic of interest to psychologists. The majority of studies have focused

---

[7] These instances have been clearly marked in Table 14.1.

on the issue of coming out and the management of a lesbian, gay or bisexual identity in a work context (Chrobot-Mason, Button & DiClementi, 2001; Day & Schoenrade, 2000; Griffin & Zukas, 1993; Rostosky & Riggle, 2002; Waldo, 1999). These studies tend to concur that it is important to be out at work. This is because not only is the concealment of one's identity considered personally detrimental, but it has also been reported to impact negatively on aspects such as job satisfaction and performance at work (Croteau, 1996; Day & Schoenrade, 2000). However, experiences of direct heterosexism (Waldo, 1999) and the absence of a non-discrimination policy (Rostosky & Riggle, 2002) have been found to be significant factors in the decision not to be out at work.

A number of other studies have focused on particular aspects of workplace discrimination. For example, van Hoye & Lievens (2003) undertook an experimental study on the effects of sexual orientation on the perceived hirability of candidates, but found no significant effects. However, studies on career development have tended to identify discrimination and a lack of social support as significant barriers to LGB and T people considering certain jobs or careers (e.g. see Fassinger, 1996; Irwin, 2002; Skelton, 1999). Likewise, LGB and T people are more likely to report discrimination when employed in organizations where there is a lack of affirmative policies and protective legislation (Ragins & Cornwell, 2001). As highlighted by Rostad and Long (Chapter 15), success for lesbians in a work context may be contingent on the presence of non-discrimination legislation, and adequate support coupled with a positive climate for LGB people. It would be reasonable to assume that this might also be true for the success of gay men, bisexual and trans people.

Psychological studies of LGB people's *experiences* at work are much scarcer. Although fairly dated now, there are a small number of papers specifically focusing on homophobic discrimination in the workplace. In one study (Levine & Leonard, 1984), 24% of respondents reported actual incidences of job-discrimination, 75% of those in the form of verbal harassment, just over a third non-verbal harassment (e.g. ostracism, vandalism, etc), and around 10% actual physical violence. Furthermore, LGB people have sometimes reported violence (e.g. see Herek & Berrill, 1990); and/or the denial of employment, promotion or being pressured to leave their jobs, because their sexual orientation had become known to employers (see Kitzinger, 1991, for a full discussion of these issues). There are, however, a number of studies exploring the 'climate' for LGB staff and students in educational settings (Evans & Broido, 2002; Sears, 2002; Taulke-Johnson & Rivers, 1999). These studies tend to suggest that homophobic acts are commonplace, and it would be reasonable to assume that this would be true of other large organizations.

In the present study, although participants were asked general questions about work, the main focus of this section of the interviews was to explore the interface between work and being LG or B. Consequently, participants were specifically asked about the relationship between their work and their sexual orientation/identity (e.g. 'did your being lesbian/gay/bisexual have any impact on your choice of career?', 'to what extent do you think your being lesbian/gay/bisexual has impacted on your work?' Have you ever had any problems as a result of being out at work?). Although there was considerable diversity in participants' responses to these questions, and the extent to which any given participant was out at work, about half reported specific (and recent) first-hand experience of homophobia in the workplace.

One participant reported that she felt her being (openly) lesbian had ultimately resulted in unfair dismissal from work: 'I've had bad experiences with being side-lined, pushed out, made redundant, got rid of because people didn't like me I felt because of being lesbian' (Donna, 28[8]). Across the interviews as a whole though, reports of these types of experiences were very uncommon. More often, participants reported incidences of being made to feel uncomfortable for being LGB but simultaneously feeling disempowered to challenge this level of homophobia. For example, Kate describes a situation where her identity as lesbian is inappropriately invoked in the guise of inclusiveness:

> it's the kind of things people say and the things that they actually think are funny . . . they're just treating it as normal. It's like one of the guys at work, John, will say 'so how's my favourite lesbian today?' and you just kind of think like you're just not getting the point of this at all are you . . . but it's just going to get his back up if I say something to him, because he actually thinks he's being really very supportive and inclusive and so it's those kind of things that really grate sometimes. (Kate, 35)

Seemingly innocuous occurrences such as being the target of gay jokes, having people speculate about their sexuality, being the object of colleagues' attempts at matchmaking, or overhearing disparaging comments about lesbians/gay men were all frequently reported. These types of incidents, while often passed off by the perpetrators as 'a joke' or 'friendly banter', represent homophobia disguised by the thin veil of humour, and are commonly reported in campus climate studies (e.g. see Evans & Broido, 2002; Taulke-Johnson & Rivers, 1999).

Homophobia in the workplace was also manifested in more deliberate attempts to silence or regulate LGB identities. Those who experienced the most difficulty in this respect were those with careers that involved working closely with young people. Without exception, these participants reported being put under pressure not to be out in the workplace:

> when I first started the job, I was told that it was okay to be 'out' with my colleagues, but not with my client group, so not with the young women – that's what the . . . strong recommendation from my boss was . . . a lot of these young women there's just rampant homophobia going on, and you're constantly in this decision well, do I tell them and risk them then refusing to work with me on that basis . . . or do I just have to pretend or divert conversations . . . my manager was worried as well that some of the parents wouldn't approve of their daughters being supported by a lesbian woman, and all that cobblers. (Leanne, 39)

Silencing LGB people in this way is clearly problematic in that it not only denies the worker the right to be open about their sexual identity, but also prevents young LGB people and those questioning their sexuality from having access to appropriate role models and adequate support.

Homophobia in relation to work with young people was not just restricted to employers discouraging employees from being out, but also in some cases preventing service users (e.g. LGBT and 'questioning' youth) from having easy access to information and advice. For example, David, who worked for an LGBT youth organization, reported that other organizations were often not willing to cooperate in proactively working with or providing resources to LGBT youth:

> I go to certain agencies [who] say it's not appropriate for me to work with people of certain ages or . . . 'there's no gay people here in this area, we don't have any gays in

---

[8] The number after the participants' names indicates their age.

> our town, but you can still come if you want to and I'll put a poster up' or you give
> them leaflets and they'll put them away in a drawer . . . so I spend a lot of time kind
> of being confronted with homophobia by sort of staff teams. (David, 30)

Employment conditions also appeared to be a significant point of discrimination. Despite
the institution of the Employment Equality (Sexual Orientation) Regulations, some of
those interviewed reported difficulties with line managers in respect of accessing the same
benefits as their heterosexual colleagues. For example, one woman recounted the way in
which her and her partner's decision to start a family had highlighted for her just how
tenuous employment equality can be:

> my partner's going through assisted conception at the moment and that's been a bit of
> a roller-coaster ride of emotions and um previously I would have been able to share
> that with my manager and had some support around, you know, needing to take some
> time off in the mornings to go for the treatment and that kind of thing . . . my current
> manager is very unsupportive of that and I know if it comes to the situation where
> we're successful I'll have a right battle on my hands to get the equivalent of paternity
> leave. (Clare, 42)

This suggests that although legislation may be put in place to protect people from
discrimination, in practice, there is still the likelihood that individuals will be discriminated against. This is a particular concern given the way in which policies can be (and
often are) merely 'paper policies' rather than 'lived policies' (Biaggio et al., 2003; Epstein
et al., 2003).

   Although the changes to legislation that prohibit discrimination on grounds of sexual
orientation may go some way to addressing these issues, legislation and its translation
into policy at the organizational level are often insufficient for addressing issues such as
implicit homophobia (e.g. jokes, invoking LGB identity in inappropriate situations) (see
Harding & Peel, Chapter 12), silencing, and censoring. It would seem then, that considerable work is needed in order for policy and legislation to be translated into effective and
equal practice. The analysis of this data indicates that not only, as others (Ragins &
Cornwell, 2001; Rostosky & Riggle, 2002) suggest, is it important to have policies that
protect LGB people from discrimination, but that these need to be 'lived'. The monitoring
of non-discrimination policy implementation, and its operationalization in practice, would
appear to be a significant priority for research.

Relationships

It has only really been since 2004, with actual and proposed legislative change in many
western countries (Canada, UK, New Zealand), that the issue of legally recognized relationships has become a focus of published LGB psychological work. In particular, the
proposal and institution of the UK Civil Partnerships Act (2005) evoked much debate and
discussion around 'marriage' versus 'civil partnership' (Clarke, Burgoyne & Burns, 2006)
and the respective advantages and disadvantages of each; and the pros and cons of different types of arguments for equality (see Clarke, Finlay & Wilkinson, 2004; Kitzinger
& Wilkinson, 2004; Peel & Harding, 2004; Wilkinson & Kitzinger, 2005).

   As highlighted by Peel and Harding (2004), these debates can be organized into
three main arguments: romance (i.e. public affirmation of love), rights (i.e. equality) and

radicalism (i.e. feminist arguments about the need for the patriarchal institution of marriage, in whatever form, to be abolished). However, with only a few exceptions (e.g. Clarke, Burgoyne & Burns, Chapter 9; Clarke et al., 2006; Harding & Peel, 2006; Lannutti, 2005; Soloman, Rothblum & Balsam, 2004, 2005; Weeks, Donovan & Heaphy, 2001; Yip, 2004) there has been little published empirical research on lesbians' and gay men's views on legal recognition (see Clarke et al., Chapter 9 for a review of the literature). Nevertheless, the amount of attention the topic has received in the LGB psychological literature is testimony enough that relationship recognition is an important issue for same-sex couples.

Across the transcripts, relationship recognition (through access to rights and legal protection) typically emerged at two points in the interviews: First, in connection with relationships (especially in relation to marriage or civil partnership) and in connection with growing old (particularly in relation to partner bereavement).

Although many participants were not keen on the idea of marriage per se, most indicated that should they legally be able to do so, they would consider 'marrying' their same-sex partner. For some this was about making a public affirmation of their commitment (e.g. 'the making of a commitment and the depth that that can bring to a relationship' – Naomi, 43), but in most cases access to rights and legal protection as a couple or family was at least one, if not the sole, reason for considering a legal union (see Clarke et al., Chapter 9). For example, participants stated that it would offer them 'the same rights for . . . pensions and benefits' (Brenda, 25); 'inheritance and tenancy rights . . . visiting rights in hospital, next of kin rights' (David, 30). This was most clearly expressed by one participant who said

> I would like to be his legal [spouse] in the sense that I would like the right to his estate and I would like rights that if he goes into hospital I'm considered family, because obviously at the moment I'm not . . . I would like the equal rights to everything that's his, and I would like <u>him</u> to have the legal rights to everything that's mine just as [we] would if we were married. (Wayne, 21)

For some participants, current or future family circumstances made this a particularly salient issue. For example, Tina (53) mentioned that her partner is disabled and doesn't work, and therefore legal recognition of their relationship is very important in terms of making her partner financially secure. Similarly, Steph (28) is considering having children in the future and although ideologically opposed to marriage, would consider it to enable her and her (future) partner both to have legal access to the children and to be financially responsible for them, particularly in the event of relationship dissolution.

For several participants, legal recognition of partnerships was seen as an important issue in relation to growing older. Although some had made legal provision (e.g. made wills; assigned their partners as power of attorney) many were particularly concerned about finances in old age, especially in the event of a partner's death (e.g. 'I am anxious about finances . . . Elizabeth would miss out on my pension', Penny, 56; '. . . worries about pension rights', James, 35). For one participant in particular, access to rights was a pertinent issue as a result of his experiences when his partner died 10 years ago:

> when Mike died . . . I was faced with these . . . I didn't inherit any of Mike's stuff, he was on a life support machine, and I didn't have any rights about whether that being turned off or not . . . I didn't have any say in the funeral . . . it was months later I thought . . . well he [was] a therapist for the NHS if we'd been a heterosexual married

couple wouldn't I have a got a widows pension or something? You don't get any thing like that I got a few clothes and one or two things from the house as I helped them go through his stuff but it was clear the financial stuff was up to the father and mother to sort out. (Francis, 49)

Although none of the other participants had experienced a partner bereavement, for Leanne, her partner giving birth to their child made her realize the importance of securing rights as a couple, even though she and her partner do not cohabitate. When discussing growing older she said 'I think my biggest worry . . . is the lack of legal status I have as a coparent, in so much as if anything happens to Theresa [Leanne's partner], Sarah [their baby] doesn't automatically come to me' (Leanne, 39).

While the dominant discourse in this study centres around access to benefits and rights, as Katzen (1997) highlights, legal recognition is not simply about entitlements but about ending discrimination, and about validation of our relationships by our families and mainstream society. However, it is interesting to note that as Peel and Harding (2004) also highlight, when talking about same-sex marriage, the rights discourse is employed by lesbians and gay men in the absence of its legal antithesis, responsibilities (but see Clarke et al., Chapter 9). The ability to obtain legal recognition will inevitably change some of the concerns expressed here, in that many of the issues raised by participants will be afforded couples on entering a civil partnership. This will, therefore, be an issue to be followed up once the civil partnerships legislation is well established.

LGB Community

Much consideration has been given to the notion of LGB community in the broader social sciences, particularly the use of and relationship to LGB spaces (Binnie & Skeggs, 2004; Holt & Griffin, 2003; Valentine & Skelton, 2003; Visser, 2003). In the psychological literature there is considerable evidence that LGB communities (i.e. groups, events, organizations, networks and spaces centred on LGB identity) play a significant role in the lives of LGB people. For example, many psychologists and sociologists (Cowie & Rivers, 2000; Dietz & Dettlaff, 1997; Esterberg, 1996; Grossman et al., 2000; Holt & Griffin, 2003; Markowe, 2002; McCarthy, 2000; Szymanski, Chung & Balsam, 2001; Vincke & van Heeringen, 2002) have consistently suggested that the LGB community provides an important reference point from which to develop and (re)affirm a positive identity as lesbian, gay or bisexual. It therefore provides a (literal and metaphorical) space within heteronormative society in which one can be authentic (i.e. be oneself) and perform LGB identity (MacBride-Stewart, 2004). As well as being a source of social interactions with other LGB people and (secondarily) relationship/sexual opportunities (D'Augelli & Garnets, 1995), it can offer a 'refuge' from heterocentric society (Binnie & Skeggs, 2004; Holt & Griffin, 2003; Kitzinger & Perkins, 1993; Liddle, 2005). Furthermore, historically 'the community' has been central to the development and maintenance of lesbian/gay/bi-centred social and support networks, the absence of which has been identified as particularly detrimental to the well-being of those who are coming out (Cowie & Rivers, 2000; Groves, 1985; Markowe, 2002; Schneider & Witherspoon, 2000) or who live in isolated rural settings (McCarthy, 2000; Oswald & Culton, 2003).

Almost without exception, those interviewed highlighted the importance to them of connecting socially with other LGB people – for example 'we share something similar, we don't necessarily have to speak about what's similar' (Naomi, 43); 'it's quite nice to go somewhere where I don't have to start off explaining the basics' (David, 30); 'sometimes it's nice to talk about things like girly sex stuff that you couldn't necessarily talk about with your heterosexual friends' (Maria, 23). Although most of the women and men interviewed had their own small circle of LGB friends, many highlighted the fact that increasingly there are fewer and fewer opportunities for them to meet socially with other LGB people outside those personal social circles.

One of the issues that many participants highlighted is the way that 'the scene' (i.e. commercialized gay pubs/clubs) and other LGB focused groups and organizations were predominantly youth focused. As Maria highlights, being LGB is typically considered synonymous with being young:

> I think it's quite an important observation and fact sadly that a lot of things like gay magazines and gay lifestyle is targeted towards younger people and kind of neglect older people and again because of the stereotype of a gay or lesbian as someone who is young not someone who is old. (Maria, 23)

While there is a need for a space for young LGB people to explore and celebrate their sexual identities, focusing primarily or solely on youth means that old/older LGB people become marginalized. Since there are few (if any) alternatives for older people, it is often difficult for them to establish a circle of LGB friends:

> the whole lesbian and gay scene seems to be very young and . . . if you're not into going into clubs . . . I think it's going to be far harder to meet up with people . . . there's the older lesbian network group in Bradford, which you can join once you hit 40 apparently . . . but if you're an older woman coming out in your 40s and 50s, I think it would be bloody hard to try and meet other people . . . when you're younger there's more activity to organize around being lesbian or gay. (Leanne, 39)

In addition to being focused on youth, 'the scene' was also heavily criticized on grounds of its atmosphere, particularly its predatory nature. It was viewed as an undesirable place to connect socially because it is 'not a very sociable place . . . not a very friendly place . . . the music's too loud [and] it's all geared around getting drunk and having one night stands' (James, 35). Scene venues were also typically described as 'seedy' (Tina, 53), 'grotty' (Penny, 56) or 'meat markets and dives' (Vanessa, 43). Although some participants saw scene venues as a place for a good night out with friends, they were not perceived as conducive to meeting new people or getting to know them on a social level.

Another issue highlighted by participants was the way in which this relative absence of community makes aged and 'well adjusted' LGB people more invisible and therefore marginalized. However, it is not just *aged* LGB people who appear to be excluded by the lack of points of contact with the community. It was especially noticeable that those who were over 25, but too young to have established a network of LGB friends at the height of second-wave feminism and/or the gay liberation movement, found it particularly difficult to connect with other LGB people. For example, although she has a number of gay male friends, Steph highlights the way in which she is excluded from the LGB community by the multiple positions she occupies (e.g. age, class, politics, etc.):

> I'm not old enough to go to the over 40s; I've also found that sometimes my politics don't sit very well with radical lesbian feminists, so I've never had that kind of, the access to the middle-class lesbian community . . . I can't afford a house in Hebden

> Bridge[9] at the moment . . . I've found that if I go out on the scene they're all
> much younger than me now . . . [so] you're looking in the free ads, you're looking in
> *Diva*,[10] how do you meet eligible middle-class lesbians that are non-scene oriented?
> (Steph, 28)

Moreover, participants tended to report that significant life events – both normative (e.g. relocation, relationship break-up, partner bereavement, coming out, having children) and non-normative (e.g. being the victim of homophobic hate crimes) – made the need to connect socially with other LGB people particularly acute.

The isolation and exclusion brought about by the absence of adequate points of contact to facilitate connection with the community is not just particular to this sample. Even a cursory glance at postings in lesbian/gay magazines (e.g. *Diva*; *Gay Times*) and chat forums on the internet (e.g. www.libertas.co.uk; www.divamag.co.uk) clearly indicate a desire/need to connect socially with other LGB people, and a lack of opportunity to do so. Despite increased integration into mainstream society, it would seem then that the LGB community has become extremely fragmented, resulting in a degree of social exclusion. The issues raised by participants in this study look remarkably similar to those raised in studies of rural LGB people (McCarthy, 2000; Oswald & Culton, 2003). That the participants in this study were almost exclusively based in and around large metropolitan areas belies the myth that isolation and exclusion are particular to those residing some distance from sizeable urban areas.

Furthermore, the analysis presented here shows a desire to connect with other LGB people outside of mainstream settings. The findings of this study therefore strongly support the assertion of others (Coleman, Strapko, Zubrzycki & Broach, 1993; Ellis, 2007; Kamano, 2005; Liddle, 2005) of the need for specifically LGB space and provision, community and connection outside of mainstream settings.

THE LIVES OF LESBIANS, GAY MEN AND BISEXUALS: BEYOND HOMOPHOBIA?

Despite major positive changes in the extent to which LGB people are included within and integrated into mainstream society legislatively and socially, the findings of this study seem to suggest that there are limitations to this inclusion. The analysis presented here identified three contemporary issues in the lives of lesbians and gay men:

1. (Homophobic) harassment and discrimination in the workplace.
2. A lack of legal and social recognition of same-sex relationships.
3. The absence of a visible LGBT community.

All three issues highlight the way in which LGB people continue to be marginalized within mainstream society. They also indicate that fundamentally, homophobia is still a significant issue in the lives of LGB people.

In the case of workplace discrimination, although relatively recent, the Employment Equality (Sexual Orientation) Regulations are designed to protect LGB people from

---

[9] Hebden Bridge is a small town in the Pennine Hills, West Yorkshire, England alleged to have the highest number of lesbians per head of population in the UK (Bindel, 2004). It has historical associations with lesbian separatism.

[10] *Diva* is a UK-based mainstream commercial magazine for lesbians.

discrimination at work. While the legislation had only just been instituted when the interviews for this study took place, it would be reasonable to assume that legislation alone is insufficient to ensure that homophobic discrimination does not occur in the workplace (see Harding & Peel, Chapter 12). Likewise, although many workplaces have developed substantive policies to support this legislation (see, for example, the documentation at http://www.shu.ac.uk/university/diversity/sexual.html) this also does not in itself ensure that harassment and discrimination will not occur, and that it will be managed appropriately when it does. Furthermore, when much of the homophobia encountered in the workplace is seen by heterosexual (and sometimes other LGB) employees as 'a joke' or 'friendly banter' it often passes unnoticed or is explained away (e.g. see Taulke-Johnson & Rivers, 1999, p. 82). When constructed in this way, it can be difficult to define such incidents as homophobia (Epstein, 1997) and consequently they often go unchecked. Specific attention therefore needs to be paid to ensuring that the workplace climate is 'LGB-friendly'. Likewise, issues such as the right to be out (or not), the right to be able to access information, and the right to equal benefits – whether covered by legislation and non-discrimination policy or not – need to be monitored if real social change is to occur.

The issue of relationship recognition has (since these interviews took place) been partially addressed by legislative change through the UK Civil Partnerships Act. This act is not ideal, however, in that it maintains an apartheid system where same-sex relationships are treated as different from, and unequal to, heterosexual relationships. As outlined by Kitzinger & Wilkinson (2004; see also Wilkinson & Kitzinger, 2005) marriage is widely recognized and socially understood, whereas civil partnership does not have a pre-existing social status and consequently is perceived as different and inferior. Nevertheless, many of the issues raised by participants in this study (e.g. pension rights, inheritance rights) will be addressed through this and other legislation. However, like discrimination at work, legal recognition alone cannot ensure that same-sex couples will be afforded *social* recognition, particularly given the uncertain and differential social status implied by the two-tier system. Although it has been argued elsewhere (Ellis, 2002) that positive change at an individual or social level is often mobilized by affirmative policy and legislation, relying solely on legal recognition to bring about social change is problematic. It is therefore imperative that homophobic discrimination is also challenged on a social level.

I now want to turn to the third issue raised in this study, the absence of a visible LGBT community. This is not a legislative issue, but one solely about social inclusion/exclusion. The analysis presented here clearly highlights both the importance of community to LGB people, and the way in which 'integrating' LGBT community into the mainstream has resulted in the maintenance of our marginalization. Our integration into mainstream society may be seen as a good thing, in that it has resulted in many mainstream services and organizations developing more inclusive practices. This has undoubtedly helped to break down some of the institutionalized prejudice that previously existed in the public, community and voluntary sectors. However, the cost of this has been the disappearance (or at best the commercialization) of specifically LGBT services, organizations and resources, and a distinct and affirming sense of community. This is tantamount to removing the mosques, halal shops and other markers of cultural and ethnic difference from Britain, and expecting ethnic minority individuals to simply blend into mainstream British society.

When we look at the impact of integration on the lives of individual LGB people our so-called 'integration' starts to look very much like what cross-cultural psychologists call assimilation (see Ghuman, 1998). The main problem is that integration buys into the notion of sameness (i.e. that lesbians and gay men are 'just like' heterosexuals) rather than celebrating difference and highlighting the way in which we are both different from – and our oppression distinguishes us from – heterosexuals. In particular, it reduces the difference between LGB people and heterosexuals to one of sexual preference, thus ignoring the very real social and structural differences between us (see Clarke, 2002a for a detailed discussion of the politics of sameness versus difference arguments). We therefore need to ask ourselves do we want to be subsumed into the mainstream or (to some extent) to be respected but separate?

In essence, LGBT community is socially and culturally distinct, and too often being 'integrated' means *being* like heterosexuals, blending in, or even 'passing'. One of the consequences of being 'included' in the mainstream is that existing power relationships are reproduced and that *real* social change is simply an illusion. Despite there being significant benefits legislatively and socially, the wholesale mainstreaming of LGB lifestyles is detrimental to our well-being, both individually and as a community, and therefore antithetical to the liberation agenda (cf. Jeffreys, 2003). This is because assimilation simply addresses the issues, needs and concerns of the dominant group, providing little opportunity to challenge that agenda and organize around LGB-centred agendas (Clarke, 2002a).

Considerable progress has been made in terms of positive social change for LGB people. Historically, we have experienced different levels of social inclusion and have responded to these by arguing for change in different ways. For example, in the 1970s, lesbians responded to their exclusion from the mainstream (both as lesbians and as women) by establishing women-centred communities; while the gay-liberation movement centred on establishing 'gay'-centred communities. With greater inclusion of LGB lifestyles and culture within mainstream society the goal-posts shifted and the need for a separate community became less salient. So, lesbians and gay men (often along with bisexuals and trans people) set aside our political differences and developed combined communities within the mainstream. Over time we have gradually become subsumed into that mainstream as a commodity (or niche market). With heightened invisibility and increased isolation perhaps it is time to re-evaluate the extent to which we want to be separate from or integrated into mainstream society.

REFERENCES

Adelman, M. (1990). Stigma, gay lifestyles, and adjustment to aging: A study of later-life gay men and lesbians. *Journal of Homosexuality*, **20**(3–4), 7–32.

Biaggio, M., Orchard, S., Larson, J., Petrino, K. & Mihara, R. (2003). Guidelines for gay/lesbian/bisexual-affirmative educational practices in graduate psychology programs. *Professional Psychology: Research and Practice*, **34**(5), 548–544.

Bindel, J. (2004). Location, location, orientation. *The Guardian*, 27 March.

Binnie, J. & Skeggs, B. (2004). Cosmopolitan knowledge and the production and consumption of sexualised space: Manchester's gay village. *The Sociological Review*, **52**(1), 39–61.

Braun, V. & Clarke, V. (2006). Using thematic analysis in psychology. *Qualitative Research in Psychology*, **3**(2), 77–101.

Chrobot-Mason, D., Button, S. B. & DiClementi, J. D. (2001). Sexual identity management strategies: An exploration of antecedents and consequences. *Sex Roles*, **45**(5–6), 321–336.

Ciasullo, A. M. (2001). Making her (in)visible: Cultural representations of lesbianism and the lesbian body in the 1990s. *Feminist Studies*, **27**(3), 577–608.

Clarke, V. (2002a). Sameness and difference in research on lesbian parenting. *Journal of Community & Applied Social Psychology*, **12**(3), 210–222.

Clarke, V. (2002b). Resistance and normalization in the construction of lesbian and gay families: A discursive analysis. In A. Coyle, & C. Kitzinger (Eds), *Lesbian & Gay Psychology: New perspectives* (pp. 98–116). Leicester: BPS Blackwell.

Clarke, V. & Kitzinger, C. (2004). Lesbian and gay parents on talk shows: Resistance or collusion in heterosexism. *Qualitative Research in Psychology*, **1**(3), 195–217.

Clarke, V., Finlay, S. J. & Wilkinson, S. (2004). Special Issue on Marriage II. *Feminism & Psychology: An International Journal*, **14**(1).

Clarke, V., Burgoyne, C. & Burns, M. (2006). Just a piece of paper? A qualitative exploration of same-sex couples' multiple conceptions of civil partnership and marriage. *Lesbian & Gay Psychology Review*, **7**(2), 141–161.

Coleman, E., Strapko, N., Zubrzycki, M. R. & Broach, C. L. (1993). Social and psychological needs of lesbian mothers. *Canadian Journal of Human Sexuality*, **2**(1), 13–17.

Cowie, H. & Rivers, I. (2000). Going against the grain: Supporting lesbian, gay and bisexual clients as they 'come out'. *British Journal of Guidance & Counselling*, **28**(4), 503–513.

Croteau, J. M. (1996). Research on the work experiences of lesbian, gay, and bisexual people: An integrative review of methodology and findings. *Journal of Vocational Behavior*, **48**(2), 195–209.

D'Augelli, A. R. (1994). *Identity Development and Sexual Orientation: Toward a model of lesbian, gay, and bisexual development*. San Francisco, CA: Jossey-Bass.

D'Augelli, A. R. & Garnets, L. D. (1995). Lesbian, gay and bisexual communities. In A. R. D'Augelli & C. J. Patterson (Eds), *Lesbian, Gay, and Bisexual Identities over the Lifespan: Psychological perspectives* (pp. 293–320). New York: Oxford University Press.

Day, N. E. & Schoenrade, P. (2000). The relationship among reported disclosure of sexual orientation, anti-discrimination policies, top management support and work attitudes of gay and lesbian employees. *Personnel Review*, **29**(3), 346–363.

Dietz, T. J. & Dettlaff, A. (1997). The impact of membership in a support group for gay, lesbian, and bisexual students. *Journal of College Student Psychotherapy*, **12**(1), 57–72.

Eliason, M. J. (1996). A survey of the campus climate for lesbian, gay, and bisexual university members. *Journal of Psychology & Human Sexuality*, **8**(4), 39–58.

Ellis, S. J. (2002). Student support for lesbian and gay human rights: Findings from a large-scale questionnaire study. In A. Coyle & C. Kitzinger (Eds), *Lesbian and Gay Psychology: New perspectives* (pp. 239–254). Leicester: BPS/Blackwell.

Ellis, S. J. (2007). Community in the 21st century: Issues arising from a study of British lesbians and gay men. *Journal of Gay & Lesbian Psychotherapy*.

Ellis, S. J. & Kitzinger, C. (2002). Denying equality: An analysis of arguments against lowering the age of consent for sex between men. *Journal of Community & Applied Social Psychology*, **12**(3), 167–180.

Epstein, D. (1997). Keeping them in their place: Hetero/sexist harassment, gender and the enforcement of heterosexuality. In A. M. Thomas & C. Kitzinger (Eds), *Sexual Harassment: Contemporary feminist perspectives* (pp. 154–171). Buckingham: Open University Press.

Epstein, D., O'Flynn, S. & Telford, D. (2003). *Silenced Sexualities in Schools and Universities*. Stoke-on-Trent: Trentham Books.

Esterberg, K. G. (1996). Gay cultures, gay communities: The social organization of lesbians, gay men and bisexuals. In R. C. Savin-Williams & K. M. Cohen (Eds), *The Lives of Lesbians, Gays and Bisexuals* (pp. 377–392). Fort Worth, TX: Harcourt Brace.

Evans, N. J. & Broido, E. M. (2002). The experiences of lesbian and bisexual women in college residence halls: Implications for addressing homophobia and heterosexism. *Journal of Lesbian Studies*, **6**(3–4), 29–42.

Fassinger, R. E. (1996). Notes from the margins: Integrating lesbian experience into the vocational psychology of women. *Journal of Vocational Behavior*, **48**(2), 160–175.

Gamson, J. (1998). *Freaks Talk Back: Tabloid talk shows and sexual nonconformity*. Chicago, IL: Chicago University Press.

Ghuman, P. A. S. (1998). Ethnic identity and acculturation of south Asian adolescents: A British perspective. *International Journal of Adolescence and Youth*, **7**(3), 227–247.

Golombok, S. & Tasker, F. (1994). Children in lesbian and gay families: Theories and evidence. *Annual Review of Sex Research*, **5**, 73–100.

Green, S. F. (1997). *Urban Amazons: Lesbian feminism and beyond in the gender, sexuality and identity battles of London*. Basingstoke: Macmillan.

Griffin, C. & Zukas, M. (1993). Coming out in psychology: Lesbian psychologists talk. *Feminism & Psychology*, **3**(1), 111–133.

Grossman, A. H., D'Augelli, A. R. & Hershberger, S. L. (2000). Social support networks of lesbian, gay, and bisexual adults 60 years of age and older. *Journals of Gerontology: Series B: Psychological Sciences and Social Sciences*, **55**(3), 171–179.

Groves, P. A. (1985). Coming out: Issues for the therapist working with women in the process of lesbian identity formation. *Women & Therapy*, **4**(2), 17–22.

Harding, R. & Peel, E. (2006). 'We do'? International perspectives on equality, legality and same sex relationships. *Lesbian & Gay Psychology Review*, **7**(2), 123–140.

Harper, G. W. & Schneider, M. (2003). Oppression and discrimination among lesbian, gay, bisexual, and transgendered people and communities: A challenge for community psychology. *American Journal of Community Psychology*, **31**(3–4), 243–252.

Hayes, N. (2000). *Doing Psychological Research: Gathering and analysing data*. Buckingham: Open University Press.

Heaphy, B., Yip, A. K. T. & Thompson, D. (2004). Ageing in a non-heterosexual context. *Ageing & Society*, **24**(6), 881–902.

Hegarty, P., Pratto, F. & Lemieux, A. F. (2004). Heterosexist ambivalence and heterocentric norms: Drinking in intergroup discomfort. *Group Processes & Intergroup Relations*, **7**(2), 119–130.

Herek, G. M. & Berrill, K. T. (1990). Documenting the victimization of lesbians and gay men: Methodological issues. *Journal of Interpersonal Violence*, **5**(3), 301–315.

Holt, M. & Griffin, C. (2003). Being gay, being straight and being yourself: Local and global reflections on identity, authenticity and the lesbian and gay scene. *European Journal of Cultural Studies*, **6**(3), 404–425.

International Gay and Lesbian Human Rights Commission (1998). *1997 year in review*. Retrieved 7 July 1998, from http://www.iglhrc.org/97review.html

Irwin, J. (2002). Discrimination against gay men, lesbians and transgendered people working in education. *Journal of Gay & Lesbian Social Services*, **14**(2), 65–77.

Jeffreys, S. (2003). *Unpacking Queer Politics*. Cambridge: Polity.

Kamano, S. (2005). Entering the lesbian world in japan: Debut stories. In E. Rothblum & P. Sablove (Eds), *Lesbian Communities: Festivals, RVs, and the internet* (pp. 11–30). Binghamton, NY: Harrington Park Press.

Katzen, H. (1997). Valuing our differences: The recognition of lesbian and gay relationships. *Australian and New Zealand Journal of Family Therapy*, **18**(1), 1–9.

Kitzinger, C. (1987). *The Social Construction of Lesbianism*. Thousand Oaks, CA: Sage.

Kitzinger, C. (1991). Lesbians and gay men in the workplace: Psychosocial issues. In M. Davidson & J. Earnshaw (Eds), *Vulnerable Workers: Psychosocial and legal issues* (pp. 224–240). London: Wiley.

Kitzinger, C. (1996). Speaking of oppression: Psychology, politics, and the language of power. In E. D. Rothblum & L. A. Bond (Eds), *Preventing Heterosexism and Homophobia* (pp. 3–19). Thousand Oaks, CA: Sage.

Kitzinger, C. & Perkins, R. (1993). *Changing our Minds: Lesbian feminism and psychology*. London: Onlywomen Press.

Kitzinger, C. & Wilkinson, S. (1995). Transitions from heterosexuality to lesbianism: The discursive production of lesbian identities. *Developmental Psychology*, **31**(1), 95–104.

Kitzinger, C. & Wilkinson, S. (2004). The re-branding of marriage: Why we got married instead of registering a civil partnership. *Feminism & Psychology*, **14**(1), 127–150.

Lannutti, P. J. (2005). For better or worse: Exploring the meanings of same-sex marriage within the lesbian, gay, bisexual and transgendered community. *Journal of Social and Personal Relationships*, **22**(1), 5–18.

Levine, M. P. & Leonard, R. (1984). Discrimination against lesbians in the work force. *Signs*, **9**(4), 700–710.

Liddle, K. (2005). More than a bookstore: The continuing relevance of feminist bookstores for the lesbian community. In E. Rothblum & P. Sablove (Eds), *Lesbian Communities: Festivals, RVs, and the internet* (pp. 145–159). Binghamton, NY: Harrington Park Press.

MacBride-Stewart, S. (2004). Dental dams: A parody of straight expectations in the promotion of 'safer' lesbian sex. In D. W. Riggs & G. A. Walker (Eds), *Out in the Antipodes: Australian and New Zealand perspectives on gay and lesbian issues in psychology* (pp. 368–391). Bentley, Western Australia: Brightfire.

Markowe, L. (2002). Coming out as lesbian. In A. Coyle & C. Kitzinger (Eds), *Lesbian and Gay Psychology: New perspectives* (pp. 63–80). Leicester: BPS Blackwell.

McCarthy, L. (2000). Poppies in a wheat field: Exploring the lives of rural lesbians. *Journal of Homosexuality*, **39**(1), 75–94.

Oswald, R. F. & Culton, L. S. (2003). Under the rainbow: Rural gay life and its relevance for family providers. *Family Relations: Interdisciplinary Journal of Applied Family Studies*, **52**(1), 72–81.

Peel, E. & Harding, R. (2004). Divorcing romance, rights and radicalism: Beyond pro and anti in the lesbian and gay marriage debate. *Feminism & Psychology*, **14**(4), 588–599.

Ragins, B. R. & Cornwell, J. M. (2001). Pink triangles: Antecedents and consequences of perceived workplace discrimination against gay and lesbian employees. *Journal of Applied Psychology*, **86**(6), 1244–1261.

Rivers, I. (1995). Mental-health issues among young lesbians and gay men bullied in school. *Health & Social Care in the Community*, **3**(6), 380–383.

Rostosky, S. S. & Riggle, E. D. B. (2002). 'Out' at work: The relation of actor and partner workplace policy and internalized homophobia to disclosure status. *Journal of Counseling Psychology*, **49**(4), 411–419.

Sanders, D., Kickler, K. & Croome, R. (1997). *Finding a place in international law*. Retrieved 24 August 1998, from http://www.ILGA.org/information/finding_a_place_in_international.htm

Schneider, M. S. (2001). *Toward a Reconceptualization of the Coming-out Process for Adolescent Females*. New York, NY: Oxford University Press.

Schneider, M. S. & Witherspoon, J. J. (2000). Friendship patterns among lesbian and gay youth: An exploratory study. *Canadian Journal of Human Sexuality*, **9**(4), 239–246.

Sears, J. T. (2002). The institutional climate for lesbian, gay and bisexual education faculty: What is the pivotal frame of reference. *Journal of Homosexuality*, **43**(1), 11–37.

Skelton, A. (1999). An inclusive higher education? Gay and bisexual make teachers and the cultural politics of sexuality. *International Journal of Inclusive Education*, **3**(3), 239–255.

Soloman, S., Rothblum, E. & Balsam, K. (2004). Pioneers in partnership: Lesbians and gay men in civil unions compared with those not in civil unions, and married heterosexual siblings. *Journal of Family Psychology*, **18**(2), 275–286.

Soloman, S., Rothblum, E. D. & Balsam, K. F. (2005). Money, housework, sex and conflict: Same-sex couples in civil unions, those not in civil unions and heterosexual married siblings. *Sex Roles*, **52**(9–10), 561–575.

Szymanski, D. M., Chung, Y. B. & Balsam, K. F. (2001). Psychosocial correlates of internalized homophobia in lesbians. *Measurement and Evaluation in Counseling and Development*, **34**(1), 27–38.

Taulke-Johnson, R. A. & Rivers, I. (1999). Providing a safe environment for lesbian, gay and bisexual students living in university accommodation. *Youth & Policy*, 64, 74–89.

Trade Unionists Against Section 28 (1989). *Out at Work: Campaigning for lesbian and gay rights*. London: Trade Unionists Against Section 28.

Valentine, G. & Skelton, T. (2003). Finding oneself, losing oneself: The lesbian and gay 'scene' as a paradoxical space. *International Journal of Urban and Regional Research*, **27**(4), 849–866.

van Hoye, G. & Lievens, F. (2003). The effects of sexual orientation on hirability ratings: An experimental study. *Journal of Business and Psychology*, **18**(1), 15–30.

van Reyk, P. (2004). Baby love: Gay donor father narratives of intimacy. In D. W. Riggs & G. A. Walker (Eds), *Out in the Antipodes: Australian and New Zealand perspectives on gay and lesbian issues in psychology* (pp. 146–166). Bentley, Western Australia: Brightfire.

Vincke, J. & van Heeringen, K. (2002). Confidant support and the mental wellbeing of lesbian and gay young adults: A longitudinal analysis. *Journal of Community & Applied Social Psychology*, **12**(3), 181–193.

Visser, G. (2003). Gay men, leisure space and South African cities: The case of Cape Town. *Geoforum*, **34**(1), 123–137.

Waites, M. (1998). Sexual citizens: Legislating the age of consent in Britain. In T. Carver & V. Mottier (Eds), *Politics of Sexuality: Identity, gender, citizenship* (pp. 25–35). London: Routledge.

Waites, M. (2005). *The Age of Consent: Young people, sexuality and citizenship*. London: Palgrave Macmillan.

Waldo, C. R. (1999). Working in a majority context: A structural model of heterosexism as minority stress in the workplace. *Journal of Counseling Psychology*, **46**(2), 218–232.

Warwick, I., Aggleton, P. & Douglas, N. (2001). Playing it safe: Addressing the emotional and physical health of lesbian and gay pupils in the UK. *Journal of Adolescence*, **24**(1), 129–140.

Weeks, J., Donovan, C. & Heaphy, B. (2001). *Same-sex Intimacies: Families of choice and other life experiments*. London: Routledge.

Weinstock, J. S. (Ed.). (1998). *Lesbian, Gay, Bisexual, and Transgender Friendships in Adulthood*. New York, NY: Oxford University Press.

Wilets, J. D. (1994). International human rights law and sexual orientation. *Hastings International and Comparative Law Review*, **18**(1), 1–120.

Wilkinson, S. & Kitzinger, C. (2005). Same-sex marriage and equality. *Psychologist*, **18**(5), 290–293.

Yip, A. K. T. (2004). Same-sex marriage: Contrasting perspectives among lesbian, gay and bisexual Christians. *Feminism & Psychology*, **14**(1), 173–180.

CHAPTER 15

Striving for Holistic Success: How Lesbians Come Out on Top

Faith Rostad
Surrey School District, British Columbia, Canada
and
Bonita C. Long
University of British Columbia, Canada

INTRODUCTION

Despite the prevalence of discrimination against employees who are lesbian, gay, bisexual and transgendered (LGBT) or simply appear to be (for a review see Croteau, 1996), some have become leaders in their field and are acknowledged as prominent, high-achieving individuals. Considering that LGBT individuals have a long history of discrimination and oppression in work and educational environments, their success is surprising. Research on the career development of LGBT populations has been limited (e.g. Chung, 1995; Lonborg & Phillips, 1996); however, theoretically-oriented writing on career development has identified several issues associated with the difficulties LGBT people may experience, including sexual identity development, barriers related to sexual orientation and sexual identity management (e.g. Fassinger, 1996; Irwin, 2002; Skelton, 2000). How LGBT individuals overcome these difficulties has remained unexplored.

As a young adult or adolescent, LGBT individuals may limit or abandon career choices as a consequence of the turmoil associated with sexual identity development (Fassinger, 1996, see also Monsen & Bailey, Chapter 19). Moreover, LGBT individuals may face external barriers to their career decision-making (e.g. discrimination, lack of social support), which may block career alternatives and restrict choices as a result of fear or need for safety (Chur-Hansen, 2004; Irwin, 2002; Morrow, Gore & Campbell, 1996; Skelton, 1999). Finally, how LGBT individuals handle self-disclosure of their sexual orientation may also affect their career success. Although some LGBT individuals may choose to 'pass' as heterosexual, others may disclose their orientation in the workplace.

Out in Psychology: Lesbian, gay, bisexual, trans and queer perspectives. Edited by Victoria Clarke and Elizabeth Peel.
© 2007 John Wiley & Sons, Ltd.

Disclosing may have major repercussions on one's career, whereas passing may affect an individuals overall well-being (Humphrey, 1999; Prince, 1995; Raven, 2001).

Although LGBT issues are increasingly visible in western popular culture, anti-LGBT attitudes are still held in North America (Yang, 1999), as they are around the world. As a consequence of this bias, individuals who are outside this norm often lack the same privileges, particularly in their work. Several studies have found that employed LGBT individuals who experienced homophobia at work had reductions in perceived productivity, job satisfaction, organizational and career commitment, and organization-based self-esteem, as well as increases in perceived health problems, psychological distress and turnover intensions (Button, 2004; Humphrey, 1999; Ragins & Cornwell, 2001; Waldo, 1999). For example, Kitzinger's (1991) study revealed that lesbian and gay individuals in the UK continually faced decisions about the safety of revealing their sexual orientation and frequently concealed their sexual identity by introducing their lovers as friends and by changing pronouns. Thus, non-affirming organizational settings where homophobia is prevalent or tolerated is likely to be a major factor in limiting occupational success.

Although LGBT persons share the experience of sexual discrimination, a lesbian's occupational experience is influenced by both sexual and gender-based marginalization. Thus, in contrast with other less visible marginalized women, such as bisexual and transgendered women, lesbians may experience sexual and gender discrimination that affects their occupational success in unique ways. Despite multiple barriers, lesbians have become successful high achievers. For example, Ellen Degeneres, the star of a popular American sitcom in which she played herself, an 'out' lesbian, has gone on to host her own successful talk show called *Ellen*. In Canada, Prime Minister Paul Martin appointed Nancy Ruth, the well-known lesbian and feminist activist, to the Senate and, in the UK, Angela Mason was appointed Director of the Women and Equality Unit, following a lifetime of campaigning for LGBT civil rights. Thus, in the present study, we focus on the occupational success of lesbians, although some of the findings may relate to gay, bisexual and transgendered individuals (e.g. Button, 2004; Croteau, 1996; Irwin, 2002).

Occupational Success

To address the confusion surrounding the terms 'career' and 'occupation,' for the purposes of this study, the term occupation refers to paid employment or work. Whereas the terms career and 'career development' are used in reference to distinct theories and subsume the terms occupation and 'occupational success'. The lack of research on lesbians' occupational success implies that their career development does not differ from that of women in general, and ignores aspects of the career process that may be unique to lesbians. In an attempt to address the existing lacunae in the career development literature, in the present study we used a qualitative research methodology to develop a theoretical framework that explicates the occupational success of notable lesbians in Canada.

The concept of occupational success has many meanings that may differ for men and women and within men and women, as well as by social class, culture and sexual orientation. Definitions of occupational success vary considerably and range from intrinsic success (e.g. job satisfaction) to extrinsic success (e.g. salary, promotion, hierarchical position). Extrinsic organizational indicators of success may tell us little about the psychological or intrinsic, subjective perceptions of women's own success (Betz & Fitzgerald, 1987). Subjective feelings of success are a combination of the evaluations of significant others, self-evaluations compared with co-workers, and self-evaluations of career expectations (Frye, 1984). Frye concluded that self-perceptions of success are more highly related to satisfaction than objective criteria of success, such as salary. However, neither extrinsic nor intrinsic indicators of success account for the impact of broader social, political and institutional contexts on LGBT individuals' work experience.

Traditional definitions of career success that reflect white, male, middle-class standards of excellence have been criticized because they are not representative of the experiences of women or other minority groups (e.g. Fassinger & Richie, 1994). To address this problem, a research programme in the USA, the National Study of Women's Achievement (Fassinger, 2002), investigated the career development of more than 100 prominent women that include black African American women as well as white women (Richie et al., 1997), Asian American women (Prosser, Chopra & Fassinger, 1998), and women with disabilities (Noonan et al., 2004). The women in these studies were identified as successful, high achieving, or prominent by national organizations or the media. To date, results of this programme of research have suggested that predominantly non-linear career paths and exceptional ability to transform a challenge into an opportunity; extensive experiences with oppression; notable perseverance; dedication to work; reliance on internal standards of judgement; a wide variety of familial, cultural, educational and socio-political influences; supportive relationships; and a myriad of strategies for stress management are all factors that effect occupational success.

Career Theories: Context

Although traditional career theorists once equated career with paid employment and neglected non-work activities (e.g. Astin, 1984), more recent theorists have expanded existing definitions of career beyond paid employment to consider contextual factors (e.g. socio-cultural and political conditions). Three models of women's career development provided by Gomez et al. (2001), Poole and Langan-Fox (1997), and Richie et al. (1997), are particularly relevant to the present investigation because they explored the interactions amongst contextual, cultural and personal variables in the career development of several diverse populations. For example, Gomez et al. (2001) investigated the career development and success of 20 notable Latinas (i.e. women of Hispanic origin). Poole and Langan-Fox (1997) examined the careers, life satisfaction, and success of young Australian women ($n = 1489$) who were at the beginning of their careers (age 17), following them to age 35. Finally, Richie et al. (1997) investigated the career development of 18 prominent, high-achieving black African American and white women in the USA. Of note, across these studies, the authors found that socio-cultural and political conditions influenced the success of the women in their studies.

Gomez et al. (2001) posited that macro- and micro-environmental factors can either limit or facilitate vocational behaviours and are helpful in understanding the unique social and political context in which women operate. For example, they found that notable Latina women experienced challenges, barriers and support systems specific to their Latina cultural background. Moreover, political movements (e.g. Chicano [an ethnic minority group of Mexican Americans], and the Women's Movement) strongly influenced and supported the career development of many Latinas. These factors are particularly important in understanding lesbians' career success because the socio-cultural and political context of their work experience differs from that of women in general and other minority groups in several ways.

As members of a stigmatized group, whose membership is not readily apparent, lesbians, as well as gay, bisexual and transgendered people must decide whether to reveal their sexual identity in the workplace or to their colleagues and clients, often fearing homophobia if they do so (Croteau, 1996; Kitzinger, 1991; Prince, 1995; Raven, 2001). This decision is complex and involves careful strategizing (Button, 2004; Cody & Welch, 1997; Kitzinger, 1991; Shachar & Gilbert, 1983; Waldo & Kemp, 1997). In contrast, those who choose to remain closeted often employ elaborate coping strategies (e.g. avoidance, passing as heterosexual) to maintain their invisibility (Cody & Welch, 1997; Griffith & Hebl, 2002; Raven, 2001; Waldo & Kemp, 1997). In addition, sexual identity development is a process that may interact with the career development process (Boatwright, Gilbert, Forrest & Ketzenberger, 1996; Button, 2004; Woods, 1993). Lesbians who are preoccupied with the exploration of their sexual identity may neglect occupational planning or minimize their occupational choices in order to accommodate their sexual identity, potentially hindering their career success (Fassinger, 1996; Tomlinson & Fassinger, 2003). In addition, their sexuality may necessitate economic self-reliance; and for lesbian families, careers are mutually developed, as gender difference is not a factor in determining employment (Dunne, 2000). Finally, lesbians may be less likely than heterosexual men to have access to mentors and role models, a factor cited by career theorists as having a negative impact on the career development of women in particular (Fassinger, 1996).

In the Canadian workforce, LGBT individuals have legal protection under the Canadian Human Rights Code and sexual orientation became a prohibited ground for discrimination in 1992 (Casswell, 1996). Similar to Canada, the New Zealand Human Rights Act includes protection based on sexual orientation, and in Australia, several states (e.g. New South Wales, South Australia) prohibit discrimination based on sexual orientation (Sexuality Information and Education Council of the United States, 1999). Currently only 12 states in the USA prohibit employment discrimination on the basis of sexual orientation (for both private and public employees). In the UK, The Employment Equality Regulations of 2003 prohibit discrimination in employment and vocational training based on sexual orientation (Department of Trade and Industry, 2005, see also Harding & Peel, Chapter 12). Despite their legal status, many employed lesbians, as well as gay men, bisexuals and transgendered persons continue to feel stigmatized and fear discrimination (e.g. Irwin, 2002; Raven, 2001).

In summary, the limited literature on lesbians' career development has identified important cultural and contextual factors that may contribute to career success; however, to date this literature has been mostly atheoretical and anecdotal and has a narrow focus on barriers and middle-class, white Americans (Croteau, 1996; Fassinger, 1996). Notably absent is attention to facilitative factors that may contribute to lesbians' (and gay men's, bisexuals' and transgendered people's) occupational success, despite the barriers they face. In the present study, we interviewed notable lesbians – women who had made an impact on their respective occupational fields. By studying lesbians who have achieved in their fields, despite multiple challenges, facilitates the identification of successful career strategies and healthy career development, despite sexual orientation.

METHOD

Grounded theory (Strauss & Corbin, 1998), a qualitative method, was chosen to describe and develop the concepts related to lesbians becoming successful in their occupations. Grounded theory is a comprehensive method of data collection and analytic procedures aimed at developing concepts and ultimately theory that is grounded in the data and developed directly from participants' experiences. We used in-depth semi-structured interviews and the grounded theory method of data analysis because we wanted to discover an emergent framework constructed from, and therefore grounded in the words and experiences of lesbians.

Participants

Volunteers were recruited from within the lesbian community in a large urban centre in Western Canada. The initial selection criteria focused on women identified by lesbian organizations as leaders in their fields (i.e. having influenced their field, community or society) and who self-identified as lesbians even though they may not have been open about their sexuality at work. All participants ($n = 15$) were attained through word of mouth, a strategy known as snowball sampling (Morse, 1991), having heard of the study from friends and individuals from the lesbian community.

The women ranged in age from 35 to 69 years ($M = 48$) and were employed in eight occupational fields (athletics, education, law/politics, business, arts, police, dentistry and medicine). The majority of the women made 2–7 occupational changes throughout their careers because of new opportunities, however, three (20.0%) women were fired, which they believed was directly related to their lesbianism, and several moved to work environments that they perceived as LGBT friendly. Thirteen (86.7%) women were white, one was First Nations (i.e. Canadian Native Indian) and one was Asian Canadian. The majority ($n = 12$; 80.0%) of these women were in relationships and considered their present work environment as LGBT friendly. Thirteen (86.7%) were out at work and two (13.3%) were selectively out at the time of the interviews. The women's annual salary ranged from $40000 (i.e. $32000 US, $41400 Australian, or £17000) to $175000 Canadian (i.e. $140200 US, $181000 Australian, or £75000) with the average $86000 ($68000 US, $90000 Australian, or £37370). Six (40.0%) participants had post-graduate degrees, five (33.3%) had undergraduate degrees or were working towards them, two (13.3%) had professional degrees (law, medicine), and two (13.3%) had only a high school education. The majority ($n = 13$; 86.7%) considered themselves privileged, because of their economic status, education level or employment.

Procedures

For the respondents who met the criteria, a convenient place (e.g. their homes, workplace) was identified where a semi-structured interview (which was audio-taped), lasting approximately 1½ hours, was held. At the beginning of each interview, participants read and signed an informed consent form. The initial interviews were conducted between February 2000 and May 2001. The interview questions were formulated from a review of the literature and experience with the phenomenon (after Hollingsworth, Tomlinson & Fassinger, 1997, see Appendix, p. 327). Open-ended questions were used to avoid imposing existing constructs and to facilitate probing deeper to uncover new dimensions of the process of lesbians becoming successful. Later interviews became more focused in order to explore particular concepts and to determine their inclusion in the evolving description of lesbians becoming successful in their occupations. Follow-up interviews were conducted with six of the initial participants who were chosen because they represented a variety of experiences. They were asked to comment on the developing categories, and whether anything was unclear or did not fit for them. Based on their responses, three paths were further articulated, *working 'in' silence, working quietly*, and *boldly 'out' spoken*.

Data Analysis

The basic principles and procedures of the grounded theory method were used to analyse the data, which included transcribed interviews and memos (Strauss & Corbin, 1998). Memos were written immediately after each interview, and when reviewing audiotapes and reading the transcriptions. Three major types of coding procedures were used: open coding, axial coding and selective coding, each level progressively represented the gleaning of a more abstract view of the data. Open coding was employed in which the text was broken down into discrete parts (e.g. phrases, sentences) and code names were generated that reflected the essence of what was articulated. Open coding was done after each interview, prior to conducting the next interview. The results of this initial coding guided the following interviews (i.e. theoretical sampling).

Code names were systematically grouped that seemed to relate to the same phenomenon but at a more abstract level. These code names were compared with one another for similarities and differences and then were grouped into categories. Axial coding was employed to determine relationships amongst the code names, and was used to group code names into higher order key categories. This process led to the development of the constructs, which in turn, generated more questions and further data collection and analysis. As the concepts that emerged from the analysis became more and more cohesive, selective coding was employed, which involved integrating and refining constructs. At this level of analysis, the focus was on constructs and relationships that seemed core to the experience. *Striving for holistic success* was eventually developed as the core or central construct.

In the following description of the model, direct quotations from the lesbians are used for illustrative purposes. Italicized words represent participants' emphasis. All participants are identified by pseudonyms they selected. Following Richie et al. (1997), responses are discussed according to the following descriptors: (1) the words *generally, most, often, the majority, typically, many*, or *the women in this study* indicate a response characteristic of the majority (eight or more) of the participants; (2) the words *some, a number of*, or *several* indicate responses from three to seven participants; and (3) the words *a few* indicate responses from one or two participants.

FINDINGS

The emergent model explained the career success of 15 notable lesbians and is illustrated in Figure 15.1. The basic core process is conceptualized as a process of *striving for holistic integration*. The specific way that the women *manage their lesbian identity at work* is the beginning of this endeavour and is represented within a circle of contextual conditions. Based on the women's strategies for managing their lesbian identity, they engaged in:

* *taking risks and coming out*
* *working 'in' silence*
* *working quietly*
* *boldly 'out' spoken*
* *facing ongoing fear*

Figure 15.1 Conceptual ordering of the process of 'striving for holistic integration'

- *handling homophobia*
- *fighting for social change*
- *holistic integration*

Striving for holistic integration consists of processes that are affected by and enacted within the following contextual conditions: (1) *changing social times* (i.e. 1930 to present), (2) *personal background*, (3) *serendipitous conditions* (e.g. being in the right place at the right time), (4) *love and support*, and (5) *a LGBT-friendly work environment*. This basic process was affected by the changing social times that exerted an influence on participants' personal background and serendipitous conditions, which in turn, affected the current context of participants' lives, which included love and support, and a LGBT-friendly work environment. These changing conditions interacted synergistically, continuously influencing lesbians striving for holistic integration.

Managing Lesbian Identity in the Workplace

For the lesbians in the present study, the first step in the process of striving for holistic integration was managing their lesbian identity as it related to their work. For many, this involved appraising the situation to determine its potential threat, harm, or loss should they reveal their lesbian identity. For example, Leona appraised the consequences of being a lesbian as 'living in a tortured world, in a well of loneliness'. Early in their careers, many participants considered coming out at work as too risky. However, several women experienced managing their lesbian identity as more of a challenge than a threat, and subsequently were truthful and open about their lesbian identity, eventually becoming advocates for other lesbians by fighting for social change.

Taking Risks and Coming Out

Taking risks and coming out reflected ways the women managed their lesbian identity in their careers. The majority of the women were out at work at the time they were first interviewed. The process of taking risks is represented by a continuum of coming out at work, ranging from working 'in' silence to the boldly 'out' spoken path. Over time, participants shifted along this continuum as conditions changed (e.g. societal attitudes towards LGBT individuals, choosing to work in a LGBT-friendly work environment, being 'outed'). For example, Jan taught at a university and had her first lesbian novel published in the 1960s when it was illegal to be a lesbian. Because of the social times and the risk of losing her university position, Jan described how she dealt with this issue, 'as long as you were decorous and didn't make a fuss and were good at your work, people turned a blind eye'. This strategy, to work quietly, enabled her to write what she chose despite living and working in a social context where criminality and lesbianism were considered synonymous. Later in her career, Jan recalled the difficult decision to be boldly 'out' spoken with a piece of lesbian non-fiction she was writing. Having the love and support of family was a condition that facilitated Jan's decision to write the book that was her official public outing, despite the consequences.

Working 'In' Silence

Working 'in' silence was a path chosen early in the careers of several participants who feared they might face discrimination because of their lesbianism. Several participants began their careers in the early 1970s, a time Leona described as 'a deeply underground life in those days when people snuck around after dark and didn't tell anybody what they were doing'. Fear of sexual orientation discrimination and anti-LGBT harassment led a few participants to hide their lesbian identity at some point along their career path.

When Aggie began her career as an educator, it was not safe to come out because of the social climate at the time. Early in her career colleagues thought she was straight because she attended events with 'boyfriends'. Although Aggie felt she had no choice but to separate her work and private life, she thought 'that it cost me, because I didn't establish relationships with people within my work sphere'. Cowgirl found herself in a sport milieu with other lesbians who were not out, and managed her lesbian identity by working 'in' silence, but feeling the unspoken support of her lesbian team mates – a 'kind of supportive club'. Leona had a sense of being in two worlds and learning two languages (i.e. LGBT and straight) as a strategy to cope with and to hide her lesbian identity at work. In the 1980s, Haze feared coming out both personally and professionally, and made her relationship invisible to the outside world:

> I didn't tell anybody for a really long time, you know that whole fear thing; it was in the '80s for God's sake. But we still ran a two-bedroom house for the longest time. It wasn't until we had the puppies six years ago [that] we went down to a one-bedroom house.

A number of the women who began their careers working 'in' silence, eventually shifted along the continuum of taking risks and coming out. Several catalysts acted to catapult a few of them out of the closet at work. For example, Cowgirl initially chose the working 'in' silence path but after being fired from her position as head coach of a national team because of her lesbianism, she followed the boldly 'out' spoken path, acting as a lesbian spokesperson in the community and telling her story on national television. Negative rumours of Leona's lesbian identity acted as the catalyst for a pivotal turn along her occupational path in the police force. To her surprise, Leona received support from close work colleagues, which encouraged her to come out to other colleagues. For Leona, coming out at work was a turning point in her career because she no longer felt she had to expend considerable energy living a secret life. Rather, coming out represented an opportunity to be truthful and to focus new found energy on work.

Working Quietly

Working quietly within the system was a strategy that did not draw attention to the women's lesbian identity and thus cause embarrassment for themselves or their colleagues. Even though they maintained the status quo, some lesbians were able to move into positions of power that allowed them to make positive changes for women and LGBT individuals. A number of the women suspected that others knew about their lesbian identity, but it remained unspoken. These women did not try to hide the fact that they were lesbian, nor did they bring it up when it was not relevant to the task or topic at hand. For example,

Artemis, the psychologist, usually did not discuss her lesbian orientation with heterosexual clients because either it was irrelevant or it could be detrimental to their therapy. Overtime, several of the women felt more comfortable with being out at work and were less inclined to broadcast their lesbian identity, but to work quietly within the system. For example, Leona, the police officer, who experienced boldly coming out to her close colleagues after facing rumours, described how she chose to quietly handle the rumours and recalled the beneficial consequences of not waving her 'rainbow' flag (i.e. a LGBT pride symbol) and announcing her lesbian status:

> It's true that I went the quieter way, and it's true it had some major potholes in it, but I never would have been comfortable just leaping out in the middle and waving my flag no matter what happened. By handling the rumours quietly, I believe I earned even more respect instead of running and screaming to human rights [abuses].

Boldly 'Out' Spoken

The majority of women were primarily boldly 'out' spoken at work at the time of their interview. However, several of the participants felt that they had been boldly 'out' spoken about their lesbian identity right from the start of their career. In the early 1970s, Kathleen felt she was in a privileged environment for coming out because she was at the University of California, which was considered a lesbian Mecca. Similarly, Stella was boldly 'out' spoken at work as soon as she recognized her lesbianism. She attributed this to being in a stereotypical LGBT-friendly work environment (e.g. beauty salon), but also she believed that her personality demanded forthrightness: 'because of who I am, I tell it like it is, no bullshit, no secrets'. Reflecting on her career, Dad, the lawyer stated: 'I never thought I was straight, never pretended I was straight, so coming out for me wasn't sudden, it was always knowing and just always dealing with life on that basis'.

Several women were in careers that made them visible to the public. This visibility propelled them even further out. As they became known as lesbians, some women appeared in international, national, provincial and local media, where they either deliberately or inadvertently came out to the public at large. For example, Jan's work as an author outed her on the international scene. When her book became a successful movie, her notoriety reached an even wider audience, which she used to advocate for LGBT rights. Nina's career took a pivotal turn when one of her occupational roles included being the media spokesperson for the LGBT community, which was engaged in a lengthy battle for LGBT rights involving book censorship. Her visibility as an out lesbian became national, provincial and local news on a regular basis for over 15 years. Mia discussed the importance of being boldly 'out' spoken and challenging stereotypes in her work:

> I think it's very important for me to be visible and to be out. Because I think that if we still have stereotypes of who gays and lesbians are, that needs to be challenged. I think people are challenged when they see an Asian lesbian and I think people are challenged when they see a woman, a lesbian in a professional capacity, or in a senior capacity who is out, especially for young people.

Many participants discussed how fortunate they were to be born into a privileged family, society, or country with considerable intelligence, personality and opportunities. For example, Dad noted how her 'gifts' (e.g. emotional strength) helped her endure and beat breast cancer without interrupting or delaying her career. Lisa described herself as having a sense of resiliency, or a feeling of 'being capable of surviving'. This privilege was considered a powerful factor that helped several women cope with difficult circumstances throughout their careers and contributed to their determination to be boldly 'out' spoken at work.

The majority of participants noted how important being true to themselves had been for their career and that it facilitated their ability to follow the boldly 'out' spoken path. The process of being true often involved taking risks and being open about their lesbianism or simply speaking their minds on important issues they passionately believed in.

Facing Ongoing Fear

Although the women managed their lesbian identity by taking risks and coming out, most of them reported *facing ongoing fear*. This involved an element of uncertainty and threat, as the women were aware of the potential for negative reactions from others in the work environment. Facing ongoing fear was a process whereby participants continually had to make decisions regarding coming out to different people in different work contexts. This ongoing fear is portrayed well by Dad's analogy, 'It's what being black probably feels like. In most cases it's fine, but you never know what you might encounter'. As Leona moved along the continuum from working 'in' silence, to boldly 'out' spoken, to working quietly, she experienced the positive effects of facing her ongoing fears, which had silenced her for many years. Moreover, feeling safe and accepted as a lesbian in her work environment facilitated facing her ongoing fears:

> You lose the fear of being ridiculed, humiliated, embarrassed and persecuted. It just isn't there. Everything is so right that it's comforting. I've lost the worry I used to have about someone else's discomfort. You don't lose fear until you feel safe. There's a direct relationship, so, for fear to go away needs to come trust or belief that where you are in a safe place. Losing fear allows you to be true to yourself; allows you to stand up and be counted.

Two older participants (aged 53 and 62) decided to be boldly 'out' spoken from the beginning of their careers. As activists, they fought for social change and were considered pioneers in their work in this regard. Their early politicization may have been a factor that explained their route to success devoid of ongoing fear. For example, Kathleen recognized that she had the protection and safety of a large activist community, which empowered her to be fearless in her work as an out lesbian. Similarly, when Lisa began her career as a physician, she was in a social milieu that facilitated her involvement as a feminist and activist for women's rights. This early politicization combined with her prestigious position in the community may have contributed to her confidence and unwillingness to be driven by fear on route to her occupational success.

In contrast, several participants lived through painful circumstances and felt rejected when they took risks and came out at work. However, these women were able to face ongoing fear by turning 'obstacles into usefulness' by dealing directly with the problems they encountered. Facing ongoing fear included *handling homophobia* and *fighting for social change*. By facing ongoing fears associated with their careers, the lesbians became empowered and transformed. This transformation happened as these women took responsibility for their own role in coming out and stood up for their rights as lesbians.

Handling Homophobia

One of the consequences of facing ongoing fears for many of the women was handling homophobia, which encompassed the ways in which participants recognized and handled prejudice or bias by their colleagues, presumably because of their lesbianism. Kathleen encapsulated the meaning of homophobia by using the term 'lesbophobia' to define homophobia specific to lesbians:

> In my usage, 'lesbophobia,' fear of and hatred toward lesbians, is expressed in attitudes and actions based on prejudice. Widespread prejudice translates into social/political/economic discrimination, whereby dominate group's benefit at the expense of minority groups, which is institutionalized prejudice.

Many of the women faced lesbophobia, which was expressed in attitudes (e.g. rumours, harassment) and actions (e.g. loss of friends and family, hate mail, workplace being bombed), some of which led to discrimination (e.g. being fired, financial ruin, censored books). In addition, a few women reported that because they anticipated discrimination their fear of homophobia silenced them. Generally, the women addressed issues of homophobia directly by challenging the source. For example, two participants were fired from their jobs in the early 1980s, a time when they had no legal recourse because LGBT individuals were not yet protected under the Canadian Charter of Rights and Freedoms. Although legal protection for LGBT people was not in place at that time, one woman handled this situation successfully by standing up for herself and settling out of court. In contrast, another participant filed a complaint against her employer and requested same sex benefits in the 1990s, a move that was perceived by her colleagues as likely to limit her career. However, her case was successfully challenged, a sign of the changing social times that reflects the progress that has been made toward equality and freedom for LGBT people.

Several women handled homophobia by being open and honest, yet respectful of others' feelings when dealing with perceived bias and discrimination. Moreover, others were unrelenting about educating people and used humour to diffuse situations. Jan identified positive benefits that went along with successfully handling homophobia, 'a lot of the places of negative judgement, of silencing, in fact turned out to be places where you could hone your skill and your nerve, and your courage and insight'. Many other women chose to reframe a negative event by 'creating something positive'. For example, participants who were fired from their positions commented on the wonderful new opportunities that opened up for them as a consequence of experiencing discrimination.

Because of the emotional support provided by others, several women were able to overcome very painful experiences at work, which gave them the confidence and determination to continue striving in the face of adversity. Long-term relationships (i.e. 5–45 years) were experienced as providing the love and support needed to handle difficulties at work and to become successful in their careers. The women also handled homophobia by expanding their community through intimate, authentic relationships with those they came out to. In addition, many women sought support from the LGBT community and professional organizations.

It is important to note that a few women felt that they had never encountered homophobia. These women did not take potentially homophobic situations seriously or personally. Wadamga, an artist, said, 'I don't really notice it. I'm kind of oblivious to it. I'm aware that if something isn't working then I need to change it, but it's not going to stop me'. In contrast, Mia, an Asian Canadian who felt that she passes as heterosexual, did not feel that she had experienced discrimination at work. Although these women were not overt targets of homophobia, they dealt with homophobia at work by the way they responded to LGBT jokes and by fighting for LGBT rights.

Fighting for Social Change

Facing ongoing fear at work also involves fighting for social change for women and LGBT people. The interaction of conditions (e.g. LGBT-friendly work environment, changing social times, love and support) and coming out at work resulted in facing ongoing fear, which motivated participants to fight for social change in unique ways. Some women did not face ongoing fears but passionately fought for social change most of their lives. For these women, fighting for social change occurred at the individual as well as the broader societal level. It was often experienced as transformational for those who moved from working 'in' silence, to speaking out, and finally to making a difference for LGBT people in the workforce. Giving back to the LGBT community enhanced these women's feelings of pride about the changes they made to the work environment. The women's activities included public advocacy, running for public office, volunteering time and money to LGBT organizations, serving as role models for younger women and lesbians, and working directly with lesbian clients.

Holistic Integration

Many participants felt as though they lived in two separate worlds, a work world and a lesbian world, a split that seemed necessary to survive in a world perceived as homophobic. By facing their ongoing fears and feelings of fragmentation, many of the women experienced a sense of holistic integration. When these women felt safe, found their voice, spoke their truth and embraced previously cut off lesbian identities, they experienced holistic integration on several levels. In contrast, for a few women who did not feel that their work and lesbian lives were separate, holistic integration occurred early in their careers. Given that they had not experienced major obstacles in the work, striving for holistic integration felt smooth and natural.

Holistic integration was a continuous process as the conditions in the women's lives changed and new environments and social times influenced how they managed their lesbian identities at work. For several women, integrating their lesbian and work worlds was the result of being outed, but with positive consequences. For example, when Haze was outed by her partner's illness, she found her relationships with colleagues to be much more honest.

Many of the women felt that their lesbian identities enhanced their courage to be themselves and engage in occupational paths that led to success. For example, Jack chose to work harder as a shield against potential homophobia and said, 'In the end you feel that you are stronger in the face of discrimination to counter any of their claims'. By being open, Haze felt that 'it ends up giving you confidence, giving you passion and conviction in the life that you have chosen. By being truthful and forthright in your life, it breaks down barriers'.

DISCUSSION

The central process that is described in the present study specifies common aspects of the experiences of lesbians becoming successful. By employing the grounded theory method, we developed concepts that originate in the experiences of lesbians, rather than from heterosexuals on whom existing theories of women's career development are based.

Similar to many of the women's career development theories, the theoretical model of the process of striving for holistic integration includes both individual and environmental influences that affect occupational success (e.g. Astin, 1984; Fitzgerald & Betz, 1994). It is also congruent with the more recently developed models of women's career development (e.g. Gomez et al., 2001; Poole & Langan-Fox, 1997). All are dynamic, interactive personenvironment models of women's career development and career success that consider personal background and individual characteristics; as well as social, cultural and contextual variables. The present study identifies individual conditions (i.e. personal background, and love and support conditions), environmental conditions (i.e. LGBT-friendly work environment, serendipitous conditions), and cultural and contextual conditions (i.e. changing social times, discrimination, homophobia) that dynamically interact and influence the central process of striving for holistic integration that facilitated participants' occupational success as they integrated their lesbian and work worlds.

Lesbians in the present study experienced unique work-related experiences by virtue of their lesbian identities. Managing their lesbian identities at work was a crucial consideration that often involved purposeful decision-making and initiated the process of striving for holistic integration. The process extends personal and environmental models of women's career development by considering the influence of purpose and meaning in the unique context of these lesbians' lives. The process of becoming successful often involved finding meaning in the face of adversity and appraising benefit from undesirable circumstances, or 'turning obstacles into usefulness'. Some lesbians let go of untenable goals (e.g. coaching at the National level) because of homophobic circumstances and formulated new goals that ultimately created positive opportunities.

Several of the women in the study began their careers concealing their lesbian identity; however, over time all of the participants came out at work to varying degrees. Findings from the present study are consistent with other studies that found a strong relationship between being open about one's sexual orientation, and greater levels of support as well as job satisfaction (Humphrey, 1999; Jordan & Deluty, 1998; Morrow, Campbell & Beckstead, 1995). Although the women were well aware of the potential for discrimination or harassment because of their lesbianism, remaining silenced and invisible was perceived as costly to them personally and professionally. The potential for job loss or discrimination was real for these participants, however, the majority of them felt that they had proven themselves in their work, had chosen or created LGBT-friendly work environments, and were surrounded by loving and supportive people that helped them face ongoing fear and to continue to take risks and come out at work.

Empirical investigations have primarily focused on the coping strategies LGBT people employ at work in order to conceal their sexual identities; however, in the present study we identified coping strategies that were facilitative for an 'out' lesbian identity at work. The women in our study used strategies to deal with challenges at work that ranged from pursuing legal avenues to assertively voicing their concerns. For the women who felt they could change the situations they were in, congruent with stress theory, they directly challenged the source of distress (Lazarus & Folkman, 1984). On the other hand, participants who worked 'in' silence reported avoiding lesbian issues, evading social contact and seeking social support. In addition, many of the women used cognitive reframing strategies that focused on finding a positive way out of a negative situation, a coping strategy that has not been revealed in the extant literature.

Meaning-based coping helps the individual relinquish untenable goals and formulate new ones, find meaning in what has happened and appraise benefit where possible, even when the events have unsatisfactory outcomes (Folkman & Greer, 2000). In addition, this type of coping generates positive affect and motivates further coping. Many of the participants in this study who initially chose the working 'in' silence path were catapulted out of the closet in their various work environments. Although these events were initially viewed as having unsatisfactory outcomes (e.g. getting fired), all of the participants who experienced such loss and pain found meaning and benefit that equipped them with further coping resources. For example, some changed occupations or work environments in order to more easily integrate their lesbian identities at work.

Pearson and Bieschke (2001), in their investigation of high-achieving African American women, found that experiences with discrimination and racism heightened the women's level of determination in their careers and the extent to which they effectively attended to and coped with racism. The narratives of the lesbians in the present study were remarkably similar. Despite obstacles and setbacks (e.g. lost their job, friends and families), they engaged in practices and political advocacy that allowed them to develop a strength and capacity to cope effectively. Their ability to reframe negative experiences and gain a broader positive perspective equipped them with unique coping resources that prepared them for dealing with homophobia at work and in society at large.

Many of the lesbians in our study actively used their lesbian identities to address societal homophobia. By fighting for social change, these women became empowered as they found their voices and the courage to fight for legal and social policy changes within the workplace and, in some cases, on a broader societal level. By actively engaging in and pioneering workplace policies for LGBT people, many of these women have been instrumental in building a LGBT community, a process that has been healing and transformational on an individual and community level.

Although there is no existing career development theory that includes the construct of holistic integration, Juntunen et al. (2001), in their study of the meaning of career for American Indians, described the concept 'living in two worlds'. The separate Native and white worlds left American Indians feeling misunderstood and often disconnected. Similarly, the lesbians in our study who lived separate private and public lives often sought refuge in the LGBT community where they felt more authentic, validated and understood. Juntunen and co-workers also found that American Indians moved along a continuum from living in two worlds, to moving between two worlds, to evolving to a holistic third world where they were able to appreciate their own culture and integrate those pieces of the majority culture that they accepted. Similarly, the lesbians in our study who moved along the continuum of coming out that led to holistic integration experienced an expansiveness that opened them to new possibilities in the work world, and established connections with heterosexual colleagues from whom they had previously been distanced. As a consequence, because the lesbians no longer had to hide a part of themselves, they experienced a renewed energy that was available for work.

Limitations of the Study

There are several limitations to this study that need to be acknowledged. The sample size is a limitation because it affects the transferability of the findings. The sample represents a limited range of ages, cultural backgrounds and professional fields. The sample size did not permit greater variability (e.g. lower social-economic status, younger women), which may have modified the findings. However, eight occupational fields were represented, including several in which lesbians are more likely to be closeted (i.e. police officer, educator). The criteria used to select successful lesbians were subjective, as there is no unambiguous definition of 'successful'. The women in the study were predominately out at the time of the interviews; therefore the experience of women who are presently closeted and successful is limited. However, because many of the participants described being closeted at some time in their past, the findings do represent a range of experiences in regard to being out or closeted at work.

All of the women in this study were living in a large metropolitan city on the west coast of Canada at the time of their interview. This region is noted for being LGBT friendly compared to many regions in Canada that are not. Therefore, the findings may not reflect the experiences of lesbians that are living in more conservative regions.

Implications for Research and Practice

The present study has only begun to illuminate the process of lesbians becoming successful in their occupations. Future research needs to increase variation in participants and data sources. The experience of women representing other demographic groups are clearly needed, such as women of colour, women with disabilities, bisexual women, transgendered, as well as working-class women. In addition, comparing lesbians from other regions of the country, and from rural areas, would contribute to our knowledge of how geography and the social, political environment may influence the process of lesbians becoming successful in their occupations.

The current sample was restricted because the majority of women were visibly out and some identifiable in the media. Further research focusing on those who are more closeted would contribute to our understanding of factors that contribute to their invisibility in the workforce and the coping strategies these women use to conceal their lesbian identities at work. Research that focuses on cognitive factors such as self-efficacy and goal mechanisms (e.g. Lent, Brown & Hackett, 1994) would be useful to better understand how lesbians cope with difficult circumstances. Greater attention to the constructs of 'taking risks and coming out' that lead to the continuum of coming out is warranted. Further research on the construct 'fighting for social change' may prove useful in illuminating the role politicization (e.g. Gomez et al., 2001) has on lesbians' occupational success. In addition, the construct 'holistic integration' has not previously been identified in the literature. Further research is needed to explore the dimensions of this category in order to further our understanding of this complex construct on both intrapersonal and interpersonal levels.

Our findings have important implications for psychological well-being and personal and interpersonal growth. Managing sexual identity at work by taking risks and coming out contributed to a sense of wholeness and balance in work and personal lives, and the majority of the women in this study no longer felt their lives were fragmented as they began to integrate their work and lesbian worlds. As they became open about their lesbian identity, they felt free to be themselves and to experience relationships with colleagues based on honesty. With this knowledge, career counsellors may be in a better position to help lesbian clients understand the psychological and vocational benefits of coming out at work and to help incorporate balance and holistic health practices into their lifestyle (Miller & Brown 2005). However, the lesbian client's personal background, love and support, work environment, social climate and serendipitous conditions need to be addressed in order to understand the complexity of the interaction between the personal and professional that leads to holistic integration and occupational success.

Concluding Remarks

The significance of this study lies in its potential to enhance current therapeutic and career counselling practices as well as its promising contribution to future career development theories that include the experiences of LGBT persons. The vocational counsellor who is familiar with the unique work issues that lesbians' face can provide competent, ethical services. Sensitivity to factors related to lesbian identity, such as minority group status, coming out and employment discrimination, is required of counsellors who seek to understand and work with lesbians. It is critical that professionals working with lesbians understand the complexity of their career paths in order to meet their vocational needs. They also need to recognize the internal and external processes and coping strategies that successful lesbians employ to overcome external barriers and achieve occupational success. In addition, career counsellors need to be aware of their own homophobic attitudes, values and prejudices regarding lesbian issues. The significance of this study lies in its potential to enhance current therapeutic and career counselling practices as well as its promising contribution to future career development theories, which include the experiences of lesbians. Finally, it is hoped that this study has rendered visibility to the uniqueness and complexity of lesbians' successful occupational experiences. These findings may facilitate an improvement in the workplace environment for both lesbians and their co-workers and empower lesbians to become the best they can be by being true to themselves.

APPENDIX

Interview Protocol

The following questions served as a guide and were modified as necessary depending on the emerging concepts and relationships between concepts.

1. Describe the path that brought you to your current position?
2. Have there been any external challenges and limitations that you have dealt with in order to achieve in your occupation? If yes, how have they affected your occupational path?
3. Tell me about your coming out process?
4. Has your coming out process affected your occupational path?
5. How have you dealt with disclosure at work?
6. Do you identify with a specific culture or community that has influenced your occupational path? If yes, how has this influenced your path?
7. Is there anything about your beliefs or values that has had an influence on your success?
8. How would you define occupational success? Based on your definition, do you consider yourself successful?
9. How do you feel about how far you have come?
10. Have you ever changed jobs or geographic locations because of your sexual orientation?
11. Has work protection for lesbians and gays influenced your career? If so, in what ways?
12. Are there any other things in your life that have had a significant influence on your occupational success?
13. Is there anything else you feel is important in relation to your occupational success that I have not asked?

REFERENCES

Astin, H. S. (1984). The meaning of work in women's lives: A sociopsychological model of career choice and work behaviour. *Counseling Psychologist*, **12**(3–4), 117–126.

Betz, N. E. & Fitzgerald, L. F. (1987). *The Career Psychology of Women*. New York, NY: Academic Press.

Boatwright, K. J., Gilbert, M. S., Forrest, L. & Ketzenberger, K. (1996). Impact of identity development upon career trajectory: Listening to the voices of lesbian women. *Journal of Vocational Behavior*, **48**(2), 210–228.

Button, S. B. (2004). Identity management strategies utilized by lesbian and gay employees. *Group & Organization Management*, **29**(4), 470–494.

Casswell, J. E. (1996). *Lesbians, Gay Men, and Canadian Law*. Toronto, ON: Emond Montgomery.

Chung, Y. B. (1995). Career decision making of lesbian, gay, and bisexual individuals. *Career Development Quarterly*, **44**(2), 178–190.

Chur-Hansen, A. (2004). Experience of being gay, lesbian or bisexual at an Australian medical school: A qualitative study. *International Journal of Inclusive Education*, **8**(3), 281–291.

Cody, P. J. & Welch, P. L. (1997). Rural gay men in northern New England: Life experiences and coping styles. *Journal of Homosexuality*, **33**(1), 51–67.

Croteau, J. M. (1996). Research on the work experiences of lesbian, gay, and bisexual people: An integrative review of methodology and findings. *Journal of Vocational Behavior*, **48**(2), 195–209.

Department of Trade and Industry (2005). *Employment relations. Equality and diversity. The employment equality regulations 2003-key questions*. Department of Trade and Industry, UK. Retrieved 4 October 2005, from http://www.dti.gov.uk/er/equality/eeregs_a.htm#b1

Dunne, G. A. (2000). Lesbians as authentic workers? Institutional heterosexuality and the reproduction of gender inequalities. *Sexualities*, **3**(2), 133–148.

Fassinger, R. E. (1996). Notes from the margins: Integrating lesbian experience into the vocational psychology of women. *Journal of Vocational Behavior*, **48**(2), 160–175.

Fassinger, R. E. (2002). *Honoring women's diversity: A new inclusive theory of career development*. Paper presented at the 110th Annual Meeting of the American Psychological Association, Chicago, IL, August.

Fassinger, R. E. & Richie, B. (1994). Being the best: Preliminary results from a national study of the achievement of prominent black and white women. *Journal of Counseling Psychology*, **41**(2), 191–204.

Fitzgerald, L. R. & Betz, N. E. (1994). Career development in cultural context: The role of gender, race, class and sexual orientation. In M. L. Savickas & R. Lent (Eds), *Convergence in Career Development Theories* (pp. 103–117). Palo Alto, CA: Consulting Psychologists Press.

Folkman, S. & Greer, S. (2000). Promoting psychological well-being in the face of serious illness: When theory, research and practice inform each other. *Psycho-Oncology*, **9**, 11–19.

Frye, J. (1984). *Success and satisfaction: Does it make a difference who you ask?* Paper presented at the convention of the American Psychological Association, Toronto, ON, August.

Gomez, M. J., Fassinger, R. E., Prosser, J., Cook, K., Mejia, B. & Luna, J. (2001). Voces abriendo caminos (voices forging paths): A qualitative study of the career development of notable Latinas. *Journal of Counseling Psychology*, **48**(3), 286–300.

Griffith, K. H. & Hebl, M. R. (2002). The disclosure dilemma for gay men and lesbians: 'Coming out' at work. *Journal of Applied Psychology*, **87**(6), 1191–1199.

Hollingsworth, M. A., Tomlinson, M. J. & Fassinger, R. E. (1997). *Working it 'out:' Career development among prominent lesbian women*. Paper presented at the annual convention of the American Psychological Association, Chicago, IL, August.

Humphrey, J. C. (1999). Organizing sexualities, organized inequalities: Lesbians and gay men in public service occupations. *Gender, Work & Organization*, **6**(3), 134–151.

Irwin, J. (2002). Discrimination against gay men, lesbians, and transgendered people working in education. *Journal of Gay & Lesbian Social Services*, **14**(2), 65–77.

Jordan, K. M. & Deluty, R. H. (1998). Coming out for lesbian women: Its relation to anxiety, positive affectivity, self-esteem, and social support. *Journal of Homosexuality*, **35**(2), 41–63.

Juntunen, C. L., Barraclough, D. J., Broneck, C. L., Seibel, G. A., Winrow, S. A. & Morin, P. M. (2001). American Indian perspectives on the career journey. *Journal of Counseling Psychology*, **48**(3), 274–285.

Kitzinger, C. (1991). Lesbians and gay men in the workplace: Psychosocial issues. In M. Davidson & J. Earnshaw (Eds), *Vulnerable Workers: Psychosocial and legal issues* (pp. 223–240). London: Wiley.

Lazarus, R. & Folkman, S. (1984). *Stress, Appraisal, and Coping*. New York, NY: Springer.

Lent, R. W., Brown, S. D. & Hackett. G. (1994). Toward a unifying social cognitive theory of career and academic interest, choice, and performance. *Journal of Vocational Behavior*, **45**, 79–122.

Lonborg, S. D. & Phillips, J. M. (1996). Investigating the career development of gay, lesbian, and bisexual people: Methodological considerations and recommendations. *Journal of Vocational Behavior*, **48**, 176–194.

Miller, M. J. & Brown, S. D. (2005). Counseling for career choice: Implications for improving interventions and working with diverse populations. In S. D. Brown & R. W. Lent (Eds), *Career Development and Counseling: Putting theory and research to work* (pp. 441–465). Hoboken, NJ: Wiley.

Morrow, S. L., Campbell, B. W. & Beckstead, A. L. (1995). *The impact of invisibility on the career directions of lesbian and bisexual women*. Paper presented at the annual convention of the American Psychological Association, New York, August.

Morrow, S. L., Gore, P. A. & Campbell, B. W. (1996). The application of a sociocognitive framework to the career development of lesbian women and gay men. *Journal of Vocational Behavior*, **48**(2), 136–148.

Morse, J. M. (1991). Strategies for sampling. In J. M. Morse (Ed.), *Qualitative Nursing Research: A contemporary dialogue* (pp. 127–145). Newbury Park, CA: Sage.

Noonan, B. M., Gallor, S. M., Hensler-McGinnis, N. F., Fassinger, R. E., Wang, S. & Goodman, J. (2004). Challenge and success: A qualitative study of the career development of highly achieving women with physical and sensory disabilities. *Journal of Counseling Psychology*, **51**(1), 68–80.

Pearson, S. M. & Bieschke, K. J. (2001). Succeeding against the odds: An examination of familial influences on the career development of professional African American women. *Journal of Counseling Psychology*, **48**(3), 301–309.

Poole, M. E. & Langan-Fox, J. (1997). *Australian Women and Careers: Psychological and contextual influences over the life course.* Melbourne: Cambridge University Press.

Prince, J. P. (1995). Influence on the career development of gay men. *Career Development Quarterly*, **44**(2), 168–177.

Prosser, J., Chopra, S. & Fassinger, R. E. (1998). *A qualitative study of the careers of prominent Asian American women.* Paper presented at the annual conference of the Association for Women in Psychology, Baltimore, MD, March.

Ragins, B. R. & Cornwell, J. M. (2001). Pink triangles: Antecedents and consequences of perceived workplace discrimination against gay and lesbian employees. *Journal of Applied Psychology*, **86**(6), 1244–1261.

Raven, A. K. (2001). Dangerous territories. *Journal of Lesbian Studies*, **5**(1–2), 157–182.

Richie, B. S., Fassinger, R. E., Linn, S. G., Johnson, J., Prosser, J. & Robinson, S. (1997). Persistence, connection, and passion: A qualitative study of the career development of highly achieving African American-Black and White women. *Journal of Counseling Psychology*, **44**(2), 133–148.

Sexuality Information and Education Council of the United States (1999). *Fact sheet: Worldwide antidiscrimination laws and policies based on sexual orientation.* Retrieved 19 September 2005, from http://www.thebody.com/siecus/report/discrimination.html

Shachar, S. & Gilbert, L. A. (1983). Working lesbians: Role conflicts and coping strategies. *Psychology of Women Quarterly*, **7**(3), 244–256.

Skelton, A. (1999). An inclusive higher education? Gay and bisexual male teachers and the cultural politics of sexuality. *International Journal of Inclusive Education*, **3**(3), 239–255.

Skelton, A. (2000). 'Camping it up to make them laugh?' Gay men teaching in higher education. *Teaching in Higher Education*, **5**(2), 181–193.

Strauss, A. L. & Corbin, J. (1998). *Basics of Qualitative Research: Techniques and procedures for developing grounded theory* (2nd edn). Thousand Oaks, CA: Sage.

Tomlinson, M. J. & Fassinger, R. E. (2003). Career development, lesbian identity development, and campus climate among lesbian college students. *Journal of College Student Development*, **44**(6), 845–860.

Waldo, C. R. (1999). Working in a majority context: A structural model of heterosexism as minority stress in the workplace. *Journal of Counseling Psychology*, **46**(2), 218–232.

Waldo, C. R. & Kemp, J. L. (1997). Should I come out to my students? An empirical investigation. *Journal of Homosexuality*, **34**(2), 79–94.

Woods, J. D. (with Lucas, J. H.). (1993). *The Corporate Closet: The professional lives of gay men in America.* New York, NY: Free Press.

Yang, A. (1999). *From Wrong to Rights: Public opinion on gay and lesbian Americans moves toward equality.* Washington, DC: National Gay and Lesbian Task Force.

PART IV

Health and Practice

Bringing LGBTQ Psychology into Mainstream Practice

Ian Rivers
Queen Margaret University College, UK

How does one practice lesbian, gay, bisexual, trans or queer (LGBTQ) psychology? Unlike clinical, health, forensic, occupational, counselling, educational (school) or, indeed, sports and exercise psychology, LGBTQ psychology has neither a unitary focus nor a restrictive remit. The practice of LGBTQ psychology is not confined to particular therapeutic or exploratory methods, it does not provide a framework for the assessment of competence or functioning, nor does it have as its goal the alleviation of pain or suffering though the application of various interventions. If one believes that sexual identity, orientation or preference is a continuum, and that sex is not simply a matter of genitalia at birth, then it becomes apparent that LGBTQ psychology is intrinsic to all aspects of professional practice. At any point in our working lives an LGBTQ client, student or colleague may walk through our door and request our support as any heterosexual client, student or colleague might. In essence, the following chapters represent a call to arms – a rallying cry – that highlights the need for LGBTQ psychology in the mainstream education and continuing professional development of *all* psychologists. It should be as common to include LGBTQ issues in the training of today's professionals as it is to include discussions of sex, race, religion, disability or age. It is a testament to the bravery, strength and commitment of those who have written and edited this book, that we are able to share and learn from their experiences, and I hope incorporate their insights and knowledge into our own professional practice.

In the following chapters, colleagues consider the practice of psychology drawing on experiences of working with clients in a variety of applied settings. These remarkable chapters discuss the complexities of working within the context of LGBTQ psychology; the different paradigms and discourses that inform our own subjective understandings of the experiences with those with whom we work, and the ways in which those understandings translate into constructive practice. In the first of these six chapters, Susan Speer (Chapter 16) explores the ways in which gender identity is mutually constructed through the observation and analysis of an interview between a psychiatrist and a pre-operative male-to-female transsexual client. In this chapter she considers how gender identity is not

Out in Psychology: Lesbian, gay, bisexual, trans and queer perspectives. Edited by Victoria Clarke and Elizabeth Peel.
© 2007 John Wiley & Sons, Ltd.

only talked about but represented and displayed, and how the professional and client interact in a meaningful way. By way of contrast, Jeffery Adams and his colleagues (Chapter 17) consider the central role 'alcohol' plays in the social lives of gay men. In particular, Adams et al. consider the health implications of a 'scene' located around bars, clubs and pubs, and the power of advertising within the gay press. They discuss various initiatives that challenge the acceptability of advertising in gay newspapers and magazines, and in the promotional literature often found in venues where gay men meet. Finally, they challenge the normalization of alcohol consumption within the lives of gay men, and identify a need for further research to better understand the ways in which public health psychology can support interventions that seek to inform those men about the dangers of alcohol.

In the next chapter, Lih-Mei Liao (Chapter 18) locates a discussion of the sexual concerns of heterosexually identified intersex women within a social constructionist framework. Based on her experience in clinical practice, Liao presents a compelling argument that illustrates how the sexual difficulties faced by heterosexually identified intersex women are often gendered and socially constructed. Subsequently, she argues that it is necessary to adopt deconstructionist approaches to better understand the concerns expressed by intersex women. Finally, she argues that, within the context of health care practice, professionals need to engage with feminist and LGBTQ discourses that challenge heteronormative assumptions and question cultural practices about sex.

Many of those cultural practices and heteronormative assumptions described by Lih-Mei Liao first appear within the classroom and school yard. Jeremy Monsen and Sydney Bailey (Chapter 19) bridge the gap between the adult and the youth, by focusing on much needed interventions to combat homophobia at school. Monsen and Bailey show what can and should be done when there is the will to challenge homophobia. Throughout this chapter, the authors provide a wealth of evidence that demonstrates that schools continue to fail to be safe places for LGB young people, and remind those of us in academia that no matter how many papers we publish on the subject, rarely does academic research translate into changes in practice. Ultimately, Monsen and Bailey task us to find better ways of supporting educational and school psychologists in challenging homophobia.

The penultimate chapter in this section addresses the often forgotten issue of lesbian health, and how a group of lesbians talk about their perceptions of health and well-being. Centred around a critique of both social constructionist and queer theory, Sara MacBride-Stewart (Chapter 20) offers us a perspective on the ways in which 16 lesbian women view their own lives in terms of the 'healthiness' of coming out, the importance of support mechanisms, and the fact that 'health' cannot always be assumed or bound to a rigid sense of 'self' (it can, for some, be found in their 'sense' of freedom and flux). In this chapter we are taken on a journey which demonstrates that lesbian sexual health risks are just as real as those for gay and bisexual men, but are less well known and, as a consequence, are often forgotten by those who provide health care.

The final chapter, by Katherine Johnson (Chapter 21), addresses the issue of transsexualism and provides an authoritative account of the development of knowledge and clinical practice in the support and treatment of those who identify as trans and may seek gender reassignment surgery. Johnson notes that although, for many people who are transsexual, surgery may be their ultimate goal, once undergone it does not bring with it a cloak of invisibility or acceptance. Past lives have to be explained, future lives have to be planned and, ultimately, an individual must learn to 'pass' in a world of their same- and opposite-sex peers. Johnson concludes that the pressing issue for us rests not in establishing an aetiology of transsexualism, but in ensuring that appropriate professional services are in place to support clients as they engage with the process of gender re-assignment and begin their lives anew.

CHAPTER 16

On Passing: The Interactional Organization of Appearance Attributions in the Psychiatric Assessment of Transsexual Patients[1]

Susan A. Speer
The University of Manchester, UK
and
Richard Green
Imperial College School of Medicine, UK

INTRODUCTION

In this chapter we do three things. First, we discuss the concept of 'passing', how it has been defined and used in the social scientific literature on LGBTQ topics, and its special relevance for those who identify as 'transsexual'. Second, we discuss how passing has been examined in two classic ethnomethodological studies of gender by Harold Garfinkel (1967) and Suzanne Kessler and Wendy McKenna (1978), and critically evaluate the contribution of these studies to what we know about the social construction of gender. Third, in an effort to update and extend the findings of these studies, we use conversation analysis (CA) and CA-inspired studies of gesture to analyse one minute of videotaped, naturally occurring interaction between a consultant psychiatrist and a pre-operative male-to-female

---

[1] The first author wrote this chapter and conducted all the analyses. The second author arranged access to the field site, coordinated the collection of data at that site, and provided brief explanation on the clinical management of patients. He is the psychiatrist whose interactions are analysed in this chapter.

Out in Psychology: Lesbian, gay, bisexual, trans and queer perspectives. Edited by Victoria Clarke and Elizabeth Peel.
© 2007 John Wiley & Sons, Ltd.

transsexual[2] patient in a British National Health Service (NHS) Gender Identity Clinic. Focusing specifically on the use by both parties of appearance attributions that implicitly or explicitly 'index' the patient's gender, we explore the role that such attributions play in the patient's attempts to pass as female, and to be treated *as* a trans woman in this distinctive institutional setting. We intend this chapter to contribute to LGBTQ research on passing, identity management and appearance, as well as conversation analytic work on how gender gets 'done', 'displayed' and 'oriented to' in interaction. Finally, we explain why we believe LGBTQ psychologists might benefit from a closer engagement with CA-inspired analyses of videotaped materials.

ON PASSING

'Passing' is a historically problematic concept that is 'fraught with all sorts of political implications' (Transsexual Roadmap, 1996–2006). Commonly understood to involve 'being accepted, or representing oneself successfully as, a member of a different ethnic, religious, or sexual group' (*Oxford English Dictionary*, 2006: passing, n.8), such a definition is problematic for at least three reasons. First, it implies deception of some kind – that the passing individual is presenting themselves as a member of a group that is *not their own*. Second, it implies a real/unreal dichotomy – that there is an original, unconstructed 'real' self, and a constructed, 'unreal', passing self. Third, it 'implies a binary of pass or fail' (Transsexual Roadmap, 1996–2006), which involves 'the denial of mixture' (Stone, 1993, p. 11), and, which 'puts the power of determining the validity of our identities in the hands of others' (Transsexual Roadmap, 1996–2006).

A broader definition of passing – and one we adopt in this chapter – treats it from within an ethnomethodological framework as involving a person 'doing something in order to be taken as she/he intends' (Kessler & McKenna, 1978, p. 19). From this perspective, passing is not about deception, inauthenticity, or the denial of mixture. Rather, it is an activity that we *all* engage in as part of our everyday lives. As Kessler and McKenna (1978, p. 19) put it, 'everyone is passing'.[3] When considered in this way, passing is not necessarily overt or explicit. Indeed, the whole idea of passing is that the practices that are deployed in order to pass go 'unnoticed'. As Stephen Whittle (1999, p. 7) puts it, trans individuals 'have always been programmed to pass and hence disappear.'

For those persons who fit the prescribed norms for heteronormative group membership, passing successfully is a routine, unthinking and relatively effortless accomplishment (Garfinkel, 1967). For those persons who do not fit such norms, however, and who wish to manage (what they take to be) certain 'stigma' or 'undisclosed' but potentially 'discrediting information about self' (Goffman, 1963, p. 42), passing can become an abiding

---

[2] Although the medicalization and treatment of transsexualism is subject to considerable debate (see Burns, 2006; Butler, 2004; Johnson, Chapter 21), transsexualism is formally designated in the Diagnostic and Statistical Manual of Mental Disorders (DSM-IV) (American Psychiatric Association, 1994) as a 'Gender Identity Disorder' (GID). Persons with GID are said to exhibit 'a strong and persistent cross-gender identification and a persistent discomfort with their sex or a sense of inappropriateness in the gender role of that sex' (The Harry Benjamin International Gender Dysphoria Association (HBIGDA) 'Standards of Care for Gender Identity Disorders', 2001, p. 4). Throughout this chapter we use the medical term 'transsexual' as opposed to the more political term, 'transgender', to describe our research participants, because this research deals specifically with individuals who seek medical treatment to change their sex. The notion of transgender is often used in a political context by transgender activists in order to avoid medical categorization.

[3] The first author is, for example, passing as a 34-year-old feminist academic, a home-owner, a competent driver and so on.

preoccupation (Lev, 2004). For example, closeted gay men and lesbians who have not yet 'come out' to others, may strive consciously to pass as heterosexual. Similarly, transsexuals who wish to keep their birth sex secret may work hard to pass as 'natural' men and women.[4] For these groups, passing involves bringing a range of features of bodily comportment and appearance under conscious and deliberate control (Atkins, 1998; Dozier, 2005; Holliday, 1999; Schrock, Reid & Boyd, 2005; Skidmore, 1999)[5]. As Seidman (2002, p. 31) notes, 'For closeted individuals, daily life acquires a heightened sense of theatricality or performative deliberateness'. Indeed, our society is one in which sexual ambiguity is not (yet) tolerated, with the consequence that not fitting prescribed norms is highly accountable.[6] Moreover, in popular consciousness gender and sexuality are inextricably linked, such that any deviations from the norm in respect to either can be *doubly* consequential. Thus, if a woman 'looks like a man' then she not only falls short of gender norms, but she is deemed to be a 'mannish' or 'butch' lesbian. Similarly if a man 'looks like a woman' he may be seen as an 'effeminate' gay man (Peel, 2005).

For persons who live with the constant fear of exposure – of being 'read' as gay or lesbian, or a member of his or her birth sex – the importance of passing cannot be underestimated. It has been noted that passing is important for a transsexual person's self-image, for validating their identity, and for 'affirming their reintegration into society' (Lev, 2004, p. 398). As Brown and Rounsley (1996, p. 135) put it, 'If transsexuals can pass, they have a far better chance of developing relationships and finding jobs'. Indeed, passing successfully as heterosexual, or as a 'genuine' male or female, may be necessary for daily survival – for avoiding public ridicule, homophobic and transphobic violence, and the psychosocial difficulties (anxiety, depression) that may result from such discrimination. At the same time, individuals can pay a 'steep price' for passing – particularly if being 'closeted' involves denying a strongly felt gay, lesbian or trans identity (Seidman, 2002). There have been a number of well-documented cases of individuals who were passing well but then 'outed' as gay, lesbian, or trans with devastating, and sometimes lethal, consequences (see Califia, 1997).

In this chapter we focus specifically on the passing practices of a person who identifies as a male-to-female transsexual.[7] In addition to the bodily transformations that transsexuals experience as a result of consuming high doses of 'cross-sex' hormones and undergoing sex reassignment surgery, male-to-female transsexuals may elect to undergo a range of treatments and training in order to enhance their physical appearance and ensure that they pass well. Such treatments and training may include, but are not limited to, breast surgery and implants, facial and body hair removal (via electrolysis or laser), and speech and language therapy (in order to work on intonation, adjust the resonance of the voice and raise its pitch). Some patients may request a referral to an ear, nose and throat specialist for

---

[4] Although it is important to note that it's in the very nature of being transsexual that passing as one's preferred gender may require less effort, and feel more 'natural' than passing as one's ascribed birth sex. This is highlighted nicely in a quote from the trans activist Jeanne B (quoted in Bell, 1995, p. 141, quoted in Namaste, 2000, p. 32) who states 'One interesting thing, a lot of people ask me: "What do you do to pass as a woman? To look, walk, and talk like a woman?" But nobody asks me: "How did you manage to live and pass as a man for so many years?"'

[5] However, it should be noted that norms for gender expression vary both historically and cross-culturally (see, for example, Hall, 1997, 2005).

[6] The fact that we typically feel it necessary to apologize for mis-attributing someone's gender – as though it is an insult to get somebody's gender wrong – is testament to the strength of this socially imposed and sanctioned norm (Butler, in More, 1999, p. 293).

[7] Male-to-female transsexuals tend to pass less easily than female-to-male transsexuals, for whom hormone treatment has a significant masculinizing effect.

vocal pitch surgery and/or a tracheal shave (to diminish a protruding Adam's apple), and a few may request referral to a cosmetic surgeon for facial feminization surgery and lipo-suction. Finally, most patients will elect to undergo image modification – hair, clothes, make-up, accessories and props, attention to bodily comportment, posture and movement (e.g. walking), speech, emotional expression and even handwriting.

Unlearning traditional sex roles and relearning new ones usually requires considerable training and practice. Consequently, teaching people how to pass is big business, with individuals making a living out of training people to look, sound and move more like men and women (see, for example, Doyle, 2002–2005). It follows that since learning the tech-niques of passing often requires considerable funds, successful passing is not an equal opportunity phenomenon.

Critical Perspectives on Passing

The transsexual person's preoccupation with passing has been subject to a wide-ranging critique. A number of radical feminists (Jeffreys, 1990, 2003; Raymond, 1979) and others with a critical agenda (MacKenzie, 1994) have argued that transsexualism is politically conservative. For these researchers, a transsexual person's adoption of the 'hyper-femi-nine' or 'hyper-masculine' actions, appearances and linguistic attributes associated with 'the opposite sex', reinforces the essentialist idea that gender dualism is biologically determined, compounds women's oppression, and makes gender diversity harder to see (Golden, 2000). Indeed, some suggest that passing 'is a product of oppression' (Feinberg, 1996, p. 89). If it were not for the existence of a patriarchal social order, individuals would not feel that they must pass, and hence 'blend unambiguously into mainstream society' (Brown & Rounsley, 1996, p. 135).

It is for precisely these reasons that some trans activists and queer theorists refuse to embrace the concept of passing, and treat the pressure to conform to social expectations regarding gender norms, with contempt. They resist this pressure by celebrating their gender ambiguity and the 'transgressive potential' of trans (Hird, 2002, p. 589). For them, it is trans visibility and the *refusal to pass* that is paramount (May, 2002). In refusing to identify as either male or female, gay or straight, many trans people consider themselves 'gender terrorists' who seek to 'radically deconstruct sex and gender' (Hird, 2002, p. 589), and who aim ultimately to render the sex and gender binary obsolete. From this perspec-tive, 'the point is not about going from man to woman or woman to man' (hence exchang-ing one set of restrictive gender norms for another), but rather to go 'from one category to being a transsexual' (Butler, in More 1999, p. 291).

Rather than seeing transsexuals' desire to pass as insufficiently radical, or as reinforcing the gendered status quo, an alternative feminist approach, and one we adopt in this chapter, is to recognize and accept that, as the editors to this volume point out, on a day-to-day level there are many transsexuals who 'identify with normative values and have no desire to be "gender terrorists"' (Clarke & Peel, Chapter 2). Although they may ultimately hope that their transition will render their trans status 'invisible', it is nonetheless the case that the very act of 'migrating' (King, 2003) from one sex and gender identity to another has the potential to radically disrupt commonsense assumptions about the natural immutabil-ity of sexual dimorphism, and 'what counts' as sex and gender (Butler, 2004; see also, Johnson, Chapter 21). As Hird (2002, p. 347; see also Butler, 2004) notes, 'to the extent that transsexual people are able to "pass" as "real" women or men, they reveal that sex and gender do not adhere to particular bodies naturally'. Certainly, for many researchers, transsexuals' passing practices offer revealing insights into familiar cultural and normative ways of *doing* sex and gender.

DOING SEX AND GENDER

Social scientists, especially symbolic interactionists, ethnomethodologists, social constructionists, post-structuralists and queer theorists, have long been concerned with the idea that sex and gender are phenomena that one *does* rather than something one *has* – a performance rather than an essence, a situated accomplishment rather than an ascribed, pre-determined role (see, for example, Butler, 1990, 1993, 2004; Fenstermaker & West, 2002; Garfinkel, 1967; Goffman, 1979; Kessler & McKenna, 1978; West & Zimmerman, 1987). One of the first publications to shed light on the actual practices that constitute the achievement of gender was Harold Garfinkel's (1967) ethnomethodological study of a pre-operative intersexed person called Agnes.[8]

Ethnomethodology takes as its topic for study 'members' methods' for producing their everyday affairs. Members' methods consist of the routinized, taken-for-granted procedures that individuals employ as they go about their everyday lives and tasks. It is because such methods are routinized and taken-for-granted that Garfinkel refers to them as '"seen but unnoticed" backgrounds of [our] everyday affairs' (1967, p. 118). Garfinkel argued that gender (what he called 'sex status') is one such 'invariant but unnoticed' (1967, p. 118) background in everyday life. It is omnirelevant, and yet its organization is something that, for most individuals who can take their sex status for granted, remains hidden. What interested Garfinkel was that for some members, such as intersexed persons, this is not the case. Far from being able to take their sex status for granted, intersexed persons are engaged in the constant 'work of achieving and making secure their rights to live in their elected sex status' (1967, p. 118). For them, the work of passing as a 'normal' or 'natural' male or female is an 'enduring practical task' (1967, p. 118), which requires constant work and 'active deliberate management' (1967, p. 139) on their part. Garfinkel believed that by studying their situation, the ethnomethodologist can render visible what culture makes invisible – the accomplishment of gender (West & Zimmerman, 1987, p. 131).

It was on the basis of his study of Agnes's more and less successful experiences of passing as an '120 per cent female' (1967, p. 129), that Garfinkel was able to demonstrate precisely how it is that 'over the temporal course of their actual engagements, and "knowing" the society only from within, members produce stable, accountable practical activities, *i.e.*, social structures of everyday activities' (1967, p. 185). He concluded that 'normally sexed persons are cultural events' and that members' practices 'produce the observable-tellable normal sexuality of persons' (1967, p. 181).

---

[8] Intersexed person are 'individuals born with anatomy or physiology that differs from contemporary ideals of what constitutes "normal" male and female' (The UK Intersex Association, nd). In the appendix to the chapter in which the Agnes study was reported, Garfinkel reveals that eight years after the study took place, Agnes admitted that she had lied to the research team, and that the feminization of her body was not due to the intersex condition known as 'testicular feminization syndrome', but rather to her having ingested female hormones that were originally prescribed for her mother. Thus, Agnes was not an intersexed person at all, but a male-to-female transsexual (see also, Johnson, Chapter 21).

Garfinkel's ideas were rather slow to seep into feminist consciousness. It was not until 1978, some 11 years after the publication of the Agnes study, that Kessler and McKenna's book, *Gender: An ethnomethodological approach*, developed Garfinkel's ideas about the social construction of sex for a feminist audience. Kessler and McKenna (1978) studied the *gender attribution process*, which describes the methodical procedures through which members come to identify others as unambiguously male or female. By examining how members 'do' gender attributions, Kessler and McKenna hoped to find out how it was that in each instance of interaction 'we produce a sense that there are *only* men and women' (1978, pp. 5–6). Kessler and McKenna argued that while the dichotomous nature of the gender attribution process is typically hidden, it comes to the fore in situations where members attempt to assign gender to 'ambiguous' individuals, or make sense of seemingly contradictory 'gender cues'. Thus, following Garfinkel, they set about exploring what transsexualism can tell us about the gender attribution process, and about 'the day-to-day social construction of gender by all persons' (1978, p. 112).

Although Kessler and McKenna shared Garfinkel's view that 'gender is omnirelevant' in interaction and that 'gender "work" is required' (1978, p. 136), unlike Garfinkel, they did not believe that most of the work was 'required of the one displaying gender' (1978, p. 136). Instead, for them, 'most of the work is done for the displayer by the perceiver' (1978, p. 136). Hence, they argued that a gender attribution is the product of an *interaction between displayer and perceiver*: 'Passing is an ongoing practice, but it is practiced by both parties' (Kessler & McKenna, 1978, p. 137). Although displayers create the first gender attribution, primarily through means of talk and physical appearance, once an attribution has been made, the perceiver's role is central to its maintenance (1978, pp. 136–137).

The approach to gender exemplified in these studies was remarkably ahead of its time. Indeed, Garfinkel's (1967, p. 181) claim that 'normally sexed persons are cultural events', can be considered a radical comment on the social construction of sex, more typically credited to the post-feminist philosopher, Judith Butler (1990), more than two decades later.[9] Unlike Butler, who does not examine concrete empirical materials, and whose theory of the discursive construction of gender is a rather abstract and decontextualized one, Garfinkel and Kessler and Mckenna were among the first to demonstrate, with reference to the real-life, lived experience of transsexual individuals, that and how sex is a situated accomplishment. Treating gender as an emergent product of social interaction, they drew attention to the local interpretative practices and socially shared, taken-for-granted methods that members use to create the social structural 'reality' of a world of two sexes (Kessler & McKenna, 1978, p. vii).

The lasting significance of the Garfinkel and Kessler and McKenna studies is evidenced in the numerous debates and discussions that have taken place since their publication.[10] Although Garfinkel has since been criticized by feminists for his 'androcentrism' (Rogers 1992a, p. 170), and for reproducing sexist stereotypes and commonsense understandings about the 'priorities and competences' of young (heterosexual) men and women (Rogers 1992a, p. 180), his analysis of 'the accomplished character' (Zimmerman, 1992, p. 197)

---

[9] As Dorothy Smith (2002, p. ix) puts it 'postmodern feminists reinvented the wheel', and 'it is tiresome to read contemporary feminist philosophers and literary theorists presenting as radically new discoveries ideas that are old hat to sociologists'

[10] For discussions of the Agnes study see contributions to *Gender & Society* by Bologh (1992), Rogers (1992a, 1992b) and Zimmerman (1992), and to *Sociological Theory* by Denzin (1990, 1991), Hilbert (1991), Lynch and Bogen (1991) and Maynard (1991). For a discussion of the Kessler and McKenna study see Crawford (2000).

of gender has been described as 'a groundbreaking work in sociology' (Bologh, 1992, p. 199), and 'a profound analysis' (Heritage, 1984, p. 181) that 'affords an unusually clear vision' of the workings of the social construction of gender (Zimmerman, 1992, p. 197). Similarly, the Kessler and McKenna study has been described as 'an extraordinary book, a prescient work' (Denny, 2000, p. 63), which provides a 'bold assault on the sanctity of the two-gender model' (Tiefer, 2000, p. 36). Despite the lasting importance and clear resonance of these studies for much contemporary feminist research, however, neither has received many follow-ups, nor the attention from LGBTQ psychologists that they deserve. As the editors to this volume point out in their introduction, LGBTQ psychologists have typically ignored gender, despite widespread recognition that gender and sexuality are mutually co-implicative.

One reason for this apparent neglect, is that it is not always clear how one might apply the findings of the Garfinkel and Kessler and McKenna studies to new interactional materials. Indeed, one of the main limitations of both studies is that although they placed great emphasis on members' 'everyday interactions' (Kessler & McKenna, 1978, p. 115), 'accounting practices' (Garfinkel, 1967, p. 1), 'witnessed displays of common talk and conduct' (1967, p. 181), 'situated indexical particulars of talk' (1967, p. 181), and 'the ways transsexuals talk about . . . transsexualism, the language they use' (Kessler & McKenna, 1978, p. 114), there is remarkably little by way of first-hand evidence of participants' accounts and interactions included in their analyses. Garfinkel's data consist of 35 hours of tape-recorded 'conversations' that he had with Agnes, which he supplemented with unspecified 'additional' materials collected by the psychiatric team at UCLA (Garfinkel, 1967, p. 121). Similarly, Kessler and McKenna's data consist of interviews with 15 trans-sexuals, letters written over a period of two years from a male-to-female transsexual friend called Rachel, and the results of a number of games and experiments. The vast proportion of the data used or cited in these texts consist of short, decontextualized (i.e. typically monologic, one speaker, one line) excerpts from transcripts of interviews with trans individuals, and the researchers' post hoc recollections and (anecdotal) reports of events. Extended examples of 'conversations' and 'interactions' are reported by Kessler and McKenna in the appendix to their book in the form of letters written by their transsexual friend, Rachel. However, like most data used in these studies, these second-hand descriptions of interactions, conversations and events are treated as first-hand, unreconstructed evidence for what actually took place in the setting – that is, as accurate reports on reality rather than situated accomplishments or *versions*. What is missing from both studies is a systematic analysis of first-hand examples of trans persons' actual language use, their situated interactions and accounts, and their contribution to those very practices of gender construction that Garfinkel and Kessler and McKenna intended to analyse.

An approach that *does* offer just the kind of systematic analytic framework advocated here, is CA. CA developed in the pioneering lectures of the American sociologist, Harvey Sacks, between 1964 and 1972 (Sacks, 1995), and has its roots in Garfinkel's (1967) ethnomethodology, Goffman's (1983) theory of the interaction order, and linguistic philosophy (Austin, 1962; Wittgenstein, 1953). Harvey Sacks and his colleagues, Emmanuel Schegloff, Gail Jefferson and Anita Pomerantz, were among the first to translate ideas from these perspectives into an empirically grounded, data-driven, and highly systematized research agenda. Conducting fine-grained, line-by-line analyses of highly detailed transcripts of audio and (where interactants are co-present) videotaped, naturally occurring interactions, CA is primarily concerned to examine and describe the oriented-to methods and practices that speakers use to coordinate their talk to produce orderly and meaningful conversational actions.

A number of feminists, inspired primarily by Emanuel Schegloff's (1991, 1997a, 1998a), remarks on the role of gender and other demographic variables in interaction, have begun to use insights from CA to interrogate the relevance of gender in talk, and to explore 'what counts' as gender or an 'orientation to gender' in an interaction. Instead of conceiving of 'male' and 'female' as 'external and constraining' (Heritage, 1984, p. 181) independent variables that condition and account for members' social practices, researchers within this tradition treat gender, sexuality and prejudice as emergent, socially constructed phenomena. From this perspective, such phenomena may or may not be made relevant in interaction, and constructed and oriented to as participants' concerns (for some examples of research within this tradition, see Fenstermaker & West, 2002; Kitzinger, 2000; Land & Kitzinger, Chapter 8; Speer 2005a; Stokoe & Smithson, 2001). This body of work has produced some extremely rich insights into how gender gets done in interaction, and is taking the field of research on gender, sexuality and language in productively new directions.

CA has a long history of working with videotaped materials of co-present interactions (see C. Goodwin, 1980, 1981, 2003; Heath, 1986, 2006; Sacks & Schegloff, 2002; Schegloff, 1984, 1998b), and feminist researchers are increasingly using video to analyse how gender gets done and displayed in interaction (e.g. see M. Goodwin, 2001, 2002, 2006). In addition, there is a broad tradition of research outside CA that investigates the relationship between sex, gender and non-verbal communication (for some classic examples, see Birdwhistell, 1970; Frances, 1979; Goffman, 1979; Henley, 1977; and Wood, 2002). The majority of contemporary research within the field of research on gender and language, however, continues to focus on speakers and speaking, and on audio-based transcripts alone. For most gender and language scholars, 'doing gender' is conceived primarily as a verbal activity, with the consequence that the role of the hearer, or the recipient of a gender display in co-constructing gender, is largely ignored. Consequently, we have no way of knowing what role the recipient of a gender display plays in members passing as male or female.[11]

In this chapter, by contrast, we adopt the view expressed by C. Goodwin and M. Goodwin, that nobody is ever building an utterance or an action alone. Rather, utterances are produced by both speakers and hearers as part of a 'multi-modal' activity system, which integrates the disparate sign systems of grammar, prosody and the body into a common course of interactive activity (Stivers & Sidnell, 2005). These sign systems interact with each other in mutually reinforcing and interesting ways. For example, speakers will often change what they are saying in the course of their ongoing talk on the basis of the looks or 'gaze' that they are getting from their recipients (C. Goodwin, 1981; C. Goodwin & M. Goodwin, 2004; M. Goodwin, 1980). From this perspective, gender is a collaborative product of the interaction between speakers and hearers.

Our aim in the remainder of this chapter is to use insights from CA and CA-inspired analyses of gesture in order to develop and extend what we know about transsexuals' passing practices. Unlike Garfinkel and Kessler and McKenna, we will not be analysing members' retrospective reports on how they passed, or our own recollections and reports

---

[11] This is somewhat ironic, given that three decades ago Kessler and McKenna (1978, pp. 136–7) stressed the central role of the recipient, or the 'perceiver' of a gender display, in transsexuals passing as male or female.

of 'passing occasions' and events. Instead, we will provide a detailed empirical analysis of one minute of videotaped and transcribed, naturally occurring interaction in which a pre-operative male-to-female transsexual patient is engaged in the act of passing with a consultant psychiatrist in the Gender Identity Clinic (GIC). We ask, what are the vocal and gestural means by which the patient works to pass as a transsexual female, and 'do gender' in this setting? How does the psychiatrist orient towards and treat these 'gender displays'? Does he co-participate in, ignore, or reject them? How does the psychiatrist's response shape the patient's next interactional move, and what is the relationship between these displays and responses? Finally, what can our analyses tell us about transsexuals' passing practices and about the social construction of gender more broadly?

Part of the distinctiveness of what we aim to show here is that gender gets done as a thoroughly embodied and *co-constructed* practice in interaction, and that an analysis of the interrelation of the talk and gestures *of both speakers and hearers* is absolutely fundamental to our understanding of how members 'do', and 'display' gender in an interaction, and pass as male or female.

PASSING IN THE GENDER IDENTITY CLINIC

Before we describe our materials and procedures and proceed to our analyses, we will first detail some features of the psychiatric assessment process in the GIC, and how this process shapes the distinctive role of passing in this setting.

In particular, it is important to note one crucial difference between what it means to 'pass' in the clinic environment, and what it means to pass outside it: As 'insiders', the psychiatrists at the GIC (just like Garfinkel and the psychiatrists in the Agnes study), will already know that the patient was not born male or female. In this sense, patients cannot possibly pass with psychiatrists in this institutional setting in the same way they might with others outside the clinic environment who do not know about their 'trans' status. Nevertheless, there are a number of features of the psychiatric assessment process that makes the GIC an ideal setting for an analysis of members' passing practices.

First, the internationally recognized Harry Benjamin International Gender Dysphoria Association's 'Standards of Care for Gender Identity Disorders' (HBIGDA, 2001) specify that, before they can obtain hormone treatment or surgery, patients must be assessed by two psychiatrists at the GIC. Psychiatrists assess the patient according to a pre-defined set of medical criteria, and aim to produce a 'differential diagnosis' (that is, to accurately diagnose the type of gender identity disorder and to determine that the patient is not suffering from some related or unrelated mental health problem). As Louise Newman (2000, p. 400) puts it, 'for the mental health clinician . . . the task is to distinguish the "true transsexual" (or primary transsexual) from others with lesser degrees of gender dysphoria or other gender issues for which surgery is not considered appropriate treatment'.[12] Psychiatrists are essentially gatekeepers to hormones and surgery (Speer & Parsons, 2006; see also Johnson, Chapter 21 and Clifford & Orford, Chapter 10). It follows that in order to obtain their desired treatment, patients must first pass with the psychiatrist in the clinic environment as a transsexual who meets all the requisite diagnostic criteria (May, 2002,

---

[12] It should be noted, however, that clinicians themselves no longer use 'true transsexual' as a diagnostic term.

p. 459). That patients are attentive to this requirement is evidenced in the reports of patients who, concerned not to delay or risk being refused surgery, quickly learnt the 'necessary life-history required for successful "passing"' (Hird, 2002, p. 583) – a life-history whose parameters they found handily spelt out in the Standards of Care (HBIGDA, 2001) and in the 'published developmental histories of transsexuals who preceded them' (Green, 1987, pp. 7–8; see also, Johnson, Chapter 21).

Second, as part of the assessment process, patients must participate in the 'Real Life Experience' (RLE – also known commonly as the 'Real Life Test'), in which they must demonstrate that they are living full-time within their preferred gender role for a period of at least a year. This will include at least one year on high doses of cross-sex hormones. When they assess the quality of the patient's Real Life Experience, clinicians review their ability 'to maintain full or part-time employment' (or 'to function as a student' or in some 'community-based volunteer activity', HBIGDA, 2001, p. 17). The patient must also provide documentary evidence that someone other than the psychiatrist (e.g. an employer) knows them to function outside of the clinic setting in their preferred gender role, and change their first name to a 'gender appropriate' one (2001, p. 17).[13]

The Standards of Care (HBIGDA, 2001) does not treat physical appearance or success in passing in the preferred gender role as a formal criterion in assessing the quality of the Real Life Experience. Moreover, in recent years there has been a 'shift in thinking toward recognizing the enormous diversity in the ways that gender and gender roles can be expressed' and, some might suggest, an associated loosening of the requirement to pass as unambiguously male or female (Brown & Rounsley, 1996). Despite this, however, there are numerous reports in the literature that gender professionals 'have judged transsexuals' authenticity on their ability to pass' (Lev, 2004, p. 264). Indeed, gender professionals have noted that 'clients often look for positive feedback on their presentation. They show off their bodily changes and boast about their new breasts or hair growth' (Lev, 2004, p. 263). Certainly, we have found that it is not uncommon (as we go on to show below), for psychiatrists (as well as patients) to comment on the patient's appearance and overall ability to pass *as* a man or a woman, during the assessment sessions. Additionally, if patients do not turn up obviously 'in role', then psychiatrists will often treat this as an accountable matter. It is hardly surprising given this context that patients will interpret their success in the RLE as dependent on them showing, through their talk, bodily comportment, appearance and gestures, that they can pass as a convincing, 'always have been, always will be', male or female, in their interactions with the psychiatrist.

DATA AND METHOD

The data excerpt we analyse below derives from a large corpus of more than 150 audio-recorded and 20 video-recorded psychiatrist–patient consultations from a large British National Health Service (NHS) Gender Identity Clinic. These data were collected by the authors as part of a large scale Economic and Social Research Council funded study of the construction of transsexual identities in medical contexts.

The clinic in our study is the largest GIC in the world. Ninety-five per cent of all NHS referrals are dealt with here, and psychiatrists at the clinic see 600 new patients each year.

---

[13] For more on the diagnosis and treatment of transsexualism see Green (2000, 2004).

The majority of patients attending this clinic self-identify as pre-operative, male-to-female transsexuals. Although statistics on such matters are notoriously problematic, this reflects the much larger incidence of transsexualism amongst males in the population (some of the latest figures from the Netherlands suggest transsexualism effects 1 in 11 900 males and 1 in 30 400 females, HBIGDA, 2001, p. 2). At the time we collected our data, there were four psychiatrists at the clinic – three male and one female. Although all four psychiatrists were involved in audio-recording their sessions with patients, two of the male psychiatrists recorded the majority of sessions for this study. One of these psychiatrists also consented to video-recording approximately 30 of his sessions for the study. Each recorded session lasts 15–60 minutes each. Although the relative infrequency of patients' appointments means that we are unable to track the progress of individual patients over time, our corpus includes examples of sessions with patients at a variety of different stages of the assessment process, from initial intake assessment interviews, to exit interviews (where they are signed off for surgery by a second psychiatrist), and post-surgery follow-ups.

Ethical approval for this study was granted by the NHS Central Office of Research Ethics Committee. Patients' participation was sought by the psychiatrist responsible for recording the session. They were provided with an information sheet and consent form, and had the opportunity to ask questions before recording commenced. Patients were advised that their decision whether or not to participate would not affect the course or outcome of their treatment, that their name and date of birth, and all names and place names referred to during the session would be changed in all reports produced by the study. They were told that stills of the videotapes may be printed in a scientific report, but that their image would be digitally disguised in order to protect their anonymity.

All data were transcribed verbatim in the first instance by a professional transcriber. Detailed transcripts were then worked up by the first author using conventions developed within CA by Gail Jefferson (2004). A simplified version of these conventions is included in the Appendix (see p. 363). Bodily movements and gestures were also noted in the margin on the transcript. Video stills have been included below to exemplify these gestures and their interlacing with the talk, where relevant to the analyses. The excerpt heading provides information about the date of the recording, and the exact location within that recording of the clip. The clip we have chosen is from an exit interview, and the patient identifies as a pre-operative male-to-female transsexual. This patient has been taking female hormones for over a year, and she presents 'in role', in traditional female attire. As we noted above, patients must be assessed by two psychiatrists before they can be referred for surgery. At her last visit to the clinic this patient obtained her first approval for surgery from one of the psychiatrists, and this interaction is taken from her session with a second psychiatrist. Four minutes prior to the start of the excerpt, the psychiatrist announces to the patient that he and his colleagues will be sending a letter to the surgeons endorsing her for surgery. This 'green light announcement' is a momentous occasion for this patient – who has been trying to obtain her surgery for 12 years (the psychiatrist tells the patient that until now she has not been deemed psychologically stable enough to proceed to surgery). The psychiatrist explains the referral process to the patient, and the risks of surgery, and informs her that she can pull out before the surgery. A minute after he first announces the clinic's approval for surgery, he states again that they will recommend her to the surgeon, subject to the condition that she is 'absolutely certain' that surgery is going to be helpful to her. The patient works to provide such assurances. The psychiatrist is at great pains to point out that genital surgery will not alter her outward appearance, and, in particular, to correct her erroneous assumption that genital surgery will prevent further loss of hair from her scalp. Indeed, he suggests that she could continue to live as a woman without the surgery. The patient responds that she would not have gone through 'all the things' she has 'been through' unless she was sure she wanted the surgery.

The excerpt we analyse below begins at this point in the interaction, one minute prior to the end of the assessment session. It begins with the psychiatrist re-issuing (now for a third time) the clinic's approval for surgery, this time subject to the patient meeting the condition (and reassuring him) that she is 'absolutely convi:nced' (lines 1–2). The whole sequence is dedicated to unpacking why the patient is 'absolutely convinced' that she wishes to go ahead with surgery, and, in particular, why she wants the surgery 'now'.

[Video 4. Clip 2. Male-to-Female Pre-op. 19.09.05. 33.30–34.30 mins. Exit interview]

```
 1    Psy:                    As long as you're absolutely convi:nced we'll let you
 2    Pat simultaneously      do it.
 3    engaged with bag              (.)
 4    Pat:                    W'll ye::ah- I mea- I mea:n there's no good puttin'
 5                            any more obstacles in the way, I might aswell j's:t
 6                            sort of get it done when I know I can sti::ll- you
 7                            know- hopefully maybe I mean,
 8    Pat sweeps hair both    I- I do: (0.4) you know people at wo:rk think I've
 9    sides of face           got a lovely figure >I mean I've got that going for
10    Psy smiles, Pat         me I (look/got)quite nice,<
11    gestures hand across chest
12                                  (0.8)
13    Psy:                    [°Okay°.
14    Pat:                    [(because/figure) slight- you know- kind of- you
15                            know- dependin',
16                                  (.)
17    Pat: Psy nods          >An- that's the men(h)< (h)ri(h)ght(h) I'm not
18                            (   ) say that (   ) so .hhh you kno::w uh:m,
19                                  (0.4)
20    Pat: Pat gestures       I mean my face is- I c'd do with putting a ba:g over
21    bag over head           my head b't .hhh uh:m,
22                                  (0.4)
23    Pat:                    .Pt as a ru:le- you know like as I say the lo:nger
24    Psy nods                I leave it the harder it's gonna ge:t,you know(°l-°)
25    Psy:                    Okay but whether or not you have the genital
26                            surgery, [sitting here right now,
27    Pat:                             [Ye:ah,
28                                  (.)
29    Pat:                    Yeah,
30                                  (.)
```

```
31   Psy:                   I don' know whether you've had surgery.
32                                  (1.0)
33   Pat:                   You don't kno:w.
34   Psy:  Psy hands out-   [(        I'm) here looking at you who]=
35   Pat:  stretched,       [Oh r:ight      yes   that's what I'm]=
36   Psy:  shakes head      =[who w'd know?=
37   Pat:  and shrugs       =[saying.        Yeah. Yeah. (Sure).
38   Psy:                   This is not a (nudist) interview.
39                                  (.)
40   Pat:                   No. Su:re. [Su:re.]
41   Psy:                              [You]    look like a woman.
42                                  (.)
43   Pat:                   Yea:h, n[o, that's right. (Yeah that's)
44   Psy:                           [You don't have to have surgery to
45                          continue looking like a woman [(of course).
46   Pat:                                                 [Yeah but- I- I- s- I-
47   Psy nods               (0.6) I- I want to have relationsh(h)ip(h) so(h)
48                          wi[th a ma:n or whatever. .h[h
49   Psy:  Psy nods         [Okay.                      [Okay.
50   Pat:                   An' (0.4) whatever.
51   Psy:  Psy nods and     [Okay.
52   Pat:  starts to get    [You know so,
53   Psy:  up. Psy stands   Okay, we will send a let[ter of referral
54   Pat:                                           [Yeah, okay,
```

ON THE ROLE OF APPEARANCE ATTRIBUTIONS
IN PASSING AS FEMALE

Like Garfinkel (1967), Kessler and Mckenna (1978, p. 136) and others (e.g. Fenstermaker, West & Zimmerman, 2002; West & Zimmerman, 1987) we are of the view that gender is *omnirelevant* in interaction. Although it is typically a 'seen but unnoticed . . . background in the texture of relevances that comprise the changing actual scenes of everyday life' (Garfinkel, 1967, p. 118), every single thing a person does or says (whether it explicitly indexes gender or not), can potentially be 'read', interpreted, or accounted for through the lens of gender.[14] The relevance of gender is particularly acute within the clinic environment, where the patient's actions are institutionally consequential: they have a direct bearing on whether or not they pass as a man or a woman, and, in turn, on whether or not the psychiatrist deems that they meet the institutionally ratified criteria to be diagnosed as transsexual.

---

[14] Fenstermaker, West and Zimmerman (2002, p. 29) note that 'an individual involved in virtually any course of action may be held accountable for her or his execution of that action as a woman or a man . . . virtually any pursuit can be evaluated in relation to its womanly or manly nature'. But compare Sacks (1972), who suggests that 'there is no cross-setting omnirelevant categorization device that has been *shown* to be omni-relevant' (Schegloff, nd: n5, emphasis in original).

As symbolic interactionists, conversation analysts and gender and language researchers have shown, gender gets 'indexed', 'displayed', or 'oriented to', through a range of vocal and gestural means (Goffman, 1979; Hopper & LeBaron, 1998; Ochs, 1992; Schegloff, 1997a). One routine conversational means through which gender gets indexed (implicitly and explicitly) in the GIC, and through which passing gets done, is via what we are calling 'appearance attributions' – that is, references to what the patient *looks* like. In our data, appearance attributions are initiated by both parties, and take a range of forms (e.g. 'I/you look *x*', 'I/you have *x appearance*', I/you are an *x looking kind of person*). Such attributions are typically evaluative, involving positive or negative assessments of some appearance-relevant attribute.[15] We have marked these appearance attributions on the transcript in bold.

We have chosen this excerpt for analysis, in part, because it contains examples of both patient-initiated and psychiatrist-initiated appearance attributions. As such, it allows us to investigate the interactional circumstances in which the patient deploys appearance attributions in order to pass as a transsexual female, *and* those circumstances in which she is apparently treated as having passed successfully by the psychiatrist. Additionally, in this excerpt we have a chain of *multiple* descriptions concerning the patient's appearance. This allows us to track how such descriptions develop incrementally over time, with each successive turn in the interaction, and in response to the recipient's actions.

We will show that appearance attributions are multi-unit phenomena that can be used by patients in an incrementally upgraded or downgraded fashion to pursue (and respond to) certain kinds of participation from the psychiatrist. In this excerpt these appearance attributions are progressively *downgraded* by the patient in order to attract a response in which the psychiatrist co-participates in her performance by treating her *as a woman*.

Let us start by taking a closer look at the first few lines of the excerpt. What can we say about the interactional environment in which the first, patient-initiated (reported) appearance attribution takes place?

THE PSYCHIATRIST'S OPENING DECLARATIVE AND THE PATIENT'S (HEDGED) RESPONSE

As we noted above, the psychiatrist's conditional declarative 'As long as you're a̲bsolutely convi:nced we'll let you do it'[16] (lines 1–2) re-issues the approval for surgery that he had given the patient just four minutes prior to the start of this excerpt. It also recycles his subsequent conditional approval in which he sought the patient's assurances that she was 'absolutely certain' that she wished to go ahead with the surgery. Now the clinic's approval is subject to the patient meeting the condition (and reassuring the psychiatrist) that she is 'a̲bsolutely convi:nced'.

In a sense, this whole exchange is dedicated from the outset to being a 'sequence-closing sequence' (Schegloff, 2007). As conversation analysts have shown, the re-mentioning of topics from prior talk is often done in closing environments, precisely in order to

---

[15] For more on the conversation analytic understanding of assessments see C. Goodwin & M. Goodwin, 1987; Heritage & Raymond, 2005; Pomerantz, 1984a.

[16] This utterance represents a clear orientation by the psychiatrist to the institutional, gatekeeping role of the psychiatrists at the clinic, and their control over the patient's destiny.

Figure 16.1   Lines 1–2, Psy: 'As long as you're absolutely convi:nced we'll let you do it'.

bring that talk to a close (Schegloff & Sacks, 1973). From the psychiatrist's initiation of a sequence that echoes, almost precisely, the topic and structure of the just-prior talk, the patient would be able to project that the psychiatrist is moving toward closure of the assessment session, just prior to the 'closing proper'. That the patient is oriented to this *as* a closing relevant environment is evident from Figure 16.1, where she is clearly in the middle of packing the paperwork that she has been showing the psychiatrist during the session into her bag.[17]

The psychiatrist's declarative makes relevant and 'prefers' (Pomerantz, 1984a)[18] a response in which the patient shows herself to agree with the formulation that she is 'absolutely convi:nced' – to produce a 'no doubts' response. Indeed, given what we have just noted about the closing relevance of the psychiatrist's declarative, this interaction could end relatively swiftly at line three with the patient saying 'of course I'm convinced'. Instead, the patient responds with the turn initial 'W'll ye::ah' (line 4). This indicates that her response will not be straightforward (Schegloff & Lerner, 2004) and treats the under-lying supposition of the question – that she may have some remaining doubts about pro-ceeding to surgery – as inapposite. She goes on to produce a (hedged) account for *why* she is convinced, and which explains *why* she needs the surgery now.[19]Although the psy-chiatrist's question does not ask the patient to produce this kind of account, it nonetheless opens up a slot in which she can unpack, and provide evidence for, precisely why his question is inapposite (the 'I mean' (line 4) is dedicated to launching this task). So what does the patient's account for 'why now' consist of?

Her 'I mea:n there's no good puttin' any more obstacles in the way' (lines 4–5) indexes the views of many patients who see the real life test as an inconvenient hoop they must jump through in order to get what they need. In lines 5–6, she seems to be having some trouble over formulating her response. She says 'I might aswell j's:t sort of get it done when I know I can sti::ll'. But still what? This turn is clearly moving toward explicating some time- or age-limited activity in which surgery would allow her to participate, but it

---

[17] Indeed as soon as the psychiatrist has finished his turn at lines 1–2, and throughout the patient's response at lines 4–7, the patient pulls the drawstring of her bag up towards her and slowly sliding it closed, before resting the bag on her lap.

[18] For more on the conversation analytic notion of preference see Sacks, 1987 and Schegloff, 2007.

[19] Indeed, as we shall see, this entire sequence builds toward an account in which the patient specifies why she needs surgery *at all* (lines 46–48).

trails off. Indeed, it may be designedly doing so in that it relies on the psychiatrist to project where the patient might be going with this turn, and specifically to infer what time- or age-limited activities she is explicitly *not* stating. The patient's 'hopefully maybe' (line 7) is taking up a stance of desire towards this world of activities that she hopes she might 'still' be able to partake in and which she has so far been unable to articulate. However, here again, the precise specification of this world of desires and possible actions is aborted in favour of further unpacking ('I mean' – line 7).

The utterance that comes exactly next is the patient's first appearance attribution 'I- I do: (0.4) you know people at wo:rk think I've got a lovely figure' (lines 8–9.) In combination, the hedging, the temporalizing of 'sti::ll' (line 6), the stance taking of 'hopefully maybe' (line 7), and the appearance attribution (lines 8–9), provide clues that help the psychiatrist indexically to fill in or infer what the patient is getting at here: that she wants the surgery now, while she is still young and attractive enough to get a partner.

Indeed, lines 5–9 can be heard as possibly 'suppressing' (Schegloff, 2003) what they're going towards, and which we arrive at only eventually after the psychiatrist's challenge, at lines 46–48: 'Yeah but- I- I- s- I- (0.6) I- I want to have relationsh(h)ip(h) so(h) with a ma:n or whatever. .hh'. The word 'relationsh(h)ip(h)' captures the patient's as-yet-unstated desire for a (hetero)*sexual* relationship. In addition, the utterance is delivered in a hesitant fashion (note the cut-offs, re-starts and the 0.6 second pause in lines 46–47), and is interpolated with laughter. This hesitation and laughter suggest that the patient is orienting toward this utterance as a delicate object (Haakana, 2001). That this matter – of having a sexual relationship with a man – is oriented to as delicate by the patient, *and* exists in a sequential environment in which it gets addressed only *after* the psychiatrist's challenge, suggests that such matters may indeed have been those that were being suppressed at lines 5–9.[20]

THE PATIENT'S (REPORTED) APPEARANCE ATTRIBUTION

Let us now take a closer look at the appearance attribution: 'I- I do: (0.4) you know people at wo:rk think I've got a lovely figure', and its launching at line 8. The first thing we wish to note is that the launching of this appearance attribution coincides precisely with a 'self-groom' in which the patient sweeps her hair away from both sides of her face, as exemplified in Figures 16.2a, 16.2b and 16.2c, below.

That this self-groom coincides so precisely with the launching of the appearance attribution at line 8 indicates to us that it may not be entirely random (i.e. that the patient's hair is in the way of her face and needs moving at just this moment). Rather, it may be a gender display that's designedly fitted to the vocal elements of the interaction. By 'designedly fitted' we mean that as a distinctly feminine, normatively recognizable way that women groom their hair (especially, perhaps, during heterosexual interactions[21]), it works as an

---

[20] Note that we are using the notion of suppression rather differently from Schegloff (2003, p. 246). According to Schegloff, evidence for suppression consists in the word/s that were suppressed (if they seem to have been projected) appearing in the immediately following talk. In the instance we discuss here, lines 46–48 are non-proximate to what we are suggesting constitutes the suppressed element in lines 5–9. Therefore, we can only infer (just as the psychiatrist may infer) that lines 46–48 constitutes the 'surfacing' of that suppressed element.

[21] Of course, the patient does not know the sexual orientation of the psychiatrist in these data, but this does not rule out the patient treating the interaction from within a heteronormative framework *as* a heterosexual interaction.

Figure 16.2a Lines 8–9, Pat: 'I- I <u>do</u>: (0.4) you know people at <u>wo</u>:rk think I've got a <u>lo</u>vely figure'

Figure 16.2b Lines 8–9 cont'd

Figure 16.2c Lines 8–9 cont'd

implicit indexing of gender, and a 'seen but unnoticed' background (Garfinkel 1967) through which the psychiatrist will frame and interpret the vocal element of what the patient is saying. In combination, we see the vocal (appearance attribution) and the visual (self-groom) here as mutually elaborative and reinforcing elements of the same phenomenon – that is, of the patient showing the psychiatrist that not only is she treated by others outside of the clinic environment as a woman, but that she is able to behave like one within it.

Indeed, the second thing we wish to note about the appearance attribution at line 8 is that the turn in which it appears is launched with 'I- I do:'. This seems to be the beginnings of some kind of positive self-assessment (e.g. it could be going towards 'I do think I look nice', or 'I do have a lovely figure'), but it is repaired[22] in favour of the participation-seeking 'you know' (which invites the psychiatrist to fill in inferences regarding what the patient is getting at here (Fox Tree & Schrock, 2002)), and the reported compliment of a third party: 'people at wo:rk think I've got a lovely figure' (lines 8–9). This repair from 'I do:' to 'people at wo:rk think' constitutes a shift in the patient's footing (Clayman, 1992). This footing shift appears to be in the service of avoiding what Pomerantz (1978) has termed 'overt self-praise' or a 'self-brag'.

Some of Sacks's (1975, p. 72) observations are pertinent here. Sacks makes a distinction between two different kinds of statement. He notes: 'For the first, if, e.g. a little girl comes home and says to her mother, *Mama, I'm pretty* or *Mama, I'm smart*, the mother could say "Who told you that?." For the second if someone says *I'm tired* or *I feel lousy*, etc., no such thing is asked. One is responsible for knowing some things on one's own behalf, in contrast to the situation in which one is treated as likely to be repeating what another has told him about himself.'

In shifting her footing and reporting the compliment of a third-party (line 9), the patient avoids the kind of self-brag associated with the first statement that Sacks identifies above. Since, for reasons of self-praise avoidance, the patient may not be at liberty to compliment herself, these third parties ('people at wo:rk' (line 8)) are, by virtue of being third parties, *entitled* (and perhaps more entitled than she is) to make an objective assessment of her appearance.

In addition to being *interactionally consequential*, it is also *clinically consequential* that the patient formulates the description of her appearance in this way. Indeed, she is currently being assessed by the psychiatrist in part for whether she has a *realistic* view of herself in her new role. If she can convince the psychiatrist that she passes with others (both men and women) outside the clinic environment who notice and comment on feminine aspects of her appearance – thus *treating her as a woman*, then she can show that she is hardly deluded about her trans status.[23]

---

[22] For more on the conversation analytic notion of repair see Schegloff, Jefferson & Sacks (1977) and Schegloff (2007).

[23] In other words, in reporting this reference to recognizably feminine *attributes*, she shows herself to *be*, and to be recognizable by others as, a *bone fide* member of the *category* 'woman' (Sacks, 1995). Of course, the appearance attribution, 'I've got a lovely figure', does not index gender explicitly, through the use of gender category terms or pronouns, for example. Nor does it get oriented to explicitly as gendered by the psychiatrist in his next turn. Indeed, this utterance could *potentially* be said by men about themselves, or by others about men. In this respect, we appear to have no analytic basis from which to suggest that such utterances constitute examples of the patient *doing gender* at all. However, if we could show that this kind of appearance attribution is regularly uttered *by women* about themselves, and by others *about women*, and that such 'ways of talking' are, outside this context, *regularly treated as, or oriented to* explicitly by members as things said normatively by and about women, then we may be justified on this occasion in treating such utterances as *possible instances of* the speaker showing that she is *doing being*, or *speaking as* a woman (and we may claim this independently of whether or not members explicitly orient towards such utterances in their next turn *as* doing femininity). For more on the notion of a 'possible x' see Schegloff (2006). For more on the relationship between attributes and categories see Schegloff (nd).

The psychiatrist's pose remains steadfast throughout this first reported appearance attribution. It is possible this steadfastness, combined with his apparent failure to respond visibly or vocally to the self-groom, the patient's repeated 'you know's, and the positive reported compliment-in-progress, may account for why the patient shifts footing again at line 9, as she unpacks what she meant by, and her stance towards, the embedded compliment. Her '>I mean I've got that going for me' (lines 9–10) indexes back directly to the assessment, 'lovely figure', shows that she affiliates with it, and holds its relevance in place.

This is followed with a second appearance attribution: 'I (look/got)quite nice, <' (line 10) – an attribution in which the patient is now assessing her own figure, and displaying what she takes to be the import of the reported compliment. As she produces this appearance attribution, she gestures her hand across her chest. This gesture comes to completion after the word 'nice' (line 10), and, here again, seems to work in a mutually elaborative fashion with the talk in order to convey what it is that the patient is getting at, and to encourage the psychiatrist to respond (see Figure 16.3).

'I (look/got)quite nice, <' (line 10) – is clearly framed as a *positive* self-assessment, but is also a *downgraded* assessment that is not as strong as 'lovely figure'. Why might the patient downgrade the assessment in this way?

As we have seen, the psychiatrist remains steadfastly non-responsive throughout lines 8 and 9. He does not coparticipate in the patient's assessments, affiliate with, or ratify what she is saying. He does smile as the patient produces her gesture at line 10, as she starts to voice her second appearance attribution, 'I (look/got)quite nice'. However, this is a 'grimacy' smile that's strongly mitigated by the hand in front of his face (see Figure 16.3). This smile appears to show that the psychiatrist is responding to what the patient is saying, but without explicitly agreeing or disagreeing with it.

In our view, each of the three components of the patient's turn in lines 8–10: the reported compliment, the displayed alignment with the reported compliment, and the downgraded self-assessment, seem to work incrementally to secure, and pursue (Pomerantz 1984b) a particular kind of response from the psychiatrist. Indeed, as conversation analysts have shown, recipients of first assessments often co-participate in those assessments by producing agreeing and upgraded second assessments (Pomerantz, 1984a; see also Heritage & Raymond, 2005). We want to suggest that, in this instance, the patient

Figure 16.3 Line 10, Pat: 'I (look/got) quite nice, <'

uses each of the three elements of her turn in lines 8–10 to exploit this normative feature of the sequential organization of assessments, and to secure just this kind of recipient uptake from the psychiatrist. In particular, with each added unit of her turn-so-far she seems to be working to encourage the psychiatrist to affiliate with, validate or ratify what she is saying.

THE PSYCHIATRIST'S RESPONSE TO THE PATIENT'S POSITIVE APPEARANCE ATTRIBUTIONS

Instead of affiliating, however, the 0.8 second gap at line 12 projects a 'dispreferred' response (Pomerantz, 1984a). Indeed, following this gap the psychiatrist says a rather quiet '°Okay°' (line 13) which, like the smile at line 10, is mitigated by his hand over his face. Just like the smile, although it does not explicitly align or disalign with what the patient has said, this '°Okay°' is certainly not doing enthusiastic uptake or acknowledgement.[24] Indeed, it is so delayed that it overlaps with the patient's continuation of her turn. This failure on the part of the psychiatrist to respond adequately to what the patient is saying seems to be oriented to by the patient, whose turn at lines 14–15 contains overt signs of trouble: it is full of false starts, perturbations, and affiliation-seeking 'you knows': '(because/figure) slight- you know- kind of- you know dependin'. Despite this, however, each part of her turn acts like a 'filler': This turn holds the import of the prior assessment in place – and most importantly – the relevance of a response *to* that assessment. Thus, the psychiatrist *could* repeat the 'Okay' or make some other visible indication of uptake or a readiness to take a turn at any point during lines 14–16, but he does not.

Then, as if orienting to the psychiatrist's lack of affiliation so far as an indication that something is problematic or needs repairing in her prior talk (Davidson 1984; Schegloff 1997a, 1997b), the patient says '>An- that's the men(h)< (h)ri(h)ght(h) I'm not ( ) say that ( )' (lines 17–18). This turn is interpolated with 'nervous' sounding laughter, and is accompanied by a hand gesture in which the patient rotates her arm away from her body toward the psychiatrist (see Figure 16.4).

Figure 16.4   Line 17, Pat: '>An- that's the men(h)< (h)ri(h)ght(h)'

---

[24] See C. Goodwin & M. Goodwin (1987) for how recipients can refuse to co-participate in assessments.

Although it is not possible to hear precisely what the patient is saying here, it appears that this utterance indexes directly back to, and is locating as a possible trouble source, her earlier reported compliment and subsequent alignment with it. Through this turn the patient clarifies that it is 'the men(h)' (at work) who say this about her, and that she is not saying this about herself. In doing so she works to deflect the potential imputation available at this time, that her assessment was produced independently (with the corresponding implication that it may be a self-brag), as opposed to being her *interpretation* of the compliment of a third party. The psychiatrist fails to respond vocally, but emits an almost imperceptible nod on completion of the word '(h)ri(h)ght(h)' (line 17) – a nod that we are taking to be an 'I've heard you' nod, rather than an affiliative or agreeing nod.

THE PATIENT'S SELF-DEPRECATION

In the absence of the kind of response from the psychiatrist that she appears to be working towards, the patient continues 'so .hhh you kno::w uh:m,' (line 18) – thus providing further opportunities for the psychiatrist to show that he is participating in which she is saying. After a further 0.4 seconds gap of silence at line 19, the patient proceeds to unpack what it is that she is getting at by providing a third appearance attribution – this time in the form of a negative assessment or *self-deprecation* of her (facial) appearance: 'I mean my face is- I c'd do with putting a ba:g over bag over head my head,' (lines 20–21). This self-deprecation is accompanied by an intricate gesture whereby she points to her face and, just ahead of vocalizing the self-deprecation, exemplifies the act of putting a bag over her head (see Figures 16.5a, 16.5b and 16.5c).

This self-deprecation does three things: First, by virtue of being a self-deprecation it works to deflect any remaining imputation that the patient is engaging in a self-brag. Second, by targetting her *facial* appearance it shows (irrespective of whether or not it is 'true') that she has a balanced, realistic view of her appearance, that she is 'aware' that although she may have a lovely figure, that there are other features of her appearance that might be problematic. That she uses the recognizably humorous 'bag over head' metaphor to communicate this self-deprecation, also shows that she is able to *mock* herself, and that

Figure 16.5a   Lines 20–21, Pat: 'I mean my face is- I c'd do with putting a ba:g over my head'

Figure 16.5b   Lines 20–21 cont'd

Figure 16.5c   Lines 20–21 cont'd

she does not take herself, or her appearance, too seriously. Third, like the two positive assessments at lines 8–10, this self-deprecation seems to be a further attempt on the part of the patient to get a more active kind of response or participation from the psychiatrist. Indeed, as CA work on negative self-assessments or self-deprecations has shown (Pomerantz, 1984a) they usually prefer some sort of *disagreement* by the recipient. Moreover, as an idiomatic and humorous reference, the 'bag over head' metaphor is instantly recognizable, and, as such, should ideally elicit some kind of jocular disagreement or humour from the psychiatrist. The 'b't .hhh uh:m' at line 21, and the 0.4 second gap at line 22 both provide further opportunities for the psychiatrist to participate. However, here again, he remains steadfastly non-responsive.

Having moved through a chain of progressively downgraded appearance attributions ranging from the very positive 'lovely figure' (line 9), through the downgraded 'quite nice' (line 10), right through to the self-deprecating 'my face is- I c'd do with putting a ba:g over my head' (lines 20–21), the patient appears to have nowhere else to go with the appearance attribution to get the kind of participation from the psychiatrist that she seems to be pursuing. Indeed, she has already worked hard in her prior talk to locate and rectify any potential sources of trouble that may account for the psychiatrist's non-participation.

Figure 16.6   Lines 23–24, Pat: 'the lo:nger I leave it the <u>h</u>arder it's gonna <u>ge</u>:t'

When she continues her turn at line 23, the patient produces a series of cliches: 'as a <u>ru</u>:le' (line 23) and 'the lo:nger I leave it the <u>h</u>arder it's gonna <u>ge</u>:t' (lines 23–24). As instantly recognizable 'truisms', these utterances are easily and perhaps normatively 'agreeable with' (especially when combined with the participation-seeking 'you knows' at lines 23 and 24). There is also something about these cliches which may alert the psychiatrist that the patient's account is coming to completion. For example, Schegloff and Sacks (1973, p. 306) suggest that such 'aphoristic' formulations can be heard as summarizing the 'moral' or 'lesson' of the speaker's perspective. And summary assessments, 'appear to be implicative of closure for a topic, and are recurrently deployed prior to various forms of topic shift' (Jefferson, 1984, p. 211, see also Holt & Drew, 2005).

There is also evidence that the patient is returning to addressing the very matter that she started with – that is, accounting for why she is convinced that she needs the surgery now. The 'as a <u>ru</u>:le' formulates the gist or overall upshot of what the patient is getting at here, while the 'like as I say the lo:nger I leave it the <u>h</u>arder it's gonna <u>ge</u>:t' (lines 23–24) explicitly marks this as returning to something that the patient has already said. Likewise, the 'it' indexes right back to the psychiatrist's reference to surgery at line 2. Finally, the temporalizing of references like 'the lo:nger I leave it', is reminiscent of the temporalizing of 'when I know I can sti::ll' (line 6), again, clearly returning to the issue of 'why surgery now'. As we noted earlier, speakers will often return to topics from prior talk in closing environments (Schegloff & Sacks, 1973). From such re-mentionings, the psychiatrist might project that on completion of her turn, the patient will have said all that she has to say on this topic, and transition of speakership is relevant. Indeed, the psychiatrist begins to nod over the word 'gonna' (line 24), which suggests that he is projecting where the patient is going with this, and with a second nod repetition over the remainder of the patient's turn at line 24, displays a readiness to take a turn (see Figure 16.6).

THE PSYCHIATRIST'S CHALLENGE

The psychiatrist immediately follows these nods with an 'O<u>k</u>ay but' at line 25, and then a hand gesture that mirrors that just used by the patient (see Figure 16.7).

In combination with the nods, the 'O<u>k</u>ay but' and gesture seem to work to bracket off (rather than to agree or affiliate with) what the patient has just said, and stop her from

Figure 16.7   Lines 25–26, Psy: 'O<u>k</u>ay but <u>wh</u>ether or not you have the <u>g</u>enital <u>s</u>urgery,'

continuing any turn possibly in progress (the barely audible '°l-°' in line 24 *might* indicate that the patient is going to continue, but could also be evidence that her turn is trailing off in order to let the psychiatrist come in). As Wayne Beach (1995) has shown, 'okay's' are often deployed by medical practitioners as a way of closing down a patient's discussion of non-clinical matters. Indeed, in many ways, this 'o<u>k</u>ay but' seems to work like an explicit acknowledgement of the psychiatrist's failure to participate in the way the patient may be working towards here. It launches a challenge to what the patient is saying, which extends over lines 25, 26 and 31: 'O<u>k</u>ay but <u>wh</u>ether or not you have the <u>g</u>enital <u>s</u>urgery, <u>s</u>itting here right <u>n</u>ow, . . . <u>I</u> don' know whether you've had surgery'. This challenge is one of a series that involve the psychiatrist voicing his 'here and now' experience of the patient in order to counter what she has been alluding to both within and prior to the start of this excerpt: First, that genital surgery may affect her outward appearance, and, second (and by implication), that she may be more able to attract a man when she has had the operation.

   Although the psychiatrist clearly *does* know that the patient is *pre*-operative, on the face of it, 'I don' know whether you've had surgery' (line 31), could be interpreted as an indirect compliment – and a proposal that the patient 'passes'. Indeed, the long, one second gap at line 32, and the patient's response, '<u>Y</u>ou don't kno:w' (line 33) indicates that she is having some trouble in understanding what the psychiatrist is getting at here. '<u>Y</u>ou don't kno:w' targets precisely the element in the psychiatrist's utterance that the patient is treating as problematic – thus prompting him to clarify. The psychiatrist responds by shaking his head and shrugging, his arms outstretched. Just after he initiates these gestures, he says: '(I'm) here looking at you who=who w'd know?' (lines 34 and 36) (see Figure 16.8).

   On seeing the onset of these gestures, and in overlap with the start of the psychiatrist's turn, the patient shows that she's 'got it': 'Oh r:ight' (line 35). And then something rather interesting happens: Instead of treating the psychiatrist's turn at lines 25–31 as something that *challenges* her account for 'why surgery now', the patient's 'yes that's what I'm=saying' (line 35), transforms it into something that potentially *aligns with*, or *ratifies* her own position. Thus, once out of overlap, she says 'Yeah. Yeah. (Sure)' (line 37). The repetition of these discrete lexical items shows further, not only that she accepts and agrees with what the psychiatrist is saying, but that she is treating what he says as something that is

Figure 16.8 Lines 34–36, Psy: '(I'm) here looking at you who= who w'd know?'

already evident to her.[25] Then, in a further effort to clarify, and as if to 'drum his position home' to the patient, the psychiatrist states: 'This is not a (nudist) interview' (line 38). The patient responds with a further repetition of three lexical items: 'No. Su:re. Su:re.' (line 40), signalling both her agreement with what the psychiatrist is saying, and that his comments are not news. The psychiatrist continues to elaborate his 'here and now' experience of the patient, this time with an *explicitly gendered* appearance attribution: 'You look like a woman' (line 41).

THE PSYCHIATRIST'S APPEARANCE ATTRIBUTION

The psychiatrist's appearance attribution differs from those of the patient in that it does not contain any subjective, assessing terms like 'lovely' or 'nice' (cf. lines 9 and 10). Instead, it is produced as an objective, *clinical* statement about the patient's appearance. However, here again, instead of treating 'You look like a woman' (line 41) as part of a challenge, the patient accepts it, transforming it into a potential compliment that validates her own, position: 'Yea:h, no, that's right. (Yeah that's)' (line 43).

In the face of this, the psychiatrist now shifts away from detailing aspects of his 'here and now' experience of the patient, towards formulating the import or upshot of these experiences for his challenge: 'You don't have to have surgery to continue looking like a woman (of course).' (lines 44–45). It is only now that the patient treats what he is saying *as* a challenge and makes her own, 'bottom line' account for why she wants surgery now explicit: 'Yeah but- I- I- s- I- (0.6) I- I want to have relationsh(h)ip(h) so(h) with a ma:n or whatever. .hh' (lines 46–48). This bottom line account alludes to what we suggested the patient might be suppressing right at the start of this excerpt: that she needs the surgery now because she wants the appropriate genital equipment for a heterosexual relationship.

That the psychiatrist now treats this account as acceptable and wishes to bring the session rapidly to a close is evidenced from his five nod repetitions – initiated at the word 'so(h)' (line 47) and just prior to each 'okay' at line 49, and his repeated, sequence closing 'okays' at lines 51 and 53 (Schegloff, 2007). The delivery, positioning and relative intensity

---

[25] For more on the function of multiple sayings see Stivers (2004).

Figure 16.9   Line 53, Psy: 'Okay, we will send a letter of referral'

of these nods and okays would allow the patient to project that the session is coming to a close, and indeed her account trails off with the generalized 'or whatever.' (line 48), the 'An' (0.4) whatever.' (line 50), and the alignment-seeking filler 'you know so,' (line 52). At line 51 the psychiatrist begins to uncross his legs and prepares to get up from his chair. He begins to stand at line 53 (see Figure 16.9), at the same time reiterating what he had said four minutes prior to the start of this excerpt: 'we will send a letter of referral', thus bringing the sequence to a close.

CONCLUSION: ON TREATING SOMEONE *AS* A WOMAN

We have analysed an excerpt that contains a chain of multiple descriptions concerning the patient's appearance. We noted that these appearance attributions are multi-unit phenomena that can be used in an incrementally upgraded or downgraded fashion in order to seek (and respond to) certain kinds of participation from the psychiatrist. In this excerpt, the patient progressively *downgrades* her descriptions in order to secure a response from the psychiatrist in which he co-participates in, and ratifies her performance by *treating her as a woman*.

Of course, one might suggest that the psychiatrist's resultant *failure* to participate in the interaction in the way that the patient appears to be working towards here, can be accounted for, in part, by reference to his status as a professional expert who is expected to exemplify just the kind of *professional distance* or *clinical neutrality* that we see here (Clayman & Heritage, 2002; Drew & Heritage, 1992; Heritage & Maynard, 2006). However, this argument cannot provide a complete explanation, because the psychiatrist's own, subsequent appearance attributions: 'You look like a woman' (line 41), and 'You don't have to have surgery to continue looking like a woman (of course)' (lines 44–45) show that he is not averse to making explicitly gendered comments about the patient, or commenting on her appearance.

So what might account for this seemingly contradictory behaviour on the part of the psychiatrist? In particular, why might he appear reluctant at first to ratify or validate the patient's position, only to subsequently state that she does indeed look like a woman? There are some sequential features of these appearance attributions that have consequences for the way in which they get produced and managed. Crucially, the patient's reported compliment (lines 8–9) and subsequent downgraded appearance attributions (lines 10 and 20–21), are relatively informal, 'lifeworld' descriptions (Mishler, 1985, pp. 81–82), which place the psychiatrist in *second position* (that is – a *responsive* position) to the patient's assessments (Sacks, 1995; Schegloff, 2007). Thus, if he were to agree with them (and to disagree with the self-deprecation), it would require him to respond by co-participating in treating the patient as a woman in a non-clinical way – agreeing with her view of her appearance.[26] By contrast, the psychiatrist's description 'You look like a woman' (line 41), devoid as it is of the kinds of evaluative terms (e.g. 'lovely' and 'nice') evidenced in the patient's life-world narrative, is delivered in *first position* in order to fulfil the *clinical*, and hence formal, professional task of informing the patient that an operation will not affect her outward appearance. Now the patient is in the responsive position, and must affiliate or disaffiliate with his (clinical) view of her appearance. This shows that the psychiatrist is not averse to telling the patient that she looks like a woman – that she 'passes'. Rather, he *is* averse to being placed in *second position* to a life-world narrative in which he must agree or disagree with, ratify or validate *her view of her appearance*. It follows that the precise composition and position of the psychiatrist's (clinical) appearance attributions, is bound up with his efforts to sustain a relatively neutral, medical definition of the situation in the face of the pursuit by the patient of 'counterthemes' (Emerson, 1970). And this order of things is very much in line with the psychiatrist's role as gate-keeper in this setting (Speer & Parsons, 2006).

We are not simply arguing that gender identities – and passing – is co-constructed. Rather, the distinctiveness of what we have tried to show here is that the precise form the patient's gender-infused descriptions, displays and passing practices take, is highly contingent on the type of participation that is shown by the psychiatrist. Clearly, parties are able to exploit the normative sequential features of interaction (e.g. whether one is in first position, initiating a course of action, or in second position, responsive to a course of action), in order to seek ratification of, or avoid being placed in the role of having to ratify, a particular identity. It remains to be seen whether we would see similar patterns of participation in other, non-institutional settings (such at dating interactions, for example), where participants strive to have their displayed identities affirmed and ratified by others.

A further important point we wish to note here is this: these appearance attributions do not exist in an interactional vacuum. When a speaker notes that someone has a 'lovely figure', or 'looks like a woman', it does not necessarily follow that they are off-loading some cognitive-perceptual experience of their recipient, or making a factual, objective statement about what their recipient looks like. When people make ontological statements about their own or others' appearance or gender, it does not necessarily follow that such statements are neutral renderings of some 'reality'. Thus, no matter how many times I might say 'I'm a man', or 'I look like a man' it does not automatically mean that I *am* one, or that I look like one. As one of us (Speer, 2005b) has demonstrated elsewhere, the task of attributing gender (and mis-attributing, or failing to attribute) is a complex interactional process that cannot be explained exclusively or primarily in terms of cognitive

---

[26] Although the patient does not know whether the psychiatrist is gay or straight, being treated as a woman *by a man* in a heteronormative culture, may be the ultimate validation of one's passing – and a testament to the mutually co-implicative relationship between gender and sexuality.

perceptual factors, or members' desire to apprehend and describe some gendered, 'out there in the world', reality. Rather, members consistently describe cognitive processes, including their factual-objective 'perceptions' of 'real world' people and events, as part of *doing* things (Edwards, 1997; Te Molder & Potter, 2005), and gender relevant appearance attributions get tailored to the interactional context in which the attributor finds themselves. It follows that the precise gendered reality that members construct is very much dependent on the local interactional concerns of the present.

Crucially, when we consider the detailed turn-by-turn construction of this interaction, it becomes clear that although gender is relevant to the interactions of both parties (as we noted above, it forms an omnirelevant background to the interaction), 'doing gender', 'indexing gender' and 'orienting to gender', is not the *primary* activity of either party, or the most salient thing about what they are doing with their talk at that moment. Neither patient nor psychiatrist is, first and foremost, engaged in the act of displaying or ratifying gender. Rather, these appearance attributions are delivered *primarily* in the service of *other, non-gendered business* (see also Kitzinger, 2007). Thus, the patient's implicitly gendered appearance attributions at lines 8–10, and 20–21, are produced in order to account for why she is 'absolutely convi:nced' (line 1) that she wants the surgery now, while the *psychiatrist's* explicitly gendered appearance attributions at lines 41 and 44–5 are deployed as part of a counter-argument designed to *challenge* the patient's account – and in particular – her alluded-to view that surgery will alter her appearance.

That the patient's attempts to pass, and be treated by the psychiatrist as a woman, may be subservient to these other activities, does not mean that gender and passing are not relevant here, or that gender is not getting done, indexed or oriented to. Indeed, in this particular setting, gender is a fairly pervasive category that gets indexed and talked about, *much of the time*. Rather, since gender is normatively a 'seen but unnoticed' phenomenon, then it makes sense that doing, indexing and orienting to gender co-exists with, and gets woven relatively seamlessly into the texture of interactional slots whose primary purpose is the accomplishment of *other* actions – even in this setting. It is this multi-layered nature of social action which accounts for how it is that in the GIC (as, perhaps, elsewhere), telling a patient that they 'look like a woman' – that they 'pass', does not necessarily involve *treating* them as one. Talking about, indexing, or doing gender on the one hand, and treating someone as gendered on the other, are very different things. Just as explicitly articulating a gender category does not automatically make gender relevant to what is going on in the talk, so too, gender can be relevant and consequential for an interaction even where a gender category is not explicitly articulated (Raymond & Heritage, 2006).

We want to end by suggesting that LGBTQ psychologists and other gender and language scholars might benefit from closer engagement with videotaped materials of interactions in real-life settings. To date LGBTQ researchers – particularly those inspired by queer theory (e.g. Butler 1990, 1993, 2004), have tended to treat gender identity as something that 'congeals' over time – an outcome of the re-iteration of a series of discrete 'performatives'. However, such theories of gender are overwhelmingly abstract and tend to be disengaged from 'the social' (Jackson 1999). Researchers within the queer theoretical tradition do not analyse 'real-life' accounts, there is no sense in their work of a peopled world in which participants interact and speak with one another, and the role of recipients in co-constructing gender – indeed *inter*subjectivity itself – is largely ignored (Speer, 2005a). Consequently, such work exists in isolation from the concrete practices of the very members whose gendered performatives it purports to illuminate.

We hope to have demonstrated in this chapter that considerable insights can be gained from examining real-life empirical materials in their turn-by-turn detail – considering both the composition of the speaker's turn, its position in a sequence of turns, and the mutually elaborative relationship of the talk with bodily gestures and movements. It is this kind of analysis, rather than abstract theorizing, that we believe offers the most promising set of tools with which to develop a systematic, empirically grounded form of LGBTQ psychology. This approach will allow us to validate our politics and theories of the workings of gender and heteronormativity in an analytically tractable fashion, in the turn-by-turn, line-by-line analysis of recorded, live interactional materials, in front of us, on the page.

APPENDIX: TRANSCRIPTION NOTATION

.	A full stop indicates falling, or stopping intonation.
,	A comma indicates a continuing intonation.
?	A question mark indicates rising intonation.
-	A dash marks a sharp cut-off of the just prior word or sound.
↑	An upward arrow immediately precedes rising pitch.
↓	A downward arrow immediately precedes falling pitch.
LOUD	Capitals mark talk that is noticeably louder than that surrounding it.
°quiet °	Degree signs enclose talk that is noticeably quieter than that surrounding it.
Underline	Underlining marks parts of words that are emphasized by the speaker.
Rea::lly	Colons mark an elongation or stretch of the prior sound. The more colons, the longer the stretch.
huh/hah	Marks full laughter tokens.
(h)	An 'h' in brackets indicates laughter particles.
.hhh	A dot before an 'h' or series of 'h's indicates an inbreath.
hhh	An 'h' or series of 'h's marks an out-breath.
>faster<	'More than' and 'less than' signs enclose speeded up talk.
=	An equals sign indicates immediate latching of successive talk.
(2.0)	The length of a pause or gap, in seconds.
(.)	A pause or gap that is hearable but too short to assign a time to.
[overlap]	Square brackets mark the onset and end of overlapping talk.
( )	Single brackets mark transcriber doubt.
(brackets)	Content of single brackets represents a possible hearing.
((laughs))	Double brackets enclose comments from the transcriber.

ACKNOWLEDGEMENTS

We gratefully acknowledge the support of the ESRC (award number RES-148-0029) for funding the research reported here. The first author would also like to acknowledge the support of an ESRC-SSRC Collaborative Visiting Fellowship, which funded her trip to the University of California at Los Angeles as a Visiting Scholar in 2005–2006. She would like to thank Candy Goodwin, Chuck Goodwin, Jon Hindmarsh, Chris Koenig, Gene

Lerner and Geoff Raymond for their helpful comments during data sessions on the extract presented here. All deficiencies are of course, our own.

REFERENCES

American Psychiatric Association (1994). *Diagnostic and Statistical Manual of Mental Disorders* (4th edn). Washington, DC: American Psychiatric Association.

Atkins, D. (Ed.) (1998). *Looking Queer: Body image and identity in lesbian, bisexual, gay, and transgendered communities.* New York, NY: Harrington Park Press.

Austin, J. L. (1962). *How to do Things with Words.* Oxford: Clarendon Press.

Beach, W. A. (1995). Preserving and constraining options: 'Okays' and 'official' priorities in medical interviews. In G. H. Morris & R. J. Cheneil (Eds), *The Talk of the Clinic: Explorations in the analysis of medical and therapeutic discourse* (pp. 259–289). Hillsdale, NJ: Lawrence Erlbaum Associates, Inc.

Bell, S. (Ed.) (1995). *Whore Carnival.* Brooklyn, NY: Autonomedia.

Birdwhistell, R. L. (1970). *Kinesics and Context.* Philadelphia, PA: University of Pennsylvania Press.

Bologh, R. W. (1992). The promise and failure of ethnomethodology from a feminist perspective: Comment on Rogers. *Gender & Society,* **6**(2), 199–206.

Brown, M. & Rounsley, C. (1996). *True Selves: Understanding transsexualism for families, friends, coworkers, and helping professionals.* San Francisco, CA: Jersey-Bass.

Burns, C. (2006). *Collected Essays in Trans Healthcare Politics: Documenting the Scandal of How Medicine Lost the Trust of Trans People.* [Online document] Retrieved September 2006, from: http://www.pfc.org.uk/files/essays-transhealth.pdf

Butler, J. (1990). *Gender Trouble: Feminism and the subversion of identity.* New York, NY: Routledge.

Butler, J. (1993). *Bodies that Matter: On the discursive limits of 'sex'.* London: Routledge.

Butler, J. (2004). *Undoing Gender.* New York, NY: Routledge.

Califia, P. (1997). *Sex Changes: The politics of transgenderism.* San Francisco, CA: Cleis Press.

Clayman, S. (1992). Footing in the achievement of neutrality: The case of news interview discourse. In P. Drew & J. Heritage (Eds) *Talk at Work: Interaction in institutional settings* (pp. 163–198). Cambridge: Cambridge University Press.

Clayman, S. & Heritage, J. (2002). *The News Interview: Journalists and public figures on the air.* Cambridge: Cambridge University Press.

Crawford, M. (Ed.) (2000). A reappraisal of *Gender: An ethnomethodological approach. Feminism & Psychology,* **10**(1), 7–72.

Davidson, J. A. (1984). Subsequent versions of invitations, offers, requests, and proposals dealing with potential or actual rejection. In J. M. Atkinson & J. Heritage (Eds), *Structures of Social Action: Studies in Conversation Analysis* (pp. 102–128). Cambridge: Cambridge University Press.

Denny, D. (2000). Rachel and me: A commentary on *Gender: An ethnomethodological approach. Feminism & Psychology,* **10**(1), 62–65.

Denzin, N. K. (1990). Harold and Agnes: A feminist narrative undoing. *Sociological Theory,* **8**(2), 198–216.

Denzin, N. K. (1991). Back to Harold and Agnes. *Sociological Theory,* **9**(2), 280–285.

Doyle, D. (2002–2005). *Fem Image: Femininity Coaching for Transsexuals and Serious Cross-dressers* [Website]. Retrieved September, from: http://www.femimage.com/

Dozier, R. (2005). Beards, breasts, and bodies: Doing sex in a gendered world. *Gender & Society,* **19**(3), 297–316.

Drew, P. & Heritage, J. (Eds) (1992). *Talk at Work: Interaction in institutional settings.* Cambridge: Cambridge University Press.

Edwards, D. (1997). *Discourse and Cognition.* London: Sage.

Emerson, J. P. (1970). Behavior in private places: Sustaining definitions of reality in gynecological examinations. *Recent Sociology,* **2**, 74–97.

Feinberg, L. (1996). *Transgender Warriors: Making history from Joan of Arc to Dennis Rodman.* Boston, MA: Beacon Press.

Fenstermaker, S. & West, C. (Eds) (2002). *Doing Gender, Doing Difference: Inequality, power, and institutional change.* New York, NY: Routledge.

Fenstermaker, S., West, C. & Zimmerman, D. H. (2002). Gender inequality: New conceptual terrain. In S. Fenstermaker & C. West, C. (Eds), *Doing Gender, Doing Difference: Inequality, power, and institutional change* (pp. 25–39). New York, NY: Routledge.

Fox Tree, J. E. & Schrock, J. C. (2002). Basic meanings of *you know* and *I mean. Journal of Pragmatics*, **34**(6), 727–747.

Frances, S. J. (1979). Sex differences in nonverbal behavior. *Sex Roles*, **5**(4), 519–535.

Garfinkel, H. (1967). *Studies in Ethnomethodology.* Englewood Cliffs, NJ: Prentice-Hall.

Goffman, E. (1963). *Stigma: Notes on the management of spoiled identity.* Englewood Cliffs, NJ: Prentice-Hall.

Goffman, E. (1979). *Gender Advertisements: Studies in the anthropology of visual communication.* New York, NY: Harper and Row.

Goffman, E. (1983). The interaction order. *American Sociological Review*, **48**(1), 1–17.

Golden, C. (2000). Still seeing differently, after all these years. *Feminism & Psychology*, **10**(1), 30–35.

Goodwin, C. (1980). Restarts, pauses and the achievement of mutual gaze at turn beginning. *Sociological Inquiry*, **50**(3/4), 272–302.

Goodwin, C. (1981). *Conversational Organization: Interaction between speakers and hearers.* New York, NY: Academic Press.

Goodwin, C. (2003). The semiotic body in its environment. In J. Coupland & R. Gwyn (Eds), *Discourses of the Body* (pp. 19–42). New York, NY: Palgrave/Macmillan.

Goodwin, C. & Goodwin, M. H. (1987). Concurrent operations on talk: Notes on the interactive organization of assessments. *IPrA Papers in Pragmatics*, **1**(1), 1–55.

Goodwin, C. & Goodwin, M. H. (2004). Participation. In A. Duranti (Ed.), *A Companion to Linguistic Anthropology* (pp. 222–244). Oxford: Basil Blackwell.

Goodwin, M. H. (1980). Processes of mutual monitoring implicated in the production of description sequences. *Sociological Inquiry*, **50**(3–4), 303–317.

Goodwin, M. H. (2001). Organizing participation in cross-sex jump-rope: Situating gender differences within longitudinal studies of activities. *Research on Language and Social Interaction*, **34**(1), 75–106.

Goodwin, M. H. (2002). Building power asymmetries in girls' interaction. *Discourse & Society*, **13**(6), 715–730.

Goodwin, M. H. (2006). *The Hidden Life of Girls: Games of stance, status, and exclusion.* Oxford: Blackwell.

Green, R. (1987). *The 'Sissy Boy Syndrome' and the Development of Homosexuality.* New Haven, CT: Yale University Press.

Green, R. (2000). Gender identity disorder in adults. In M. Gelder, J. Lopez-Ibor, & N. Andreasen (Eds), *The New Oxford Textbook of Psychiatry* (pp. 913–917). Oxford: Oxford University Press.

Green, R. (2004). Transsexualism: Historical to contemporary notes. *Sexologies*, **13**(47), 22–25.

Haakana, M. (2001). Laughter as a patient's resource: Dealing with delicate aspects of medical interaction. *Text*, **21**, 187–219.

Hall, K. (1997). Go suck your husband's sugarcane! Hijras and the use of sexual insult. In A. Livia & K. Hall (Eds), *Queerly Phrased: Language, gender, and sexuality* (pp. 430–460). New York: Oxford University Press.

Hall, K. (2005). Intertextual sexuality: Parodies of class, identity, and desire in liminal Delhi. *Journal of Linguistic Anthropology*, **15**(1), 125–144.

HBIGDA (2001). The Harry Benjamin International Gender Dysphoria Association *Standards of Care for Gender Identity Disorders*, Sixth Version. Retrieved September 2006, from: <http://www.hbigda.org/Documents2/socv6.pdf>

Heath, C. (1986). *Body Movement and Speech in Medical Interaction.* Cambridge: Cambridge University Press.

Heath, C. (2006). Body work: The collaborative production of the clinical object. In J. Heritage & D. Maynard (Eds), *Communication in Medical Care: Interactions between primary care physicians and patients* (pp. 185–213). Cambridge: Cambridge University Press.

Henley, N. M. (1977). *Body Politics: Power, Sex, and Nonverbal Communication*. Englewood Cliffs, NJ: Prentice Hall.

Heritage, J. (1984). *Garfinkel and Ethnomethodology*. Cambridge: Polity Press.

Heritage, J. & Maynard, D. (Eds) (2006). *Communication in Medical Care: Interactions between primary care physicians and patients*. Cambridge: Cambridge University Press.

Heritage, J. & Raymond, G. (2005). The terms of agreement: Indexing epistemic authority and subordination in talk-in-interaction. *Social Psychology Quarterly*, **68**(1), 15–38.

Hilbert, R. A. (1991). Norman and Sigmund: Comment on Denzin's 'Harold and Agnes'. *Sociological Theory*, **9**(2), 264–268.

Hird, M. (2002). For a sociology of transsexualism. *Sociology*, **36**(3), 577–595.

Holliday, R. (1999). The comfort of identity. *Sexualities*, **2**(4), 475–491.

Holt, E. & Drew, P. (2005). Figurative pivots: The use of figurative expressions in pivotal topic transitions. *Research on Language & Social Interaction*, **38**(1), 35–61.

Hopper, R. & LeBaron, C. (1998). How gender creeps into talk. *Research on Language & Social Interaction*, **31**(1), 59–74.

Jackson, S. (1999). Feminist sociology and sociological feminism: Recovering the social in feminist thought. *Sociological Research Online*, **4**(3). Retrieved September 2006, from: http://www.socresonline.org.uk/socresonline/4/3/jackson.html

Jefferson, G. (1984). On stepwise transition from talk about a trouble to inappropriately next-positioned matters. In J. M. Atkinson & J. Heritage (Eds), *Structures of Social Action: Studies in conversation analysis* (pp. 191–222). Cambridge: Cambridge University Press.

Jefferson, G. (2004). Glossary of transcript symbols with an introduction. In G. H. Lerner (ed.) *Conversation Analysis: Studies from the first generation* (pp. 13–31). Amsterdam: John Benjamins.

Jeffreys, S. (1990). *Anticlimax: A feminist perspective on the sexual revolution*. London: Women's Press.

Jeffreys, S. (2003). *Unpacking Queer Politics: A lesbian feminist perspective*. Malden, MA: Blackwell Publishers.

Kessler, S. J. & McKenna, W. (1978). *Gender: An ethnomethodological approach*. New York, NY: John Wiley & Sons.

King, D. (2003). Gender migration: A sociological analysis (or the leaving of Liverpool). *Sexualities*, **6**(2), 173–194.

Kitzinger, C. (2000). Doing feminist conversation analysis. *Feminism & Psychology*, **10**(2), 163–193.

Kitzinger, C. (2007). Is 'woman' always relevantly gendered? *Gender & Language*.

Lev, A. I. (2004). *Transgender Emergence: Therapeutic guidelines for working with gender-variant people and their families*. Binghampton, NY: The Haworth Clinical Practice Press.

Lynch, M. & Bogen, D. (1991). In defense of dada-driven analysis. *Sociological Theory*, **9**(2), 269–276.

MacKenzie, G. (1994). *Transgender Nation*. Bowling Green, OH: State University Popular Press.

May, K. (2002). Becoming women: Transgendered identities, psychosexual therapy and the challenge of metamorphosis. *Sexualities*, **5**(4), 449–464.

Maynard, D. W. (1991). Goffman, Garfinkel, and games. *Sociological Theory*, **9**(2), 277–279.

Mishler, E. G. (1985). *Discourse of Medicine: Dialectics of Medical Interviews*. Norwood, NJ: Ablex.

More, K. (1999). Never mind the bollocks: 2. Judith Butler on Transsexuality. In K. More & S. Whittle (Eds), *Reclaiming Genders: Transsexual Grammars at the fin de siècle* (pp. 285–302). London: Cassell.

Namaste, V. K. (2000). *Invisible Lives: The erasure of transsexual and transgendered people*. Chicago, IL: The University of Chicago Press.

Newman, L. K. (2000). Transgender Issues. In J. Ussher (Ed.), *Women's Health: Contemporary international perspectives* (pp. 394–404). Leicester: BPS Books.

Ochs, E. (1992). Indexing gender. In A. Duranti & C. Goodwin (Eds), *Rethinking Context: Language as an interactive phenomenon* (pp. 335–358). Cambridge: Cambridge University Press.

Oxford English Dictionary (2006). *The Oxford English Dictionary*. Retrieved July 2006, from: http://www.oed.com/

Peel, E. (2005). Effeminate 'fudge nudgers' and tomboyish 'lettuce lickers': Language and the construction of sexualities in diversity training. *Psychology of Women Section Review*, **7**(2), 22–34.

Pomerantz, A. (1978). Compliment responses: Notes on the co-operation of multiple constraints. In J. Schenkein (Ed.), *Studies in the Organization of Conversational Interaction* (pp. 79–112). London: Academic Press.

Pomerantz, A. (1984a). Agreeing and disagreeing with assessments: Some features of preferred/dispreferred turn shapes. In J. M. Atkinson & J. Heritage (Eds), *Structures of Social Action: Studies in Conversation Analysis* (pp. 79–112). Cambridge: Cambridge University Press.

Pomerantz, A. (1984b). Pursuing a response. In J. M. Atkinson & J. Heritage (Eds), *Structures of Social Action: Studies in conversation analysis* (pp. 152–163). Cambridge: Cambridge University Press.

Raymond, J. (1979). *The Transsexual Empire: The making of the she-male*. New York, NY: Teachers College Press.

Raymond, G. & Heritage, J. (2006). The epistemics of social relationships: Owning grandchildren. *Language in Society*, **35**(5), 677–705.

Rogers, M. F. (1992a). They were all passing: Agnes, Garfinkel, and company. *Gender & Society*, **6**(2), 169–191.

Rogers, M. F. (1992b). Resisting the enormous either/or: A response to Bologh and Zimmerman. *Gender & Society*, **6**(2), 207–214.

Sacks, H. (1972). An initial investigation of the usability of conversational data for doing sociology. In D. Sudnow (Ed.) *Studies in Social Interaction* (pp. 31–74). New York: Free Press.

Sacks, H. (1975). Everyone has to lie. In M. Sanches & B. Blount (Eds), *Sociocultural Dimensions of Language Use* (pp. 57–80). New York, NY: Academic Press.

Sacks, H. (1987). On the preferences for agreement and contiguity in sequences in conversation. In G. Button & J. R. E. Lee (Eds), *Talk and Social Organisation* (pp. 54–69). Clevedon: Multilingual Matters.

Sacks, H. (1995). *Lectures on Conversation* (vols 1 and 2 combined, G. Jefferson, ed.). Oxford: Blackwell.

Sacks, H. & Schegloff, E. A. (2002). Home position. *Gesture*, **2**(2), 133–146.

Schegloff, E. A. (1984). On some gestures' relation to talk. In J. M. Atkinson & J. Heritage (Eds), *Structures of Social Action: Studies in conversation analysis* (pp. 266–298). Cambridge: Cambridge University Press.

Schegloff, E. A. (1991). Reflections on talk and social structure. In D. Boden & D. Zimmerman (Eds), *Talk and Social Structure* (pp. 44–70). Cambridge: Polity Press.

Schegloff, E. A. (1997a). Whose text? Whose context? *Discourse & Society*, **8**(2), 165–187.

Schegloff, E. A. (1997b). Practices and actions: Boundary cases of other-initiated repair, *Discourse Processes*, **23**(3), 499–545.

Schegloff, E. A. (1998a). Reply to Wetherell. *Discourse & Society*, **9**(3), 413–416.

Schegloff, E. A. (1998b). Body Torque. *Social Research*, **65**(3), 535–596.

Schegloff, E. A. (2003). The Surfacing of the Suppressed. In P. Glenn, C. D. LeBaron & J. Mandelbaum (Eds), *Studies in Language and Social Interaction: In honor of Robert Hopper* (pp. 241–262). Mahweh, NJ: Lawrence Erlbaum.

Schegloff, E. A. (2006). On possibles. *Discourse Studies*, **8**(1), 141–157.

Schegloff, E. A. (2007). *Sequence Organization in Interaction: A primer in conversation analysis, Vol I*. Cambridge: Cambridge University Press.

Schegloff, E. A. (No date) A tutorial on membership categorization.

Schegloff, E. A. & Lerner, G. (2004). Beginning to respond. Paper presented at the *Annual Meeting of the National Communication Association*, Chicago, IL, November.

Schegloff, E. A. & Sacks, H. (1973). Opening up closings. *Semiotica*, **8**(4), 289–327.

Schegloff, E. A., Jefferson, G. & Sacks, H. (1977). The preference for self-correction in the organization of repair in conversation. *Language*, **53**(2), 361–382.

Schrock, D., Reid, L. & Boyd, E. M. (2005). Transsexuals' embodiment of womanhood. *Gender & Society*, **19**(3), 317–335.

Seidman, S. (2002). *Beyond the Closet: The Transformation of Gay and Lesbian Life*. London: Routledge.

Skidmore, P. (1999). Dress to impress: Employer regulation of gay and lesbian appearance. *Social & Legal Studies*, **8**(4), 509–529.

Smith, D. E. (2002). Foreword. In S. Fenstermaker & C. West (Eds), *Doing Gender, Doing Difference: Inequality, power, and institutional change* (pp. i–xv). New York, NY: Routledge.

Speer, S. A. (2005a) *Gender Talk: Feminism, discourse and conversation analysis*. London: Routledge.

Speer, S. A. (2005b). The interactional organization of the gender attribution process. *Sociology*, **39**(1), 67–87.

Speer, S. A. & Parsons, C. (2006). Gatekeeping gender: Some features of the use of hypothetical questions in the psychiatric assessment of transsexual patients. *Discourse & Society*, **17**(6), 785–812.

Stivers, T. (2004). 'No no no' and other types of multiple sayings in social interaction. *Human Communication Research*, **30**(2), 260–293.

Stivers, T. & Sidnell, J. (2005). Introduction: Multi-modal interaction. *Semiotica*, **156**(1/4), 1–20.

Stone, S. (1993). The 'empire' strikes back: A posttranssexual manifesto. Retrieved September 2006, from http://sandystone.com/empire-strikes-back.

Stokoe, E. & Smithson, J. (2001). Making gender relevant: Conversation analysis and gender categories in interaction. *Discourse & Society*, **12**(2), 217–244.

Te Molder, H. & Potter, J. (Eds) (2005). *Conversation and Cognition*. Cambridge: Cambridge University Press.

The UK Intersex Association (nd). [Webpage]. Retrieved September 2006, from http://www.ukia.co.uk

Tiefer, L. (2000). Agreeing to disagree: Multiple views on gender laws and transsex. *Feminism & Psychology*, **10**(1), 36–40.

Transsexual Roadmap (1996–2006). *Passing*. Retrieved September 2006, from http://www.tsroadmap.com/early/passing.html

West, C. & Zimmerman, D. (1987). Doing gender. *Gender & Society*, **1**(2), 125–151.

Whittle, S. (1999). Introduction 2. In K. More & S. Whittle (Eds), *Reclaiming Genders: Transsexual grammars at the fin de siècle* (pp. 6–11). London: Cassell.

Wittgenstein, L. (1953). *Philosophical Investigations*. Oxford: Blackwell.

Wood, J. T. (2002.) *Gendered Lives: Communication, gender and culture* (5th edn). Belmont, CA: Wadsworth.

Zimmerman, D. H. (1992). They were all doing gender, but they weren't all passing: Comment on Rogers. *Gender & Society*, **6**(2), 192–198.

CHAPTER 17

Alcohol and Gay Men: Consumption, Promotion and Policy Responses

Jeffery Adams
The University of Auckland, Aotearoa New Zealand
Tim McCreanor
Te Ropu Whariki and Centre for Social and Health Outcomes Research and Evaluation, Massey University, Aotearoa New Zealand
and
Virginia Braun
The University of Auckland, Aotearoa New Zealand

INTRODUCTION

Alcohol has been consumed in most societies for as long as history has been recorded, and drinking is woven into the fabric of social existence (Mandlebaum, 1965). Today alcohol is consumed in almost all societies (Roche, 2001), and in many countries it is the most widely used drug (see, for example, Field & Casswell, 1999). Alcohol has important cultural and symbolic meanings and is used in various ways including as a means of socialization, an instrument of hospitality and as an intoxicant (Babor et al., 2003). While the harmful effects of alcohol consumption are significant at the population level, they are also particularly significant for some sub-populations, including gay men. In this chapter, we focus on gay men and alcohol, arguing that alcohol use is a significant health issue for gay men. We review recent research on the marketing and promotion of alcohol (see, for example, Babor et al., 2003; Casswell, 2004; McCreanor et al., 2005), identifying a new area of concern – the *public health* implications of alcohol marketing directed at gay men. Exemplars of how gay communities are 'targetted' by alcohol companies promoting their products are provided and we also discuss how gay communities have responded to alcohol use by gay men. We conclude that specific gay health issues, such as alcohol use, remain under-researched within psychology (and elsewhere) and that further research is required so that effective health promotion strategies can be developed.

Out in Psychology: Lesbian, gay, bisexual, trans and queer perspectives. Edited by Victoria Clarke and Elizabeth Peel.
© 2007 John Wiley & Sons, Ltd.

Most current mainstream alcohol research ignores issues of (gay male) sexual orientation, perhaps reflecting the negative positioning of gay men relative to other groups in society (Adams, Braun & McCreanor, 2007). The specific focus on gay men in this chapter reflects our position as collaborators engaged in research on gay men's health issues. The first author is a gay man currently researching gay men's health issues for a PhD in critical health psychology. The other authors are heterosexual, with experience in research about/ with gay men, and have reflected on their involvement in such projects elsewhere (Braun, 2004; McCreanor, 1996, 2004). There are also specific aspects of the topic of the consumption and promotion of alcohol that we identify as supporting this focus on gay men (and which we develop through this chapter). These include: an established, if limited, tradition in psychology addressing 'homosexual' men and alcoholism; some research focusing on gay men's consumption patterns; and a substantial body of advertising and alcohol promotion aimed directly at gay men. Our discussion may, in part, be applicable to lesbian, bisexual, transgender and queer (LBTQ) communities, but in general we agree with Wilkinson (2002) that gay and lesbian health issues are likely to be most usefully addressed and advanced separately (e.g. MacBride Stewart, Chapter 20). We argue that a specific focus on gay men is necessary to recognize the complexities that are apparent in gay men's health (Adams et al., 2007).

PSYCHOLOGY, GAY MEN AND ALCOHOL

Psychology has had a long-standing interest in the relationship between 'homosexuality' and alcohol, including psychoanalyst Abraham's linking of alcoholism and homosexuality at the turn of the twentieth century (Israelstam & Lambert, 1983). Historically, alcoholism and homosexuality were viewed as diseases to be cured and there was a great deal of interest in alcohol abuse by 'homosexual' men (Israelstam & Lambert, 1983). Such studies fit the pattern of early psychology in presenting homosexuality as a form of pathology (Coyle & Wilkinson, 2002). In more recent times there has been an increased recognition of the legitimacy of gay (and LBTQ) research in psychology (Kitzinger, 1997; Kitzinger & Coyle, 2002), and much research into alcohol use no longer presumes that gay men, in particular, have a problem with alcohol.

Most psychological research on alcohol and gay men is located within health psychology. Health psychology expands understandings of health and illness, and contributes to the task of improving the health of society (Murray, 2004a). However, Murray and others (e.g. Crossley, 2000; Marks, 2002) are critical of mainstream health psychology, arguing that to be useful it needs to incorporate more than individualistic explanations of ill-health (Campbell, 2004; Murray, 2004a; see also MacBride-Stewart, Chapter 20). Instead, they advocate an approach that moves beyond the individual and considers interpersonal and social qualities (Murray, 2004b). Albee and Fryer (2003) explicitly identify the usefulness of a 'public health psychology' paradigm, where the skills of psychology are brought to focus on improving social and physical environments rather than improving outcomes at the individual level. Our approach to gay men and alcohol is located within critical health psychology and public health psychology. We focus on structural (rather than individual) explanations of health, drawing from critical approaches to (health) psychology that reject individual-focused epistemologies (Lee, 2000; Ussher, 2000), and which recognize that health and illness are socially and politically located (Stam, 2004). This is consistent with the population-level focus we incorporate from public health (Hepworth, 2004). Although we acknowledge the importance of mainstream positivist psychology – for establishing comprehensive prevalence data for example – we, nonetheless, agree that (health) psychology needs to focus more on being an 'agent for promoting health through varied methods of social rather than individual change' (Murray, 2004a, p. 228). We also draw on a developing body of psychological research on consumer culture, which in part looks at how advertising and consumption affect personal, social and ecological well-being (Kasser & Kanner, 2004). Thus, our concerns with alcohol use by gay men transcend individual gay men's use of alcohol, and incorporate and acknowledge the role of economic, political and social factors, both locally and globally (Hepworth, 2004; Morgan, Spicer & Reid, 2002; Murray & Campbell, 2003).

ALCOHOL AS A PUBLIC HEALTH ISSUE

Alcohol is a significant public health issue. It is a major cause of avoidable mortality and disability; the fifth highest risk factor worldwide in terms of burden of disease, rising to the third in industrial countries (World Health Organization, 2002). It has causal relationships with more than 60 types of disease and injury (World Health Organization, 2004a). The alcohol-related burden of disease is particularly acute among men, who overall are more likely to use alcohol than women and to consume at much higher rates (World Health Organization, 2004b). As well as being a burden in terms of disease, there are considerable economic costs incurred through alcohol consumption. In Aotearoa New Zealand, with a population of four million, the annual direct cost of alcohol misuse is estimated at NZ$2.9b (Easton, 1997). In the USA (population nearly 296 million), the cost of misuse per annum is estimated at US$148b (Harwood, Fountain & Livermore, 1998). In the UK (population over 60 million), annual costs related to alcohol misuse include: crime and public disorder (£7.3b); work place productivity (£6.4b); and health (£1.7b) (Prime Minister's Strategy Unit, 2003).

The dangers associated with alcohol are multiple and varied. Alcohol consumption has a variety of adverse effects on individuals, including impaired physical coordination, cognition and attention, as well as effects on nearly every organ of the body. It is also implicated with an increased incidence of infectious diseases and mental health issues (Room, 2002). In addition to individual effects, alcohol has the potential to impair a drinker's performance in family, work and social roles and can therefore affect bystanders, and acquaintances, friends and family of the drinker (Room, 2002). There is evidence for some positive effects of consuming alcohol, such as protection against diabetes and gallstones (Ashley et al., 2000). Many studies indicate alcohol's protective factor for coronary heart disease, although this appears to come from very low levels of consumption – one drink every *other* day (World Health Organization, 2004c). However, overall, many studies suggest that from a personal health perspective drinking is not advised, with more associated harm than benefits (Edwards et al., 1994; Rehm, Ashley & Dubois, 1997). From a public health perspective, it is the effects on the population as a whole that are the main concern. The premise of the 'new public health approach' to alcohol is that there is a diversity of alcohol problems, fairly widely distributed among the population of drinkers, and, therefore, alcohol-related harm is not just confined to a relatively small number of heavy drinkers (World Health Organization, 2004a).

ALCOHOL AND GAY COMMUNITIES

Around the world gay bars have historically been, and currently are, significant in the development and maintenance of gay communities (see Ellis, Chapter 14). For many gay men, socializing often involves alcohol and bars (Weinberg, 1994). Bars and clubs are a safe social space for gay men, providing an opportunity for men to construct and enact openly gay lives. As one of the few places a gay identity is completely accepted, bars have been described as 'induction' centres for gay men and as de-facto community centres (Malinowitz, 1995; Stall & Purcell, 2000). Many gay communities worldwide have as a focal point a specific geographic area or commercial centre (Bell, 2000; Higgs, 1999), often with numerous bars and clubs. One such area is Oxford Street in Sydney, Australia, where there are multiple gay pubs, clubs and sex venues (some of which serve alcohol), but, according to Schembri (2001), few other venues where men can meet and socialize. While bars and clubs serve positive functions, they are also places where alcohol (as well as tobacco and other drug) use is most likely to occur (Kus & Latcovich, 1995).

Much is made of the central role of bars in gay male culture, but this role is also contested as commercial venues do not cater for everyone (see Bennett & Coyle, Chapter 7). Many men find bars smoky and noisy, and some are not interested in the public gay scene (Moore, 1998). For other gay men, however, gay bars remain important, and the central role of bars potentially shapes the way gay men use alcohol (Greenwood et al., 2001). Although gay bars provide a 'safe' place for gay men to socialize, and attachment to (bar-focused) gay communities is likely to be positive for individual gay men, in terms of social interaction and support, it is also risk-inducing as far as alcohol and other drug use is concerned.

GAY MEN'S ALCOHOL CONSUMPTION

Since the 1970s, psychological research has examined the prevalence of alcohol use by gay men. Early studies, which were US-based, found significant levels of alcohol abuse among gay men. For example, one study found a rate of 'alcoholism' of about 29% amongst gay men (Lohrenz, Connelly, Coyne & Spare, 1978), a rate considerably higher than the 10% usually ascribed to the general population (Stall & Purcell, 2000). Other studies reported similar rates. However, these early studies have been subsequently criticized, primarily on methodological grounds, because the samples were drawn from bar patrons (Bux, 1996; Trocki, Drabble & Midanik, 2005). With the advent of the AIDS crisis in the mid-1980s, more representative sampling of gay men was undertaken and some of these studies included questions about substance abuse (Stall & Purcell, 2000). Bux's (1996) review of the literature found that the rates of substance abuse among gay men decreased from levels found in the 1970s. He concluded that gay men have a similar risk from heavy drinking as heterosexual men, but are less likely to abstain from alcohol. Altogether, this reported decline in prevalence is likely to result from methodological improvements in sampling and data collection, an increasing number of gay-focused treatment programmes, and the availability of other leisure options for gay men including cafés and gyms (Crosby, Stall, Paul & Barrett, 1998). Others suggest that the 1970s and 1980s were times of exceptionally *high* alcohol and other drug use within gay communities (Martin, Dean, Garcia & Hall, 1989; Ostrow et al., 1993).

Our review of the literature had identified four issues that we feel need further attention: (1) spread of consumption; (2) amount of consumption; (3) age and consumption; and (4) associations with risky sex. We now briefly discuss each of these areas in turn.

Spread of Consumption

Recent research indicates widespread use of alcohol by gay men. Skinner (1994) reported lifetime use of alcohol at high levels for gay men in the USA, with 98.5% ever having used alcohol, 88.5% having used over the past year and 76.0% having used in the last month. A study from Victoria (Australia) reported that about nine out of 10 gay, bisexual, queer (GBQ) men aged 20–59 use alcohol, a rate considerably higher than the seven out of 10 men in the overall population (Murnane et al., 2000). Stall et al. (2001) reported similar results in four large US cities, with 87% of gay men having used alcohol within the previous six months. Concurrently, reported rates of alcohol abstinence are consistently lower among gay men than the general population. For instance, a review of US national survey data found abstinence amongst gay men at a rate of 14% compared with 34% amongst heterosexual men (Drabble, Midanik & Trocki, 2005). Other US studies (e.g. McCabe, Boyd, Hughes & d'Arcy, 2003; McKirnan & Peterson, 1989; Skinner & Otis, 1992, 1996) have found a similar relationship between gay and straight male consumption. Skinner and Otis (1992), for example, reported that 21% of gay men had not consumed alcohol in the month prior to the survey, compared with 40% of men in the general population. Swedish research indicates rate of abstinence as the major point of difference between gay men and men in general, with abstinence at 3.2% and 9.2% respectively (Bergmark, 1999).

Amount of Consumption

As indicated above, the research on amount of consumption is split. Some US research suggests that when gay men use alcohol, it is used heavily and sometimes, but not always, at levels higher than men in general. Heavy alcohol use was confirmed by Stall and Wiley (1988) with 18.7% of gay men reporting having used alcohol heavily, compared with 11.3% of heterosexual men. Similarly, McKirnan and Peterson (1989) reported that 17% of gay men used alcohol heavily, although Crosby et al. (1998) reported a decrease in heavy levels of use among gay men (25–29 years) from 17.4% (in 1984) to 14.7% (in 1992). Rates of heavy alcohol consumption have been reported to be as high as 46% in HIV+ men in Australia (Guinan, Hall, Clarke & Gold, 1992). However, two other studies have reported few differences with regard to heavy drinking and use of alcohol between gay men and men in the general population (McKirnan & Peterson, 1989; Skinner & Otis, 1996). Among a sample of undergraduate students, the level of heavy episodic drinking in the past two weeks was 30% among gay undergraduate students, but 48% among other male undergraduate students (McCabe et al., 2003). Although there is some variance and disagreement in the literature over prevalence rates and differences between gay and heterosexual men's alcohol use, it is apparent that substantial numbers of gay men use alcohol heavily (Hughes & Eliason, 2002).

Age and Consumption

There are various 'demographic' factors in the research literature associated with alcohol consumption by gay men, with age the most salient (others, such as race/ethnicity, or class, are either less significant or under-researched). Unlike men in the general population, research suggests that gay men do not reduce their drinking as they get older (Bergmark, 1999; Murnane et al., 2000). In a study by Murnane et al. (2000), drinking by GBQ men in Australia remained relatively constant across age categories (20–29, 93.5% drinking; 50–59, 89.1% drinking). However, at the present time, we only have access to data from cross-sectional rather than longitudinal studies, which only reflect a snapshot in time. Longitudinal research on drinking patterns will be necessary to ascertain how drinking changes throughout the lifespan of gay men.

Alcohol use by young gay men is a recent focus for health research. Early onset alcohol consumption is of particular concern, as the risk of alcohol misuse throughout life increases when drinking starts young (Casswell, 1996; Chou & Pickering, 1992). In one Australian study, 65% of same-sex attracted youth aged 14–18 were drinking, a rate higher than for young people in the general population (Hillier et al., 1998). Research from the USA has similarly reported that same-sex attracted school students (Blake et al., 2001; DeBord, Wood, Sher & Good, 1998; Faulkner & Cranston, 1998; Rostosky, Owens, Zimmerman & Riggle, 2003) and gay/bisexual undergraduates (McCabe et al., 2003) are heavier users than their heterosexual counterparts. Another Australian study (Smith, Lindsay & Rosenthal, 1999) reported same-sex attracted males were twice as likely as heteroscxual males to be involved in hazardous drinking. Higher levels of binge drinking by young gay males have also been found in the USA (Caldwell, Kivel, Smith & Hayes, 1998), with 15% of same-sex attracted students reporting heavy drinking, compared with 3.8% of heterosexual students (Faulkner & Cranston, 1998). However, there is also some evidence to suggest that alcohol use among gay young men has decreased over time (Crosby et al., 1998).

Risky Sex and Other Health Issues

Alcohol use by gay men is linked with a number of negative health outcomes such as chronic diseases, violence and sexually transmitted infections (Gay and Lesbian Medical Association and LGBT health experts, 2001). In the context of research on gay men's health, alcohol (and other drug use) is often discussed in relation to its role in HIV infection, and is specifically linked to unsafe and risky sex – principally unprotected anal intercourse (McInnes, Hurley, Prestage & Hendry, 2001; Slavin, 2001). However, while numerous studies report an association between drinking and sexual risk behaviour in the general community (Maisto et al., 2004), the relationship between alcohol and unsafe sex remains a contested and complex issue for gay men (Stall & Purcell, 2000).

Alcohol use by gay men before and during sex has been associated with unsafe sex (Dolezal, Carballo-Dieguez, Nieves-Rosa & Diaz, 2000; Purcell et al., 2001; Stall et al.,

1986), with some indication that the greater the problem with alcohol use (and with other drugs) the greater the association with unsafe sex (Ross et al., 2001). In one study, 36% of HIV infected gay men who had had unsafe sex nominated alcohol as a factor (Guinan et al., 1992). Another study of young men (aged 15–22) who have sex with men found both unprotected receptive and insertive anal intercourse was positively associated with being under the influence of alcohol (Celentano et al., 2006). However, other studies (e.g. Leigh, 1990; McManus & Weatherburn, 1994; Reilly & Woo, 2001; Weatherburn et al., 1993) report no association between alcohol and unsafe sex. Weatherburn et al. (1993) found that condom use is not related to alcohol use and another study concluded that 'contrary to popular belief, the consumption of alcohol does not appear to make individuals more likely to engage in unsafe sex' (McManus & Weatherburn, 1994, p. 115). Blake et al.'s (2001) research on GLB youth reported higher use of alcohol (than heterosexual youth) but similar rates of condom use across the sample.

In sum, the literature suggests that alcohol is used differently by gay and heterosexual men, and may impact on risky sex behaviours among gay men (Donovan & McEwan, 1995). The relationship between alcohol and risky sex is a complex one, and probably cannot be fully understood without taking account of the meanings attached to alcohol use and the context of alcohol use, including the use of alcohol to heighten sexual pleasure (Kippax et al., 1998). Thus, not only is alcohol risky for its physiological impacts, but also because of behaviours and practices associated with it.

ALCOHOL PROMOTION

In this section of the chapter we consider socio-cultural contexts that shape why and how gay men are encouraged to drink alcohol. We explore alcohol advertising as one particular facet of socio-cultural contexts. To understand effectively gay men's relationship with alcohol, we need to look at the way it is promoted to gay men. We focus on the cultural precepts of the alcohol industry, which views gay men as a niche market ripe for exploitation, and the targetted advertising of alcohol that seeks to profit from the 'pink market'.

Since the early 1990s gay men have been an important niche market for many companies (Sender, 2004), with a range of products and services actively targetting gay male consumers (Badgett, 2001; Binnie, 1995; Dotson, 1999). This recognition by advertisers, particularly in the case of cigarette and alcohol promotions, pays scant attention to health consequences. Alcohol marketing is perhaps the most crowded category in international gay marketing (Commercial Closet Association, 2001). Alcohol industries, whose primary agenda is to maintain and expand their markets and maximize profits (Giesbrecht, 2000), are driven by the imperative for sales and profit. Alcohol advertising frequently portrays drinking as socially desirable, promoting pro-alcohol attitudes, and thereby recruiting new drinkers and increasing consumption among current drinkers (World Health Organization, 2004a). This is in fundamental conflict with the public health goal of reducing hazardous drinking and alcohol-related harm (McCreanor, Casswell & Hill, 2000).

The rationale for targeting gay markets comes from research that has shown that alcohol advertising does have a small but contributory impact on drinking behaviour (Edwards et al., 1994), especially by young people. Brand promotion advertising can target niche markets and desired lifestyles (Hill & Casswell, 2004; Wyllie, Zhang & Casswell, 1998), and there is increasing evidence that exposure to advertising shapes positive perceptions of drinking and can increase heavier drinking (World Health Organization, 2004a). A range of sophisticated marketing practices (e.g. in the print media, on the internet, and through event promotion and sponsorship) portray alcohol in an unproblematic way. These practices rarely show the harmful consequences of alcohol use (Babor et al., 2003; McCreanor et al., 2005), and aim to normalize alcohol use in everyday life (Hill & Casswell, 2004). We suggest that the effects of these practices may well be reflected in the widespread use of alcohol by gay men. Although alcohol companies often claim they promote moderate consumption of their products through the use of, for instance, 'drink responsibly' tag-lines in advertising, such messages in isolation from other measures (such as taxation and advertising controls) are not effective strategies to minimize adverse health effects (Babor et al., 2003).

Alcohol companies make deliberate decisions to target gay markets (Kilbourne, 1999), and a range of market research supports the commercial importance of gay consumers. In the USA, for example, it is estimated that there are 8.7 million gay men with a purchasing power of US$337b (Brown & Washton, 2004). Contemporary marketing theory suggests that communities are likely to respond positively to marketing that is sensitive to their identity and values (Brown & Washton, 2004; Cova & Cova, 2002; Godin, 1999; Lukenbill, 1999). Thus gay focused product promotion can be effective as it creates and expands feelings of brand loyalty (Stevens, Carlson & Hinman, 2004). Since the early 1980s, two brands – ABSOLUT vodka and Miller beer – have been prominent in the gay press and are recognized as being among the brands with high gay loyalty (Wilke, 2001). ABSOLUT is regarded as one of the most 'venerable' brands in the gay market, appearing consistently in gay publications many years before other major advertisers (Commercial Closet Association, 2001). It has targetted the gay market from the very beginning of its USA marketing campaign (Baker, 1997; Lewis, 1996), including advertising in the *Advocate* (US gay magazine) from 1981. The continued presence of alcohol advertising in the US print media reflects gay men's high readership of gay print magazines and newspapers (Brown & Washton, 2004), and shows that gay print media is cost-effective advertising (Yin, 2003). Much of this media (especially magazines) is widely available in other gay marketplaces, including in Australia, New Zealand and the UK.

Vodka and the Spirit of Gay Men

ABSOLUT vodka provides a good example of sophisticated, innovative marketing practices aimed at gay men. These practices include print advertising, sponsorship, internet promotions, branded events and billboards. ABSOLUT print advertisements are aimed specifically at gay consumers, through placement in appropriate media, and through featuring gay imagery and relevant text. ABSOLUT HARING (*Advocate*, US, 1986, back cover) was an early advertisement in the gay press. Featuring the artwork of Keith Haring, a well-know gay ('subway graffiti') artist (Lewis, 1996), it depicts an ABSOLUT bottle on a bright yellow background surrounded with bold lined, cartoon-like people with hands-raised, as if in celebration. Another advertisement featuring an ABSOLUT bottle sitting inside a gold crown with the words ABSOLUT QUEEN underneath it, directly appropriated colloquial gay language to associate the product and gay identity (*BlueMode*, Australian gay fashion magazine, 2003, inside back cover). ABSOLUT is involved with gay targetted sponsorship (including gay film festivals), is supportive of AIDS organizations, and is a corporate sponsor of GLAAD (Gay & Lesbian Alliance Against Defamation, US) and has sponsored the GLAAD media awards since its inception in 1990. ABSOLUT created a specific advertisement for GLAAD consisting of an ABSOLUT bottle presented as a lava lamp with the GLAAD logo shape forming the 'blobs' inside the lamp. ABSOLUT has also used billboard promotion (ABSOLUT OUT, 2003) in 'gay neighbourhoods' in San Francisco and New York, which played on 'closeted sexuality'. The promotion featured nine closets complete with items donated by gay celebrities such as Billy Bean (a former US major league baseball player), that were later available for purchase via live and online auctions. Internet promotion by ABSOLUT has included an interactive pop-up ad on gay.com (a US gay male lifestyle website), which required the user to manipulate a lemon squeezer to fill an ABSOLUT CITRON bottle. In 2004 ABSOLUT produced a planning guide for gay commitment ceremonies which was distributed as an insert in gay magazines including the *Advocate* and *OUT* and is also available online (http://www. absolutcommitment.com). It is clear that the gay community has been targetted by ABSOLUT as an important niche market for its products.

Miller beer has used print advertisements to support a number of gay-related causes – including HIV/AIDS issues, gay pride and the gay community more broadly. Other companies have also placed print advertisements focusing on gay markets and using gay themes and imagery in gay magazines and newspapers. US (gay) Olympic swimmer Bruce Hayes was used to promote Coors beer (*Genre*, US gay magazine, 2001, back cover). Other companies have used stereotypically attractive men – an example of this is the use of a naked male torso to promote Witchmount Estates's Kleenskin 04 Chardonnay (*Melbourne Star,* Australian gay and lesbian newspaper, 2005, p. 2) (Figure 17.1). Another popular strategy is the use of gay focused text – such as the phrase 'Drink it straight or gay', set on a pink background, to promote 42 BELOW vodka (*Jack*, New Zealand gay magazine, 2005, back cover) (Figure 17.2). As well as using gay focused and themed advertisements, many companies have also placed mainstream advertisements in the gay press.

In addition to traditional print advertising, a range of marketing practices and media drawing explicitly on gay imagery and themes have been used to promote alcohol to gay men. Many of these promotions are placed in media or other places where gay men are likely to access them. For instance there was a Miller beer promotion in 2002 on the website gay.com, where men could search for a gay bar and club by entering in a US zip code. Email is another such marketing tool – 42 BELOW promoted its product with a 'viral' marketing campaign using a 'movie' laden with gay images, including gay 'icons' like the 'Village People' and Liberace (Australia, 2003; US, 2005). 42 BELOW also developed a viral 'slideshow style' to promote Auckland's gay and lesbian Hero party (New Zealand, 2006), of which it was a sponsor. See Figure 17.3 for an example of the use of radio.

Sponsorship of organizations and events is also an important marketing practice. Examples of this include sponsorship of the International Gay Rodeo Association (US and Canada, sponsored by BudLight and Bacardi Silver, 2005), San Francisco's 'Folsom Street' and 'Up Your Alley' Fairs (US, sponsored by Miller, Finlandia, Southern Comfort, 2004), and Brighton Pride (UK, sponsored by Pimm's and Smirnoff, 2005). The alcohol industry has a high profile at Pride events throughout North America, particularly through BudLight sponsorship and on-site promotion in the US. See Figure 17.4 for an example of the use of an over-sized inflatable BudLight bottle at an entrance to the 2004 Los Angles Pride festival. The Budweiser company also had a presence at the 2003 Los Angles Pride

Figure 17.1 Kleenskin 04 Chardonnay, Witchmount Estate
Reproduced by permission of Witchmount Estate Winery.

parade (see Figure 17.5). In Canada, Toronto Pride 2005 was sponsored by Labatt Blue beer and Polar Ice vodka, with a visible presence including banners at gay bars (see Figure 17.6 and Figure 17.7).

Kim Crawford Wines in New Zealand have acknowledged the New Zealand gay community's support of their business, through the creation of a wine called Pansy! Rosé. The 2003 label proclaims: 'Pansy! is for the gay community: their glamour and generosity inspired it!' Pansy! Rosé was also the 'Official wine' of New Mardi Gras, Sydney (2005). Similarly, in Australia, Redd Wines have targetted the gay community with the release of the irreverently named Cock Wine brand. Also in Australia, brewers Lion Nathan repackaged a mainstream beer (Hahn Ice) for the Sydney gay market during Mardi Gras (1997) – with the neck label asserting that the beer 'Goes down a treat' (B. Guerin, pers. comm., 21 October, 2005).

Television has not been used extensively to promote alcohol products directly to gay men, perhaps reflecting that print advertisements are more easily targetted to specific audiences. One appearance of gay men on television advertising was via Miller Lite's *Switcheroo* advertisement (US, 2001), which featured two women in a bar sending a beer over to an attractive male bar patron. When the boyfriend of the man arrives, the women

Figure 17.2 42 BELOW vodka print advertisement
Reproduced by permission of 42 BELOW Ltd.

---

42 BELOW vodka ad text

 (NB for radio ad it was read at speed, in a 'stereotypical', high pitched
and camp manner. In the email video promotion the voice-over was
more neutral).

"Calling all gay men. Put down your fluffy little dog and your fabric
samples and mince your backless leather chaps onto the street. Join with
other men, who like kissing other men, in fancifully dressed harmony ...
because we, the manufacturers of 42 BELOW vodka, want you to give
us your mighty pink dollar. We don't care if you're the Indian, the Biker,
the Cop, Cowboy or Construction Worker ... whenever you're out
cruising for casual man/man rumpy pumpy we want you to wrap your
manicured fingers around our fine product. Because at 42 BELOW
Vodka, greed comes before conservatism. In an effort to prevent sexual
stereotypes this ad was run past two fags and a queer – neither of them
were me."

Figure 17.3 42 BELOW vodka text for viral email movie promotion (Australia and US) and
radio advertisement (New Zealand). Reproduced by permission of 42 BELOW Ltd.

Figure 17.4   LA Pride fair entrance 2004
Photo by: Richard E. Settle. Reproduced by permission of Richard E. Settle.

Figure 17.5   LA Pride parade 2003
Reproduced by permission of Westhollywood.com.

concluded the advertisement with the comment that: 'well at least he is not married'. According to Sender (2004), consumer research found that gay men appreciated inclusion in this advertisement. This advertisement highlights that the presence of gay men in advertising is acceptable to some sections of (the presumed heterosexual) mainstream television audience. The relatively new development of gay television channels, such as Pride TV in Canada, which has featured advertising by Polar Ice vodka and Labatt Blue beer, offers a potentially new outlet for gay targeted advertising and promotion. Labatt was also a prominent sponsor of the 1st World Outgames (Montreal, 2006).

Although the promotion of alcohol to gay men does have some 'positive' elements, such as securing funding for worthwhile organizations (like GLAAD and AIDS charities)

Figure 17.6 Toronto Pride 2005
Photo by Virginia Braun. Reproduced by permission of Virginia Braun.

Figure 17.7 Toronto Pride 2005
Photo by Virginia Braun. Reproduced by permission of Virginia Braun.

and (at times) presenting positive images of gay men to wider audiences, the overall purpose of alcohol marketing is to promote products and encourage consumption. Sponsorship of gay events by alcohol companies has also been subject to critique, for example, the visibility of BudLight at Pride Events arguably exaggerates the importance of alcohol to the LGBTQ community (Ventura County Behavioral Health Department, 2004). Further, with a marketing imperative of maximizing sales and markets (Babor et al., 2003; Giesbrecht, 2000), gay images and ideas are not always handled in a sensitive way and are at times considered offensive or inappropriate by gay consumers. One example of this is the 42 BELOW viral email promotion that contained many gay images and references that can be interpreted negatively, including camp stereotypical presentations of the celebrities, (simulated) anal sex between two 'teletubbies' (UK children's television characters), and a male face moving toward a vodka bottle as if to perform fellatio on it. The advertisement was criticized by a gay New York City bar owner who found it offensive and viewed it as a desperate act 'begging for the gay dollar' (Crysell, 2005).

Alcohol promotions to mainstream audiences have also portrayed gay men in negative ways. An example is a billboard advertisement in Grey Lynn, a suburb within Auckland's 'gay ghetto' (Stevens, 2004). This advertisement was one of a series of billboard advertisements for Speight's beer that star two 'real southern' (unreconstructed) men (a father and son). The billboard featured the following commentary: 'Interesting part of town' [son]; 'Keep yer back to the billboard boy' [father]. Another example of a problematic billboard advertisement comes from an extensive series of billboards advertising Tui beer (Dominion Breweries) in New Zealand. This series of advertisements play 'to a young masculinity, working on a discursive orientation to the sceptical and ironic' (McCreanor et al., 2005). The billboards often employ sexist slogans, such as 'Her butt walked into my hand. Yeah right' and 'I didn't notice her moustache. Yeah right'. On another billboard, displayed at the edge of Ponsonby, the heart of gay Auckland, the text read: 'Dad's new boyfriend seems nice. Yeah right'. In the US, a BudLight television advertisement (*Opener*, US, 2001) featured a man's 'butt' being used as an opener for beer bottles which, claims commercialcloset.org, makes negative comparisons to gay male sex (specifically anal intercourse).

In summary, gay men are likely to be exposed to the mainstream marketing of alcohol products, but may *also* be exposed to gay specific marketing, including marketing that uses both gay imagery and is placed in gay specific media and other related contexts. This marketing is often highly visible, such as that in gay magazines, or that prominently displayed at LGBTQ events and venues. The internet has also provided an opportunity to target alcohol advertisements at those men who use the internet but may not access traditional gay media or attend community events, because of a desire to maintain anonymity or discretion around their sexuality (Sender, 2004). Although there are some benefits of such marketing to gay communities, these are arguably outweighed by the health costs arising from increased promotion of, and continued consumption of, alcohol among gay men.

COMMUNITY RESPONSES TO ALCOHOL USE BY GAY MEN

Alcohol promotion and use do not occur in a vacuum – communities 'talk back' and respond to the implications of alcohol use in and on their communities. In this final section we consider community responses to alcohol use by gay men. The responses we have been able to identify tend to come from organizations or communities in cities, with a concentration of LGBTQ citizens. Although we have been unable to locate such responses from more geographically dispersed areas (and potentially quite different LGBTQ communities), it is likely that these communities are engaging with issues associated with gay men and alcohol use in some way.

Although health issues for gay men in recent years have been focused mainly on HIV/ AIDS (Saxton, Hughes & Robinson, 2002; Scarce, 1999), there has been some recognition of alcohol-related issues for gay men, including the development of gay-friendly and gay-specific treatment for alcohol (mis)use at the individual level. Gay AA meetings have been available in the USA since the 1940s (Paul, Stall & Bloomfield, 1991), and other treatment options are also accessible, such as the Antidote LBGT programme (Hungerford Drug Project, London) and the Alcohol, Tobacco, and Other Drugs Prevention Program (Los Angeles Gay and Lesbian Center). MacEwan (1994) pointed out that gay specific treatment offers not just the potential of increased effectiveness over general programmes (e.g. by factoring issues to do with sexuality, society and culture into gay treatment programmes), but also an increased uptake of services by gay men, with gay specific programmes being more likely to attract gay clients than mainstream programmes. This approach, however, runs the risk of allowing mainstream health care providers to sidestep the issue of ensuring their services are appropriate to all people, and are not heterosexist in their focus, assumptions and practice.

Increasingly, gay communities are becoming aware of the wider public health implications of alcohol misuse, and are addressing alcohol (mis)use at community as well as individual treatment levels. This recognition is consistent with knowledge that individual interventions, such as alcohol treatment, are not adequate to reduce population-level alcohol problems (Holder, 1997). The Gay and Lesbian Medical Association (1998) in the USA has a policy of restricting the support it will accept from events or organizations linked with alcohol companies. The AIDS Council of New South Wales, Australia (a health promotion organization based in GLBT communities) has a drug strategy aimed at reducing harm associated with alcohol (and other drug) use (AIDS Council of NSW, 2002). Some gay commercial organizations also have recognized the public health implications of alcohol misuse within the gay community, including *XY* magazine, which refuses to accept alcohol advertising. This magazine views alcohol, tobacco and drug cultures as subverting young people from healthy relationships and social life (Elliot, 1997). Other gay media organizations, such as the *Advocate*, have also considered the appropriateness of carrying alcohol advertisements, but continue to accept advertising revenue from alcohol companies (Sender, 2004). Alcohol-free gay venues have been established in some places, such as the Auckland Pride Centre (New Zealand), and other venues strictly control the use of alcohol at their premises (for example, the DeFrank LGBT Center in San Jose, California). Alcohol-free events have also been organized, such as 'Club Freedom', an alcohol (and tobacco and drug) free event held in conjunction with LA Pride (2004). The cost of refusing sponsorship from alcohol companies can be high, however, particularly as money from alcohol companies is a readily available form of sponsorship (Chasin, 2000).

As well as gay community acknowledgement of alcohol-related issues, there has been some acknowledgement of gay men's alcohol issues by mainstream health promotion agencies. For example, New Zealand's National Alcohol Strategy includes the objective to reduce the likelihood of alcohol-related harm among LGBTQ people (Alcohol Advisory Council of New Zealand and Ministry of Health, 2001). In Scotland, problems such as access to appropriate and sensitive alcohol-related services by gay men have been noted (Scottish Executive, 2002). In Chicago, a taskforce of local gay community and the public health officials have recently developed recommendations for policy and programmes around substance abuse (Office of LGBT Health, 2005). In contrast to these initiatives, however, a number of national alcohol strategies (e.g. from England, Northern Ireland, Finland and Australia) do not address issues of alcohol use by gay men, but typically do address other 'high-risk' groups such as young people.

What remains clear from the discussion above is that, given significant investments in gay markets by alcohol companies, there is a need for both LGBTQ communities and 'main-stream' health agencies to engage more thoroughly with gay men's alcohol consumption.

CONCLUSION

In this chapter, we have examined the issue of alcohol and gay men's health from a variety of angles including prevalence and effects research, strategies of alcohol promotion and community responses to such strategies. One of the aims of the chapter has been to inter-rogate some aspects of gay men's lives and communities that may often be taken for granted, such as alcohol consumption, promotion and sponsorship.

Despite disagreements over prevalence rates, we have argued that alcohol misuse is a particularly significant issue for gay men as a sub-population. Alcohol remains firmly embedded in gay culture, and is important in the lives of many gay men. Alcohol compa-nies work vigorously to maintain this position, by targeting the niche market of drinkers (and potential drinkers) available to them. Therefore, alcohol constitutes a continued threat to the health of gay men (Crosby et al., 1998). However, we need to do more than consider the impacts of alcohol use among gay men (whether at levels similar to or higher than the overall population). We must also to take into account barriers to gay men accessing appropriate health care and health services (see, for example, Dodds, Keogh & Hickson, 2005; Gay and Lesbian Medical Association and LGBT health experts, 2001).

Most research on alcohol use continues to ignore issues of (gay male) sexual orientation. There are methodological and other difficulties related to researching sensitive issues in gay communities, especially when representative quantitative data are sought (Clatts & Sotheran, 2000; Hughes & Eliason, 2002; Sell & Becker, 2001). However, there is a need for better information about the drinking patterns and behaviours of gay men to ensure that more robust data about alcohol use is available to policy makers. Clearly, national studies of alcohol use need to address issues of sexual orientation and adequately sample gay male populations (Drabble et al., 2005). Although some national health behaviour surveys in New Zealand, for instance, now collect such data, this is not yet standard practice internationally.

Further, effective health promotion for any group is dependent on a detailed understand-ing of their culture and social practices (Adams, Braun & McCreanor, 2004). This require-ment needs to be addressed more vigorously within public health research programmes. As Stall et al. (2001) note, the factors influencing alcohol use are complex and include individual, interpersonal and socio-cultural factors. Quantitative research, therefore, cannot be relied on to offer an understanding of the complexity of gay men's lives. There is also a need for in-depth qualitative research. Alcohol research should not only focus on epidemiology of drinking patterns and effects at the individual (or even population) level; it should also develop a broader focus on environmental influences, such as alcohol pro-motion (McCreanor et al., 2000). Qualitative research is needed to better understand the role of alcohol in gay men's lives, to investigate meanings associated with alcohol, with drinking and not drinking, and to consider how drinking amongst gay men is similar to, and different from, other men's (and from LBTQ people's) drinking. Future research should not only focus on gay men as individuals, but as embedded members of communities and societies. This research needs to recognize that alcohol companies continue to target gay consumers and alcohol remains normalized in gay life. Environmental factors, such as these, that encourage gay male alcohol consumption at harmful levels must be understood before public health psychology can contribute to the development of appropriate responses to the issues associated with gay men's alcohol use.

REFERENCES

Adams, J., Braun, V. & McCreanor, T. (2004). Framing gay men's health: A critical review of policy documents. In D. W. Riggs & G. Walker (Eds), *Out in the Antipodes: Australian and New Zealand perspectives on gay and lesbian issues in psychology* (pp. 212–246). Perth: Brightfire Press.

Adams, J., Braun, V. & McCreanor, T. (2007). Warning voices in a policy vacuum: Professional accounts of gay men's health in Aotearoa, New Zealand. *Social Policy Journal of New Zealand*, **30**.

AIDS Council of NSW (2002). *Drug Strategy*. Sydney: AIDS Council of NSW.

Albee, G. W. & Fryer, D. M. (2003). Towards a public health psychology. *Journal of Community & Applied Social Psychology*, **13**(1), 71–75.

Alcohol Advisory Council of New Zealand and Ministry of Health (2001). *National Alcohol Strategy*. Wellington: Alcohol Advisory Council of New Zealand and Ministry of Health.

Ashley, M. J., Rehm, J., Bondy, S., Single, E. & Rankin, J. (2000). Beyond ischemic heart disease: Are there other health benefits from drinking alcohol? *Contemporary Drug Problems*, **27**(4), 735–777.

Babor, T., Caetano, R., Casswell, S., Edwards, G., Giesbrecht, N., Graham, K. et al. (2003). *Alcohol: No ordinary commodity*. Oxford: Oxford University Press.

Badgett, M. V. L. (2001). *Money, Myths, and Change: The economic lives of lesbians and gay men*. Chicago, IL: The University of Chicago Press.

Baker, D. (1997). A history in ads: The growth of the gay and lesbian market. In A. Gluckman & B. Reed (Eds), *Homo Economics: Capitalism, community, and lesbian and gay life* (pp. 11–20). New York, NY: Routledge.

Bell, D. (2000). Farm boys and wild men: Rurality, masculinity, and homosexuality. *Rural Sociology*, **65**(4), 547–561.

Bergmark, K. H. (1999). Drinking in the Swedish gay and lesbian community. *Drug and Alcohol Dependence*, **56**(2), 133–143.

Binnie, J. (1995). Trading places: Consumption, sexuality and the production of queer space. In D. Bell & G. Valentine (Eds), *Mapping Desire: Geographies of sexualities* (pp. 182–199). London: Routledge.

Blake, S. M., Ledsky, R., Lehman, T., Goodenow, C., Sawyer, R. & Hack, T. (2001). Preventing sexual risk behaviors among gay, lesbian, and bisexual adolescents: The benefits of gay-sensitive HIV instruction in schools. *American Journal of Public Health*, **91**(6), 940–946.

Braun, V. (2004). Assumptions, assumptions and yet more assumptions: Identity in sexuality research and teaching. *Lesbian & Gay Psychology Review*, **5**(2), 55–58.

Brown, R. & Washton, R. (2004). *The U.S. Gay and Lesbian Market*. New York, NY: Market Research.com.

Bux, D. A. (1996). The epidemiology of problem drinking in gay men and lesbians: A critical review. *Clinical Psychology Review*, **16**(4), 277–298.

Caldwell, L. L., Kivel, B. D., Smith, E. A. & Hayes, D. (1998). The leisure context of adolescents who are lesbian, gay male, bisexual and questioning their sexual identities: An exploratory study. *Journal of Leisure Research*, **30**(3), 341–355.

Campbell, C. (2004). Health psychology and community action. In M. Murray (Ed.), *Critical health psychology* (pp. 203–221). Houndmills, Basingstoke: Palgrave Macmillan.

Casswell, S. (1996). Alcohol use: Growing up and learning about drinking - children in Dunedin in the 1980s. In P. A. Silva & W. R. Stanton (Eds), *From Child to Adult: The Dunedin multidisciplinary health and development study* (pp. 206–224). Oxford: Oxford University Press.

Casswell, S. (2004). Alcohol brands in young peoples' everyday lives: New developments in marketing. *Alcohol and Alcoholism*, **39**(6), 471–476.

Celentano, D. D., Valleroy, L. A., Sifakis, F., MacKellar, D. A., Hylton, J., Thiede, H. et al. (2006). Associations between substance use and sexual risk among very young men who have sex with men. *Sexually Transmitted Diseases*, **33**(4), 265–271.

Chasin, A. (2000). *Selling Out: The gay and lesbian movement goes to market*. New York, NY: St Martin's Press.

Chou, S. P. & Pickering, R. B. (1992). Early onset of drinking as a risk factor for lifetime alcohol related problems. *British Journal of Addiction*, **87**(8), 1199–1204.

Clatts, M. C. & Sotheran, J. L. (2000). Challenges in research on drug and sexual risk practices of men who have sex with men: Applications of ethnography in HIV epidemiology and prevention. *AIDS and Behavior*, **4**(2), 169–179.

Commercial Closet Association (2001). ABSOLUT GLAAD. Retrieved 11 September 2001, from http://www.commercialcloset.org/cgi-bin/iowa/portrayals.html?record=526.

Cova, B. & Cova, V. (2002). Tribal marketing: The tribalisation of society and its impact on the conduct of marketing. *European Journal of Marketing*, **36**(5), 595–620.

Coyle, A. & Wilkinson, S. (2002). Social psychological perspectives on lesbian and gay issues in Europe: The state of the art. *Journal of Community & Applied Social Psychology*, **12**(3), 147–152.

Crosby, G. M., Stall, R. D., Paul, J. P. & Barrett, D. C. (1998). Alcohol and drug use patterns have declined between generations of younger gay-bisexual men in San Francisco. *Drug and Alcohol Dependence*, **52**(2), 177–182.

Crossley, M. L. (2000). *Rethinking Health Psychology*. Buckingham: Open University Press.

Crysell, M. (2005). The drink talking. On *Sunday (12 June 2005)*, Television New Zealand, New Zealand.

DeBord, K. A., Wood, P. K., Sher, K. J. & Good, G. E. (1998). The relevance of sexual orientation to substance abuse and psychological distress among college students. *Journal of College Student Development*, **39**(2), 157–168.

Dodds, C., Keogh, P. & Hickson, F. (2005). *It Makes Me Sick: Heterosexism, homophobia and the health of gay men and bisexual men*. London: Sigma Research.

Dolezal, C., Carballo-Dieguez, A., Nieves-Rosa, L. & Diaz, F. (2000). Substance use and sexual risk behavior: Understanding their association among four ethnic groups of Latino men who have sex with men. *Journal of Substance Abuse*, **11**(4), 323–336.

Donovan, C. & McEwan, R. (1995). A review of the literature examining the relationship between alcohol use and HIV-related sexual risk-taking in young people. *Addiction*, **90**(3), 319–328.

Dotson, E. W. (1999). *Behold the Man: The hype and selling of male beauty in media and culture*. New York, NY: Harrington Park Press.

Drabble, L., Midanik, L. T. & Trocki, K. (2005). Reports of alcohol consumption and alcohol-related problems among homosexual, bisexual and heterosexual respondents: Results from the 2000 National Alcohol Survey. *Journal of Studies on Alcohol*, **66**(1), 111–120.

Easton, B. H. (1997). *The Social Costs of Tobacco Use and Alcohol Misuse*. Wellington: Department of Public Health, Wellington School of Medicine.

Edwards, G., Anderson, P., Babor, T. F., Casswell, S., Ferrence, R., Giesbrecht, N. et al. (1994). *Alcohol Policy and the Public Good*. Oxford: Oxford University Press.

Elliot, S. (1997). A campaign urges gay men and lesbians to resist tobacco ads. *New York Times* (4 June 1997).

Faulkner, A. H. & Cranston, K. (1998). Correlates of same-sex sexual behavior in a random sample of Massachusetts high school students. *American Journal of Public Health*, **88**(2), 262–266.

Field, A. & Casswell, S. (1999). *Drugs in New Zealand: National survey, 1998*. Auckland: Alcohol & Public Health Research Unit, University of Auckland.

Gay and Lesbian Medical Association (1998). Conflict of interest/Corporate support policy (101-98-101). Retrieved 22 March 2004, from http://services.glma.org/policy.

Gay and Lesbian Medical Association and LGBT health experts (2001). *Healthy People 2010 Companion Document for Lesbian, Gay, Bisexual, and Transgender (LGBT) Health.* San Francisco, CA: Gay and Lesbian Medical Association.

Giesbrecht, N. (2000). Roles of commercial interests in alcohol policies: Recent developments in North America. *Addiction*, **95**(12, Suppl 4), S581–595.

Godin, S. (1999). *Permission Marketing: Turning strangers into friends, and friends into customers.* New York, NY: Simon & Schuster.

Greenwood, G. L., White, E. W., Page-Shafer, K., Bein, E., Osmond, D. H., Paul, J. et al. (2001). Correlates of heavy substance use among young gay and bisexual men: The San Francisco Young Men's Health Study. *Drug and Alcohol Dependence*, **61**(2), 105–112.

Guinan, J. G., Hall, W., Clarke, J. C. & Gold, J. (1992). Alcohol and recreational drug use by HIV-seropositive homosexual men. *Drug and Alcohol Review*, **11**(4), 355–362.

Harwood, H., Fountain, D. & Livermore, G. (1998). *The Economic Costs of Alcohol and Drug Abuse in the United States, 1992. Report prepared for the National Institute on Drug Abuse and the National Institute on Alcohol Abuse and Alcoholism.* Rockville, MD: National Institute on Drug Abuse.

Hepworth, J. (2004). Public health psychology: A conceptual and practical framework. *Journal of Health Psychology*, **9**(1), 41–54.

Higgs, D. (1999). Introduction. In D. Higgs (Ed.), *Queer Sites: Gay urban histories since 1600* (pp. 1–9). London: Routledge.

Hill, L. & Casswell, S. (2004). Alcohol advertising and sponsorship: commercial freedom or control in the public interest? In N. Heather & T. Stockwell (Eds), *The Essential Handbook of Treatment and Prevention of Alcohol Problems* (pp. 339–359). Chichester: John Wiley.

Hillier, L., Dempsey, D., Harrison, L., Beale, L., Matthews, L. & Rosenthal, D. (1998). *Writing Themselves In: A national report on the sexuality, health and well-being of same-sex attracted young people.* Melbourne: Australian Research Centre in Sex, Health and Society.

Holder, H. D. (1997). Can individually directed interventions reduce population-level alcohol-involved problems? *Addiction*, **92**(1), 5–7.

Hughes, T. L. & Eliason, M. J. (2002). Substance use and abuse in lesbian, gay, bisexual and transgender populations. *The Journal of Primary Prevention*, **22**(3), 263–298.

Israelstam, S. & Lambert, S. (1983). Homosexuality as a cause of alcoholism: A historical review. *The International Journal of the Addictions*, **18**(8), 1085–1107.

Kasser, T. & Kanner, A. D. (Eds.), (2004) *Psychology and Consumer Culture: The struggle for a good life in a materalistic world.* Washington DC: American Psychological Association.

Kilbourne, J. (1999). *Deadly Persuasion: Why women and girls must fight the addictive power of advertising.* New York, NY: Free Press.

Kippax, S., Campbell, D., Van de Ven, P., Crawford, J., Prestage, G., Knox, S. et al. (1998). Cultures of sexual adventurism as markers of HIV seroconversion: A case control study in a cohort of Sydney gay men. *AIDS Care*, **10**(6), 677–688.

Kitzinger, C. (1997). Lesbian and gay psychology: A critical analysis. In D. Fox & I. Prilleltensky (Eds), *Critical Psychology: An introduction* (pp. 202–216). London: Sage.

Kitzinger, C. & Coyle, A. (2002). Introducing lesbian and gay psychology. In A. Coyle & C. Kitzinger (Eds), *Lesbian & Gay Psychology: New perspectives* (pp. 1–29). Oxford: Blackwell.

Kus, R. J. & Latcovich, M. A. (1995). Special interest groups in Alcoholics Anonymous: A focus on gay men's groups. In R. J. Kus (Ed.), *Addiction and Recovery in Gay and Lesbian Persons* (pp. 41–55). Binghampton, NY: Harrington Park Press.

Lee, C. (2000). Psychology of women's health: A critique. In J. M. Ussher (Ed.), *Women's Health: Contemporary international perspectives* (pp. 26–40). Leicester: BPS Books.

Leigh, B. C. (1990). The relationship of substance use during sex to high-risk sexual behavior. *Journal of Sex Research*, **27**, 199–213.

Lewis, R. S. (1996). ABSOLUT BOOK. The ABSOLUT Vodka advertising story. Boston: Journey Editions.

Lohrenz, L., Connelly, J., Coyne, L. & Spare, K. (1978). Alcohol problems in several midwest homosexual populations. *Journal of Studies on Alcohol*, **39**(11), 1959–1963.

Lukenbill, G. (1999). *Untold Millions: Secret truth about marketing to gay and lesbian consumers.* New York: Harrington Press.

MacEwan, I. (1994). Differences in assessment and treatment approaches for homosexual clients. *Drug and Alcohol Review*, **13**(1), 57–62.

Maisto, S. A., Carey, M. P., Carey, K. B., Gordon, C. M., Schum, J. L. & Lynch., K. G. (2004). The relationship between alcohol and individual differences variables on attitudes and behavioral skills relevant to sexual health among heterosexual young adult men. *Archives of Sexual Behavior*, **33**(1), 571–584.

Malinowitz, H. (1995). *Textual Orientations: Lesbian and gay students and the making of discourse communities.* Portsmouth, NH: Boynton/Cook.

Mandlebaum, D. G. (1965). Alcohol and culture. *Current Anthropology*, **6**(3), 281–294.

Marks, D. F. (2002). Freedom, responsibility and power: Contrasting approaches to health psychology. *Journal of Health Psychology*, **7**(1), 5–19.

Martin, J. L., Dean, L., Garcia, M. & Hall, W. (1989). The impact of AIDS on a gay community: Changes in sexual behavior, substance use, and mental health. *American Journal of Community Psychology*, **17**(3), 269–293.

McCabe, S. E., Boyd, C., Hughes, T. L. & d'Arcy, H. (2003). Sexual identity and substance use among undergraduate students. *Substance Abuse*, **24**(2), 77–91.

McCreanor, T. (1996). 'Why strengthen the city wall when the enemy has poisoned the well?' An assay of anti-homosexual discourse in New Zealand. *Journal of Homosexuality*, **31**(4), 75–105.

McCreanor, T. (2004). The city wall: Intersections of heterosexism and racism in Aotearoa New Zealand. *Lesbian & Gay Psychology Review*, **5**(2), 59–63.

McCreanor, T., Casswell, S. & Hill, L. (2000). ICAP and the perils of partnership (Editorial). *Addiction*, **92**(2), 179–185.

McCreanor, T., Greenaway, A., Moewaka Barnes, H., Borell, S. & Gregory, A. (2005). Youth identity formation and contemporary alcohol marketing. *Critical Public Health*, **15**(3), 251–262.

McInnes, D., Hurley, M., Prestage, G. & Hendry, O. (2001). *Enacting Sexual Contexts: Negotiating the self, sex and risk in sex on premises venues.* Sydney: University of Western Sydney.

McKirnan, D. J. & Peterson, P. L. (1989). Alcohol and drug use among homosexual men and women: Epidemiology and population characteristics. *Addictive Behaviours*, **14**(5), 545–533.

McManus, T. J. & Weatherburn, P. (1994). Alcohol, AIDS and immunity. *British Medical Bulletin*, **50**(4), 115–123.

Moore, C. (1998). Behaving outrageously: Contemporary gay masculinity. *Journal of Australian Studies*, **56**, 158–168.

Morgan, M., Spicer, J. & Reid, M. (2002). Sociological and psychological investigations. In R. Detels, J. McEwen, R. Beaglehole & H. Tanaka (Eds), *Oxford Textbook of Public Health*, Vol. 2 (pp. 781–806). Oxford: Oxford University Press.

Murnane, A., Smith, A., Crompton, L., Snow, P. & Munro, G. (2000). *Beyond Perceptions: A report on alcohol and other drug use among gay, lesbian, bisexual and queer communities in Victoria.* Melbourne: The ALSO Foundation & Centre for Youth Drug Studies.

Murray, M. (2004a). Conclusion: Towards a critical health psychology. In M. Murray (Ed.), *Critical Health Psychology* (pp. 222–229). Basingstoke: Palgrave Macmillan.

Murray, M. (2004b). Introduction: Criticizing health psychology. In M. Murray (Ed.), *Critical Health Psychology* (pp. 1–11). Basingstoke: Palgrave Macmillan.

Murray, M. & Campbell, C. (2003). Living in a material world: Reflecting assumptions of health psychology. *Journal of Health Psychology*, **8**(2), 231–236.

Office of LGBT Health (2005). *The Chicago Taskforce on LGBT Substance Use and Abuse.* Chicago, IL: Chicago Department of Public Health.

Ostrow, D. G., Beltran, E. D., Joseph, J. G., DiFranceisco, W., Wesch, J. & Chmiel, J. S. (1993). Recreational drugs and sexual behavior in the Chicago MACS/CCS cohort of homosexually active men. *Journal of Substance Abuse*, **5**(4), 311–325.

Paul, J. P., Stall, R. & Bloomfield, K. A. (1991). Gay and alcoholic: Epidemiologic and clinical issues. *Alcohol Health and Research World*, **15**(2), 151–160.

Prime Minister's Strategy Unit (2003). *Strategy Unit Alcohol Harm Reduction Project: Interim analytical report*. London: Her Majesty's Stationery Office.

Purcell, D. W., Parsons, J. T., Halkitis, P. N., Mizuno, Y. & Woods, W. J. (2001). Substance use and sexual transmission risk behavior of HIV-positive men who have sex with men. *Journal of Substance Abuse*, **13**(1/2), 185–200.

Rehm, J., Ashley, M. J. & Dubois, G. (1997). Alcohol and health: Individual and population perspectives. *Addiction*, **92**, S109–S115.

Reilly, T. & Woo, G. (2001). Predictors of high-risk sexual behavior among people living with HIV/AIDS. *AIDS and Behavior*, **5**(3), 205–217.

Roche, A. M. (2001). Drinking behavior: A multifaceted and multiphasic phenomenon. In E. Houghton & A. M. Roche (Eds), *Learning about Drinking* (pp. 1–33). Philadelphia, PA: Brunner-Routledge.

Room, R. (2002). Alcohol. In R. Detels, J. McEwen, R. Beaglehole & H. Tanaka (Eds), *Oxford Textbook of Public Health*, Vol. 3 (pp. 1521–1531). Oxford: Oxford University Press.

Ross, M. W., Rosser, B. R. S., Bauer, G. R., Bockting, W. O., Robinson, B. B. E., Rugg, D. L. et al. (2001). Drug use, unsafe sexual behavior, and internalized homonegativity in men who have sex with men. *AIDS and Behavior*, **5**(1), 97–103.

Rostosky, S. S., Owens, G. P., Zimmerman, R. S. & Riggle, E. D. B. (2003). Associations among sexual attraction status, school belonging, and alcohol and marijuana use in rural high school students. *Journal of Adolescence*, **26**(6), 741–751.

Saxton, P. J., Hughes, A. J. & Robinson, E. M. (2002). Sexually transmitted diseases and hepatitis in a national sample of men who have sex with men in New Zealand. *The New Zealand Medical Journal*, 115. Retrieved 21 November 2006, from http://www.nzma.org.nz/journal/115-1158/1106/.

Scarce, M. (1999). *Smearing the Queer: Medical bias in the health care of gay men*. New York, NY: Haworth Press.

Scottish Executive (2002). *Plan for Action on Alcohol Problems*. Edinburgh: Scottish Executive.

Schembri, A. M. (2001). Reality check: Lesbian and gay health and welfare in Sydney. In C. Johnston & P. van Reyk (Eds), *Queer City: Gay and lesbian politics in Sydney* (pp. 193–210). Annandale, NSW: Pluto Press.

Sell, R. L. & Becker, J. B. (2001). Sexual orientation data collection and progress toward Healthy People 2010. *American Journal of Public Health*, **91**(6), 876–882.

Sender, K. (2004). *Business, not Politics: The making of the gay market*. New York: Columbia University Press.

Skinner, W. F. (1994). The prevalence and demographic predictors of illicit and licit drug use among lesbians and gay men. *American Journal of Public Health*, **84**(3), 1307–1310.

Skinner, W. F. & Otis, M. D. (1992). Drug use among lesbian and gay people: Findings, research design, insights, and policy issues from the Trilogy project. In R. Kelly (Ed.), *The Research Symposium on Alcohol and Other Drug Problem Prevention among Lesbians and Gay Men* (pp. 34–60). Sacramento, CA: EMT Group, Inc.

Skinner, W. F. & Otis, M. D. (1996). Drug and alcohol use among lesbian and gay people in a Southern US sample: Epidemiological, comparative, and methodological findings from the Trilogy project. *Journal of Homosexuality*, **30**(3), 59–91.

Slavin, S. (2001). Recreational use of amyl nitrite. *Venereology*, **14**(2), 81–82.

Smith, A. M. A., Lindsay, J. & Rosenthal, D. A. (1999). Same-sex attraction, drug injection and binge drinking among Australian adolescents. *Australian and New Zealand Journal of Public Health*, **23**(6), 643–646.

Stall, R. & Purcell, D. W. (2000). Intertwining epidemics: A review of research on substance use among men who have sex with men and its connection to the AIDS epidemic. *AIDS and Behavior*, **4**(2), 181–192.

Stall, R. & Wiley, J. (1988). A comparison of alcohol and drug use patterns of homosexual and heterosexual men: The San Francisco men's health study. *Drug and Alcohol Dependence*, **22**(1/2), 63–73.

Stall, R., McKusick, L., Wiley, J., Coates, T. J. & Ostrow, D. G. (1986). Alcohol and drug use during sexual activity and compliance with safe sex guidelines for AIDS: The AIDS behavioral research project. *Health Education Quarterly*, **13**(4), 359–371.

Stall, R., Paul, J. P., Greenwood, G., Pollack, L. M., Bein, E., Crosby, G. M. et al. (2001). Alcohol use, drug use and alcohol-related problems among men who have sex with men: The urban men's health study. *Addiction*, **96**(11), 1589–1601.

Stam, H. J. (2004). A sound mind in a sound body: A critical historical analysis of health psychology. In M. Murray (Ed.), *Critical Health Psychology* (pp. 15–30). Basingstoke: Palgrave Macmillan.

Stevens, M. (2004). Saturday night's alright for dancing. In I. Cater, D. Craig & S. Matthewman (Eds), *Almighty Auckland?* (pp. 225–239). Palmerston North: Dunmore Press.

Stevens, P., Carlson, L. M. & Hinman, J. M. (2004). An analysis of tobacco industry marketing to lesbian, gay, bisexual, and transgender (LGBT) populations: Strategies for mainstream tobacco control and prevention. *Health Promotion Practice*, **5**(3), 129S–134S.

Trocki, K. F., Drabble, L. & Midanik, L. (2005). Use of heavier drinking contexts among heterosexuals, homosexuals and bisexuals: Results from a national household probability survey. *Journal of Studies on Alcohol*, **66**(1), 105–110.

Ussher, J. M. (2000). Women's health: Contemporary concerns. In J. M. Ussher (Ed.), *Women's Health: Contemporary international perspectives* (pp. 1–25). Leicester: BPS Books.

Ventura County Behavioral Health Department (2004). Pride and alcohol problem prevention. *Prevention File*, **Winter**, 3.

Weatherburn, P., Davies, P. M., Hickson, F. C. I., Hunt, A. J., McManus, T. J. & Coxon, A. P. M. (1993). No connection between alcohol use and unsafe sex among gay and bisexual men. *AIDS*, **7**(1), 115–119.

Weinberg, T. S. (1994). *Gay Men, Drinking, and Alcoholism*. Carbondale, IL: Southern Illinois University Press.

Wilke, M. (2001). Are gays really brand loyal? Retrieved 13 September 2001, from http://www.commercialcloset.org.

Wilkinson, S. (2002). Lesbian health. In A. Coyle & C. Kitzinger (Eds), *Lesbian & Gay Psychology: New perspectives* (pp. 117–134). Oxford: Blackwell.

World Health Organization (2002). *The World Health Report 2002: Reducing risks, promoting healthy life*. Geneva: World Health Organization.

World Health Organization (2004a). *Global Status Report on Alcohol 2004*. Geneva: World Health Organization.

World Health Organization (2004b). *Global Status Report: Alcohol policy*. Geneva: World Health Organization.

World Health Organization (2004c). *Neuroscience of Psychoactive Substance Use and Dependence: Summary*. Geneva: World Health Organization.

Wyllie, A., Zhang, J. F. & Casswell, S. (1998). Positive responses to televised beer advertisements associated with drinking and problems reported by 18 to 29-year-olds. *Addiction*, **93**(5), 749–760.

Yin, S. (2003). Coming out in print. *American Demographics*, **25**(1), 18–21.

CHAPTER 18

Towards a Clinical-Psychological Approach to Address the Heterosexual Concerns of Intersexed Women

Lih-Mei Liao

University College London, UK

INTRODUCTION

In the first ever British edited and authored lesbian and gay psychology text, Kitzinger and Coyle (2002) clarified a misconception about lesbian and gay psychology, that is, despite its name, it 'has also historically included work on bisexual, transgender and – indeed – *hetero*sexual issues'. They pointed out that 'lesbian and gay issues have always been deeply implicated with notions of gender', and drew attention to the importance of 'cross-fertilization' (p. 4) between feminist psychology and lesbian and gay psychology (see also Clarke & Peel, 2005). This cross-fertilization is crucial for understanding how 'intersex' is responded to. In turn, intersex can contribute to the examination of gendered sexual practices and their ramifications for our social context.

The aim of this chapter is threefold. First, I argue that the heterosexual practice difficulties of intersexed women are gendered and socially constructed. Second, I highlight the potentially important contributions of deconstructionist approaches for addressing the sexuality concerns expressed by these women. Third, I suggest that a health care psychology for intersex needs to engage with feminist and LGBTQ psychological interrogation of heteronormative discourses in cultural practices relating to sex, practices that could be detrimental to many groups, including heterosexuals.

I work in a women's health care context where virtually all of my clients self-identify as female and most as heterosexual. The experiences of self-identified heterosexual women are the focus of this chapter. I consider myself a feminist psychological practitioner with a strong interest in social constructionism. As such I question ideas about 'normal' bodies (as categorically and mutually exclusively male or female) and 'normal' sexual practices (as heterosexual intercourse) that underpin 'corrective' interventions for intersex. My

Out in Psychology: Lesbian, gay, bisexual, trans and queer perspectives. Edited by Victoria Clarke and Elizabeth Peel.
© 2007 John Wiley & Sons, Ltd.

conversations with intersexed women, however, have sensitized me to the possibility that criticism of these discourses is at risk of being misunderstood as criticism of individuals who feel bound by them. As a clinician, my role is to assist people to develop their own responses to atypical anatomical sexual characteristics. These responses may involve 'normalizing' the body to fit with cultural norms/ideals and I do not minimize individuals' reasons for their choices. Rather, I highlight the constraints that heteronormative discourses impose on intersexed women. This is an important consideration for the development of a critical health care psychology for intersex. Finally, as a member of a multi-disciplinary clinical team, I have a role in shaping service delivery.

In order to analyse traditional medical practice and challenge its negative aspects, I have engaged with the medical literature on its own terms. I draw on strands of different literatures and my clinical experience to develop the argument that medical/surgical interventions alone are not an adequate professional response to intersex, that critical psychological approaches are important in care delivery in specific ways.

This chapter is divided into three main parts. The first part outlines what intersex is and the standard approach to its management. Most often, surgery is carried out to 'feminize' intersexed genitals, a process that is governed by powerful heteronormative discourses that serve to regulate a male-female dichotomy and corresponding sexual practices. A main criterion for successful feminization is the production of a functioning vagina – that is, a vagina capable of coitus. In the second part, I draw on relevant research and my clinical experience to problematize the pragmatics of stabilizing heterosexual female gender identity through achieving 'normal sex', that is, coitus. The conflation of sex and coitus does not only organize the provision of services for intersexed women (and men), it likewise underpins diagnosis and treatment of sexual problems in general. The high personal costs of the 'coital imperative' to intersexed women, in terms of surgical interventions for instance, serve to render more visible its tyranny. In the third part of the chapter, I outline a way of working psycho-sexually with intersexed women that decentralizes coitus and encourages a broader exploration of sexual relating. Two literatures inform this aspect of my clinical work: feminist deconstructionist critiques of mainstream approaches to sexual problems (e.g. Tiefer, 1995) and reflexive psycho-therapeutic approaches (e.g. Jones, 1995). I suggest that such an alternative model of psycho-sexual counselling is also relevant for work with non-intersexed and non-heterosexual populations.

DEFINING 'INTERSEX'

Assignment of newborns to male or female is primarily determined by genital appearance. The smoothness with which this transaction operates on most occasions belies painful institutional and individual responses to the challenges posed by genital ambiguity. The stability of dimorphic sexual categories obscures the fact that all human embryos begin with a common set of reproductive and genital structures. Regular sexual differentiation begins at about six weeks of embryonic life, and an undifferentiated foetus gradually assumes the anatomical structures and appearance of what we think of as male or female (see Cameron & Smith, 2004). A number of genetic conditions, however, can disrupt the process, resulting in developmental outcomes that do not clearly correspond to one of the two mutually exclusive sexual categories. That is to say, the usual markers of sex – gonads, genitalia and karyotype – are neither all male nor all female. Such developmental out-comes fall within western medical classification of 'intersex' or, previously, 'hermaphro-ditism' (see Dreger et al., 2005). Intersexed individuals may have both male-typical and female-typical and/or ambiguous reproductive-genital characteristics.

Using a very broad definition, prevalence of intersexed live births has been estimated to be as high as one in 200 (Blackless, Charuvastra, Derryck & Fausto-Sterling, 2000). Prevalence depends of course on inclusion criteria. In Rokitansky syndrome, for example, the womb and part of the vagina are absent in a girl with otherwise normative physical development. This is one of a number of conditions which are sometimes classified as intersex and sometimes not (see Hughes, 2002). In a recent consensus statement, 'disor-ders of sex development' (DSD) was put forward as an umbrella term to denote a broader range of diagnoses, that is, to include all 'congenital conditions in which development of chromosomal, gonadal or anatomical sex is atypical' (Hughes, Houk, Ahmed & Lee, 2006). This new terminology has, perhaps inevitably, received mixed responses; it remains to be seen to what extent it will be adopted in the literatures. The analysis in this chapter is based on work with women with atypical sex development that is sometimes referred to as 'intersex' and sometimes not. I make use of both terms where applicable while acknowledging that all terminologies are potentially pejorative.

In the women's health service context where I work, two broad scenarios in presentation are common. The first concerns individuals who present standard external female genitalia at birth. Most of these individuals would not have had their sex doubted or come under medical attention until adolescence or adulthood. These women may have a male (46XY) or female (46XX) genetic karyotype. One of the best known conditions associated with the former is complete androgen insensitivity syndrome (CAIS). A foetus with CAIS produces normative quantities of androgens (virilizing hormones) but lacks receptors to decode them and do not virilize. Internally, individuals with CAIS are without a womb or cervix and have abdominal testes and a smaller than average vagina. Virtually all of these women are reared and identify unambiguously as female (see Hines, 2004). Many women with CAIS present themselves during adolescence for medical investigations because their periods have not started as expected, though a few may have presented to paediatricians prompted, for example, by the discovery of protruding testes in the pelvic area.

The second presentation scenario concerns individuals who present visible genital ambiguity at birth. Because of this, most of them would have come under medical man-agement from birth and been subjected to surgical feminizing of the genitalia in infancy and childhood. These individuals may also have a so-called male (46XY) or female (46XX) genetic karyotype. In partial androgen insensitivity syndrome, for example, due to a degree of receptivity to androgens, the XY infant may present partially masculinized external genitalia. Erectile/penetrative potential of the phallus is a major consideration in male sex assignment; any child with a penis of stretched length of less than 2.5 cm may be assigned female regardless of the underlying diagnosis or karyotype (Donaghoe, 1991). 'Under virilized males' suddenly become 'over virilized females', for whom feminizing treatments ensue. Many surgeons favour female sex assignment largely because of techni-cal difficulties in penile reconstructive surgery – multiple procedures may produce a penis that is relatively normative in appearance, but the capacity for erection and penetration is usually limited. As some surgeons have crudely put it, it is easier to dig a hole than to build a pole (see Chase, 1998a).

A larger group that presents external genital ambiguity at birth comprises individuals with a so-called female karyotype (46XX) and a condition known as congenital adrenal hyperplasia (CAH). In this instance, the adrenal gland of the foetus produces unusually large amounts of androgens. The physiological events have metabolic consequences relating to salt loss and dehydration, which can be fatal without effective endocrine management. They also result in a variable degree of virilization of the infant's external genitalia. That is to say, she may present a clitoris that is bigger than average, and/or labia that are fused and perhaps with somewhat rippled skin giving a scrotal appearance, and/or the absence of a vaginal opening. Internally she has ovaries, womb and usually an internal (upper) vagina. She would also have fertility potential, which, being an important deciding factor in sex assignment, means that the majority of girls with CAH are assigned female. As for XY individuals assigned female, feminizing treatment is likely to follow.[1] Research suggests that the majority of individuals so managed tend also to identify as female (see Hines, 2004).

FEMINIZING GENITAL SURGERY

Feminizing of the genitals may include surgery to the external and internal genitalia. Where genital ambiguity is detected at birth, surgery is commonly performed in the first year or two of life. Feminizing could be thought of as comprising three sets of procedures. Gonadectomy – removal of the testes or pre-testes, is routinely carried out for XY individuals to prevent (any) further production of testosterone and/or prevent the gonads from becoming cancerous. The second set of feminizing procedures is concerned with cosmetic alteration to the sexed appearance of the external genitalia. This often involves surgery to the clitoris (or previously 'phallus' for some individuals) to reduce its size and is controversial especially in childhood. The third set of procedures aims to make the female genitalia 'functional', that is, receptive to an erect penis. Since the surgically constructed vagina has no purpose for baby girls, this is especially controversial when carried out on children.

As noted above, surgical feminizing of infants and young children is increasingly criticized (e.g. Chase, 1998b; Kessler, 1998; Kipnis & Diamond, 1998), not least because children cannot give consent, and because surgery is not reversible should the individuals change their mind about the assigned sex later in life. The Intersex Society of North America (see www.isna.org) argues that parental distress about ambiguous genitalia should not be treated by performing surgery on their child. Childhood surgery is also challenged on scientific grounds, because evidence founded on authoritative long-term follow-up work is currently absent (see Creighton & Liao, 2004).

Clitoral Surgery

For women with DSDs, surgery to reduce the size of the clitoris is essentially a cosmetic procedure. Implicit in this widespread practice are the assumptions that there is a normal size for the clitoris, that decision makers and service providers know what it is, and that it is safely achievable or at least the benefits far outweigh the risks. Recent work suggests

---

[1] Note that CAH also affects individuals with XY karyotype, but they are not considered intersex because their genitals are congruent with maleness.

that female genital structure and appearance vary considerably in the general population (Lloyd et al., 2005). Furthermore, questions have been raised concerning the impact of clitoral surgery on future sexual experiences. These questions have, however, only been asked relatively recently – paediatric surgeons in the past have been insistent that future sexual functions were unimpaired, though without offering a creditable rationale (Rink & Adams, 1998), especially given current knowledge (e.g. Baskin et al., 1999). A recent study compared women born with ambiguous genitalia who had undergone feminizing genital surgery with those who had not (Minto et al., 2003a). While self-reported sexual function was impaired for both groups compared to normative data, inorgasmia was significantly more frequently reported by women who had undergone clitoral surgery. Recent work in genital sensation testing has found that for women with CAH who had undergone clitoral surgery, there was marked impairment to sensitivity thresholds at the site of surgical incision (Crouch et al., 2004). Feminists are divided on the place of orgasm in female sexuality. On one hand, it has been highlighted that female sexual pleasure and orgasm is sidelined in mainstream treatment models of sexual difficulties that centralizes coitus (see Boyle, 1993). On the other hand, discourses that privilege female orgasm can create negative self-evaluations in women who do not tend to experience orgasm (see Densmore, 1973; Lavie & Willig, 2004; Nicholson & Burr, 2003). Nevertheless, information on the risk of loss of sensation as a result of genital surgery must be made available to those considering clitoral surgery for themselves or their children. Sensation loss, however, is not the only risk that could raise concerns, there are also the less documented problems associated with clitoral surgery including, for example, pain on arousal (Ansell & Rajfer, 1981; Minto et al., 2003a).

Vaginoplasty

Surgery to (re)construct a vagina may involve dissection and lining of a neovaginal space, usually either with skin grafts (taken from the thigh or buttock) or a section of the intestine (Minto & Creighton, 2003).[2] These are major procedures and post-operative complications can include contracture in the case of skin graft (Klingele et al., 2003) and/or offensive discharge in the case of gut (Syed, Malone & Hitchcock, 2001). Scarring is to be expected. Malignant change in the neovagina has also been reported (Munkara, Malone, Budev & Evans, 1994). As for sexual outcome, studies have reported 'normal' sexual function in 80–90% of women following surgery (Cali & Pratt, 1968; Martinez-Mora, Isnard, Castellevi & Lopez-Ortiz, 1992), but no report is available on how 'normal' was determined. The figures probably reflected the surgeons' opinions, perhaps based on an absence of complaints. An absence of complaints in medical consultations, however, does not mean that sexual experiences are positive (Kessler, 1998). As a research participant in a study that colleagues and I have recently conducted suggests:

> Whenever I used to see the doctor, there would always be at least eight white coats sitting behind me, you know, scribbling down notes, and that's not really a time that you can then sit there and say, 'is it going to affect my orgasms?' because I could just imagine, you know, all the eyes glancing at one another and you, you just don't do it. (quoted in Boyle, Smith & Liao, 2005, p. 578)

---

[2] Vaginal reconstruction is also relatively commonly carried out for women whose vagina has been damaged as a result of childbirth, accidents or medical treatments (e.g. pelvic irradiation).

There are very few evaluations of vaginal construction specific to DSD. The few studies involving adults have examined the appearance of the vagina of women with CAH. One study did examine the cosmetic results of early vaginal surgery as rated by doctors (Alizai et al., 1999). In this study, unsatisfactory outcome was reported for 28–46% of the sample. I know of no systematic investigation of treatment satisfaction from the recipients' perspectives, although in my work context, dissatisfaction and seeking of further procedures to improve appearance is common. In another recent study, cosmetic results were again judged to be poor by surgeons in 41% of the adolescent and adult patients who had been operated on as children (Creighton, Minto & Steele, 2001). The authors concluded that nearly all of the participants required further procedures to improve the appearance of the genitals and/or to permit tampon use or coitus. Tracking of paediatric case notes enabled the authors to conclude that in 89% of the genitoplasties that had been planned as one-stage procedures in childhood, one or more further major operations had been needed by adolescence to improve appearance and/or function. It has been known for some time that a dilation regime is usually required to prevent stenosis (shrinkage) of the neovagina (e.g. Klingele et al., 2003). This means that, unless dilation of a child's vagina by adults is considered acceptable, it is puzzling why childhood vaginoplasty could ever have been expected to achieve the targeted functional outcome in the longer term. Early surgery means that the number of operations over the lifespan could be considerable. Newer techniques involving keyhole surgery are less invasive with a quicker recovery period (Ismail-Pratt, Cutner & Creighton, 2006). These procedures again require a self-managed dilation regime and, as yet, psychological and sexual outcomes are unknown.

Vaginal Dilation

Pressure dilation involves insertion into the vaginal space cylindrical shapes that graduate in width and length.[3] The shapes are usually made of plastic, glass, or Perspex. The technique was first described by Frank (1938), who treated six young women born without a vagina. The women had to dilate two to three times per day and throughout the night. Frank reported that for five of his six patients vaginal lengths of 6.5–7 cm were achieved within six to eight weeks, and that three of the women had heterosexual intercourse post-treatment. Since then more variations of the technique have been reported (e.g. Ingram, 1981), though the underlying treatment principle of gradual stretch of vaginal tissue remains unchanged. As far as intersexed women are concerned, patient satisfaction with and adherence to such a regime is, not surprisingly, low (Minto, Liao, Conway & Creighton, 2003b). In the light of the uncertainties surrounding surgical reconstruction of the vagina, which in most circumstances requires a dilation regime to be maintained by the patient afterwards, it may make more sense to recommend pressure dilation, where appropriate, as the first line approach. As for surgical reconstruction, however, reliable outcome data for dilation treatment on its own are scant. Success rates of up to 80% have been claimed (Costa et al., 1997) but, as with the surgical studies, no attempt was made to systematically assess subsequent sexual experiences. There is also no published data on optimal

---

[3] The technique is also commonly applied to non-intersexed women who attend psycho-sexual services for vaginal penetration difficulties.

frequency and duration of insertion plotted against size increase for different patient groups. Generally, women are advised to dilate daily for some months and thereafter less frequently to keep the vagina open unless they engage in regular vaginal penetrative sex.

In an attempt to minimize the need for and the number of vaginoplasties and their attendant risks, a psychology-led protocol has been developed to improve dilation treatment adherence. My own observations and a recent pilot study carried out to aid protocol design suggest that emotional barriers to treatment adherence are considerable (Liao, Doyle, Crouch & Creighton, 2006). Follow-up psycho-sexual data will give useful information about sexual experiences in the longer term.

Accountability

The overriding emphasis on appearance and function of female genitals – defined in terms of a non-protruding exterior and a penetrable interior – in the medical literature and, the related disregard for the quality of women's sexual experiences, betray outrageous (hetero)sexist notions. Clearly these practices do not just reflect the (hetero)sexism of a few maverick doctors but are informed by dominant cultural discourses of sex, womanhood and manhood. In my experience, two concerns most frequently expressed by heterosexual intersexed (and non-intersexed) women in relation to vaginal construction are: whether their genitals look normal on the outside, and whether the vagina would feel normal to penetrate (e.g. whether the angle would feel 'right' for male partners, or whether male partners could tell that it was not a standard vagina). Despite the potential risks and unanswered questions relating to genital surgery, many women do choose to 'normalize'. It should be pointed out, however, that women who do not choose to normalize may be less likely to present themselves at the clinic to my service context.

The vagina is clearly of considerable import in women's gendered identity (see Braun & Wilkinson, 2005). Some intersexed women that I see have sought vaginoplasty despite a professed disinterest in heterosexual sexual activity and relationships. And, some seek further surgery even though they have derived no tangible benefit from previous operations. These observations are not just based on my work with intersexed women. One of my non-intersexed clients who had survived pelvic cancer in childhood for example, will, contrary to advice from her gynaecological oncologist, undergo a thirteenth (albeit minor) procedure to her vagina because her male partner has not been able to penetrate 'all the way'. Where repeat operations have not resulted in a penetrable vagina, I notice that very few women express regret about the operations. If the vagina indeed 'signifies womanhood pure and simple' (Braun & Wilkinson, 2005, p. 511), then an orifice signifying the vagina would be preferable to an absence, regardless of its functional status. In this limited sense, it is easy to see how surgeons could claim such a high rate of 'success' without producing evidence of positive sexual experiences in the recipients of their interventions.

Can surgical accountability, however, be founded on an absence of regret? Arguably it ought to take account of the reasons behind people's acceptance of what are invasive and sometimes risky procedures. The apparent straightforwardness with which surgery is offered and accepted is at least partly to do with its imagined ability to confer normality and sexual entitlement. In an interview study, my colleagues and I talked to women with XY karyotype who had undergone (mainly first time) vaginal construction in adulthood.

One of the participants reported her reasons for seeking this help as follows: 'I expected that I would have an ordinary heterosexual relationship' (Boyle, Smith & Liao, 2005, p. 577). This participant could be speaking for the majority of women seeking genital surgery. Many women who have a DSD speak of feeling like outsiders and feeling unentitled to relationships until they have had surgery to remove the obstacles for 'normal sex'. These women are not just looking to surgeons for an orifice, they are seeking 'normality' in identity, relationships and sexual practices. Chase (1998b) reminds us though, that surgery is much more effective in obliteration than construction (something that is rarely appreciated in the public realm). Even the most perfectly feminized genitals, it would seem, at best begin the project of normalcy, a project that needs to be completed by the woman herself through 'successful' coitus.

DOING 'NORMAL'

In this section, I explore the distress and some of the negative sexual experiences associated with the pursuit of heteronormative sexuality. It is, of course, possible for intersexed women to have positive heterosexual experiences, and many have accessed them. However, I argue that a project of narrowly pursuing 'normal' heterosex devalues a range of sexual practices, thereby limiting rather than optimizing opportunities for positive sexual relating.

Challenging Heterosexism

In the section above I highlighted some of the risks of surgery such as scarring and sensation loss. These problems are, of course, not the only barriers to positive sexual experiences. Intersexed women who have not had genital surgery have also reported sexual difficulties (Minto, Liao, Conway & Creighton, 2003b). This is not surprising given that positive sexual experiences involve interpersonal processes that may be especially challenging to individuals whose social context devalues their difference. The following comment by an intersexed woman provides an eloquent summary of this issue:

> I felt . . . like [ ] I hadn't learned all the social sort of skills that were needed to [ ] you know to-to establish a relationship and that maybe that was the main problem, and having a vagina wouldn't really help . . . there's more going on than just vaginal length. (Boyle et al., 2005, p. 579)

The lip-service paid to psychological factors in the medical literature on sexual outcomes, in contrast to detailed discussion of the relative merits of corrective techniques, betrays not inconsiderable professional naivety about the dynamics of social and sexual relating. In their qualitative study, May, Boyle and Grant (1996) focused on psychological perspectives in sexual experiences. They compared the sexual experiences of two groups of adult women who had attended the same children's hospital. The first group comprised women diagnosed with CAH (the majority of whom had had one or more episodes of genital surgery), the second group comprised women diagnosed with insulin dependent diabetes, a condition that also requires lifelong endocrine management and is associated with some sexual difficulties (due to a degree of nerve and vascular changes over time for some women). Over half of the (mainly heterosexual) CAH sample reported considerable anxiety about sexual intimacy. Furthermore, in contrast to the comparison group, women with CAH were less sexually experienced and emphasized enjoyment less when giving reasons for sexual activity (e.g. to keep their vagina open or to find out what the surgeons had done). The CAH group also reported a greater degree of passivity in the face of difficulty (e.g. they were less likely to have tried using a lubricant to deal with problems of dryness). And finally, they were more preoccupied with successful vaginal intercourse when asked what would improve their sexual life. The authors explained their differential observations in terms of the way in which the two conditions are managed. For example, the women with diabetes knew where to get information, expected potential sexual difficulties and negotiated these with their partners. Importantly, the women with diabetes would not have been subjected to repeated scrutiny of their genitals or become preoccupied with 'sex' as a result of their medical condition.

For many of the women that I see in clinical practice and research, reconstruction is taken up to enable them to 'have sex' or, more precisely, to engage in genital intercourse. The fact that women seek reconstruction despite being already capable of sex in the sense of arousal and pleasure reflects a strong linguistic and conceptual conflation of 'sex' and coitus in society (Boyle et al., 2005). The desire for a vagina capable of being penetrated by a penis is strongly related to the psychological meanings of this act, meanings that are, of course, cultural rather than unique to the person. Intercourse has historically been seen as a psychologically transformative event, particularly for women (Boyle, 1993). A woman is deemed a virgin despite being sexually experienced, provided that her vagina has not been 'used' – as evident in an intact hymen. And, of course, vaginal intercourse is needed for the consummation of heterosexual marriage. In intersex, the conflation of sex and coitus is often reinforced in medical encounters in which clinicians take for granted that women with vaginal hypoplasia require reconstruction in order to 'have sex'. Some women to whom I have spoken remembered being told by doctors to return for medical reviews when they were about to get married or had a boyfriend or were considering relationships. 'Successful' vaginal intercourse may to an extent resolve some of the identity issues for heterosexual women with a DSD but, just as intercourse is attributed transformative powers, it also represents high risk. A woman could become a 'normal' (heterosexual) woman through the process of 'normal sex', or they could, conversely, be 'found out' and have all their fears confirmed about their 'freakishness'.

Preoccupation with penetrability can be counter-productive. For clients who are not currently sexually active, heightened anxiety means that some of them could be preoccupied with thoughts about relationships, while simultaneously withdraw from opportunities to avoid the risk of humiliation in case vaginal intercourse was to ensue and then 'fail'. Fear and avoidance of relationships may be related to experiences of not being in control in clinical encounters in the past. For women who have not discovered or do not value other forms of physical and sexual intimacy, idealized notions about relationships may be maintained and psychological barriers to relationships further heightened. Some women have described to me how they had been spectator to their own performance and their partners' reactions during (potentially) sexual encounters. Arousal mechanisms are hindered by anxiety and the women's self-doubt can be self-fulfilling. The 'ordinary heterosexual relationship' may continue to elude some people despite a 'good' surgical result. As one person said post-surgery: 'But then I still, even though that . . . part of the problem had been taken away, that, you know, penetrative sex could be possible, I still had all the other hang-ups, the shit that I was still carrying around' (Boyle et al., 2005, p. 579).

In general, in our psycho-therapeutic conversations, relatively few heterosexual women allude to pleasure as the reason for wishing to engage in sex or consider non-penetrative sexual activities as equally valid forms of sexual expression. Despite documentation of the importance of non-penetrative sexual activities in (heterosexual) women's experiences of sexual pleasure in the general population (e.g. Hite, 1981, 2000), coitus continues to possess the status of 'proper', 'real' or 'full' sex in our social context. In their in-depth interview study involving 30 men and women, McPhillips, Braun and Gavey (2001) found that the 'coital imperative' was alive and well and remained 'a strong and normative feature of heterosexual practice' (p. 239). Amongst their socially privileged informants, only limited discursive space in their talk could be located for accounts of alternative, non-heteronormative sexual practices.

The normalization/naturalization of vaginal intercourse frames an entire range of sexual activities and experiences as 'other'. The cultural positioning of penis–vagina intercourse as real/full sex vastly limits the construction of other sexual experiences as satisfying or affirming. Epistemic issues aside, on a purely practical level, the immutability of vaginal intercourse in heterosexual relations produces anxiety and leads to self-surveillance, which can negatively affect sexual responses. Negative experiences in turn affirm sexual inadequacy and perpetuate a sense of non-entitlement. Needless to say, discourses that centralize coitus likewise produce sexual distress and concerns in heterosexual women and men outside the DSD context.

Clinicians and heterosexual women with a DSD may be preoccupied with 'successful' intercourse but it is not always clear what this is supposed to entail. The concerns expressed to me in my clinical context suggest that 'success' would involve: (1) full penetration of the vagina to orgasm for the male partner; (2) the male partner's enjoyment being at least equal to his previous experiences with female partners; and (3) absence of detectable difference in his sensations compared to his previous experiences in vaginal penetration. For the women, however, passing as 'normal' appears to take precedence over other aspects of sexual experiences. In the following section, I explore these observations further in the context of some psycho-sexual research that I have been involved in.

Performing Gender Through 'Sex'

In this section I examine the complexities in sexual problems reported by currently sexually active intersexed women. Recent studies that colleagues and I have carried out with women who have CAIS and CAH (with and without a history of clitoral surgery) suggest that clinically significant levels of sexual difficulties were common for these women (Minto et al., 2003a; Minto et al., 2003b). Table 18.1 combines data obtained in separate studies using the same standardized psycho-sexual measure (Rust & Golombok, 1986). It provides the percentages of women in each group whose scores fell within 'normal' and 'dysfunctional' ranges. As we can see from Table 18.1, the prevalence of 'dysfunction' was high across nearly all of the problem dimensions assessed including: 'infrequency', 'non-communication', 'avoidance', 'vaginal penetration difficulties', 'anorgasmia' and 'non-sensuality'. The only domain dimension on which impairment was relatively uncommon for our samples was 'dissatisfaction'. In our current studies using different

Table 18.1 Problems and non-problems of currently heterosexually active samples of intersexed women (percentage reporting normative sexual functioning [N] and sexual difficulty [D])

	CAH (SURGERY) (N = 18)		CAH (NO SURGERY) (N = 10)		CAIS (N = 59)	
Sexual problem dimensions	N	D	N	D	N	D
Infrequency	27.8	72.2	30.0	70.0	33.9	66.1
Non-communication	27.8	72.2	20.0	80.0	49.2	50.8
Avoidance	27.8	72.2	20.0	80.0	50.8	49.2
Vaginal penetration difficulties	33.3	66.7	33.3	66.7	41.4	58.6
Anorgasmia	38.9	61.1	60.0	40.0	66.1	33.9
Non-sensuality	22.2	77.8	80.0	20.0	57.6	42.4
Dissatisfaction	61.1	38.9	80.0	20.0	86.4	13.6

Source: Combined data from Minto et al., 2003a; Minto et al., 2003b.

psycho-sexual measures, similar patterns of findings are becoming evident, that is, where sexual problems are common, satisfaction remains relatively uncompromised.

I have noticed that intersexed women would often blame themselves for any sexual difficulty and find it extremely difficult to raise issues with partners. If intercourse was painful or uncomfortable or not enjoyable, then a degree of sexual avoidance might be expected. Successful avoidance, as manifested in sexual infrequency and non-communication, might even be welcomed. Where sample size permitted statistical analysis, the associations between these dimensions were significant (Minto et al., 2003b). It is also possible that heterosexual women who have a DSD have lowered expectations about their sexual lives. Perhaps the cultural context that devalues their difference has taught some of them to be satisfied with less than positive sexual experiences. Another possible explanation for the discrepancy between the reported difficulties *and* expression of satisfaction is that the latter is informed by the fulfillment of gendered expectations. My interpretation of our empirical data is that engagement in heterosexual relations and performance of vaginal intercourse, albeit infrequently, mitigate the dilemmatic sexual identity so characteristic of intersexed women. Problems such as discomfort or absence of sensual or erotic pleasure may not be as central to the appraisal of sexual experiences.

Sexual performance en*genders* identity and, through this, constructs enjoyment. Intersexed women and service providers subscribe, consciously or non-consciously, to the notion that the ability to 'have sex' in the way that meets the perceived criteria of heterosexual relations is crucial for stabilizing the women's sexual identity. In that sense intersexed women's participation in (hetero)sex resonates with a performative account of gender (Butler, 1990). The discrepancy between perceived problems and satisfaction sheds light on why early reports of surgical outcomes are more positive than what my observations would suggest, why so few women have complained about what experts consider poor surgical outcome, and why some women seek more procedures despite previously poor outcome in terms of genital appearance and function.

Given the context outlined so far, an important role for psychologists then, is to work with the multi-disciplinary team to minimize the number of operations and the risks and complications associated with surgery, and to assist in research to improve the evidence base in intersex, not least to inform decision making for patients and parents. But a crucial role for psychologists is also to develop appropriate psycho-therapeutic responses to the sexual distress and concerns, if alongside genital reconstruction. This development is the focus of the rest of the chapter.

FORMULATING THERAPEUTIC RESPONSES

So far, I have argued that powerful heteronormative discourses have shaped individual, professional and scientific responses to atypical genitalia. These responses reveal that coitus remains a benchmark for heterosexual relations in general, so that bodies that cannot accomplish this must be altered. 'Successful' coitus separates functional from dysfunctional, normal from abnormal, adequate from inadequate heterosexual activity. In this part of the chapter, I discuss how I have been developing alternative clinical-psychological responses to DSD. This work draws largely on feminist critiques of traditional approaches to sexual distress and on psychotherapies that emphasize reflexivity. The aim here is to affirm differences and co-create new possibilities. Finally, I suggest alternative therapeutic goals and processes that could open up helpful conversations with heterosexuals and non-heterosexuals, whether or not they have a DSD.

A Feminist Conceptualization of Women's Sexual Problems

In westernized societies, medical classification predominates in theory and practice relating to human sexual problems. Within the predominant classification system (Diagnostic and Statistical Manual-IV) (American Psychiatric Association, 1994), four main categories of sexual dysfunction are conceptualized for women: sexual desire disorders, sexual arousal disorders, orgasmic disorders and sexual pain disorders. Classification has been revised over the years and aspects of its current structure continue to be criticized even by mainstream sexologists (e.g. Bancroft, Graham & McCord, 2001). The most cogent opposition to a medicalized model of women's sexual distress, however, has come from feminists and other critical sexologists, who argue for a paradigm shift away from pathologizing women's negative sexual experiences towards an approach that emphasizes the context of women's lives. Recently, a working group of clinicians and social scientists have published a critique of the American Psychiatric Association (APA) nomenclature (see Kaschak & Tiefer, 2001). The group first of all challenged the assumption of sexual equivalence between men and women in the DSM-IV (an assumption based on the work of Masters and Johnson [1970]):

> Women's accounts do not fit neatly into the Masters and Johnson model; for example, women generally do not separate 'desire' from 'arousal', women care less about physical than subjective arousal, and women's sexual complaints frequently focus on 'difficulties' that are absent from the DSM. (Kaschak & Tiefer, 2001, p. 3)

Importantly, the group further argued that the diagnostic system erased important relational aspects of sexuality and levelled differences amongst women:

> All women are not the same, and their sexual needs, satisfactions, and problems do not fit neatly into categories of desire, arousal, orgasm or pain. Women differ in their values, approaches to sexuality, social and cultural backgrounds, and current situations, and these differences cannot be smoothed over into an identical notion of 'dysfunction' – or an identical one-size-fits-all treatment. (Kaschak & Tiefer, 2001, p. 3)

These workers argue for a formal re-classification of sexual difficulties into those that relate to: (1) socio-cultural, political or economic factors (e.g. overworked, inadequate access to services); (2) partner and relationship factors (e.g. discrepancies in desire or preference, relationship conflict); (3) psychological factors (e.g. depression, experience of abuse); and (4) medical factors (e.g. neurological diseases, side effect of drugs). A more in-depth appreciation of the social context though, does not in itself lead to social change. This means that treatment often continues to focus on fixing body parts because 'there are no magic bullets for the socio-cultural, political, psychological, social or relational bases of women's sexual problems' (Kaschak & Tiefer, 2001, p. 4).

Moving the Therapeutic Goal Post

Sex researchers may subscribe to medical nomenclature, especially those whose interests lie in physical factors (e.g. effects of illness or its treatments), but most practitioners would be wary of a pure biomedical approach to treatment. Most therapists would routinely take account of intrapersonal and interpersonal issues. In practice, the work carried out by the majority of therapists today can be said to be aligned to a biopsychosocial framework (see Liao, 2004). Within this framework, bodily pathology (e.g. hormonal deficiencies, side effects of drugs, ill health) is seen to 'interact' with the individual's psychological diatheses (e.g. anxiety, depression, low self-esteem, poor body image). Psychological diatheses could include past events (e.g. past history of abuse, punitive parenting) or present circumstances (e.g. unemployment, bereavement), or relate to the quality of the relationship issues (e.g. marital discord). The social part of the formulation is conceptualized as environmental stress, religious prohibition and so on. But even these more sophisticated, multi-theoretical models often fail to take account of the social meanings assigned to sex, the strategic functions of sex in social transactions and the ways in which discourses construct experiences as satisfactory or unsatisfactory, adequate or inadequate, normal or abnormal.

Many psycho-sexual therapists continue to valorize pathologizing discourses. Most practitioners subscribe to the view that there are real and distinguishable deficits or abnormalities that can be uncovered, categorized and treated. Furthermore, the broadly behaviouristic programme outlined by Masters and Johnson (1970) remains the cornerstone of most therapy programmes (see Hawton, 1985, for a discussion of the programmes). Bancroft (2002) argues that, although there are weaknesses to Masters and Johnson's work, their approach to treating sexual problems (in heterosexual relationships) nevertheless 'seeks out the aspects of lovemaking that the woman needs to enjoy sex as well as the man' (p. 454). This 'fair deal' in heterosexual activities may be less straightforward than it would seem (Braun, Gavey & McPhillips, 2003), but it is important to acknowledge that practitioners increasingly subscribe to the notion of women's right to sexual pleasure.

LoPiccolo (1994) suggested that sex therapists in the post-Masters and Johnson era should provide more than education and skills development. They should explore the ways in which sexual difficulties may regulate distance and closeness and power relationships between some couples, ward off what are perceived to be socially unacceptable sexual urges such as those involving same-sex partners, defend against intrapsychic conflict, or drive toward success in other (compensatory) life goals. Such rhetoric certainly represents positive changes. But what needs to be contested much more energetically by therapists is the goal of sex therapy. In her criticism of DSM narratives, Tiefer (1995) writes:

> Full *genital performance during heterosexual intercourse is the essence of sexual functioning*, which excludes and demotes nongenital possibilities for pleasure and expression. Involvement or non-involvement of the nongenital body parts becomes incidental, of interest only as it impacts on genital responses identified in the nosology. (p. 53, emphasis original)

The centrality of coitus in the assessment and treatment frameworks for heterosexuals has remained stable. Coital frequency, duration and satisfaction form the most important benchmark for measuring heterosexual sexual experiences and remain by and large the accepted treatment outcome for service users and providers alike.

An Alternative Approach for Women's Heterosexual Concerns

Feminist sex therapists, then, face considerable challenges, not least because the women (and men) that they treat would not welcome their problems being attributed to oppressive cultural constructions. Feminist therapists, however, are not alone in their struggle to reconcile diverse philosophical stances and social values in clinical practice. In the broader field of psychological service provision, constructionist and critical realist theorists have challenged practitioners' pathologization and individualization of human suffering, and for positioning themselves as scientific wizards 'able to identify and expose the processes leading to the patient's disorder and manipulate them such that the abnormalities are repaired' (Smail, 2001, p. 57). Criticisms that strike at the ideological buttresses of clinical psychological practice have paved the way for interrogations of traditional formulations of presenting difficulties based solely on intrinsic, individual factors. Therapists committed to work with 'race' and culture issues have assisted in this development by their insistence in emphasizing the social context in clinical formulations of individuals' difficulties (see Patel et al., 2000). Likewise for therapists who are committed to work critically with LGBT issues, who further challenge social and sexual conformity as a desirable therapeutic outcome (e.g. Neal & Davies, 2000). Continued development in these directions is needed to pave the way for radical revisions to clinical formulations of human sexuality problems, and for these changes to be taken on board in mainstream sexology.

Exploring problems of sexuality with heterosexual women (and men) within a deconstructionist framework, however, is complicated by many clients' reluctance to relinquish their normatively gendered aspirations. The experience of distress and the desire for socially acceptable solutions are not always within the individual's control (Smail, 2001).

Nevertheless, the future remit of sex therapy must surely include a greater appreciation of the potentially high costs of doing gender through sex and an exploration of alternative perspectives. In the meantime, it is of course important to validate clients' realities and demonstrate our respect for these realities even when working within a deconstructionist framework (see Fredman, 2004).

In DSD management, surgical interventions represent an attempt to stabilize gendered identity through achieving a more clearly gendered body that permits clearly gendered (hetero) sexual acts. This has been a physically and psychologically costly project for some individuals and one that has sidelined other possibilities. In psycho-sexual counselling, I work to emphasize sensate focus rather than gender performance. Such a model offers more scope for clients to take in pleasure as they explore what works best for them and to become more open to opportunities for good-enough enjoyment and positive sexual relating. In recommending sensate focus, however, I do not mean to reproduce Masters and Johnson's approach (1970), which involved banning coitus to remove tension and to rediscover sensual pleasure as a step towards reintroducing coitus. Instead, I recommend that sensate focus replaces coitus altogether as a goal, that coitus becomes *incidental* to the process of renegotiating optimal sexual lives. In emphasizing choice, entitlement, enjoyment and discovery, individuals may reclaim their right to redefine what they want 'sex' to mean for them, even if this can never be entirely free of cultural influence.

With clients' permission to explore such an approach, our conversations might explore the developmental trajectories of the following (not in any particular order): (1) gender positioning of self; (2) gender(s) of preferred partners; (3) body perceptions; (4) sexual experiences and fantasies; (5) sexual and relationship aspirations; and (6) knowledge and attitude relating to a range of sexual activities. If therapy continues, we may move towards one or more of the following goals: (1) expanding our shared understanding of past and present influences on the identified problem(s); (2) increasing awareness of variations in male and female sexualities; (3) decision not to pursue sexual activities – alone or partnered – as appropriate to the clients; (4) self-permission to explore a range of sexual activities – alone or partnered – with or without erotic material or mechanical aids; (5) de-centralizing vaginal intercourse; and (6) increasing control over social and sexual situations. Through such an approach, which must be made transparent to client(s), it may be possible eventually to uncouple 'sex' and genital intercourse conceptually and linguistically, and validate other sexual activities (or inactivity) that have otherwise been constructed as inadequate or abnormal.

CONCLUSION

Clinical management of atypical sex development brings into sharp focus salient issues relating to human sexuality. Practices underpinned by heteronormative discourses are limiting for people with DSDs, as for many social groups. While the importance of psychological support is frequently alluded to in the literature, its delivery (remit, scope, theories, methods, accountability) has never been coherently articulated, perhaps, at least partly, because it is not obvious how such support may fit with the centrality of corrective surgery in clinical practice.

ACKNOWLEDGEMENTS

I am grateful to the clients and research participants who have offered their insights, to my medical and nursing colleagues for their clinical and research collaboration, to Paul Chadwick and Mary Boyle for stimulating discussions over the years, and to Victoria Clarke and Liz Peel for their indispensable editorial recommendations.

REFERENCES

Alizai, N. K., Thomas, D. F. M., Lilford, R. J., Batchelor, A. G. G. & Johnson, N. (1999). Feminizing genitoplasty for congenital adrenal hyperplasia: What happens at puberty? *Journal of Urology*, **161**(5), 1588–1591.

American Psychiatric Association (APA) (1994). *Diagnostic and Statistical Manual of Mental Disorders* (4th edn). Washington, DC: APA Press.

Ansell, J. & Rajfer, J. (1981). A new simplified method for concealing the hypertrophied clitoris. *Journal of Paediatric Surgery*, **16**(5), 681–684.

Bancroft, J. (2002). The medicalization of female sexual dysfunction: the need for caution. *Archives of Sexual Behaviour*, **31**(5), 451–455.

Bancroft, J., Graham, C. A. & McCord, C. (2001). Conceptualizing women's sexual problems. *Journal of Sex & Marital Therapy*, **27**(2), 95–104.

Baskin, L. S., Erol, A., Li, Y. W., Liu, W. H., Kurzrock, E. & Cunha, G. R. (1999). Anatomical studies of the human clitoris. *Journal of Urology*, **162**(3 pt 2), 1015–1020.

Blackless, M., Charuvastra, A., Derryck, A. & Fausto-Sterling, A. (2000). How sexually dimorphic are we? Review and synthesis. *American Journal of Human Biology*, **12**(2), 151–166.

Boyle, M. (1993). Sexual dysfunction or heterosexual dysfunction? *Feminism & Psychology*, **3**(1), 73–88.

Boyle, M., Smith, S. & Liao, L. M. (2005). Adult genital surgery for intersex: A solution to what problem? *Journal of Health Psychology*, **10**(4), 573–584.

Braun, V., Gavey, N. & McPhillips, K. (2003). The 'fair deal'? Unpacking accounts of reciprocity in heterosex. *Sexualities*, **6**, 237–261.

Braun, V. & Wilkinson, S. (2005). Vagina equals woman? On genitals and gendered identity. *Women's Studies International Forum*, **28**(6), 509–522.

Butler, J. (1990). Gender trouble, feminist theory and psychoanalytic discourse. In L. J. Nicholson (Ed.) *Feminism/Postmodernism*, (pp. 324–340). London: Routledge.

Cameron, F. & Smith, G. (2004). Embryology of the female genital tract. In A. Balen, S. M. Creiighton, M. C. Davies, J. MacDougall & R. Stanhope (Eds), *Paediatric and Adolescent Gynaecology: A multi-disciplinary approach* (pp. 3–8). Cambridge, UK: Cambrige University Press.

Cali, R. W. & Pratt, J. H. (1968). Congenital absence of the vagina: Long term results of vaginal reconstruction in 175 cases. *American Journal of Obstetrics & Gynecology*, **100**(6), 752–763.

Chase, C. (1998a). Hermaphrodites with attitude: Mapping the emergence of intersex political activism. *GLQ: A Journal of Lesbian and Gay Studies*, **4**(2), 189–211.

Chase, C. (1998b). Surgical progress is not the answer to intersexuality. *Journal of Clinical Ethics*, **9**(4), 385–392.

Clarke, V. & Peel, E. (2005). LGBT psychology and feminist psychology: Bridging the divide. *Psychology of Women Section Review,* **7**(2), 4–10.

Costa, E. M., Mendonca, B. B., Inacio, M., Arnhold, I. J., Silva, F. A. & Lodovici, O. (1997). Management of ambiguous genitalia on pseudohermaphrodites: New perspectives on vaginal dilation. *Fertility and Sterility*, **67**(2), 229–232.

Creighton, S. M. & Liao, L. M. (2004). Changing attitudes to sex assignment in intersex. *British Journal of Urology International*, **93**(5), 659–664.

Creighton, S., Minto, C. & Steele, S. J. (2001). Feminising childhood surgery in ambiguous genitalia: Objective cosmetic and anatomical outcomes in adolescence. *Lancet*, **358**(9276), 124–125.

Crouch, N. L., Minto, C. L., Liao, L. M., Woodhouse, C. R. J. & Creighton, S. M. (2004). Genital sensation following feminising genitoplasty for congenital adrenal hyperplasia: A pilot study. *British Journal of Urology International*, **93**(1), 135–138.

Densmore, D. (1973). Independence from the sexual revolution. In A. Koedt, E. Levine & A. Rapone (Eds), *Radical Feminism* (pp. 107–118). New York: Quadrangle Books.

Donaghoe, P. (1991). Clinical management of intersex abnormalities. *Current Problems in Surgery*, **28**(8), 513–579.

Dreger, A. D., Chase, C., Sousa, A., Gruppusso, P. A. & Frader, J. (2005). Changing the nomenclature/taxonomy of intersex: A scientific and clinical rationale. *Journal of Pediatric Endocrinology & Metabolism*, **18**(8), 735–738.

Frank, R. T. (1938). The formation of an artificial vagina without operation. *American Journal of Obstetrics & Gynecology*, **35**, 1053.

Fredman, G. (2004). *Transforming Emotion: Conversations in counselling and psychotherapy*. London: Whurr.

Hawton, K. (1985). *Sex Therapy: A practical guide*. Oxford: Oxford University Press.

Hines, M. (2004). *Brain Gender*. New York, NY: Oxford University Press.

Hite, S. (1981). *The Hite Report: A nationwide study of female sexuality*. New York, NY: Dell.

Hite, S. (2000). *The New Hite Report: The revolutionary report on female sexuality updated*. London: Hamlyn.

Hughes, I. A. (2002). Intersex. *British Journal of Urology International*, **90**(8), 769–776.

Hughes, I. A., Houk, C., Ahmed, S. F. & Lee, P. A. (2006). Consensus statement on management of intersex disorders. *Archives of Diseases of Childhood*, **91**(7), 554–563.

Ingram, J. M. (1981). The bicycle seat stool in the treatment of vaginal agenesis and stenosis: A preliminary report. *American Journal of Obstetrics & Gynecology*, **140**(8), 867–873.

Ismail-Pratt, I. S., Cutner, A. S. & Creighton, S. M. (2006). Laparoscopic vaginoplasty: Alternative techniques in vaginal reconstruction. *British Journal of Obstetrics & Gynaecology*, **113**(3), 340–343.

Jones, E. (1995). The Construction of Gender in Family Therapy. In C. Burck & B. Speed (Eds), *Gender, Power and Relationships* (pp. 7–35). London: Routledge.

Kaschak, E. & Tiefer, L. (Eds) (2001). *A New View of Women's Sexual Problems*. New York, NY: Haworth Press.

Kessler, S. J. (1998). *Lessons from the Intersexed*. New Brunswick, NJ: Rutgers University Press.

Kipnis, K. & Diamond, M. (1998). Pediatric ethics and the surgical assignment of sex. *The Journal of Clinical Ethics*, **9**(4), 398–410.

Kitzinger, C. & Coyle, A. (2002). Introducing Lesbian and Gay Psychology. In A. Coyle & C. Kitzinger (Eds), *Lesbian and Gay Psychology: New perspectives* (pp. 1–29). London: BPS Blackwell.

Klingele, C. J., Gebhart, J. B., Croak, A. J., DiMarco, C. S., Lesnick, T. G. & Lee, R. A. (2003). McIndoe procedure for vaginal agenesis: Long term outcome and effect on quality of life. *American Journal of Obstetrics and Gynecology*, **189**(6), 1569–1573.

Lavie, M. & Willig, C. (2004). 'I don't feel like melting butter': An interpretative phenomenological analysis of the experience of 'inorgasmia'. *Psychology & Health*, **12**(3), 18–19.

Liao, L. M. (2004). Development of Sexuality: Psychological Perspectives. In A. Balen, S. Creighton, M. Davies, J. MacDougall & R. Stanhope (Eds), *Paediatric & Adolescent Gynaecology: A multi-disciplinary approach* (pp. 77–93). Cambridge: Cambridge University Press.

Liao, L. M., Doyle, J., Crouch, N. S. & Creighton, S. M. (2006). Dilation as treatment for vaginal agenesis and hypoplasia: A pilot exploration of benefits and barriers as perceived by patients. *Journal of Obstetrics & Gynecology*, **26**(2), 144–148.

Lloyd, J., Crouch, N. S., Minto, C. L., Liao, L. M. & Creighton, S. M. (2005). Female genital appearance: 'Normality' unfolds. *British Journal of Obstetrics & Gynaecology*, **112**(5), 643–646.

LoPiccolo, J. (1994). The evolution of sex therapy. *Sexual & Marital Therapy*, **9**(1), 5–7.

Masters, W. H. & Johnson, V. E. (1970). *Human Sexual Inadequacy.* London: Churchill.

Martinez-Mora, J., Isnard, R., Castellevi, A. & Lopez-Ortiz, P. (1992). Neovagina in vaginal agenesis: Surgical methods and long-term results. *Journal of Pediatric Surgery*, **27**(1), 10–14.

May, B., Boyle, M. & Grant, D. (1996). A comparative study of sexual experiences: Women with diabetes and women with congenital adrenal hyperplasia due to 21-hydroxylase deficiency. *Journal of Health Psychology*, **1**(4), 479–492.

McPhillips, K., Braun, V. & Gavey, N. (2001). Defining (hetero)sex: how imperative is the 'coital imperative'. *Women's Studies International Forum*, **24**(2), 229–240.

Minto, C. L. & Creighton, S. M. (2003). Vaginoplasty. *The Obstetrician & Gynecologist*, **5**(2), 84–89.

Minto, C. L., Liao, L. M., Woodhouse, C. R. J., Ransley, P. G. & Creighton, S. M. (2003a). Adult outcomes of childhood clitoral surgery for ambiguous genitalia. *Lancet*, **361**(9365), 1252–1257.

Minto, C. L., Liao, K. L. M., Conway, G. S. & Creighton, S. M. (2003b). Sexual function and complete androgen insensitivity syndrome. *Fertility and Sterility*, **80**(1), 157–164.

Munkarah, A., Malone, J., Budev, H. & Evans, T. (1994). Mucinous adenocarcinoma arising in a neovagina. *Gynecologic Oncology*, **52**(2), 272–275.

Neal, C. & Davies, D. (Eds) (2000). *Issues in Therapy with Lesbian, Gay, Bisexual and Transgender Clients.* Milton Keynes: Open University Press.

Nicholson, P. & Burr, J. (2003). What is 'normal' about women's (hetero)sexual desire and orgasm?: a report of an in-depth interview study. *Social Science & Medicine*, **57**(9), 1735–1745.

Patel, N., Bennett, L., Dennis, M., Dosanjh, N., Mahtani, A., Miller, A. & Nadishaw, Z. (Eds) (2000). *Clinical Psychology, 'Race' and Culture: A Training Manual.* Oxford: BPS Books.

Rink, R. C. & Adams, M. C. (1998). Feminizing genitoplasty: state of the art. *World Journal of Urology*, **16**(3), 212–218.

Rust, J. & Golombok, S. (1986). The Golombok Rust Inventory of Sexual Satisfaction (GRISS). In D. Milne (Ed.), *Interpersonal Difficulties* (pp. 51–59). Windsor: NFER-Nelson.

Smail, D. (2001). *The Nature of Unhappiness.* London: Robinson.

Syed, H. A., Malone, P. S. J. & Hitchcock, R. J. (2001). Diversion colitis in children with colovaginoplasty. *British Journal of Urology International*, **87**(9), 857–860.

Tiefer, L. (1995). *Sex is not a Natural Act and Other Essays.* Oxford: Westview Press.

CHAPTER 19

Educational Psychology Practice with LGB Youth in Schools: Individual and Institutional Interventions

Jeremy J. Monsen
University College London, UK
and
Sydney Bayley
Educational Psychologist, Essex Local Education Authority, UK

INTRODUCTION

The following requests, made by two head teachers (school principals), to one of the authors, give a flavour of the kinds of issues that educational psychologists (school psychologists) in the United Kingdom are consulted about when school problems are linked to sexuality.

Case Example One

Matthew, a 15-year-old boy, attends a large inner city co-educational secondary school (high school). School staff had recently noticed that Matthew did not appear to be his usual self, his work had suffered and he seemed to be depressed. The form tutor [teacher responsible for a cohort of students] had planned to have a quiet word with him but never got around to it. Matters came to a dramatic head when school staff found Matthew collapsed and crying uncontrollably in the corridor. He was covered in spit and the word 'gay' had been written in felt-pen on his shirt. When Matthew had calmed down he talked about how he had no friends and that everyone was ignoring him and continually calling him names. School staff felt uncomfortable talking about these issues and so contacted their link educational psychologist.[1]

---

[1] In the UK every state (public) primary and secondary school has cost-free access to an educational psychologist.

Out in Psychology: Lesbian, gay, bisexual, trans and queer perspectives. Edited by Victoria Clarke and Elizabeth Peel.
© 2007 John Wiley & Sons, Ltd.

Case Example Two

Alice is an 11-year-old girl who lives with her mother and her mother's female partner. School staff viewed Alice as being polite and hardworking and until recently they had had no problems with her. A few weeks ago Alice sent a love-letter to another girl in her class – Rebecca. Alice told the class-teacher that she wanted to be just like her mum and have a girlfriend. Subsequently, the head teacher was approached by a number of parents, including Rebecca's, who strongly objected to Alice's behaviour and wanted something done about it or else they would remove their children from the school because they felt that they 'would be made lesbians'. School staff did not know how to handle the situation and so contacted their link educational psychologist.

Some readers may be perplexed by the schools' perceived need to even involve educational psychologists in issues that seemingly could and should be adequately addressed by them. Others may be surprised that scenarios of pupil violence and parental threat, centred on issues of homophobia, are occurring in educational institutions in the twenty-first century (McInnes, 2004). This chapter is written by two practicing educational psychologists working in the UK and focuses on the dilemmas associated with the development of a lesbian, gay or bisexual (LGB) identity in school and the practice implications of these dilemmas.[2] This chapter is not intended as a theoretical critique or a review of the literature (see Rivers, 2002), rather it is an exploration of practice, grounded in the lives of real adolescents and practitioners and the actual dilemmas (and possibilities) stemming from homophobic discourses in schools (Epstein, 1994; McInnes, 2004). In this chapter, we draw heavily on our own experiences and develop recommendations for best practice based on our own ways of working. We discuss two levels of intervention – individual interventions (with LGB pupils) and institutional interventions (working within, and attempting to change, the homophobic environment), and highlight the importance of the latter level. Such an 'applied common sense approach' draws on a liberal framework that aims to support the creation of truly inclusive schools (Frederickson & Cline, 2002).

We acknowledge Dadds's (1997) caution that educational institutions are fundamentally conservative establishments, which are just beginning to grapple with an important human rights issue, namely how education can be accessed by all without prejudice, violence or fear (Day, 1997; Talburt, Rofes & Rasmussen, 2004). We begin by focusing on some of the dilemmas associated with developing an LGB identity. We then highlight that educational psychologists, as officers of the local education authority, are legally bound to prioritize inclusive practice (Education Act 1996). This duty places educational psychologists in a pivotal front-line role when working with schools to manage the outcomes of homophobia and opening up new possibilities for framing the experiences of young LGB people. The chapter emphasizes the role that educational psychologists have in contributing to the reduction of prejudice (Robertson & Monsen, 2001; Ryan, 2001). There is a need for educational psychologists and educational institutions to move from a sole reliance on LGB awareness raising training (see Kitzinger & Peel, 2005; Peel, 2001; Peel, 2002) to the active engagement of school staff in accessible dialogues focused on the generation of new ways of responding to LGB issues (Cameron & Monsen, 1998; Robinson, 1993).

---

[2] This chapter does not specifically focus on the experiences of transgender youth. The main reason for this is that we have had little experience of transgender issues in relation to our school-based practice, and want to avoid 'empty inclusivity'. That is, adding 'T' onto LGB, but not actually addressing the (specific) experiences and perspectives of transgender people.

There is also a need for more applied research which has a *direct* bearing on the questions that educational psychologists, school staff, parents/carers and LGB youth want answered and that extend the possibilities associated with the development of a LGB identity. With a few noteworthy exceptions, LGB identity development has been a much-overlooked area of research, particularly in the UK (Coyle & Kitzinger, 2002; Comley, 1993; Crowley, Harré & Lunt, 2007; Ellis & High, 2004; Trenchard & Warren, 1984). The existing research has tended to be North American, theoretical, or reliant on retrospective case studies (Remafedi, Farrow & Deisher 1991; Savin-Williams, 1990, 1994; Savin-Williams & Cohen, 1996). Although these endeavours are helpful in moving thinking forward they have little relevance to and direct impact on the challenges faced by school staff and educational psychologists in the UK (Rofes, 2004).

LGB YOUTH: VICTIMS OR ACTIVE AGENTS

Research focused on sexualities and schooling (D'Augelli, 1992, 1996; D'Augelli & Patterson, 2001; Epstein, 1994, 2000; Herek, 2004; Ryan, 2001; Savin-Williams, 1995a; Savin-Williams & Cohen, 1996) has detailed the discrimination experienced by LGB youth and investigated the functions and consequences of homophobia alongside the hegemony of the heterosexual assumption. Recent thinking and research has brought into question the victimized and pathologized positions that are often ascribed to LGB youth (Talburt et al., 2004; Youdell, 2004). This new work has asked whether, and under what conditions, a positive non-heterosexual experience of school might be possible and has actively fought against perpetuating a narrative of LGB youth that frames them as victims in need of tolerance and understanding (D'Emilio, 2002; Youdell, 2004).

One of the consequences of an applied commonsense approach is that much educational psychology practice in the UK emanates from a set of implicit 'givens' where tolerance, understanding, equity and inclusion for LGB youth is emphasized under a broader agenda of building inclusive schools and practices (Frederickson & Cline, 2002; Slee, Weiner & Tomlinson, 1998). It is hard for us to imagine practitioners (let alone the public) holding an image of LGB youth as vital, empowered, strong and sexual. Such an image is very difficult to accommodate for many schools, parents/carers and support workers. Instead the default position has been to portray LGB youth as 'victims' of prejudice and bullying, 'at risk' of HIV/AIDS, substance abuse, alcoholism, depression and suicide, homelessness, violence, dropping out of school and failing to reach their potential (D'Augelli & Patterson, 2001; Fikar, 1992; Garofalo et al., 1998; Savin-Williams, 1995a; Savin-Williams & Cohen, 1996). This is understandable because educational psychologists are often involved, as the opening scenarios testify, in engaging with 'real world messes and dilemmas' (Argyris, & Schön, 1974). Educational psychologists' attempts to work and build alliances with school staff, parents/carers and the young people themselves need not necessarily support the status quo, but can create new dialogues and practices that position LGB youth as active agents rather than passive victims.

Attitudes of Family, School and Peers

In this section, we outline some of the real world messes and dilemmas that LGB youth experience and that educational psychologists are often called on to manage. For many young people, a fear of rejection by parents appears to be well founded. A now classic British survey of LGB youth in London (Trenchard & Warren, 1984) revealed that approximately 40% of parents reacted badly to a child's disclosure of homosexuality, with the most extreme consequence being that some young people left home (11%). Another common parental response was to send their son or daughter to a doctor (10%) or to a psychiatrist (15%). In Wallace and Monsen's (pers. comm.) 2004 study, conducted in London, they found that, in comparison with 1984, more young people were being rejected by family members when they came out (32%) and more were being thrown out of home (27% of those who disclosed to parents/carers were thrown out). Of those young people who reported experiencing violence from family members as a result of their sexual orientation, over half still lived with the violent family member(s). Finally, 23% of the 2004 sample were 'out' to their doctor, 5% had attended a psychiatric unit and a further 42% reported that they had received a clinical diagnosis from medical staff focused around anxiety disorders and depression.

As well as experiencing rejection from their families, many LGB youth receive direct abuse from prejudiced and intolerant peers (Reid, Monsen & Rivers, 2004; Rivers & Carragher 2003; Rivers & D'Augelli, 2001; Rivers, 2003). There is particular pressure to conform to certain sex-role stereotypes in adolescence. Gonsiorek (1988) observed that failure to conform could result in cruel behaviour from peers. Savin-Williams (1995b) found that adolescents (particularly boys and young men) are frequently intolerant of difference in others and may actively punish and ostracise peers, particularly if the perceived difference concerns their sexuality (Gough, 2002; Phoenix, Frosh & Pattman, 2003).

In Trenchard and Warren's (1984) survey, 58% of respondents reported verbal abuse and 21% reported some kind of experience of physical assault. In a survey conducted by the LGB political lobbying group Stonewall (Mason & Palmer, 1996), 48% of respondents aged under 18 had experienced violence and 90% name-calling because of their sexuality. Of the violent attacks reported, 50% involved fellow students and 40% took place within school. In Wallace and Monsen's (pers. comm.) study, about 66% of respondents indicated that they had experienced bullying at school because of their sexual orientation. Ellis and High (2004) found similar patterns in their partial replication of Trenchard and Warren's (1984) survey. About 31% of respondents indicated teasing, 37% had been verbally abused and 15% had been physically assaulted. These figures confirm that the fear of violence, intimidation and rejection reported by many LGB youth is indeed justified (Bontempo & D'Augelli, 2002; Garofalo et al., 1998).

A Psychological Constraint to Development: Internalized Homophobia

One of the most pernicious constraints on some LGB young people developing a vital sense of themselves is internalized homophobia. This can occur when an individual incorporates negative attitudes toward homosexuals as part of their own self-image and wishes that they had been born 'straight'. During conversations with Matthew (case example one) he expressed such feelings on a number of occasions: 'I wish I could have been born like everyone else . . . you know, like the other boys . . . I never feel that I belong . . . I always feel like . . . an outsider . . . and I worry about being lonely when I grow up'.

One of Matthew's on-going dilemmas was reconciling how he could be both a 'nice person' and gay when the images he had of homosexuals were as follows: 'well they get

AIDS . . . and are lonely and camp . . . weak people'. This dilemma created a great deal of anxiety and fear: 'my father will think I'm like that'. Most adolescents can usually rely on the support and understanding of their family and friends when they experience feelings of self-doubt and anxiety; however, for some LGB youth, this 'buffer zone' of family support may not be so readily available. Matthew was particularly fearful and ashamed of the reactions of his family and was worried that they would: 'throw me out . . . what would I do?'. Such thinking, which, as we noted above, is often realistic (Ellis & High, 2004; Trenchard & Warren, 1984), can make some young LGB persons more susceptible to their own negative self-talk and to the effects of victimization by family, peers, teachers and others. The experience of rejection by family and peers can have damaging and long-lasting effects on these adolescents. In addition to the direct consequences of victimization by peers, Rivers (2000; 2001) found that such experiences could lead to poor school performance and emotional and behavioural difficulties.

Over the course of our work with Matthew, he slowly tried to reconstruct a more positive and open image of himself as a young gay man. Much of this work was done through attendance at a homework club and supported via family meetings.[3] What we tried to do in Matthew's case was to develop cognitive strategies that fostered positive self-acceptance (Beck, 1995; Graham, 2005; Neenan, & Dryden, 2000; Stallard, 2005). This involved not only working with Matthew but with school staff and his parents. Hershberger and D'Augelli (1995) found that self-acceptance was the single best predictor of current and future mental health among LGB youths, rather than the degree of victimization or level of family support. They concluded that: 'a general sense of personal worth, coupled with a positive view of their sexual orientation, appears to be critical for the youths' mental health' (p. 72).

EDUCATIONAL PSYCHOLOGY PRACTICE WITH LGB YOUTH IN THE UK

The following section outlines the ways in which educational psychologists intervene both at the level of the individual (LGB youth) and at the level of the (homophobic) institution in order to create positive change.

Individual Interventions

Schneider (1998) provided a useful framework for thinking through the issues associated with managing the needs of LGB youth at an individual level. First, young people may seek assistance to obtain support for issues (such as confusion, isolation and distress) directly related to their developing sexual identity. These young people require connection with other young people like themselves so they can construct a positive identity. Second, adolescents may present with general issues that are related to and exacerbated by fears

---

[3] When working with Matthew we assisted the school in refocusing its anti-bullying policy and practices. This incident, along with others that had occurred in the area, prompted us and the local children and adolescent mental health worker to set up a monthly homework club for LGB and questioning youth in the area. Matthew was invited and attended this group regularly.

and tensions surrounding their developing sexual identity (such as family and relationship problems). Educational psychologists need to facilitate the management of the immediate dilemma, in the broader context of distress associated with possible undisclosed sexual identity. Third, young people may present with issues unrelated to their sexual identity.

There is little or no information about the incidence of requests for referrals to educational psychology services for LGB adolescents in the UK, and little in the way of specific recommendations for suitable interventions for this age group (Comely, 1993; King & Bartlett, 1999; Radkowsky & Siegel, 1997; Smith, Bartlett & King, 2004). It is unlikely (although not unknown) that a pupil will be referred to the school's link educational psychologist as a result of concerns *directly* related to their sexuality. It is more likely that LGB adolescents will be referred due to concerns regarding their behaviour, emotional well-being and/or schoolwork.

When an adolescent is referred because of concerns about their self-acceptance, behaviour, bullying or a sudden decline in schoolwork, educational psychologists, drawing on their knowledge of adolescent development (including psychosexual development), need to develop initial guiding hypotheses within their general analysis of the situation. These hypotheses should allow for the possibility that sexual orientation *may be* an important aspect to explore, even if not explicitly mentioned (Monsen, Graham, Frederickson & Cameron, 1998; Monsen, 2001). Other adolescents may disclose their sexual identity to educational psychologists, in which case the psychologist must be sensitive to issues of confidentiality, especially because the pupil might not have (and might have no desire to) come out to their family, school staff or their peers.

Self-Acknowledgement Leading to Self-Acceptance and Resilience

Savin-Williams (1995b) argued that for:

> youth struggling with a stigmatising sexual identity, adolescence can be a time of conflict and distress. With pressures from family and peers to be heterosexual, gay male, lesbian and bisexual youths face unique hurdles in their efforts to forge a healthy sense of self (p. 174).

'Coming out' is a process by which an individual incorporates a same-gender sexual identity into their sense of 'who they are' and in doing so makes a transition into a more integrated view of themselves as a LGB youth. Ryan (2001) suggests that, until relatively recently, most LGB youth 'came-out' in their late teens or early 20s when they were either working or attending college or university, rather than when they were at secondary school (see also Clarke & Broughton, 2005). More young people are 'coming-out' while at secondary school, and, with few exceptions (for example, the charities Family and Friends of Lesbian and Gay Men, in the UK, and Parents, Friends and Family of Lesbians and Gays, in North America), school and community support services have not kept pace with this apparent cultural change.

Returning to our work with Matthew – he wanted to downplay the significance of the assault and was initially reluctant to talk much about it. The head teacher interviewed the boys who had attacked him and they said they did it because Matthew was a 'poof'. In subsequent sessions with the psychologist it took a great deal of time for Matthew to express 'his little secret' as he was frightened that the feelings he had were 'bad . . .

embarrassing'. He was also concerned that if his parents (especially his father) found out why the boys had 'really bullied' and attacked him, he 'just could not cope' because of the violence and rejection he thought would result. Such feelings can act as a defence against self-recognition for young LGB people, and delay the process of constructing a congruent sense of themselves. Initially Matthew just wanted to be left alone and allowed to be who he was: 'I just want to do my work . . . I'm not interested in sex or anything like that'.

When working with Matthew and other LGB young people, as well as using generic psychological practice frameworks (i.e. problem-analysis, Monsen et al., 1998; Woolfson, Whaling, Stewart & Monsen, 2003), we have found stage models of sexual identity formation (Cass, 1979, 1996; Troiden, 1988), as well as ideas from Cognitive Behaviour Therapy (CBT) (Beck, 1995; Graham, 2005; Neenan, & Dryden, 2000; Stallard, 2005) helpful. These various models have helped us to view psychosexual adjustment pragmatically, as being a series of developmental problem-solving tasks through which adolescents navigate their way.

During subsequent sessions with Matthew he indicated that he liked boys and men but vehemently rejected any definition of himself as being gay, which peers and others had labelled him since primary school. It was useful to share with him (and others) an adapted version of some of the phases and tasks described by Cass and Troiden, and ideas informed from CBT in the form of a series of task focused worksheets within a broader workbook entitled 'All About Me: My Journey'. This workbook used language, concepts and tasks accessible to adolescents (i.e. timeline activity[4], simulations, drama, drawing, writing and a range of homework tasks). When working with secondary school aged pupils we tend to focus on the following five main tasks: (1) 'how to manage my internal confusion and self doubts'; (2) 'how to feel okay with being different'; (3) 'how to feel okay with me and how to tell others when I am ready'; (4) 'how to acknowledge/accept who I am and all that this means'; and (5) 'my future . . .'. Because some of Matthew's peers had actually physically attacked him, one of his 'worst nightmares', during sessions work was also done around keeping himself safe, managing future dilemmas, developing resilience and helpful ways of thinking about oneself, others and the world (Beck, 1995; Graham, 2005; Jackson & Martin, 1998).

In educational institutions in the UK, educational psychologists are beginning to lead discussions around challenging pathologizing constructions of LGB youth. Such critical dialogues can suggest new possibilities but also introduce new risks of reinscribing the 'martyr-target-victim' story within the inclusive education debate (Rofes, 2004). Discussions around LGB young people in the UK are moving toward an examination of the concept of resilience and the ways that many LGB young people have thrived and succeeded in difficult circumstances. Resilience as a descriptor is a useful construct that can be used strategically to develop awareness, understanding and possibilities for change in the lives of LGB adolescents. However, there is some concern that it could be dismissed as the latest 'bandwagon' – a fashionable term used without due understanding of the complexities involved.

To sum up, in terms of interventions at an individual level, evidence suggests that working to increase feelings of self-worth is more likely to reduce self-destructive attitudes

---

[4] This activity involves the young person drawing on large pieces of paper their life story so far, highlighting key life events and feelings from their perspective.

and behaviour. Much of our work with individuals is focused on creating a safe and supportive environment so that they can feel good about themselves. There is also an emphasis on finding social groups that can enhance self-acceptance and help the young person to understand that the stigma they experience is not intrinsic to them, and on building coping skills and resilient attitudes and behaviours (including assertion and problem-solving skills).

There are limitations when working at an individual level – for instance, sexual identity is perceived as being fixed. An educational psychologist could say to a young LGB person, 'yes, it's okay that you're LGB and this is an acceptable LGB identity for you to inhabit'. This kind of intervention prompts (and requires) a coming out story that leads to a declaration of lesbianism, gayness or bisexuality. A story with an end point is seen as more conducive to the development and maintenance of positive mental health than a story that is about 'becoming' and never quite getting to 'out'. Another limitation is that most educational psychologists (except for those working within specialized services) are unlikely to have time to work closely with one pupil (and their family) over an extended period. In practice, most tend to work through those adults who have daily contact with the adolescent to develop supportive groups, and provide access to information and services designed for LGB pupils, such as youth groups, mentoring programmes and help-lines (Crowley, Hallam, Harré & Lunt, 2001). The most effective way for educational psychologists to increase self-acceptance and resilience in LGB pupils (both those who are 'out' and those still in the 'closet') is by directly working with school staff to challenge unhelpful practices. The next section discusses the main focus of educational psychology practice with LGB youth in the UK – working with educational institutions.

Institutional Interventions

Research in the UK suggests that many schools do very little to counter prejudice associated with LGB issues, either directly through mentoring, counselling and equal opportunities policies, or indirectly through the curriculum and the general ethos of the school (Adams, Cox & Dunstan, 2004; Douglas, Warwick, Kemp & Whitty, 1997). Until Section 28 of the Local Government Act[5] was repealed in 2003, many schools in England and Wales[6] used this legislation to justify a failure to address issues of homosexuality. For instance, Manchester City Council's Guide to Section 28 (1992) pointed out that no court had defined what 'promoting homosexuality' entailed, but legal advisers suggested it would involve 'encouraging people who are not homosexual to become lesbian or gay' (p. 3). However, in 1999, the Department for Education and Employment stated clearly in Circular 10/99 that:

> The emotional distress caused by bullying in whatever form – be it racial, or as a result of a child's appearance, behaviour or special educational needs, or related to sexual orientation – can prejudice school achievement, lead to lateness or truancy and in extreme cases end in suicide . . . Head teachers have a legal duty to take measures to prevent all forms of bullying among pupils. All teaching and non-teaching staff,

---

[5] Section 28 of the Local Government Act was a piece of legislation introduced by the Conservative Government (1979–1997) that made it illegal for local authorities to 'promote the teaching in any maintained school of the acceptability of homosexuality as a pretended family relationship'.

[6] Scotland and Northern Ireland had their own versions of this legislation, both of which have now been repealed.

including lunchtime supervisors, should be alert to signs of bullying and act promptly
and firmly (pp. 24–25).

Section 28 would not have prevented an objective discussion of homosexuality within the
classroom, or the counselling of students concerning their sexuality (Department for
Education and Science Circular, 5/94). This said, in practice, Section 28 delivered the
message that there were 'legal restrictions on the discussion of sexuality in schools and
in reproducing inequality and prejudice more widely in society' (Epstein, 2000, p. 387;
see also Ellis & High, 2004). Even though Section 28 has now been repealed, a significant
number of schools (and local authorities) still operate as if it is still in place and seem
unaware that their activities are not as restricted as they might believe (Adams et al.,
2004).

The Response of Local Education Authority Educational Psychology Services

Educational psychology services need to ensure that they are fully aware of issues
related to psychosexual development in childhood and adolescents and that they have
appropriate policies and codes of conduct and practice in place. Ryan (2001) points out
that, with few exceptions, most support staff working with schools lack knowledge about
LGB people, are usually ambivalent about the needs of LGB people, and may hold
stereotyped attitudes and beliefs. Educational psychologists need to demonstrate competence not only in working with sexuality issues but in questioning their own assumptions
and biases about LGB people.[7] At the time of writing, the Association of Educational
Psychologists (equivalent to the American School Psychology Association) and the British
Psychological Society have not issued any guidance or discussion papers on these issues
for educational psychologists.

Educational psychologists can work to improve provision for LGB pupils through publicly raising the issue of homosexuality and normalizing it with school staff, parents/carers
and other practitioners. They can also provide advice and guidance, consultation, individual, group- and family-based work and training related to:

- making sexuality an explicit item on the inclusion agenda in discussions with schools
  and community groups;
- raising awareness among school staff, school Governors and parents/carers of the needs
  of sexual minority students;
- raising the possibility that behavioural, educational, self-acceptance and emotional difficulties may be related to issues of sexual orientation;
- developing comprehensive equal opportunities and pastoral care policies that challenge
  heteronormalcy, homophobia and intolerance;
- advising on materials and resources that lead to a greater understanding of discrimination against LGB pupils and that give guidance about how to deal with it;

---

[7] The practice of homophobia is not confined to any specific portion of society, with all social institutions being capable of
communicating bias in subtle ways. It is important that educational psychologists recognize that they too are liable to this
form of prejudice, and need to take steps to reduce homophobia, in the same way that they reflect on their collusion in
racism and sexism. This is often done through the medium of professional practice supervision where a psychologist's work
is regularly scrutinized by a 'critical–friend-colleague'.

- addressing pupils needs through sex education lessons and the general curriculum;
- supporting pupils through the availability of relevant literature;
- encouraging the school to work with available community support groups.

These suggestions highlight the need for educational psychologists to work closely with school systems to effect changes for LGB young people.

From Staff Training Towards Accessible Dialogues

It is important that educational psychology services have a robust equality policy as a starting point for their work in the area of sexual orientation. The educational psychology service in which one of us works has had such a policy for over 10 years and as far as we are aware it is the only service in the UK to do so. This policy document is based on four central tenets: commitment, process, content and outcomes. In the document, there is an initial statement asserting the *commitment* of the educational psychology service to equal opportunities for all. The document lists those groups for whom there may need to be positive action taken, and then those *process* and *content* issues that might need to be addressed in working with other organizations, such as schools, and within organizations. A formal working group enacted the policy through the development and monitoring of an 'equalities action plan'. This plan includes guidelines and procedures for challenging racist, sexist and other problematic attitudes encountered in day-to-day work. The equality policy and action plan are developmental in the sense that, since their inception, there has been a working group that meets formally six times a year to monitor and update them. Another innovation, within this local authority, has been to have a standing item on 'equalities issues' on all meeting agendas.

One of the process issues was to address discrimination as part of a professional development programme of awareness raising and training. Staff training has focused on the following objectives: raising awareness of the needs of LGB pupils; sharing experiences in relation to the population of LGB youth (to identify implications for educational psychology work in schools); and identifying the professional development needs of educational psychologists (Imich, Bayley & Farley, 2001). Professional practice guidance was produced which included specifications on effective working as well as basic information about: professional psychological codes of conduct and ethics; current legislation; relevant Government documents; relevant research findings; major teaching union views; and contact information of voluntary groups and help-lines in the area.[8]

Training can give people permission to talk publicly about issues related to sexuality, and this is an important first step, which many services in the UK are only just beginning to acknowledge (see Harding & Peel, Chapter 12). Educational psychologists who received the training described above reported that they were much more likely to think about sexual identity as a possible issue in a referral or request. Although staff training is useful in sharing information, raising awareness of issues, debating ideas and practices, training alone is not an effective way of developing staff competence in dealing with complex issues in their practice (Day, 1997; Eraut, 1996; Guzzo & Dickson, 1996; Harland &

---

[8] Unfortunately, this folder was never actually issued because, in spite of many amendments, initial legal advice from the local authority solicitor was that it might be seen as 'promoting homosexuality' within the terms of Section 28. Even after the repeal of Section 28, the Local Authority was reluctant to pursue the guidance.

Kinder, 1997; Lacey, 1996; Peel, 2002). Day (1997) summarized the findings of several investigations into the efficacy of staff training and concludes that though it is a:

> popular means of promoting professional development – [it] may not properly be able to promote the necessary range of outcomes essential to continuing high quality professional developments, since they are predominately limited to information, awareness (p. 44).

Awareness raising training for school staff and educational psychologists is often seen as an adequate sole strategy for grappling with LGB issues; however it should be seen as a necessary starting point in an ongoing process. The challenge for educational institutions, if they are serious about developing staff competence with LGB issues, is to realize that structural and technical changes *also* require behavioural changes (i.e. in the ways that staff think about and perceive LGB issues), which are not produced 'by a simple process of exposing people to new truths' (Bell, 1979, p. 58). Staff not only need awareness raising but also support in being able to translate new knowledge into action. Accessible dialogue, as a communications framework, has been particularly helpful in guiding our critical discussions with school staff, parents/carers and young people themselves (Cameron & Monsen, 1998; Robinson 1993), and it is to this framework that we now turn.

Developing Accessible Dialogues

Discussions between educational psychologists and school staff (and others) can be limited to rather superficial stereotypes about the lives of LGB people. Argyris and Schön (1974, 1996) have characterized these as 'single-loop' exchanges. Such dialogues encourage people to act in ways that are consistent with their current (often implicit, untested and stereotyped) view of LGB people. If left unchallenged, such discussions discourage systematic self and other review of thinking, planning and practice. Argyris and Schön (1974, 1996) advocated the need for school staff to move towards more 'double-loop' dialogues if they truly want to resolve what they see as difficult and intransigent problems of practice. Double-loop dialogue involves the systematic exploration of a teacher's intentions and practices, which are made explicit and open to public testing and debate. An important aim of educational psychologists work with schools is to encourage a relationship where teachers are able to talk honestly about their theories (of why they did what they did) and their practices (what they actually did and how they did it). Educational psychologists should work skilfully with staff to enable them to systematically explore the match or mismatch between their intentions and their actions so that they can generate new ways of dealing with situations they find problematic (Eraut, 1996).

In its simplest form, accessible dialogue outlines four key principles that can be used to inform and enhance interpersonal communications between an educational psychologist and a teacher. These are the need to: increase valid information for both participants, promote freedom of informed choice, enhance commitment and responsibility, and do this in such a manner which increases the likelihood that the other will listen and not become defensive. Robinson (1993) has summarized the process as: being clear and saying exactly what you think (within the terms of your role); making the reasoning and evidence base which led you to think in terms of 'x' or 'y' explicit; and fully checking out possible faulty premises, based on overgeneralization, unsupported assumptions or inappropriate attributions. An accessible dialogue should be focused (as far as possible) on concrete events and evidence. Consider, for example, the following questions that we asked the head teachers and parents involved in the cases of Matthew and Alice:

- 'When you declared that there was no homophobia or bullying operating in your school, does this mean that we won't explore the specific and broader issues surrounding what *actually* happened to Matthew . . . so that we can learn from this . . . and make sure that things like this do not happen again?'
- 'How do you think your daughter (Alice) will be made into a lesbian by receiving a letter from another pupil?'
- 'Would it be helpful if I outlined what the research tells us about how people develop their sexual orientation?'

Such a reality-based approach removes the possibility of discussion taking place at philosophical, abstract or emotional levels, where the chances of resolving difficulties are reduced and the likelihood of emotional argument and heated debate are increased. Accessible dialogue aims to enhance interpersonal communication by making thinking and reasoning as explicit and as open as possible.

The scenario involving Alice and her family was a fraught and emotionally charged one. We first met with school staff and then with the group of parents who were complaining to try and understand their perceptions of the issues. The school staff were embarrassed because they had never had to deal with 'these problems before' and did not know what to do. Alice was perceived as being a 'nice polite girl' but staff had never really 'felt comfortable with working with two mums . . . but we got used to it'. When the themes in the staff members' talk were carefully and strategically reflected back to them it was apparent that they had inadvertently colluded with the view that basically there was something wrong with Alice, her mother and her girlfriend: 'well it is a bit unusual . . . and I can see why they would have got upset . . .'. The parent group had perceived three main problems: Alice's behaviour was wrong ('Well . . . it's not normal is it?'); Alice would 'spread lesbianism in the school' and taint their children; and standards at school were 'going to the dogs' and not being appropriately managed.

We facilitated a joint meeting between school staff and the parent group, and employing accessible dialogue strategies, asked participants to imagine what they would have thought, felt and done if Alice had written a love-letter to a boy in her class. This exercise enabled everyone to reflect on the behaviour at issue and slowly highlighted how untenable some current emotional positions were. Unfortunately, in Alice's case, one set of parents decided to remove their daughter from the school, however for those who remained there were no further problems. This incident prompted the school to re-look at its equality policy and set in motion staff training and a parent awareness evening. It was made clear, via a positively worded and prominently displayed charter that the school was firmly committed to challenging prejudice.

CONCLUSIONS

As noted above there is a need for further research specifically related to educational psychology practice with LGB youth. The very real concerns of LGB young people have only recently been publicly aired and discussed within applied educational psychology practice in the UK (Monsen, 2001). Research from the USA has provided useful information about the experiences of LGB adolescents, but much of this research needs to be replicated in the UK and related to the development of rational policies and services to meet the needs of LGB youth. Robinson (1993) argued that although many academic researchers want their work to make a difference to practice it rarely does. An indication of such motivations is often found in the introduction and discussion sections of papers. The introductory section forges a link with an important problem 'out there', with young people, families, schools and the discussion section outlines recommendations for practice. If researchers really want to make a difference to practice, if they want school staff (and others) to take notice, then there are some issues they need to consider. There is a need for more local research focused on applied practice, such research demands dialogue between researchers and school staff about staff's perception of the problems to be solved by research (Robinson, 1993; Ryan, 2001). Problem based methodology (PBM) developed by Robinson (1993) incorporates the accessible dialogue strategy and provides a methodology to facilitate such conversations.

PBM constitutes a combination of three main elements: first, PBM views people's practices as their solutions to real world messes that incorporates a theory of the problem and of what it means to solve it. Second, PBM engages with the normative requirements of practice. It deals with the 'shoulds' of practice, because school staff are constantly having to make decisions about what is more or less desirable, and to defend their positions. If research cannot engage with the process of practitioner decision making, then it is disconnected from a key feature of applied practice. Finally, problems of practice are solved and resolved by school staff and not by researchers. Therefore, PBM is designed to understand, change and improve practice and incorporates a social enquiry process, designed to produce agreement about: the nature of the problem, the nature of the solution and the adequacy of it.

Educational psychologists are in a pivotal position to contribute to the growing understanding of adolescent sexuality and to help school systems manage the needs of LGB pupils more effectively. Educational psychology services can bridge the gap between the provisions of public health and social services agencies and educational institutions, thus ensuring that these are combined to meet the needs of LGB youth.[9] By working closely with agencies specifically devoted to LGB youth, educational psychologists can provide LGB pupils (and school staff) with opportunities to gain further advice, information and support. Within schools, educational psychologists can not only raise awareness of important issues and normalize these, but also constructively challenge (through accessible dialogue) attitudes and practices that constrain the experiences and possibilities of LGB young people. Although individual interventions are vital, education psychologists can most effectively challenge homophobic thinking and practice in schools (and in the broader social context) by intervening at an institutional level.

ACKNOWLEDGEMENTS

The authors wish to thank Dr Viv Ellis (University of Oxford) and Andre Imich (DfES) for their helpful comments and reflections. We would also like to thank the school staff

---

[9] In fact, in the UK, a Government-led review of public services is currently underway, which could lead to increased multi-agency practice and a more holistic approach to working with LGB youth.

parents/carers and the many LGB clients we have worked with over the years who have taught us so much.

REFERENCES

Adams, N., Cox, T. & Dunstan, L. (2004). 'I am the hate that dare not speak its name': Dealing with homophobia in secondary schools. *Educational Psychology in Practice*, **20**(3), 259–269.

Argyris, C. & Schön, D. A. (1974). *Theory in Practice*. San Francisco, CA: Jossey-Bass.

Argyris, C. & Schön, D. A. (1996). *Organisational Learning II: Theory, method, and practice*. Reading, MA: Addison-Wesley Longman.

Beck, J. S. (1995). *Cognitive Therapy: Basics and beyond*. London: The Guilford Press.

Bell, L. A. (1979). A discussion of some of the implications of using consultants in schools. *British Educational Research Journal*, **5**(1), 55–62.

Bontempo, D. E. & D'Augelli, A. R. (2002). Effects of at school victimisation and sexual orientation on lesbian, gay or bi-sexual youths. *Journal of Adolescent Health*, **30**(5), 364–374.

Cameron, R. J. & Monsen, J. J. (1998). Coaching and critical dialogue in educational psychology practice. *Educational and Child Psychology*, **15**(4), 112–126.

Cass, V. (1979). Homosexual identity formation: A theoretical model. *Journal of Homosexuality*, **4**(3), 210–235.

Cass, V. (1996). Sexual orientation identity formation: A western phenomenon. In R. Gabaj & T. Stein (Eds), *Textbook of Homosexuality and Mental Health* (pp. 227–252). Washington, DC: American Psychiatric Press.

Clarke, V. & Broughton, J. (2005). Focus on Activism: Parents' pride – Victoria Clarke in conversation with Jenny Broughton. *Lesbian & Gay Psychology Review*, **6**(1), 56–60.

Comely, L. (1993). Lesbian and gay teenagers at school: How can educational psychologists help? *Educational and Child Psychology*, **10**(3), 22–24.

Coyle, A. & Kitzinger, C. (Eds) (2002). *Lesbian and Gay Psychology: New perspectives*. Oxford: BPS Blackwell.

Crowley, C., Hallam, S., Harré, R. & Lunt, I. (2001). Study support for young people with same-sex attraction – views and experiences from a pioneering peer support initiative in the north of England. *Educational and Child Psychology*, **18**(1), 108–124.

Crowley, C., Harré, R. & Lunt, I. (2007) Safe spaces and sense of identity: Experiences of lesbian, gay and bisexual young people. In E. Peel, V. Clarke & J. Drescher (Eds), *British LGB Psychologies: Theory, research and practice*. New York, NY: Haworth Press.

Dadds, M. (1997). Continuing professional development: nurturing the expert within. *British Journal of In-Service Education*, **23**(1), 31–38.

D'Augelli, A. R. (1992). Lesbian and gay male undergraduate experiences of harassment and fear on campus. *Journal of Interpersonal Violence*, **7**(3), 383–395.

D'Augelli, A. R. (1996). Enhancing the development of lesbian, gay, and bisexual youths. In E. D. Rothblum & L. A. Bond (Eds), *Preventing Heterosexism and Homophobia* (pp. 124–150). Thousand Oaks, CA: Sage.

D'Augelli, A. R., & Patterson, C. J. (Eds) (2001). *Lesbian, Gay and Bisexual Identities and Youth: Psychological perspectives*. New York, NY: Oxford University Press.

Day, C. (1997). In-service teacher education in Europe: Conditions and themes for development in the 21st century. *British Journal of In-Service Education*, **23**(1), 39–54.

Department for Education and Employment (DfEE) (1999). *Social Exclusion: Pupil support*. Circular 10/99. London: DfEE.

Department for Education (DfE) (1994). *Education Act 1993: Sex education in schools*. Circular 5/94. London: DfE.

D'Emilio, J. (2002). *The World Turned: Essays on gay history, politics, and culture*. Durham, NC: Duke University Press.

Douglas, N., Warwick, I., Kemp, S. & Whitty, G. (1997). *Playing it Safe: Responses of secondary school teachers to lesbian, gay and bisexual pupils, bullying, HIV and AIDS education and section 28*. London: University of London.

Epstein, D. (Ed) (1994). *Challenging Lesbian and Gay Inequalities in Education*. Buckingham: Open University Press.

Epstein, D. (2000). Sexualities and education: Catch 28. *Sexualities*, **3**(4), 387–394.

Ellis, V. & High, S. (2004). Something more to tell you: Gay, lesbian or bisexual young people's experience of secondary schooling. *British Educational Research Journal*, **30**(2), 213–225.

Eraut, M. (1996). *Developing Professional Knowledge and Competence*. London & Washington DC: The Falmer Press.

Fikar, C. R. (1992). Gay teens and suicide. *Paediatrics*, **89**(3), 519–520.

Frederickson, N. & Cline, T. (2002). *Special Educational Needs, Inclusion and Diversity: A textbook*. Buckingham: Open University Press.

Garofalo, R., Wolf, R. C., Kessel, S., Palfrey, J. & DuRant, R. H. (1998). The association between health risk behaviours and sexual orientation among a school-based sample of adolescents. *Pediatrics*, **101**(5), 895–902.

Gonsiorek, J. C. (1988). Mental health issues of lesbian and gay adolescents. *Journal of Adolescent Health Care*, **9**(2), 114–122.

Gough, B. (2002). 'I've always tolerated it but . . . !: Heterosexual masculinity and thediscursive reproduction of homophobia. In A. Coyle & C. Kitzinger (Eds.), *Lesbian and Gay Psychology: New perspectives* (pp. 255–274). Oxford: BPS Blackwell.

Graham, P. (Ed) (2005). *Cognitive Behaviour Therapy for Children and Families* (2nd edn). Cambridge: Cambridge University Press.

Guzzo, R. A. & Dickson, M. W. (1996). Teams in organisations: Recent research on performance and effectiveness. *Annual Review of Psychology*, **47**(1), 307–338.

Harland, J. & Kinder, K. (1997). Teachers' continuing professional development: Framing a model of outcomes. *British Journal of In-Service Education*, **23**(1), 71–84.

Herek, G. M. (2004). Beyond 'homophobia': Thinking about sexual prejudice and stigma in the twenty-first century. *Sexuality Research and Social Policy*, **1**(2), 6–24.

Hershberger, S. K. & D'Augelli, A. R. (1995). The impact of victimisation on the mental health and suicidality of lesbian, gay and bisexual youths. *Developmental Psychology*, **31**(1), 65–74.

Imich, A., Bayley S. & Farley, K. (2001). Equalities and lesbian and gay young people: Implications for educational psychologists. *Educational Psychology in Practice*, **17**(4), 375–384.

Jackson, S. & Martin, P. (1998). Surviving the care system: Education and resilience. *Journal of Adolescence*, **21**(15), 569–583.

King, M. & Bartlett, A. (1999). British psychiatry and homosexuality. *British Journal of Psychiatry*, **175**(2), 106–113.

Kitzinger, C. & Peel, E. (2005). The de-gaying and re-gaying of AIDS: Contested homophobias in lesbian and gay awareness training. *Discourse & Society*, **16**(2), 173–197.

Lacey, P. (1996). Training for collaboration. *British Journal of In-Service Education*, **22**(1), 67–80.

Manchester City Council (1992). *Section 28 of the Local Government Act: A Guide for Workers in the Education Service*. Manchester: Manchester City Council.

Mason, A. & Palmer, A. (1996). *Queer Bashing: A national survey of hate crimes against lesbians and gay men*. London: Stonewall.

McInnes, D. (2004). Melancholy and the productive negotiations of power in sissy boy experience. In M. L. Rasmussen, E. Rofes. & S. Talburt (Eds), *Youth and Sexualities: Pleasure, subversion in and out of schools* (pp. 223–241). Basingstoke: Palgrave MacMillan.

Monsen, J. J. (2001). Editorial - Lesbian and gay identities: working with young people, their families and school. *Educational and Child Psychology*, **18**(1), 4–9.

Monsen, J. J., Graham, B., Frederickson, N. & Cameron, S. (1998). Problem analysis and professional training in educational psychology: An accountable model of practice. *Educational Psychology in Practice*, **13**(4), 234–249.

Neenan, M. & Dryden, W. (2000). *Essential Rational Emotive Behaviour Therapy*. London: Whurr.

Peel, E. (2001). 'I am what I am'? Using stereotypes in anti-heterosexism training. *Lesbian & Gay Psychology Review*, **2**(2), 50–56.

Peel, E. (2002). Lesbian and gay awareness training: Homophobia, liberalism, and managing stereotypes. In A. Coyle & C. Kitzinger (Eds), *Lesbian and Gay Psychology: New perspectives* (pp. 255–274). Oxford: BPS Blackwell.

Phoenix, A., Frosh, S. & Pattman, R. (2003). Producing contradictory masculine subject positions: Narratives of threat, homophobia and bullying in 11–14 year old boys. *Journal of Social Issues*, **59**(1), 179–195.

Radkowsky, M. & Siegel, L. J. (1997). The gay adolescent: Stressors, adaptations and psychological interventions. *Clinical Psychology Review*, **17**(2), 191–216.

Reid, P., Monsen, J. J. & Rivers, I. (2004). Psychology's contribution to understanding and managing bullying in schools. *Educational Psychology in Practice*, **20**(3), 241–258.

Remafedi, G., Farrow, J. A. & Deisher, R. W. (1991). Risk factors for attempted suicide in gays. *Paediatrics*, **87**(6), 869–875.

Rivers, I. (2000). Social exclusion, absenteeism and sexual minority youth. *Support for Learning*, **15**(1), 13–18.

Rivers, I. (2001). The bullying of sexual minorities at school: Its nature and long-term correlates. *Educational and Child psychology*, **18**(1), 32–46.

Rivers, I. (2002). Developmental issues for lesbian and gay youth. In A. Coyle & C. Kitzinger (Eds), *Lesbian and Gay Psychology: New perspectives* (pp. 30–44). Oxford: BPS Blackwell.

Rivers, I. (2003). Bullying: Implications for mental health. *Paper presented at the child mental health research networking day*, postgraduate medical education centre, York, January.

Rivers, I. & Carragher, D. J. (2003). Social-development factors affecting lesbian and gay youth: A review of cross-national research findings. *Children & Society*, **17**(5), 374–385.

Rivers, I. & D'Augelli, A. R. (2001). The victimisation of lesbian and gay and bisexual youths: Implications for interventions. In A. D'Augelli & C. Patterson (Eds), *Lesbian, Gay and Bisexual Identities and Youth: Psychological perspectives* (pp. 199–223). New York: Oxford University Press.

Robertson, L. & Monsen, J. J. (2001). Issues in the development of a homosexual identity: Practice implications for educational psychologists. *Educational and Child Psychology*, **18**(1), 13–32.

Robinson, V. (1993). *Problem-based Methodology: Research for the improvement of practice.* Oxford: Pergamon Press.

Rofes, E. (2004). Martyr-target-victim: Interrogating narratives of persecution and suffering among queer youth. In M. L. Rasmussen, E. Rofes & S. Talburt (Eds), *Youth and Sexualities: Pleasure, subversion in and out of schools* (pp. 41–62). Basingstoke: Palgrave MacMillan.

Ryan, C. (2001). Counselling lesbian, gay and bisexual youths. In A. R. D'Augelli & C. J. Patterson (Eds), *Lesbian, Gay and Bisexual Identities and Youth: Psychological perspectives* (pp. 224–250). New York: Oxford University Press.

Savin-Williams, R. C. (1990). *Lesbian and Gay Youth: Expressions of identity.* Washington DC: Hemisphere.

Savin-Williams, R. C. (1994). Verbal and physical abuse as stressors in the lives of lesbian, gay male and bisexual youths: Associations with school problems, running away, substance abuse, prostitution and suicide. *Journal of Consulting and Clinical Psychology*, **62**(2), 261–269.

Savin-Williams, R. C. (1995a). An exploratory study of pubertal maturation timing and self esteem among gay and bisexual male youths. *Developmental Psychology*, **31**(1), 56–64.

Savin-Williams, R. C. (1995b). Lesbian, gay male and bisexual adolescents. In A. R. D'Augelli & C. J. Patterson (Eds), *Lesbian, Gay and Bisexual Identities and Youth: Psychological perspectives* (pp. 165–189). New York: Oxford University Press.

Savin-Williams, R. C. & Cohen, K. M. (1996). *The Lives of Lesbians, Gays, and Bisexuals: Children to adults.* Fort Worth: Harcourt Brace.

Schneider, M. (1998). Pride, prejudice and lesbian, gay, bi-sexual youth. In M. Schneider (Ed.), *Pride and Prejudice: Working with lesbian, gay and bi-sexual youth* (pp. 11–27). Toronto: Central Toronto Youth Service.

Slee, R., Weiner, G. & Tomlinson, S. (Eds) (1998). *School Effectiveness for Whom? Challenges to the school effectiveness and school improvement movements.* London: Falmer Press.

Smith, G., Bartlett, A. & King, M. (2004). Treatments of homosexuality in Britain since the 1950s – an oral history: The experience of patients. *British Medical Journal*, **328**(7437), 427–429.

Stallard, P. (2005). *A Clinician's Guide to Think Good – Feel Good: Using CBT with children and young people*. Chichester: John Wiley & Son.

Talburt, S., Rofes, E. & Rasmussen, M. L. (2004). Transforming discourses of queer youth and educational practices surrounding gender, sexuality, and youth. In M. L. Rasmussen, E. Rofes & S. Talburt (Eds), *Youth and Sexualities: Pleasure, subversion in and out of schools* (pp. 1–13). Basingstoke: Palgrave MacMillan.

Trenchard, L. & Warren, H. (1984). *Something to Tell You*. London: London Gay Teenage Group.

Troiden, R. R. (1988). Homosexual identity development. *Journal of Adolescent Health Care*, **9**(2), 105–113.

Woolfson, L., Whaling, R., Stewart, A. & Monsen, J. J. (2003). An integrated framework to guide educational psychologist practice. *Educational Psychology in Practice*, **19**(4), 283–302.

Youdell, D. (2004). Bent as a ballet dancer: The possibilities for and limits of legitimate homomasculinity in school. In M. L. Rasmussen, E. Rofes & S. Talburt (Eds), *Youth and Sexualities: Pleasure, subversion in and out of schools* (pp. 201–222). Basingstoke: Palgrave MacMillan.

CHAPTER 20

Que(e)rying the Meaning of Lesbian Health: Individual(izing) and Community Discourses

Sara MacBride-Stewart
Cardiff University, UK

INTRODUCTION

Health is often conceived of in individual (and individualizing) terms – something that adheres in individuals and that can be achieved by individuals. This chapter explores lesbians' accounts of health and, in particular, their conceptions of what it means to be healthy (as a lesbian), drawing on interview data from a broader study of lesbian health conducted in New Zealand. My argument is that research and practice in lesbian health is limited by a lack of engagement with lesbians' own definitions of health (and of being a healthy lesbian). Lesbians' own conceptions of health may shape (and, more importantly, constrain) their access to, and engagement with, health and health care. If a lesbian conceives of her sexuality negatively, this may limit her engagement with lesbian health care provision, and lead to poorer health (Wilkinson, 2002). Through exploring lesbians' own accounts of health, I challenge (or query) individualizing constructions and practices of and around lesbian health. A specific focus on lesbian health (rather than, say, lesbian and gay health or LGBTQ health) is important because this is a neglected area in health research, and because of the broader neglect and marginalization of (specifically) lesbian experience (and gender) within the field of 'gay affirmative' psychology (Kitzinger, 2001). Wilkinson (2002) argues for the need to 'disaggregate "lesbian and gay health" . . . in order to identify the full range of health needs and concerns of a wide variety of lesbians' (p. 129). Gender has a special significance in relation to health, not least because women have (some) different health concerns from men and a greater need for health services.[1] In the section that follows, I outline the current status (and limitations)

---

[1] It may be that some of my arguments in this chapter are also applicable to the experiences of bisexual and trans women.

Out in Psychology: Lesbian, gay, bisexual, trans and queer perspectives. Edited by Victoria Clarke and Elizabeth Peel.
© 2007 John Wiley & Sons, Ltd.

of research on lesbian health, and consider constructionist and queer challenges to individualizing frameworks within lesbian and gay psychology. I then outline the method of
the study and present an analysis of two intersecting discourses of lesbian health – first
a discourse that emphasizes the psychological health gains of coming out (and staying
out), which represents an individual(izing) conception of health. Second, a discourse that
emphasizes the sexual (and physical) health gains of not having sex with men, and as such
represents a conception of lesbian health that is informed by understandings and beliefs
about what might constitute a 'lesbian community'.

From Lesbian Sickness To Lesbian Health

Prior to the removal of homosexuality per se from the second edition of the American
Psychiatric Association's Diagnostic and Statistical Manual (DSM) in 1973, and the
development of an affirmative lesbian and gay psychology, lesbians and sickness were
inextricably linked. Psychologists, psychiatrists, psychoanalysts and sexologists paraded
and promoted a range of images of the psychologically immature, overly masculine,
sexually perverted and fundamentally 'sick' lesbian in their work. The removal of homosexuality per se from the DSM promoted the development of an affirmative gay psychology, which brought about a reversal of this view – once sick, in the new frontier world of
gay psychology, lesbians were now healthy. Much early affirmative research focused
on proving the psychological health of lesbians (and gay men), and their similarities to
heterosexuals. Although, as this volume testifies, the field has moved away from a narrow
focus on proving health and sameness, a defining discourse of gay affirmative, lesbian
and gay, LGB and now LGBTQ psychology is one that positions lesbianism as a healthy
life choice. This discourse is particularly evident in research on lesbian health, and, specifically, in research that aims to speak to mainstream health professionals about lesbian
health, including research on lesbians' health care preferences (Bradford & Ryan, 1987;
Lucas, 1993; Robertson, 1993; Smith, Johnson & Guenther, 1985; Stevens & Hall, 1988;
Trippet & Bain, 1993), lesbians' experiences of health care services (Bradford, Ryan &
Rothblum, 1994; Robertson, 1993; Stevens, 1993, 1996; Stevens & Hall, 1988; Trippet &
Bain, 1993), and health care providers' attitudes to lesbians (Douglas, Kalman & Kalman,
1985; Eliason, Donelan & Randall, 1993; Johnson, Guenther, Laube & Keettel, 1981;
Rothblum, 1994; Stevens, 1993, 1996).

As Wilkinson (2002) outlines, lesbian health first appeared as a distinctive area of
research in the USA in the 1970s with the emergence of 'second wave' feminism and early
critiques of the male dominated health professions. Since then, research has focused
mainly on descriptions of lesbian health issues, the use of demographic surveys and attitude research, and mental health and nursing. There has been an emphasis on: (1) the
social (rather than physical) causes of poor health; (2) the promotion of health services
for lesbians and other equality issues; and (3) educating health professionals about lesbian
health concerns (Johnson et al., 1981; MacBride-Stewart, 2001). In the 1990s only a small
number of empirical/epidemiological investigations into health risks for lesbians and the
prevalence of physical and mental illness among lesbians were carried out. Although the
findings of this (and other lesbian health) research has been widely disseminated, it
appears to have had little practical impact on lesbians' reported health care experiences
(Stevens, 1993; Trippet & Bain, 1993).

In the lesbian health literature, the focus has been on the difficulties that lesbians face in accessing appropriate and effective health care (Wilkinson, 2002). As early as 1981, Johnson et al. found that participants in lesbian health care research were more concerned about issues relating to their interactions with health care professionals than issues about specific illnesses. It was also widely reported that health care providers appeared uncertain about what constituted lesbian health concerns, and that lesbian women felt seriously disenfranchized from health care (Stevens, 1993). These findings were supported by research that explored negative attitudes held by nurses and other health care providers toward homosexuality. For example, Rose (1993) found that a quarter of lesbian nurses asked about their experiences of homophobia in the workplace had encountered another nurse refusing to care for a homosexual patient, and 'most had heard lesbianism being referred to as an illness, or as deviant, and described as sinful by other nurses' (p. 51). It has been consistently argued in the literature that poor health outcomes and a limited uptake of health care by lesbians is an effect of their exclusion or invisibility (Wilkinson, 2002). 'Prejudice', either in the form of a presumption of heterosexuality or in the form of hostility, is argued to be key to lesbians' experiences of exclusion (Wilkinson, 2002). In a review of 20 years of studies on health provider attitudes to lesbians, Stevens (1993) concluded that prejudice about lesbians and lesbianism among health professional groups had a significant negative impact on the care provided to lesbian women. She argued that 'deeply entrenched prejudicial meanings about lesbian health remain influential in the education of health care providers, the quality of care they deliver, their comfort in interacting with clients and the institutional policies under which they work' (p. 24). This evidence suggests that despite claims that the removal of homosexuality per se from DSM-II led to a significant shift in perceptions of homosexuality, a view of lesbian sexuality as sick or deficit persists in relation to professional attitudes toward lesbianism and lesbians (see Garnets et al., 1991; Rothblum, 1994).

Despite the need for improvement in lesbian health research, there appears to be some real limits to its effectiveness in terms of improving the delivering of health care to lesbians and improving the health of lesbians. This is probably due, at least in part, to an enduring gap in professional knowledge about specific lesbian health concerns. It is often assumed that filling this gap and improving research and education will necessarily produce better health outcomes for lesbians. However, the desire for concrete actions (better research, further education of health professionals) is based on insecure interpretations that assume that research and education can be directly translated into practice. One factor that may mediate the relationship between research, practice and outcome is lesbians' perceptions of what constitutes health. What, therefore, is missing from our current body of knowledge is an appreciation of how lesbians conceive of and account for health and what it means to be a healthy lesbian. Research and practice is also limited by an individual(izing) conception of health (and of lesbianism) – there is a need to move away from liberal and bio-medical frameworks to a more social understanding of the achievement and embodiment of health. In the next section, I consider two challenges to the individualism that underpins lesbian health research and the broader field of lesbian and gay psychology.

Constructionist And Queer Critiques Of Individualism

This section considers challenges to the individualizing (and essentializing) conceptions of lesbianism, and lesbian health that dominate psychological research. The first challenge comes from social constructionism, and in particular, from Celia Kitzinger's (1987) classic, radical lesbian feminist infused, social constructionist analysis of the (then) emerging field of gay affirmative psychology. The second, more recent, challenge comes from queer theory, and most notably, from the work of Eve Sedgwick and Judith Butler.

Constructionist Critiques

Kitzinger (1987) argued for the importance of radical feminism and social constructionism to the (then) developing field of lesbian and gay psychology. Her text was an analysis of the role played by psychology in the shift away from understanding lesbianism as a sickness to understanding lesbianism as a 'lifestyle', as a healthy (individual) choice. She argued this shift relied on the liberal humanist conception of lesbians as fundamentally no different from heterosexual women. Psychological research on lesbianism and homosexuality has progressively supplanted the notion of the homosexual as 'sick' with that of the homophobe as 'sick' (Kitzinger, 1987). The notion of lesbian 'health' is simply a reversal of the historic discourse of lesbian 'sickness'. This reversal replaces the conceptualization of the bad, sick lesbian by the conceptualization of the good, happy, healthy lesbian. As such, this reversal leaves intact the underlying health/sickness binary. The emergence and promotion of the discourse of the 'healthy lesbian' does not challenge the structures, apparatuses and institutions that support the oppressive notion of the 'sick' lesbian. Kitzinger (1987) argued that a liberal-humanistic discourse of lesbian health represents at best short-term gain, and a failure to challenge the institutions and practices that lie at the heart of lesbian oppression. The triumph of liberal-humanistic discourses represents the undermining of radical feminist theories of lesbianism. The notion of the healthy lesbian also relies on an individualized conception of health, as an achievable, stable outcome for lesbians (MacBride-Stewart, 2004a). It is my proposition that after an initial rush of research arguing that lesbians to be just as mentally healthy as heterosexual women, a competing account of lesbians as sexually healthier than heterosexual women came to dominate discourses about lesbian health. Both 'just as healthy' and 'even healthier' discourses are grounded in the assumption that the achievement of health for lesbians represents an individual triumph over the social forces of homophobia.

Queer Critiques

Judith Butler (1990, 1993, 2004) goes further than Kitzinger and exposes the limits of identity-based theorizing and action. Whereas Kitzinger's constructionist/radical critique retained lesbian identity (while acknowledging its constructed status) as a basis for theorizing and action, Butler queried the fiction of unified identity categories. Butler argued that identity categories such as 'woman' and 'lesbian' are regulatory fictions rather than innate or essential identities that reproduce heteronormative relations between sex and gender and naturalize heterosexuality. In relation to lesbian health research, this analysis shows that woman is a fractured category, that not all women share the same health concerns (see Wilkinson, 2002, MacBride-Stewart, 2004b). Assumptions about 'normal' health for women reveal the heteronormativity embedded in the category woman (MacBride-Stewart, 2004c).

Eve Sedgwick (1990), one of queer theory's earliest proponents, intervened into debates about the relationship between lesbian and gay oppression and theories of the aetiology of homosexuality. Sedgwick queried the value of the essentialist or social constructionist debate over which theory of homosexuality is more likely to bring about the end of lesbian and gay oppression. Both sexual essentialists and constructionists have claimed that their theory will lead to the ending of oppression, and there appears to be no necessary relationship between essentialism (or constructionism) and political effectiveness (see also Kitzinger, 1995). Sedgwick offered up a new binary – that of minoritizing/universalizing. She argued that lesbian and gay political activism is organized in one of two ways: first, around the shared experience of lesbians and gay men (universalizing). Second, around the distinct and separate experiences of lesbians and gay men, which result from the apparently fundamental differences between women and men (minoritizing). Bristow (1997) explains the minoritizing/universalizing view in the following way: there is:

> on the one hand, a gender 'separatist' standpoint underscoring the specific experiences of what it means to be male or female. One manifestation of this minoritizing position would be the lesbian separatist position of the kind that developed in the 1970s . . . On the other hand there are 'universalizing' attitudes that celebrate the liminality or transitivity of gender . . . [including] styles of political campaigning such as solidarity between lesbians and gay men (p. 208).

Sedgwick's argument was that lesbianism/homosexuality is meaningful to those who adopt it as an identity category of their own (minoritizing view) or, to those who accept it as one half of a gender binary (universalizing view). By emphasizing the role of culture, according to Turner (2000), Sedgwick was able to ask 'how does the constitution of lesbian/gay, or "homosexual" identity contribute to the power knowledge regimes through which all persons come to be constituted in this culture' (p. 130). Similarly, we could ask how the constitution of lesbian 'identity' might contribute to the ways in which lesbians are constituted as 'healthy' or 'sick' in western cultures. Sedgwick (1990) emphasized the importance of representations and meanings about sexuality and gender, which are enabled or constrained by the surrounding institutions or cultures. In relation to understanding the meanings of sexuality and gender, there is a need to shift attention away from scientific/medical discourse about sexed bodied towards the lived experiences of what it means to be male or female (heterosexual or homosexual). Likewise, there is a need to shift attention away from medical/psychological discourses of lesbian health, towards lesbians' own accounts of being a healthy lesbian. Vance (1998) similarly argued that there exists an irresolvable tension between queer and lesbian and gay approaches to action, between 'on one hand attack[ing] a naturalised system of sexual hierarchy which categorises and stabilises desires and privileges some over others and on the other hand defend[ing] the interests of "lesbian and gay people"' (p. 169). A broader shift from understanding the aetiology of lesbianism towards the politics and meanings of sexuality and the unpacking of identity categories (male/female, homosexual/heterosexual, healthy/sick) could have a significant impact on research on lesbian health.

Radical feminism and queer theory approach are often considered to be fundamentally at odds. However, as Jackson (1999) noted, both queer and social constructionist perspectives 'question the ways in which male dominated heterosexuality is routinely normalised and both assume that neither gender divisions nor the heterosexual/homosexual divide are fixed by nature' (para 6.5). Queer theory emerged out of the perceived limitations of social constructionist perspectives on sexuality. Jackson (1999) argued that queer theory has something to learn from its predecessors about 'the constraints of material inequalities and the idea of the reflexive social self' (para 7.2). Queer theory also needs to attend to 'the reflexive, social self [that] comes into play in all those mundane everyday situations in which we "do" gender and sexuality, in which the existing gender and sexual order is sometimes affirmed, sometimes re-negotiated, sometimes contested' (para 7.3).

Neither Kitzinger's critique of lesbian health and gay affirmative research, nor the analysis of oppression by queer theorists has made a significant impact on research into lesbian health. Rather, their influence appears to be at the periphery of the field, in areas such as lesbian violence (see Mason, 2002) or transgender (Butler, 2004) (see also Wilton, 1995). Here the focus of the research has been on the experience of 'lesbians' who are living with violence, and are regarded as sick or unhealthy; this research usually reflects a concern with developing an understanding about who, rather than what, people are. Lesbian health research has painted a picture of health as a positive, achievable and essential quality of lesbian experience. But lesbians often have a tenuous relation to health and the health professions have often been key sites of lesbian oppression. As Miller, Rosga & Satterthwaite (1995) commented, 'it might be said that "lesbian health" is something of an oxymoron' (p. 431). Gay liberationist and radical feminist scholarship and activists sought to conceptualize and to address lesbian and gay oppression. For example, academics have contributed to the promotion of research, rights and education and to campaigns, such as the one that led to the removal of homosexuality per se from the DSM-II. Much research on lesbian sexuality has, until relatively recently, explicitly or implicitly reflected concerns of aetiology. Questions about aetiology have always been central to lesbian health research, partly because models that attempt to theorize sexual orientation have also queried the antecedents of a homosexual identity (Kitzinger, 1995). Perspectives on aetiology often cohere around the question of whether sexuality is constructed or natural. Since the 1990s queer theorists have been arguing for the importance of exploring the social construction of gender and sexuality and the limits of identity-based practice. Such analysis – it has been argued - will have a greater impact on understanding oppression and theorizing sexuality than pursuing irresolvable debates about aetiology.

RESEARCHING LESBIANS' ACCOUNTS OF HEALTH

The analysis of lesbians' accounts of health is based on semi-structured interviews conducted with 16 self-identified lesbian women in Hamilton, New Zealand. The women were aged 20–59 years of age and had been 'out' from periods of between 11 months and 25 years. Participants chose their own pseudonyms. The interviews were conducted and transcribed by the author.[2] I use a discursive approach to explore talk about lesbian health – this approach allows for the possibility that there are multiple, competing and contradictory ways of making meaning of the world, and as such there are many ways of understanding 'health' across time and place (Fox, 1997). From this perspective, the experience of 'being lesbian' or 'being healthy' is partly a product of the socio-cultural discourses

---

[2] All interviews were transcribed using the following system: *wor-* an abrupt change in word/sentence; *[word]* additional text added for clarification; [. . .] full quote has been shortened for publication, but original meaning is retained; *word* emphasis made by participant (unless otherwise stated).

that surround and constitute those concepts/experiences in a particular context. In western contexts, lesbian health is no longer understood only as an individual or a shared community quality; rather it is the beliefs, practices and expressions that are carried out to achieve (or not) a particular health outcome or mode of being. This chapter explores the discourses that produce the notion of lesbian health, as a positive and achievable state of being for individual lesbians. By paying attention to the discursive practices that surround and produce the lived experience of lesbian health, it is possible to explore the various resources that lesbians draw on as they come to understand themselves as healthy. The focus of the analysis was on identifying discourses surrounding and producing the notion of lesbian health.

I used an interpretative and textual approach to analyse the participants' understandings and concepts about what constituted lesbian health (Grace, 1998). This approach attempts to make sense of the participants' accounts and is informed by the researcher's theoretical position. The analysis was constituted by a number of stages. In the first stage, I identified all sections of the text across the 16 transcripts that related to 'health' understandings and meanings. I collated in a word file any text relevant to lesbian health issues, references to a relationship between 'being lesbian' and 'health', and answers to the statement 'a healthy lesbian is . . .'. In the next (interpretative) stage of analysis, this collated material was organized into categories and these categories were read closely to build an interpretation of the emerging discourses. From this process, three accounts were identified (two main accounts and one minor account): (1) 'an out lesbian is a healthy lesbian' (coming out); (2) 'a healthy lesbian does not have sex with men' (difference); and (3) 'lesbians have a responsibility to keep other lesbians healthy' (adjustment).

The first account – coming out – was comprised of statements about the way in which coming out may be experienced as a process of adjustment, culminating in a sense of completion in which participants saw themselves as making choices about their state of mental and physical well-being. This account then could be categorized under Sedgwick's notion of 'universalizing' lesbian and gay experiences. The second account – difference – focused on the positive physical benefits of not having sex with men. This account also emphasized an array of social and physical differences between lesbians and heterosexual women and between lesbians and gay men. This account fits Sedgwick's notion of a minoritizing of lesbian and gay experience. Interestingly, both of these main accounts were subject to the same limitation – neither accounted for the experiences of lesbian women who had not adjusted to a healthy lesbian lifestyle, and who represented the stereotype of lesbian women as having poor mental health. However, the third account – adjustment – proposed that any failure to achieve health is attributable to individual makeup and is not 'inherently' lesbian; this account departs significantly from the view that any health gains attributable to being lesbian are achievable by all lesbians. These themes structure the analysis that follows.

Analysis

'An Out Lesbian is a Healthy Lesbian'

The first account was focused on the idea that coming to terms with one's sexuality produces a sense of being (psychologically) healthy. Health is about personal acceptance of and comfort with lesbian sexuality. Coming out and the processes constructed as facilitating and maintaining it – such as moving away from home, finding contacts on the lesbian scene, dealing with sadness over the loss of contact with members of their family or making peace with them – were regarded as important contributors to health.

> *Toni:* Like the coming out process is very hard on any women. [. . .] there's so much you've got to do in yourself. That transition because *you're actually doing a lot of grieving and giving up society's expectation* [. . .] I think my observation is that a lot of people grow within their self and do more work on themselves than the rest of the community.

Toni comments that coming out involves grieving and giving up social expectations around heterosexuality. The participants did not view the difficulties of coming out as wholly negative; rather they were viewed as challenges to be overcome, which lead to personal development and growth. The participants' talk emphasized the importance of 'staying out', in doing so, their talk reflected an expectation that managing their grief and 'working on' themselves would produce positive and enduring psychological benefits. The participants' talked about the contextual processes that facilitated their coming out. Therefore, their accounts were suggestive of a social constructionist account of coming out, one that rejects the essentialist notion of coming out as a process of developing an awareness of what was there all along (Kitzinger & Wilkinson, 1995). Coming out involves 'a mixture of personal re-evaluation, practical necessity, political values, chance and opportunity' (Kitzinger & Wilkinson, 1995, p. 96).

The participants' talk conforms in part with Jeffrey Weeks's (1977) definition of coming out as 'a personal process, the acceptance, and public demonstration of the validity of one's homosexuality' (p. i). Yet the participants' talk did not emphasize public demonstrations of sexuality or, as Mason (2002) has defined it, 'those times when individuals deliberately say or do something to indicate to others that they are gay or lesbian' (p. 143). Rather, the participants' accounts reflected Weeks's emphasis on coming out by individuals as 'the gradual emergence of a homosexual identity and public presence' (Weeks, 1977, p. i), where coming out is an intensely personal process. Angela, for instance, represented coming out as involving psychological shift:

> *Angela:* I've always been a healthy person. I'm no more or less healthy physically than I was before, but mentally, I think I'm more healthy than I was before [. . .] I actually think that knowing who I am, and acknowledging who I am was a major breakthrough mentally for me.

'Health' was conceptualized as the internal and individual stability achieved through the acceptance of one's sexuality. Angela viewed coming out as a psychological necessity to achieve acceptance of the self (see Jansen, 2004), such an account eschews any suggestion that oppression or other political factors must be first overcome. Her account appears depoliticized, as if the acknowledgement of self is an experience potentially but equally shared and gained by all women, and not mediated by other social or political factors. Angela differed from other participants, like Toni, who claimed that the oppression experienced by lesbians has to be addressed to achieve the same psychological outlook as other (heterosexual) women. Sedgwick (1990) argued that in western culture having secrets is believed to attract shame, guilt and sickness. Anxieties about remaining 'in the closet' reveal as much about the heteronormative social meanings of secrecy and concealment as they do about the simplification of the experience of homosexual oppression (Eadie, 2004).

The inability to acknowledge one's sexuality often is represented as an individual rather than a social failure.

> *Toni*: Psychologically I would say that [lesbians can be healthier]. They're a lot freer [. . .] I think women, lesbian women have to do a lot of work on themselves to live in the community, and so I think in that way we are a lot healthier and more aware of ourselves. And I think a lot of heterosexual women can actually lay back and not have to do anything, they're supported by the community, by society at large [. . .] I've often had heterosexual women say that they find lesbian women very strong, very sure of themselves, and we've had to do it to exist in that community.

Toni comments that lesbians 'have had to work *on themselves*' to facilitate the transition towards coming out and being out. She emphasizes that it is the responsibility of lesbians to access community support, whereas, heterosexual women enjoy support by virtue of their heterosexuality. Toni's assertion that lesbians appear sure and strong to her heterosexual friends is presented as a vindication for the personal work done by lesbian women (including herself presumably), to achieve a better state of health (in a heteronormative social context). The elements of liberal discourse that emphasizes individuality and heterosexuality as the norm for equality allow a presentation of social differences as surmountable, and resulting in 'healthier' people.

> *Ellen:* I would have to say I'm healthier than most heterosexual women that I know [. . .] possibly we do a little bit more talking. And talking about real things. Talking about things like health, and what's going on in our heads.

Ellen's talk suggests that the privileged status of lesbian health ('being healthier') cannot be expected or assumed; lesbians' better health is the result of their harder work. The women in this study could have only told stories about the struggles and challenges associated with coming out and being lesbian, however, in the context of a discussion about 'health' they were strongly focused on stories of pride and acceptance. I suggest that, in line with cultural narratives, they (re)told their life stories in ways that presented themselves as happy, healthy lesbians.

> *Deb:* A healthy lesbian has to feel strong in her sexual orientation. Really strong, and feels – not necessarily clear that they're always going to be lesbian – but clear and strong and okay that at this particular point in time; 'I am a lesbian and I am a happy lesbian, and I will do all the other things that every person has to about maintaining that place, balance', whatever.

The participants presented coming out as if it involved a number of stages, culminating in a sense of completion. The production of a well-adjusted lesbian is seen as both a possible and desirable outcome of the coming out process. This understanding echoes scholarly representations such as Cass's coming out as a stage process (Cass, 1979). Yet, as Kitzinger and Wilkinson (1995) note, from a social constructionist standpoint, 'completing transition from a heterosexual to a lesbian identity does not mean the achievement of a static identity' (p. 101). Deb's claim of being a happy, healthy lesbian is grounded in fluidity rather than rigidity, and echoes a social constructionist account of lesbian sexuality. Deb reflects on how health and well-being is achieved through the ability to maintain a sense of self, even when that sense of self is in flux. The participants' repeated talk about 'being strong', 'being sure' and 'being real' draws on the idea that personal growth and maturity are key aspects for achieving lesbian health. For Deb, 'strength' includes a realization that the meanings about being 'lesbian' can shift and change.

Overall, the participants articulated the view that self-awareness is positive because a self-aware person has the capacity to take care of their future health demands and manage ongoing societal pressures. The (negative) implication is that if a lesbian has not come to terms with herself (as lesbian) then she is unable to properly access resources or care for herself. This has the effect of rendering the period prior to coming out as 'unhealthy', the 'not out' lesbian is conceived of as not yet having come to a full realization of her self. Underpinning the participants' talk was an assumption that lesbians play an active role in producing lesbian health – they manage their coming out and their ongoing personal development. The participants also seemed to accept that society has a role in creating personal meanings about health, as in Toni's acknowledgement that heteronormative assumptions require lesbians but not heterosexuals to come out or seek support. Autonomy was presented by the participants both as necessary for the achievement of lesbian health and as an outcome of being a healthy lesbian in heterosexual culture. This latter view was evident in the accounts of lesbians as strong and engaged with a sense of what is 'real' (for example, see the earlier extract from Ellen). However, a particular notion of agency is being taken up here. As Carl Ratner (2000) argues, the role of 'individual agency is fostered by, adapts to, and functions to perpetuate specific social relations [which] demonstrates that it is socially intentional' (p. 426). The limits of individual autonomy mean that participants' experience of themselves as healthy is defined in terms of the social context in which lesbian health occurs.

This emphasis on autonomy is limited because in order to achieve a lesbian identity, women must be liberated and endure a personal struggle to achieve success (see Kitzinger & Wilkinson, 1995). The discourse claiming 'an out lesbian is a healthy lesbian' was relatively consistent across the interviews. The participants appeared to have similar experiences, and their understandings of lesbian health did not transcend normative cultural patterns. Such patterns require lesbians to 'come out' and/or defend their psychological adjustment (see Ratner, 2000).

'A Healthy Lesbian Does Not Have Sex With Men'

This account focused on the differences between lesbians and heterosexual women, and particularly the notion that lesbians are healthier because they are not involved sexually with men. Fewer women used this account than the previous one; however, it is interesting because it draws attention to differences between lesbian, heterosexual and bisexual women and between lesbians and gay men, and it focuses primarily on sexual/physical (rather than mental) health. Further, whereas the previous account emphasized women's individual responsibility for their psychological health, this account casts women's sexual health as a community (as well as an individual) responsibility.

> Ellen: [. . .] having sex with women is safer than having sex with men.
>
> Ariah: Because heterosexuals are probably *more* unsafe. They know that it's more available for them to be safe, but they [are]n't!

As the talk from Ellen and Ariah demonstrates, 'safer' lesbian sexual health was presented as a consequence of the absence of sexual contact with men, because men are assumed to be the cause or carriers of sexually transmitted infections. This account constitutes men as vectors of (sexual) disease and presents lesbians as healthier than both heterosexual women and gay men. This account draws on a difference model of lesbian identity. As Clarke (2002) notes in relation to research on lesbian parenting, a lesbian feminist account of difference rejects the assumption that difference equals deficit. Instead, in lesbian feminist accounts of lesbian parenting difference is celebrated and given political significance. This account of lesbian health is potentially transformative because it emphasizes an explicit sexual (health) advantage of being lesbian.

> *Ariah:* With heterosexual people, one of their pastimes, you know, [is to] drink as much as you can and get laid if that's what happens [. . .] Therefore it makes it more important for you to ask safe sex questions before you get involved [with a woman] 'cause if they've just come out as bisexual possibly they have lived the typical heterosexual lifestyle.

As well as drawing on an assumption of heterosexual sex as unsafe, the participants' talk about 'sexual health' suggested that both men and women who have been sexual with men are potentially less healthy. Ariah constructs a very particular notion of what it means to be heterosexual by positioning bisexual or heterosexual women (in contrast to lesbians) as engaging in potentially risky sexual practices. She implies that attitudes in heterosexual 'culture' towards safer sex (and related issues such as alcohol use) reflect poor judgement, and place women who have sex with men (and lesbians who have sex with bisexual women) at risk. Any lesbians who have had a 'heterosexual past' are assumed to be potentially sexually unhealthy or unsafe, and are often dismissed by lesbians (who have not had such a past) as 'bisexual', and, like men, as potential vectors of disease.

> *Deb:* I suppose I think the safe sex issue is a major [one] for lesbians because of the-the ramifications of bisexuality, of how long a woman's been out and away from maybe heterosexual partners, or [hypodermic] needles. You know, like there could be specific lesbian issues when it comes to the sexual- sexual side of it. I do think it needs to be dealt with. I don't think it's been particularly sufficient in the amount of education around this. I mean it is generally said that lesbians are less likely to contract AIDS because they're lesbian.

Deb suggests that 'the ramifications of bisexuality' decrease the longer a woman has been out as lesbian. The participants constituted bisexuality as damaging both to the sexual health of lesbian communities and to individual lesbians. Lesbianism was viewed as providing women with a sexual safety net – lesbians have less sexual health risks precisely '*because* they're lesbian'. The rejection of lesbians who have had sex with men as bisexual is challenged by the relatively consistent research finding that most lesbians have had sex with men at some point in their lives (see Kitzinger & Wilkinson, 1995). Rust (1995) argued that there is an overwhelming silence about bisexuality in lesbian accounts of sexuality, and when bisexuality is discussed it is in strongly negative terms. Rust (1995) emphasized that bisexuality is considered by lesbians to be a passing phase in the process of becoming lesbian and is not seen as a legitimate sexual identity in its own right. In the accounts of my participants, it seems that the possibility of any lesbian having a heterosexual past is ignored in order to produce an account of lesbians as healthy and healthier than heterosexual women. This particularly utopian view of lesbian health (as dependent on not having sex with men) challenges and counters the notion that lesbian sex is perverse and psychological unhealthy, and presents a positive image of lesbianism.

The possibility of having sex without the need for precautions like condoms or the contraceptive pill, to protect against pregnancy or sexually transmitted infections, was used to highlight the constraints on heterosexual women's sexual pleasure.

> *Jo:* [. . .] there are heterosexual women that are just as promiscuous as lesbian women, but [. . .] you could get pregnant that's like a life threat – I mean, that's going to alter your whole life-

The participants' accounts reflected uncertainty about which sexual practices might be regarded as safe and healthy and which ones might not.

> *Ellen* I still I think, have a belief, that having sex with women is safer than having sex with men. And how wrong that is. But in terms of sexual practices I'm pretty ignorant.

> *Lee* I mean, you don't really know what problems people [lesbians] do have anyway. That's specifically the issue. I've never heard of them.

As these accounts suggest that it may not be possible to know what constitutes a sexual health risk for lesbians. Lesbian invisibility influences understandings about lesbian sexual health. Some authors claim that the notion that lesbians have little or no risk of contracting sexual transmitted infections is primarily the result of their exclusion from research on sexual health (O'Sullivan & Parmar, 1992). Lesbians' invisibility in relation to health checks and in discussions about sexual or gynaecological health also leads to the claim that lesbians are healthier than heterosexual women – the reasoning is then if lesbians are not being written about in the health literature, they must simply not be at risk.

> *Jade:* [in a workshop on safe sex] we talked about the different categorizations of sexuality on the spectrum of, you know, how you can get it – gay, heterosexual, lesbian [. . .] and she said lesbians might be the lowest to get – catch HIV– to become HIV positive, but it doesn't mean like they're at the other end, it's just that they're, you know, further way from the highest highest risk – whatever that means.

Jade refers to lesbians as having the lowest risk for contracting HIV. Yet there is an evident tension between the expressed advantage of lesbian health and the potentially constructed nature of HIV risk, which is reflected in what Jade refers to as the 'different categorizations of sexuality on the spectrum of how you get it'. McNay (2000) suggests that such tension is important for realizing autonomy. In effect, lesbian health is conceived here not merely as an effect of specific medical practices related to the categorization of disease. Rather, it is politically agentic. In the negotiation between the medical categorization of risk and the political status of lesbian sexuality it is impossible to determine what is materially real or constructed about lesbian health. However, the reflexivity of the participants' talk reflects a movement towards an active rather than a passive engagement with meanings about lesbian health, which in this context reinforce an image of lesbians as 'healthier'.

This account highlights the differences between lesbians and heterosexual (and bisexual) women (and between lesbians and gay men). Women who are or have been sexually active with men are viewed as unhealthy (because men are unhealthy). This account echoes a particular radical feminist account of lesbianism and focuses on constructing a positive identity for lesbians as a result of their refusal of sexual contact with men. This account suggests that to be able to account for lesbians as 'healthier', it is necessary to draw on meanings about individual sexual activity, which is also conceived as contributing to the health of the lesbian community overall.

'Lesbians Have a Responsibility to Keep Other Lesbians Healthy'

The first two accounts detailed how the participants constructed lesbian health, in the context of mental and sexual (physical) health. In this section I highlight the potential limitations of both of these accounts in relation to explaining individual failures in achieving health. Both accounts reject the notion that lesbians are inherently healthy; instead lesbian health relies on individual autonomy and political agency. When health is no longer assumed to be intrinsic to lesbians, or it has the appearance of a 'base or default state, health instead becomes something to work toward . . . and an accomplishment in and of itself' (Clarke et al., 2003, p. 172). This is a moral perspective; so we can assume that individuals who do not learn to overcome societal pressures may be viewed as irresponsible or failing in some way for not achieving 'health'.

> *Toni:* [. . .] And also there is the other side [of coming out]. There's the one, the person that stays locked away inside and uses drug or alcohol abuse to keep the secret, so there is two camps.

In the participants' talk about coming out there was an alternative account that contrasted with the image of the well-adjusted lesbian who has overcome societal oppression. Toni referred to this as the 'other side' of coming out – the person who 'stays locked away' and 'keep[s] the secret' presumably of the closet. The reference to substance abuse is particularly important here, because it suggests that the inherent failure (and poor health) of the individual who is always still in the process of coming to their full identity.

Substance abuse, particularly alcoholism, is well researched in the area of lesbian health (Bradford et al., 1994). Early studies attempting to determine the prevalence of alcohol problems in lesbians suggested that alcohol problems affected 30% of lesbians compared with 10% of the general population (Hall, 1993). However, the relationship between lesbianism and alcohol is hard to determine because of the historical co-diagnosis of lesbianism and alcoholism (Hall, 1993). Hall (1993) suggested that alcohol consumption has contradictory meanings for lesbians. Her explanation of this paradox relies on individual, social and cultural explanations of alcohol use:

> drinking alcohol and gathering in lesbian bars symbolizes positive self-expression and communality for lesbians, and lesbian alcohol use represents societal repression, as does the virtual ghettoization of lesbians in bar environments. Thus alcohol use has paradoxical meanings for lesbians: self-affirmation and nonconformity to heterosexual expectations versus isolation, repression, and self-deprecation (p. 114).

This view is reflected in the experiences of Hine:

> *Hine:* So I guess in my early days of being a lesbian, that's how we all met [at a lesbian nightclub or party]. I don't know whether it's the early stages of being a lesbian that you drink a lot, but I know it's certainly not in the later stages because I don't see it as much as I used to [. . .] No actually I'll take that back [. . .] a good friend of mine [. . .] I haven't seen her for years [. . .] and she still drinks about the same amount, so– it might be an individual thing too.

It is possible to find elements of Hall's reflection on alcohol use in Hine's account of her youth – at a time when, according to dominant ideologies, self-expression is paramount. The belief that the communality provided by lesbian bars represents an early 'stage' of being lesbian was frequently raised in the participants' talk about health. Now older, and presumably more mature, Hine suggests that heavy drinking is not a necessary part of being a lesbian, nor does it represent a healthy behaviour for an older lesbian. Although socializing around alcohol may just be part of an 'early stage' of being lesbian when other interests or connections have not yet developed, Hine implies that due to alcohol abuse, her friend has not moved beyond this state.

The notion that health is a consequence of individual achievement is reflected in the construction of other 'lesbians' as either still in the process of coming to a full identity (i.e. youth) or as 'predisposed' to risky practices (i.e. substance abuse). The failure of some lesbians to adjust, to come out or to simply stop drinking is, however, presented as a consequence of alcoholism (rather than as a specifically lesbian health issue). In contrast to the suggestion that the (healthy) individual can change, act on, or manage their environment, the failure of the alcoholic is presented as inherent and enduring. Although social environments that lesbians socialize in may establish precipitating factors, alternative accounts of lesbian health imply that not all lesbians are predisposed to abuse alcohol. The participants' talk about lesbian health was not as coherent or consistent as it might first have appeared. Some participants suggested that women could fail to overcome social pressure and, after 'coming out', still be heavy drinkers and socialize around bars. In the context of this research, alcoholism was highlighted as an individual failure that did not assist in the process of overcoming social pressures.

CONCLUSIONS

In contrast to a lengthy history of lesbians being constructed as sick in psychology, psychiatry, sexology and psychoanalysis, the participants' accounts of lesbian health reflected an understanding that individual lesbians and lesbian communities can fashion themselves as healthy. The psychological (individualizing) account presented lesbian health as achieved through a process of self-reflection, personal growth and navigating the pressures and expectations of a heterosexual society. The community account presented lesbians at an advantage in relation to sexual (physical) health, and heterosexual (and bisexual) women (and men) at a disadvantage. Neither of these accounts entertained the possibility that there are lesbians who endure poor health. However, the third (minor) account revealed possible limits in individuals' autonomous ability to become healthy lesbians. The various representations of lesbian health that emerged from this analysis are consistent with Sedgwick's (1990) attempts to make sense of lesbian (and gay) visibility. Consistent with Sedgwick's emphasis on understanding which meanings about sexuality are enabled or constrained by the context in which it sexuality is experienced, lesbians' accounts of lesbian health are not concerned with the aetiology of lesbianism. Rather understandings of lesbian health are informed by the ways in which lesbian sexuality is experienced in relation to others as well as by assumptions about lesbian sexuality. The accounts of lesbian health emphasize the social (rather than the physical) dimensions of health. Lesbian health is presented as a consequence of, or as emerging from, lesbians' experiences in the social world.

The lack of focus on medical or scientific discourses about health in the participants' accounts seems at odds with the increasing emphasis on biology and science in clinical medicine (Clarke at al., 2003). The processes of biomedicalization can also be understood as the extension of medical jurisdiction over health, such that illness becomes an individual moral responsibility (that requires improved access to knowledge, self-surveillance and risks assessment). As Clarke at al. (2003, p. 184) explain: 'biomedicalization engages the concepts of structure and agency, stratification, and the complex intersectionalities of culture, political economy, organisation, and technoscience . . . the processes and experiences of biomedicalisation illustrate the importance of interaction and contingency in social life'. Do the participants' accounts of lesbian health (and the emphasis on the social dimensions of health) suggest that what it means to be a healthy lesbian incorporates new meanings about (individual) health? These new meanings about health potentially connect us in different ways (strategic and resistive) to the institutions from which researchers in lesbian health often like to claim we have been liberated. In this analysis, the notion of 'being a healthy lesbian' was used as a starting place for examining lesbians' experiences and understandings of health. This analysis was facilitated by looking at the relationship between lesbian (social) identities and new modes of medical intervention, particularly in the domain of sexual health. This chapter represents a shift in researching lesbian health, and the potential to direct our thinking toward alternative questions about, for instance, the role of biomedicialization for determining new and legitimate health identities.

ACKNOWLEDGEMENTS

I would like to thank all the women who participated in this study; without your willingness to share your experiences, this project could not have been possible. This research was supported by funding from the University of Waikato, Hamilton, New Zealand, and the New Zealand Federation of University Women. I would like to acknowledge the time and support provided by Cardiff University in bringing this work to publication, and for ongoing discussion and support of Chris Brickell, Victoria Clarke and Hernan Pulido-Martinez.

REFERENCES

Bristow, J. (1997). *Sexualities*. London: Routledge.
Bradford, J., Ryan, C. & Rothblum, E. D. (1994). National lesbian health care survey: Implications for mental health care. *Journal of Consulting and Clinical Psychology*, **62**(2), 228–242.
Butler, J. (1990). *Gender Trouble: Feminism and the subversion of identity*. New York, NY: Routledge.
Butler, J. (1993). *Bodies that Matter: On the discursive limits of sex*. New York, NY: Routledge.
Butler, J. (2004). *Undoing Gender*. London: Routledge.
Cass, V. (1979). Homosexual identity formation: A theoretical model. *Journal of Homosexuality*, **4**(3), 219–241.
Clarke, V. (2002). Sameness and difference in research on lesbian parenting. *Journal of Community & Applied Social Psychology*, **12**(3), 210–222.
Clarke, A. E., Shim, J. K., Mamo, L., Fosket, J. R. & Fishman, J. R. (2003). Biomedicalization: Technoscientific transformations of health, illness, and U.S. biomedicine. *American Sociological Review*, **68**(2), 161–194.

Douglas, C. J., Kalman, C. M. & Kalman, T. P. (1985). Homsphobia amongst physicians and nurses: An empirical study. *Hospital and Community Psychiatry, 36*(12), 1309–1311.

Eadie, J. (2004). Closet. In J. Eadie (Ed.), *Sexualities: The essential glossary* (pp. 32–35). London: Arnold.

Eliason, M., Donelan, C. & Randall, C. (1993). Lesbian stereotypes. In P. N. Stern (Ed.), *Lesbian Health: What are the issues?* (pp. 41–54). Washington, DC: Taylor & Fancis.

Fox, N. J. (1997). Is there life after Foucault? Texts, frames and differends. In A. Petersen & R. Bunton (Eds), *Foucault: Health and Medicine* (pp. 31–50). London: Routledge.

Garnets, L., Hancock, K., Cochran, S., Goodchilds, J. & Peplau, L. (1991). Issues in psychotherapy with lesbians and gay men: A survey of psychologists. *American Psychologist, 46*(9), 964–972.

Grace, V. (1998). Researching women's encounters with doctors: Discourse analysis and method. In R. Du Plessis & L. Alice (Eds), *Feminist Thought in Aotearoa/New Zealand: Differences and connections* (pp. 111–119). Auckland: Oxford University Press.

Hall, J. M. (1993). Lesbians and alcohol: Patterns and paradoxes in medical notions and lesbians health beliefs. *Journal of Psychoactive Drugs, 25*(2), 109–119.

Jackson, S. (1999). Feminist sociology and sociological feminism: Recovering the social in feminist thought. *Sociological Research Online, 4*(3), para 1.1–7.4. Available at www.socresonline.org.uk/socresonline/4/3/jackson.html

Jansen, H. (2004). Narratives of coming out: Developing understandings of same sex identifications. In D. W. Riggs & G. A. Walker (Eds), *Out in the Antipodes: Australian and New Zealand perspectives on gay and lesbian issues in psychology* (pp. 306–335). Bentley, WA: Brightfire Press.

Johnson, S. R., Guenther, S. R., Laube, D. W. & Keettel, W. (1981). Factors influencing lesbian gynaecological care: A preliminary study. *American Journal of Obstetrics & Gynecology, 140*, 20–28.

Kitzinger, C. (1987). *The Social Construction of Lesbianism.* London: Sage.

Kitzinger, C. (1995). Social constructionism: Implications for lesbian and gay psychology. In A. R. D'Augelli & C. J. Patterson (Eds), *Lesbian, Gay and Bisexual Identities over the Lifespan: Psychological perspectives* (pp. 136–161). Oxford: Oxford University Press.

Kitzinger, C. (2001). Sexualities. In R. K. Unger (Ed.), *Handbook of the Psychology of Women and Gender* (pp. 272–285). New York, NY: Wiley.

Kitzinger, C. & Wilkinson, S. (1995). Transitions from heterosexuality to lesbianism: The discursive production of lesbian identities. *Developmental Psychology, 31*(1), 95–104.

Lucas, V. A. (1993). An investigation of the health care preferences of the lesbian population. In P. N. Stern (Ed.), *Lesbian health: What are the issues?* (pp. 131–138). Washington: Taylor & Francis.

MacBride-Stewart, S. (2004a). Kitzinger's pivotal text on 'The Social Construction of Lesbianism'. *Feminism & Psychology, 14*(4), 522–526.

MacBride-Stewart, S. (2004b). 'Neither of us uses contraception'. Heteronormative expectations affecting lesbian experiences of cervical screening. In N. Gavey, A. Potts & A. Wetherall (Eds), *Sex and the Body* (pp. 165–182). Palmerston North: Dunmore Press.

MacBride-Stewart, S. (2004c). Dental dams: A parody of straight expectations in the promotion of 'safer' lesbian sex. In D. W. Riggs & G. A. Walker (Eds), *Out in the Antipodes: Australian and New Zealand Perspectives on Gay and Lesbian Issues in Psychology* (pp. 368–391). Bentley, WA: Brightfire Press.

Mason, G. (2002). *The Spectacle of Violence: Homophobia, gender and knowledge.* London: Routledge.

McNay, L. (2000). *Gender and Agency: Reconfigurations of the subject in feminist and social theory.* Oxford: Polity Press.

Miller, A., Rosga, A. & Satterthwaite, M. (1995). Health, human rights and lesbian existence. *Health and Human Rights, 1*(4), 428–448.

O'Sullivan, S. & Parmar, P. (1992). *Lesbians Talk Safer Sex.* London: Scarlet Press.

Ratner, C. (2000). Agency and culture. *Journal for the Theory of Social Behaviour, 30*(4), 413–434.

Robertson, M. M. (1993). Lesbians as an invisible minority in the health services arena. In P. N. Stern (Ed.), *Lesbian Health: What are the issues?* (pp. 65–74). Washington: Taylor & Francis.

Rose, P. (1993). Out in the open? *Nursing Times*, **89**(30), 50–52.

Rothblum, E. D. (1994). 'I only read about myself on bathroom walls': The need for research on the mental health of lesbians and gay men. *Journal of Consulting and Clinical Psychology*, **62**(2), 213–220.

Rust, P. (1995). *Bisexuality and the Challenge to Lesbian Politics: Sex, loyalty and revolution*. New York, NY: New York University Press.

Sedgwick, E. K. (1990). *Epistemology of the Closet*. Berkeley: University of California Press.

Smith, E., Johnson, S. & Guenther, S. (1985). Health care attitudes and experiences during gynecologic care among lesbians and bisexuals. *American Journal of Public Health*, **75**(9), 1085–1087.

Stevens, P. E. (1993). Lesbian health care research: A review of the literature from 1970 to 1990. In P. N. Stern (Ed.), *Lesbian Health: What are the issues?* (pp. 1–30). Washington: Taylor & Francis.

Stevens, P. E. (1996). Lesbians and doctors: Experiences of solidarity and domination in health care settings. *Gender and Society,* **10**(1), 24–42.

Stevens, P. E. & Hall, J. M. (1988). Stigma, health beliefs, and experiences with health care in lesbian women. *Image: Journal of Nursing Scholarship*, **20**(2), 69–73.

Trippet, S. & Bain, J. (1993). Physical health problems and concerns of lesbians. *Women & Health*, **20**(2), 59–70.

Turner, W. B. (2000). *A Genealogy of Queer Theory*. Philadelphia, PA: Temple University Press.

Vance, C. (1998). Social construction theory: Problems in the history of sexuality. In P. M. Nardi & B. E. Schneider (Eds), *Social Perspectives in Lesbian and Gay Studies* (pp. 160–170). New York, NY: Routledge.

Weeks, J. (1977). *Coming Out: Homosexual politics in Britain from the nineteenth century to the present*. London: Quartet Books.

Wilkinson, S. (2002). Lesbian health. In A. Coyle & C. Kitzinger (Eds), *Lesbian and Gay Psychology: New perspectives* (pp. 117–134). Oxford: BPS Blackwell.

Wilton, T. (1995). *Lesbian Studies: Setting an agenda*. London: Routledge.

CHAPTER 21

Transsexualism: Diagnostic Dilemmas, Transgender Politics and the Future of Transgender Care

Katherine Johnson

University of Brighton, UK

> What is at stake here is who has the power to determine how one's body is treated . . . As transgender medical services are currently delivered in the United States, it is the psychotherapist, not the transsexual, who ultimately determines what will happen to the transsexual's body. This is an unacceptable situation (Stryker, 1997, p. 244).

Since the 1970s, there have been a series of shifts in the psychiatric conceptualization of transsexualism. Taking a social constructionist perspective this chapter provides a historical overview of the emergence of transsexualism as a new diagnostic and 'identity' category, distinct from 'transvestism' and 'homosexuality', and explores the reconceptualizations of that category within subsequent psychiatric literature. It outlines three areas of contention that underpin clinical practitioners' engagement with transsexualism: (1) regulating diagnosis; (2) legitimizing reassignment surgery as the treatment of choice; and (3) controlling access to surgery. These issues are discussed in light of recent conceptual and political developments concerning the ontological status of 'sex', 'gender' and 'identity' itself, which unsettle the ongoing search for an etiological understanding of the transsexual phenomenon. These developments have primarily originated outside of psychology. The key focus for debate is the (psychiatric) contention that a desire to transform the sexed body is indicative of 'mental illness'. The psychomedical understanding of transsexualism has been increasingly contested by postmodern theorists and this has shaped campaigns for the removal of the term 'gender dysphoria' and other references to Gender Identity Disorders (GID) from the Diagnostic and Statistical Manual-IV (DSM) (e.g. Stryker, 1994) and the formation of alternative models of transgenderism (e.g. Denny, 2004). The idea of freeing an identity from the pathologizing psychiatric discourse that surrounds it is not new. Most of the arguments utilized by trans-activists and their supporters are similar to arguments made by the lesbian and gay advocates who fought for the removal

Out in Psychology: Lesbian, gay, bisexual, trans and queer perspectives. Edited by Victoria Clarke and Elizabeth Peel.
© 2007 John Wiley & Sons, Ltd.

of homosexuality from the DSM-III in the 1970s. However, the defining difference between removing homosexuality and gender identity disorders from DSM concerns the radical change to the transsexual body – and who sanctions this. As Pauly (1992) pointed out, an individual who identifies as lesbian, gay or bisexual has no need to engage with the medical or psychiatric profession in order to be able to pursue his or her lifestyle. Conversely, at the moment, if an individual identifies as 'transsexual', first they have to convince a psychiatrist/psychologist or psychotherapist they are 'genuine' in order to receive a referral for sex reassignment surgery. Second, they are reliant on the surgical skills of the surgeon for the final outcome of their treatment. This chapter reflects on the regulation and treatment of gender identity disorders in the context of the emergence of transsexual politics and concludes by assessing the future role of psychological and medical professions in transgender care.

THE MAKING OF A NEW DIAGNOSTIC CATEGORY

Harry Benjamin MD coined the term 'transsexual' in 1953, and is frequently credited with the title 'father of transsexualism' (e.g. Califia, 1997; MacKenzie, 1994; Szasz, 1990). His article was issued in response to the widespread media coverage of Christine Jorgensen's sex reassignment operation that was conducted by a team of surgeons in Denmark (Hamburger, Sturup & Dahl-Iversen, 1953). In his paper and subsequent book, Benjamin argued for a distinction to be drawn between 'transvestites' and 'transsexuals'. However, while Benjamin thought these to be discrete identifications, he did consider both transsexualism and transvestism to be symptomatic of the same underlying psychopathological condition, which he defined as 'sex or gender role disorientation or indecision' (1966, p. 17). For him, the contrast lay in the transsexual's greater degree of sex and gender disorientation coupled with greater emotional disturbances than the transvestite. Moreover, as was common with much research in this historical period, there was no acknowledgment of the specificity of female experiences of gender uncertainty. Thus, 'transsexual disorientation' was only attributed to biological men and took the form of feelings of disgust and hate towards male sex organs, hair distribution, masculine habits, male dress and male (hetero)sexuality.

As well as drawing a distinction between 'transvestites' and 'transsexuals', Benjamin also attempted to distinguish between homosexuality and transsexualism. He proposed that a psychiatrist's diagnosis of 'homosexuality' could be problematic for the transsexual, arguing: 'The "gay" life . . . is no solution for the transsexual. He does not like it. He actually dislikes homosexuals and feels he has nothing in common with them' (1966, p. 65).

This notion that the 'true' transsexual was not homosexual became one of the central tenets for what became know as the *Benjamin Criteria* for sex reassignment candidates. In fact, up until the late 1980s individuals were turned away from this form of treatment if they stated their post-operative sexual preference as lesbian or gay (Bockting & Coleman, 1992; Nataf, 1996). However, it is important to put into context Benjamin's theoretical stance on homosexuality. Having cited Kinsey, Pomeroy and Martin's (1948) estimate that 4% of the adult male population are exclusively homosexual, Benjamin appeared to resist the idea of homosexuality as a personal identity and preferred a more fluid interpretation of sexual orientation. He expressed dislike for the term 'homosexual', which is 'applied too often', preferring to speak 'merely of homosexual behaviour, inclinations, and more or less frequent activities' (1966, p. 25). Concluding strongly that transsexualism and homosexuality are very different 'problems' – gender and sex problems respectively – the idea that a post-operative transsexual may want to engage in sexual activity with a member of the same genital sex appears to have completely failed him. We can only speculate reasons why, but attention can be drawn to two factors, the McCarthyism of the 1950s and his research focus on male-to-female transsexuals.

Much of Benjamin's research and theorizing took place against a political back drop of growing McCarthy hysteria that constructed the homosexual as a 'sexually perverted' bogeyman, eager to betray the American government and harm the American family (MacKenzie, 1994). For me, there is no doubt that Benjamin had considerable sympathy for the plight of his patients. Given the political climate, and the status of homosexuality at this time as a mental disorder, it is possible that less stigma would be afforded to transsexuals who were diagnosed in terms of a treatable medical condition, if some distance could be put between them and the 'homosexual'. Secondly, Benjamin's research was principally concerned with male-to-female transsexuals, because at this point in time far fewer cases of female-to-male transsexuals had been reported. As this research took place against a historical legacy that theorized lesbians as 'masculine' (e.g. Ellis, 1936) or 'mannish' (Krafft-Ebing, 1908), the idea that any man who took the drastic measures of having sex reassignment surgery to become 'feminine' would then enter into lesbian sexual relations may have appeared improbable, if not implausible. Richard Green supports this assumption in his early work. Describing one of his first meetings with a male-to-female transsexual who did not identify as heterosexual after surgery, he says:

> An additional complication described by one male seeking sex reassignment was that his erotic attractions are only to women. Males are not sexually stimulating him. This patient's primary motive in seeking sex reassignment appeared to be a gender one: that is, he wished to lead the social life of a woman but not the sexual one. He found himself in the rare situation of anticipating a life of lesbianism after surgery. (Green, 1969, p. 288)

Thus, while embedded in the discourses of sexology that reveal the interconnection of gender and sexuality theory, the early classification 'transsexual' was dependent on the creation of a diagnostic criteria that was separate from 'transvestism' and 'homosexuality'. Benjamin (1966) also saw a clear distinction in terms of who should provide 'treatment' for these forms of non-conformity and the key differential related to the role of the medical profession. As he put it, the transsexual 'puts all his faith and future into the hands of the doctor, particularly the surgeon', while the transvestite 'wants to be left alone' (p.14). He clearly believed that the medical professions should have the greatest influence in determining the life paths of those who present as transsexual. He saw psychological intervention as ineffective and argued that most attempts to use psychotherapy to cure transsexuals had proven futile, often resulting in:

> Some of them probably languishing in mental institutions, some in prisons, and the majority as miserable, unhappy members of the community, unless they have committed suicide. Only because of the recent advances in endocrinology and surgical techniques has the picture changed. (1966, p. 14)

This enthusiasm for surgical intervention is outlined in the Preface to *The Transsexual Phenomenon* (Benjamin, 1966). Referring to Hamburger et al. (1953), Benjamin praises 'the courageous and compassionate Danish physicians who, for the first time, dared to violate the taboo of a supposedly inviolate sex and gender concept' (1966, p. viii). The latter sections of this chapter demonstrate how the division between psychological and biomedical conceptions of transsexualism has remained an important theme in current debates about diagnosis and treatment. However, it is Christine Jorgensen that Benjamin credits for publicizing both the transsexual 'condition' and sex reassignment as the favoured therapeutic intervention.

The case of Christine Jorgensen was of crucial importance in the creation of current understanding of transsexual identity and highlights the continuing tensions between the medical profession and those seeking to create new forms of sex/gender expression. The widespread media attention of the Jorgensen story in 1952, culminating in the publication of her autobiography in 1967, was greeted with varying reactions from other physicians and the wider general public. Billed on the front cover as 'The candid and courageous story of an outstanding woman who pioneered an age of sexual awareness through her own astonishing sex transformation!' Jorgensen narrated her path from confused youth to celebrity show-girl and film maker. Possibly the most interesting revelation in the book was that she was already self-administrating ethinyl-oestradiol, a female hormone, before she approached physicians about her 'condition'.

Jorgensen is not the only person who self-administrated hormones before presenting themselves to medical professionals. Bernice Hausman (1995) documents the case of Agnes, a young woman who in 1958 appeared at the Department of Psychiatry of the University of California, seeking plastic surgery to remedy an apparent endocrine abnormality. Agnes appeared as a typically 'feminine' woman, with breast development, wide hips and small waist, long hair and smooth skin, but nevertheless had a fully developed penis and atrophic scrotum. Working with a medical team, the UCLA researchers involved in the case, psychoanalyst Robert Stoller, sociologist Harold Garfinkel and psychologist Alexander Rosen could find no physiological explanation for her genital aberration. Instead, they hypothesized that she suffered from 'testicular feminization syndrome, that is extreme feminization of the male body (breasts, no body and facial hair, feminine skin and subcutaneous fat distribution) due to oestrogens produced by the testes' (Stoller, 1968, p. 365). In due course, Agnes was given surgical treatment to remove the penis and testes and create a vagina. After the operation, Agnes was given oestrogen replacement therapy, as the testes, her perceived source of oestrogen had been removed. It was to the shock of the research team involved that eight years after first presenting at UCLA Agnes revealed that she had actually been self-administrating her mother's hormone replacement tablets since the age of 12 (Hausman, 1995). Thinking they were dealing with an intersexed patient, a 'natural mistake', the research team had been outwitted and carried out sex reassignment surgery on a biological male.

The processes revealed in these cases are compelling because they illustrate the reliance on the medical profession for the construction of a transsexual identity (Hausman, 1995), as both Jorgensen and Agnes could only go so far in their desire to transition. Yet, despite being dependent on medical practices, one cannot overlook the revelation that Jorgensen and Agnes had been able to move some way towards transition *unsupervised*. This distinction points to the key issue of transsexual agency and the question of who defines a person as 'transsexual'. As Benjamin noted, the media coverage of Jorgensen's case 'caused emotions to run high among those similarly effected. Suddenly they understood and "found" themselves and saw hope for a release from an unhappy existence' (1966, p. viii). Drawing on the ideas of Ken Plummer (1995), it could be argued that these individuals did not 'find' their true self, rather they 'found' a story to tell about themselves that allowed them to experience themselves in different ways, and they were able to do this because they identified similarities between Jorgensen's narrative and their own life histories (Mason-Schrock, 1996). Through this identification with Jorgensen's past experience, they could conclude that they, like her, were transsexual, and thus re-position themselves in the discourses of gender transformation contained in Jorgensen's story. This would be particularly applicable after the publication of her autobiography in 1967. This possibility of 'self-identification' or 'self-diagnosis', whichever way it is put, has remained one of central concern throughout the literature on transsexualism. In the following sections, I trace the ensuing dialogue between medical practitioners, trans-activists and other critics of the psychomedical model in an attempt to further unpack contentions in the practice of diagnosis and treatment that underpin 'who has the power to determine how one's body is treated' (Stryker, 1997 p. 244).

Regulating Diagnosis

The term 'transsexual' is unusual as a diagnostic category because it names the method of treatment and rehabilitation (i.e. moving from one sex to the other) rather than the underlying 'syndrome' (gender dysphoria). Furthermore, without a known cause, transsexualism is open to self-definition through personal suffering. Clinicians, however, have constructed a set of criteria that a patient must fulfil before they will accept what has been described as a 'self-defined illness' (Money, 1986). In 1973, Fisk summarized the following guidelines for recognizing the 'true transsexual':

> A life-long sense or feeling of being a member of the 'other sex'; the early and persistent behaviouristic phenomenon of cross-dressing, coupled with a strong emphasis upon a total lack of erotic feelings associated with cross-dressing; and a disdain or repugnance for homosexual behaviour (Fisk, 1973, p. 8).

Not only did this criteria determine who is, or who can be a 'true' transsexual it also provided justification for the category itself, as Benjamin proposed, by eliminating any overlap with transvestite and homosexual behaviour. Yet, given the lack of organic indications of a 'disease' and the self-diagnostic nature of transsexualism, it is argued that clinicians depend on the accuracy and honesty of the patients' statements for diagnoses, as well as for their understanding of the disorder (Billings & Urban, 1995). This has been problematic. As early as 1968, Kubie and Mackie wrote that patients demanding surgery 'tailor their views of themselves and their personal histories to prevailing "scientific" fashions' (1968, p. 435). Having consulted the guidelines as to what constitutes a 'textbook' transsexual, and knowing that reputable clinics only treated 'textbook' cases, candidates had little choice but to present as a 'textbook' case. As the psychiatrist's job is to assess how well patients' self-reported life histories fit the diagnostic criteria for transsexualism, it was not long before they caught on to the lack of variation in prospective reassignment candidates' personal accounts. As Fisk stated:

> Soon it became conspicuously and disturbingly apparent that far too many patients presented a pat, almost rehearsed history, and seemingly were well versed in precisely

what they should or should not say or reveal. Only later did we learn that there did and does exist a very effective grape-vine (Fisk, 1973 p. 8).

The threat of deception had become so strong that Stoller also complained:

> Those of us faced with the task of diagnosing transsexualism have an additional burden these days, for most patients who request sex-reassignment are in complete command of the literature and know the answers before the questions are asked (1973a, p. 53).

In 'The socio-medical construction of transsexualism', Dwight Billings and Thomas Urban (1995, p. 108) describe this as 'the con', arguing physicians reinforced this process by granting surgery to those who complied with the established criteria and turning away those who gave 'honest' but non-revised subjective histories. The construction of a rigid clinical classification and its uptake by those positioning their experience within it reveals the circulatory nature of discourse and how diagnostic practices serve to both legitimize and perpetuate the institutional conditions that created them (Foucault, 1973). However, labelling this a 'con' poses the question of whether it is ever possible to give an accurate subjective account of one's past. For example, other developments within social constructionist perspectives suggest that the analysis of self-reported accounts such as narratives or memories tells us more about the ways in which people will attempt to construct their memories, in order to support their current situation and create a cohesive life story, than the truth of their past experiences (e.g. Crawford et al., 1992). Billings and Urban (1995) do, nevertheless, make an important point in arguing that the medical image of a stable life-long transsexual identification does not adequately represent some individual's experiences and motivations. This notion of a fixed, monadic, identity is clearly contradicted by the self-reflexive fluidity in sexuality and gender identities expressed by 'a (male-to-female) patient . . . whose lover was also a post-operative male-to-female transsexual': 'I thought I was a homosexual at one time; then I got married and had a child so I figured I was a heterosexual; then because of cross-dressing I thought I was a transvestite. Now [post-operatively] I see myself as bisexual' (pp. 111–112).

Legitimating Reassignment Surgery

A second problem that has beleaguered the study of transsexualism can loosely be defined as the 'morality debate'. Here, bolstered by the inclusion of diagnostic references in various forms to 'gender identity disorders' in the DSM since 1980, critics take issue with whether physical treatment of what are considered healthy bodies should be offered to those who, arguably, have a psychological disorder. Thomas Szasz, who described transsexualism as 'a condition tailor-made for our surgical-technological age' (1990, p. 86), was, as ever, critical of the psychiatric profession. He went on to argue that 'instead of scrutinizing the nature of "transsexualism", sexologists are now busily attacking and defending sex-change operations' (1990, p. 89). This has certainly been the case. News that a prominent centre for the surgical treatment of transsexualism had been set up at The John Hopkins University, sparked off a wave of opposition within medicine in the late 1960s (Billings & Urban, 1995). This attack was led by psychoanalysts in private practice, who labelled transsexuals as 'all border-line psychotics' and charged surgeons with 'collaboration with psychosis'

(Meerloo, 1967, p. 263). In response, it was necessary for 'sex-change' proponents to legitimize surgical treatment. Billings and Urban (1995) propose this was achieved by two methods: constructing an etiological theory that stressed the non-psychopathic character of the illness, and rationalizing diagnostic and treatment strategies.

While many proponents of sex-reassignment favoured a biological predisposition for transsexualism (e.g. Benjamin, 1966), it was the psychoanalyst Robert Stoller (1967, 1973b, 1975) who, by spearheading early socialization, provided the greatly needed non-pathologizing, etiological justification for cross-gender identification (although his theory is problematic in other ways). Stoller claimed the male transsexual was the outcome of an over-intense physical relationship between the boy and his mother, coupled with the 'absence and lack of emotional involvement of the father' who would have interrupted the process of feminization (1975, p. 94). Furthermore, Stoller conceptualized transsexualism as a gender identity disorder, rather than a neurotic perversion, such as transvestism. As such, he argued that, due to parental factors, the male transsexual over-identifies with his mother to the extent that he believes he is the same as her, despite having different genitals. Stoller's theory is based on the notion of a 'core gender identity', which is formed early in life. Despite proposing that this identity can vacillate at times between masculine and feminine expressions, he did suggest that its basis, the 'core', would always remain the same. Thus, he argued that psychotherapy is pointless for the transsexual, as there is no psychological conflict. The distress they exhibit is the result of their core gender identity *never* corresponding to their biological sex (Stoller, 1975).

Benjamin (1966) was also in favour of permitting physical intervention via the alteration of visible genitalia and secondary sex characteristics, if it had an advantageous effect on the individual's life. Frequently, the benefit gained is described in terms of reducing the risk of a transsexual individual committing suicide. Thus, the early defences of sex reassignment surgery, in particular, stressed the patient's intense anguish and the duty of physicians 'to ease the existence of these fellow-men' (Hamburger et al., 1953, p. 373). Bockting and Coleman (1992), both clinicians currently working in the field, argue that this had the useful effect of swinging the treatment pendulum from attempting to 'cure' the transsexual with psychoanalysis or aversion therapy to facilitating acceptance and management of gender role transition. However, they also point out negative aspects of such a stance. For instance, Benjamin's initial emphasis on the intensity of the suffering of the transsexual often resulted in less severe co-morbid psychopathology being over-looked when decisions were taken regarding treatment and sex reassignment. Thus, depression and anxiety came to be seen as symptoms of the gender disturbance, which would be alleviated by the sex reassignment. However, 13 years after Benjamin's work, a widely publicized study by Meyer and Reter (1979) indicated that, contrary to Benjamin's assertions, sex reassignment did not decrease distress and suicide among transsexuals, or improve their general life functioning.

Jon Meyer, director of John Hopkins University's Gender Clinic was already becoming unsympathetic to the plight of transsexuals. In 1973, he complained that 'the label "trans-sexual" has come to cover such a "multitude of sins"' (Meyer, 1973, p. 35). A year later he stated that amongst the patients who had requested, and on occasions received, surgery at John Hopkins were 'sadists', 'homosexuals', 'schizoids', 'masochists', 'homosexual prostitutes' and 'psychotic depressives' (Meyer & Hoopes, 1974). These findings were employed to support the decision at John Hopkins University in 1979 to decline further sex reassignment services. Based on the grounds that the patients they had operated on were no better off than a sample of transsexual patients who received psychotherapy but no surgery (Meyer & Reter, 1979), this decision presented a mighty blow to those in favour of medical treatment. Recent studies have reported more favourable follow-up findings, but indicate that satisfaction with life after transitioning is more likely when individuals have successful professional lives, good support networks and are emotionally stable (Carroll, 1999; Green & Fleming, 1990; Ross & Need, 1989). Despite this, whether or not to advocate hormonal and surgical sex reassignment remains deeply controversial.

Regulating Access to Surgery

A third contention for the clinical engagement with transsexualism is closely related to those already outlined and focuses on the complicated relationship between diagnosis and treatment. I have already pointed to one unusual feature of transsexuality; that is, the diagnosis 'transsexual' is defined in terms of the treatment: to be 'transsexual' presumes movement across or between sexes. Hence, the flipside to this is that if a patient says 'I am a transsexual', it already implies the course of treatment. For this reason, not only do the psychiatric profession have a problem in regulating the diagnosis of the disorder, they are also concerned that the self-diagnosed transsexual may have already decided that sex reassignment surgery is the only viable treatment. Considerable attention has been paid to this problem in the clinically based literature, and significant effort has been made by clinicians to regain control of both diagnosis and prescribed treatments. As Ross stated:

> Unfortunately, many who present for treatment . . . request gender reassignment as the 'cure'. It is necessary, however, for the professional to set aside this self-diagnosis and prescription for treatment, and to determine a diagnosis from a careful history and from other appropriate investigations. (Ross, 1986a, p. 1)

Bockting and Coleman also supported this view. They argued that:

> For many clients as well as professionals, this diagnosis [transsexualism] presupposes sex reassignment as the treatment of choice. Implying sex reassignment early on precludes the exploration of co-morbid psychopathology and of the various dynamics and motivations for sex reassignment. This approach has potentially disastrous consequences given the irreversibility of hormonal and surgical sex reassignment. (Bockting & Coleman, 1992, p. 136)

Ross (1986a) has suggested that it is not uncommon for individuals who are gay to present as transsexuals, predominantly because they are unable to accept their homosexuality. Morgan (1978) gave the harsher summary that of those presenting to clinics as 'transsexual', 10% will have a major mental illness, 30% will be homophobic homosexuals, and 20–25% will be 'sexually inadequate' individuals with ambiguous gender identity. Both these explanations assume some level of psychopathology. However, of the many transsexuals presenting for treatment, it has been argued that gender reassignment may not always be the most common or appropriate treatment. Lothstein and Levine (1981), who began the discussion of the importance of recognizing co-morbid psychopathology in the assessment and treatment of individuals with gender identity disorders, suggested that up to 70% of transsexual patients reject gender reassignment treatment following long-term psychotherapy. Within this interpretation it appears that expressed gender non-conformity itself is not indicative of a mental disorder, but that it can manifest in some individuals as a symptom of other emotional problems. Thus, whether or not individuals choose to embrace or reject reassignment surgery as a treatment, the opportunity to enter a therapeutic relationship might have benefits for long-term adjustment.

THE CLINICAL RESPONSE: EXIT THE TRANSSEXUAL

It has been argued that the clinical professions' response to these debates has been to attempt to regulate and control access to reassignment through the re-labelling, re-categorization and re-classification of transsexualism. If we trace the entrance of the term 'transsexualism' into the DSM III in 1980, its replacement with 'gender dysphoria' with a cross reference to transsexualism in 1987, to the altogether replacement of transsexualism with Gender Identity Disorders (GIDs) in 1994 (American Psychiatric Association, 1980, 1987, 1994) there certainly seems some support for this claim. Billings and Urban (1995) asserted that, rather than questioning the conceptual, clinical and diagnostic substructure of the 'disease', practitioners in the wake of Fisk (1973) simply replaced the term 'transsexual' with 'gender dysphoria syndrome'. Hence, critics have argued that the category 'gender dysphoria' was created by the medical profession in order to reclaim the act of diagnosis, while proponents suggest that it provides an effective method of weeding out cases that present for sex reassignment inappropriately. In this format, the mental health professions have come to regard transsexualism as a symptom of an underlying disorder rather than the disorder itself. Gender dysphoria is now seen as the underlying psychiatric disorder, while transsexualism, the belief that one is, or should be, a member of the opposite biological sex, is the presenting symptom.

Clinicians might respond that changes in classifications are a result of greater knowledge about the 'condition' and the range of experiences expressed by those presenting. For example, one change in the classification that is particularly welcome involves the recognition of different sexualities. Heterosexuality used to be one of the defining characteristics of 'what it meant to be a transsexual'. Gender reassignment would certainly not have been permitted if candidates had indicated any same-sex inclinations. This view has slowly changed over the years, and now it is widely recognized that many (estimates of up to 50%) post-operative male-to-female transsexuals pursue relationships with other women, while estimates for female-to-male transsexuals suggest in the region of 25% identify as gay (Nataf, 1996). After important changes to the terminology employed in DSM-IV, transsexual relationships are now recognized in terms of *gender status*, rather than the genetic composition of the individuals involved. As recently as 1987, in DSM-III-R, a post-operative male-to-female transsexual and her lesbian partner would have been referred to as 'heterosexual'. More usefully, this has now been replaced with the far simpler 'sexually attracted to females'.

Some clinicians have begun to debate the relevance of sexual orientation at all in understanding their client's gender identity and dysphoria, suggesting the current classification system overemphasizes sexual orientation (Coleman, Bockting & Gooren, 1993). They disagree with many theories of sexual and gender identity development, particularly the notion that a same-sex sexual orientation implies a certain degree of cross-gender identification, correctly arguing that such theoretical frameworks imply a stereotypical view of lesbian and gay people. Instead, it is suggested that future revisions of the DSM should stop defining gender identity disorders in relation to a person's sexual orientation. They believe that this distinction has been used to discriminate against natal female gender dysphoric individuals who might be candidates for reassignment but are attracted to men, and hence would become, post-operatively, gay men (Coleman et al., 1993). In fact, Bockting and Coleman (1992) advocated:

> A clear separation of gender identity, social sex role and sexual orientation, which allows a wide spectrum of sexual identities and prevents limiting access to sex reassignment services to those who conform to a heterosexist paradigm of mental health. (p. 149)

Having highlighted specific dilemmas faced by clinicians it is apparent that a common thread links all of these issues. This is itself the greatest problem in understanding transsexualism as a 'mental disorder' and concerns the lack of an etiological basis for the classification.

The Search for an Etiological Basis

It is not an unusual occurrence for a diagnosable psychological disorder to lack an etiological basis, even when methods used to treat it have been found to be effective – depression, for example (Clark, Beck & Alford, 1999). The problem specific to transsexualism appears to be the invasive and controversial nature of the treatment of a healthy body, coupled with the question of whether a post-operative transsexual has any claim or right to be recognized as a 'real' man or woman. Critics of the procedure would say no. For example, Janice Raymond (1980) in *The Transsexual Empire* provided a scathing account of male-to-female transsexuals as 'misguided and mistaken men' who 'are not women'. In her view 'they are deviant males' (p. 183). Thomas Szasz (1990) argued along similar lines that the medical procedure is 'simply turning men into fake women, and women into fake men' (p. 87). Meyer and Hoopes (1974) also expressed this view in an elaborate description of a disappointed post-operative male-to-female transsexual's situation:

> In a thousand subtle ways, the reassignee has the bitter experience that he is not – and never will be – a real girl but is, at best, a convincing simulated female. Such an adjustment cannot compensate for the tragedy of having lost all chance to be male and of having, in the final analysis, no way to be really female. (p. 450)

Throughout the history of transsexualism the question of 'what causes it' has been unequivocally tied to what constitutes 'sex' and 'gender', and underpinned by an epistemological orientation towards either biological or psychosocial explanations. Although not conclusive, prior to the late 1980s, evidence seems to support psychological, social and environmental explanations (Coleman, Gooren & Ross, 1989; Ross, 1986b). Some supported Stoller's (1975) non-pathologizing, psychoanalytic etiological account of transsexualism (e.g. Lothstein, 1979). Here Stoller claimed that the biological sex of a person has a tendency to *augment* rather than determine the appropriate gender identity for that sex, such that gender is primarily the result of post-natal psychological influences. Stoller's theory gained support from some feminists as it upheld the notion of a 'sex/gender system' (Rubin, 1975), which was gaining favour at this time, but many applicants appeared not to have had the dysfunctional family dynamics upon which the theory is based. Moreover,

Stoller had little to say in the way of an explanation for the developmental pattern of female-to-male transsexualism. This is the case with much of the clinical and psychiatric literature, where female-to-male transsexualism remains under-theorized and under-represented with the better accounts found outside of psychological disciplines (e.g. Devor, 1997, 2004; Rubin, 2003).

It has also been argued that transsexuals have very rigid views on gender roles (McCauley & Erhardt, 1977), but this may be less revealing than it seems. There is no guarantee that this is because male-to-female transsexuals *do* have rigid ideas about what it means to be a woman, since they may *express* rigid, stereotypical notions because they need to justify their own position as a 'real' woman. However, Ross, Wålinder, Lundström and Thuwe (1981) claimed, after a comparative study in Australia and Sweden, that in a society with more rigid gender roles and more hostile to homosexuality (Australia) there were three times more clinical consultations by individuals who labelled themselves as 'transsexual' than in a less restrictive society (Sweden). Similarly, in an epidemiological study of transsexualism, Hoenig and Kenna (1973) indicated that most transsexuals come from lower socio-economic families, where gender roles are, reportedly, more fixed. Again, favouring a psychosocial explanation, Ross, Rogers and McCulloch (1978) argued that in some instances transsexuals are homosexual males who rationalize their preference for a male partner into the socially acceptable form of a heterosexual relationship by altering their gender. Ross (1986b) drew support for this suggestion from Lothstein (1979) who stated that society usually accepts a transsexual adaptation more readily than a homosexual one. How valid these conclusions are today is debatable. It should be remembered that these articles were written in the shadow of the removal of homosexuality per se from the DSM in the USA in 1973. One might like to think that acceptance of homosexuality has progressed sufficiently during the past 30 years for men not to recourse to their own surgical castration in order to have same-sex relations, but homophobia and discrimination against lesbians and gay men is endemic in society.

While psychosocial accounts are certainly inconclusive, prior to the 1990s, there was even less evidence to support a biological explanation (Coleman et al., 1989). In his article 'How does transsexualism develop and why?', Michael Ross (1986b) surmised that there was no evidence to suggest genetic and endocrinological factors feature amongst the causes of gender 'disorientation'. However, there has been some more recent indication that there may be some difference in the brain structure of transsexuals (Swaab, Zhou, Fodor & Hofman, 1997; Swaab & Hofman, 1995; Zhou, Hofman, Gooren & Swaab, 1995). These findings have been greeted enthusiastically by the media and some members of the transsexual community and serve as an example of what Lynne Segal (1999, p. 79) describes as 'a new form of fundamentalism in the social sciences and media world'. Yet, the findings can also be discredited in terms of the study's own epistemological underpinnings: the reporting of a minute region of the hypothalamus as smaller in six, post-operative male-to-female transsexuals than in 'normal' men, while being *similar* in size to 'normal' women, is hardly conclusive that these transsexuals had the brain structure of a female all along. It should be noted that these findings were based on the autopsies of male-to-female transsexual subjects who had died from a range of illnesses including AIDS and alcohol-related liver disease, and they had all been consuming known and, presumably in some cases, unknown quantities of hormones, alcohol and medication during their lifespan. All these factors could influence the structure of the hypothalamus, rather than supporting the claim that male-to-female transsexuals (and biological women) have an inherently different brain structure from biological men.

Furthermore, as Ross et al. (1981) argued, if there was a biological basis for transsexualism, occurrences would be expected to be fairly stable across similar western cultures. However, to recall their study comparing prevalence rates in Sweden and Australia, they found marked variations in the incidence of transsexualism, indicating there could be plausible sociocultural explanations. The existence of a genetic or biological basis as an explanation for cross-gender identity may seem attractive to some transsexuals, as is does to many lesbians and gay men, as a means of defending themselves against discrimination. Yet, it is relevant to bear in mind that feminists have argued that there are dangers in grounding identity and personal narratives in biological difference. As Jennifer Terry (1997) states, 'biological explanations have historically been deployed to keep women in a subordinate position to men' (p. 281). This might be heeded if we are to contest the pathologizing language of the scientific community that suggests evidence points 'to a neurobiological basis of gender identity disorder' (Kruijver et al., 2000, p. 2034) rather than interpreting their research as evidence of gender variation beyond a binary gender system of simply 'male' or 'female'.

It is apparent from the tenor of the debates surrounding the search for an etiological basis of transsexualism that the determinants of the 'disorder' remain hypothetical and controversial. The lack of an etiological justification for the diagnosis and treatment of transsexuals means that clinicians have yet to solve the diagnostic dilemmas outlined above. However, biological explanations have grown in popularity over the past decade and this trend is exacerbated by an increasing division in the types of research questions asked by those studying gender identifications and behaviour. Medical approaches toward transsexualism have continued to focus on finding the causes for cross-gender identification and its relationship to same-sex desire, predominantly through neurobiology (e.g. Kruijver et al., 2000; Swaab et al., 1997), or through developing new surgical techniques to transform physical appearance (e.g. Hage, 1996). In contrast, accounts that offer causal explanations for gender identity variation from within a psychosocial framework are harder to find. This might be explained by debates outside of the medical sciences that have had the dramatic effect of reformulating our understanding of gender, self, identity and the body. Here, there has been a marked shift away from an engagement with questions of 'causation', to a greater, critical focus on the performative, a function of language that describes and pathologizes variation as 'disorder', plus a growing interest in the subjective accounts of those who experience themselves as outside of the gender system (see Clifford and Orford, Chapter 10). Theorists such as Thomas Laqueur and Judith Butler have led the field in questioning the 'truth' of the western belief that there are only two biological sexes, suggesting that this is a 'reality effect' produced by powerful medical and scientific discourses.

Laqueur (1990), in *Making Sex*, claimed that the shift from a pre-enlightenment understanding of a 'one-sex' model (where woman was seen as inferior to man, but nonetheless of the same-kind) to the 'two-sex' model accepted today, is the product of cultural change, rather than scientific discovery. Judith Butler (1993), in *Bodies that Matter*, similarly argued that our understanding of 'sex' as a naturalized category is a fiction that has become established as truth through the repetition of the very discursive practices that construct it as so. There is no 'real' male or female body, just an unattainable idea for us all to aspire to become. Anthropological and cross-cultural research has also been used to demonstrate the limitations of a western understanding of a binary gender system through ethnomethodological and participant-observation research into transsexualism (e.g. Bolin, 1988; Kessler & McKenna, 1978) and accounts of a 'third sex': for example through analysis of gender categories that are produced by the Berdache of North America, or the Hijras in India (Herdt, 1993), that seem to be beyond or between 'male' and 'female'.

Moreover, uncertainty in the biological assumption that there are only two sexes (male-masculine, female-feminine) has not been restricted to the humanities and social sciences. In 1993, the feminist biologist, Anne Fausto-Sterling published a paper suggesting that the two-sex system should be replaced with a five-sex system. The motivation behind this was to highlight the level of biological variation in birth genitals by presenting examples of intersex cases. Her work has played an important role in challenging the problematic practice of the medical management of intersexuality that has, until recently, set out to operate on these 'biological anomalies' and reinstate the truth of a two-sex system.

Therefore, intersexuality also raises questions about how gender identity and the sexed body can be experienced beyond a medicalized notion of a binary sex/gender system. However, given transsexualism lacks the 'tangible', biological evidence that defines intersexuality, these are slightly different questions from the ones it raises for our understanding of transsexualism. Specifically, intersexuality poses questions about the fixed nature of 'sex', whilst transsexualism raises issues about the fixed nature of 'gender' and its relationship to the category 'sex'. In line with Butler's (1990) thesis, transsexualism leads us to ask if a male gender identity has to follow from a male body. Does a female gender identity have to follow from a female body? And what role does the medical profession play in maintaining the notion of a binary gender system? As Billings and Urban (1995) conclude in their critique of the socio-medical construction of transsexualism 'by substituting medical terminology for political discourse, the medical profession has tamed and transformed a potential wildcat strike at the gender factory' (p. 115).

This position has also been supported by feminist critics (e.g. Hausman, 1995; Jeffreys, 2000; Raymond, 1980). In feminist analyses, however, it is often transsexuals themselves who are seen as the enemy, rather than the medical establishment. Lorber (1995), for example, states 'transvestites and transsexualism do nothing to challenge the social construction of gender. Their goal is to be masculine men and feminine women' (p. 20–21). However, detailed research into transgender phenomena that is sensitive to the lived experiences of transsexual and transgendered people reveals that the material grounding of their new gender experiences can also unravel the certainty of particular pervasive discourses (e.g. Elliot & Roen, 1998; Halberstam, 1998; Rubin, 2003; Stryker, 1998). For example, the clinically established notion of 'changing sex' does help to regulate a binary gender system, but the subsequent state of gender ambiguity in which some transsexuals reside, exemplified through the risk of not 'passing', challenges, threatens and undoes the belief in gender certainty for all of us (Johnson, 2007b). Equally, analysis of the narratives of individuals who identify as transsexual or transgendered reveals considerable variation in the discourses they draw on to conceptualize what it means to be transsexual (Johnson 2001) and offers challenges to some feminist interpretations and critiques (Johnson, 2005; 2007a).

TRANSGENDER POLITICS AND THE CHANGING ROLE OF THE MEDICAL PROFESSION

In recent years we have seen a greater acknowledgement of this variation in transsexual subjectivity through the growing politicization of transsexual people and the emergence of a newly labelled 'transgendered' community. This has occurred alongside other actions that aim to shake off the stigma of the pathologizing connotations of the identity 'transsexual' and its reliance on the psychiatric professions. The growth in political action also coincided with an increase in interest in transgender issues in the academy. This was undoubtedly due to the influence of Butler's (1990) notion of gender performativity and subsequent debates that provided a forum in which transgendered individuals, often also academics, could draw on and contest 'performativity' when theorizing trans experiences (e.g. Bornstein, 1994; Prosser, 1998; Whittle, 1995). Stryker (1994, 1998) provides a detailed account of the newly emerging area 'trans-studies' suggesting that the transsexual body is not simply a creation of modern science, and the medically constructed nature of transsexual bodies does not preclude them from being viable sites for subjectivity. Moreover, although medical science may enable the very means to transsexual embodiment, Stryker argues this does not *guarantee* the transsexual subject's complicity with a conservative and heteronormative agenda that upholds sex reassignment surgery as the establishment's treatment of choice. Encouragingly, the medical professions have responded to transgender activism by revising guidelines for clinical practice. In the preface to a gender dysphoria special issue in the *Journal of Psychology and Human Sexuality*, the editors commented:

> In the context of a growing political movement in transgender communities across North America and Europe arguing for a depathologization of cross gender behavior (including removal of transvestism and transsexualism from DSM classification), the task of the clinician remains to provide up-to-date health care and ongoing support for gender dysphoric clients. This includes, but is not limited to, providing professional consultation regarding sex reassignment procedures. An interdisciplinary approach to treatment, research and education is essential for continuing progress. (Bockting & Coleman, 1992, p. xix)

The diagnostic criteria and treatment practices for transsexualism have undergone significant change since 1980 and are now encompassed within the term 'transgender care'. The emphasis is no longer on surgical intervention as a cure-all for gender dysphoria, and transsexualism is now seen as 'the most extreme form of gender dysphoria' for which 'sex reassignment is an effective method to treat' it (Kuiper & Cohen-Kettenis, 1998, p. 1). In addition, the distinction between the transsexual subject and the clinical or academic expert is no longer so easy to discern. For example, transsexual and transgendered identified people now serve on the steering committees of organizations such as *The Harry Benjamin International Gender Dysphoria Association* (HBIGDA), which outlines the Standards of Care for professions working in the area. Yet, for many individuals seeking gender reassignment, the clinical and medical professions often remain in the position of 'gate-keeper', regulating their passage to new gender identities. What might seem like successive attempts to regulate and control access to surgical intervention have frequently been underpinned by a genuine concern to provide the gender dysphoric individual with choices and strategies for living with a complex and fragmented gender identification (Di Ceglie & Freeman, 1999).

In contrast to transgender activists such as Susan Stryker (1994), who was involved in organizing a disruption and protest at the American Psychiatric Association's 1993 annual meeting, clinicians believe that 'gender identity disorders' *do* have a place in classification systems of psychiatric disorders (Pauly 1990a, 1990b, 1992). This is because many individuals who partake in cross-dressing or cross-gender behaviour present with significant levels of psychological distress due to their gender non-conformity. However, the experience of anxiety associated with gender non-conformity should not be conflated with gender non-conformity itself being a mental disorder. The first large-scale study of sexuality and mental health in the UK has recently demonstrated that lesbians, gay men and bisexuals experience higher levels of psychological distress than a comparative group of heterosexuals (King et al., 2003). These findings have been explained in relation to the higher levels of discrimination they have encountered (Warner et al., 2004). It would be reasonable to suggest that 'trans' identified people experience similar aspects of discrimination and some studies support this (e.g. Cole, Denny, Eyler & Samons, 2000; Jones & Hill, 2002). Others argue that it is the affirmation of the new gender identity, through a range of social relationships including partners and family, that is crucial for a positive sense of mental health (Bolin, 1988; Johnson, 2007b; Nuttbrock, Rosenblum & Blumenstein, 2002).

Thus, in the light of postmodern accounts of gender it is difficult to claim that gender non-conformity is a psychological disorder and, certainly, there is little evidence to suggest that psychotherapy can 'cure' profound gender dysphoria (Stoller, 1975). But gender dysphoric feelings, and the complexities of life that ensue for the transgendered or transsexual individual, can be explored in a psychotherapeutic setting. *The Standards of Care For Gender Identity Disorders* (HBIGDA, 2001) recommends that each individual presenting with gender dysphoria should undergo a period of psychotherapy before commencing other forms of treatment such as hormone therapy. From a study of the responses of 93 trans identified people (70 female-to-male and 23 male-to-female), Katherine Rachlin (2002) suggests that 87% of respondents reported positive change in their lives as a result of psychotherapy. It is therefore of some concern that many trans identified people do not have this opportunity. Of the participants in my research in the UK, few benefited from this opportunity. Though many had had contact with mental health professions at some point in their life, this was rarely with a practitioner who was authoritative in gender issues. After deciding to transition, most had approached the same private practice psychiatrist who specialized in referrals for reassignment and were prescribed hormones on either their first or second visit. This is concerning given the recent revelation that this psychiatrist has been charged by the General Medical Council of serious professional misconduct as he 'allegedly breached standards of care by inappropriately prescribing sex-changing hormones to patients and referring them for genital surgery without adequate assessment' (Batty, 2004). However, the charges against him are led by doctors of the 'old-guard', working at the NHS Gender Identity Clinic, Charing Cross Hospital (Batty, 2004). Less publicized are the serious criticisms of the treatment provided at Charing Cross, made by those who have been referred and by General Practitioners who have made the referrals (West, 2004). Christine Burns (2004) has also catalogued a list of complaints from patients 'who had recently completed their treatment (and therefore had less to fear)'. These included: 'Aggressive and rude handling, punitive rules, threats to withdraw treatment, appointments cancelled without notice, different therapists at each appointment, notes getting lost'. In contrast, the leading private practice psychiatrist has found favour amongst the transsexual and transgender community (e.g. Burns, 2004) for his less 'ortho-dox' approach to treatment, including providing prescriptions for hormones prior to tran-sitioning. Thus, while he acknowledges the agency and subjectivity of the trans-identified individual, he is open to criticism for providing a fast-track route to transition and rarely asking for evidence that HBIGDA (2001) criteria, such as Real Life Experience or psy-chotherapy, have been met. Yet, if we look at the services available to people in the vul-nerable state of transition it is clear that the level of care currently on offer in both systems is seriously lacking.

CONCLUSION

Thus, we return to the theme that has been discussed throughout this chapter: who regu-lates diagnosis and access to reassignment surgery? As Stryker (1997) set out, in the current climate it is still the psychiatrist or psychologist who makes the final decision on what happens to the transsexual's body. This is because whether treatment is publicly or privately funded a psychiatric 'diagnosis' is required in order to proceed with the physical transformation. Some transsexual and transgendered individuals continue to campaign for the removal of Gender Identity Disorders from the DSM, and with the next edition not due until at least 2010 (PsyWeb, 2005), it is not yet apparent whether classification will change any further. Despite supporting the depathologization of gender non-conformity I suggest there might still be a place for psychological professionals in the process of transi-tion. This, however, is not as 'gate-keepers', but as professionals that work *with* people to explore a range of choices (see Speer, Chapter 16). It should be heeded that some people are left in a distressed state post-transition and a small number request reversal procedures (Kuiper & Cohen-Kettenis, 1998). Yet, unless a system is in place for gender displaced individuals to discuss the options available to them with a therapist skilled in gender issues, reassignment surgery will remain the dominant trajectory and not always the best outcome for some. Moreover, psychotherapy and other therapeutic models currently have an undervalued role for individuals post-transition. As I have argued elsewhere (Johnson, 2007b), many transsexuals cannot simply 'disappear' into their new gender identities. The aftermath of such a radical shift unleashes its own set of problems; particularly questions of how to negotiate previous gender history and past social relations and how to live in the new gender role when you do not always 'pass'. These types of issues can raise anxiety in the transsexual subject and ongoing access to psychotherapy may facilitate some degree of relief from these stresses as well as providing access to new strategies for living. Thus, rather than debating the etiological basis of transsexualism, the range of medical and social support available to transgendered people are the pressing issues for future research and practice.

ACKNOWLEDGEMENTS

Thank you to the many people who have contributed to developing the ideas presented in this chapter and particularly the participants who provided the original stories on which my argument is based.

REFERENCES

American Psychiatric Association. (1980). *Diagnostic and Statistical Manual of Mental Disorders* (3rd edn). Washington, DC: APA.

American Psychiatric Association. (1987). *Diagnostic and Statistical Manual of Mental Disorders* (3rd edn, revised). Washington, DC: APA.

American Psychiatric Association. (1994). *Diagnostic and Statistical Manual of Mental Disorders* (4th edn). Washington, DC: APA.

Batty, D. (2004). 'GMC inquiry into gender change expert', *The Guardian*, 20 January. Retrieved 21 November 2006, from http://society.guardian.co.uk/mentalhealth/story/0,,1126985,00.html

Benjamin, H. (1953). Transvestism and transsexualism. *International Journal of Sexology*, **7**(1), 12–14.

Benjamin, H. (1966). *The Transsexual Phenomenon*. New York, NY: Julian Press.

Billings, D. B. & Urban, T. (1995/1982). The Socio-Medical Construction of Transsexualism: An interpretation and critique. In R. Ekins & D. King (Eds), *Blending Genders: Social aspects of cross dressing and sex-changing* (pp. 99–117). London: Routledge.

Bockting, W. O. & Coleman, E. (1992). A comprehensive approach to the treatment of gender dysphoria. *Journal of Psychology & Human Sexuality*, **5**(4), 131–155.

Bolin, A. (1988). *In search of Eve: Transsexual rites of passage*. South Hadley, MA: Bergin and Harvey.

Bornstein, K. (1994). *Gender Outlaw: On men, women and the rest of us*. London: Routledge.

Burns, C. (2004) 'Something rotten in the state of the profession'. Retrieved 1 February 2005, from http://www.annasplace.me.uk/journal.php?archive=2004_11_01_archive.xml

Butler, J. (1990). *Gender Trouble: Feminism and the subversion of identity*. New York: Routledge.

Butler, J. (1993). *Bodies That Matter: On the discursive limits of 'sex'*. New York, NY: Routledge.

Califia, P. (1997). *Sex Changes: The politics of transgenderism*. San Francisco, CA: Cleis Press.

Carroll, R. (1999). Outcomes of treatment for gender dysphoria. *Journal of Sex Education and Therapy*, **24**(3), 128–136.

Clark, D. A., Beck, A. T. & Alford, B. A. (1999). *Scientific Foundations of Cognitive Theory and Therapy of Depression*. Chichester: John Wiley.

Cole, S., Denny, D., Eyler, A. & Samons, S. (2000). Issues in transgender. In L. Szuchman & F. Muscarella (Eds), *Psychological Perspectives on Human Sexuality* (pp. 149–168). New York, NY: John Wiley.

Coleman, E., Gooren, L. & Ross, M. (1989). Theories of gender transpositions: A critique and suggestions for further research. *The Journal of Sex Research*, **26**(4), 525–538.

Coleman, E., Bockting, W. & Gooren, L. (1993). Homosexual and bisexual identity in sex-reassigned female-to-male transsexuals. *Archives of Sexual Behavior*, **22**(1), 37–50.

Crawford, J., Kippax, S., Onyx, J., Gault, U. & Benton, P. (1992). *Emotion and Gender: Constructing meaning from memory*. London: Sage.

Denny, D. (2004). Changing models of transsexualism. *Journal of Gay & Lesbian Psychotherapy*, **8**(1–2), 25–40.

Devor, A. H. (1997). *FTM: Female-to-Male Transsexuals in Society*. Bloomington, IN: Indiana University Press.

Devor, A. H. (2004). Witnessing and mirroring: A fourteen stage model of transsexual identity formation. *Journal of Gay & Lesbian Psychotherapy*, **8**(1/2), 41–67.

Di Ceglie, D. & Freeman, D. (Eds) (1999). *A Stranger In My Own Body: Atypical gender identity development and mental health*. London: Karnac Books.

Elliot, P. & Roen, K. (1998). Transgenderism and the question of embodiment: Promising queer politics. *GLQ: A Journal of Lesbian and Gay Studies*, **4**(2), 231–261.

Ellis, H. (1936). *Sexual Inversion, Studies in Psychology of Sex* (Vol. 2). New York, NY: Random House.

Fausto-Sterling, A. (1993). 'The Five Sexes'. *The Sciences*, **March/April**, 20–25.

Fisk, N. (1973). Gender dysphoria syndrome. In D. Laub & P. Gandy (Eds), *Proceedings of the Second Interdisciplinary Symposium on Gender Dysphoria Syndrome* (pp. 7–14). Palo Alto, CA: Stanford University Press.

Foucault, M. (1973). *The Birth of the Clinic* (trans. A. M. Sheridan). London: Tavistock.

Green, R. (1969). Psychiatric Management of Special Problems in Transsexualism. In R. Green & J. Money (Eds), *Transsexualism and Sex Reassignment* (pp. 279–291). Baltimore: John Hopkins University Press.

Green, R. & Fleming, D. (1990). Transsexual surgery follow-up: Status in the 1990's. *Annual Review of Sex Research*, **1**(1), 163–174.

Hage, J. J. (1996). Metoidioplasty: An alternative phalloplasty technique in transsexuals. *Plastic and Reconstructive Surgery*, **97**(1), 161–167.

Halberstam, J. (1998). *Female Masculinity*. London: Duke University Press.

Hamburger, C., Sturup, C. K. & Dahl-Iversen, E. (1953). Transvestism, hormonal, psychiatric and surgical treatment. *Journal of the American Medical Association*, **12**(6), 391–394.

Harry Benjamin International Gender Dysphoria Association, (2001). *The Standards of Care for Gender Identity Disorders*, Sixth Version. Retrieved 7 December 2004, from http://www.symposion.com/ijt/soc_2001/

Hausman, B. L. (1995). *Changing Sex: Transsexualism, technology, and the idea of gender.* London: Duke University Press.

Herdt, G. (Ed.) (1993). *Third Gender, Third Sex: Beyond sexual dimorphism in culture and history.* New York, NY: Zone Books.

Hoenig, J. & Kenna, J. (1973). Epidemiological aspects of transsexualism. *Psychiatrica Clinica*, **6**(2), 65–80.

Jeffreys, S. (2000). 'Body art' and social status: Cutting, tattooing and piercing from a feminist perspective. *Feminism & Psychology*, **10**(4), 409–429.

Johnson, K. (2001). Studying transsexual identity. In F. Haynes & T. McKenna (Eds), *Unseen Genders: Beyond the binaries* (pp. 143–156). New York, NY: Peter Lang.

Johnson, K. (2005). From gender to transgender: 30 years of feminism. *Social Alternatives*, **24**(2), 36–39.

Johnson, K. (2007a). Fragmented identities, frustrated politics: transsexuals, lesbians and 'queer'. *Journal of Lesbian Studies*, **11**(1–2), 123–141.

Johnson, K. (2007b). Changing sex, changing self: Transitions in embodied subjectivity. *Men and Masculinities*, **10**(1).

Jones, B. & Hill, M. (2002). Mental health issues in lesbian, gay, bisexual, and transgender communities. *Review of Psychology*, **21**, 15–31.

Jorgensen, C. (1967). *Christine Jorgensen: A Personal Autobiography.* New York, NY: P. S. Eriksson.

Kessler, S. & McKenna, W. (1978). *Gender: An ethnomethodological approach.* New York, NY: John Wiley.

King, M., McKeown, E., Warner, J., Ramsay, A., Johnson, K., Cort, C., Wright, L., Blizard, R. & Davidson, O. (2003). Mental health and quality of life of gay men and lesbians in England and Wales: Controlled, cross-sectional study. *British Journal of Psychiatry*, **183**(December), 552–558.

Kinsey, A. C., Pomeroy, W. B. & Martin, C. E. (1948). *Sexual Behaviour in the Human Male.* Philadelphia, PA: W. B. Saunders.

Krafft-Ebing, R. von (1908). *Psychopathia Sexualis with Especial Reference to the Aantipathic Sexual Instinct*, trans., F. J. Rebmab. Brooklyn, NY: Physicians and Surgeons Book Co.

Kruijver, F. P. M., Zhou, J. N., Pool, C. W., Hofman, M. A., Gooren, L. J. G. & Swaab, D. F. (2000). Male-to-female transsexuals have female neuron numbers in a limbic nucleus. *The Journal of Clinical Endocrinology & Metabolism*, **85**(5), 2034–2041.

Kubie, L. S. & Mackie, J. B. (1968). Critical issues raised by operations for gender transmutation. *Journal of Nervous and Mental Diseases*, **147**(5), 431–443.

Kuiper, A. J. & Cohen-Kettenis, P. T. (1998). Gender role reversal among postoperative transsexuals. *The International Journal of Transgenderism*, **2**(3). Retrieved 26 January 2005, from http://www.symposion.com/ijt/ijtc0502.htm

Laqueur, T. (1990). *Making Sex: Body and Gender from the Greeks to Freud.* Cambridge, MA: Harvard University Press.

Lorber, J. (1995). *Paradoxes of Gender.* New Haven, CT: Yale University Press.

Lothstein, L. M. (1979). Psychodynamics and sociodynamics of gender dysphoric states. *American Journal of Psychotherapy,* **33**(2), 214–238.

Lothstein, L. M. & Levine, S. B. (1981). Expressive psychotherapy with gender-dysphoric patients. *Archives of General Psychiatry,* **38**(8), 924–929.

McCauley, E. A. & Erhardt, A. A. (1977). Role expectations and definitions: A comparison of female transsexuals and lesbians. *Journal of Homosexuality,* **3**(2), 137–147.

MacKenzie, G. O. (1994). *Transgender Nation.* Bowling Green, OH: Bowling Green State University Popular Press

Mason-Schrock, D. (1996). Transsexuals' narrative construction of the "true self". *Social Psychology Quarterly,* **59**, 176–192.

Meerloo, J. A. M. (1967). Change of sex and collaboration with the psychosis. *American Journal of Psychiatry,* **124**(2), 263–264.

Meyer, J. K. (1973). Some thoughts on nosology and motivation among 'transsexuals'. In D. Laub & P. Gandy (Eds), *Proceedings of the Second Interdisciplinary Symposium on Gender Dysphoria Syndrome* (pp. 31–33). Palo Alto, CA: Stanford University Press.

Meyer, J. K. & Hoopes, J. E. (1974). The gender dysphoria syndromes: A position statement on so-called transsexualism. *Plastic and Reconstructive Surgery,* **54**(October), 444–451.

Meyer, J. K. & Reter, D. J. (1979). Sex reassignment follow-up. *Archives of General Psychiatry,* **36**(9), 1010–1015.

Money, J. (1986). *LOVEMAPS: Clinical concepts of sexual/erotic health and pathology, paraphilia, and gender transposition in childhood, adolescence and maturity.* New York, NY: Irvington.

Morgan, A. J. (1978). Psychotherapy for Transsexual candidates screened out of surgery. *Archives of Sexual Behavior,* **7**(4), 273–283.

Nataf, Z. I. (1996). *Lesbians Talk Transgender.* London: Scarlet Press.

Nuttbrock, L., Rosenblum, A. & Blumenstein, R. (2002). Transgender identity affirmation and mental health. *The International Journal of Transgenderism,* **6**(4) http://www.symposion.com/ijt/ijtvo06no04_03.htm

Pauly, I. (1990a). Gender identity disorders: Evaluation and treatment. *Journal of Sex Education and Therapy,* **16**(1), 2–24.

Pauly, I. (1990b). Gender identity disorders: Update. In F. J. Bianco & R. H. Serrano (Eds), *Sexology: An independent field* (pp. 63–84). Amsterdam: Elsevier.

Pauly, I. (1992). Terminology and classification of gender identity disorders. *Journal of Psychology & Human Sexuality,* **5**(4), 1–14.

Plummer, K. (1995). *Telling Sexual Stories: Power, change and social worlds.* London: Routledge.

Prosser, J. (1998). *Second Skins: The body narratives of transsexuality.* New York, NY: Columbia University Press.

PsyWeb. (2005). *Disorders Diagnostic Criteria (DSM-IV™ Made Easy).* Retrieved 2 February 2005, from http://www.psyweb.com/Mdisord/DSM_IV/dsm_iv.html

Rachlin, K. (2002). Transgender Individuals' Experiences of Psychotherapy. *International Journal of Transgenderism,* **6**(1). Retrieved 21 November 2006, from http://www.symposion.com/ijt/ijtvo06no01_03.htm

Raymond, J. G. (1980). *The Transsexual Empire. The making of the She-Male.* London: The Women's Press.

Ross, M. W. (1986a). Gender Identity: male, female or third gender. In W. A. W. Walters & M. W. Ross (Eds), *Transsexualism and Sex Reassignment* (pp. 1–8). Oxford: Oxford University Press.

Ross, M. W. (1986b). Causes of gender dysphoria: How does transsexualism develop and why? In W. A. W. Walters & M. W. Ross (Eds), *Transsexualism and Sex Reassignment* (pp. 16–25). Oxford: Oxford University Press.

Ross, M. W. & Need, J. A. (1989). Effects of adequacy of gender reassignment surgery on psychological adjustment: A follow-up of fourteen male-to-female patients. *Archives of Sexual Behavior,* **18**(2), 145–153.

Ross, M. W., Rogers, L. J. & McCulloch, H. (1978). Stigma, sex and society: A new look at gender differentiation and sexual variation. *Journal of Homosexuality*, **3**(4), 315–330.

Ross, M. W., Wålinder, J., Lundström, B. & Thuwe, I. (1981). Cross-cultural approaches to transsexualism: A comparison between Sweden and Australia. *Acta Psychiatrica Scandinavica*, **63**(1), 75–82.

Rubin, G. (1975). The traffic in women: notes on the 'political economy of sex'. In R. R. Reiter (Ed.), *Toward an Anthropology of Women* (pp. 157–210). New York: Monthly Review Press.

Rubin, H. (2003). *Self-made Men: Identity and embodiment among transsexual men*. Nashville, TN: Vanderbilt University Press.

Segal, L. (1999). *Why Feminism? Gender, psychology, politics*. Oxford: Polity Press.

Stoller, R. (1967). Etiological factors in male transsexualism. *Transactions of the New York Academy of Sciences*, **86**(4), 365–366.

Stoller, R. J. (1968). A further contribution to the study of gender identity. *International Journal of Psycho-Analysis*, **49**(2), 365–366.

Stoller, R. J. (1973a). Male transsexualism: Uneasiness. *American Journal of Psychiatry*, **22**(5), 47–64.

Stoller, R. J. (1973b). The male transsexual as 'experiment'. *International Journal of Psycho-Analysis*, **54**(2), 215–225.

Stoller, R. J. (1975). *Sex and Gender, Volume II: The transsexual experiment*. New York, NY: Jason Aronson.

Stryker, S. (1994). My words to Victor Frankenstein above the village of Chamounix: Performing transgender rage. *GLQ: A Journal of Lesbian and Gay Studies*, **1**, 237–254.

Stryker, S. (1997). Over and Out in Academe: Transgender Studies Come of Age. In G. E. Israel & D. E. Tarver (Eds), *Transgender Care: Recommended guidelines, practical information & personal accounts* (pp. 214–244). Philadelphia, PA: Temple University Press.

Stryker, S. (1998). The transgender issue: An introduction. *GLQ: A Journal of Lesbian and Gay Studies*, **4**(2), 145–148.

Swaab, D. F. & Hofman, M. A. (1995). Sexual differentiation of the human hypothalamus in relation to gender and sexual orientation. *Trends in Neurosciences*, **18**(6), 264–270.

Swaab, D. F., Zhou, J-N., Fodor, M. & Hofman, M. A. (1997). Sexual differentiation of the human hypothalamus: Differences according to sex, sexual orientation, and transsexuality In L. Ellis & L. Ebertz (Eds), *Sexual Orientation: Toward biological understanding* (pp. 130–150). Westport, CT: Praeger.

Szasz, T. (1990). *Sex by Prescription: The Startling Truth about Today's Sex Therapy*. Syracuse, NY: Syracuse University Press.

Terry, J. (1997). The Seductive Power of Science in the Making of Deviant Subjectivity In V. A. Rosario (Ed.), *Science and Homosexualities* (pp. 271–296). London: Routledge.

Warner, J., McKeown, E., Griffin, M., Johnson, K., Ramsay, A., Cort, C. & King, M. (2004). Rates and predictors of mental illness in gay men, lesbians and bisexual men and women. Results from a survey based in England and Wales. *British Journal of Psychiatry*, **185**(December), 479–485.

West, P. (2004). Report into the medical and related needs of transgender people in Brighton and Hove: The case for a local integrated service. Retrieved 24 January 2005, from http://www.pfc.org.uk/medical/spectrum.pdf.

Whittle S. (1995). Gender fucking or fucking gender? In D. King & R. Ekins (Eds), *Blending Genders: Social aspects of cross dressing and sex changing* (pp. 196–214). London: Routledge.

Zhou, J. N., Hofman, M. A., Gooren, L. J. & Swaab, D. F. (1995). A sex difference in the human brain and its relation to transsexuality. *Nature*, **378**(6552), 68–70.

Index